COMPLETE
Handbook of
SPANISH
VERBS

Judith Noble • Jaime Lacasa

PASSPORT BOOKS
a division of *NTC Publishing Group*
Lincolnwood, Illinois USA

1995 Printing

This edition first published in 1984 by National Textbook Company,
a division of NTC Publishing Group, 4255 West Touhy Avenue,
Lincolnwood (Chicago), Illinois 60646-1975 U.S.A.,
which has been granted exclusive worldwide reprint rights.
Manufactured in the United States of America.
Original copyright © 1980 The Iowa State University Press.

4 5 6 7 8 9 ML 9 8 7

Table of Contents

Introduction

About This Book

Section I of the *Complete Handbook of Spanish Verbs* lists more than 4,500 Spanish infinitives. In addition, more than 5,500 forms of irregular verbs are included to help users identify the infinitives of irregular verbs and to help them locate their complete conjugation or the model for their conjugation.

The verbs in this list were selected for two reasons—first of all, to illustrate regular and irregular conjugations and, secondly, to create a convenient reference to the verbs most frequently used in Spanish. Each Spanish infinitive listed is followed by one or more English equivalents, as well as by a reference number that indicates its conjugation chart or the model verb whose pattern it follows. Reflexive verbs are also accompanied by an additional reference number (4), referring users to the chart containing a model conjugation of a reflexive verb.

Section II (p. 53) contains charts listing English translations for Spanish verb tenses, as well as the meanings of the subject pronouns of verbs.

Section III (p. 55) consists of charts outlining model conjugations for regular *-ar*, *-er*, and *-ir* verbs.

Sections IV–X (p. 60) presents charts that show the full conjugation of a series of model verbs, each followed by a list entitled "Verbs of This Category," which identifies all the verbs in this book that follow this particular model.

Section IV outlines regular verb patterns, including the progressive tenses, reflexive verbs, and the passive voice.

Section V (p. 74) consists of charts displaying model orthographic-changing (spelling-changing) verbs that are regular in *sound* but that undergo changes in certain written forms. At the end of this section, a chart summarizes the types and locations of all changes.

Section VI (p. 138) presents charts that summarize patterns for radical-changing (stem-changing) verbs. These verbs undergo a change in the stem vowel in certain forms. The change is always in the next-to-the-last (penultimate) vowel of the infinitive. The change that the stem vowel undergoes is shown in parentheses after the infinitive. A summary chart gives the user an overview of the types and locations of all stem changes.

Section VII (p. 154) summarizes verbs that have *both* spelling and stem changes.

Section VIII (p. 188) consists of verbs that undergo a shift in accent in certain forms—from the vowel where it would normally fall to another vowel.

Section IX (p. 200) is made up of charts of irregular verbs. They are grouped, first of all, according to infinitive ending. Then they appear individually in a list. Some of these verbs are unique; some provide a model for other verbs. At the end of this section, a chart summarizes the location of all spelling and stem changes, as well as the irregularities occurring in irregular verbs.

Section X (p. 302) features defective verbs, that is, verbs that do not have the full range of forms of an ordinary verb.

Finally, *Section XI* (p. 322) lists, in alphabetical order, the English translations of Spanish infinitives found in the list at the beginning of the book. This section was not designed to serve as a dictionary of English verbs. The English equivalents of Spanish verbs are simply repeated here in alphabetical order.

How to Use This Book

Verb forms that evidence changes and/or irregularities from the usual patterns are printed in bold type in the charts. In compound tenses, the auxiliary verb *haber*, which is irregular in many forms, appears in regular type, since the focus in the charts is on changes or irregularities in the model verb only.

To find the conjugation pattern of a verb, first look up the infinitive in Section I and turn to the chart number immediately following it. If it is not a regular verb, all changes and/or irregularities are shown in bold type.

If you do not know the infinitive form of a verb, look for one of the forms you *do* know or for an infinitive that it resembles. If the form is irregular, it should appear in the list of irregular verb forms. The infinitive will be given in that list. (When the irregular forms in a particular tense closely resemble one another, only one person is given, followed by "etc.")

Beneath the heading "Verbs of This Category," the user will find a list of verbs having all the characteristics of the model verb. These verbs may be followed by one or more numbers, along with a letter code. A number that is *higher* than the number of the chart you are consulting indicates that this particular verb has other changes and/or irregularities. The chart with the higher number shows a model verb with the same changes and irregularities as the verb you are interested in. The letter code, explained in footnotes, identifies the general category of the model verb indicated by the chart number.

I. Spanish-English Alphabetical Verb List

A

abalance, etc. (abalanzar)
abalancé (abalanzar)
abalanzar (11), to balance, to hurl
abalanzarse (11) (4), to rush upon
abandonar (1), to abandon
abanicar (8), to fan
abanique, etc. (abanicar)
abaniqué (abanicar)
abaniquear (1), to fan
abaratar (1), to cheapen
abarcar (8), to include, to embrace, to monopolize
abarque, etc. (abarcar)
abarqué (abarcar)
abarquillar (1), to curl up
abarrotar (1), to overstock
abarse (115) (4), to move aside, to get out of the way
abastecer (73), to supply
abastezca, etc. (abastecer)
abastezco (abastecer)
abatir (3), to knock down
abdicar (8), to abdicate
abdique, etc. (abdicar)
abdiqué (abdicar)
abducir (67), to abduct
abduje (abducir)
abdujera, etc. (abducir)
abdujere, etc. (abducir)
abdujeron (abducir)
abdujese, etc. (abducir)
abdujimos (abducir)
abdujiste (abducir)
abdujisteis (abducir)
abdujo (abducir)
abduzca, etc. (abducir)
abduzco (abducir)
abellacar (8), to make mean
abellacarse (8) (4), to become mean
abellaque, etc. (abellacar)
abellaqué (abellacar)
aberrar (1), to err
abierto (abrir)
abigarrar (1), to paint in motley colors
abisagrar (1), to put hinges on
abismar (1), to overwhelm
abjurar (1), to abjure
ablandar (1), to soften
ablandecer (73), to soften
ablandezca, etc. (ablandecer)
ablandezco (ablandecer)
abnegar (ie) (50), to renounce
abnegué (abnegar)
abneguemos, etc. (abnegar)
abniega, etc. (abnegar)
abniego (abnegar)
abniegue, etc. (abnegar)
abobar (1), to make stupid
abobarse (1) (4), to become stupid
abocar (8), to transfer by pouring
abocetar (1), to sketch
abochornar (1), to make blush
abochornarse (1) (4), to blush
abofetear (1), to slap in the face
abogar (9), to plead
abogue, etc. (abogar)
abogué (abogar)
abolir (116), to abolish, to revoke
abolsar (1), to form pockets

abollar (1), to dent
abombar (1), to make convex
abombarse (1) (4), to become convex
abominar (1), to abominate
abonar (1), to fertilize, to pay
aboque, etc. (abocar)
aboqué (abocar)
abordar (1), to board
aborrascarse (8) (4), to get stormy
aborrasque, etc. (aborrascarse)
aborrasqué (aborrascarse)
aborrecer (73), to hate
aborrezca, etc. (aborrecer)
aborrezco (aborrecer)
abortar (1), to abort
abotonar (1), to button
aboyar (1), to mark with buoys
abrace, etc. (abrazar)
abracé (abrazar)
abrasar (1), to burn
abrazar (11), to embrace
abrevar (1), to water (cattle)
abreviar (1), to abbreviate
abrigar (9), to shelter
abrigarse (9) (4), to take shelter, to wrap oneself up
abrigue, etc. (abrigar)
abrigué (abrigar)
abrillantar (1), to polish, to shine, to brighten
abrir (75), to open, to unlock
abrochar (1), to fasten, to button
abrogar (9), to abrogate, to annul, to repeal
abrogue, etc. (abrogar)
abrogué (abrogar)
abrumar (1), to oppress, to overwhelm
absolver (ue) (70), to absolve
absorber (2), to absorb
abstendré, etc. (abstenerse)
abstendría, etc. (abstenerse)
abstenerse (ie) (108) (4), to abstain
abstenga, etc. (abstenerse)
abstengo (abstenerse)
abstente (abstenerse)
abstiene, etc. (abstenerse)
abstraer (109), to abstract
abstraerse (109) (4), to be absorbed
abstraiga, etc. (abstraer)
abstraigo (abstraer)
abstraje (abstraer)
abstrajera, etc. (abstraer)
abstrajere, etc. (abstraer)
abstrajeron (abstraer)
abstrajese, etc. (abstraer)
abstrajimos (abstraer)
abstrajiste (abstraer)
abstrajisteis (abstraer)
abstrajo (abstraer)
abstrayendo (abstraer)
abstuve, etc. (abstenerse)
abstuviera, etc. (abstenerse)
abstuviere, etc. (abstenerse)
abstuvieron (abstenerse)
abstuviese, etc. (abstenerse)
abstuvimos (abstenerse)
abstuviste (abstenerse)
abstuvisteis (abstenerse)
abstuvo (abstenerse)
absuelto (absolver)
absuelva, etc. (absolver)

absuelve, etc. (absolver)
absuelvo (absolver)
abuchear (1), to boo
abultar (1), to bulge
abundar (1), to abound
abuñolar (ue) (36), to fry (eggs) fluffy and brown
abuñuela, etc. (abuñolar) (abuñuelar)
abuñuelar (1), to fry (eggs) fluffy and brown
abuñuele, etc. (abuñolar) (abuñuelar)
abuñuelo (abuñolar) (abuñuelar)
aburguesarse (1)(4), to become bourgeois
aburrir (3), to bore
aburrirse (3) (4), to get bored
abusar (1), to abuse
acaballonar (1), to furrow
acabar (1), to end, to finish, to complete
academice, etc. (academizar)
academicé (academizar)
academizar (11), to make academic
academizarse (11) (4), to become academic
acaecer (73), to happen
acaezca, etc. (acaecer)
acalambrarse (1) (4), to contract with cramps (muscles)
acalorarse (1) (4), to get excited
acallar (1), to silence
acampar (1), to camp
acanalar (1), to corrugate, to channel
acantalear (1), to hail large hail stones
acantonar (1), to quarter (troops)
acaparar (1), to monopolize
acapice, etc. (acapizarse)
acapicé (acapizarse)
acapizarse (11) (4), to come to grips
acaramelar (1), to caramelize
acardenalar (1), to make black and blue
acardenalarse (1) (4), to become black and blue
acariciar (1), to caress
acarrear (1), to cart
acartonarse (1) (4), to dry up like cardboard
acatar (1), to show respect and submission
acatarrarse (1) (4), to catch cold
acaudalar (1), to accumulate
acaudillar (1), to lead
acceder (2), to accede, to agree
accidentarse (1) (4), to have an accident
accionar (1), to gesticulate
acece, etc. (acezar)
acecé (acezar)
acechar (1), to lurk
aceitar (1), to oil
acelerar (1), to accelerate
acensuar (62), to tax a possession
acentuar (62), to accentuate, to stress
aceptar (1), to accept
acerarse (1) (4), to harden
acercar (8), to bring near or nearer
acercarse (8)(4), to approach, to get closer
acerque, etc. (acercar)
acerqué (acercar)
acerrojar (1), to bolt
acertar (ie)(37), to hit upon, to guess right
acezar (11), to pain, to gasp
acibarar (1), to embitter
acicalarse (1) (4), to get dressed up

acidificar (8), to acidify
acidifique, etc. (acidificar)
acidifiqué (acidificar)
acidular (1), to make sour
acierta, etc. (acertar)
acierte, etc. (acertar)
acierto (acertar)
aclarar (1), to brighten, to make clear
aclimatar (1), to acclimatize
aclocarse (ue) (44), to brood, to squat
acloqué (aclocar)
acloquemos, etc. (aclocar)
aclueca, etc. (aclocar)
aclueco (aclocar)
aclueque (aclocar)
acocear (1), to kick (said of horses)
acodiciar (1), to covet
acodillar (1), to bend into an elbow
acoger (15), to receive, to welcome
acogerse (15) (4), to take refuge
acogotar (1), to subdue
acoja, etc. (acoger)
acojinar (1), to quilt
acojo (acoger)
acolchar (1), to quilt
acolitar (1), to serve as an acolyte, to assist
acometer (2), to attack
acomodar (1), to accommodate, to be suitable
acomodarse (1) (4), to make oneself comfortable
acompañar (1), to accompany, to come along
acompasar (1), to keep time (rhythm)
acomunar (1), to join forces
acondicionar (1), to condition
acongojar (1), to grieve
aconsejar (1), to advise
acontecer (73), to happen
acontezca, etc. (acontecer)
acopiar (1), to gather together
acoplar (1), to couple
acoquinar (1), to intimidate
acorace, etc. (acorazar)
acoracé (acorazar)
acorazar (11), to armor-plate
acordar (ue) (36), to agree
acordarse (ue) (36) (4), to remember
acordonar (1), to cordon off, to lace
acornar (ue) (36), to butt
acornear (1), to butt, to gore
acorralar (1), to corral
acorrucarse (8) (4), to huddle up
acorruque, etc. (acorrucarse)
acorruqué (acorrucarse)
acortar (1), to shorten
acosar (1), to pursue relentlessly, to harass
acostar (ue) (36), to lay down, to put to bed
acostarse (ue) (36) (4), to lie down, to go to bed
acostumbrar (1), to accustom
acostumbrarse (1) (4), to get used to, to become accustomed
acotar (1), to mark off
acrecentar (ie) (37), to increase
acrecer (73), to increase
acrecienta, etc. (acrecentar)
acreciente, etc. (acrecentar)
acreciento (acrecentar)
acreditar (1), to accredit, to credit
acrezca, etc. (acrecer)
acrezco (acrecer)
acribillar (1), to riddle
acriminar (1), to incriminate

acrisolar (1), to purify
acromatice, etc. (acromatizar)
acromaticé (acromatizar)
acromatizar (11), to rid of color
activar (1), to activate
actuar (62), to act
acuantiar (61), to fix or set amount of
acuartelar (1), to quarter (troops)
acuatice, etc. (acuatizar)
acuaticé (acuatizar)
acuatizar (11), to alight on water
acuciar (1), to goad, to prod, to urge
acuclillarse (1) (4), to squat
acuchillar (1), to knife, to cut
acudir (3), to come, to come to the rescue
acuerda, etc. (acordar)
acuerde, etc. (acordar)
acuerdo (acordar)
acuerna, etc. (acornar)
acuerne, etc. (acornar)
acuerno (acornar)
acuesta, etc. (acostar)
acueste, etc. (acostar)
acuesto (acostar)
acular (1), to back up (said of a horse)
acumular (1), to accumulate
acunar (1), to rock in a cradle
acuñar (1), to coin
acurrucar (8), to wrap up
acurrucarse (8) (4), to huddle up
acurruque, etc. (acurrucar)
acurruqué (acurrucar)
acusar (1), to accuse
achacar (8), to attribute
achantarse (1) (4), to hide from danger
achaque, etc. (achacar)
achaqué (achacar)
achatar (1), to flatten
achicar (8), to make smaller, to drain
achicharrar (1), to scorch
achique, etc. (achicar)
achiqué (achicar)
achisparse (1) (4), to get tipsy
acholarse (1) (4), to be abashed
achuchar (1), to incite
adaptar (1), to adapt
adargar (9), to shield
adargue, etc. (adargar)
adargué (adargar)
adecentar (1), to make decent, to clean up
adecentarse (1) (4), to dress up
adecuar (1), to adapt
adelantar (1), to move forward
adelantarse (1) (4), to move forward, to be fast, to gain (said of clocks)
adelgace, etc. (adelgazar)
adelgacé (adelgazar)
adelgazar (11), to make thin
adelgazarse (11) (4), to get thin
adentrar (1), to go into
adentrarse (1) (4), to go into
aderece, etc. (aderezar)
aderecé (aderezar)
aderezar (11), to prepare, to adorn, to garnish
adeudar (1), to owe
adherir (ie, i) (41), to adhere
adherirse (ie, i) (41) (4), to adhere
adhiera, etc. (adherir)
adhiere, etc. (adherir)
adhiero (adherir)
adhiramos, etc. (adherir)
adhiriendo (adherir)
adhiriera, etc. (adherir)
adhiriere, etc. (adherir)
adhirieron (adherir)

adhiriese, etc. (adherir)
adhirió (adherir)
adicionar (1), to add
adiestrar (1), to train
adietar (1), to put on a diet
adir (121), to accept an inheritance
adivinar (1), to guess
adjetivar (1), to use as an adjective
adoctrinar (1), to indoctrinate
adolecer (73), to suffer (from illness, defect, etc.)
adolezca, etc. (adolecer)
adolezco (adolecer)
adonice, etc. (adonizarse)
adonicé (adonizarse)
adonizarse (11) (4), to doll up
adoptar (1), to adopt
adoquinar (1), to pave with cobblestones
adorar (1), to worship, to adore
adormecer (73), to make sleepy
adormecerse (73) (4), to get sleepy, to get numb
adormezca, etc. (adormecer)
adormezco (adormecer)
adormilarse (1) (4), to doze
adosar (1), to lean
adquiera, etc. (adquirir)
adquiere, etc. (adquirir)
adquiero (adquirir)
adquirir (ie) (76), to acquire
adscribir (69), to assign
adscrito (adscribir)
aducir (67), to adduce
adueñarse (1) (4), to take possession
aduje (aducir)
adujera, etc. (aducir)
adujere, etc. (aducir)
adujeron (aducir)
adujese, etc. (aducir)
adujimos (aducir)
adujiste (aducir)
adujisteis (aducir)
adujo (aducir)
adular (1), to flatter
adulce, etc. (adulzar)
adulcé (adulzar)
adulterar (1), to adulterate
adulzar (11), to sweeten
aduzca, etc. (aducir)
aduzco (aducir)
advén (advenir)
advendré, etc. (advenir)
advendría, etc. (advenir)
advenga, etc. (advenir)
advengo (advenir)
advenir (ie, i) (111), to come, to arrive
advertir (ie, i) (41), to notice, to warn
adviene, etc. (advenir)
advierta, etc. (advertir)
advierte, etc. (advertir)
advierto (advertir)
advine (advenir)
adviniendo (advenir)
adviniera, etc. (advenir)
adviniere, etc. (advenir)
advinieron (advenir)
adviniese, etc. (advenir)
advinimos (advenir)
adviniste (advenir)
advinisteis (advenir)
advino (advenir)
advirtamos, etc. (advertir)
advirtiendo (advertir)
advirtiera, etc. (advertir)
advirtiere, etc. (advertir)
advirtieron (advertir)

advirtiese, etc. (advertir)
advirtió (advertir)
aerear (1), to aerate, to vent
afamar (1), to make famous
afanarse (1) (4), to strive to
afear (1), to make ugly, to blame
afectar (1), to affect
afeitar (1), to shave
afeminar (1), to effeminate
aferrar (1), to seize
aferrarse (1) (4), to insist
afiance, etc. (afianzar)
afiancé (afianzar)
afianzar (11), to guarantee
aficionar (1), to cause to like
aficionarse (1) (4), to become fond of
afilar (1), to sharpen
afiliar (1) or (61), to affiliate
afinar (1), to perfect, to tune, to sing or
    play in tune
afincar (8), to buy up real estate
afinque, etc. (afincar)
afinqué (afincar)
afirmar (1), to strengthen, to affirm
afligir (16), to afflict
afligirse (16) (4), to grieve
aflija, etc. (afligir)
aflijo (afligir)
aflojar (1), to slacken, to loosen
afluir (71), to flow
afluya, etc. (afluir)
afluye, etc. (afluir)
afluyendo (afluir)
afluyera, etc. (afluir)
afluyere, etc. (afluir)
afluyeron (afluir)
afluyese, etc. (afluir)
afluyo (afluir)
afluyó (afluir)
aforar (1), to measure, to appraise
aforrar (1), to line
afoscarse (8) (4), to become misty or hazy
afosque, etc. (afoscarse)
afosqué (afoscarse)
afrentar (1), to affront
afrentarse (1) (4), to be ashamed
afrontar (1), to confront
agachar (1), to lower
agacharse (1) (4), to crouch, to squat
agarrar (1), to grasp
agasajar (1), to shower with attentions
agazaparse (1) (4), to crouch, to squat
agenciar (1), to manage
agigantar (1), to make huge
agilitar (1), to make agile
agitar (1), to agitate, to stir
aglomerar (1), to agglomerate
aglutinar (1), to agglutinate, to stick to-
    gether
agobiar (1), to overburden
agolparse (1) (4), to throng
agonice, etc. (agonizar)
agonicé (agonizar)
agonizar (11), to be in the throes of death,
    to agonize
agorar (ue) (48), to predict
agostar (1), to burn up
agotar (1), to exhaust
agraciar (1), to grace
agradar (1), to please
agradecer (73), to thank
agradezca, etc. (agradecer)
agradezco (agradecer)
agrandar (1), to enlarge
agravar (1), to aggravate
agraviar (1), to offend

agraviarse (1) (4), to be offended
agredir (116), to attack
agregar (9), to add
agregarse (9) (4), to join
agregue, etc. (agregar)
agregué (agregar)
agriarse (1) or (61) (4), to sour
agrietarse (1) (4), to crack
agrumar (1), to clot, to curd
agrupar (1), to group
aguantar (1), to hold, to bear
aguantarse (1) (4), to restrain oneself
aguar (10), to water, to spoil
aguardar (1), to wait
aguce, etc. (aguzar)
agucé (aguzar)
agudice, etc. (agudizar)
agudicé (agudizar)
agudizar (11), to sharpen, to make more
    acute
agudizarse (11) (4), to become aggra-
    vated, to get worse
agüe, etc. (aguar)
agüé (aguar)
agüera, etc. (agorar)
agüere, etc. (agorar)
agüero (agorar)
aguerrir (116), to inure to war
aguijar (1), to urge on
aguijonear (1), to spur
agujerear (1), to make a hole or holes in
aguzar (11), to sharpen
aherrumbrar (1), to rust
ahija, etc. (ahijar)
ahijar (34), to adopt
ahíje, etc. (ahijar)
ahijo (ahijar)
ahíla, etc. (ahilar)
ahilar (34), to line up, to go single file
ahilarse (34) (4), to faint from hunger
ahíle, etc. (ahilar)
ahílo (ahilar)
ahincar (8), to urge, to press
ahínca, etc. (ahincar)
ahínco, etc. (ahincar)
ahínque, etc. (ahincar)
ahinqué (ahincar)
ahinquemos, etc. (ahincar)
ahíta, etc. (ahitar)
ahitar (34), to gorge to the point of feeling
    sick
ahíte, etc. (ahitar)
ahíto (ahitar)
ahocicar (8), to win out over someone in a
    discussion
ahocique, etc. (ahocicar)
ahociqué (ahocicar)
ahogar (9), to choke
ahogarse (9) (4), to drown
ahogue, etc. (ahogar)
ahogué (ahogar)
ahondar (1), to deepen
ahorcajarse (1) (4), to sit astride
ahorcar (8), to hang
ahornar (1), to put in the oven
ahornarse (1) (4), to burn on the outside
    (in the oven) with the inside not yet done
ahorque, etc. (ahorcar)
ahorqué (ahorcar)
ahorrar (1), to save, to spare
ahoyar (1), to dig holes in
ahúcha, etc. (ahuchar)
ahuchar (34), to stash away (in a piggy
    bank or safe place)
ahúche, etc. (ahuchar)
ahúcho (ahuchar)

ahuecar (8), to hollow
ahueque, etc. (ahuecar)
ahuequé (ahuecar)
ahúma, etc. (ahumar)
ahumar (34), to smoke
ahúme, etc. (ahumar)
ahúmo (ahumar)
ahuyentar (1), to chase away
ahuyentarse (1) (4), to run away
airar (63), to anger
airarse (63) (4), to get angry
airear (1), to air, to ventilate
aislar (63), to isloate
ajar (1), to wither
ajornalar (1), to hire by the day
ajuiciar (1), to bring to one's senses
ajumarse (1) (4), to get drunk
ajustar (1), to fit
ajusticiar (1), to punish with death
alabar (1), to praise
alabarse (1) (4), to boast
alambicar (8), to distill, to scrutinize
alambique, etc. (alambicar)
alambiqué (alambicar)
alambrar (1), to fence with wire
alancear (1), to spear
alardear (1), to boast
alargar (9), to lengthen
alargarse (9) (4), to go away
alargue, etc. (alargar)
alargué (alargar)
alarmar (1), to alarm
alarmarse (1) (4), to get alarmed
albergar (9), to shelter
albergarse (9) (4), to take shelter
albergue, etc. (albergar)
albergué (albergar)
alborear (1), to dawn
alboroce, etc. (alborozar)
alborocé (alborozar)
alborotar (1), to make a racket
alborotarse (1) (4), to get excited
alborozar (11), to overjoy
alcance, etc. (alcanzar)
alcancé (alcanzar)
alcanzar (11), to catch up, to reach
alce, etc. (alzar)
alcé (alzar)
alear (1), to alloy
aleccionar (1), to teach
alegar (9), to allege
alegrar (1), to cheer
alegrarse (1) (4), to rejoice, to be glad, to
    be happy
alegue (alegar)
alegué (alegar)
alejar (1), to move away
alelar (1), to stupefy
alentar (ie) (37), to encourage
alertar (1), to alert
aletargar (9), to make lethargic
aletargarse (9) (4), to become lethargic
aletargue, etc. (aletargar)
aletargué (aletargar)
aletear (1), to beat or flap wings or fins
alfabetice, etc. (alfabetizar)
alfabeticé (alfabetizar)
alfabetizar (11), to alphabetize
alfeñicarse (8) (4), to be finical
alfeñique, etc. (alfeñicarse)
alfeñiqué (alfeñicarse)
alfilerar (1), to pin
alfombrar (1), to carpet
alforce, etc. (alforzar)
alforcé (alforzar)
alforzar (11), to pleat

aliar (61), to ally
aliarse (61 (4), to become allied
alienar (1), to alienate
alienarse (1) (4), to become alienated
alienta, etc. (**alentar**)
aliente, etc. (**alentar**)
aliento (**alentar**)
aligerar (1), to lighten, to hasten
alijar (1), to sandpaper
alimentar (1), to feed
alindar (1), to mark off
alisar (1), to smooth
alistar (1), to enlist
alistarse (1) (4), to get ready
aliviar (1), to alleviate
almacenar (1), to store
almibarar (1), to preserve in syrup
almidonar (1), to starch
almohadillar (1), to pad, to cushion
almonedar (1), to auction
almorcé (**almorzar**)
almorcemos (**almorzar**)
almorzar (ue) (46), to eat lunch
almuerce, etc. (**almorzar**)
almuerza, etc. (**almorzar**)
almuerzo (**almorzar**)
alojar (1), to lodge
alongar (9), to lengthen
alongue, etc. (**alongar**)
alongué (**alongar**)
aloquecerse (73) (4), to go crazy
aloquezca, etc. (**aloquecerse**)
aloquezco (**aloquecerse**)
alquilar (1), to rent
alquilarse (1) (4), to hire oneself out, to be for rent
alquitranar (1), to tar
alterar (1), to alter
alterarse (1) (4), to get irritated
altercar (8), to argue
alternar (1), to alternate
alterque, etc. (**altercar**)
alterqué (**altercar**)
altivecerse (73) (4), to become haughty
altivezca, etc. (**altivecerse**)
altivezco (**altivecerse**)
alucinar (1), to hallucinate
aludir (3), to allude
alumbrar (1), to illuminate
alumbrarse (1) (4), to get tipsy
alzar (11), to raise
alzarse (11) (4), to rise
allanar (1), to level
allegar (9), to gather
allegarse (9) (4), to approach
allegue, etc. (**allegar**)
allegué (**allegar**)
amaestrar (1), to train, to tame
amagar (9), to hint
amague, etc. (**amagar**)
amagué (**amagar**)
amalgamar (1), to amalgamate
amamantar (1), to nurse
amancillar (1), to stain
amanecer (73), to dawn
amanezca (**amanecer**)
amansar (1), to tame
amar (1), to love
amarar (1), to alight on water
amargar (9), to make bitter
amargarse (9) (4), to become bitter
amargue, etc. (**amargar**)
amargué (**amargar**)
amarillear (1), to show yellow
amarillecer (73), to become yellow
amarillezca, etc. (**amarillecer**)

amarillezco (**amarillecer**)
amarrar (1), to tie up
amartelar (1), to make jealous
amartillar (1), to hammer
amasar (1), to knead, to amass
ambicionar (1), to earnestly desire
ambientar (1), to give atmosphere to
ambular (1), to walk, to move about
amedrentar (1), to frighten
amedrentarse (1) (4), to get scared
amelgar (9), to plow regularly
amelgue, etc. (**amelgar**)
amelgué (**amelgar**)
amenace, etc. (**amenazar**)
amenacé (**amenazar**)
amenazar (11), to threaten
amenguar (10), to diminish
amengüe, etc. (**amenguar**)
amengüé (**amenguar**)
amenice, etc. (**amenizar**)
amenicé (**amenizar**)
amenizar (11), to make agreeable
amentar (ie) (37), to fasten with a strap
americanice, etc. (**americanizar**)
americanicé (**americanizar**)
americanizar (11), to Americanize
ametrallar (1), to machine-gun
amienta, etc. (**amentar**)
amiente, etc. (**amentar**)
amiento (**amentar**)
amilanar (1), to intimidate
aminorar (1), to diminish
amistarse (1) (4), to become friends
amnistiar (61), to grant amnesty
amoblar (ue) (36), to furnish
amodorrarse (1) (4), to become drowsy
amodorrecer (73), to make drowsy
amodorrezca, etc. (**amodorrecer**)
amodorrezco (**amodorrecer**)
amohecer (73), to mold
amohezca, etc. (**amohecer**)
amohezco (**amohecer**)
amohína, etc. (**amohinar**)
amohinar (34), to annoy
amohinarse (34) (4), to get annoyed
amohíne, etc. (**amohinar**)
amohíno (**amohinar**)
amolar (ue) (36), to sharpen
amoldar (1), to mold
amonedar (1), to coin
amonestar (1), to admonish
amontonar (1), to pile
amoratar (1), to make black and blue
amoratarse (1) (4), to become black and blue
amordace, etc. (**amordazar**)
amordacé (**amordazar**)
amordazar (11), to muzzle
amorrar (1), to hang one's head
amorrarse (1) (4), to sulk
amortace, etc. (**amortazar**)
amortacé (**amortazar**)
amortazar (11), to shroud
amortecer (73), to tone down
amortezca, etc. (**amortecer**)
amortezco (**amortecer**)
amortice, etc. (**amortizar**)
amorticé (**amortizar**)
amortiguar (10), to soften, to moderate
amortigüe, etc. (**amortiguar**)
amortigüé (**amortiguar**)
amortizar (11), to amortize
amoscarse (8) (4), to become annoyed
amosque, etc. (**amoscarse**)
amosqué (**amoscarse**)
amostace, etc. (**amostazar**)

amostacé (**amostazar**)
amostazar (11), to anger
amotinar (1), to incite to riot or mutiny
amover (ue) (38), to remove
amparar (1), to protect
ampararse (1) (4), to seek protection
ampliar (61), to amplify
amplificar (8), to amplify
amplifique, etc. (**amplificar**)
amplifiqué (**amplificar**)
ampollarse (1) (4), to blister
amputar (1), to amputate
amuebla, etc. (**amoblar**) (**amueblar**)
amueblar (1), to furnish
amueble, etc. (**amoblar**) (**amueblar**)
amueblo (**amoblar**) (**amueblar**)
amuela, etc. (**amolar**)
amuele, etc. (**amolar**)
amuelo (**amolar**)
amueva, etc. (**amover**)
amueve, etc. (**amover**)
amuevo (**amover**)
amunicionar (1), to supply with ammunition
amurallar (1), to wall
amurcar (8), to hit with the horns
amurque, etc. (**amurcar**)
amurqué (**amurcar**)
amusgar (9), to throw back the ears (said of animals), to squint to see better
amusgue, etc. (**amusgar**)
amusgué (**amusgar**)
anadear (1), to waddle
analice, etc. (**analizar**)
analicé (**analizar**)
analizar (11), to analyze
anarquice, etc. (**anarquizar**)
anarquicé (**anarquizar**)
anarquizar (11), to spread anarchism
anatomice, etc. (**anatomizar**)
anatomicé (**anatomizar**)
anatomizar (11), to anatomize
anclar (1), to anchor
ancorar (1), to anchor
anchar (1), to widen
andar (77), to walk, to go, to run (clock)
anduve (**andar**)
anduviera, etc. (**andar**)
anduviere, etc. (**andar**)
anduvieron (**andar**)
anduviese, etc. (**andar**)
anduvimos (**andar**)
anduviste (**andar**)
anduvisteis (**andar**)
anduvo (**andar**)
aneblar (ie) (37), to cloud
anegar (ie) (50), to flood
anegué (**anegar**)
aneguemos, etc. (**anegar**)
anestesiar (1), to anesthetize
anexar (1), to annex
angostar (1), to narrow
angustiar (1), to afflict
anhelar (1), to desire eagerly
anidar (1), to nestle
aniebla, etc. (**aneblar**) (**anieblar**)
anieblar (1), to cloud
anieble, etc. (**aneblar**) (**anieblar**)
anieblo (**aneblar**) (**anieblar**)
aniega, etc. (**anegar**)
aniego (**anegar**)
aniegue, etc. (**anegar**)
anillar (1), to make into rings
animalice, etc. (**animalizar**)
animalicé (**animalizar**)
animalizar (11), to animalize

animar (1), to encourage

aniñarse (1) (4), to act childishly, to become childish

aniquilar (1), to annihilate

anochecer (73), to grow dark (day)

anochezca (anochecer)

anonadar (1), to overwhelm, to destroy

anotar (1), to note

anquilosarse (1) (4), to become stiff in the joints

ansiar (1) or (61), to long for, to yearn to

anteceder (2), to precede

antedecir (i, i) (84), to predict

antedí (antedecir)

antedice, etc. (antedecir)

antediciendo (antedecir)

antedicho (antedecir)

antediga, etc. (antedecir)

antedigo (antedecir)

antedije (antedecir)

antedijera, etc. (antedecir)

antedijere, etc. (antedecir)

antedijeron (antedecir)

antedijese, etc. (antedecir)

antedijimos (antedecir)

antedijiste (antedecir)

antedijisteis (antedecir)

antedijo (antedecir)

antediré, etc. (antedecir)

antediría, etc. (antedecir)

antepagar (9), to pay in advance

antepague, etc. (antepagar)

antepagué (antepagar)

antepón (anteponer)

antepondré, etc. (anteponer)

antepondría, etc. (anteponer)

anteponer (98), to place in front, to prefer

anteponga, etc. (anteponer)

antepongo (anteponer)

antepuesto (anteponer)

antepuse (anteponer)

antepusiera, etc. (anteponer)

antepusiere, etc. (anteponer)

antepusieron (anteponer)

antepusiese, etc. (anteponer)

antepusimos (anteponer)

antepusiste (anteponer)

antepusisteis (anteponer)

antepuso (anteponer)

antevea, etc. (antever)

anteveo (antever)

anteveía, etc. (antever)

antever (112), to foresee

antevisto (antever)

anticipar (1), to anticipate, to advance (money), to lend, to cause to happen before the regular time

anticiparse (1) (4), to act or happen before the regular time

anticuar (1) or (62), to antiquate

anticuarse (1) or (62) (4), to become acquainted

antiguarse (10) (4), to attain seniority

antigüe, etc. (antiguarse)

antigüé (antiguarse)

antipatice, etc. (antipatizar)

antipaticé (antipatizar)

antipatizar (11), to arouse a strong dislike

antojarse (124), to strike

anublar (1), to cloud, to obscure

anublarse (1) (4), to become cloudy

anudar (1), to know, to tie

anudarse (1) (4), to get knotted

anular (1), to annul

anunciar (1), to announce, to advertise

añadir (3), to add

añascar (8), to gather together bit by bit

añasque, etc. (añascar)

añasqué (añascar)

añejar (1), to age

añilar (1), to use bluing (on clothes)

añorar (1), to long for

añusgar (9), to choke

añusgue, etc. (añusgar)

añusgué (añusgar)

aojar (1), to cast the evil eye

aovillarse (1) (4), to shrink

apabullar (1), to crush

apacentar (ie) (37), to pasture

apacentarse (ie) (37) (4), to feed on

apacienta, etc. (apacentar)

apaciente, etc. (apacentar)

apaciento (apacentar)

apaciguar (10), to pacify

apaciguarse (10) (4), to calm down

apacigüe, etc. (apaciguar)

apacigüé (apaciguar)

apachurrar (1), to crush

apadrinar (1), to act as a godfather, to be best man, to back

apagar (9), to put out, to extinguish, to turn off

apague, etc. (apagar)

apagué (apagar)

apalabrar (1), to speak for, to reserve

apalancar (8), to move or raise with a crowbar

apalanque, etc. (apalancar)

apalanqué (apalancar)

apalear (1), to shovel, to beat (with a stick)

apandar (1), to swipe

apandillarse (1) (4), to band together

apantanar (1), to make swampy

apantanarse (1) (4), to get swampy, to get stuck in the mud

apañar (1), to pick up, to repair

apañarse (1) (4), to scheme, to maneuver

aparcar (8), to park

aparear (1), to make even, to pair

aparecer (73), to appear

aparejar (1), to prepare, to harness

aparentar (1), to pretend, to look to be

aparezca, etc. (aparecer)

aparezco (aparecer)

aparque, etc. (aparcar)

aparqué (aparcar)

aparroquiar (1), to get customers

apartar (1), to separate

apasionar (1), to arouse passion

apasionarse (1) (4), to become impassioned

apayasarse (1) (4), to clown around

apear (1), to dismount

apearse (1) (4), to get off, to get out

apedace, etc. (apedazar)

apedacé (apedazar)

apedazar (11), to piece out, to mend, to patch

apedrear (1), to stone

apegarse (9) (4), to become attached

apegue, etc. (apegarse)

apegué (apegarse)

apelar (1), to appeal, to have recourse

apelmace, etc. (apelmazar)

apelmacé (apelmazar)

apelmazar (11), to compress

apelotonar (1), to bunch together, to pile up

apellidar (1), to call by one's surname

apenar (1), to cause sorrow

apenarse (1) (4), to grieve

apercibir (3), to prepare, to provide

apercibirse (3) (4), to get ready

apercollar (ue) (36), to grab by the neck

apercuella, etc. (apercollar)

apercuelle, etc. (apercollar)

apercuello (apercollar)

apersonarse (1) (4), to appear in person

apesadumbrar (1), to grieve

apestar (1), to stink

apetecer (73), to crave

apetezca, etc. (apetecer)

apetezco (apetecer)

apiadar (1), to move to pity

apiadarse (1) (4), to have pity

apilar (1), to pile

apiñar (1), to squeeze together

apisonar (1), to roll with a roller

aplacar (8), to placate, to satisfy

aplace, etc. (aplacer) (aplazar)

aplacé (aplazar)

aplacer (73), to please

aplanar (1), to level, to astound

aplaque, etc. (aplacar)

aplaqué (aplacar)

aplastar (1), to smash, to leave someone speechless

aplaudir (3), to applaud

aplazar (11), to postpone

aplazca, etc. (aplacer)

aplazco (aplacer)

aplicar (8), to apply

aplicarse (8) (4), to apply oneself, to devote oneself

aplique, etc. (aplicar)

apliqué (aplicar)

aplomar (1), to plumb, to make straight with a plumb

aplomarse (1) (4), to collapse, to fall to the ground

apocar (8), to lessen, to humiliate, to humble

apocopar (1), to apocopate

apodar, (1), to nickname

apoderarse (1) (4), to take possession

apolillarse (1) (4), to become moth-eaten

apologice, etc. (apologizar)

apologicé (apologizar)

apologizar (11), to praise, to defend

apoltronarse (1) (4), to sprawl in a chair, to become lazy

apoque, etc. (apocar)

apoqué (apocar)

aporrear (1), to club

aportar (1), to contribute, to bring

aposentar (1), to lodge

aposentarse (1) (4), to take lodging

aposesionar (1), to give possession

aposesionarse (1) (4), to take possession

apostar (ue) (36), to bet

apostatar (1), to apostatize

apostillar (1), to comment, to note

apoyar (1), to lean, to support

apreciar (1), to appreciate, to appraise, to esteem

aprehender (2), to apprehend

apremiar (1), to urge, to harass

aprender (2), to learn

aprensar (1), to press

apresar (1), to seize, to capture

aprestar (1), to make ready

aprestarse (1) (4), to get ready

apresurar (1), to hurry

apretar (ie) (37), to press, to squeeze, to fit tightly

apretujar (1), to jam, to press hard

aprieta, etc. (apretar)

apriete, etc. (apretar)

aprieto (apretar)
apriscar (8), to gather (sheep) into the fold
aprisionar (1), to imprison
aprisque, etc. **(apriscar)**
aprisqué (apriscar)
aprobar (ue) (36), to approve, to pass an examination
aprontar (1), to prepare quickly, to hand over without delay
apropiar (1) (4), to appropriate
aprovechar (1), to make use, to be useful
aprovecharse (1)(4), to take advantage of
aprovisionar (1), to supply
aproximar (1), to bring near
aproximarse (1) (4), to get near
aprueba, etc. **(aprobar)**
apruebe, etc. **(aprobar)**
apruebo (aprobar)
apuesta, etc. **(apostar)**
apueste, etc. **(apostar)**
apuesto (apostar)
apuntalar (1), to prop
apuntar (1), to point at, to point out, to take note, to aim, to prompt, to begin to show
apuñalar (1), to stab
apuñetear (1), to punch with the fist
apurar (1), to exhaust, to hurry
apurarse (1) (4), to worry, to hurry
aquejar (1), to afflict
aquejarse (1) (4), to complain
aquietar (1), to quiet
aquietarse (1) (4), to quiet down
aquilatar (1), to assay, to appraise, to appreciate (in value)
arabice, etc. **(arabizar)**
arabicé (arabizar)
arabizar (11), to make Arabic, to Arabize
arañar (1), to scratch
arar (1), to plow
arbitrar (1), to referee
arcar (8), to arch, to beat (wool)
arcillar (1), to improve soil by adding clay
archivar (1), to file
arder (1), to burn
arenar (1), to spread sand
arengar (9), to harangue
arengue, etc. **(arengar)**
arengué (arengar)
argentar (1), to silver
argüir (72), to argue
argumentar (1), to argue
arguya, etc. **(argüir)**
arguye, etc. **(argüir)**
arguyendo (argüir)
arguyera, etc. **(argüir)**
arguyere, etc. **(argüir)**
arguyeron (argüir)
arguyese, etc. **(argüir)**
arguyo, etc. **(argüir)**
arguyó (argüir)
aridecerse (73) (4), to become arid, to become dry
aridezca, etc. **(aridecerse)**
armar (1), to arm, to assemble
arponear (1), to harpoon
arque, etc. **(arcar)**
arqué (arcar)
arquear (1), to arch
arracimarse (1) (4), to cluster
arraigar (9), to take root
arraigue, etc. **(arraigar)**
arraigué (arraigar)
arramblar (1), to sweep away
arrancar (8), to pull out, to start
arranque, etc. **(arrancar)**

arranqué (arrancar)
arrasar (1), to level, demolish
arrasarse (1) (4), to clear up (said of the sky)
arrastrar (1), to drag
arrastrarse (1) (4), to crawl
arrear (1), to urge on (horses, etc.)
arrearse (1) (4), to be ruined, to lose all one's money
arrebañar (1), to clean up (usually a plate, bowl, etc., with a piece of bread)
arrebolarse (1) (4), for clouds to become reddish
arreciar (1), to grow worse
arrecirse (116) (4), to grow stiff with cold
arreglar (1), to fix, to repair
arrellanarse (1)(4), to sprawl in one's seat
arremangar (9), to turn up (sleeves), to tuck up
arremangarse (9) (4), to turn up one's sleeves, to tuck one's dress
arremangue, etc. **(arremangar)**
arremangué (arremangar)
arrematar (1), to finish
arremeter (2), to rush forth
arremolinarse (1) (4), to whirl, to form a crowd, to crowd
arrendar (ie) (37), to rent
arrepentirse (ie, i) (41) (4), to repent, to back down
arrepienta, etc. **(arrepentirse)**
arrepiente, etc. **(arrepentirse)**
arrepiento (arrepentirse)
arrepintamos, etc. **(arrepentirse)**
arrepintiendo (arrepentirse)
arrepintiera, etc. **(arrepentirse)**
arrepintiere, etc. **(arrepentirse)**
arrepintieron (arrepentirse)
arrepintiese, etc. **(arrepentirse)**
arrepintió (arrepentirse)
arrestar (1), to arrest
arrestarse (1) (4), to rush ahead boldly
arrezagar (9), to tuck up
arrezague, etc. **(arrezagar)**
arrezagué (arrezagar)
arriar (61), to lower
arribar (1), to arrive
arrienda, etc. **(arrendar)**
arriende, etc. **(arrendar)**
arriendo (arrendar)
arriesgar (9), to risk
arriesgarse (9) (4), to take a risk
arriesgue, etc. **(arriesgar)**
arriesgué (arriesgar)
arrimar (1), to bring close
arrimarse (1) (4), to come close
arrinconar (1), to corner, to abandon
arrodillarse (1), to kneel
arrojar (1), to throw, to emit
arrollar (1), to trample upon
arromper (104), to plow (untilled ground)
arropar (1), to wrap up (with clothing)
arrostrar (1), to face
arroto (arromper)
arrugar (1), to wrinkle
arruinar (1), to ruin
arruinarse (1) (4), to go to ruin
arrullar (1), to coo
arrumbar (1), to lay aside (as useless)
articular (1), to articulate
asaetear (1), to shoot with arrows
asalariar (1), to fix a salary
asalariarse (1) (4), to work for a salary
asaltar (1), to assault
asar (1), to roast
asarse (1) (4), to be extremely hot

ascender (ie) (39), to promote, to ascend, to be promoted, to amount to
ascienda, etc. **(ascender)**
asciende, etc. **(ascender)**
asciendo (ascender)
asear (1), to clean up
asearse (1) (4), to get cleaned up
asediar (1), to besiege
asegurar (1), to make secure, to assure, to assert, to insure
asegurarse (1) (4), to make oneself sure, to get insured
asemejar (1), to make like
asemejarse (1) (4), to be similar
asentar (ie) (37), to seat
asentir (ie, i) (41), to assent
aserrar (ie) (37), to saw
asesinar (1), to assassinate
asesorar (1), to advise
asesorarse (1) (4), to seek advice
asestar (1), to aim, to deal a blow
aseverar (1), to assert
asfaltar (1), to asphalt
asfixiar (1), to asphyxiate
asfixiarse (1) (4), to be asphyxiated
asga, etc. **(asir)**
asgo (asir)
asienta, etc. **(asentar) (asentir)**
asiente, etc. **(asentar) (asentir)**
asiento (asentar) (asentir)
asierra, etc. **(aserrar)**
asierre, etc. **(aserrar)**
asierro (aserrar)
asignar (1), to assign
asilar (1), to give refuge, to place in an asylum, to silo
asilarse (1) (4), to take refuge
asimilar (1), to assimilate
asimilarse (1) (4), to resemble
asintamos, etc. **(asentir)**
asintiendo (asentir)
asintiera, etc. **(asentir)**
asintiere, etc. **(asentir)**
asintieron (asentir)
asintiese, etc. **(asentir)**
asintió (asentir)
asir (78), to grasp
asirse (78) (4), to take hold
asistir (3), to assist, to attend
asociar (1), to associate
asolar (ue) (36), to raze
asolear (1), to sun
asolearse (1) (4), to get suntanned
asomar (1), to show something out through an opening or from behind something
asomarse (1) (4), to lean out, to go out
asombrar (1), to astonish, to amaze
asombrarse (1)(4), to be astonished, to be amazed
asordar (1), to deafen
asosegar (ie) (50), to calm
asosegué (asosegar)
asoseguemos, etc. **(asosegar)**
asosiega, etc. **(asosegar)**
asosiego (asosegar)
asosiegue, etc. **(asosegar)**
aspirar (1), to inhale, to aspire
asquear (1), to disgust, to nauseate
astillar (1), to splinter
astringir (16), to constrict
astrinja, etc. **(astringir)**
astrinjo (astringir)
asuela, etc. **(asolar)**
asuele, etc. **(asolar)**
asuelo (asolar)
asumir (3), to assume

asustar (1), to scare
asustarse (1) (4), to get scared
atacar (8), to attack
atajar (1), to intercept, to take a shortcut
atañendo (atañer)
atañer (28), to concern
atañera, etc. **(atañer)**
atañere, etc. **(atañer)**
atañeron (atañer)
atañese, etc. **(atañer)**
atañó (atañer)
ataque, etc. **(atacar)**
ataqué (atacar)
atar (1), to tie
atarse (1) (4), to get tied up
atarantar (1), to stun
atardecer (73), to draw towards evening, to grow late, to grow dark (day)
atardezca (atardecer)
atarear (1), to assign a task
atarearse (1) (4), to busy oneself, to be very busy
atarugar (9), to make someone be quiet, to nail something down with wooden pegs
atarugarse (9) (4), to get confused
atarugue, etc. **(atarugar)**
atarugué (atarugar)
atascar (8), to stop up, to plug up
atascarse (8) (4), to get stuck, to get stopped up
atasque, etc. **(atascar)**
atasqué (atascar)
ataviar (61), to attire, to adorn
ataviarse (61) (4), to dress up
atece, etc. **(atezarse)**
atecé (atezarse)
atediar (1), to bore
atediarse (1) (4), to get bored
atemorice, etc. **(atemorizar)**
atemoricé (atemorizar)
atemorizar (11), to frighten
atemorizarse (11) (4), to get frightened
atemperar (1), to temper
atender (ie) (39), to attend, to pay attention, to take care, to take into account, to wait on
atenderé, etc. **(atenerse)**
atendría, etc. **(atenerse)**
atenebrarse (1) (4), to become dark
atenerse (ie) (108) (4), to abide (by)
atenga, etc. **(atenerse)**
atengo (atenerse)
atentar (1), to attempt
atente (atenerse) (atentar)
atenuar (62), to lessen, to tone down
aterirse (116) (4), to become stiff with cold
aterrar (1), to terrify
aterrar (ie) (37), to cover with earth
aterrarse (1) (4), to become frightened
aterrice, etc. **(aterrizar)**
aterricé (aterrizar)
aterrizar (11), to land
aterrorice, etc. **(aterrorizar)**
aterroricé (aterrorizar)
aterrorizar (11), to terrify
atesorar (1), to treasure, to hoard up
atestar (1), to attest, to cram, to stuff
atestar (ie) (37), to cram, to stuff
atestiguar (10), to testify, to attest
atestigüe, etc. **(atestiguar)**
atestigüé (atestiguar)
atezarse (11) (4), to become tanned
atiborrar (1), to stuff
atiborrarse (1) (4), to gorge
atice, etc. **(atizar)**
aticé (atizar)

atienda, etc. **(atender)**
atiende, etc. **(atender)**
atiendo (atender)
atiene, etc. **(atenerse)**
atierra, etc. **(aterrar)** (ie) (37)
atierre, etc. **(aterrar)** (ie) (37)
atierro (aterrar) (ie) (37)
atiesar (1), to stiffen
atiesta, etc. **(atestar)** (ie) (37)
atieste, etc. **(atestar)** (ie) (37)
atiesto (atestar) (ie) (37)
atildar (1), to spruce up
atinar (1), to guess right
atiriendo (aterirse)
atiriera, etc. **(aterirse)**
atiriere, etc. **(aterirse)**
atirieron (aterirse)
atiriese, etc. **(aterirse)**
atirió (aterirse)
atisbar (1), to look cautiously, to catch a glimpse
atizar (11), to stir up, to poke (a fire), to rouse, to let have it (slap, kick, etc.)
atolondrar (1), to confuse
atolondrarse (1) (4), to get confused
atollarse (1) (4), to get stuck
atomice, etc. **(atomizar)**
atomicé (atomizar)
atomizar (11), to atomize
atontar (1), to stupefy
atontarse (1) (4), to become stupefied
atorar (1), to obstruct
atormentar (1), to torment
atornillar (1), to screw
atosigar (9), to poison, to urge with insistence
atosigue, etc. **(atosigar)**
atosigué (atosigar)
atracar (8), to cram, to approach land, to hold up
atracarse (8) (4), to over eat
atraer (109), to attract
atragantar (1), to choke
atraiga, etc. **(atraer)**
atraigo (atraer)
atraje (atraer)
atrajera, etc. **(atraer)**
atrajere, etc. **(atraer)**
atrajeron (atraer)
atrajese, etc. **(atraer)**
atrajimos (atraer)
atrajiste (atraer)
atrajisteis (atraer)
atrajo (atraer)
atramparse (1) (4), to be trapped
atrancar (8), to bar, to obstruct
atrancarse (8) (4), to get stuck
atranque, etc. **(atrancar)**
atranqué (atrancar)
atrapar (1), to trap
atraque, etc. **(atracar)**
atraqué (atracar)
atrasar (1), to slow down, to set back, to delay
atrasarse (1) (4), to go slow, to fall behind
atravesar (ie) (37), to put or lay across, to cross, to pierce, to go through
atraviesa, etc. **(atravesar)**
atraviese, etc. **(atravesar)**
atravieso (atravesar)
atrayendo (atraer)
atreverse (2) (4), to dare
atribuir (71), to attribute
atribular (1), to afflict
atribuya, etc. **(atribuir)**
atribuye, etc. **(atribuir)**

atribuyendo (atribuir)
atribuyera, etc. **(atribuir)**
atribuyere, etc. **(atribuir)**
atribuyeron (atribuir)
atribuyese, etc. **(atribuir)**
atribuyo (atribuir)
atribuyó (atribuir)
atrofiar (1), to atrophy
atronar (ue) (36), to deafen or disturb with thunderlike noise
atropellar (1), to run over, to offend
atropellarse (1) (4), to move, talk or act hastily
atruena, etc. **(atronar)**
atruene, etc. **(atronar)**
atrueno (atronar)
atufarse (1) (4), to get angry
aturdir (3), to stun
aturdirse (3) (4), to be stunned
atusar (1), to trim, to smooth hair with hand or comb
atusarse (1) (4), to dress too fancily
atuve, etc. **(atenerse)**
atuviera, etc. **(atenerse)**
atuviere, etc. **(atenerse)**
atuvieron (atenerse)
atuviese, etc. **(atenerse)**
atuvimos (atenerse)
atuviste (atenerse)
atuvisteis (atenerse)
atuvo (atenerse)
augurar (1), to augur, to foretell
aullar (65), to howl
aumentar (1), to increase
aunar (65), to unite
auscultar (1), to examine with a stethoscope
ausentar (1), to send away
ausentarse (1) (4), to absent oneself, to leave
auspiciar (1), to support
autenticar (8), to authenticate
autentique, etc. **(autenticar)**
autentiqué (autenticar)
autografiar (61), to autograph
autorice, etc. **(autorizar)**
autoricé (autorizar)
autorizar (11), to authorize
auxiliar (1) or (61), to help
avalar (1), to guarantee with a letter of credit or similar document
avalorar (1), to estimate
avaluar (62), to appraise
avance, etc. **(avanzar)**
avancé (avanzar)
avanzar (11), to advance
avasallar (1), to dominate
avece, etc. **(avezar)**
avecé (avezar)
avecindar (1), to reside
avecindarse (1) (4), to take up residence (in a city or town)
avén (avenir)
avendré (avenir)
avendría, etc. **(avenir)**
avenga, etc. **(avenir)**
avengo (avenir)
avenir (ie, i) (111), to reconcile
avenirse (ie, i) (111) (4), to agree
aventajar (1), to excel
aventajarse (1) (4), to get ahead of
aventar (ie) (37), to fan
aventurar (1), to adventure
avergoncé (avergonzar)
avergoncemos, etc. **(avergonzar)**
avergonzar (ue) (49), to shame

avergonzarse (ue) (49) (4), to be ashamed
avergüence, etc. **(avergonzar)**
avergüenza, etc. **(avergonzar)**
avergüenzo (avergonzar)
averiar (61), to damage
averiarse (61) (4), to become damaged
averiguar (10), to find out
averigüe, etc. **(averiguar)**
averigüé (averiguar)
avezar (11), to accustom
avezarse (11) (4), to become accustomed
aviar (61), to prevent, to prepare something for the road, to get ready, to prepare, to provide
aviene, etc. **(avenir)**
avienta, etc. **(aventar)**
aviente, etc. **(aventar)**
aviento (aventar)
avinagrar (1), to sour
avinagrarse (1) (4), to turn sour
avine (avenir)
aviniendo (avenir)
aviniera, etc. **(avenir)**
aviniere, etc. **(avenir)**
avinieron (avenir)
aviniese, etc. **(avenir)**
avinimos (avenir)
aviniste (avenir)
avinisteis (avenir)
avino (avenir)
avisar (1), to inform, to let know
avistar (1), to glimpse
avistarse (1) (4), to meet
avivar (1), to enliven
ayudar (1), to help
ayunar (1), to fast
azararse (1) (4), to get rattled
azorarse (1) (4), to be abashed
azotar (1), to whip
azucarar (1), to sugar
azuce, etc. **(azuzar)**
azucé (azuzar)
azular (1), to color blue
azularse (1) (4), to turn blue
azulejar (1), to tile
azuzar (11), to sick, to incite

B

babear (1), to slobber
bailar (1), to dance
bajar (1), to lower, to take down, to come down, to go down, to get off, to go downstairs
balancear (1), to rock, to swing
balar (1), to bleat
balbucear (1), to stammer, to stutter, to babble
balbucir (118), to stammer, to stutter, to babble
balbuzca (balbucir)
balbuzco (balbucir)
baldar (1), to cripple
baldear (1), to wash with pails of water (decks, floors, etc.)
baldonar (1), to affront
baldosar (1), to tile
balear (1), to shoot
balice, etc. **(balizar)**
balicé (balizar)
balizar (11), to mark with buoys or flares
bambolear (1), to sway
bandearse (1) (4), to shift for oneself
bañar (1), to bathe
bañarse (1) (4), to take a bath
barajar (1), to shuffle

baratear (1), to sell at a bargain
barnice, etc. **(barnizar)**
barnicé (barnizar)
barnizar (11), to varnish
barrenar (1), to drill
barrer (2), to sweep
barruntar (1), to guess
basar (1), to base
basarse (1) (4), to base one's judgment
bastar (11), to be enough
batallar (1), to battle
batear (1), to bat
batir (3), to beat
bautice, etc. **(bautizar)**
bauticé (bautizar)
bautizar (11), to baptize
beber (2), to drink
beberse (2) (4), to drink up
becar (8), to grant a scholarship or fellowship
befar (1), to scoff
bendecir (i, i) (79), to bless
bendice, etc. **(bendecir)**
bendiciendo (bendecir)
bendiga, etc. **(bendecir)**
bendigo (bendecir)
bendije (bendecir)
bendijera, etc. **(bendecir)**
bendijere, etc. **(bendecir)**
bendijeron (bendecir)
bendijese, etc. **(bendecir)**
bendijimos (bendecir)
bendijiste (bendecir)
bendijisteis (bendecir)
bendijo (bendecir)
beneficiar (1), to benefit
beneficiarse (1) (4), to profit
beque, etc. **(becar)**
bequé (becar)
besar (1), to kiss
bienquerer (ie) (101), to like
bienquerré, etc. **(bienquerer)**
bienquerría, etc. **(bienquerer)**
bienquiera, etc. **(bienquerer)**
bienquiere, etc. **(bienquerer)**
bienquiero (bienquerer)
bienquise (bienquerer)
bienquisiera, etc. **(bienquerer)**
bienquisiere, etc. **(bienquerer)**
bienquisieron (bienquerer)
bienquisiese, etc. **(bienquerer)**
bienquisimos (bienquerer)
bienquisiste (bienquerer)
bienquisisteis (bienquerer)
bienquiso (bienquerer)
bienquistar (1), to reconcile
bienquistarse (1) (4), to become reconciled
bifurcar (8), to divide into two (branches, roads, etc.)
bifurque, etc. **(bifurcar)**
bifurqué (bifurcar)
bilocar (8), to be in two places at the same time
biloque, etc. **(bilocar)**
biloqué (bilocar)
birlar (1), to filch
bisecar (8), to bisect
biselar (1), to bevel
biseque, etc. **(bisecar)**
bisequé (bisecar)
blandear (1), to soften
blandir (116), to brandish
blanquear (1), to whiten
blanquecer (73), to whiten
blanquezca, etc. **(blanquecer)**

blanquezco (blanquecer)
blasfemar (1), to blaspheme
blasonar (1), to boast
blindar (1), to armor-plate
bloquear (1), to block
bobear (1), to talk nonsense
bogar (9), to row
bogue, etc. **(bogar)**
bogué (bogar)
boicotear (1), to boycott
bolear (1), to shoot billiard balls (but not as part of a game), to bowl, to tell lies
bombardear (1), to bomb
bombear (1), to pump
bordear (1), to border, to stay on the edge
borrar (1), to erase
botar (1), to throw away, to bounce, to launch
boxear (1), to box
bracear (1), to swing one's arms
bramar (1), to bellow
bravear (1), to boast
bregar (9), to struggle
bregue, etc. **(bregar)**
bregué (bregar)
brillar (1), to shine
brincar (8), to hop, to jump
brindar (1), to toast, to offer
brinque, etc. **(brincar)**
brinqué (brincar)
bromear (1), to joke
broncear (1), to tan
brotar (1), to sprout
bruñendo (bruñir)
bruñera, etc. **(bruñir)**
bruñere, etc. **(bruñir)**
bruñeron (bruñir)
bruñese, etc. **(bruñir)**
bruñir (29), to polish
bruñó (bruñir)
brutalice (brutalizar)
brutalicé (brutalizar)
brutalizar (11), to brutalize
bucear (1), to dive
bufar (1), to snort, to blow
bufonear (1), to clown
bullendo (bullir)
bullera, etc. **(bullir)**
bullere, etc. **(bullir)**
bulleron (bullir)
bullese, etc. **(bullir)**
bullir (27), to boil
bulló (bullir)
burbujear (1), to bubble
burilar (1), to engrave with a burin
burlar (1), to mock, to deceive
burlarse (1) (4), to make fun
buscar (8), to look for, to provoke
busque, etc. **(buscar)**
busqué (buscar)

C

cabalgar (9), to ride horseback, to gallop
cabalgue, etc. **(cabalgar)**
cabalgué (cabalgar)
cabecear (1), to bob the head, to nod (in sleep)
cabellar (1), to grow hair, to put on false hair
caber (80), to fit, to have enough room
cablegrafiar (61), to cable
cabré, etc. **(caber)**
cabría, etc. **(caber)**
cacarear (1), to cackle, to exaggerate
cace, etc. **(cazar)**

cacé (cazar)
cachear (1), to frisk
cachondear (1), to arouse sexually
cachondearse (1) (4), to make fun of someone, to become sexually aroused
caducar (8), to dote, to be in one's dotage, to expire
caduque, etc. (caducar)
caduqué (caducar)
caer (81), to fall, to be located
cagar (9), to defecate, to spoil
cague, etc. (cagar)
cagué (cagar)
caiga, etc. (caer)
caigo (caer)
calafatear (1), to caulk
calar (1), to soak through, to pierce, to size up a person
calarse (1) (4), to become soaked
calcar (8), to trace, to copy
calce, etc. (calzar)
calcé (calzar)
calcificar (8), to calcify
calcifique, etc. (calcificar)
calcifiqué (calcificar)
calcinar (1), to calcine
calcular (1), to calculate
caldear (1), to heat up
caldearse (1) (4), to become heated
caldrá, etc. (caler)
caldría, etc. (caler)
calecer (73), to become hot
calefaccionar (1), to heat
calentar (ie) (37), to heat, to warm, to annoy
caler (110), to be necessary, to be worthwhile
calezca, etc. (calecer)
calezco (calecer)
calga, etc. (caler)
calibrar (1), to calibrate
calienta, etc. (calentar)
caliente, etc. (calentar)
caliento (calentar)
calificar (8), to qualify, to rate, to grade, to mark (exam paper)
califique, etc. (calificar)
califiqué (calificar)
calque, etc. (calcar)
calqué (calcar)
calzar (11), to put shoes on, to wear (a certain size of shoe), to block up
callar (1), to silence, not to mention
callarse (1) (4), to become silent
callejear (1), to loaf around the streets
cambalachear (1), to barter, to swap
cambiar (1), to change, to exchange
camelar (1), to cajole, to flirt
caminar (1), to walk, to go
campanear (1), to ring the bells
campar (1), to camp, to stand out
campear (1), to be in the field, to go to pasture, to grow green, to be prominent
camuflar (1), to camouflage
canalice, etc. (canalizar)
canalicé (canalizar)
canalizar (11), to canalize
cancelar (1), to cancel
canjear (1), to exchange
canonice, etc. (canonizar)
canonicé (canonizar)
canonizar (11), to canonize
cansar (1), to tire
cansarse (1) (4), to get tired
cantar (1), to sing
canturrear (1), to sing in a low voice

cañonear (1), to cannonade
capacitar (1), to enable, to qualify
capacitarse (1) (4), to become qualified, to become capacitated
capar (1), to castrate
capear (1), to duck, to beguile
capitalice, etc. (capitalizar)
capitalicé (capitalizar)
capitalizar (11), to capitalize, to compound (interest)
capitanear (1), to lead
capitular (1), to capitulate
capotear (1), to beguile, to duck
captar (1), to attract
capturar (1), to capture
caracolear (1), to caper
caracterice, etc. (caracterizar)
caractericé (caracterizar)
caracterizar (11), to characterize
caramelice, etc. (caramelizar)
caramelicé (caramelizar)
caramelizar (11), to caramelize
carbonatar (1), to carbonate
carbonear (1), to make charcoal
carbonice, etc. (carbonizar)
carbonicé (carbonizar)
carbonizar (11), to carbonize, to char
cardar (1), to card
carduce, etc. (carduzar)
carducé (carduzar)
carduzar (11), to card
carear (1), to bring face to face
carecer (73), to lack
carezca, etc. (carecer)
carezco (carecer)
cargar (9), to load, to charge (battery), to bore
cargue, etc. (cargar)
cargué (cargar)
cariar (61), to decay
cariarse (61) (4), to become decayed
caricaturice, etc. (caricaturizar)
caricaturicé (caricaturizar)
caricaturizar (11), to caricature
carnear (1), to slaughter, to butcher
carretear (1), to cart
casar (1), to marry
casarse (1) (4), to get married
cascabelear (1), to jingle
cascar (8), to crack
casque, etc. (cascar)
casqué (cascar)
castañetear (1), to snap one's fingers, to click castanets, to chatter (teeth)
castigar (9), to punish
castigue, etc. (castigar)
castigué (castigar)
castrar (1), to castrate
catar (1), to taste
catear (1), to flunk, to fail (a student)
catequice, etc. (catequizar)
catequicé (catequizar)
catequizar (11), to catechize
causar (1), to cause
cauterice, etc. (cauterizar)
cautericé (cauterizar)
cauterizar (11), to cauterize
cautivar (1), to capture, to charm
cavar (1), to dig
cavilar (1), to cavil, to quibble
cayendo (caer)
cayera, etc. (caer)
cayere, etc. (caer)
cayeron (caer)
cayese, etc. (caer)
cayó (caer)

cazar (11), to hunt
cebar (1), to fatten, to prime (a pump, a furnace), to bait (a fishhook)
cecear (1), to lisp, to pronounce Spanish s like c (before e or i) and z
ceder (2), to yield, to give up
cegar (ie) (50), to blind, to plug
cegarse (ie) (50) (4), to go blind
cegué (cegar)
ceguemos, etc. (cegar)
cejar (1), to back up
celar (1), to keep an eye or check on, to conceal
celebrar (1), to celebrate
cellisquear (1), to sleet
cementar (1), to cement
cenar (1), to have supper, to eat dinner
cencerrear (1), to jingle cowbells continuously, to rattle
centellear (1), to sparkle
centrar (1), to center
centrifugar (9), to centrifuge
centrifugue, etc. (centrifugar)
centrifugué (centrifugar)
centuplicar (8), to centuple
centuplique, etc. (centuplicar)
centupliqué (centuplicar)
ceñir (i, i) (60), to gird, to encircle
ceñirse (i, i) (60) (4), to limit oneself
cepillar (1), to brush, to plane
cercar (8), to encircle, to fence in, to lay seige to, to surround
cercenar (1), to trim, to cut down
cerciorar (1), to assure
cerciorarse (1) (4), to ascertain
cerner (ie) (39), to sift
cernerse (ie) (39) (4), to hover, to hang over, to threaten
cernir (ie) (85), to sift
cerque, etc. (cercar)
cerqué (cercar)
cerrar (ie) (37), to close, to lock
certificar (8), to certify, to certificate, to register (a letter)
certifique, etc. (certificar)
certifiqué (certificar)
cesar (1), to cease, to stop, to quit
ciar (19), to back water (nautical)
cicatear (1), to be stingy
cicatrice, etc. (cicatrizar)
cicatricé (cicatrizar)
cicatrizar (11), to close (a wound), to scar, to heal
ciega, etc. (cegar)
ciego (cegar)
ciegue, etc. (cegar)
cierna, etc. (cerner) (cernir)
cierne, etc. (cerner) (cernir)
cierno (cerner) (cernir)
cierra, etc. (cerrar)
cierre, etc. (cerrar)
cierro (cerrar)
cifrar (1), to cipher
cimbrear (1), to place a long, flexible thing in vibrating motion
cimbrearse (1) (4), to vibrate, to shake
cimentar [(ie) (37)] or (1), to found, to lay the foundation
cimienta, etc. (cimentar)
cimiente, etc. (cimentar)
cimiento (cimentar)
cincelar (1), to carve, to chisel
cinchar (1), to cinch
cinematografiar (61), to film
ciña, etc. (ceñir)
ciñe, etc. (ceñir)

ciñendo (ceñir)
ciñera, etc. (ceñir)
ciñere, etc. (ceñir)
ciñeron (ceñir)
ciñese, etc. (ceñir)
ciño (ceñir)
ciñó (ceñir)
circuir (73), to circle
circular (1), to circulate
circuncidar (1), to circumcise
circundar (1), to surround
circunnavegar (9), to circumnavigate
circunnavegue, etc. (circunnavegar)
circunnavegué (circunnavegar)
circunscribir (69), to circumscribe
circunscrito (circunscribir)
circunvalar (1), to surround
circunvolar (ue) (36), to fly around
circunvuela, etc. (circunvolar)
circunvuele, etc. (circunvolar)
circunvuelo (circunvolar)
circuya, etc. (circuir)
circuye, etc. (circuir)
circuyendo (circuir)
circuyera, etc. (circuir)
circuyere, etc. (circuir)
circuyeron (circuir)
circuyese, etc. (circuir)
circuyo (circuir)
circuyó (circuir)
citar (1), to make an appointment with, to cite
civilice, etc. (civilizar)
civilicé (civilizar)
civilizar (11), to civilize
cizañar (1), to sow discord
clamar (1), to cry out for
clarear (1), to clarify, to clear up
clarearse (1) (4), to show through, to be transparent (said of fabric)
clarecer (73), to dawn
clarezca (clarecer)
clarificar (8), to clarify
clarifique, etc. (clarificar)
clarifiqué (clarificar)
clasificar (8), to classify
clasifique, etc. (clasificar)
clasifiqué (clasificar)
claudicar (8), to yield, to weaken, to give up
claudique, etc. (claudicar)
claudiqué (claudicar)
clausurar (1), to close
clavar (1), to nail
clavetear (1), to stud, to nail
clocar (ue) (44), to cluck
cloqué (clocar)
cloquear (1), to cluck
cloquemos, etc. (clocar)
cloroformice, etc. (cloroformizar)
cloroformicé (cloroformizar)
cloroformizar (11), to chloroform
clueca, etc. (clocar)
clueco (clocar)
clueque, etc. (clocar)
coacervar (1), to heap up, to pile
coactar (1), to coerce
coadunar (1), to join closely together
coadyuvar (1), to help
coagular (1), to coagulate
coartar (1), to limit
cobardear (1), to be or act cowardly
cobijar (1), to cover
cobrar (1), to collect, to charge, to cash (check)
cocear (1), to kick (said of horses)

cocer (ue) (54), to cook, to boil, to bake, to fire (bricks)
cocinar (1), to cook
codear (1), to elbow
codearse (1) (4), to hobnob, to rub elbows with someone
codiciar (1), to covet
codificar (8), to codify
codifique, etc. (codificar)
codifiqué (codificar)
coercer (12), to coerce
coerza, etc. (coercer)
coerzo (coercer)
coexistir (3), to coexist
coextender (2), to coextend
coger (15), to seize, to pick, to catch, to get, to hold
cohabitar (1), to live together
cohechar (1), to bribe, to take a bribe
cohíba, etc. (cohibir)
cohíbe, etc. (cohibir)
cohibir (34), to restrain, to repress
cohíbo (cohibir)
coincidir (3), to coincide
coja, etc. (coger)
cojear (1), to limp, to wobble
cojo (coger)
colaborar (1), to collaborate
colacionar (1), to collate
colar (ue) (36), to strain
colarse (ue) (36) (4), to slip or sneak in
colchar (1), to quilt
colear (1), to wag the tail
coleccionar (1), to collect
colectar (1), to collect
colectivice, etc. (colectivizar)
colectivicé (colectivizar)
colectivizar (11), to collectivize
colectivizarse (11) (4), to become collectivized
colegir (i, i) (57), to gather, to infer
colgar (ue) (45), to hang, to dangle
colgué (colgar)
colguemos, etc. (colgar)
coligarse (9) (4), to join forces
colige, etc. (colegir)
coligiendo (colegir)
coligiera, etc. (colegir)
coligiere, etc. (colegir)
coligieron (colegir)
coligiese, etc. (colegir)
coligió (colegir)
coligue, etc. (coligar)
coligué (coligar)
colija, etc. (colegir)
colijo (colegir)
colindar (1), to border
colmar (1), to fill to the brim, to overwhelm, to shower with
colocar (8), to place
colocarse (8) (4), to get placed, to find a job
coloque, etc. (colocar)
coloqué (colocar)
colonice, etc. (colonizar)
colonicé (colonizar)
colonizar (11), to settle, to colonize
colorar (1), to color
colorear (1), to color
colorearse (1) (4), to redden
colorir (116), to color
coludir (3), to be in collusion
columbrar (1), to glimpse, to guess
columpiar (1), to swing
comadrear (1), to go around gossiping
comandar (1), to command

comanditar (1), to invest in (an undertaking) as a silent partner
comarcar (8), to border
comarque, etc. (comarcar)
comarqué (comarcar)
combar (1), to bend
combarse (1) (4), to warp
combatir (3), to combat
combinar (1), to combine
comediar (1), to divide into equal parts
comedirse (i, i) (42) (4), to be moderate, to be polite, to be obliging
comencé (comenzar)
comencemos, etc. (comenzar)
comentar (1), to comment, to gossip
comenzar (ie) (51), to begin, to start
comer (2), to eat
comercialice, etc. (comercializar)
comercialicé (comercializar)
comercializar (11), to commercialize
comerciar (1), to trade
comerse (2) (4), to eat up
cometer (2), to commit
comida, etc. (comedirse)
comide, etc. (comedirse)
comido (comedirse)
comidiendo (comedirse)
comidiera, etc. (comedirse)
comidiere, etc. (comedirse)
comidieron (comedirse)
comidiese, etc. (comedirse)
comidió (comedirse)
comience, etc. (comenzar)
comienza, etc. (comenzar)
comienzo (comenzar)
comisionar (1), to commission
compadecer (73), to pity, to feel sorry for
compadezca, etc. (compadecer)
compadezco (compadecer)
compadrar (1), to contract and/or have the relationship of father-godfather (with respect to each other), to be or become cronies
compadrear (1), to contract and/or have the relationship of father-godfather (with respect to each other), to be or become cronies
compaginar (1), to put in order
compaginarse (1) (4), to agree
comparar (1), to compare
comparecer (73), to appear
comparezca, etc. (comparecer)
comparezco (comparecer)
compartir (3), to divide, to share
compasar (1), to measure with a compass
compeler (2), to compel
compendiar (1), to summarize
compenetrarse (1) (4), to interpenetrate, to have the same thoughts and feelings
compensar (1), to compensate
competer (2), to belong, to be incumbent on
competir (i, i) (42), to compete
compilar (1), to compile
compita, etc. (competir)
compite, etc. (competir)
compito (competir)
compitiendo (competir)
compitiera, etc. (competir)
compitiere, etc. (competir)
compitieron (competir)
compitiese, etc. (competir)
compitió (competir)
complacer (73), to please
complacerse (73) (4), to be pleased
complazca, etc. (complacer)

complazco (complacer)
complementar (1), to complement
completar (1), to complete
complicar (8), to complicate, to involve
complicarse (8) (4), to become complicated, to become entangled
complique, etc. **(complicar)**
compliqué (complicar)
complotar (1), to plot
compón (componer)
compondré, etc. **(componer)**
compondría, etc. **(componer)**
componer (98), to fix, to compose
componga, etc. **(componer)**
compongo (componer)
comportar (1), to tolerate, to bear
comportarse (1) (4), to behave
comprar (1), to buy
comprender (2), to comprehend, to understand
comprimir (3), to compress
comprimirse (3) (4), to become compressed
comprobar (ue) (36), to verify, to check, to prove
comprometer (2), to compromise
comprometerse (2) (4), to become compromised
comprueba, etc. **(comprobar)**
compruebe, etc. **(comprobar)**
compruebo (comprobar)
compuesto (componer)
compungir (16), to make remorseful
compungirse (16) (4), to feel remorse
compunja, etc. **(compungir)**
compunjo (compungir)
compuse (componer)
compusiera, etc. **(componer)**
compusiere, etc. **(componer)**
compusieron (componer)
compusiese, etc. **(componer)**
compusimos (componer)
compusiste (componer)
compusisteis (componer)
compuso (componer)
computar (1), to compute
comulgar (9), to take communion
comulgue, etc. **(comulgar)**
comulgué (comulgar)
comunicar (8), to communicate
comunicarse (8) (4), to get in touch
comunice, etc. **(comunizar)**
comunicé (comunizar)
comunique, etc. **(comunicar)**
comuniqué (comunicar)
comunizar (11), to communize
comunizarse (11) (4), to become communistic
concadenar (1), to link together
concatenar (1), to link together
concebir (i, i) (42), to conceive
conceder (2), to concede, to grant
concentrar (1), to concentrate
conceptuar (62), to judge (form a concept of something)
concernir (ie) (85), to concern
concertar (ie) (37), to arrange, to conclude, to harmonize
concertarse (ie) (37) (4), to come to terms
conciba, etc. **(concebir)**
concibe, etc. **(concebir)**
concibiendo (concebir)
concibiera, etc. **(concebir)**
concibiere, etc. **(concebir)**
concibieron (concebir)
concibiese, etc. **(concebir)**

concibió (concebir)
concibo (concebir)
concierna, etc. **(concernir)**
concierne, etc. **(concernir)**
concierno (concernir)
concierta, etc. **(concertar)**
concierte, etc. **(concertar)**
concierto (concertar)
conciliar (1), to conciliate
concitar (1), to incite
concluir (71), to conclude, to finish
concluya, etc. **(concluir)**
concluye, etc. **(concluir)**
concluyendo (concluir)
concluyera, etc. **(concluir)**
concluyere, etc. **(concluir)**
concluyeron (concluir)
concluyese, etc. **(concluir)**
concluyo (concluir)
concluyó (concluir)
concordar (ue) (36), to agree
concretar (1), to concrete
concretarse (1) (4), to limit oneself
concuerda, etc. **(concordar)**
concuerde, etc. **(concordar)**
concuerdo (concordar)
conculcar (8), to trample underfoot, to violate
conculque, etc. **(conculcar)**
conculqué (conculcar)
concurrir (3), to concur, to gather
conchabar (1), to join
condecorar (1), to decorate (with honors, medals, etc.)
condenar (1), to condemn
condensar (1), to condense
condescender (ie) (39), to condescend
condescienda, etc. **(condescender)**
condesciende, etc. **(condescender)**
condesciendo (condescender)
condicionar (1), to condition
condimentar (1), to season
condoler (ue) (38), to sympathize
condonar (1), to condone
conducir (67), to conduct, to drive
conducirse (67) (4), to behave
conduela, etc. **(condoler)**
conduele, etc. **(condoler)**
conduelo (condoler)
conduje (conducir)
condujera, etc. **(conducir)**
condujere, etc. **(conducir)**
condujeron (conducir)
condujese, etc. **(conducir)**
condujimos (conducir)
condujiste (conducir)
condujisteis (conducir)
condujo (conducir)
conduzca, etc. **(conducir)**
conduzco (conducir)
conectar (1), to connect
conexionar (1), to connect
confabular (1), to chat
confabularse (1) (4), to connive, to scheme
confederar (1), to confederate
conferenciar (1), to confer
conferir (ie, i) (41), to bestow, to compare
confesar (ie) (37), to confess
confiar (61), to entrust, to confide
confiarse (61) (4), to trust, to become confident
confiera, etc. **(conferir)**
confiere, etc. **(conferir)**
confiero (conferir)
confiesa, etc. **(confesar)**

confiese, etc. **(confesar)**
confieso (confesar)
configurar (1), to shape, to form
configurarse (1) (4), to take shape, to take form
confinar (1), to confine, to border
confinarse (1) (4), to keep oneself confined
confiramos, etc. **(conferir)**
confiriendo (conferir)
confiriera, etc. **(conferir)**
confiriere, etc. **(conferir)**
confirieron (conferir)
confiriese, etc. **(conferir)**
confirió (conferir)
confirmar (1), to confirm
confiscar (8), to confiscate
confisque, etc. **(confiscar)**
confisqué (confiscar)
confitar (1), to preserve, to candy
confluir (71), to come together
confluya, etc. **(confluir)**
confluye, etc. **(confluir)**
confluyendo (confluir)
confluyera, etc. **(confluir)**
confluyere, etc. **(confluir)**
confluyeron (confluir)
confluyese, etc. **(confluir)**
confluyo (confluir)
confluyó (confluir)
conformar (1), to conform
confortar (1), to comfort
confraternar (1), to be brotherly
confraternice, etc. **(confraternizar)**
confraternicé (confraternizar)
confratenizar (11), to fraternize
confrontar (1), to confront
confundir (3), to confuse
confundirse (3) (4), to become confused
congelar (1), to freeze
congeniar (1), to get along
congestionar (1), to congest
conglomerar (1), to conglomerate
congraciar (1), to win the favor of someone
congraciarse (1) (4), to get into the good graces (of)
congratular (1), to congratulate
congregar (9), to congregate
congregue, etc. **(congregar)**
congregué (congregar)
conjeturar (1), to guess
conjugar (9), to conjugate
conjugue, etc. **(conjugar)**
conjugué (conjugar)
conjurar (1), to conspire, to conjure
conmemorar (1), to commemorate
conmensurar (1), to make commensurate
conminar (1), to threaten
conmover (ue) (38), to stir, to shake, to affect
conmoverse (ue) (38) (4), to be affected
conmueva, etc. **(conmover)**
conmueve, etc. **(conmover)**
conmuevo (conmover)
conmutar (1), to exchange
connaturalice, etc. **(connaturalizar)**
connaturalicé (connaturalizar)
connaturalizar (11), to make natural
connaturalizarse (11) (4), to become accustomed
connotar (1), to connote
connumerar (1), to enumerate
conocer (73), to know, to meet
conozca, etc. **(conocer)**
conozco (conocer)
conquistar (1), to conquer, to win over

consagrar (1), to consecrate, to devote
consagrarse (1) (4), to devote oneself
conseguir (i, i) (58), to obtain, to get
consentir (ie, i) (41), to allow, to consent
conservar (1), to conserve
considerar (1), to consider
consienta, etc. (consentir)
consiente, etc. (consentir)
consiento (consentir)
consiga, etc. (conseguir)
consignar (1), to consign
consigo (conseguir)
consigue, etc. (conseguir)
consiguiendo (conseguir)
consiguiera, etc. (conseguir)
consiguiere, etc. (conseguir)
consiguieron (conseguir)
consiguiese, etc. (conseguir)
consiguió (conseguir)
consintamos, etc. (consentir)
consintiendo (consentir)
consintiera, etc. (consentir)
consintiere, etc. (consentir)
consintieron (consentir)
consintiese, etc. (consentir)
consintió (consentir)
consistir (3), to consist
consolar (ue) (36), to console
consolidar (1), to consolidate
consonar (ue) (36), to be in harmony
conspirar (1), to conspire
constar (1), to consist, to be on the record, to be certain
constatar (1), to verify
consternar (1), to terrify
constiparse (1) (4), to catch cold
constituir (71), to constitute, to set up
constituya, etc. (constituir)
constituye, etc. (constituir)
constituyendo (constituir)
constituyera, etc. (constituir)
constituyere, etc. (constituir)
constituyeron (constituir)
constituyese, etc. (constituir)
constituyo (constituir)
constituyó (constituir)
constreñir (i, i) (60), to constrain
constriña, etc. (constreñir)
constriñe, etc. (constreñir)
constriñendo (constreñir)
constriñera, etc. (constreñir)
constriñere, etc. (constreñir)
constriñeron (constreñir)
constriñese, etc. (constreñir)
constriño (constreñir)
constriñó (constreñir)
construir (71), to construct, to build
construya, etc. (construir)
construye, etc. (construir)
construyendo (construir)
construyera, etc. (construir)
construyere, etc. (construir)
construyeron (construir)
construyese, etc. (construir)
construyo (construir)
construyó (construir)
consuela, etc. (consolar)
consuele, etc. (consolar)
consuelo (consolar)
consuena, etc. (consonar)
consuene, etc. (consonar)
consueno (consonar)
consultar (1), to consult
consumar (1), to consummate
consumir (3), to consume
contagiar (1), to infect, to contaminate

contagiarse (1) (4), to become infected, to become contaminated
contaminar (1), to contaminate
contaminarse (1) (4), to become contaminated
contar (ue) (36), to count, to relate
contemplar (1), to contemplate
contemporice, etc. (contemporizar)
contemporicé (contemporizar)
contemporizar (11), to comply
contén (contener)
contender (ie) (39), to contend, to compete
contendré, etc. (contener)
contendría, etc. (contener)
contener (ie) (108), to contain
contenerse (ie) (108) (4), to control oneself
contenga, etc. (contener)
contengo (contener)
contentar (1), to contend
contestar (1), to answer
contextuar (62), to back with quotations
contienda, etc. (contender)
contiende, etc. (contender)
contiendo (contender)
contiene, etc. (contener)
continuar (62), to continue
contorcerse (ue) (53) (4), to writhe
contornear (1), to trace the contour of, to go around
contornearse (1) (4), to strut
contorzamos, etc. (contorcerse)
contraatacar (8), to counterattack
contraataque, etc. (contraatacar)
contraataqué (contraatacar)
contrabalancear (1), to counterbalance
contrabandear (1), to smuggle
contradecir (i, i) (84), to contradict
contradí (contradecir)
contradice, etc. (contradecir)
contradiciendo (contradecir)
contradicho (contradecir)
contradiga, etc. (contradecir)
contradigo (contradecir)
contradije (contradecir)
contradijera, etc. (contradecir)
contradijere, etc. (contradecir)
contradijeron (contradecir)
contradijese, etc. (contradecir)
contradijimos (contradecir)
contradijiste (contradecir)
contradijisteis (contradecir)
contradijo (contradecir)
contradiré, etc. (contradecir)
contradiría, etc. (contradecir)
contraer (109), to contract
contrahacer (90), to copy, to counterfeit
contrahaga, etc. (contrahacer)
contrahago (contrahacer)
contraharé, etc. (contrahacer)
contraharía, etc. (contrahacer)
contrahaz (contrahacer)
contrahecho (contrahacer)
contrahíce (contrahacer)
contrahiciera, etc. (contrahacer)
contrahiciere, etc. (contrahacer)
contrahicieron (contrahacer)
contrahiciese, etc. (contrahacer)
contrahicimos (contrahacer)
contrahiciste (contrahacer)
contrahicisteis (contrahacer)
contrahízo (contrahacer)
contraiga, etc. (contraer)
contraigo (contraer)
contraje (contraer)
contrajera, etc. (contraer)
contrajere, etc. (contraer)

contrajeron (contraer)
contrajese, etc. (contraer)
contrajimos (contraer)
contrajiste (contraer)
contrajisteis (contraer)
contrajo (contraer)
contramarcar (8), to place a second mark on something for reverification
contramarchar (1), to countermarch
contramarque, etc. (contramarcar)
contramarqué (contramarcar)
contrapesar (1), to counterbalance
contrapón (contraponer)
contrapondré, etc. (contraponer)
contrapondría, etc. (contraponer)
contraponer (98), to oppose, to compare
contraponga, etc. (contraponer)
contrapongo (contraponer)
contrapuesto (contraponer)
contrapuse (contraponer)
contrapusiera, etc. (contraponer)
contrapusiere, etc. (contraponer)
contrapusieron (contraponer)
contrapusiese, etc. (contraponer)
contrapusimos (contraponer)
contrapusiste (contraponer)
contrapusisteis (contraponer)
contrapuso (contraponer)
contrariar (61), to oppose, to irritate
contrarrestar (1), to resist
contrastar (1), to contrast, to resist
contratar (1), to contract
contravén (contravenir)
contravendré, etc. (contravenir)
contravendría, etc. (contravenir)
contravenga, etc. (contravenir)
contravengo (contravenir)
contravenir (ie, i) (111), to transgress
contraviene, etc. (contravenir)
contravine (contravenir)
contraviniendo (contravenir)
contraviniera, etc. (contravenir)
contraviniere, etc. (contravenir)
contravinieron (contravenir)
contraviniese, etc. (contravenir)
contravinimos (contravenir)
contraviniste (contravenir)
contravino (contravenir)
contrayendo (contraer)
contribuir (71), to contribute
contribuya, etc. (contribuir)
contribuye, etc. (contribuir)
contribuyendo (contribuir)
contribuyera, etc. (contribuir)
contribuyere, etc. (contribuir)
contribuyeron (contribuir)
contribuyese, etc. (contribuir)
contribuyo (contribuir)
contribuyó (contribuir)
contristar (1), to sadden
controlar (1), to control
controvertir (ie, i) (41), to dispute
controvierta, etc. (controvertir)
controvierte, etc. (controvertir)
controvierto (controvertir)
controvirtamos, etc. (controvertir)
controvirtiendo (controvertir)
controvirtiera, etc. (controvertir)
controvirtiere, etc. (controvertir)
controvirtieron (controvertir)
controvirtiese, etc. (controvertir)
controvirtió (controvertir)
contuerce, etc. (contorcerse)
contuerza, etc. (contorcerse)
contuerzo (contorcerse)

contundir (3), to contuse
conturbar (1), to upset
contusionar (1), to contuse
contuve, etc. (**contener**)
contuviera, etc. (**contener**)
contuviere, etc. (**contener**)
contuvieron (**contener**)
contuviese, etc. (**contener**)
contuvimos (**contener**)
contuviste (**contener**)
contuvisteis (**contener**)
contuvo (**contener**)
convalecer (73), to recover from an illness
convalezca, etc. (**convalecer**)
convalezco (**convalecer**)
convalidar (1), to confirm
convén (**convenir**)
convencer (12), to convince
convendré, etc. (**convenir**)
convendría, etc. (**convenir**)
convenga, etc. (**convenir**)
convengo (**convenir**)
convenir (ie, i) (111), to agree, to convene, to be convenient
convenza, etc. (**convencer**)
convenzo (**convencer**)
converger (15), to converge
convergir (16), to converge
converja, etc. (**converger**) (**convergir**)
converjo (**converger**) (**convergir**)
conversar (1), to converse
convertir (ie, i) (41), to convert
convidar (1), to invite
conviene, etc. (**convenir**)
convierta, etc. (**convertir**)
convierte, etc. (**convertir**)
convierto (**convertir**)
convine (**convenir**)
conviniendo (**convenir**)
conviniera, etc. (**convenir**)
conviniere, etc. (**convenir**)
convinieron (**convenir**)
conviniese, etc. (**convenir**)
convinimos (**convenir**)
conviniste (**convenir**)
convinisteis (**convenir**)
convino (**convenir**)
convirtamos, etc. (**convertir**)
convirtiendo (**convertir**)
convirtiera, etc. (**convertir**)
convirtiere, etc. (**convertir**)
convirtieron (**convertir**)
convirtiese, etc. (**convertir**)
convirtió (**convertir**)
convivir (3), to live together
convocar (8), to convoke
convoque, etc. (**convocar**)
convoqué (**convocar**)
convulsionar (1), to convulse
coñearse (1) (4), to make fun of
cooperar (1), to cooperate
coordinar (1), to coordinate
copar (1), to corner
copear (1), to have a drink, to sell wine and liquor by the glass
copiar (1), to copy, to copy down
copular (1), to join one thing with another
copularse (1) (4), to copulate
coquetear (1), to flirt
corcovar (1), to bend
corcovear (1), to buck (said of horses)
corear (1), to choir, to answer in chorus
cornear (1), to butt
coronar (1), to crown, to cap
corregir (i, i) (57), to correct
correlacionar (1), to correlate

correr (2), to run, to embarrass
correrse (2) (4), to become embarrassed
corresponder (2), to correspond, to reciprocate, to belong to
corretear (1), to run around, to romp
corrige, etc. (**corregir**)
corrigiendo (**corregir**)
corrigiera, etc. (**corregir**)
corrigiere, etc. (**corregir**)
corrigieron (**corregir**)
corrigiese, etc. (**corregir**)
corrigió (**corregir**)
corrija, etc. (**corregir**)
corrijo (**corregir**)
corroborar (1), to corroborate
corroer (103), to corrode
corroiga, etc. (**corroer**)
corroigo (**corroer**)
corromper (2), to corrupt, to spoil, to rot
corromperse (2) (4), to become spoiled, to rot
corroya, etc. (**corroer**)
corroyendo (**corroer**)
corroyera, etc. (**corroer**)
corroyere, etc. (**corroer**)
corroyeron (**corroer**)
corroyese, etc. (**corroer**)
corroyo (**corroer**)
corroyó (**corroer**)
corrugar (9), to corrugate
corrugue, etc. (**corrugar**)
corrugué (**corrugar**)
cortar (1), to cut, to cut off, to omit
cortarse (1) (4), to become confused, to chap, to curdle
cortejar (1), to court
cosechar (1), to harvest
coser (2), to sew
cosquillear (1), to tickle
costar (ue) (36), to cost
costear (1), to defray or pay cost, to navigate along the coast
costearse (1) (4), to pay for itself
cotejar (1), to confront, to compare
cotice, etc. (**cotizar**)
coticé (**cotizar**)
cotillear (1), to gossip
cotizar (11), to quote (price), to contribute one's share
cotorrear (1), to chatter, to gossip
cozamos, etc. (**cocer**)
crear (1), to create
crecer (73), to grow, to swell (stream)
crecerse (73) (4), to become or feel important
creer (20), to believe, to think
crepitar (1), to crackle
creyendo (**creer**)
creyera, etc. (**creer**)
creyere, etc. (**creer**)
creyeron (**creer**)
creyese, etc. (**creer**)
creyó (**creer**)
crezca, etc. (**crecer**)
crezco (**crecer**)
criar (19), to raise, to rear, to breed, to bring up
cribar (1), to sieve
crispar (1), to put on edge, to contract (muscles)
cristalice, etc. (**cristalizar**)
cristalicé (**cristalizar**)
cristalizar (11), to crystallize
cristianice, etc. (**cristianizar**)
cristianicé (**cristianizar**)
cristianizar (11), to Christianize

criticar (8), to criticize
critique, etc. (**criticar**)
critiqué (**criticar**)
croar (1), to croak
cronometrar (1), to clock
cruce, etc. (**cruzar**)
crucé (**cruzar**)
crucificar (8), to crucify, to vex
crucifique, etc. (**crucificar**)
crucifiqué (**crucificar**)
crujir (3), to creak, to grate (one's teeth)
cruzar (11), to cross
cuadrar (1), to square, to balance (books)
cuadrarse (1) (4), to stand at attention
cuadricular (1), to divide into squares
cuadruplicar (8), to quadruple
cuadruplique, etc. (**cuadruplicar**)
cuadrupliqué (**cuadruplicar**)
cuajar (1), to coagulate, to materialize, to be well received
cuartear (1), to quarter
cubicar (8), to cube (math), to determine the volume of
cubierto (**cubrir**)
cubique, etc. (**cubicar**)
cubiqué (**cubicar**)
cubrir (82), to cover, to cover up
cubrirse (82) (4), to put one's hat on
cucharear (1), to spoon
cuchufletear (1), to make fun, to joke
cuece, etc. (**cocer**)
cuela, etc. (**colar**)
cuele, etc. (**colar**)
cuelga, etc. (**colgar**)
cuelgo (**colgar**)
cuelgue, etc. (**colgar**)
cuelo (**colar**)
cuenta, etc. (**contar**)
cuente, etc. (**contar**)
cuento (**contar**)
cuesta, etc. (**costar**)
cueste, etc. (**costar**)
cuestionar (1), to discuss a doubtful point
cuesto (**costar**)
cueza, etc. (**cocer**)
cuezo (**cocer**)
cuidar (1), to take care of, to watch over, to take good care of
culebrear (1), to wiggle
culminar (1), to culminate
culpar (1), to blame
cultivar (1), to cultivate
cumplir (3), to fulfill, to fulfill an obligation, to keep (a promise)
cundir (3), to spread, to yield abundantly, to propagate
cupe (**caber**)
cupiera, etc. (**caber**)
cupiere, etc. (**caber**)
cupieron (**caber**)
cupiese, etc. (**caber**)
cupimos (**caber**)
cupiste (**caber**)
cupisteis (**caber**)
cupo (**caber**)
curar (1), to cure, to treat (a sick person), to heal
curarse (1) (4), to get well, to get drunk
curiosear (1), to snoop, to browse around
cursar (1), to take a course or courses in, to send something on its way through channels
curtir (3), to tan, to make used to difficulty
curtirse (3) (4), to become tanned, to become used to difficulty
custodiar (1), to watch over, to guard

CH

chacotear (1), to laugh and make a lot of noise
chacharear (1), to chatter
chafar (1), to flatten
chaflanar (1), to chamfer
chalar (1), to make someone lose his head
chalarse (1) (4), to lose one's head
chamuscar (8), to singe
chamusque, etc. (chamuscar)
chamusqué (chamuscar)
chancar (8), to crush (stones)
chancear (1), to joke
chancletear (1), to go around in slippers
chanque, etc. (chancar)
chanqué (chancar)
chantar (1), to put on
chapalear (1), to splash
chaparrear (1), to rain hard, to pour at intervals
chapotear (1), to splash
chapuce, etc. (chapuzar)
chapucé (chapuzar)
chapucear (1), to do or make something fast and poorly, to deceive
chapurrear (1), to speak (a language) brokenly
chapuzar (11), to duck under water, to dive
charlar (1), to chat
charlatanear (1), to chatter
charlotear (1), to chatter
charolar (1), to varnish, to polish
chascar (8), to click (the tongue)
chascarse (8) (4), to crack (break with a sharp noise)
chasque, etc. (chascar)
chasqué (chascar)
chasquear (1), to play a trick on
chicotear (1), to lash, to whip
chicharrar (1), to scorch
chicharrear (1), to chirp (said of a cicada)
chichear (1), to hiss
chiflar (1), to whistle
chiflarse (1) (4), to lose one's head
chillar (1), to scream
chinchar (1), to bother
chiripear (1), to win by a fluke
chirlar (1), to talk fast and loud
chirriar (61), to squeak
chismear (1), to gossip
chismorrear (1), to gossip
chispar (1), to gossip
chispear (1), to spark, to sparkle, to rain gently
chisporrotear (1), to throw off sparks
chistar (1), to mumble
chitar (1), to mumble
chocar (8), to collide, to shock, to fight
chocarrear (1), to tell coarse jokes
chochear (1), to act senile, to become childish
choque, etc. (chocar)
choqué (chocar)
chorrear (1), to spout, to drip
chotear (1), to make fun of, to jeer
chufletear (1), to jest
chungar (9), to jest
chungue, etc. (chungar)
chungué (chungar)
chupar (1), to suck
chuparse (1) (4), to get drunk
chupetear (1), to suck gently and by starts
churrasquear (1), to barbecue

churruscarse (8) (4), to become burnt (food)
churrusque, etc. (churruscarse)
churrusqué (churruscarse)
chutar (1), to kick a ball

D

dance, etc. (danzar)
dancé (danzar)
danzar (11), to dance
dañar (1), to hurt, to harm, to damage
dañarse (1) (4), to spoil, to get hurt, to get damaged
dar (83), to give, to yield, to hit, to hand
darse (83) (4), to devote oneself, to give up
datar (1), to date (a document, etc.)
dé (dar)
deambular (1), to walk, to move about
debatir (3), to debate
debatirse (3) (4), to struggle
deber (2), to owe, must, to have to
debilitar (1), to weaken
debutar (1), to make one's debut
decaer (81), to decay
decaiga, etc. (decaer)
decaigo (decaer)
decantar (1), to decant, to exaggerate
decapitar (1), to behead
decayendo (decaer)
decayera, etc. (decaer)
decayere, etc. (decaer)
decayeron (decaer)
decayese, etc. (decaer)
decayó (decaer)
decepcionar (1), to disappoint
decidir (3), to decide
decir (i, i) (84), to tell, to say
decirse (i, i) (84) (4), to be said
declamar (1), to declaim
declarar (1), to declare
declinar (1), to decline
decomisar (1), to confiscate
decorar (1), to decorate
decrecer (73), to decrease
decrepitar (1), to crackle
decretar (1), to decree
decrezca, etc. (decrecer)
decrezco (decrecer)
decuplicar (8), to multiply by ten
decuplique, etc. (decuplicar)
decupliqué (decuplicar)
dedicar (8), to dedicate
dedicarse (8) (4), to apply oneself
dedique, etc. (dedicar)
dediqué (dedicar)
deducir (67), to deduce, to deduct
deduje (deducir)
dedujera, etc. (deducir)
dedujere, etc. (deducir)
dedujeron (deducir)
dedujese (deducir)
dedujimos (deducir)
dedujiste (deducir)
dedujisteis (deducir)
dedujo (deducir)
deduzca, etc. (deducir)
deduzco (deducir)
defecar (8), to defecate
defeccionar (1), to desert, to defect
defender (ie) (39), to defend, to protect
defeque, etc. (defecar)
defequé (defecar)
deferir (ie, i) (41), to defer (yield)
defienda, etc. (defender)
defiende, etc. (defender)

defiendo (defender)
defiera, etc. (deferir)
defiere, etc. (deferir)
defiero (deferir)
definir (3), to define
defiramos, etc. (deferir)
defiriendo (deferir)
defiriera, etc. (deferir)
defiriere, etc. (deferir)
defirieron (deferir)
defiriese, etc. (deferir)
defirió (deferir)
deformar (1), to deform
deformarse (1) (4), to become deformed
defraudar (1), to defraud, to disappoint
degenerar (1), to degenerate
deglutir (3), to swallow
degollar (ue) (48), to behead
degradar (1), to degrade
degüella, etc. (degollar)
degüelle, etc. (degollar)
degüello (degollar)
degustar (1), to taste
deificar (8), to deify
deifique, etc. (deificar)
deifiqué (deificar)
dejar (1), to leave, to abandon, to lend, to let
delatar (1), to denounce
delegar (9), to delegate
delegue, etc. (delegar)
delegué (delegar)
deleitar (1), to delight
deletrear (1), to spell
deliberar (1), to deliberate
delimitar (1), to delimit
delinca, etc. (delinquir)
delinco (delinquir)
delinear (1), to delineate, to draw
delinquir (18), to transgress
delirar (1), to be delirious
deludir (3), to delude
demandar (1), to demand
demarcar (8), to demarcate
demarque, etc. (demarcar)
demarqué (demarcar)
democratice, etc. (democratizar)
democraticé (democratizar)
democratizar (11), to democratize
demoler (ue) (38), to demolish
demorar (1), to delay
demostrar (ue) (36), to demonstrate
demudar (1), to change
demuela, etc. (demoler)
demuele, etc. (demoler)
demuelo (demoler)
demuestra, etc. (demostrar)
demuestre, etc. (demostrar)
demuestro (demostrar)
denegar (ie) (50), to deny
denegrecer (73), to blacken
denegrecerse (73) (4), to become black
denegrezca, etc. (denegrecer)
denegrezco (denegrecer)
denegrir (116), to blacken
denegué (denegar)
deneguemos, etc. (denegar)
deniega, etc. (denegar)
deniego (denegar)
deniegue, etc. (denegar)
denigrar (1), to denigrate
denominar (1), to name, to call
denostar (ue) (36), to insult
denotar (1), to denote
dentar (ie) (37), to tooth
denudar (1), to denude

denuesta, etc. (**denostar**)
denueste, etc. (**denostar**)
denuesto (**denostar**)
denunciar (1), to denounce
deparar (1), to provide
departir (3), to converse, to talk
depender (2), to depend
depilar (1), to depilate
deplorar (1), to deplore
depón (**deponer**)
depondré, etc. (**deponer**)
depondría, etc. (**deponer**)
deponer (98), to remove from office, to depose
deponga, etc. (**deponer**)
depongo (**deponer**)
deportar (1), to deport
depositar (1), to deposit
depravar (1), to deprave
deprecar (8), to implore
depreciar (1), to depreciate
depreque, etc. (**deprecar**)
deprequé (**deprecar**)
deprimir (3), to depress
depuesto (**deponer**)
depurar (1), to purify
depuse (**deponer**)
depusiera, etc. (**deponer**)
depusiere, etc. (**deponer**)
depusieron (**deponer**)
depusiese (**deponer**)
depusimos (**deponer**)
depusiste (**deponer**)
depusisteis (**deponer**)
depuso (**deponer**)
derivar (1), to derive
derogar (9), to revoke
derogue, etc. (**derogar**)
derogué (**derogar**)
derramar (1), to spill
derramarse (1) (4), to overflow
derrengar (ie) (50), to cripple
derrengué (**derrengar**)
derrenguemos, etc. (**derrengar**)
derretir (i, i) (42), to melt
derretirse (i, i) (42) (4), to melt down
derribar (1), to tear down
derrienga, etc. (**derrengar**)
derriengo (**derrengar**)
derriengue, etc. (**derrengar**)
derrita, etc. (**derretir**)
derrite, etc. (**derretir**)
derritiendo (**derretir**)
derritiera, etc. (**derretir**)
derritiere, etc. (**derretir**)
derritieron (**derretir**)
derritiese, etc. (**derretir**)
derritió (**derretir**)
derrito (**derretir**)
derrocar [(ue) (44)] or (8), to overthrow, to fling down
derrochar (1), to squander
derroque, etc. (**derrocar**)
derroqué (**derrocar**)
derroquemos, etc. (**derrocar**)
derrotar (1), to defeat
derrueca, etc. (**derrocar**)
derrueco (**derrocar**)
derrueque, etc. (**derrocar**)
derruir (71), to tear down
derrumbar (1), to knock down
derruya, etc. (**derruir**)
derruye, etc. (**derruir**)
derruyendo (**derruir**)
derruyera, etc. (**derruir**)
derruyere, etc. (**derruir**)

derruyeron (**derruir**)
derruyese, etc. (**derruir**)
derruyo (**derruir**)
derruyó (**derruir**)
des, etc. (**dar**)
desabollar (1), to knock the dents out
desabotonar (1), to unbutton
desabrigar (9), to deprive of shelter, to take off outer clothing (coat, sweater, etc.)
desabrigue, etc. (**desabrigar**)
desabrigué (**desabrigar**)
desabrirse (3) (4), to become embittered
desabrochar (1), to unfasten, to unbutton
desacatar (1), to show disrespect and lack of submission
desacertar (ie) (37) to miss, to make a mistake
desacierta, etc. (**desacertar**)
desacierte, etc. (**desacertar**)
desacierto (**desacertar**)
desacreditar (1), to discredit
desafiar (61), to defy
desafinar (1), to play or sing out of tune
desafinarse (1) (4), to get out of tune
desagradar (1), to displease
desagradecer (73), to be ungrateful
desagradezca, etc. (**desagradecer**)
desagradezco (**desagradecer**)
desagraviar (1), to make amends
desaguar (10), to drain
desagüe, etc. (**desaguar**)
desagüé (**desaguar**)
desahíja, etc. (**desahijar**)
desahijar (34), to separate young from their mothers (in a herd)
desahíje, etc. (**desahijar**)
desahíjo (**desahijar**)
desahogar (9), to relieve from pain or trouble, to give rein to (passions, desires)
desahogarse (9) (4), to find relief or release
desahogue, etc. (**desahogar**)
desahogué (**desahogar**)
desahuciar [see special note on (34)], to declare a patient past recovery, to evict
desajustar (1), to put out of adjustment
desajustarse (1) (4), to get out of adjustment
desalentar (ie) (37), to discourage
desalentarse (ie) (37) (4), to become discouraged
desalienta, etc. (**desalentar**)
desaliente, etc. (**desalentar**)
desaliento (**desalentar**)
desalojar (1), to dislodge, to evict, to oust
desamoblar (ue) (36), to remove the furniture
desamuebla, etc. (**desamoblar**)
desamueble, etc. (**desamoblar**)
desamueblo (**desamoblar**)
desandar (77), to retrace
desanduve (**desandar**)
desanduviera, etc. (**desandar**)
desanduviere, etc. (**desandar**)
desanduvieron (**desandar**)
desanduviese, etc. (**desandar**)
desanduvimos (**desandar**)
desanduviste (**desandar**)
desanduvisteis (**desandar**)
desanduvo (**desandar**)
desangrar (1), to bleed copiously
desanimar (1), to discourage
desanudar (1), to unknot, to untie
desaparecer (73), to disappear
desaparejar (1), to unharness

desaparezca, etc. (**desaparecer**)
desaparezco (**desaparecer**)
desapretar (ie) (37), to loosen
desaprieta, etc. (**desapretar**)
desapriete, etc. (**desapretar**)
desaprieto (**desapretar**)
desaprobar (ue) (36), to disapprove
desaprovechar (1), to use to no advantage
desaprueba, etc. (**desaprobar**)
desapruebe, etc. (**desaprobar**)
desapruebo (**desaprobar**)
desarmar (1), to disarm
desarraigar (9), to root out
desarraigue, etc. (**desarraigar**)
desarraigué (**desarraigar**)
desarreglar (1), to mess up
desarrollar (1), to unroll, to develop
desarropar (1), to take off clothing
desarroparse (1) (4), to take off one's clothing
desarrugar (9), to unwrinkle
desarrugue, etc. (**desarrugar**)
desarrugué (**desarrugar**)
desarticular (1), to disjoint
desasga, etc. (**desasir**)
desasgo (**desasir**)
desasir (78), to let go
desasirse (78) (4), to let loose, to get rid of
desasistir (3), to abandon
desasnar (1), to give good manners to
desasnarse (1) (4), to acquire good manners
desasociar (1), to disassociate
desasosegar (ie) (50), to disquiet
desasosegarse (ie) (50 (4), to become disquieted
desasosegué (**desasosegar**)
desasoseguemos, etc. (**desasosegar**)
desasosiega, etc. (**desasosegar**)
desasosiego (**desasosegar**)
desasosiegue, etc. (**desasosegar**)
desatar (1), to untie, to unknot
desatarse (1) (4), to come untied, to break loose
desatascar (8), to pull out of the mud, to get out of a difficult or tight spot, to unclog
desatasque, etc. (**desatascar**)
desatasqué (**desatascar**)
desatender (ie) (39), to disregard
desatienda, etc. (**desatender**)
desatiende, etc. (**desatender**)
desatiendo (**desatender**)
desatinar (1), to talk nonsense, to blunder
desatrancar (8), to unbar, to remove obstructions from
desatranque, etc. (**desatrancar**)
desatranqué (**desatrancar**)
desautorice, etc. (**desautorizar**)
desautoricé (**desautorizar**)
desautorizar (11), to deprive of authority or credit, to discredit, to unauthorize
desavén (**desavenir**)
desavendré, etc. (**desavenir**)
desavendría, etc. (**desavenir**)
desavenga, etc. (**desavenir**)
desavengo (**desavenir**)
desavenir (ie, i) (111), to bring disagreement
desavenirse (ie, i) (111) (4), to disagree
desaviar (61), to mislead, to lead astray, to deprive someone of something necessary
desaviene, etc. (**desavenir**)
desavine (**desavenir**)

desaviniendo (desavenir)
desaviniera, etc. **(desavenir)**
desaviniere, etc. **(desavenir)**
desavinieron (desavenir)
desaviniese, etc. **(desavenir)**
desavinimos (desavenir)
desaviniste (desavenir)
desavinisteis (desavenir)
desavino (desavenir)
desayunar (1), to breakfast, to eat breakfast
desayunarse (1) (4), to breakfast, to eat breakfast
desbandar (1), to disband
desbandarse (1) (4), to disband
desbarajustar (1), to disorder
desbaratar (1), to destroy, to upset
desbaratarse (1), (4), to fall into pieces
desbarrar (1), to talk nonsense
desbastar (1), to rough out, to educate and polish
desbocarse (8) (4), to run away, to break loose (said of a horse)
desboque, etc. **(desbocarse)**
desboqué (desbocarse)
desbordar (1), to overflow
desbravar (1), to tame, to break in
desbravecer (73), to tame, to break in
desbravecerse (73) (4), to become less wild, to calm down
desbravezca, etc. **(desbravecer)**
desbravezco (desbravecer)
desbroce, etc. **(desbrozar)**
desbrocé (desbrozar)
desbrozar (11), to remove grass, rotten branches, leaves on the ground
descabalgar (9), to dismount
descabalgue, etc. **(descabalgar)**
descabalgué (descabalgar)
descabece, etc. **(descabezar)**
descabecé (descabezar)
descabezar (11), to behead, to top (chop off the tip or head of)
descaecer (73), to decrease
descaezca, etc. **(descaecer)**
descaezco (descaecer)
descalabrar (1), to hit in the head, to ruin
descalabrarse (1) (4), to fracture one's skull, to hurt one's head
descalce, etc. **(descalzar)**
descalcé (descalzar)
descalzar (11), to take shoes off, to remove wedges or chocks from
descansar (1), to rest
descararse (1) (4), to speak or behave in an impudent or insolent manner
descargar (9), to unload, to discharge
descargue, etc. **(descargar)**
descargué (descargar)
descarriar (61), to mislead, to lead astray
descarriarse (61) (4), to go astray
descarrilar (1), to derail
descartar (1), to discard
descascarar (1), to shell
descender (ie) (39), to lower, to descend, to come from
descentrar (1), to put off center
descentrarse (1) (4), to get off center
descerrajar (1), to break or tear off the lock of
descienda, etc. **(descender)**
desciende, etc. **(descender)**
descendiendo (descender)
descifrar (1), to decipher, to make out
desclavar (1), to unnail
descolgar (ue) (45), to unhang

descolgarse (ue) (45) (4), to climb down, to drop in
descolgué (descolgar)
descolguemos (descolgar)
descolorar (1), to discolor
descolorir (120), to discolor
descollar (ue) (36), to excel
descomedirse (i, i) (42) (4), to be disrespectful
descomida, etc. **(descomedirse)**
descomide, etc. **(descomedirse)**
descomidiendo (descomedirse)
descomidiera, etc. **(descomedirse)**
descomidiere, etc. **(descomedirse)**
descomidieron (descomedirse)
descomidiese, etc. **(descomedirse)**
descomidió (descomedirse)
descomido (descomedirse)
descompón (descomponer)
descompondré, etc. **(descomponer)**
descompondría, etc. **(descomponer)**
descomponer (98), to decompose, to put out of order, to upset
descomponerse (98) (4), to rot, to get out of order, to become upset
descomponga, etc. **(descomponer)**
descompongo (descomponer)
descompuesto (descomponer)
descompuse (descomponer)
descompusiera, etc. **(descomponer)**
descompusiere, etc. **(descomponer)**
descompusieron (descomponer)
descompusiese, etc. **(descomponer)**
descompusimos (descomponer)
descompusiste (descomponer)
descompusisteis (descomponer)
descompuso (descomponer)
desconcertar (ie) (37), to disconcert
desconcertarse (ie) (37) (4), to get out of order
desconcierta, etc. **(desconcertar)**
desconcierte, etc. **(desconcertar)**
desconcierto (desconcertar)
desconectar (1), to disconnect
desconfiar (61), to distrust
descongelar (1), to defrost
descongestionar (1), to decongest
desconocer (73), to fail to recognize
desconozca, etc. **(desconocer)**
desconozco (desconocer)
desconsolar (ue) (36), to grieve
desconsolarse (ue) (36) (4), to become grieved
desconsuela, etc. **(desconsolar)**
desconsuele, etc. **(desconsolar)**
desconsuelo (desconsolar)
descontar (ue) (36), to discount
descontarse (ue) (36) (4), to miscount
descontentar (1), to displease, to dissatisfy
descontinuar (62), to discontinue
descorazonar (1), to dishearten
descorchar (1), to uncork
descorrer (2), to draw (a curtain)
descortece, etc. **(descortezar)**
descortecé (descortezar)
descortezar (11), to remove bark, bread crust; to civilize
descoser (2), to unstitch
descoyuntar (1), to dislocate
describir (69), to describe
descrito (describir)
descuartice, etc. **(descuartizar)**
descuarticé (descuartizar)
descuartizar (11), to quarter (divide into pieces)

descubierto (descubrir)
descubrir (82), to discover, to uncover, to invent
descubrirse (82) (4), to take off one's hat, etc.
descuelga, etc. **(decolgar)**
descuelgo (descolgar)
descuelgue, etc. **(descolgar)**
descuella, etc. **(descollar)**
descuelle, etc. **(descollar)**
descuello (descollar)
descuenta, etc. **(descontar)**
descuente, etc. **(descontar)**
descuento (descontar)
descuidar (1), to neglect
desdecir (i, i) (84), to retract
desdentar (ie) (37), to pull or break the teeth of
desdeñar (1), to disdain
desdí (desdecir)
desdice, etc. **(desdecir)**
desdiciendo (desdecir)
desdicho (desdecir)
desdienta, etc. **(desdentar)**
desdiente, etc. **(desdentar)**
desdiento (desdentar)
desdiga, etc. **(desdecir)**
desdigo (desdecir)
desdije (desdecir)
desdijera, etc. **(desdecir)**
desdijere, etc. **(desdecir)**
desdijeron (desdecir)
desdijese, etc. **(desdecir)**
desdijimos (desdecir)
desdijiste (desdecir)
desdijisteis (desdecir)
desdijo (desdecir)
desdiré, etc. **(desdecir)**
desdiría, etc. **(desdecir)**
desear (1), to desire
desecar (8), to dessicate
desechar (1), to discard, to reject
desedificar (8), to give a bad example to
desedifique, etc. **(desedificar)**
desedifiqué (desedificar)
desembalar (1), to unpack
desembarace, etc. **(desembarazar)**
desembaracé (desembarazar)
desembarazar (11), to disembarrass
desembarazarse (11) (4), to free oneself
desembarcar (8), to disembark
desembargar (9), to lift an embargo, to remove impediments from
desembargue (desembargar)
desembargué (desembargar)
desembarque, etc. **(desembarcar)**
desembarqué (desembarcar)
desembarrancar (8), to set afloat, to disentangle
desembarranque, etc. **(desembarrancar)**
desembarranqué (desembarrancar)
desembocar (8), to flow, to lead
desembolsar (1), to disburse
desemboque, etc. **(desembocar)**
desemboqué (desembocar)
desemborrachar (1), to sober up
desembragar (9), to disengage, to unclutch
desembrague, etc. **(desembragar)**
desembragué (desembragar)
desempacar (8), to unpack
desempaque, etc. **(desempacar)**
desempaqué (desempacar)
desemparejar (1), to make uneven
desempatar (1), to break the tie between

desempeñar (1), to perform, to carry out, to fulfill
desempolvar (1), to dust
desemporqué (**desemporcar**)
desemporquemos, etc. (**desemporcar**)
desempuerca, etc. (**desemporcar**)
desempuerco (**desemporcar**)
desempuerque, etc. (**desemporcar**)
desencadenar (1), to unchain
desencadenarse (1) (4), to break loose, to break out with fury (storm)
desencajar (1), to dislocate
desencantar (1), to disillusion, to disenchant
desenchufar (1), to unplug
desenfadarse (1) (4), to calm down
desenganchar (1), to unhitch, to disengage
desengañar (1), to disillusion, to disappoint
desengañarse (1) (4), to become disillusioned, to become disappointed
desenjaular (1), to take out of the cage
desenlace, etc. (**desenlazar**)
desenlacé (**desenlazar**)
desenlazar (11), to untie, to unravel
desenmarañar (1), to disentangle
desenmascarar (1), to unmask
desenredar (1), to disentangle
desenrollar (1), to unroll
desenroscar (8), to unbolt
desenrosque, etc. (**desenroscar**)
desenrosqué (**desenroscar**)
desentenderse (ie) (39) (4), to ignore, to pretend not to know
desenterrar (ie) (37), to unearth
desentienda, etc. (**desentenderse**)
desentiende, etc. (**desentenderse**)
desentiendo (**desentenderse**)
desentierra, etc. (**desenterrar**)
desentierre, etc. (**desenterrar**)
desentierro (**desenterrar**)
desentonar (1), to be out of tune
desentumecer (73), to relieve of numbness
desentumecerse (73) (4), to shake off the numbness
desentumezca, etc. (**desentumecer**)
desentumezco (**desentumecer**)
desenvainar (1), to unsheath
desenvolver (ue) (70), to unwrap
desenvolverse (ue) (70) (4), to be forward, to manage the situation
desenvuelto (**desenvolver**)
desenvuelva, etc. (**desenvolver**)
desenvuelve, etc. (**desenvolver**)
desenvuelvo (**desenvolver**)
deseque, etc. (**desecar**)
desequé (**desecar**)
desequilibrar (1), to unbalance
desertar (1), to desert
desesperar (1), to despair
desestimar (1), to hold in low esteem
desfalcar (8), to embezzle
desfalque, etc. (**desfalcar**)
desfalqué (**desfalcar**)
desfallecer (73), to grow weak, to faint
desfallezca, etc. (**desfallecer**)
desfallezco (**desfallecer**)
desfavorecer (73), to disfavor
desfavorezca, etc. (**desfavorecer**)
desfavorezco (**desfavorecer**)
desfigurar (1), to disfigure, to distort
desfilar (1), to parade, to march
desfogarse (9) (4), to vent one's anger
desfogue (**desfogarse**)

desfogué (**desfogarse**)
desfrenar (1), to take the brakes off
desganarse (1) (4), to lose one's appetite, to become indifferent
desgarrar (1), to tear
desgastar (1), to wear away
desgastarse (1) (4), to wear down or away
desgranar (1), to remove the grain from
desguace, etc. (**desguazar**)
desguacé (**desguazar**)
desguazar (11), to break (a ship down)
deshabituar (62), to disaccustom, to break a habit
deshacer (90), to undo, to take apart, to untie
deshacerse (90) (4), to dissolve
deshaga, etc. (**deshacer**)
deshago (**deshacer**)
desharé, etc. (**deshacer**)
desharía, etc. (**deshacer**)
deshaz (**deshacer**)
deshecho (**deshacer**)
deshelar (ie) (37), to thaw
desherbar (ie) (37), to weed
desheredar (1), to disinherit
deshice (**deshacer**)
deshiciera, etc. (**deshacer**)
deshiciere, etc. (**deshacer**)
deshicieron (**deshacer**)
deshiciese, etc. (**deshacer**)
deshicimos (**deshacer**)
deshiciste (**deshacer**)
deshicisteis (**deshacer**)
deshidratar (1), to dehydrate
deshiela, etc. (**deshelar**)
deshiele, etc. (**deshelar**)
deshielo (**deshelar**)
deshierba, etc. (**desherbar**)
deshierbe, etc. (**desherbar**)
deshierbo (**desherbar**)
deshilachar (1), to ravel, to fray
deshilar (1), to unravel
deshilvanar (1), to unbaste
deshinchar (1), to deflate
deshizo (**deshacer**)
deshojar (1), to defoliate
deshonorar (1), to dishonor
deshonrar (1), to affront, to insult, to seduce (a woman)
deshuesa, etc. (**deshuesar**) (**desosar**)
deshuesar (1), to bone
deshuese, etc. (**deshuesar**) (**desosar**)
deshueso (**deshuesar**) (**desosar**)
deshumanice, etc. (**deshumanizar**)
deshumanicé (**deshumanizar**)
deshumanizar (11), to dehumanize
deshumedecer (73), to dehumidify
deshumedezca, etc. (**deshumedecer**)
deshumedezco (**deshumedecer**)
designar (1), to designate
desigualar (1), to make unequal
desilusionar (1), to disappoint
desinfectar (1), to disinfect
desinflamar (1), to remove the inflamation from
desinflamarse (1) (4), to lose its inflamation
desinflar (1), to deflate
desinteresarse (1) (4), to lose interest
desistir (3), to desist
desleír (i, i) (59), to dilute, to dissolve
deslía, etc. (**desleír**)
deslice, etc. (**deslizar**)
deslicé (**deslizar**)
deslíe, etc. (**desleír**)
desliendo (**desleír**)

desliera, etc. (**desleír**)
desliere, etc. (**desleír**)
deslieron (**desleír**)
desliese, etc. (**desleír**)
desligar (9), to untie
desligue, etc. (**desligar**)
desligué (**desligar**)
deslindar (1), to mark boundaries of
deslío (**desleír**)
deslió (**desleír**)
deslizar (11), to slide
deslucir (74), to tarnish
deslucirse (74) (4), to do poorly
deslumbrar (1), to dazzle, to bewilder
deslustrar (1), to tarnish
deslusca, etc. (**deslucir**)
desluzco (**deslucir**)
desmandarse (1) (4), to lose moderation or self-control, to be impudent
desmantelar (1), to dismantle
desmayarse (1) (4), to faint
desmedirse (i, i) (42) (4), to be impudent
desmejorar (1), to impair, to make worse
desmembrar (ie) (37), to dismember
desmentir (ie, i) (41), to contradict, to give the lie to
desmenuce, etc. (**desmenuzar**)
desmenucé (**desmenuzar**)
desmenuzar (11), to crumble
desmerecer (73), to become unworthy
desmerezca, etc. (**desmerecer**)
desmerezco (**desmerecer**)
desmida, etc. (**desmedirse**)
desmide, etc. (**desmedirse**)
desmido (**desmedirse**)
desmidiendo (**desmedirse**)
desmidiera, etc. (**desmedirse**)
desmidiere, etc. (**desmedirse**)
desmidieron (**desmedirse**)
desmidiese, etc. (**desmedirse**)
desmidió (**desmedirse**)
desmiembra, etc. (**desmembrar**)
desmiembre, etc. (**desmembrar**)
desmiembro (**desmembrar**)
desmienta, etc. (**desmentir**)
desmiente, etc. (**desmentir**)
desmiento (**desmentir**)
desmilitarice, etc. (**desmilitarizar**)
desmilitaricé (**desmilitarizar**)
desmilitarizar (11), to demilitarize
desmintamos, etc. (**desmentir**)
desmintiendo (**desmentir**)
desmintiera, etc. (**desmentir**)
desmintiere, etc. (**desmentir**)
desmintieron (**desmentir**)
desminitiese (**desmentir**)
desmintió (**desmentir**)
desmochar (1), to chop off (the top or tip)
desmontar (1), to dismount, to take apart
desmoralice, etc. (**desmoralizar**)
desmoralicé (**desmoralizar**)
desmoralizar (11), to demoralize
desmoronar (1), to crumble
desmoronarse (1) (4), to crumble down
desmovilice, etc. (**desmovilizar**)
desmovilicé (**desmovilizar**)
desmovilizar (11), to demobilize
desnatar (1), to skim
desnaturalice, etc. (**desnaturalizar**)
desnaturalicé (**desnaturalizar**)
desnaturalizar (11), to denaturalize
desnivelar (1), to make uneven
desnivelarse (1) (4), to become uneven
desnucar (8), to break the neck of
desnudar (1), to undress
desnuque, etc. (**desnucar**)

desnuqué (desnucar)
desnutrirse (3) (4), to become undernourished
desobedecer (73), to disobey
desobedezca, etc. (desobedecer)
desobedezco (desobedecer)
desocupar (1), to empty, to vacate
desoiga, etc. (desoír)
desoigo (desoír)
desoír (95), not to hear, to turn a deaf ear, to refuse
desolar (ue) (36), to make desolate
desollar (ue) (36), to skin
desordenar (1), to throw in disorder
desorganice, etc. (desorganizar)
desorganicé (desorganizar)
desorganizar (11), to disorganize
desorientar (1), to misdirect, to confuse
desorientarse (1) (4), to lose one's way, to become confused
desosar (ue) (47), to bone
desovar (1), to spawn
desovillar (1), to unwind (a ball of string, yarn, etc.)
desovillarse (1) (4), to become unwound (a ball of string, yarn, etc.)
desoye, etc. (desoír)
desoyendo (desoír)
desoyera, etc. (desoír)
desoyere, etc. (desoír)
desoyeron (desoír)
desoyese, etc. (desoír)
desoyó (desoír)
despachar (1), to dispatch, to wait on, to attend to
despachurrar (1), to smash, to squash
desparramar (1), to scatter
despavorir (116), to be terrified
despedace, etc. (despedazar)
despedacé (despedazar)
despedazar (11), to break to pieces
despedir (i, i) (42), to fire (dismiss), to give off, to see off
despedirse (i, i) (42) (4), to say good-bye
despegar (9), to unglue, to take off
despegarse (9) (4), to come off
despegue, etc. (despegar)
despegué (despegar)
despeinar (1), to mess up the hair
despejar (1), to clear, to remove obstacles
despejarse (1) (4), to clear up
despellejar (1), to skin
despeñar (1), to fling down a precipice
despeñarse (1) (4), to fall down a precipice
despepitar (1), to remove seeds
desperdiciar (1), to waste
desperdigar (9), to scatter
desperdigue, etc. (desperdigar)
desperdigué (desperdigar)
desperece, etc. (desperezarse)
desperecé (desperezarse)
desperezarse (11) (4), to stretch
despertar (ie) (37), to wake up, to waken
despertarse (ie) (37) (4), to wake up, to awaken
despida, etc. (despedir)
despide, etc. (despedir)
despidiendo (despedir)
despidiera, etc. (despedir)
despidiere, etc. (despedir)
despidieron (despedir)
despidiese, etc. (despedir)
despidió (despedir)
despido (despedir)
despierta, etc. (despertar)
despierte, etc. (despertar)

despierto (despertar)
despilfarrar (1), to squander
despistar (1), to throw off the trail or course
desplace, etc. (desplacer) (desplazar)
desplacé (desplazar)
desplacer (73), to displease
desplazar (11), to displace (nautical), to take someone or something from its place in order to put it in another
desplazarse (11) (4), to shift
desplazca, etc. (desplacer)
desplazco (desplacer)
desplegar (ie) (50), to unfold, to display
desplegué (desplegar)
despleguemos, etc. (desplegar)
despliega, etc. (desplegar)
despliego (desplegar)
despliegue, etc. (desplegar)
desplomarse (1) (4), to collapse
desplumar (1), to pluck
despoblar (ue) (36), to depopulate
despojar (1), to despoil, to deprive of
desportillar (1), to chip the edge of
desposar (1), to marry
despotice, etc. (despotizar)
despoticé (despotizar)
despotizar (11), to tyrannize
despotricar (8), to talk without restraint
despotrique, etc. (despotricar)
despotriqué (despotricar)
despreciar (1), to despise
desprender (2), to loosen, to unfasten, to emit
despreocuparse (1) (4), to divert one's mind
desprestigiar (1), to discredit
desproporcionar (1), to disproportion
desproveer (99), to deprive of essentials
desproveyendo (desproveer)
desproveyera, etc. (desproveer)
desproveyere, etc. (desproveer)
desproveyeron (desproveer)
desproveyese, etc. (desproveer)
desproveyó (desproveer)
desprovisto (desproveer)
despuebla, etc. (despoblar)
despueble, etc. (despoblar)
despueblo (despoblar)
despuntar (1), to blunt, to bud or sprout, to excel
desquitarse (1) (4), to get even
destacar (8), to make stand out
destacarse (8) (4), to stand out
destapar (1), to uncover, to open
destaparse (1) (4), to get uncovered
destaque, etc. (destacar)
destaqué (destacar)
destejar (1), to untile (roofing tiles), to remove roofing tiles
destellar (1), to twinkle
desteñir (i, i) (60), to discolor, to fade
desteñirse (i, i) (60) (4), to discolor, to fade
desterrar (ie) (37), to exile
destetar (1), to wean
destierra, etc. (desterrar)
destierre, etc. (desterrar)
destierro (desterrar)
destilar (1), to distill
destinar (1), to destine
destiña, etc. (desteñir)
destiñe, etc. (desteñir)
destiñendo (desteñir)
destiñera, etc. (desteñir)
destiñere, etc. (desteñir)
destiñeron (desteñir)

destiñese, etc. (desteñir)
destiño (desteñir)
destiñó (desteñir)
destituir (71), to deprive, to dismiss from office
destituya, etc. (destituir)
destituye, etc. (destituir)
destituyendo (destituir)
destituyera, etc. (destituir)
destituyere, etc. (destituir)
destituyeron (destituir)
destituyese, etc. (destituir)
destituyo (destituir)
destituyó (destituir)
destornillar (1), to unscrew
destroce, etc. (destrozar)
destrocé (destrozar)
destronar (1), to dethrone
destrozar (11), to shatter
destruir (71), to destroy
destruya, etc. (destruir)
destruye, etc. (destruir)
destruyendo (destruir)
destruyera, etc. (destruir)
destruyere, etc. (destruir)
destruyeron (destruir)
destruyese, etc. (destruir)
destruyo (destruir)
destruyó (destruir)
desuela, etc. (desolar)
desuele, etc. (desolar)
desuelo (desolar)
desuella, etc. (desollar)
desuelle, etc. (desollar)
desuello (desollar)
desvaír (117), to empty, to vacate
desvalijar (1), to rob
desvalorar (1), to devaluate
desvalorice, etc. (desvalorizar)
desvaloricé (desvalorizar)
desvalorizar (11), to devaluate
desvanecerse (73) (4), to vanish, to faint
desvanezca, etc. (desvanecerse)
desvanezco (desvanecerse)
desvariar (61), to rave, to talk nonsense
desvayendo (desvaír)
desvayera, etc. (desvaír)
desvayere, etc. (desvaír)
desvayeron (desvaír)
desvayese, etc. (desvaír)
desvayó (desvaír)
desvelar (1), to keep awake, to reveal
desvergoncé (desvergonzarse)
desvergoncemos (desvergonzarse)
desvergonzarse (ue) (49) (4), to speak or act in an impudent or insolent manner
desvergüence, etc. (desvergonzarse)
desvergüenza, etc. (desvergonzarse)
desvergüenzo (desvergonzarse)
desvestir (i, i) (42), to undress
desviar (61), to deviate
desvirtuar (62), to diminish the quality or value of
desvista, etc. (desvestir)
desviste, etc. (desvestir)
desvistiendo (desvestir)
desvistiera, etc. (desvestir)
desvistiere, etc. (desvestir)
desvistieron (desvestir)
desvistiese, etc. (desvestir)
desvistió (desvestir)
desvisto (desvestir)
desvivirse (3) (4), to be crazy about, to do one's best for
detallar (1), to detail
detectar (1), to detect

detén (detener)
detendré, etc. (detener)
detendría, etc. (detener)
detener (ie) (108), to stop, to detain
detenga, etc. (detener)
detengo (detener)
deteriorar (1), to deteriorate
determinar (1), to determine, to cause
detestar (1), to detest
detiene, etc. (detener)
detonar (1), to detonate
detractar (1), to detract, to defame
detraer (109), to detract, to defame
detraiga, etc. (detraer)
detraigo (detraer)
detraje (detraer)
detrajera, etc. (detraer)
detrajere, etc. (detraer)
detrajeron (detraer)
detrajese, etc. (detraer)
detrajimos (detraer)
detrajiste (detraer)
detrajisteis (detraer)
detrajo (detraer)
detrayendo (detraer)
detuve, etc. (detener)
detuviera, etc. (detener)
detuviere, etc. (detener)
detuvieron (detener)
detuviese, etc. (detener)
detuvimos (detener)
detuviste (detener)
detuvisteis (detener)
detuvo (detener)
devastar (1), to devastate
devolver (ue) (70), to give back, to return, to vomit
devorar (1), to devour
devuelto (devolver)
devuelva, etc. (devolver)
devuelve, etc. (devolver)
devuelvo (devolver)
di (dar) (decir)
diafanice, etc. (diafanizar)
diafanicé (diafanizar)
diafanizar (11), to make diaphanous
diagnosticar (8), to diagnose
diagnostique, etc. (diagnosticar)
diagnostiqué (diagnosticar)
dialogar (9), to dialogue
dialogue, etc. (dialogar)
dialogué (dialogar)
dibujar (1), to draw
dice, etc. (decir)
diciendo (decir)
dictaminar (1), to pass judgment
dictar (1), to dictate, to lecture
dicho (decir)
dienta, etc. (dentar)
diente, etc. (dentar)
diento (dentar)
diera, etc. (dar)
diere, etc. (dar)
dieron (dar)
diese, etc. (dar)
diezmar (1), to decimate, to tithe
difamar (1), to defame
diferenciar (1), to differentiate
diferenciarse (1) (4), to differ
diferir (ie, i) (41), to defer, to differ
dificultar (1), to make difficult
difiera, etc. (diferir)
difiere, etc. (diferir)
difiero (diferir)
difiramos, etc. (diferir)
difiriendo (diferir)

difiriera, etc. (diferir)
difiriere, etc. (diferir)
difirieron (diferir)
difiriese, etc. (diferir)
difirió (diferir)
difundir (3), to diffuse, to speak, to broadcast
diga, etc. (decir)
digerir (ie, i) (41), to digest
digiera, etc. (digerir)
digiere, etc. (digerir)
digiero (digerir)
digiramos, etc. (digerir)
digiriendo (digerir)
digiriera, etc. (digerir)
digiriere, etc. (digerir)
digirieron (digerir)
digiriese, etc. (digerir)
digirió (digerir)
dignarse (1) (4), to condescend
dignificar (8), to dignify
dignificarse (8) (4), to become dignified
dignifique, etc. (dignificar)
dignifiqué (dignificar)
digo (decir)
dije (decir)
dijera, etc. (decir)
dijere, etc. (decir)
dijeron (decir)
dijese, etc. (decir)
dijimos (decir)
dijiste (decir)
dijisteis (decir)
dijo (decir)
dilapidar (1), to dilapidate
dilatar (1), to dilate, to defer
diligenciar (1), to take steps to accomplish
dilucidar (1), to elucidate
diluir (71), to dilute
diluya, etc. (diluir)
diluye, etc. (diluir)
diluyendo (diluir)
diluyera, etc. (diluir)
diluyere, etc. (diluir)
diluyeron (diluir)
diluyese, etc. (diluir)
diluyo (diluir)
diluyó (diluir)
diluviar (1), to rain hard, to pour
dimanar (1), to emanate, to spring up
diminuir (71), to diminish
diminuya, etc. (diminuir)
diminuye, etc. (diminuir)
diminuyendo (diminuir)
diminuyera, etc. (diminuir)
diminuyere, etc. (diminuir)
diminuyeron (diminuir)
diminuyese, etc. (diminuir)
diminuyo (diminuir)
diminuyó (diminuir)
dimitir (3), to resign
dimos (dar)
dinamitar (1), to dynamite
dio (dar)
diputar (1), to delegate, to empower
diré, etc. (decir)
diría, etc. (decir)
dirigir (16), to direct, to steer, to address
dirigirse (16) (4), to go
dirija, etc. (dirigir)
dirijo (dirigir)
discernir (ie) (85), to distinguish, to discern
discierna, etc. (discernir)
discierne, etc. (discernir)
discierno (discernir)

disciplinar (1), to discipline
discontinuar (62), to discontinue
disconvén (disconvenir)
disconvendré, etc. (disconvenir)
disconvendría, etc. (disconvenir)
disconvenga, etc. (disconvenir)
disconvengo (disconvenir)
disconvenir (ie, i) (111), to disagree
disconviene, etc. (disconvenir)
disconvine (disconvenir)
disconviniendo (disconvenir)
disconviniera, etc. (disconvenir)
disconviniere, etc. (disconvenir)
disconvinieron (disconvenir)
disconviniese, etc. (disconvenir)
disconvinimos (disconvenir)
disconviniste (disconvenir)
disconvinisteis (disconvenir)
disconvino (disconvenir)
discordar (ue) (36), to disagree, to be out of tune
discrepar (1), to disagree
discriminar (1), to discriminate against
discuerda, etc. (discordar)
discuerde, etc. (discordar)
discuerdo (discordar)
disculpar (1), to excuse, to pardon
disculparse (1) (4), to apologize
discurrir (3), to reason, to flow
discursear (1), to make speeches
discutir (3), to discuss, to argue
disecar (8), to stuff and mount
diseminar (1), to disseminate
disentir (ie, i) (41), to dissent
diseñar (1), to sketch
diseque, etc. (disecar)
disequé (disecar)
disertar (1), to discourse
disfrace, etc. (disfrazar)
disfracé (disfrazar)
disfrazar (11), to disguise
disfrutar (1), to enjoy
disgregar (9), to disintegrate
disgregue, etc. (disgregar)
disgregué (disgregar)
disgustar (1), to displease
disgustarse (1) (4), to be displeased
disidir (3), to dissent
disienta, etc. (disentir)
disiente, etc. (disentir)
disiento (disentir)
disimular (1), to hide one's feelings
disintamos, etc. (disentir)
disintiendo (disentir)
disintiera, etc. (disentir)
disintiere, etc. (disentir)
disintieron (disentir)
disintiese, etc. (disentir)
disintió (disentir)
disipar (1), to dissipate
dislocar (8), to dislocate
disloque, etc. (dislocar)
disloqué (dislocar)
disminuir (71), to diminish
disminuya, etc. (disminuir)
disminuye, etc. (disminuir)
disminuyendo (disminuir)
disminuyera, etc. (disminuir)
disminuyere, etc. (disminuir)
disminuyeron (disminuir)
disminuyese, etc. (disminuir)
disminuyo (disminuir)
disminuyó (disminuir)
disociar (1), to disassociate
disolver (ue) (70), to dissolve
disonar (ue) (36), to be discordant

disparar (1), to shoot
dispararse (1) (4), to go off, to dash off
disparatar (1), to talk nonsense
dispensar (1), to excuse, to grant
dispersar (1), to disperse
displacer = desplacer
displazca, etc. (displacer)
displazco (displacer)
dispón (disponer)
dispondré, etc. (disponer)
dispondría, etc. (disponer)
disponer (98), to dispose, to order
disponerse (98) (4), to get ready
disponga, etc. (disponer)
dispongo (disponer)
dispuesto (disponer)
dispuse (disponer)
dispusiera, etc. (disponer)
dispusiere, etc. (disponer)
dispusieron (disponer)
dispusiese, etc. (disponer)
dispusimos (disponer)
dispusiste (disponer)
dispusisteis (disponer)
dispuso (disponer)
disputar (1), to dispute, to argue
distanciar (1), to place at a distance
distar (1), to be far, to be different
diste (dar)
disteis (dar)
distender (ie) (39), to distend
distienda, etc. (distender)
distiende, etc. (distender)
distiendo (distender)
distinga, etc. (distinguir)
distingo (distinguir)
distinguir (17), to distinguish
distraer (109), to distract
distraiga, etc. (distraer)
distraigo (distraer)
distraje (distraer)
distrajera, etc. (distraer)
distrajere, etc. (distraer)
distrajeron (distraer)
distrajese, etc. (distraer)
distrajimos (distraer)
distrajiste (distraer)
distrajisteis (distraer)
distrajo (distraer)
distrayendo (distraer)
distribuir (71), to distribute
distribuya, etc. (distribuir)
distribuye, etc. (distribuir)
distribuyendo (distribuir)
distribuyera, etc. (distribuir)
distribuyere, etc. (distribuir)
distribuyeron (distribuir)
distribuyese, etc. (distribuir)
distribuyo (distribuir)
distribuyó (distribuir)
disturbar (1), to disturb
disuadir (3), to dissuade
disuelto (disolver)
disuelva, etc. (disolver)
disuelve, etc. (disolver)
disuelvo (disolver)
disuena, etc. (disonar)
disuene, etc. (disonar)
disueno (disonar)
divagar (9), to digress
divague, etc. (divagar)
divagué (divagar)
divergir (16), to diverge
diverja, etc. (divergir)
diverjo (divergir)
diversificar (8), to diversify

diversifique, etc. (diversificar)
diversifiqué (diversificar)
divertir (ie, i) (41), to amuse
divertirse (ie, i) (41) (4), to have a good time
divierta, etc. (divertir)
divierte, etc. (divertir)
divierto (divertir)
divinice, etc. (divinizar)
divinicé (divinizar)
divinizar (11), to deify
divirtamos, etc. (divertir)
divirtiendo (divertir)
divirtiera, etc. (divertir)
divirtiere, etc. (divertir)
divirtieron (divertir)
divirtiese, etc. (divertir)
divirtió (divertir)
divisar (1), to sight, to distinguish
divorciar (1), to divorce
divulgar (9), to make public
divulgarse (9) (4), to become widespread
divulgue, etc. (divulgar)
divulgué (divulgar)
diz, says, it is said (apocope of dice, dícese from decir, decirse)
doblar (1), to bend, to double, to turn, to fold
doblegar (9), to bend
doblegue, etc. (doblegar)
deblegué (doblegar)
documentar (1), to document
dogmatice, etc. (dogmatizar)
dogmaticé (dogmatizar)
dogmatizar (11), to dogmatize
doler (ue) (38), to ache, to cause grief
domar (1), to tame
domeñar (1), to tame
domesticar (8), to domesticate
domestique, etc. (domesticar)
domestiqué (domesticar)
dominar (1), to dominate, to handle perfectly, to have a thorough knowledge of
dominarse (1) (4), to control oneself
donar (1), to donate
dorar (1), to gild
dormir (ue, u) (40), to sleep
dormirse (ue, u) (40) (4), to fall asleep
dosificar (8), to measure out the doses of
dosifique, etc. (dosificar)
dosifiqué (dosificar)
dotar (1), to endow, to give a dowry to, to equip
doy (dar)
dragar (9), to dredge
drague, etc. (dragar)
dragué (dragar)
dramatice, etc. (dramatizar)
dramaticé (dramatizar)
dramatizar (11), to dramatize
drenar (1), to drain
driblar (1), to dribble
drogar (9), to drug
drogue, etc. (drogar)
drogué (drogar)
duchar (1), to give a shower
ducharse (1) (4), to take a shower
dudar (1), to doubt
duela, etc. (doler)
duele, etc. (doler)
duelo (doler)
duerma, etc. (dormir)
duerme, etc. (dormir)
duermo (dormir)
dulcificar (8), to sweeten
dulcifique, etc. (dulcificar)

dulcifiqué (dulcificar)
duplicar (8), to duplicate
duplique, etc. (duplicar)
dupliqué (duplicar)
durar (1), to last, to wear well
durmamos, etc. (dormir)
durmiendo (dormir)
durmiera, etc. (dormir)
durmiere, etc. (dormir)
durmieron (dormir)
durmiese, etc. (dormir)
durmió (dormir)

E

eclipsar (1), to eclipse, to outshine
economice (economizar)
economicé (economizar)
economizar (11), to economize
echar (1), to throw, to expel, to pour
edificar (8), to build
edifique, etc. (edificar)
edifiqué (edificar)
editar (1), to publish, to edit
educar (8), to educate, to bring up
eduque, etc. (educar)
eduqué (educar)
efectuar (62), to effect
efectuarse (62 (4), to take place
ejecutar (1), to execute, to perform
ejemplificar (8), to exemplify
ejemplifique, etc. (ejemplificar)
ejemplifiqué (ejemplificar)
ejercer (12), to practice, to exert
ejercitar (1), to exercise, to practice
ejerza, etc. (ejercer)
ejerzo (ejercer)
elaborar (1), to elaborate
elastificar (8), to make elastic
elastifique, etc. (elastificar)
elastifiqué (elastificar)
electrice, etc. (electrizar)
electricé (electrizar)
electrificar (8), to electrify
electrifique, etc. (electrificar)
electrifiqué (electrificar)
electrizar (11), to electrify
electrizarse (11)(4), to become electrified
electrocutar (1), to electrocute
electrolice, etc. (electrolizar)
electrolicé (electrolizar)
electrolizar (11), to electrolyze
elegantice, etc. (elegantizar)
eleganticé (elegantizar)
elegantizar (11), to make elegant
elegir (i, i) (57), to elect, to choose
elevar (1), to elevate
elevarse (1) (4), to rise
elige, etc. (elegir)
eligiendo (elegir)
eligiera, etc. (elegir)
eligiere, etc. (elegir)
eligieron (elegir)
eligiese, etc. (elegir)
eligió (elegir)
elija, etc. (elegir)
elijo (elegir)
eliminar (1), to eliminate
elogiar (1), to praise
eludir (3), to elude
emanar (1), to emanate
emancipar (4), to emancipate
emanciparse (1) (4), to become emancipated
embadurnar (1), to daub
embaír (117), to trick, to deceive

[22]

embalar embalar   encanecerse

embalar (1), to bale
embaldosar (1), to pave with tile
embalsamar (1), to embalm
embalsar (1), to dam
embalsarse (1) (4), to dam up
embarace, etc. (embarazar)
embaracé (embarazar)
embarazar (11), to embarass, to make pregnant
embarazarse (11) (4), to become embarrassed
embarcar (8), to embark, to ship, to launch (an enterprise)
embargar (9), to embargo, to paralyze, to impede, to restrain
embargue, etc. (embargar)
embargué (embargar)
embarque, etc. (embarcar)
embarqué (embarcar)
embarrancarse (8) (4), to run aground, to entangle
embarranque, etc. (embarrancarse)
embarranqué (embarrancarse)
embarrar (1), to stain or smear with mud
embarullar (1), to make a mess of, to do in a disorderly way
embastar (1), to baste, to stitch
embaucar (8), to bamboozle
embaular (1) or (65), to pack into a trunk
embauque, etc. (embaucar)
embauqué (embaucar)
embayendo (embaír)
embayera, etc. (embaír)
embayere, etc. (embaír)
embayeron (embaír)
embayese, etc. (embaír)
embayó (embaír)
embeber (2), to imbibe
embelesar (1), to charm
embelesarse (1) (4), to be charmed
embellecer (73), to beautify
embellezca, etc. (embellecer)
embellezco (embellecer)
embestir (i, i) (42), to attack
embista, etc. (embestir)
embiste, etc. (embestir)
embistiendo (embestir)
embistiera, etc. (embestir)
embistiere, etc. (embestir)
embistieron (embestir)
embistiese, etc. (embestir)
embistió (embestir)
embisto (embestir)
emblandecer (73), to soften
emblandezca, etc. (emblandecer)
emblandezco (emblandecer)
emblanquecer (73), to whiten
emblanquezca, etc. (emblanquecer)
emblanquezco (emblanquecer)
embobar (1), to enchant, to fascinate
embodegar (9), to store away
embodegue, etc. (embodegar)
embodegué (embodegar)
emborrachar (1), to intoxicate
emborracharse (1) (4), to get drunk
emborronar (1), to blot
emboscar (8), to ambush
embosque, etc. (emboscar)
embosqué (emboscar)
emboce, etc. (embozar)
embocé (embozar)
embotar (1), to dull
embozar (11), to cover the face with a cloak or muffler
embragar (9), to engage or throw in the clutch

embrague, etc. (embragar)
embragué (embragar)
embravecer (73), to infuriate
embravezca, etc. (embravecer)
embravezco (embravecer)
embrear (1), to cover or soak with tar
embriagar (9), to intoxicate, to enrapture
embriagarse (9) (4), to get drunk
embriague, etc. (embriagar)
embriagué (embriagar)
embrollar (1), to embroil
embromar (1), to tease
embrujar (1), to bewitch
embrutecer (73), to brutalize
embrutezca, etc. (embrutecer)
embrutezco (embrutecer)
embutir (3), to insert, to stuff
emerger (15), to emerge
emerja, etc. (emerger)
emerjo (emerger)
emigrar (1), to emigrate, to migrate
emitir (3), to emit
emocionar (1), to cause emotion
emocionarse (1) (4), to be touched, to be moved
empacar (8), to pack
empachar (1), to impede, to give indigestion
empadronar (1), to register in the census
empajar (1), to fill or cover with straw
empalagar (9), to cloy, to annoy
empalague, etc. (empalagar)
empalagué (empalagar)
empalar (1), to impale
empalice, etc. (empalizar)
empalicé (empalizar)
empalizar (11), to stockade
empalmar (1), to splice, to connect
empanar (1), to bread
empantanar (1), to swamp
empantanarse (1) (4), to become swampy
empañar (1), to fog, to tarnish
empapar (1), to soak
empapelar (1), to paper, to wallpaper
empaque, etc. (empacar)
empaqué (empacar)
empaquetar (1), to pack
emparejar (1), to pair
emparentar (ie) (37), to become related by marriage
emparienta, etc. (emparentar)
empariente, etc. (emparentar)
empariento (emparentar)
empastar (1), to cover with paste, to fill a tooth
empatar (1), to tie (in games, etc.)
empecé (empezar)
empecemos, etc. (empezar)
empecer (73), to damage
empedernir (116), to harden
empedrar (ie) (37), to pave with stones
empellendo (empeller)
empeller (26), to push
empellera, etc. (empeller)
empellere, etc. (empeller)
empelleron (empeller)
empellese, etc. (empeller)
empelló (empeller)
empeñar (1), to pawn, to pledge
empeñarse (1) (4), to insist, to go in debt
empeorar (1), to make worse
empeorarse (1) (4), to get worse
empequeñecer (73), to make smaller
empequeñezca, etc. (empequeñecer)
empequeñezco (empequeñecer)
emperejilar (1), to dress up

emperrarse (1) (4), to get stubborn
empezar (ie) (51), to begin
empezca, etc. (empecer)
empezco (empecer)
empiedra, etc. (empedrar)
empiedre, etc. (empedrar)
empiedro (empedrar)
empieza, etc. (empezar)
empiezo (empezar)
empinar (1), to raise
empinarse (1) (4), to rise high
emplace, etc. (emplazar)
emplacé (emplazar)
emplastar (1), to apply a plaster
emplazar (11), to place
emplear (1), to use, to employ
emplumar (1), to feather, to adorn with feathers
empobrecer (73), to impoverish
empobrezca, etc. (empobrecer)
empobrezco (empobrecer)
empolvar (1), to cover with dust, to powder
empollar (1), to hatch
emporcar (ue) (44), to soil, to dirty
emporcarse (ue) (44) (4), to get filthy
emporqué (emporcar)
emporquemos, etc. (emporcar)
empotrar (1), to embed
emprender (2), to undertake
empuerca, etc. (emporcar)
empuerco (emporcar)
empuerque, etc. (emporcar)
empujar (1), to push
empuñar (1), to hold tightly with the fist
emular, to emulate
enajenar (1), to alienate, to enrapture
enaltecer (73), to exalt
enaltecerse (73) (4), to be exalted
enaltezca, etc. (enaltecer)
enaltezco (enaltecer)
enamarillecer (73), to become yellow
enamarillezca, etc. (enamarillecer)
enamarillezco (enamarillecer)
enamorar (1), to enamor
enamorarse (1) (4), to fall in love
enarbolar (1), to raise on high
enardecer (73), to excite
enardecerse (73) (4), to get excited
enardezca, etc. (enardecer)
enardezco (enardecer)
encabece, etc. (encabezar)
encabecé (encabezar)
encabezar (11), to head, to put a heading
encabritarse (1) (4), to rear (said of a horse), to rise up on the hind legs (said of a horse)
encadenar (1), to chain
encajar (1), to fit into
encajonar (1), to box
encajonarse (1) (4), to run through a narrow ravine
encalaboce, etc. (encalabozar)
encalabocé (encalabozar)
encalabozar (11), to throw into jail
encalar (1), to whitewash
encalvecer (73), to become bald
encalvezca, etc. (encalvecer)
encalvezco (encalvecer)
encallar (1), to run aground, to get entangled
encaminar (1), to show the way
encaminarse (1) (4), to be on the way to
encanecerse (73) (4), to become gray-haired, to become old

encanezca, etc. (encanecerse)
encanezco (encanecerse)
encantar (1), to charm
encapotar (1), to cloak
encapotarse (1) (4), to become cloudy, to put on one's cloak
encapricharse (1) (4), to whimsically set one's mind upon, to be persistent in fulfilling a whim
encaramar (1), to raise
encaramarse (1) (4), to climb, to get on top
encarar (1), to face
encararse (1) (4), to come face to face
encarcelar (1), to incarcerate
encarecer (73), to raise the price of, to extol, to urge
encarecerse (73) (4), to rise in price
encarezca, etc. (encarecer)
encarezco (encarecer)
encargar (9), to entrust, to order, to ask for
encargue, etc. (encargar)
encargué (encargar)
encariñarse (1) (4), to become fond of
encarnice (encarnizar)
encarnicé (encarnizar)
encarnizar (11), to infuriate
encarnizarse (11) (4), to fight with fury, to get furious, to show cruelty
encarrilar (1), to put on the right track, to direct
encasillar (1), to pigeonhole
encauce, etc. (encauzar)
encaucé (encauzar)
encauzar (11), to direct, to channel (stream)
encender (ie) (39), to light, to set on fire, to turn on
encerar (1), to wax
encerrar (ie) (37), to lock up, to contain
encienda, etc. (encender)
enciende, etc. (encender)
enciendo (encender)
encierra, etc. (encerrar)
encierre, etc. (encerrar)
encierro (encerrar)
encoger (15), to shrink
encoja, etc. (encoger)
encojo (encoger)
encolar (1), to glue
encolerice, etc. (encolerizar)
encolericé (encolerizar)
encolerizar (11), to anger
encolerizarse (11 (4), to become angry
encomendar (ie) (37), to recommend, to entrust
encomiar (1), to praise
encomienda, etc. (encomendar)
encomiende, etc. (encomendar)
encomiendo (encomendar)
enconarse (1) (4), to become inflamed (said of the area surrounding a wound), to become irritated or aggravated (said of the resentment against someone)
encontrar (ue) (36), to find, to meet
encontrarse (ue) (36) (4), to meet
encopetarse (1) (4), to get well groomed, to get conceited
encornar (ue) (36), to gore
encornudar (1), to make a cuckold, to grow horns
encorvar (1), to bend
encorvarse (1) (4), to bend over
encrespar (1), to ruffle, to irritate
encuadernar (1), to bind (a book)
encuadrar (1), to frame, to fit

encubierto (encubrir)
encubrir (82), to hide
encuentra, etc. (encontrar)
encuentre, etc. (encontrar)
encuentro (encontrar)
encuerna, etc. (encornar)
encuerne, etc. (encornar)
encuerno (encornar)
encumbrar (1), to raise
encumbrarse (1) (4), to rise
encunar (1), to put in the cradle
encharcar (8), to turn into a puddle
encharque, etc. (encharcar)
encharqué (encharcar)
enchilar (1), to season with chili
enchufar (1), to plug, to connect
endentar (ie) (37), to indent, to furnish with teeth
enderece, etc. (enderezar)
enderecé (enderezar)
enderezar (11), to straighten, to put in order
endeudarse (1) (4), to get into debt
endienta, etc. (endentar)
endiente, etc. (endentar)
endiento (endentar)
endiosar (1), to deify
endiosarse (1) (4), to be stuck-up
endomingarse (9) (4), to dress up in one's Sunday (best) clothes
endomingue, etc. (endomingarse)
endomingué (endomingarse)
endorsar (1), to endorse
endosar (1), to endorse
endulce, etc. (endulzar)
endulcé (endulzar)
endulzar (11), to sweeten
endurar (1), to endure
endurecer (73), to harden
endurezca, etc. (endurecer)
endurezco (endurecer)
enemistar (1), to cause emnity between
enervar (1), to unnerve
enfadar (1), to anger
enfadarse (1) (4), to get angry
enfangar (9), to soil with mud
enfangarse (9) (4), to get soiled with mud
enfangue, etc. (enfangar)
enfangué (enfangar)
enfermar (1), to become ill
enfervorice, etc. (enfervorizar)
enfervoricé (enfervorizar)
enfervorizar (11), to arouse
enfervorizarse (11) (4), to become fervorous or heated
enflaquecer (73), to make thin
enflaquecerse (73) (4), to get thin
enflaquezca, etc. (enflaquecer)
enflaquezco (enflaquecer)
enfocar (8), to focus
enfoque, etc. (enfocar)
enfoqué (enfocar)
enfrascarse (8) (4), to become entangled or involved
enfrasque, etc. (enfrascarse)
enfrasqué (enfrascarse)
enfrenar (1), to bridle
enfrentar (1), to confront
enfrentarse (1) (4), to meet face to face
enfriar (61), to cool
enfundar (1), to put in a case
enfurecer (73), to infuriate
enfurecerse (73) (4), to become infuriated
enfurezca, etc. (enfurecer)
enfurezco (enfurecer)
enfurruñarse (1) (4), to get angry

engalanar (1), to adorn, to deck out
enganchar (1), to hook
engañar (1), to deceive
engañarse (1) (4), to be mistaken
engarce, etc. (engarzar)
engarcé (engarzar)
engarzar (11), to string (mainly jewelry)
engastar (1), to enchase
engatusar (1), to cajole
engendrar (1), to engender, to produce
englobar (1), to include, to lump together
engolfarse (1) (4), to become deeply absorbed
engolosinar (1), to allure
engomar (1), to gum
engordar (1), to fatten
engordarse (1) (4), to get fat
engranar (1), to gear
engrandecer (73), to enlarge, to enhance, to extol
engrandezca, etc. (engrandecer)
engrandezco (engrandecer)
engrapar (1), to staple
engrasar (1), to lubricate, to grease
engreír (i, i) (59), to make vain
engreírse (i, i) (59) (4), to become vain
engría, etc. (engreír)
engríe, etc. (engreír)
engriendo (engreír)
engriera, etc. (engreír)
engriere, etc. (engreír)
engrieron (engreír)
engriese, etc. (engreír)
engringarse (9) (4), to follow foreign customs
engringue, etc. (engringarse)
engringué (engringarse)
engrío (engreír)
engrió (engreír)
engrosar (ue) (36), to enlarge
engruesa, etc. (engrosar)
engruese, etc. (engrosar)
engrueso (engrosar)
engrumecerse (73) (4), to curdle
engrumezca, etc. (engrumecerse)
engrumezco (engrumecerse)
engullendo (engullir)
engullera, etc. (engullir)
engullere, etc. (engullir)
engulleron (engullir)
engullese, etc. (engullir)
engullir (27), to gulp down
engulló (engullir)
enhebrar (1), to thread
enhestar (ie) (37), to erect, to raise
enhiesta, etc. (enhestar)
enhieste, etc. (enhestar)
enhiesto (enhestar)
enjabelgar (9), to whitewash
enjabelgue, etc. (enjabelgar)
enjabelgué (enjabelgar)
enjabonar (1), to soap
enjaece, etc. (enjaezar)
enjaecé (enjaezar)
enjaezar (11), to harness
enjaular (1), to cage
enjuagar (9), to rinse
enjuague, etc. (enjuagar)
enjuagué (enjuagar)
enjugar (9), to dry
enjugue, etc. (enjugar)
enjugué (enjugar)
enjuiciar (1), to pass judgment on, to sue
enlace, etc. (enlazar)
enlacé (enlazar)
enladrillar (1), to pave with bricks

enlatar (1), to can
enlazar (11), to link, to lasso, to connect
enlodace, etc. (enlodazar)
enlodacé (enlodazar)
enlodar (1), to muddy
enlodarse (1) (4), to get muddied
enlodazar (11), to muddy
enloquecer (73), to madden, to craze
enloquecerse (73) (4), to become crazy
enloquezca, etc. (enloquecer)
enloquezco (enloquecer)
enlosar (1), to pave with slabs
enlustrecer (73), to polish
enlustrezca, etc. (enlustrecer)
enlustrezco (enlustrecer)
enlutar (1), to put in mourning, to dress in
  mourning
enmarañar (1), to entangle, to tangle
enmarañarse (1) (4), to become entangled, to get tangled
enmarcar (8), to frame
enmarque, etc. (enmarcar)
enmarqué (enmarcar)
enmascarar (1), to mask
enmascararse (1) (4), to put on a mask, to
  masquerade
enmendar (ie) (37), to correct, to amend
enmienda, etc. (enmendar)
enmiende, etc. (enmendar)
enmiendo (enmendar)
enmohecerse (73) (4), to get moldy
enmohezca, etc. (enmohecerse)
enmohezco (enmohecerse)
enmudecer (73), to silence
enmudezca, etc. (enmudecer)
enmudezco (enmudecer)
ennegrecer (73), to blacken, to darken
ennegrezca, etc. (ennegrecer)
ennegrezco (ennegrecer)
ennoblecer (73), to ennoble
ennoblezca, etc. (ennoblecer)
ennoblezco (ennoblecer)
enojar (1), to anger
enojarse (1) (4), to get angry
enorgullecer (73), to make proud
enorgullecerse (73) (4), to be proud
enorgullezca, etc. (enorgullecer)
enorgullezco (enorgullecer)
enraecer (73) to rarefy
enraezca, etc. (enraecer)
enraezco (enraecer)
enraíce, etc. (enraizar)
enraicé (enraizar)
enraizar (64), to take root
enredar (1), to catch in a net, to tangle up,
  to romp around
enriquecer (73), to enrich
enriquecerse (73) (4), to get rich
enriquezca, etc. (enriquecer)
enriquezco (enriquecer)
enristrar (1), to string (onions, etc.), to
  couch (the lance)
enrojecer (73), to make red, to make red-
  hot, to blush
enrojezca, etc. (enrojecer)
enrojezco (enrojecer)
enrollar (1), to roll up
enronquecer (73), to make hoarse
enronquecerse (73) (4), to get hoarse
enronquezca, etc. (enronquecer)
enronquezco (enronquecer)
enroscar (8), to twist, to screw a nut on a
  bolt
enrosque (enroscar)
enrosqué (enroscar)
ensacar (8), to bag, to sack

ensalce, etc. (ensalzar)
ensalcé (ensalzar)
ensalzar (11), to extol
ensamblar (1), to assemble, to joint
ensanchar (1), to widen
ensangrentar (ie) (37), to stain with blood
ensangrienta, etc. (ensangrentar)
ensangriente, etc. (ensangrentar)
ensangriento (ensangrentar)
ensañar (1), to enrage
ensañarse (1) (4), to exult in cruelty
ensaque, etc. (ensacar)
ensaqué (ensacar)
ensartar (1), to string (beads, etc.), to run
  through
ensayar (1), to rehearse, to try out
enseñar (1), to teach, to show
enseñorear (1), to lord
enseñorearse (1) (4), to take possession
ensilar (1), to ensilage
ensillar (1), to saddle
ensimismarse (1) (4), to become absorbed
  in thought
ensoberbecer (73), to make proud
ensoberbezca, etc. (ensoberbecer)
ensoberbezco (ensoberbecer)
ensombrecer (73), to darken
ensombrecerse (73) (4), to become sad
  and gloomy
ensombrezca, etc. (ensombrecer)
ensombrezco (ensombrecer)
ensordecer (73), to deafen
ensordezca, etc. (ensordecer)
ensordezco (ensordecer)
ensortijar (1), to curl
ensuciar (1), to dirty, to soil
ensuciarse (1) (4), to get dirty, to soil oneself
entablar (1), to board, to start (a conversation)
entallar (1), to carve, to engrave
entarimar (1), to floor with boards
entender (ie) (39), to understand
entenebrecer (73), to make dark
entenebrezca, etc. (entenebrecer)
entenebrezco (entenebrecer)
enterar (1), to inform
enterarse (1) (4), to find out
enternecer (73), to move to pity
enternecerse (73) (4), to be moved to pity
enternezca, etc. (enternecer)
enternezco (enternecer)
enterrar (ie) (37), to bury
entibiar (1), to make lukewarm
entibiarse (1) (4), to cool down
entienda, etc. (entender)
entiende, etc. (entender)
entiendo (entender)
entierra, etc. (enterrar)
entierre, etc. (enterrar)
entierro (enterrar)
entoldar (1), to cover with an awning
entonar (1), to intone, to sing in tune
entontecer (73), to make foolish
entontezca, etc. (entontecer)
entontezco (entontecer)
entornar (1), to half-close (door, eyes)
entorpecer (73), to stupefy, to dull, to obstruct
entorpezca, etc. (entorpecer)
entorpezco (entorpecer)
entrampar (1), to trap, to trick
entrañar (1), to contain
entrar (1), to bring in, to enter
entrarse (1) (4), to slip in
entreabierto (entreabrir)

entreabrir (75), to half-open (door, eyes)
entregar (9), to deliver, to hand over, to
  hand
entregarse (9) (4), to surrender
entregue, etc. (entregar)
entregué (entregar)
entrelace, etc. (entrelazar)
entrelacé (entrelazar)
entrelazar (11), to entwine
entremeter (2), to insert
entremeterse (2) (4), to butt in, to intrude
entrenar (1), to train
entreoiga, etc. (entreoír)
entreoigo (entreoír)
entreoír (95), to hear vaguely
entreoye, etc. (entreoír)
entreoyendo (entreoír)
entreoyera, etc. (entreoír)
entreoyere, etc. (entreoír)
entreoyeron (entreoír)
entreoyese, etc. (entreoír)
entreoyó (entreoír)
entresacar (8), to pick out
entresaque, etc. (entresacar)
entresaqué (entresacar)
entretallar (1), to carve, to engrave
entretallarse (1) (4), to fit together
entretejer (2), to weave together
entretén (entretener)
entretendré, etc. (entretener)
entretendría, etc. (entretener)
entretener (ie) (108), to entertain, to delay
entretenga, etc. (entretener)
entretengo (entretener)
entretiene, etc. (entretener)
entretuve (entretener)
entretuviera, etc. (entretener)
entretuviere, etc. (entretener)
entretuvieron (entretener)
entretuviese, etc. (entretener)
entretuvimos (entretener)
entretuviste (entretener)
entretuvisteis (entretener)
entretuvo (entretener)
entrevea, etc. (entrever)
entreveía, etc. (entrever)
entreveo (entrever)
entrever (112), to see vaguely, to see imperfectly, to suspect
entrevistar (1), to interview
entrevistarse (1) (4), to talk with
entrevisto (entrever) (entrevistar)
entristecer (73), to sadden
entristezca, etc. (entristecer)
entristezco (entristecer)
entrometer (2), to insert
entrometerse (2) (4), to butt in, to intrude
entroncar (8), to show or prove the relationship between, to be connected
entronice, etc. (entronizar)
entronicé (entronizar)
entronizar (11), to enthrone
entronque, etc. (entroncar)
entronqué (entroncar)
entumecer (73), to make numb
entumecerse (73), (4), to become numb
entumezca, etc. (entumecer)
entumezco (entumecer)
enturbiar (1), to make turbid
enturbiarse (1) (4), to become turbid
entusiasmar (1), to enthuse
enumerar (1), to enumerate
enunciar (1), to enunciate
envalentonar (1), to make cocky
envalentonarse (1) (4), to get cocky
envanecer (73), to make vain

envanecerse (73) (4), to become vain
envanezca, etc. (**envanecer**)
envanezco (**envanecer**)
envasar (1), to package in a container, to bottle
envejecer (73), to make old, to make look old
envejecerse (73) (4), to grow old
envejezca, etc. (**envejecer**)
envejezco (**envejecer**)
envenenar (1), to poison
enviar (61), to send
enviciar (1), to vitiate
envidiar (1), to envy
envilecer (73), to vilify
envilezca, etc. (**envilecer**)
envilezco (**envilecer**)
envinagrar (1), to put vinegar on or in
envinagrarse (1) (4), to turn sour
enviudar (1), to be widowed
envolver (ue) (70), to wrap, to imply, to involve
envuelto (**envolver**)
envuelva, etc. (**envolver**)
envuelve, etc. (**envolver**)
envuelvo (**envolver**)
enyesar (1), to plaster
enzarce, etc. (**enzarzarse**)
enzarcé (**enzarzarse**)
enzarzarse (11) (4), to be entangled among brambles, to become involved in difficulties
epilogar (9), to recapitulate
epilogue, etc. (**epilogar**)
epilogué (**epilogar**)
epitomar (1), to epitomize
equilibrar (1), to balance
equipar (1), to equip
equiparar (1), to compare
equivál (**equivaler**)
equivaldré, etc. (**equivaler**)
equivaldría, etc. (**equivaler**)
equivaler (110), to be equivalent, to equal
equivalga, etc. (**equivaler**)
equivalgo (**equivaler**)
equivocar (8), to mistake
equivocarse (8) (4), to be mistaken, to make a mistake
equivoque, etc. (**equivocar**)
equivoqué (**equivocar**)
erguir (ie, i) (86), to erect, to set up straight, to set upright
era, etc. (**ser**)
eres (**ser**)
erice, etc. (**erizar**)
ericé (**erizar**)
erigir (16), to erect
erija, etc. (**erigir**)
erijo (**erigir**)
erizar (11), to bristle
erosionar (1), to erode
erradicar (8), to eradicate
erradique, etc. (**erradicar**)
erradiqué (**erradicar**)
errar (ie) (52), to err, to miss, to wander
eructar (1), to belch
es (**ser**)
esboce, etc. (**esbozar**)
esbocé (**esbozar**)
esbozar (11), to sketch
escabechar (1), to pickle
escabullendo (**escabullirse**)
escabullera, etc. (**escabullirse**)
escabullere, etc. (**escabullirse**)
escabulleron (**escabullirse**)
escabullese, etc. (**escabullirse**)

escabullirse (27) (4), to slip away
escabulló (**escabullirse**)
escalar (1), to scale, to climb
escaldar (1), to scald
escalfar (1), to poach (eggs)
escalonar (1), to step
escamar (1), to scale, to cause suspicion
escamotear (1), to swindle, to make disappear by sleight of hand
escampar (1), to clear out, to ease up, to stop raining
escanciar (1), to pour wine, to serve wine
escandalice, etc. (**escandalizar**)
escandalicé (**escandalizar**)
escandalizar (11), to scandalize
escapar (1), to escape
escaramuce, etc. (**escaramuzar**)
escaramucé (**escaramuzar**)
escaramuzar (11), to skirmish
escarbar (1), to scratch up, to pry into
escarchar (1), to frost
escardar (1), to weed out
escarmentar (ie) (37), to punish as a lesson, to learn by one's experience
escarmienta, etc. (**escarmentar**)
escarmiente, etc. (**escarmentar**)
escarmiento (**escarmentar**)
escarnecer (73), to ridicule
escarnezca, etc. (**escarnecer**)
escarnezco (**escarnecer**)
escasear (1), to be scarce
escatimar (1), to skimp
escenificar (8), to stage
escenifique, etc. (**escenificar**)
escenifiqué (**escenificar**)
esclarecer (73), to lighten, to make clear, to dawn
esclarezca, etc. (**esclarecer**)
esclarezco (**esclarecer**)
esclavice, etc. (**esclavizar**)
esclavicé (**esclavizar**)
esclavizar (11), to enslave
escobillar (1), to brush
escocer (ue) (54), to smart
escoger (15), to choose, to select
escoja, etc. (**escoger**)
escojo (**escoger**)
escoltar (1), to escort
escombrar (1), to clear out (debris, rubbish)
esconder (2), to hide
escozamos, etc. (**escocer**)
escribir (69), to write
escrito (**escribir**)
escrutar (1), to scrutinize
escuchar (1), to listen to, to heed
escudriñar (1), to pry into
escuece, etc. (**escocer**)
escueza, etc. (**escocer**)
escuezo (**escocer**)
esculpir (3), to sculpture
escupir (3), to spit
escurrir (3), to drain, to wring, to drip, to slide
escurrirse (3) (4), to slip away
esforcé (**esforzar**)
esforcemos, etc. (**esforzar**)
esforzar (ue) (46), to encourage
esforzarse (ue) (46) (4), to try hard
esfuerce, etc. (**esforzar**)
esfuerza, etc. (**esforzar**)
esfuerzo (**esforzar**)
esfumar (1), to tone down
esfumarse (1) (4), to disappear
esgrimir (3), to brandish, to fence
eslabonar (1), to link

esmaltar (1), to enamel, to adorn with bright colors
esmerarse (1) (4), to do one's best, to take pains
espabilar (1), to snuff
espaciar (1), to space
espantar (1), to scare, to frighten away
esparcir (13), to scatter
esparza, etc. (**esparcir**)
esparzo (**esparcir**)
especificar (8), to specify
especifique, etc. (**especificar**)
especifiqué (**especificar**)
especular (1), to speculate
esperar (1), to hope, to expect, to wait
espesar (1), to thicken
espiar (61), to spy
espigar (9), to form ears (said of cereals)
espigarse (9) (4), to grow tall
espigue, etc. (**espigar**)
espigué (**espigar**)
espirar (1), to exhale
espiritualice, etc. (**espiritualizar**)
espiritualicé (**espiritualizar**)
espiritualizar (11), to spiritualize
espolear (1), to spur
espolvorear (1), to sprinkle with powder
espolvorice, etc. (**espolvorizar**)
espolvoricé (**espolvorizar**)
espolvorizar (11), to sprinkle with powder
esponjar (1), to make fluffy
esponjarse (1) (4), to become fluffy
esposar (1), to handcuff
espumar (1), to foam
esquematice, etc. (**esquematizar**)
esquematicé (**esquematizar**)
esquematizar (11), to sketch, to outline
esquiar (61), to ski
esquilar (1), to sheer
esquivar (1), to dodge
está, etc. (**estar**)
estabilice, etc. (**estabilizar**)
estabilicé (**estabilizar**)
estabilizar (11), to stabilize
estabilizarse (11) (4), to become stabilized
establecer (73), to establish
establezca, etc. (**establecer**)
establezco (**establecer**)
estacionar (1), to park, to station
estafar (1), to swindle, to defraud
estallar (1), to explode
estampar (1), to stamp
estampillar (1), to stamp
estancar (8), to staunch
estancarse (8) (4), to stagnate
estandardice, etc. (**estandardizar**)
estandardicé (**estandardizar**)
estandardizar (11), to standardize
estanque, etc. (**estancar**)
estanqué (**estancar**)
estañar (1), to solder
estar (87), to be
estatuir (71), to establish
estatuya, etc. (**estatuir**)
estatuye, etc. (**estatuir**)
estatuyendo (**estatuir**)
estatuyera, etc. (**estatuir**)
estatuyere, etc. (**estatuir**)
estatuyeron (**estatuir**)
estatuyese, etc. (**estatuir**)
estatuyo (**estatuir**)
estatuyó (**estatuir**)
esté, etc. (**estar**)
estereotipar (1), to stereotype
esterilice, etc. (**esterilizar**)
esterilicé (**esterilizar**)

esterilizar (11), to sterilize
estigmatice, etc. (estigmatizar)
estigmaticé (estigmatizar)
estigmatizar (11), to stigmatize
estilarse (1) (4), to be in style
estilice, etc. (estilizar)
estilicé (estilizar)
estilizar (11), to stylize
estimar (1), to esteem, to estimate
estimular (1), to stimulate
estipular (2), to stipulate
estirar (1), to stretch, to tense
estofar (1), to stew
estorbar (1), to be in the way, to obstruct, to annoy
estornudar (1), to sneeze
estoy (estar)
estrangular (1), to strangle
estratificar (8), to stratify
estratifique, etc. (estratificar)
estratifiqué (estratificar)
estrechar (1), to narrow
estrellar (1), to shatter
estrellarse (1) (4), to crash
estremecer (73), to shake
estremezca, etc. (estremecer)
estremezco (estremecer)
estrenar (1), to use for the first time, to do or wear for the first time
estrenarse (1) (4), to begin to act in some capacity
estreñir (i, i) (60), to constipate
estreñirse (i, i) (60) (4), to become constipated
estriar (61), to striate, to groove, to flute
estribar (1), to rest on, to be based on
estriña, etc. (estreñir)
estriñe, etc. (estreñir)
estriñendo (estreñir)
estriñera, etc. (estreñir)
estriñere, etc. (estreñir)
estriñeron (estreñir)
estrinese, etc. (estreñir)
estriño (estreñir)
estriñó (estreñir)
estropear (1), to spoil
estructurar (1), to organize
estrujar (1), to squeeze
estudiar (1), to study
estuve (estar)
estuviera, etc. (estar)
estuviere, etc. (estar)
estuvieron (estar)
estuviese, etc. (estar)
estuvimos (estar)
estuviste (estar)
estuvisteis (estar)
estuvo (estar)
eternice, etc. (eternizar)
eternicé (eternizar)
eternizar (11), to make endless
eternizarse (11) (4), never to finish
etiquetear (1), to tag
evacuar (1), to evacuate
evadir (3), to evade
evaluar (62), to evaluate
evangelice, etc. (evangelizar)
evangelicé (evangelizar)
evangelizar (11), to evangelize
evaporar (1), to evaporate
evaporice, etc. (evaporizar)
evaporicé (evaporizar)
evaporizar (11), to vaporize
evidenciar (1), to make evident
evitar (1), to avoid
evocar (8), to evoke

evoque, etc. (evocar)
evoqué (evocar)
evolucionar (1), to evolve
exacerbar (1), to exacerbate
exagerar (1), to exaggerate
exaltar (1), to exalt
exaltarse (1) (4), to become excited
examinar (1), to examine, to inspect
examinarse (1) (4), to take an examination
excavar (1), to excavate
exceder (2), to exceed
exceptuar (62), to except
excitar (1), to excite
excitarse (1) (4), to become excited
exclamar (1), to exclaim
excluir (71), to exclude
excluya, etc. (excluir)
excluye, etc. (excluir)
excluyendo (excluir)
excluyera, etc. (excluir)
excluyere, etc. (excluir)
excluyeron (excluir)
excluyese, etc. (excluir)
excluyo (excluir)
excluyó (excluir)
excogitar (1), to think out, to devise
excomulgar (9), to excommunicate
excomulgue, etc. (excomulgar)
excomulgué (excomulgar)
excusar (1), to excuse, to avoid, to exempt
excusarse (1) (4), to apologize
exhalar (1), to emit, to exhale
exhibir (3), to exhibit
exhibirse (3) (4), to show off
exhortar (1), to exhort
exhumar (1), to exhume
exigir (16), to require, to demand
exija, etc. (exigir)
exijo (exigir)
eximir (3), to exempt
exonerar (1), to exonerate
exorcice, etc. (exorcizar)
exorcicé (exorcizar)
exorcizar (11), to exorcise
expansionar (1), to expand
expansionarse (1) (4), to open one's heart
expatriar (61), to expatriate
expedir (i, i) (42), to expedite, to issue, to ship
experimentar (1), to experience, to experiment
expiar (61), to atone for, to expiate
expida, etc. (expedir)
expide, etc. (expedir)
expidiendo (expedir)
expidiera, etc. (expedir)
expidiere, etc. (expedir)
expidieron (expedir)
expidiese, etc. (expedir)
expidió (expedir)
expido (expedir)
expirar (1), to expire
explanar (1), to level, to explain
explayar (1), to extend
explayarse (1) (4), to discourse at large
explicar (8), to explain
explique, etc. (explicar)
expliqué (explicar)
explorar (1), to explore
explotar (1), to exploit, to explode
expón (exponer)
expondré, etc. (exponer)
expondría, etc. (exponer)
exponer (98), to expose, to show
exponga, etc. (exponer)
expongo (exponer)

exportar (1), to export
expresar (1), to express
exprimir (3), to squeeze
expropiar (1), to expropriate
expuesto (exponer)
expugnar (1), to take by storm
expulsar (1), to expel
expurgar (9), to expurgate
expurgue, etc. (expurgar)
expurgué (expurgar)
expuse (exponer)
expusiera, etc. (exponer)
expusiere, etc. (exponer)
expusieron (exponer)
expusiese, etc. (exponer)
expusimos (exponer)
expusiste (exponer)
expusisteis (exponer)
expuso (exponer)
extasiar (61), to delight
extasiarse (61) (4), to be in ecstasy
extender (ie) (39), to extend, to draw up (a document)
extenuar (62), to extenuate
exteriorice, etc. (exteriorizar)
exterioricé (exteriorizar)
exteriorizar (11), to make manifest
exterminar (1), to exterminate
extienda, etc. (extender)
extiende, etc. (extender)
extiendo (extender)
extinga, etc. (extinguir)
extingo (extinguir)
extinguir (17), to extinguish
extinguirse (17) (4), to be extinguished, to go out
extirpar (1), to destroy completely, to root out
extorsionar (1), to extort
extractar (1), to abstract (a writing)
extraer (109), to extract
extraiga, etc. (extraer)
extraigo (extraer)
extraje (extraer)
extrajera, etc. (extraer)
extrajere, etc. (extraer)
extrajeron (extraer)
extrajese, etc. (extraer)
extrajimos (extraer)
extrajiste (extraer)
extrajisteis (extraer)
extrajo (extraer)
extralimitarse (1) (4), to overstep
extranjerice, etc. (extranjerizarse)
extranjericé (extranjerizarse)
extranjerizarse (11) (4), to adopt foreign ways
extrañar (1), to miss, to banish
extrañarse (1) (4), to be surprised
extrapolar (1), to extrapolate
extraviar (61), to mislead, to misplace
extraviarse (61) (4), to go astray, to get lost
extrayendo (extraer)
extremar (1), to carry to an extreme
extremarse (1) (4), to exert oneself to the utmost
eyacular (1), to ejaculate

F

fabricar (8), to manufacture, to fabricate
fabrique, etc. (fabricar)
fabriqué (fabricar)
facilitar (1), to facilitate, to supply
facturar (1), to check baggage, to invoice

fajar (1), to girdle
falsear (1), to misrepresent
falsificar (8), to falsify, to counterfeit, to forge
falsifique, etc. **(falsificar)**
falsifiqué (falsificar)
faltar (1), to be lacking, to be absent, to offend
fallar (1), to fail, to misfire
fallecer (73), to die
fallezca, etc. **(fallecer)**
fallezco (fallecer)
familiarice, etc. **(familiarizar)**
familiaricé (familiarizar)
familiarizar (11), to familiarize
familiarizarse (11) (4), to become familiar
fanatice, etc. **(fanatizar)**
fanaticé (fanatizar)
fanatizar (11), to make fanatical
fanfarronear (1), to brag
fantasear (1), to daydream, to imagine
farolear (1), to brag
fascinar (1), to fascinate
fastidiar (1), to annoy
fatigar (9), to fatigue, to tire
fatigarse (9) (4), to get tired
fatigue, etc. **(fatigar)**
fatigué (fatigar)
favorecer (73), to favor
favorezca, etc. **(favorecer)**
favorezco (favorecer)
fecundar (1), to fecundate
fecundice, etc. **(fecundizar)**
fecundicé (fecundizar)
fecundizar (11), to fecundate
fechar (1), to date (a document, etc.)
felicitar (1), to congratulate
fermentar (1), to ferment
fertilice, etc. **(fertilizar)**
fertilicé (fertilizar)
fertilizar (11), to fertilize
festejar (1), to feast, to celebrate, to court
fiar (19), to trust, to confide, to sell on credit
fiarse (19) (4), to place confidence in
figurar (1), to figure, to represent
figurarse (1) (4), to imagine
fijar (1), to fix
fijarse (1) (4), to pay attention
filmar (1), to film
filosofar (1), to philosophize
filtrar (1), to filter
finalice, etc. **(finalizar)**
finalicé (finalizar)
finalizar (11), to finalize, to finish, to end
financiar (1), to finance
fingir (16), to pretend
finja, etc. **(fingir)**
finjo (fingir)
firmar (1), to sign
fisgar (9), to pry, to snoop
fisgue, etc. **(fisgar)**
fisgué (fisgar)
flagelar (1), to whip
flamear (1), to flame
flanquear (1), to flank
flaquear (1), to weaken
fletar (1), to charter
flirtear (1), to flirt
flojear (1), to slacken, to weaken, to be lazy
florear (1), to decorate with flowers
florecer (73), to blossom, to flourish
florecerse (73) (4), to become moldy
florezca, etc. **(florecer)**
florezco (florecer)

flotar (1), to float
fluctuar (62), to fluctuate
fluir (71), to flow
fluya, etc. **(fluir)**
fluye, etc. **(fluir)**
fluyendo (fluir)
fluyera, etc. **(fluir)**
fluyere, etc. **(fluir)**
fluyeron (fluir)
fluyese, etc. **(fluir)**
fluyo (fluir)
fluyó (fluir)
fomentar (1), to foment, to promote
forcé (forzar)
forcemos, etc. **(forzar)**
forjar (1), to forge
formalice, etc. **(formalizar)**
formalicé (formalizar)
formalizar (11), to formalize, to formulate, to legalize
formar (1), to form
formular (1), to formulate
fornicar (8), to fornicate
fornique, etc. **(fornicar)**
forniqué (fornicar)
forrar (1), to line, to cover
fortalecer (73), to strengthen
fortalezca, etc. **(fortalecer)**
fortalezco (fortalecer)
fortificar (8), to fortify
fortifique, etc. **(fortificar)**
fortifiqué (fortificar)
forzar (ue) (46), to force, to rape
fotograbar (1), to photoengrave
fotografiar (61), to photograph
fracasar (1), to fail
fraccionar (1), to divide into fractions
fracturar (1), to fracture
fragmentar (1), to break into fragments
fragmentarse (1) (4), to fragment
fraguar (10), to forge, to scheme
fraguarse (10) (4), to set (cement)
fragüe, etc. **(fraguar)**
fragüé (fraguar)
franquear (1), to frank (a letter), to exempt, to free
frasear (1), to phrase
fraternice, etc. **(fraternizar)**
fraternicé (fraternizar)
fraternizar (11), to fraternize
frecuentar (1), to frequent
fregar (ie) (50), to rub, to scrub, to wash (dishes), to annoy
fregué (fregar)
freguemos, etc. **(fregar)**
freír (i, i) (88), to fry
frenar (1), to brake, to restrain
fresar (1), to drill, to mill
fría, etc. **(freír)**
fríe, etc. **(freír)**
friccionar (1), to rub, to massage
friega, etc. **(fregar)**
friego (fregar)
friegue, etc. **(fregar)**
friendo (freír)
friera, etc. **(freír)**
friere, etc. **(freír)**
frieron (freír)
friese, etc. **(freír)**
frío (freír)
frió (freír)
frito (freír)
frisar (1), to frizzle, to be near to
frotar (1), to rub
fructificar (8), to bear fruit
fructifique, etc. **(fructificar)**

fructifiqué (fructificar)
fruir (71), to enjoy oneself
fruncir (13), to wrinkle
frunza, etc. **(fruncir)**
frunzo (fruncir)
frustrar (1), to frustrate
fruya, etc. **(fruir)**
fruye, etc. **(fruir)**
fruyendo (fruir)
fruyera, etc. **(fruir)**
fruyere, etc. **(fruir)**
fruyeron (fruir)
fruyese, etc. **(fruir)**
fruyo (fruir)
fruyó (fruir)
fue (ser) (ir)
fuera, etc. **(ser) (ir)**
fuerce, etc. **(forzar)**
fuere, etc. **(ser) (ir)**
fueron (ser) (ir)
fuerza, etc. **(forzar)**
fuerzo (forzar)
fuese, etc. **(ser) (ir)**
fugarse (9) (4), to flee, to escape
fugue, etc. **(fugarse)**
fugué (fugarse)
fui (ser) (ir)
fuimos (ser) (ir)
fuiste (ser) (ir)
fuisteis (ser) (ir)
fulgurar (1), to flash
fulminar (1), to detonate, to shout (decrees, etc.) thunderously
fumar (1), to smoke
fumigar (9), to fumigate
fumigue, etc. **(fumigar)**
fumigué (fumigar)
funcionar (1), to function, to work, to run
fundar (1), to found, to establish, to base
fundarse (1) (4), to base one's opinion
fundir (3), to smelt, to fuse
fusilar (1), to execute by shooting
fusionar (1), to fuse, to merge
fustigar (9), to whip, to censure severely
fustigue, etc. **(fustigar)**
fustigué (fustigar)

G

galantear (1), to court
galardonar (1), to reward
galopar (1), to gallop
galvanice, etc. **(galvanizar)**
galvanicé (galvanizar)
galvanizar (11), to galvanize
gallardear (1), to act with grace
gambetear (1), to caper and prance
ganar (1), to earn, to gain, to win, to beat
gandulear (1), to loaf, to idle
gangrenarse (1) (4), to gangrene
garabatear (1), to scribble
garantice, etc. **(garantizar)**
garanticé (garantizar)
garantir (116), to guarantee
garantizar (11), to guarantee
gargajear (1), to expectorate phlegm
gargarear (1), to gargle
gargarice, etc. **(gargarizar)**
gargaricé (gargarizar)
gargarizar (11), to gargle
garlopar (1), to plane
garrapatear (1), to scribble
garuar (62), to drizzle
gasificar (8), to gasify
gasifique, etc. **(gasificar)**
gasifiqué (gasificar)

gastar (1), to spend, to waste, to wear, to wear out, to use up
gatear (1), to crawl
gemir (i, i) (42), to moan, to whine
generalice, etc. (**generalizar**)
generalicé (**generalizar**)
generalizar (11), to generalize
generalizarse (11) (4), to become generalized
generar (1), to generate
germinar (1), to germinate
gesticular (1), to gesture
gestionar (1), to manage
gima, etc. (**gemir**)
gime, etc. (**gemir**)
gimiendo (**gemir**)
gimiera, etc. (**gemir**)
gimiere, etc. (**gemir**)
gimieron (**gemir**)
gimiese, etc. (**gemir**)
gimió (**gemir**)
gimo (**gemir**)
gimotear (1), to whine
girar (1), to revolve; to turn; to send, issue or draw checks
gloriarse (61) (4), to boast, to be proud
glorificar (8), to glorify
glorifique, etc. (**glorificar**)
glorifiqué (**glorificar**)
gobernar (ie) (37), to govern, to steer
gobierna, etc. (**gobernar**)
gobierne, etc. (**gobernar**)
gobierno (**gobernar**)
golpear (1), to strike, to bruise, to knock
goce, etc. (**gozar**)
gocé (**gozar**)
gorjear (1), to warble
gotear (1), to drip, to sprinkle
gozar (11), to enjoy
grabar (1), to engrave, to tape-record
graduar (62), to graduate, to grade
graduarse (62) (4), to graduate
granar (1), to start forming kernels or seeds
granice (**granizar**)
granizar (11), to hail
granjearse (1) (4), to get, to win (as the good will of another)
granular (1), to granulate
gratificar (8), to gratify, to reward
gratifique, etc. (**gratificar**)
gratifiqué (**gratificar**)
gravar (1), to burden
gravitar (1), to gravitate, to rest
graznar (1), to croak, to cackle
grillarse (1) (4), to shoot, to sprout
gritar (1), to shout
gruñendo (**gruñir**)
gruñera, etc. (**gruñir**)
gruñere, etc. (**gruñir**)
gruñeron (**gruñir**)
gruñese, etc. (**gruñir**)
gruñir (29), to grunt, to growl, to grumble, to creak (door)
gruñó (**gruñir**)
guardar (1), to guard, to keep, to watch over
guarecer (73), to give shelter
guarecerse (73) (4), to take shelter
guarezca, etc. (**guarecer**)
guarezco (**guarecer**)
guarnecer (73), to garnish
guarnezca, etc. (**guarnecer**)
guarnezco (**guarnecer**)
guerrear (1), to war

guerrillear (1), to engage in guerrilla warfare
guiar (19), to guide, to steer
guillotinar (1), to guillotine
guiñar (1), to wink
guisar (1), to cook
guitarrear (1), to play the guitar
gustar (1), to taste, to be pleasing, to like
guturalice, etc. (**guturalizar**)
guturalicé (**guturalizar**)
guturalizar (11), to make guttural sounds

H

ha (**haber**)
habéis (**haber**)
haber (89), to have (auxiliary)
habilitar (1), to enable
habitar (1), to inhabit, to live
habituar (62), to habituate, to accustom
hablar (1), to speak, to talk
habré, etc. (**haber**)
habría, etc. (**haber**)
hacendarse (ie) (37) (4), to acquire property
hacer (90), to do, to make
hacienda, etc. (**hacendarse**)
haciende, etc. (**hacendarse**)
haciendo (**hacendarse**) (**hacer**)
haga, etc. (**hacer**)
hago (**hacer**)
halagar (9), to flatter, to gratify
halague, etc. (**halagar**)
halagué (**halagar**)
hallar (1), to find
hallarse (1) (4), to find oneself, to be
hambrear (1), to starve
han (**haber**)
haranganear (1), to loaf
haré, etc. (**hacer**)
haría, etc. (**hacer**)
hartar (1), to satiate, to satisfy, to tire, to make fed up
has (**haber**)
hastiar (61), to annoy
haya, etc. (**haber**)
haz (**hacer**)
he (**haber**)
hechice, etc. (**hechizar**)
hechicé (**hechizar**)
hechizar (11), to bewitch, to charm
hecho (**hacer**)
heder (ie) (39), to stink
helar (ie) (37), to freeze, to congeal, to astonish
hemos (**haber**)
henchir (i, i) (42), to fill
hender (ie) (39), to cleave
herborice, etc. (**herborizar**)
herboricé (**herborizar**)
herborizar (11), to gather herbs
heredar (1), to inherit
herir (ie, i) (41), to wound, to hurt
hermanar (1), to harmonize, to join
hermosear (1), to beautify
herrar (ie) (37), to shoe (a horse, etc.)
hervir (ie, i) (41), to boil
hibernar (1), to hibernate
hice (**hacer**)
hiciera, etc. (**hacer**)
hiciere, etc. (**hacer**)
hicieron (**hacer**)
hiciese, etc. (**hacer**)
hicimos (**hacer**)
hiciste (**hacer**)

hicisteis (**hacer**)
hidratar (1), to hydrate
hidrogenar (1), to hydrogenate
hidrolice, etc. (**hidrolizar**)
hidrolicé (**hidrolizar**)
hidrolizar (11), to hydrolize
hieda, etc. (**heder**)
hiede, etc. (**heder**)
hiedo (**heder**)
hiela, etc. (**helar**)
hiele, etc. (**helar**)
hielo (**helar**)
hienda, etc. (**hender**)
hiende, etc. (**hender**)
hiendo (**hender**)
hiera, etc. (**herir**)
hiere, etc. (**herir**)
hiero (**herir**)
hierra, etc. (**herrar**)
hierre, etc. (**herrar**)
hierro (**herrar**)
hierva, etc. (**hervir**)
hierve, etc. (**hervir**)
hiervo (**hervir**)
higienice, etc. (**higienizar**)
higienicé (**higienizar**)
higienizar (11), to make hygienic
hilar (1), to spin (thread, etc.)
hilvanar (1), to baste (sewing)
hincar (8), to drive (into)
hincarse (8) (4), to kneel down
hincha, etc. (**henchir**) (**hinchar**)
hinchar (1), to swell
hinche, etc. (**henchir**) (**hinchar**)
hinchiendo (**henchir**)
hinchiera, etc. (**henchir**)
hinchiere, etc. (**henchir**)
hinchieron (**henchir**)
hinchiese, etc. (**henchir**)
hinchió (**henchir**)
hincho (**henchir**) (**hinchar**)
hinque, etc. (**hincar**)
hinqué (**hincar**)
hiperbolice, etc. (**hiperbolizar**)
hiperbolicé (**hiperbolizar**)
hiperbolizar (11), to express with hyperbole
hipnotice, etc. (**hipnotizar**)
hipnoticé (**hipnotizar**)
hipnotizar (11), to hypnotize
hiramos, etc. (**herir**)
hiriendo (**herir**)
hiriera, etc. (**herir**)
hiriere, etc. (**herir**)
hirieron (**herir**)
hiriese, etc. (**herir**)
hirió (**herir**)
hirvamos, etc. (**hervir**)
hirviendo (**hervir**)
hirviera, etc. (**hervir**)
hirviere, etc. (**hervir**)
hirvieron (**hervir**)
hirviese, etc. (**hervir**)
hirvió (**hervir**)
hizo (**hacer**)
hoce (**hozar**)
hocé (**hozar**)
hocicar (8), to nuzzle
hocique, etc. (**hocicar**)
hociqué (**hocicar**)
hociquear (1), to nuzzle
hojear (1), to leaf through (a book, etc.)
holgar (ue) (45), to rest, to loaf, to be needless or useless, to take pleasure or satisfaction

holgarse (ue) (45) (4), to be glad
holgué (holgar)
holguemos, etc. (holgar)
hollar (ue) (36), to tread upon, to humiliate
homogeneice, etc. (homogeneizar)
homogeneicé (homogeneizar)
homogeneizar (11), to homogenize
homogenice, etc. (homogenizar)
homogenicé (homogenizar)
homogenizar (11), to homogenize
homologar (9), to make equal
homologue, etc. (homologar)
homologué (homologar)
honrar (1), to honor
honrarse (1) (4), to be honored
horadar (1), to perforate
hormiguear (1), to swarm
hornear (1), to bake
horrorice, etc. (horrorizar)
horroricé (horrorizar)
horrorizar (11), to horrify
horrorizarse (11) (4), to be horrified
hospedar (1), to lodge
hospitalice, etc. (hospitalizar)
hospitalicé (hospitalizar)
hospitalizar (11), to hospitalize
hostigar (9), to harass
hostigue, etc. (hostigar)
hostigué (hostigar)
hozar (11), to nuzzle
hube (haber)
hubiera, etc. (haber)
hubiere, etc. (haber)
hubieron (haber)
hubiese, etc. (haber)
hubimos (haber)
hubiste (haber)
hubisteis (haber)
hubo (haber)
huela, etc. (oler)
huele, etc. (oler)
huelga, etc. (holgar)
huelgo (holgar)
huelgue, etc. (holgar)
huelo (oler)
huella, etc. (hollar)
huelle, etc. (hollar)
huello (hollar)
huir (71), to flee
humanice, etc. (humanizar)
humanicé (humanizar)
humanizar (11), to humanize
humear (1), to smoke
humedecer (73), to humidify, to moisten, to wet
humedecerse (73) (4), to become moist, to become damp
humedezca, etc. (humedecer)
humedezco (humedecer)
humillar (1), to humiliate
hundir (3), to sink
hurgar (9), to poke
hurgue, etc. (hurgar)
hurgué (hurgar)
hurtar (1), to steal
husmear (1), to scent, to nose
huya, etc. (huir)
huye, etc. (huir)
huyendo (huir)
huyera, etc. (huir)
huyere, etc. (huir)
huyeron (huir)
huyese, etc. (huir)
huyo (huir)
huyó (huir)

I

iba, etc. (ir)
ice, etc. (izar)
icé (izar)
idealice, etc. (idealizar)
idealicé (idealizar)
idealizar (11), to idealize
idear (1), to devise, to form an idea
identificar (8), to identify
identifique, etc. (identificar)
identifiqué (identificar)
idolatrar (1), to idolize, to worship
ignorar (1), not to know
igualar (1), to equalize, to even
iluminar (1), to illuminate
ilusionar (1), to fascinate
ilusionarse (1) (4), to get one's hopes up
ilustrar (1), to illustrate
imaginar (1), to imagine
imaginarse (1) (4), to imagine
imanar (1), to magnetize
imanarse (1) (4), to become magnetized
imantar (1), to magnetize
imbuir (71), to imbue
imbuya, etc. (imbuir)
imbuye, etc. (imbuir)
imbuyendo (imbuir)
imbuyera, etc. (imbuir)
imbuyere, etc. (imbuir)
imbuyeron (imbuir)
imbuyese, etc. (imbuir)
imbuyo (imbuir)
imbuyó (imbuir)
imitar (1), to imitate
impacientar (1), to make impatient
impartir (3), to impart
impedir (i, i) (42), to prevent
impeler (2), to impel
imperar (1), to prevail, to rule
impermeabilice, etc. (impermeabilizar)
impermeabilicé (impermeabilizar)
impermeabilizar (11), to make waterproof
impetrar (1), to beg for
impida, etc. (impedir)
impide, etc. (impedir)
impidiendo (impedir)
impidiera, etc. (impedir)
impidiere, etc. (impedir)
impidieron (impedir)
impidiese (impedir)
impidió (impedir)
impido (impedir)
implicar (8), to imply
implique, etc. (implicar)
impliqué (implicar)
impón (imponer)
impondré, etc. (imponer)
impondría, etc. (imponer)
imponer (98), to impose
imponga, etc. (imponer)
impongo (imponer)
impopularice, etc. (impopularizar)
impopularicé (impopularizar)
impopularizar (11), to make unpopular
impopularizarse (11) (4), to become unpopular
importar (1), to import, to be worth, to imply, to concern
importunar (1), to importune
imposibilitar (1), to make impossible, to prevent, to disable
imprecar (8), to imprecate

impregnar (1), to impregnate
impreque, etc. (imprecar)
imprequé (imprecar)
impresionar (1), to impress
impreso (imprimir)
imprimir (91), to print
improbar (ue) (36), to disapprove
improvisar (1), to improvise
imprueba, etc. (improbar)
impruebe, etc. (improbar)
impruebo (improbar)
impuesto (imponer)
impugnar (1), to impugn
impuse (imponer)
impusiera, etc. (imponer)
impusiere, etc. (imponer)
impusieron (imponer)
impusiese, etc. (imponer)
impusimos (imponer)
impusiste (imponer)
impusisteis (imponer)
impuso (imponer)
imputar (1), to attribute
inaugurar (1), to inaugurate, to open the first time (store, bridge, etc.)
incapacitar, to incapacitate
incautar (1), to seize
incendiar (1), to set on fire
incendiarse (1) (4), to catch fire
incensar (ie) (37), to incense, to flatter
inciensa, etc. (incensar)
inciense, etc. (incensar)
incienso (incensar)
incinerar (1), to incinerate
incitar (1), to incite
inclinar (1), to incline, to bow
inclinarse (1) (4), to lean
incluir (71), to include, to enclose
incluya, etc. (incluir)
incluye, etc. (incluir)
incluyendo (incluir)
incluyera, etc. (incluir)
incluyere, etc. (incluir)
incluyeron (incluir)
incluyese, etc. (incluir)
incluyo (incluir)
incluyó (incluir)
incoar (122), to initiate
incomodar (1), to inconvenience
incomodarse (1) (4), to get annoyed
incomunicar (8), to isolate
incomunique, etc. (incomunicar)
incomuniqué (incomunicar)
incorporar (1), to incorporate
incorporarse (1) (4), to incorporate, to sit up (from a reclining position)
incrementar (1), to increase
increpar (1), to reprehend
incriminar (1), to incriminate
incrustar (1), to incrust
incubar (1), to incubate
inculcar (8), to inculcate
inculpar (1), to accuse
inculque, etc. (inculcar)
inculqué (inculcar)
incumbir (3), to concern
incurrir (3), to incur
indagar (9), to investigate
indague, etc. (indagar)
indagué (indagar)
indemnice, etc. (indemnizar)
indemnicé (indemnizar)
indemnizar (11), to indemnify
independice, etc. (independizar)
independicé (independizar)

independizar (11), to free
independizarse (11) (4), to become independent
indicar (8), to indicate
indigestarse (1) (4), to cause indigestion, to have indigestion
indignar (1), to anger
indignarse (1) (4), to become angry
indique, etc. (**indicar**)
indiqué (**indicar**)
indisciplinarse (1) (4), to become undisciplined
indispón (**indisponer**)
indispondré, etc. (**indisponer**)
indispondría, etc. (**indisponer**)
indisponer (98), to upset, to indispose
indisponerse (98) (4), to get upset, to get indisposed
indisponga, etc. (**indisponer**)
indispongo (**indisponer**)
indispuesto (**indisponer**)
indispuse (**indisponer**)
indispusiera, etc. (**indisponer**)
indispusiere, etc. (**indisponer**)
indispusieron (**indisponer**)
indispusiese, etc. (**indisponer**)
indispusimos (**indisponer**)
indispusiste (**indisponer**)
indispusisteis (**indisponer**)
indispuso (**indisponer**)
individualice, etc. (**individualizar**)
individualicé (**individualizar**)
individualizar (11), to individualize
inducir (67), to induce
induje (**inducir**)
indujera, etc. (**inducir**)
indujere, etc. (**inducir**)
indujeron (**inducir**)
indujese, etc. (**inducir**)
indujimos (**inducir**)
indujiste (**inducir**)
indujisteis (**inducir**)
indujo (**inducir**)
indultar (1), to pardon
industrialice, etc. (**industrializar**)
industrialicé (**industrializar**)
industrializar (11), to industrialize
industrializarse (11) (4), to become industrialized
induzca, etc. (**inducir**)
induzco (**inducir**)
infamar (1), to defame
infatuar (62), to infatuate
infectar (1), to infect
inferir (ie, i) (41), to infer, to imply
infestar (1), to infest
inficionar (1), to infect, to corrupt
infiera, etc. (**inferir**)
infiere, etc. (**inferir**)
infiero (**inferir**)
infiltrar (1), to infiltrate
infiramos, etc. (**inferir**)
infiriendo (**inferir**)
infiriera, etc. (**inferir**)
infiriere, etc. (**inferir**)
infirieron (**inferir**)
infiriese, etc. (**inferir**)
infirió (**inferir**)
inflamar (1), to inflame
inflar (1), to inflate, to exaggerate
infligir (16), to inflict
inflija, etc. (**infligir**)
inflijo (**infligir**)
influir (71), to influence
influya, etc. (**influir**)
influye, etc. (**influir**)

influyendo (**influir**)
influyera, etc. (**influir**)
influyere, etc. (**influir**)
influyeron (**influir**)
influyese, etc. (**influir**)
influyo (**influir**)
influyó (**influir**)
informar (1), to inform
infringir (16), to infringe
infrinja, etc. (**infringir**)
infrinjo (**infringir**)
infundir (3), to infuse, to instill
ingeniar (1), to conceive, to think up
ingeniarse (1) (4), to manage
ingerir (ie, i) (41), to ingest
ingerirse (ie, i) (41) (4), to interfere
ingiera, etc. (**ingerir**)
ingiere, etc. (**ingerir**)
ingiero (**ingerir**)
ingiramos, etc. (**ingerir**)
ingiriendo (**ingerir**)
ingiriera, etc. (**ingerir**)
ingiriere, etc. (**ingerir**)
ingirieron (**ingerir**)
ingiriese, etc. (**ingerir**)
ingirió (**ingerir**)
ingresar (1), to enter, to deposit (money)
inhabilitar (1), to incapacitate
inhalar (1), to inhale
inhibir (3), to inhibit
inhumar (1), to inhume
iniciar (1), to initiate
iniciarse (1) (4), to be initiated
injerir (ie, i) (41), to ingest, to take in
injerirse (ie, i) (41) (4), to interfere
injertar (1), to graft
injiera, etc. (**injerir**)
injiere, etc. (**injerir**)
injiero (**injerir**)
injiramos, etc. (**injerir**)
injiriendo (**injerir**)
injiriera, etc. (**injerir**)
injiriere, etc. (**injerir**)
injirieron (**injerir**)
injiriese, etc. (**injerir**)
injirió (**injerir**)
injuriar (1), to insult, to injure
inmergir (16), to immerse
inmerja, etc. (**inmergir**)
inmerjo (**inmergir**)
inmigrar (1), to immigrate
inmiscuir (23), to mix
inmiscuirse (23) (4), to interfere
inmiscuya, etc. (**inmiscuir**)
inmiscuye, etc. (**inmiscuir**)
inmiscuyendo (**inmiscuir**)
inmiscuyera, etc. (**inmiscuir**)
inmiscuyere, etc. (**inmiscuir**)
inmiscuyeron (**inmiscuir**)
inmiscuyese, etc. (**inmiscuir**)
inmiscuyo (**inmiscuir**)
inmiscuyó (**inmiscuir**)
inmolar (1), to immolate
inmortalice, etc. (**inmortalizar**)
inmortalicé (**inmortalizar**)
inmortalizar (11), to immortalize
inmovilice, etc. (**inmovilizar**)
inmovilicé (**inmovilizar**)
inmovilizar (11), to immobilize
inmunice, etc. (**inmunizar**)
inmunicé (**inmunizar**)
inmunizar (11), to immunize
inmutar (1), to change
innovar (1), to innovate
inocular (1), to inoculate
inquiera, etc. (**inquirir**)

inquiere, etc. (**inquirir**)
inquiero (**inquirir**)
inquietar (1), to worry, to disturb
inquirir (ie) (76), to inquire
insalivar (1), to insalivate
inscribir (69), to inscribe
inscribirse (69) (4), to enroll, to register
inscripto (**inscribir**)
inscrito (**inscribir**)
inseminar (1), to inseminate
insensibilice, etc. (**insensibilizar**)
insensibilicé (**insensibilizar**)
insensibilizar (11), to make insensible
insensibilizarse (11) (4), to become insensible
insertar (1), to insert
insidiar (1), to plot against
insinuar (62), to insinuate
insistir (3), to insist
insolentar (1), to make insolent
insonorice, etc. (**insonorizar**)
insonoricé (**insonorizar**)
insonorizar (11), to soundproof
inspeccionar (1), to inspect
inspirar (1), to inspire, to inhale
instalar (1), to install
instalarse (1) (4), to become installed, to settle
instar (1), to urge, to insist
instaurar (1), to restore
instigar (9), to instigate
instigue, etc. (**instigar**)
instigué (**instigar**)
instilar (1), to instill
instituir (71), to institute
instituya, etc. (**instituir**)
instituye, etc. (**instituir**)
instituyendo (**instituir**)
instituyera, etc. (**instituir**)
instituyere, etc. (**instituir**)
instituyeron (**instituir**)
instituyese, etc. (**instituir**)
instituyo (**instituir**)
instituyó (**instituir**)
instruir (71), to instruct
instruya, etc. (**instruir**)
instruye, etc. (**instruir**)
instruyendo (**instruir**)
instruyera, etc. (**instruir**)
instruyere, etc. (**instruir**)
instruyeron (**instruir**)
instruyese, etc. (**instruir**)
instruyo (**instruir**)
instruyó (**instruir**)
insubordinar (1), to incite to insubordination
insubordinarse (1) (4), to rebel
insultar (1), to insult
insurreccionar (1), to incite to rebellion
insurreccionarse (1) (4), to rebel
integrar (1), to integrate, to make up
intensificar (8), to intensify
intensifique, etc. (**intensificar**)
intensifiqué (**intensificar**)
intentar (1), to attempt, to intend
intercalar (1), to place between
intercambiar (1), to exchange
interceder (2), to intercede
interceptar (1), to intercept
interconectar (1), to interconnect
interdecir (i, i) (84), to interdict
interdí (**interdecir**)
interdice, etc. (**interdecir**)
interdiciendo (**interdecir**)
interdicho (**interdecir**)
interdiga, etc. (**interdecir**)

interdigo (interdecir)
interdije (interdecir)
interdijera, etc. (interdecir)
interdijere, etc. (interdecir)
interdijeron (interdecir)
interdijese, etc. (interdecir)
interdijimos (interdecir)
interdijiste (interdecir)
interdijisteis (interdecir)
interdijo (interdecir)
interdiré (interdecir)
interdiría, etc. (interdecir)
interesar (1), to interest
interferir (ie, i) (41), to interfere
interfiera, etc. (interferir)
interfiere, etc. (interferir)
interfiero (interferir)
interfiramos, etc. (interferir)
interfiriendo (interferir)
interfiriera, etc. (interferir)
interfiriere, etc. (interferir)
interfirieron (interferir)
interfiriese, etc. (interferir)
interfirió (interferir)
interlinear (1), to write between lines
intermediar (1), to intermediate
intermitir (3), to intermit
internacionalice, etc. (internacionalizar)
internacionalicé (internacionalizar)
internacionalizar (11), to internationalize
internar (1), to intern
interpaginar (1), to insert a page or pages
interpelar (1), to appeal to, to demand explanations
interpolar (1), to interpolate
interpón (interponer)
interpondré, etc. (interponer)
interpondría, etc. (interponer)
interponer (98), to place between
interponga, etc. (interponer)
interpongo (interponer)
interpretar (1), to interpret
interpuesto (interponer)
interpuse (interponer)
interpusiera, etc. (interponer)
interpusiere, etc. (interponer)
interpusieron (interponer)
interpusiese, etc. (interponer)
interpusimos (interponer)
interpusiste (interponer)
interpusisteis (interponer)
interpuso (interponer)
interrogar (9), to question, to interrogate
interrogue, etc. (interrogar)
interrogué, etc. (interrogar)
interrumpir (3), to interrupt
intervén (intervenir)
intervendré, etc. (intervenir)
intervendría, etc. (intervenir)
intervenga, etc. (intervenir)
intervengo (intervenir)
intervenir (ie, i) (111), to intervene
interviene, etc. (intervenir)
intervine (intervenir)
interviniendo (intervenir)
interviniera, etc. (intervenir)
interviniere, etc. (intervenir)
intervinieron (intervenir)
interviniese, etc. (intervenir)
intervinimos (intervenir)
interviniste (intervenir)
intervinisteis (intervenir)
intervino (intervenir)
intimar (1), to intimate

intimidar (1), to intimidate
intoxicar (8), to poison, to intoxicate
intoxique, etc. (intoxicar)
intoxiqué (intoxicar)
intranquilice, etc. (intranquilizar)
intranquilicé (intranquilizar)
intranquilizar (11), to disquiet, to worry
intrigar (9), to intrigue
intrigue, etc. (intrigar)
intrigué (intrigar)
intrincar (8), to entangle
intrinque, etc. (intrincar)
intrinqué (intrincar)
introducir (67), to introduce, to insert
introducirse (67) (4), to gain access, to interfere
introduje (introducir)
introdujera, etc. (introducir)
introdujere, etc. (introducir)
introdujeron (introducir)
introdujese, etc. (introducir)
introdujimos (introducir)
introdujiste (introducir)
introdujisteis (introducir)
introdujo (introducir)
introduzca, etc. (introducir)
introduzco (introducir)
intuir (71), to know or perceive by intuition
intuya, etc. (intuir)
intuye, etc. (intuir)
intuyendo (intuir)
intuyera, etc. (intuir)
intuyere, etc. (intuir)
intuyeron (intuir)
intuyese, etc. (intuir)
intuyo (intuir)
intuyó (intuir)
inundar (1), to inundate
inutilice, etc. (inutilizar)
inutilicé (inutilizar)
inutilizar (11), to make useless
inutilizarse (11) (4), to become useless
invadir (3), to invade
invalidar (1), to invalidate
inventar (1), to invent
invernar (ie) (37), to winter
invertir (ie, i) (41), to invert, to invest
investigar (9), to investigate
investigue, etc. (investigar)
investigué (investigar)
investir (i, i) (42), to invest
invierna, etc. (invernar)
invierne, etc. (invernar)
invierno (invernar)
invierta, etc. (invertir)
invierte, etc. (invertir)
invierto (invertir)
invirtamos, etc. (invertir)
invirtiendo (invertir)
invirtiera, etc. (invertir)
invirtiere, etc. (invertir)
invirtieron (invertir)
invirtiese, etc. (invertir)
invirtió (invertir)
invista, etc. (investir)
inviste, etc. (investir)
invistiendo (investir)
invistiera, etc. (investir)
invistiere, etc. (investir)
invistieron (investir)
invistiese (investir)
invistió (investir)
invisto (investir)
invitar (1), to invite
invocar (8), to invoke
invoque, etc. (invocar)

invoqué (invocar)
inyectar (1), to inject
ionice, etc. (ionizar)
ionicé (ionizar)
ionizar (11), to ionize
ir (92), to go, to walk, to move
irga, etc. (erguir)
irgo (erguir)
irgue (erguir)
irguiendo (erguir)
irguiera, etc. (erguir)
irguiere, etc. (erguir)
irguieron (erguir)
irguiese, etc. (erguir)
irguió (erguir)
irradiar (1), to radiate, to irradiate
irrigar (9), to irrigate
irrigue, etc. (irrigar)
irrigué (irrigar)
irritar (1), to irritate
irrumpir (3), to invade, to break into
iterar (1), to iterate
izar (11), to hoist, to haul up

J

jabonar (1), to soap
jacarear (1), to go serenading
jactarse (1) (4), to boast
jadear (1), to pant
jalar (1), to pull
jalear (1), to cheer (dancers), to encourage
jaranear (1), to go merrymaking
jeringar (9), to annoy, to inject with a syringe
jeringue, etc. (jeringar)
jeringué (jeringar)
jilotear (1), to sprout ears (corn)
jorobar (1), to annoy, to bother
jubilar (1), to retire, to rejoice
jubilarse (1) (4), to retire
juega, etc. (jugar)
juego (jugar)
juegue, etc. (jugar)
jugar (ue) (93), to play
jugarse (ue) (93) (4), to risk, to gamble (one's life, money, etc.)
jugué (jugar)
juguemos, etc. (jugar)
juntar (1), to join, to gather, to half-close
jurar (1), to swear
justificar (8), to justify
justifique, etc. (justificar)
justifiqué (justificar)
juzgar (9), to judge
juzgue, etc. (juzgar)
juzgué (juzgar)

L

laborar (1), to work
laborear (1), to work
labrar (1), to plow, to till, to carve, to work
lace, etc. (lazar)
lacé (lazar)
lacerar (1), to lacerate
lactar (1), to nurse, to feed with milk
ladear (1), to tilt, to deviate
ladrar (1), to bark
ladrillar (1), to pave with bricks
ladronear (1), to go around thieving
lagrimar (1), to weep
lagrimear (1), to weep easily
laicice, etc. (laicizar)
laicicé (laicizar)
laicizar (11), to laicize

lamentar (1), to regret, to lament
lamer (2), to lick
laminar (1), to laminate
lance, etc. (**lanzar**)
lancé (**lanzar**)
languidecer (73), to languish
languidezca, etc. (**languidecer**)
languidezco (**languidecer**)
lanzar (11), to throw, to launch
lapidar (1), to stone to death
largar (9), to let go
largarse (9) (4), to go away, to leave
largue, etc. (**largar**)
largué (**largar**)
lastimar (1), to hurt, to offend
latir (3), to throb, to beat
lavar (1), to wash
lavarse (1) (4), to wash oneself
lazar (11), to lasso
leer (20), to read
legalice, etc. (**legalizar**)
legalicé (**legalizar**)
legalizar (11), to legalize
legar (9), to be bequeath
legislar (1), to legislate
legitimar (1), to legitimate
legrar (1), to scrape a bone
legue, etc. (**legar**)
legué (**legar**)
lesionar (1), to injure
levantar (1), to raise, to lift, to elevate
levantarse (1) (4), to stand up, to rebel, to get up
levar (1), to weigh (anchor)
leyendo (**leer**)
leyera, etc. (**leer**)
leyere, etc. (**leer**)
leyeron (**leer**)
leyese, etc. (**leer**)
leyó (**leer**)
liar (19), to tie, to embroil
liarse (19) (4), to bind oneself
liberalice, etc. (**liberalizar**)
liberalicé (**liberalizar**)
liberalizar (11), to liberalize
liberar (1), to free
libertar (1), to liberate
librar (1), to free, to exempt
licenciar (1), to license
licuefacer (68), to liquefy
licuefaga, etc. (**licuefacer**)
licuefago (**licuefacer**)
licuefaré, etc. (**licuefacer**)
licuefaría, etc. (**licuefacer**)
licuefaz (**licuefacer**)
licuefecho (**licuefacer**)
licuefice (**licuefacer**)
licueficiera, etc. (**licuefacer**)
licueficiere, etc. (**licuefacer**)
licueficieron (**licuefacer**)
licueficiese, etc. (**licuefacer**)
licueficimos (**licuefacer**)
licueficiste (**licuefacer**)
licueficisteis (**licuefacer**)
licuefizo (**licuefacer**)
lidiar (1), to fight (bulls)
ligar (9), to tie, to join
ligue, etc. (**ligar**)
ligué (**ligar**)
limar (1), to file
limitar (1), to limit, to bound
limpiar (1), to clear
lindar (1), to border
liquidar (1), to liquefy, to liquidate
lisiar (1), to cripple
lisonjear (1), to flatter

litigar (9), to litigate
litigue, etc. (**litigar**)
litigué (**litigar**)
litografiar (61), to lithograph
loar (1), to praise
lobreguecer (73), to make gloomy, to grow dark, to make dark
lobreguezca, etc. (**lobreguecer**)
lobreguezco (**lobreguecer**)
localice, etc. (**localizar**)
localicé (**localizar**)
localizar (11), to localize, to locate, to find out where
lograr (1), to get, to obtain
lonchear (1), to lunch
loquear (1), to have a high time
lotear (1), to divide into lots
lozanear (1), to look fresh and luxuriant
lubricar (8), to lubricate
lubrique, etc. (**lubricar**)
lubriqué (**lubricar**)
lucir (74), to shine, to show off, to out shine
lucirse (74) (4), to come off well
lucrarse (1) (4), to profit
luchar (1), to fight, to struggle, to wrestle
lustrar (1), to polish, to shine
luzca, etc. (**lucir**)
luzco (**lucir**)

LL

llamar (1), to call
llamear (1), to flame
llegar (9), to arrive, to come, to reach, to go as far as
llegue, etc. (**llegar**)
llegué (**llegar**)
llenar (1), to fill, to stuff
llevar (1), to carry, to take
llorar (1), to cry, to weep
lloriquear (1), to whine
llover (ue) (38), to rain
lloviznar (1), to drizzle
llueva (**llover**)
llueve (**llover**)

M

macanear (1), to joke, to exaggerate
macear (1), to mace
macerar (1), to macerate
machacar (8), to crush
machaque, etc. (**machacar**)
machaqué (**machacar**)
machihembrar (1), to feather (carpentry), to mortise (carpentry)
machucar (8), to crush, to bruise
machuque, etc. (**machucar**)
machuqué (**machucar**)
madrugar (9), to rise early, to get up early
madrugue, etc. (**madrugar**)
madrugué (**madrugar**)
madurar (1), to ripen, to mature
magnetice, etc. (**magnetizar**)
magneticé (**magnetizar**)
magnetizar (11), to magnetize
magnificar (8), to magnify
magnifique, etc. (**magnificar**)
magnifiqué (**magnificar**)
magullar (1), to bruise
malbaratar (1), to squander, to undersell
malcasar (1), to mismate in marriage
malcriar (61), to spoil (a child)
maldecir (i, i) (79), to curse
maldice, etc. (**maldecir**)
maldiciendo (**maldecir**)

maldiga, etc. (**maldecir**)
maldigo (**maldecir**)
maldije (**maldecir**)
maldijera, etc. (**maldecir**)
maldijere, etc. (**maldecir**)
maldijeron (**maldecir**)
maldijese, etc. (**maldecir**)
maldijimos (**maldecir**)
maldijiste (**maldecir**)
maldijisteis (**maldecir**)
maldijo (**maldecir**)
malear (1), to corrupt, to spoil
malgastar (1), to misspend, to waste, to squander
malherir (ie, i) (41), to wound badly
malhiera, etc. (**malherir**)
malhiere, etc. (**malherir**)
malhiero (**malherir**)
malhiramos, etc. (**malherir**)
malhiriendo (**malherir**)
malhiriera, etc. (**malherir**)
malhiriere, etc. (**malherir**)
malhirieron (**malherir**)
malhiriese, etc. (**malherir**)
malhirió (**malherir**)
malograr (1), to waste, to spoil
malograrse (1) (4), to spoil, to become spoiled, to have an untimely end
malquerer (ie) (101), to dislike
malquerré, etc. (**malquerer**)
malquerría, etc. (**malquerer**)
malquiera, etc. (**malquerer**)
malquiere, etc. (**malquerer**)
malquiero (**malquerer**)
malquise (**malquerer**)
malquisiera, etc. (**malquerer**)
malquisiere, etc. (**malquerer**)
malquisieron (**malquerer**)
malquisiese, etc. (**malquerer**)
malquisimos (**malquerer**)
malquisiste (**malquerer**)
malquisisteis (**malquerer**)
malquiso (**malquerer**)
malquistar (1), to alienate
maltraer (109), to abuse, to use roughly, to mistreat
maltraiga, etc. (**maltraer**)
maltraigo (**maltraer**)
maltraje (**maltraer**)
maltrajera, etc. (**maltraer**)
maltrajere, etc. (**maltraer**)
maltrajeron (**maltraer**)
maltrajese, etc. (**maltraer**)
maltrajimos (**maltraer**)
maltrajiste (**maltraer**)
maltrajisteis (**maltraer**)
maltrajo (**maltraer**)
maltratar (1), to abuse, to use roughly, to mistreat
maltrayendo (**maltraer**)
malvender (2), to undersell
malversar (1), to embezzle, to misapply funds
mamar (1), to suckle, to suck
mamarse (1) (4), to get drunk
manar (1), to pour forth
mancar (8), to maim
mancillar (1), to dishonor
mancomunar (1), to unite, to pool (resources)
mancornar (ue) (36), to down (a steer) and hold his horns on the ground, to join two things of the same species
mancuerna, etc. (**mancornar**)
mancuerne, etc. (**mancornar**)
mancuerno (**mancornar**)

manchar (1), to stain
mandar (1), to order, to command, to send
manducar (8), to eat
manduque, etc. (manducar)
manduqué (manducar)
manejar (1), to manage, to handle, to drive
mangonear (1), to meddle (pretending to have authority)
maniatar (1), to tie the hands
manifestar (ie) (37), to declare, to manifest
manifiesta, etc. (manifestar)
manifieste, etc. (manifestar)
manifiesto (manifestar)
maniobrar (1), to maneuver
manipular (1), to manipulate
manir (116), to keep meat until it becomes gamy
manosear (1), to repeatedly touch or handle something
manotear (1), to strike with the hands, to gesture
manque, etc. (mancar)
manqué (mancar)
mantear (1), to toss in a blanket
mantén (mantener)
mantendré, etc. (mantener)
mantendría, etc. (mantener)
mantener (ie) (108), to maintain, to keep up
mantenga, etc. (mantener)
mantengo (mantener)
mantiene, etc. (mantener)
mantuve (mantener)
mantuviera, etc. (mantener)
mantuviere, etc. (mantener)
mantuvieron (mantener)
mantuviese, etc. (mantener)
mantuvimos (mantener)
mantuviste (mantener)
mantuvisteis (mantener)
mantuvo (mantener)
manufacturar (1), to manufacture
manumitir (3), to emancipate, to free from slavery
manuscribir (69), to write by hand
manuscrito (manuscribir)
maquinar (1), to plot, to scheme
marcar (8), to mark, to stamp, to brand, to dial, to score
marchar (1), to march, to run, to work, to go
marcharse (1) (4), to go away, to leave
marchitarse (1) (4), to wilt, to wither
marear (1), to annoy
marearse (1) (4), to become nauseated, to become seasick
marginar (1), to leave a margin on, to write marginal notes
marinar (1), to marinate
mariposear (1), to flutter around
marque, etc. (marcar)
marqué (marcar)
marquear (1), to mark a plot of ground for planting
marrar (1), to miss, to go astray
martillar (1), to hammer
martillear (1), to hammer
martirice, etc. (martirizar)
martiricé (martirizar)
martirizar (11), to martyrize
mascar (8), to chew
mascullar (1), to mumble
masque, etc. (mascar)
masqué (mascar)
masticar (8), to chew

mastique, etc. (masticar)
mastiqué (masticar)
masturbarse (1) (4), to masturbate
matar (1), to kill, to butcher
matear (1), to drink maté
materialice, etc. (materializar)
materialicé (materializar)
materializar (11), to materialize
materializarse (11) (4), to become materialistic
matice, etc. (matizar)
maticé (matizar)
matizar (11), to give special tint to, to blend colors
matricular (1), to register, to enroll, to matriculate
matricularse (1) (4), to register, to enroll, to matriculate
maullar (65), to meow
mayar (1), to meow
mear (1), to urinate
mecanice, etc. (mecanizar)
mecanicé (mecanizar)
mecanizar (11), to mechanize
mecanografiar (61), to type
mecer (14), to rock
mechar (1), to lard
mediar (1), to mediate, to intervene
medir (i, i) (42), to measure
medirse (i, i) (42) (4), to be moderate, to act with moderation
meditar (1), to mediate, to contemplate
medrar (1), to thrive, to prosper
mejorar (1), to make better, to improve
mejorarse (1) (4), to get better
melindrear (1), to be finicky
mellar (1), to notch, to nick, to dent
memorar (1), to remember
mencionar (1), to mention
mendigar (9), to beg
mendigue, etc. (mendigar)
mendigué (mendigar)
menear (1), to stir, to shake, to wag, to move
menguar (10), to diminish
mengüe, etc. (menguar)
mengüé (menguar)
menoscabar (1), to diminish, to impair
menospreciar (1), to underestimate, to scorn
menstruar (62), to menstruate
mensurar (1), to measure
mentar (ie) (37), to mention
mentir (ie, i) (41), to lie
menudear (1), to do frequently, to tell in detail, to sell at retail
mercadear (1), to deal, to trade
mercar (8), to buy
merecer (73), to deserve, to be worth
merendar (ie) (37), to have an afternoon snack
merengar (9), to whip (cream)
merengue, etc. (merengar)
merengué (merengar)
merezca, etc. (merecer)
merezco (merecer)
merienda, etc. (merendar)
meriende, etc. (merendar)
meriendo (merendar)
mermar (1), to decrease
merodear (1), to maraud
merque, etc. (mercar)
merqué (mercar)
mesar (1), to pull out hair
mesurarse (1) (4), to act with restraint
metalice, etc. (metalizarse)

metalicé (metalizarse)
metalizarse (11) (4), to become mercenary, to become metalized
meter (2), to put, to insert, to place
meza, etc. (mecer)
mezca, etc. = meza, etc.
mezclar (1), to mix, to blend
mezco = mezo
mezo (mecer)
mida, etc. (medir)
mide, etc. (medir)
midiendo (medir)
midiera, etc. (medir)
midiere, etc. (medir)
midieron (medir)
midiese, etc. (medir)
midió (medir)
mido (medir)
mienta, etc. (mentar) (mentir)
miente, etc. (mentar) (mentir)
miento (mentar) (mentir)
migar (9), to crumb, to put crumbles in (a liquid)
migue, etc. (migar)
migué (migar)
militar (1), to serve in the army, to militate (for or against)
militarice, etc. (militarizar)
militaricé (militarizar)
militarizar (11), to militarize
mimar (1), to pamper, to spoil a child
mimbrear (1), to sway
mimeografiar (61), to mimeograph
minar (1), to mine, to undermine
mintamos, etc. (mentir)
mintiendo (mentir)
mintiera, etc. (mentir)
mintiere, etc. (mentir)
mintieron (mentir)
mintiese, etc. (mentir)
mintió (mentir)
mirar (1), to look at, to watch
misionar (1), to do missionary work
mitigar (9), to mitigate
mitigue, etc. (mitigar)
mitigué (mitigar)
moblar (ue) (36), to furnish
modelar (1), to model
moderar (1), to moderate, to control
moderarse (1) (4), to control oneself
modernice, etc. (modernizar)
modernicé (modernizar)
modernizar (11), to modernize
modificar (8), to modify
modifique, etc. (modificar)
modifiqué (modificar)
modular (1), to modulate
mofar (1), to mock, to scoff, to jeer
mojar (1), to wet
moldear (1), to mold, to cast
moler (ue) (38), to grind
molestar (1), to disturb, to bother
molestarse (1) (4), to be annoyed, to be bothered
molificar (8), to soften
molifique, etc. (molificar)
molifiqué (molificar)
molliznar (1), to drizzle
molliznear (1), to drizzle
momificar (8), to mummify
momifique, etc. (momificar)
momifiqué (momificar)
mondar (1), to peel
monear (1), to monkey around, to make faces
monologar (9), to engage in a monologue

monologue, etc. (monologar)
monologué (monologar)
monopolice, etc. (monopolizar)
monopolicé (monopolizar)
monopolizar (11), to monopolize
montar (1), to mount, to get onto, to ride, to set up, to amount to
moralice, etc. (moralizar)
moralicé (moralizar)
moralizar (11), to moralize
morar (1), to live, to dwell
morder (ue) (38), to bite, to nibble
mordiscar (8), to nibble at
mordisque, etc. (mordiscar)
mordisqué (mordiscar)
morir (ue, u) (94), to die, to die away
mortificar (8), to mortify
mortifique, etc. (mortificar)
mortifiqué (mortificar)
mosconear (1), to annoy
mostrar (ue) (36), to show
motear (1), to speckle
motejar (1), to call names
motivar (1), to motivate
motorice, etc. (motorizar)
motoricé (motorizar)
motorizar (11), to motorize
mover (ue) (38), to move, to stir, to wag
movilice, etc. (movilizar)
movilicé (movilizar)
movilizar (11), to mobilize
mudar (1), to change, to move
muebla, etc. (moblar)
mueble, etc. (moblar)
mueblo (moblar)
muela, etc. (moler)
muele, etc. (moler)
muelo (moler)
muera, etc. (morir)
muerda, etc. (morder)
muerde, etc. (morder)
muerdo (morder)
muere, etc. (morir)
muero (morir)
muerto (morir)
muestra, etc. (mostrar)
muestre, etc. (mostrar)
muestro (mostrar)
mueva, etc. (mover)
mueve, etc. (mover)
muevo (mover)
mugir (16), to moo
muja, etc. (mugir)
mujo (mugir)
multigrafiar (61), to multigraph
multiplicar (8), to multiply
multiplique, etc. (multiplicar)
multipliqué (multiplicar)
mullendo (mullir)
mullera, etc. (mullir)
mullere, etc. (mullir)
mulleron (mullir)
mullese, etc. (mullir)
mullir (27), to fluff, to beat up
mulló (mullir)
muramos, etc. (morir)
muriendo (morir)
muriera, etc. (morir)
muriere, etc. (morir)
murieron (morir)
muriese, etc. (morir)
murió (morir)
murmurar (1), to murmur, to mutter
mutilar (1), to mutilate

N

nacer (73), to be born, to originate
nacionalice, etc. (nacionalizar)
nacionalicé (nacionalizar)
nacionalizar (11), to nationalize, to naturalize
naturalice, etc. (naturalizar)
naturalicé (naturalizar)
naturalizar (11), to naturalize
naturalizarse (11) (4), to become naturalized
naufragar (9), to be shipwrecked, to sink
naufrague, etc. (naufragar)
naufragué (naufragar)
navegar (9), to navigate, to move about
navegue, etc. (navegar)
navegué (navegar)
nazca, etc. (nacer)
nazco (nacer)
necesitar (1), to need, to necessitate
negar (ie) (50), to deny, to refuse
negociar (1), to negotiate
negué (negar)
neguemos, etc. (negar)
neutralice, etc. (neutralizar)
neutralicé (neutralizar)
neutralizar (11), to neutralize
nevar (ie) (37), to snow
neviscar (8), to snow lightly, to sleet
nevisque (neviscar)
niega, etc. (negar)
niego (negar)
niegue, etc. (negar)
nieva (nevar)
nieve (nevar)
nimbar (1), to encircle with a halo
niñear (1), to act like a child
nivelar (1), to level, to even
nombrar (1), to appoint, to name
nominalice, etc. (nominalizar)
nominalicé (nominalizar)
nominalizar (11), to nominalize
nominar (1), to appoint
normalice, etc. (normalizar)
normalicé (normalizar)
normalizar (11), to normalize, to standardize, to regulate
notar (1), to note, to notice
notificar (8), to notify
notifique, etc. (notificar)
notifiqué (notificar)
novelice, etc. (novelizar)
novelicé (novelizar)
novelizar (11), to novelize, to fictionalize, to tell stories
nublar (1), to cloud, to obscure
nublarse (1) (4), to become cloudy
numerar (1), to numerate, to number
nutrir (3), to nourish

O

obedecer (73), to obey
obedezca, etc. (obedecer)
obedezco (obedecer)
objetar (1), to object, to raise (difficulties)
obligar (9), to obligate, to force, to compel
obligarse (9) (4), to bind oneself
obligue, etc. (obligar)
obligué (obligar)
obrar (1), to work, to act
obscurecer (73), to darken, to dim, to grow dark

obscurecerse (73) (4), to cloud over, to become dark
obscurezca, etc. (obscurecer)
obscurezco (obscurecer)
obsequiar (1), to treat, to give a present
observar (1), to observe
obsesionar (1), to obsess
obstaculice, etc. (obstaculizar)
obstaculicé (obstaculizar)
obstaculizar (11), to put obstacles, to prevent
obstar (1), to stand in the way
obstinarse (1) (4), to be obstinate
obstruir (71), to obstruct
obstruya, etc. (obstruir)
obstruye, etc. (obstruir)
obstruyendo (obstruir)
obstruyera, etc. (obstruir)
obstruyere, etc. (obstruir)
obstruyeron (obstruir)
obstruyese, etc. (obstruir)
obstruyo (obstruir)
obstruyó (obstruir)
obtén (obtener)
obtendré, etc. (obtener)
obtendría, etc. (obtener)
obtener (ie) (108), to obtain
obtenga, etc. (obtener)
obtengo (obtener)
obtiene, etc. (obtener)
obturar (1), to plug, to stop up
obtuve (obtener)
obtuviera, etc. (obtener)
obtuviere, etc. (obtener)
obtuvieron (obtener)
obtuviese, etc. (obtener)
obtuvimos (obtener)
obtuviste (obtener)
obtuvisteis (obtener)
obtuvo (obtener)
obviar (1), to stand in the way
ocasionar (1), to cause
ociar (1), to idle
ocluir (71), to occlude
ocluya, etc. (ocluir)
ocluye, etc. (ocluir)
ocluyendo (ocluir)
ocluyera, etc. (ocluir)
ocluyere, etc. (ocluir)
ocluyeron (ocluir)
ocluyese, etc. (ocluir)
ocluyo (ocluir)
ocluyó (ocluir)
ocultar (1), to hide, to conceal
ocupar (1), to occupy, to keep busy
ocurrir (3), to happen, to occur
ofender (2), to offend
ofenderse (2) (4), to take offense
oficiar (1), to officiate
ofrecer (73), to offer
ofrendar (1), to present offerings
ofrezca, etc. (ofrecer)
ofrezco (ofrecer)
ofuscar (8), to obfuscate
ofusque, etc. (ofuscar)
ofusqué (ofuscar)
oiga, etc. (oír)
oigo (oír)
oír (95), to hear, to listen to
ojear (1), to eye
oler (ue) (55), to smell, to sniff out
olfatear (1), to smell, to sniff
olvidar (1), to forget
omitir (3), to omit, to neglect

ondear (1), to wave
ondular, to wave (the hair), to undulate
opacar (8), to darken
opacarse (8) (4), to become cloudy, to become obscure
opaque, etc. (opacar)
opaqué (opacar)
operar (1), to operate, to work
opinar (1), to express an opinion, to think, to pass a judgment
opón (oponer)
opondré, etc. (oponer)
opondría, etc. (oponer)
oponer (98), to oppose
oponerse (98) (4), to disapprove
oponga, etc. (oponer)
opongo (oponer)
oprimir (3), to oppress, to squeeze
optar (1), to choose
opuesto (oponer)
opugnar (1), to attack
opuse (oponer)
opusiera, etc. (oponer)
opusiere, etc. (oponer)
opusieron (oponer)
opusiese, etc. (oponer)
opusimos (oponer)
opusiste (oponer)
opusisteis (oponer)
opuso (oponer)
ordenar (1), to arrange, to order
ordeñar (1), to milk
organice, etc. (organizar)
organicé (organizar)
organizar (11), to organize
orientar (1), to orientate, to orient
orientarse (1) (4), to find one's way around
originar (1), to originate
orillar (1), to put a border or edge
orinar (1), to urinate
orlar (1), to trim with a fringe
ornamentar (1), to ornament, to adorn
orquestar (1), to orchestrate
osar (1), to dare
oscilar (1), to oscillate, to hesitate
oscurecer = obscurecer
oscurecerse = obscurecerse
oscurezca, etc. (oscurecer)
oscurezco (oscurecer)
osificar (8), to ossify
osifique, etc. (osificar)
osifiqué (osificar)
ostentar (1), to exhibit, to boast, to show off
otorgar (9), to grant
otorgue, etc. (otorgar)
otorgué (otorgar)
ovillar (1), to form into a ball (yarn, string, etc.)
oxidar (1), to oxidize
oxigenar (1), to oxigenate
oye, etc. (oír)
oyendo (oír)
oyera, etc. (oír)
oyere, etc. (oír)
oyeron (oír)
oyese, etc. (oír)
oyó (oír)

P

pacer (73), to pasture, to graze
pacificar (8), to pacify
pacificarse (8) (4), to calm down

pacifique, etc. (pacificar)
pacifiqué (pacificar)
pactar (1), to agree upon, to stipulate
padecer (73), to suffer, to endure
padezca, etc. (padecer)
padezco (padecer)
pagar (9), to pay, to pay for
pague, etc. (pagar)
pagué (pagar)
paladear (1), to relish
palear (1), to shovel
paletear (1), to row ineffectively
paliar (1), to palliate, to extenuate, to excuse
palidecer (73), to turn pale
palidezca, etc. (palidecer)
palidezco (palidecer)
paliquear (1), to chat, to gossip
palmear (1), to clap
palmotear (1), to clap
palpar (1), to touch, to feel, to to grope
palpitar (1), to throb
panderetear (1), to play the tambourine
panegirice, etc. (panegirizar)
panegiricé (panegirizar)
panegirizar (11), to eulogize
panificar (8), to make into bread, to make bread
panifique, etc. (panificar)
panifiqué (panificar)
pantanice, etc. (pantanizar)
pantanizarse (11) (4), to become marshy or swampy
papar (1), to eat without chewing
papelear (1), to look through papers
parafrasear (1), to paraphrase
paralice, etc. (paralizar)
paralicé (paralizar)
paralizar (11), to paralyze
paralizarse (11) (4), to become paralyzed
parangonar (1), to compare
parapetarse (1) (4), to hide behind a parapet, to protect oneself
parar (1), to stop, to place in an upright position
pararse (1) (4), to stop, to stand up
parcelar (1), to parcel out
parchar (1), to patch
parear (1), to match
parearse (1) (4), to pair off
parecer (73), to seem, to appear
parecerse (73) (4), to look alike, to resemble each other
parezca, etc. (parecer)
parezco (parecer)
parir (3), to give birth
parodiar (1), to parody
parpadear (1), to blink
parquear (1), to park
parrandear (1), to go out on a spree
participar (1), to participate, to share, to communicate, to notify
particularice, etc. (particularizar)
particularicé (particularizar)
particularizar (11), to particularize
particularizarse (11) (4), to have as a characteristic, to be distinguished
partir (3), to split, to divide, to depart
pasar (1), to pass, to cross, to take across, to send, to swallow
pasear (1), to stroll, to promenade, to walk, to take a walk
pasearse (1) (4), to take a walk
pasmar (1), to astound, to stun

pasmarse (1) (4), to be stunned
pasterice, etc. (pasterizar)
pastericé (pasterizar)
pasterizar (11), to pasteurize
pasteurice, etc. (pasteurizar)
pasteuricé (pasteurizar)
pasteurizar (11), to pasteurize
pastorear (1), to shepherd
patalear (1), to stamp the feet
patear (1), to kick, to treat roughly
patentar (1), to patent
patentice, etc. (patentizar)
patenticé (patentizar)
patentizar (11), to make evident, to reveal
patinar (1), to skate, to skid, to slip
patrocinar (1), to sponsor
patronar (1), to skipper
patronear (1), to skipper
patrullar (1), to patrol
pausar (1), to pause
pavimentar (1), to pave
pavonearse (1) (4), to strut, to show off
payasear (1), to clown
pazca, etc. (pacer)
pazco (pacer)
pecar (8), to sin
pedalear (1), to pedal
pedantear (1), to be pedantic
pedir (i, i) (42), to ask, to ask for, to demand, to order
peer (20), to break the wind
pegar (9), to hit, to beat, to stick, to glue
pegue, etc. (pegar)
pegué (pegar)
peinar (1), to comb
peinarse (1) (4), to comb one's hair
pelar (1), to peel, to skin, to husk, to hull, to shell, to peel bark, to cut (hair), to pluck
pelarse (1) (4), to peel off, to get a haircut
pelear (1), to fight, to quarrel, to struggle
peligrar (1), to be in danger
pelotear (1), to knock a ball around (without playing a game, without effort or interest)
pellizcar (8), to pinch, to take a pinch of
pellizque, etc. (pellizcar)
pellizqué (pellizcar)
penar (1), to suffer, to penalize, to punish
pender (2), to dangle, to hang, to depend, to be pending
penetrar (1), to penetrate
pensar (ie) (37), to think, to think over, to plan
pensionar (1), to pension
peque, etc. (pecar)
pequé (pecar)
percatar (1), to take notice, to warn
percatarse (1) (4), to realize
percibir (3), to perceive, to collect
perder (ie) (39), to lose, to waste, to miss
perderse (ie) (39) (4), to get lost
perdonar (1), to pardon, to excuse
perdurar (1), to last a long time
perecer (73), to perish, to die
peregrinar (1), to go on a pilgrimage, to travel around foreign lands
perezca, etc. (perecer)
perezco (perecer)
perfeccionar (1), to perfect, to improve
perfilar (1), to profile, to polish, to perfect
perfilarse (1) (4), to show one's profile
perforar (1), to perforate
perfumar (1), to perfume
perifonear (1), to broadcast (by radio)

perifrasear (1), to paraphrase
perjudicar (8), to damage, to hurt
perjudique, etc. (**perjudicar**)
perjudiqué (**perjudicar**)
perjurar (1), to commit perjury, to swear
permanecer (73), to remain, to stay
permanezca, etc. (**permanecer**)
permanezco (**permanecer**)
permitir (3), to permit, to allow
permutar (1), to change thoroughly, to barter, to rearrange the order or sequence of
pernoctar (1), to spend the night
perorar (1), to make an impassioned speech
perpetrar (1), to perpetrate
perpetuar (62), to perpetuate
perpetuarse (62) (4), to be perpetuated
perseguir (i, i) (58), to persecute, to pursue, to importune
perseverar (1), to persevere
persiga, etc. (**perseguir**)
persignarse (1) (4), to make the sign of the cross (on oneself)
persigo (**perseguir**)
persigue, etc. (**perseguir**)
persiguiendo (**perseguir**)
persiguiera, etc. (**perseguir**)
persiguiere, etc. (**perseguir**)
persiguieron (**perseguir**)
persiguiese, etc. (**perseguir**)
persiguió (**perseguir**)
persistir (3), to persist
personalice, etc. (**personalizar**)
personalicé (**personalizar**)
personalizar (11), to personalize
personarse (1) (4), to appear personally
personificar (8), to personify
personifique, etc. (**personificar**)
personifiqué (**personificar**)
perspirar (1), to perspire, to sweat
persuadir (3), to persuade
persuadirse (3) (4), to become convinced
pertenecer (73), to belong, to pertain
pertenezca, etc. (**pertenecer**)
pertenezco (**pertenecer**)
pertrechar (1), to supply, to equip, to prepare
perturbar (1), to perturb, to disturb, to confuse
pervertir (ie, i) (41), to pervert
pervierta, etc. (**pervertir**)
pervierte, etc. (**pervertir**)
pervierto (**pervertir**)
pervirtamos (**pervertir**)
pervirtiendo (**pervertir**)
pervirtiera, etc. (**pervertir**)
pervirtiere, etc. (**pervertir**)
pervirtieron (**pervertir**)
pervirtiese, etc. (**pervertir**)
pervirtió (**pervertir**)
pesar (1), to weigh, to have weight, to be heavy, to cause sorrow
pescar (8), to fish, to catch (fish), to catch
pespuntar (1), to backstitch
pesque, etc. (**pescar**)
pesqué (**pescar**)
pestañear (1), to blink
petardear (1), to backfire (a car), to set off petards, to swindle
peticionar (1), to petition
petrificar (8), to petrify
petrifique, etc. (**petrificar**)
petrifiqué (**petrificar**)
peyendo (**peer**)
peyera, etc. (**peer**)

peyere, etc. (**peer**)
peyeron (**peer**)
peyese, etc. (**peer**)
peyó (**peer**)
piafar (1), to paw, to stamp (said of a horse)
piar (19), to chirp, to whine
picar (8), to itch, to bite, to sting, to peck, to chop up, to pique
picarse (8) (4), to be piqued, to begin to rot
picotear (1), to strike with the beak
pida, etc. (**pedir**)
pide, etc. (**pedir**)
pidiendo (**pedir**)
pidiera, etc. (**pedir**)
pidiere, etc. (**pedir**)
pidieron (**pedir**)
pidiese, etc. (**pedir**)
pidió (**pedir**)
pido (**pedir**)
piensa, etc. (**pensar**)
piense, etc. (**pensar**)
pienso (**pensar**)
pierda, etc. (**perder**)
pierde, etc. (**perder**)
pierdo (**perder**)
pifiar (1), to miss, to err
pigmentar (1), to pigment
pignorar (1), to give as a security, pledge
pilotar (1), to pilot
pilotear (1), to pilot
pillar (1), to catch
pincelar (1), to paint, to portray
pinchar (1), to puncture, to prick
pintar (1), to paint, to depict, to be important
pintarrajear (1), to daub, to smear with paint
pipiar (61), to peep, to chirp
pique, etc. (**picar**)
piqué (**picar**)
pirarse (1) (4), to go away, to flee
piratear (1), to pirate
piropear (1), to compliment, to throw a bouquet
piruetear (1), to pirouette
pisar (1), to step on, to trample underfoot
pisotear (1), to trample underfoot, to tread all over
pitar (1), to blow a whistle, to whistle, to hiss
pitear (1), to blow a whistle, to whistle, to hiss
pitorrear (1), to jeer, to scoff
piular (1), to peep, to chirp
pivotar (1), to pivot
pizcar (8), to pinch
pizque, etc. (**pizcar**)
pizqué (**pizcar**)
placer (96), to please
plagar (9), to plague, to infest
plagiar (1), to plagiarize
plague, etc. (**plagar**)
plagué (**plagar**)
planchar (1), to iron, to press (clothes), to smooth out, to leave someone waiting, to surprise by defeating or outsmarting
planear (1), to plan, to glide
planificar (8), to plan
planifique, etc. (**planificar**)
planifiqué (**planificar**)
plantar (1), to plant, to leave dumbfounded, to throw (into the street, prison)
plantarse (1) (4), to stand, to take a stand
plantear (1), to plan, to state, to raise (an issue)

plantificar (8), to plan, to outline
plantifique, etc. (**plantificar**)
plantifiqué (**plantificar**)
plañendo (**plañir**)
plañera, etc. (**plañir**)
plañere, etc. (**plañir**)
plañeron (**plañir**)
plañese, etc. (**plañir**)
plañir (29), to lament, to grieve, to bewail
plañó (**plañir**)
plasmar (1), to mold, to shape
platear (1), to plate with silver
platicar (8), to chat, to talk, to converse
platique, etc. (**platicar**)
platiqué (**platicar**)
plazca, etc. (**placer**)
plazco (**placer**)
plega (**placer**)
plegar (ie) (50), to fold, to pleat
plegue (**placer**)
plegué (**plegar**)
pleguemos, etc. (**plegar**)
pleitear (1), to litigate
pliega, etc. (**plegar**)
pliego (**plegar**)
pliegue, etc. (**plegar**)
pluguiera (**placer**)
pluguieran (**placer**)
pluguiere (**placer**)
pluguieren (**placer**)
pluguieron (**placer**)
pluguiese (**placer**)
pluguiesen (**placer**)
plugo (**placer**)
pluralice, etc. (**pluralizar**)
pluralicé (**pluralizar**)
pluralizar (11), to pluralize
poblar (ue) (36), to populate
poder (ue) (97), to be able, can, may
podré, etc. (**poder**)
podría, etc. (**poder**)
podrir = **pudrir**
poetice, etc. (**poetizar**)
poeticé (**poetizar**)
poetizar (11), to poetize
polarice, etc. (**polarizar**)
polaricé (**polarizar**)
polarizar (11), to polarize
polemice, etc. (**polemizar**)
polemicé (**polemizar**)
polemizar (11), to start a polemic
polinice, etc. (**polinizar**)
polinicé (**polinizar**)
polinizar (11), to pollinate
politiquear (1), to play politics, to talk politics
polvorear (1), to sprinkle with dust or powder
pon (**poner**)
ponderar (1), to ponder, to ponder over, to exaggerate
pondré, etc. (**poner**)
pondría, etc. (**poner**)
poner (98), to put, to place, to set (the table), to arrange
ponerse (98) (4), to become, to get, to turn, to set (said of the sun), to dress, to put on
ponga, etc. (**poner**)
pongo (**poner**)
pontificar (8), to pontificate
pontifique, etc. (**pontificar**)
pontifiqué (**pontificar**)
popularice, etc. (**popularizar**)
popularicé (**popularizar**)
popularizar (11), to popularize
popularizarse (11) (4), to become popular

porfiar (61), to persist, to argue stubbornly
pormenorice, etc. (**pormenorizar**)
pormenoricé (**pormenorizar**)
pormenorizar (11), to tell in detail, to itemize
portar (1), to carry, to bear
portarse (1) (4), to behave, to conduct oneself
portear (1), to carry on one's back, to transport (for a price)
posar (1), to lodge, to pose (a model), to perch
posarse (1) (4), to settle (sediment), to perch (birds)
posdatar (1), to add a postscript to a letter
poseer (20), to own, to possess, to have
posesionar (1), to give possession
posesionarse (1) (4), to take possession
poseyendo (**poseer**)
poseyera, etc. (**poseer**)
poseyere, etc. (**poseer**)
poseyeron (**poseer**)
poseyese, etc. (**poseer**)
poseyó (**poseer**)
posibilitar (1), to make possible
pospón (**posponer**)
pospondré, etc. (**posponer**)
pospondría, etc. (**posponer**)
posponer (98), to postpone, to put off, to put after
posponga, etc. (**posponer**)
pospongo (**posponer**)
pospuesto (**posponer**)
pospuse (**posponer**)
pospusiera, etc. (**posponer**)
pospusiere, etc. (**posponer**)
pospusieron (**posponer**)
pospusiese, etc. (**posponer**)
pospusimos (**posponer**)
pospusiste (**posponer**)
pospusisteis (**posponer**)
pospuso (**posponer**)
postergar (9), to delay, to pass over (disregard seniority)
postergue, etc. (**postergar**)
postergué (**postergar**)
postrar (1), to prostrate
postular (1), to postulate
potabilice, etc. (**potabilizar**)
potabilicé (**potabilizar**)
potabilizar (11), to make drinkable
practicar (8), to practice
practique, etc. (**practicar**)
practiqué (**practicar**)
precaucionarse (1) (4), to be cautious
precautelar (1), to caution
precaver (2), to prevent
precaverse (2) (4), to be on one's guard
preceder (2), to precede
preceptuar (62), to give or issue a precept
preciar (1), to appraise
preciarse (1) (4), to boast of being
percintar (1), to strap, to bind, to seal
precipitar (1), to rush, to precipitate
precisar (1), to state precisely, to need
preconcebir (i, i) (42), to preconceive
preconciba, etc. (**preconcebir**)
preconcibe, etc. (**preconcebir**)
preconcibo (**preconcebir**)
preconcibiendo (**preconcebir**)
preconcibiera, etc. (**preconcebir**)
preconcibiere, etc. (**preconcebir**)
preconcibieron (**preconcebir**)
preconcibiese, etc. (**preconcebir**)
preconcibió (**preconcebir**)
preconice, etc. (**preconizar**)

preconicé (**preconizar**)
preconizar (11), to proclaim
preconocer (73), to know in advance
preconozca, etc. (**preconocer**)
preconozco (**preconocer**)
predecir (i, i) (84), to predict, to foretell
predestinar (1), to predestine
predí (**predecir**)
predicar (8), to preach
predice, etc. (**predecir**)
prediciendo (**predecir**)
predicho (**predecir**)
prediga, etc. (**predecir**)
predigo (**predecir**)
predije (**predecir**)
predijera, etc. (**predecir**)
predijere, etc. (**predecir**)
predijeron (**predecir**)
predijese, etc. (**predecir**)
predijimos (**predecir**)
predijiste (**predecir**)
predijisteis (**predecir**)
predijo (**predecir**)
predique, etc. (**predicar**)
prediqué (**predicar**)
prediré (**predecir**)
prediría, etc. (**predecir**)
predispón (**predisponer**)
predispondré, etc. (**predisponer**)
predispondría, etc. (**predisponer**)
predisponer (98), to predispose
predisponga, etc. (**predisponer**)
predispongo (**predisponer**)
predispuesto (**predisponer**)
predispuse (**predisponer**)
predispusiera, etc. (**predisponer**)
predispusiere, etc. (**predisponer**)
predispusieron (**predisponer**)
predispusiese, etc. (**predisponer**)
predispusimos (**predisponer**)
predispusiste (**predisponer**)
predispusisteis (**predisponer**)
predispuso (**predisponer**)
predominar (1), to predominate, to stand out
preelegir (i, i) (57), to elect beforehand
preelige, etc. (**preelegir**)
preeligiendo (**preelegir**)
preeligiera, etc. (**preelegir**)
preeligiere, etc. (**preelegir**)
preeligieron (**preelegir**)
preeligiese, etc. (**preelegir**)
preeligió (**preelegir**)
preelija, etc. (**preelegir**)
preelijo (**preelegir**)
preexistir (3), to preexist
prefabricar (8), to prefabricate
prefabrique, etc. (**prefabricar**)
prefabriqué (**prefabricar**)
preferir (ie, i) (41), to prefer
prefiera, etc. (**preferir**)
prefiere, etc. (**preferir**)
prefiero (**preferir**)
prefijar (1), to prefix
prefiramos, etc. (**preferir**)
prefiriendo (**preferir**)
prefiriera, etc. (**preferir**)
prefiriere, etc. (**preferir**)
prefirieron (**preferir**)
prefiriese, etc. (**preferir**)
prefirió (**preferir**)
pregonar (1), to proclaim
preguntar (1), to ask, to inquire
prejuzgar (9), to prejudge
prejuzgue, etc. (**prejuzgar**)
prejuzgué (**prejuzgar**)

preludiar (1), to prelude
premeditar (1), to premeditate
premiar (1), to reward
premorir (ue, u) (94), to die first
premuera, etc. (**premorir**)
premuere, etc. (**premorir**)
premuero (**premorir**)
premuerto (**premorir**)
premuramos, etc. (**premorir**)
premuriendo (**premorir**)
premuriera, etc. (**premorir**)
premuriere, etc. (**premorir**)
premurieron (**premorir**)
premuriese, etc. (**premorir**)
premurió (**premorir**)
prendar (1), to charm, to pawn
prendarse (1) (4), to take a liking to or for, to fall in love
prender (2), to catch, to arrest, to catch fire, to take root, to turn on, to pin
prenotar (1), to note in advance
prensar (1), to press
prenunciar (1), to announce in advance
preocupar (1), to preoccupy
preocuparse (1) (4), to worry, to become preoccupied
preparar (1), to prepare
prepararse (1) (4), to get prepared, to get ready
prepón (**preponer**)
preponderar (1), to prevail
prepondré, etc. (**preponer**)
prepondría, etc. (**preponer**)
preponer (98), to put before
preponga, etc. (**preponer**)
prepongo (**preponer**)
prepuesto (**preponer**)
prepuse (**preponer**)
prepusiera, etc. (**preponer**)
prepusiere, etc. (**preponer**)
prepusieron (**preponer**)
prepusiese, etc. (**preponer**)
prepusimos (**preponer**)
prepusiste (**preponer**)
prepusisteis (**preponer**)
prepuso (**preponer**)
presagiar (1), to predict
prescindir (3), to do without, to leave out
prescribir (69), to prescribe
prescrito (**prescribir**)
presenciar (1), to witness
presentar (1), to present, to introduce
presentarse (1) (4), to appear
presentir (ie, i) (41), to have a presentiment of
preservar (1), to preserve
presidir (3), to preside over
presienta, etc. (**presentir**)
presiente, etc. (**presentir**)
presiento (**presentir**)
presintamos, etc. (**presentir**)
presintiendo (**presentir**)
presintiera, etc. (**presentir**)
presintiere, etc. (**presentir**)
presintieron (**presentir**)
presintiese, etc. (**presentir**)
presintió (**presentir**)
presionar (1), to put pressure (on a person)
prestar (1), to lend, to pay (attention), to render (a service), to keep (silence)
prestarse (1) (4), to offer or lend oneself
presumir (3), to presume, to boast
presupón (**presuponer**)
presupondré, etc. (**presuponer**)
presupondría, etc. (**presuponer**)
presuponer (98), to presuppose

presuponga, etc. (**presuponer**)
presupongo (**presuponer**)
presupuestar (1), to budget
presupuesto (**presuponer**) (**presupuestar**)
presupuse (**presuponer**)
presupusiera, etc. (**presuponer**)
presupusiere, etc. (**presuponer**)
presupusieron (**presuponer**)
presupusiese, etc. (**presuponer**)
presupusimos (**presuponer**)
presupusiste (**presuponer**)
presupusisteis (**presuponer**)
presupuso (**presuponer**)
pretender (2), to pretend
preterir (ie, i) (119), to do without, to overlook
pretextar (1), to use as a pretext
prevál (**prevaler**)
prevaldré, etc. (**prevaler**)
prevaldría, etc. (**prevaler**)
prevalecer (73), to prevail
prevaler (110), to prevail
prevalezca, etc. (**prevalecer**)
prevalezco (**prevalecer**)
prevalga, etc. (**prevaler**)
prevalgo (**prevaler**)
prevaricar (8), to prevaricate
prevarique, etc. (**prevaricar**)
prevariqué (**prevaricar**)
prevea, etc. (**prever**)
preveía, etc. (**prever**)
prevén (**prevenir**)
prevendré, etc. (**prevenir**)
prevendría, etc. (**prevenir**)
prevenga, etc. (**prevenir**)
prevengo (**prevenir**)
prevenir (ie, i) (111), to prevent, to prepare, to warn
prevenirse (ie, i) (111) (4), to get prepared
preveo (**prever**)
prever (112), to foresee
previene, etc. (**prevenir**)
previne (**prevenir**)
previniendo (**prevenir**)
previniera, etc. (**prevenir**)
previniere, etc. (**prevenir**)
previnieron (**prevenir**)
previniese, etc. (**prevenir**)
previnimos (**prevenir**)
previniste (**prevenir**)
previnisteis (**prevenir**)
previno (**prevenir**)
previsto (**prever**)
principiar (1), to begin
pringar (9), to spot or stain with grease
pringue, etc. (**pringar**)
pringué (**pringar**)
privar (1), to deprive, to be in vogue
privilegiar (1), to privilege
probar (ue) (36), to test, to try, to try out, to prove, to taste, to sample
probarse (ue) (36) (4), to try on (clothes)
proceder (2), to procede, to originate
procesar (1), to indict, to sue, to prosecute
proclamar (1), to proclaim, to acclaim
procrastinar (1), to procrastinate
procrear (1), to procreate
procurar (1), to endeavor, to manage, to procure
prodigar (9), to lavish, to squander
prodigue, etc. (**prodigar**)
prodigué (**prodigar**)
producir (67), to produce, to yield, to cause

producirse (67) (4), to take place, to happen
produje (**producir**)
produjera, etc. (**producir**)
produjere, etc. (**producir**)
produjeron (**producir**)
produjese, etc. (**producir**)
produjimos (**producir**)
produjiste (**producir**)
produjisteis (**producir**)
produjo (**producir**)
produzca, etc. (**producir**)
produzco (**producir**)
profanar (1), to desecrate, to dishonor
proferir (ie, i) (41), to utter
profesar (1), to profess
profetice, etc. (**profetizar**)
profeticé (**profetizar**)
profetizar (11), to prophesy
profiera, etc. (**proferir**)
profiere, etc. (**proferir**)
profiero (**proferir**)
profiramos, etc. (**proferir**)
profiriendo (**proferir**)
profiriera, etc. (**proferir**)
profiriere, etc. (**proferir**)
profirieron (**proferir**)
profiriese, etc. (**proferir**)
profirió (**proferir**)
profundice, etc. (**profundizar**)
profundicé (**profundizar**)
profundizar (11), to make deeper, to get to the bottom, to go deep
profundizarse (11) (4), to become deep
programar (1), to program
progresar (1), to progress
prohíba, etc. (**prohibir**)
prohíbe, etc. (**prohibir**)
prohibir (34), to prohibit, to forbid
prohíbo (**prohibir**)
prohíja, etc. (**prohijar**)
prohijar (34), to adopt
prohíje, etc. (**prohijar**)
prohíjo (**prohijar**)
proletarice, etc. (**proletarizar**)
proletaricé (**proletarizar**)
proletarizar (11), to proletarianize
prologar (9), to write a preface (for)
prologue, etc. (**prologar**)
prologué (**prologar**)
prolongar (9), to prolong, to extend
prolongue, etc. (**prolongar**)
prolongué (**prolongar**)
promediar (1), to average, to mediate
prometer (2), to promise
promover (ue) (38), to promote
promueva, etc. (**promover**)
promueve, etc. (**promover**)
promuevo (**promover**)
promulgar (9), to promulgate, to proclaim
promulgue, etc. (**promulgar**)
promulgué (**promulgar**)
pronosticar (8), to foretell, to prognosticate
pronostique, etc. (**pronosticar**)
pronostiqué (**pronosticar**)
pronunciar (1), to pronounce, to deliver (a speech)
propagar (9), to propagate, to spread, to broadcast
propague, etc. (**propagar**)
propagué (**propagar**)
propalar (1), (to divulge)
propasarse (1) (4), to go too far, to take undue liberty

propender (2), to tend
propiciar (1), to propitiate
propinar (1), to give a tip, to give (beating, kick, slap)
propón (**proponer**)
propondré, etc. (**proponer**)
propondría, etc. (**proponer**)
proponer (98), to propose, to name, to present (a candidate)
proponerse (98) (4), to resolve
proponga, etc. (**proponer**)
propongo (**proponer**)
proporcionar (1), to provide, to proportion
propuesto (**proponer**)
propugnar (1), to defend, to protect
propulsar (1), to propel
propuse (**proponer**)
propusiera, etc. (**proponer**)
propusiere, etc. (**proponer**)
propusieron (**proponer**)
propusiese, etc. (**proponer**)
propusimos (**proponer**)
propusiste (**proponer**)
propusisteis (**proponer**)
propuso (**proponer**)
prorratear (1), to prorate, to distribute proportionally
prorrogar (9), to defer, to postpone
prorrogue, etc. (**prorrogar**)
prorrogué (**prorrogar**)
prorrumpir (3), to break forth, burst out
proscribir (69), to proscribe
proscripto (**proscribir**)
proscrito (**proscribir**)
proseguir (i, i) (58), to continue, to proceed
prosiga, etc. (**proseguir**)
prosigo (**proseguir**)
prosigue, etc. (**proseguir**)
prosiguiendo (**proseguir**)
prosiguiera, etc. (**proseguir**)
prosiguiere, etc. (**proseguir**)
prosiguieron (**proseguir**)
prosiguiese, etc. (**proseguir**)
prosiguió (**proseguir**)
prosperar (1), to prosper
prosternarse (1) (4), to prostrate oneself
prostituir (71), to prostitute
prostituya, etc. (**prostituir**)
prostituye, etc. (**prostituir**)
prostituyendo (**prostituir**)
prostituyera, etc. (**prostituir**)
prostituyere, etc. (**prostituir**)
prostituyeron (**prostituir**)
prostituyese, etc. (**prostituir**)
prostituyo (**prostituir**)
prostituyó (**prostituir**)
proteger (15), to protect
proteja, etc. (**proteger**)
protejo (**proteger**)
protestar (1), to protest
proveer (99), to provide
provén (**provenir**)
provendré, etc. (**provenir**)
provendría, etc. (**provenir**)
provenga, etc. (**provenir**)
provengo (**provenir**)
provenir (i, ie) (111), to come, to originate, to arise
proveyendo (**proveer**)
proveyera, etc. (**proveer**)
proveyere, etc. (**proveer**)
proveyeron (**proveer**)
proveyese, etc. (**proveer**)
proveyó (**proveer**)

proviene, etc. (**provenir**)
provine (**provenir**)
proviniendo (**provenir**)
proviniera, etc. (**provenir**)
proviniere, etc. (**provenir**)
provinieron (**provenir**)
proviniese, etc. (**provenir**)
provinimos (**provenir**)
proviniste (**provenir**)
provinisteis (**provenir**)
provino (**provenir**)
provisto (**proveer**)
provocar (8), to provoke, to promote, to incite
provoque, etc. (**provocar**)
provoqué (**provocar**)
proyectar (1), to project, to plan
prueba, etc. (**probar**)
pruebe, etc. (**probar**)
pruebo (**probar**)
psicoanalice, etc. (**psicoanalizar**)
psicoanalicé (**psicoanalizar**)
psicoanalizar (11), to psychoanalyze
puar (19), to put teeth on (e.g. comb)
publicar (8), to publish, to publicize
publique, etc. (**publicar**)
publiqué (**publicar**)
pude (**poder**)
pudiendo (**poder**)
pudiera, etc. (**poder**)
pudiere, etc. (**poder**)
pudieron (**poder**)
pudiese, etc. (**poder**)
pudimos (**poder**)
pudiste (**poder**)
pudisteis (**poder**)
pudo (**poder**)
pudrir (100), to rot
puebla, etc. (**poblar**)
pueble, etc. (**poblar**)
pueblo (**poblar**)
pueda, etc. (**poder**)
puede, etc. (**poder**)
puedo (**poder**)
puesto (**poner**)
pugnar (1), to fight, to struggle, to strive
pujar (1), to push ahead, to outbid
pulir (3), to polish, to finish
pulsar (1), to feel the pulse (of), to play (harp, lyre, etc.), to sound out
pulsear (1), to hand-wrestle
pulular (1), to swarm
pulverice, etc. (**pulverizar**)
pulvericé (**pulverizar**)
pulverizar (11), to pulverize, to atomize, to spray
punce, etc. (**punzar**)
puncé (**punzar**)
pungir (16), to sting, to prick
punja, etc. (**pungir**)
punjo (**pungir**)
puntear (1), to dot, to stitch
puntualice, etc. (**puntualizar**)
puntualicé (**puntualizar**)
puntualizar (11), to give a detailed account (of), to fix in one's mind
puntuar (62), to punctuate
punzar (11), to prick, to perforate
purgar (9), to purge, to purify
purgarse (9) (4), to take a laxative
purgue, etc. (**purgar**)
purgué (**purgar**)
purificar (8), to purify
purifique, etc. (**purificar**)
purifiqué (**purificar**)

puse (**poner**)
pusiera, etc. (**poner**)
pusiere, etc. (**poner**)
pusieron (**poner**)
pusiese, etc. (**poner**)
pusimos (**poner**)
pusiste (**poner**)
pusisteis (**poner**)
puso (**poner**)

Q

quebrantar (1), to break, to violate (a law)
quebrar (ie) (37), to break
quedar (1), to remain, to be left, to be left over, to turn out, to be
quedarse (1) (4), to stay
quejarse (1) (4), to complain, to whine
quemar (1), to burn, to kindle, to parch, to be hot
quepa, etc. (**caber**)
quepo (**caber**)
querellarse (1) (4), to complain
querer (ie) (101), to want, to wish, to desire, to like, to love
querré, etc. (**querer**)
querría, etc. (**querer**)
quiebra, etc. (**quebrar**)
quiebre, etc. (**quebrar**)
quiebro (**quebrar**)
quiera, etc. (**querer**)
quiere, etc. (**querer**)
quiero (**querer**)
quijotear (1), to act quixotically
quise (**querer**)
quisiera, etc. (**querer**)
quisiere, etc. (**querer**)
quisieron (**querer**)
quisiese, etc. (**querer**)
quisimos (**querer**)
quisiste (**querer**)
quisisteis (**querer**)
quiso (**querer**)
quitar (1), to remove, to take away, to clear (the table)
quitarse (1) (4), to take off (article of clothing)

R

rabiar (1), to rage, to rave, to have rabies, to get mad
raciocinar (1), ratiocinate
racionalice, etc. (**racionalizar**)
racionalicé (**racionalizar**)
racionalizar (11), to rationalize
racionar (1), to ration
radiar (1), to radio, to irradiate, to radiate
radicar (8), to be located
radicarse (8) (4), to settle down
radiodifundir (3), to radio broadcast
radiografiar (61), to radiograph
radiotelefonear (1), to radiotelephone
radiotelegrafiar (61), to radiotelegraph
radique, etc. (**radicar**)
radiqué (**radicar**)
raer (102), to scrape, to scrape off, to wipe out
raerse (102) (4), to become worn
raiga, etc. (**raer**)
raigo (**raer**)
rajar (1), to split, to crack
rajarse (1) (4), to back down
rallar, to grate
ramificar (8), to ramify

ramifique, etc. (**ramificar**)
ramifiqué (**ramificar**)
ramonear (1), to nibble grass, twigs or leaves; to browse
ranurar (1), to groove
rapar (1), to shave, to cut the hair very short
rapiñar (1), to plunder, to steal
raposear (1), to be wily
raptar (1), to kidnap
rarefacer (68), to rarefy
rarefaga, etc. (**rarefacer**)
rarefago (**rarefacer**)
rarefaré, etc. (**rarefacer**)
rarefaría, etc. (**rarefacer**)
rarefaz (**rarefacer**)
rarefecho (**rarefacer**)
rarefice (**rarefacer**)
rareficiera, etc. (**rarefacer**)
rareficiere, etc. (**rarefacer**)
rareficieron (**rarefacer**)
rareficiese, etc. (**rarefacer**)
rareficimos (**rarefacer**)
rareficiste (**rarefacer**)
rareficisteis (**rarefacer**)
rarefizo (**rarefacer**)
rarificar (8), to rarefy
rarifique, etc. (**rarificar**)
rarifiqué (**rarificar**)
rascar (8), to scratch, to scrape
rasgar (9), to tear, to rip
rasgarse (9) (4), to become torn
rasgue, etc. (**rasgar**)
rasgué (**rasgar**)
rasguear (1), to twang (e.g. a guitar), to make flourishes (on the guitar, with a pen)
rasguñar (1), to scratch
raspar (1), to scrape, to scrape off
rasque, etc. (**rascar**)
rasqué (**rascar**)
rastrear (1), to track, to trail, to drag, to dredge
rastrillar (1), to rake
rastrojar (1), to clear of stubble
rasurar (1), to shave
ratear (1), to filch, to distribute proportionally
ratificar (8), to ratify
ratifique, etc. (**ratificar**)
ratifiqué (**ratificar**)
raya (**raer**) (**rayar**)
rayar (1), to line, to make lines on, to scratch (mar), to border on
rayera, etc. (**raer**)
rayere, etc. (**raer**)
rayeron (**raer**)
rayese, etc. (**raer**)
rayo (**raer**) (**rayar**)
rayó (**raer**) (**rayar**)
razonar (1), to reason, to document or support with evidence
reabierto (**reabrir**)
reabrir (75), to reopen
reaccionar (1), to react
reacondicionar (1), to recondition
reactivar (1), to reactivate
readaptar (1), to readapt
readmitir (3), to readmit
reafirmar (1), to reaffirm
reagravar (1), to make worse again
reagravarse (1) (4), to get worse again
reajustar (1), to readjust
realce, etc. (**realzar**)
realcé (**realzar**)

realice, etc. (realizar)
realicé (realizar
realizar (11), to fulfill, to make real
realzar (11), to emphasize, to make promi-
    nent
reanimar (1), to revive, to comfort
reanudar (1), to renew, to resume
reaparecer (73), to reappear
reaparezca, etc. (reaparecer)
reaparezco (reaparecer)
rearmar (1), to rearm
reasegurar (1), to reinsure
reasumir (3), to reassume, to resume
reavivar (1), to revive
rebajar (1), to lower, to reduce
rebajarse (1) (4), to lose weight
rebalsar (1), to dam, to dam back
rebanar (1), to slice
rebañar = arrebañar
rebasar (1), to overflow, to exceed
rebatir (3), to refute, to rebut
rebelar (1), to rebel, to resist
reblandecer (73), to soften
reblandezca, etc. (reblandecer)
reblandezco (reblandecer)
reboce, etc. (rebozar)
rebocé (rebozar)
rebosar (1), to abound, to burst with
rebotar (1), to bounce back, to rebound
rebozar (11), to cover with batter
rebrotar (1), to sprout
rebujar (1), to jumble together
rebujarse (1) (4), to wrap oneself all up
rebullendo (rebullir)
rebullera, etc. (rebullir)
rebullere, etc. (rebullir)
rebulleron (rebullir)
rebullese, etc. (rebullir)
rebullir (27), to stir, to begin to move, to
    give signs of life
rebulló (rebullir)
rebuscar (8), to seek after, to glean
rebusque, etc. (rebuscar)
rebusqué (rebuscar)
rebutir (3), to stuff, to insert
rebuznar (1), to bray, to talk nonsense
recabar (1), to obtain, to gain by entreaty
recaer (81), to relapse, to fall again
recaiga, etc. (recaer)
recaigo (recaer)
recalcar (8), to stress (one's words)
recalentar (ie) (37), to reheat, to overheat
recalienta, etc. (recalentar)
recaliente, etc. (recalentar)
recaliento (recalentar)
recalque, etc. (recalcar)
recalqué (recalcar)
recamar (1), to embroider in relief
recapacitar (1), to run over in one's mind,
    to refresh one's memory
recapitular (1), to recapitulate
recargar (9), to recharge, to overcharge, to
    reload
recargue, etc. (recargar)
recargué (recargar)
recatarse (1) (4), to be reserved
recauchutar (1), to recap
recaudar (1), to collect (taxes, rent, mon-
    ey)
recayendo (recaer)
recayera, etc. (recaer)
recayere, etc. (recaer)
recayeron (recaer)
recayese, etc. (recaer)
recayó (recaer)
rece, etc. (rezar)

recé (rezar)
recelar (1), to suspect, to fear
recetar (1), to prescribe
recibir (3), to receive, to welcome, to meet
reciprocar (8), to reciprocate
reciproque, etc. (reciprocar)
reciproqué (reciprocar)
recitar (1), to recite
reclamar (1), to reclaim
recluir (71), to seclude, to intern
recluirse (71) (4), to go into seclusion
reclutar (1), to recruit
recluya, etc. (recluir)
recluye, etc. (recluir)
recluyendo (recluir)
recluyera, etc. (recluir)
recluyere, etc. (recluir)
recluyeron (recluir)
recluyese, etc. (recluir)
recluyo (recluir)
recluyó (recluir)
recobrar (1), to recover
recocer (ue) (54), to cook again, to cook a
    lot (to excess)
recoger (15), to pick up, to gather
recogerse (15) (4), to take shelter, to retire
    (go to bed)
recoja, etc. (recoger)
recojo (recoger)
recomendar (ie) (37), to recommend
recomienda, etc. (recomendar)
recomiende, etc. (recomendar)
recomiendo (recomendar)
recompensar (1), to recompense, to re-
    ward
recompón (recomponer)
recompondré, etc. (recomponer)
recompondría, etc. (recomponer)
recomponer (98), to mend, to recompose
recomponga, etc. (recomponer)
recompongo (recomponer)
recompuesto (recomponer)
recompuse (recomponer)
recompusiera, etc. (recomponer)
recompusiere, etc. (recomponer)
recompusieron (recomponer)
recompusiese, etc. (recomponer)
recompusimos (recomponer)
recompusiste (recomponer)
recompusisteis (recomponer)
recompuso (recomponer)
reconcentrar (1), to concentrate
reconciliar (1), to reconcile
reconfortar (1), to comfort
reconocer (73), to recognize, to admit
reconocerse (73) (4), to recognize one's
    own faults, errors, etc.; to know oneself
reconozca, etc. (reconocer)
reconozco (reconocer)
reconquistar (1), to recover, to recon-
    quest
reconsiderar (1), to reconsider
reconstituir (71), to reconstitute
reconstituya, etc. (reconstituir)
reconstituye, etc. (reconstituir)
reconstituyendo (reconstituir)
reconstituyera, etc. (reconstituir)
reconstituyere, etc. (reconstituir)
reconstituyeron (reconstituir)
reconstituyese, etc. (reconstituir)
reconstituyo (reconstituir)
reconstituyó (reconstituir)
reconstruir (71), to rebuild
reconstruya, etc. (reconstruir)
reconstruye, etc. (reconstruir)
reconstruyendo (reconstruir)

reconstruyera, etc. (reconstruir)
reconstruyere, etc. (reconstruir)
reconstruyeron (reconstruir)
reconstruyese, etc. (reconstruir)
reconstruyo (reconstruir)
reconstruyó (reconstruir)
recontar (ue) (36), to recount
reconvén (reconvenir)
reconvendré, etc. (reconvenir)
reconvendría, etc. (reconvenir)
reconvenga, etc. (reconvenir)
reconvengo (reconvenir)
reconvenir (ie, i) (111), to reproach
reconviene, etc. (reconvenir)
reconvine (reconvenir)
reconviniendo (reconvenir)
reconviniera, etc. (reconvenir)
reconviniere, etc. (reconvenir)
reconvinieron (reconvenir)
reconviniese, etc. (reconvenir)
reconvinimos (reconvenir)
reconviniste (reconvenir)
reconvinisteis (reconvenir)
reconvino (reconvenir)
recopilar (1), to compile
recordar (ue) (36), to remember, to remind
recorrer (2), to go over, to travel, to resort,
    to tour
recortar (1), to trim, to cut out
recortarse (1) (4), to stand out
recoser (2), to sew again, to mend
recostar (ue) (36), to recline, to lean
recozamos, etc. (recocer)
recrear (1), to recreate, to amuse
recriminar (1), to recriminate
rectificar (8), to rectify
rectifique, etc. (rectificar)
rectifiqué (rectificar)
recubierto (recubrir)
recubrir (82), to cover, to recover (cover
    again)
recuece, etc. (recocer)
recuenta, etc. (recontar)
recuente, etc. (recontar)
recuento (recontar)
recuerda, etc. (recordar)
recuerde, etc. (recordar)
recuerdo (recordar)
recuesta, etc. (recostar)
recueste, etc. (recostar)
recuesto (recostar)
recueza, etc. (recocer)
recuezo (recocer)
recular (1), to back up
recuperar (1), to recuperate, to recover
recurrir (3), to resort, to have recourse
rechace, etc. (rechazar)
rechacé (rechazar)
rechazar (11), to drive back, to reject
rechinar (1), to squeak, to gnash
redactar (1), to write up
redar (1), to net
redecir (i, i) (84), to say over and over
    again
redí (redecir)
redice, etc. (redecir)
rediciendo (redecir)
redicho (redecir)
rediga, etc. (redecir)
redigo (redecir)
redije (redecir)
redijera, etc. (redecir)
redijere, etc. (redecir)
redijeron (redecir)
redijese, etc. (redecir)
redijimos (redecir)

redijiste (redecir)
redijisteis (redecir)
redijo (redecir)
redimir (3), to redeem
rediré, etc. (redecir)
rediría, etc. (redecir)
redoblar (1), to roll a drum, to double
redondear (1), to make round, to round off
reducir (67), to reduce
reducirse (67) (4), to confine oneself
reduje (reducir)
redujera, etc. (reducir)
redujere, etc. (reducir)
redujeron (reducir)
redujese, etc. (reducir)
redujimos (reducir)
redujiste (reducir)
redujisteis (reducir)
redujo (reducir)
redundar (1), to overflow, to redound
reduzca, etc. (reducir)
reduzco (reducir)
reedificar (8), to rebuild
reedifique, etc. (reedificar)
reedifiqué (reedificar)
reeducar (8), to reeducate
reeduque, etc. (reeducar)
reeduqué (reeducar)
reelegir (i, i) (57), to reelect
reelige, etc. (reelegir)
reeligiendo (reelegir)
reeligiera, etc. (reelegir)
reeligiere, etc. (reelegir)
reeligieron (reelegir)
reeligiese, etc. (reelegir)
reeligió (reelegir)
reelija, etc. (reelegir)
reelijo (reelegir)
reembarcar (8), to reembark
reembarque, etc. (reembarcar)
reembarqué (reembarcar)
reembolsar (1), to reimburse, to refund
reembolsarse (1) (4), to collect a debt
reempacar (8), to repack
reempaque, etc. (reempacar)
reempaqué (reempacar)
reemplace, etc. (reemplazar)
reemplacé (reemplazar)
reemplazar (11), to substitute, to replace
reencarnar (1), to reincarnate
reencender (ie) (39), to rekindle, to relight
reencienda, etc. (reencender)
reenciende, etc. (reencender)
reenciendo (reencender)
reencuadernar (1), to rebind
reenganchar (1), to reenlist, to recouple
reengendrar (1), to regenerate
reexaminar (1), to reexamine
refaccionar (1), to repair
referir (ie, i) (41), to refer, to tell
referirse (ie, i) (41) (4), to refer
refiera, etc. (referir)
refiere, etc. (referir)
refiero (referir)
refinar (1), to refine
refiramos, etc. (referir)
refiriendo (referir)
refiriera, etc. (referir)
refiriere, etc. (referir)
refirieron (referir)
refiriese, etc. (referir)
refirió (referir)
refirmar (1), to ratify, to support
reflejar (1), to reflect, to show
reflexionar (1), to think, to reflect
reflorecer (73), to blossom or flower again

reflorezca, etc. (reflorecer)
reflorezco (reflorecer)
refocilarse (1) (4), to abandon oneself to voluptuous living
reforcé (reforzar)
reforcemos, etc. (reforzar)
reformar (1), to reform, to mend
reforzar (ue) (46), to reinforce, to strengthen
refractar (1), to refract
refregar (ie) (50), to rub, to upbraid
refregué (refregar)
refreguemos, etc. (refregar)
refreír (i, i) (88), to fry again, to fry well, to refry
refrenar (1), to restrain, to rein
refrendar (1), to legalize
refrescar (8), to refresh, to cool
refresque, etc. (refrescar)
refresqué (refrescar)
refría, etc. (refreír)
refríe, etc. (refreír)
refriega, etc. (refregar)
refriego (refregar)
refriegue, etc. (refregar)
refriendo (refreír)
refriera, etc. (refreír)
refriere, etc. (refreír)
refrieron (refreír)
refriese, etc. (refreír)
refrigerar (1), to refrigerate
refrío (refreír)
refrió (refreír)
refrito (refreír)
refuerce, etc. (reforzar)
refuerza, etc. (reforzar)
refuerzo (reforzar)
refulgir (16), to be resplendent, to shine
refulja, etc. (refulgir)
refuljo (refulgir)
refundir (3), to remelt, to recast, to adapt (a play, a novel), to revise (a book)
refunfuñar (1), to grumble
refutar (1), to refute
regalar (1), to give as a present
regañar (1), to scold, to grumble
regañendo (regañir)
regañera, etc. (regañir)
regañere, etc. (regañir)
regañeron (regañir)
regañese, etc. (regañir)
regañir (29), to yelp, to yowl
regañó (regañar) (regañir)
regar (ie) (50), to water, to irrigate
regatear (1), to haggle over, to bargain, to dribble (soccer)
regenerar (1), to regenerate
regentar (1), to rule, to manage, to direct
regimentar (ie) (37), to regiment
regimienta, etc. (regimentar)
regimiente, etc. (regimentar)
regimiento (regimentar)
regir (i, i) (57), to rule, to govern, to direct, to manage, to be in force (a rule, a law)
registrar (1), to search, to record
registrarse (1) (4), to register, to be recorded
reglar (1), to rule (paper), to regulate
regocijar (1), to gladden, to cheer
regocijarse (1) (4), to rejoice
regodearse (1) (4), to take delight, to joke
regoldar (ue) (48), to belch
regolfar (1), to flow back
regomar (1), to recap, to retread
regraciar (1), to show gratitude (for)
regresar (1), to return

regué (regar)
regüelda, etc. (regoldar)
regüelde, etc. (regoldar)
regüeldo (regoldar)
reguemos, etc. (regar)
regular (1), to regulate
regularice, etc. (regularizar)
regularicé (regularizar)
regularizar (11), to regularize
regurgitar (1), to regurgitate
rehabilitar (1), to rehabilitate
rehacer (90), to do over, to make over, to remake, to renovate
rehacerse (90) (4), to recover oneself
rehaga, etc. (rehacer)
rehago (rehacer)
reharé, etc. (rehacer)
reharía, etc. (rehacer)
rehaz (rehacer)
rehecho (rehacer)
rehenchir (i, i) (42), to refill, to stuff (furniture)
rehíce (rehacer)
rehiciera, etc. (rehacer)
rehiciere, etc. (rehacer)
rehicieron (rehacer)
rehiciese, etc. (rehacer)
rehicimos (rehacer)
rehiciste (rehacer)
rehicisteis (rehacer)
rehíla, etc. (rehilar)
rehilar (34), to twist too much, to stagger, to reel, to whiz
rehíle, etc. (rehilar)
rehílo (rehilar)
rehíncha, etc. (rehenchir)
rehinchamos, etc. (rehenchir)
rehínche, etc. (rehenchir)
rehinchemos, etc. (rehenchir)
rehinchiendo (rehenchir)
rehinchiera, etc. (rehenchir)
rehinchiere, etc. (rehenchir)
rehinchieron (rehenchir)
rehinchiese, etc. (rehenchir)
rehinchió (rehenchir)
rehíncho (rehenchir)
rehízo (rehacer)
rehuir (71), to decline, to shun
rehundir (34), to sink (something) to the bottom
rehúsa, etc. (rehusar)
rehusar (34), to refuse, to turn down
rehúse, etc. (rehusar)
rehúso (rehusar)
rehuya, etc. (rehuir)
rehuye, etc. (rehuir)
rehuyendo (rehuir)
rehuyera, etc. (rehuir)
rehuyere, etc. (rehuir)
rehuyeron (rehuir)
rehuyese, etc. (rehuir)
rehuyo (rehuir)
rehuyó (rehuir)
reimpreso (reimprimir)
reimprimir (91), to reprint
reinar (1), to reign, to prevail
reincidir (3), to relapse (into vice or error), to repeat an offense
reintegrar (1), to reintegrate, to restore, to pay back
reinvertir (ie, i) (41), to reinvest
reinvierta, etc. (reinvertir)
reinvierte, etc. (reinvertir)
reinvierto (reinvertir)
reinvirtamos, etc. (reinvertir)
reinvirtiendo (reinvertir)

reinvirtiera, etc. (**reinvertir**)
reinvirtiere, etc. (**reinvertir**)
reinvirtieron (**reinvertir**)
reinvirtiese, etc. (**reinvertir**)
reinvirtió (**reinvertir**)
reír (i, i) (59), to laugh
reírse (i, i) (59) (4), to laugh
reiterar (1), to reiterate, to repeat
reivindicar (8), to lay hold of, to demand (one's rights)
reivindique, etc. (**reivindicar**)
reivindiqué (**reivindicar**)
rejonear (1), to jab a bull with a short lance, breaking it off at its notch
rejuvenecer (73), to rejuvenate
rejuvenecerse (73) (4), to rejuvenate, to become rejuvenated
rejuvenezca, etc. (**rejuvenecer**)
rejuvenezco (**rejuvenecer**)
relacionar (1), to relate
relajar (1), to relax, to slacken, to debauch
relamer (2), to lick again
relamerse (2) (4), to lick one's lips, to relish
relampaguear (1), to lightning, to sparkle
releer (20), to reread
relegar (9), to relegate
relegue, etc. (**relegar**)
relegué (**relegar**)
relevar (1), to relieve, to replace
relevarse (1) (4), to stand out in relief
releyendo (**releer**)
releyera, etc. (**releer**)
releyere, etc. (**releer**)
releyeron (**releer**)
releyese, etc. (**releer**)
releyó (**releer**)
relinchar (1), to neigh
relucir (74), to shine, to glitter
relumbrar (1), to shine, to glitter
reluzca, etc. (**relucir**)
reluzco (**relucir**)
rellenar (1), to refill, to fill up, to stuff
remachar (1), to clinch (a driven nail), to rivet
remallar (1), to mend (by reweaving: stockings, nets, etc.)
remansar (1), to back up (water)
remar (1), to row
remarcar (8), to stress, to mark again
remarque, etc. (**remarcar**)
remarqué (**remarcar**)
rematar (1), to kill off, to finish off, to put an end to, to knock down, to auction
remecer (14), to swing, to shake
remedar (1), to imitate, to ape, to mimic
remediar (1), to remedy, to help, to prevent
rememorar (1), to remember, to recall
remendar (ie) (37), to mend, to patch, to repair
remesar (1), to ship, to remit
remeza, etc. (**remecer**)
remezca, etc. = remeza, etc. (**remecer**)
remezco = remezo (**remecer**)
remezo (**remecer**)
remienda, etc. (**remendar**)
remiende, etc. (**remendar**)
remiendo (**remendar**)
remilgarse (9) (4), to be overnice, prudish or finical
remilgue, etc. (**remilgarse**)
remilgué (**remilgarse**)
remitir (3), to remit, to send, to refer
remoce, etc. (**remozar**)
remocé (**remozar**)

remojar (1), to soak, to dip, to celebrate with a drink
remolcar (8), to tow
remolinar (1), to whirl about, to eddy
remolinarse (1) (4), to whirl about, to eddy
remolonear (1), to duck work or effort
remolque, etc. (**remolcar**)
remolqué (**remolcar**)
remorder (ue) (38), to cause remorse (to), to bite again
remover (ue) (38), to remove, to stir
remozar (11), to rejuvenate
remuerda, etc. (**remorder**)
remuerde, etc. (**remorder**)
remuerdo (**remorder**)
remueva, etc. (**remover**)
remueve, etc. (**remover**)
remuevo (**remover**)
remullendo (**remullir**)
remullera, etc. (**remullir**)
remullere, etc. (**remullir**)
remulleron (**remullir**)
remullese, etc. (**remullir**)
remullir (27), to fluff, to beat up (a pillow)
remulló (**remullir**)
remunerar (1), to remunerate
renacer (73), to be born again, to bloom again
renazca, etc. (**renacer**)
renazco (**renacer**)
rendir (i, i) (42), to surrender, to yield
rendirse (i, i) (42) (4), to surrender, to give up
renegar (ie) (50), to deny intensely, to abhor, to curse
renegué (**renegar**)
reneguemos, etc. (**renegar**)
renguear (1), to limp
reniega, etc. (**renegar**)
reniego (**renegar**)
reniegue, etc. (**renegar**)
renovar (ue) (36), to renovate, to renew
renquear (1), to limp
rentar (1), to produce income, to rent
renueva, etc. (**renovar**)
renueve, etc. (**renovar**)
renuevo (**renovar**)
renunciar (1), to renounce, to resign
reñir (i, i) (60), to scold, to fight
reordenar (1), to rearrange
reorganice, etc. (**reorganizar**)
reorganicé (**reorganizar**)
reorganizar (11), to reorganize
repagar (9), to repay, overpay
repague, etc. (**repagar**)
repagué (**repagar**)
repantigarse (9) (4), to sprawl out
repantigue, etc. (**repantigarse**)
repantigué (**repantigarse**)
reparar (1), to repair, to notice, to consider
repartir (3), to distribute, to deal (cards)
repasar (1), to review, to check over
repatriar (61), to repatriate
repechar (1), to go uphill
repeler (2), to repel, to repulse
repensar (ie) (37), to think over again
repercutir (3), to have repercussion, to rebound, to reverberate
repesar (1), to weigh with great care
repetir (i, i) (42), to repeat
repicar (8), to ring bells
repiensa, etc. (**repensar**)
repiense, etc. (**repensar**)
repienso (**repensar**)
repique, etc. (**repicar**)

repiqué (**repicar**)
repiquetear (1), to ring gaily
repita, etc. (**repetir**)
repite, etc. (**repetir**)
repitiendo (**repetir**)
repitiera, etc. (**repetir**)
repitiere, etc. (**repetir**)
repitieron (**repetir**)
repitiese, etc. (**repetir**)
repitió (**repetir**)
repito (**repetir**)
replantear (1), to plan or outline again, to restate
replegar (ie) (50), to fold over and over
replegarse (ie) (50) (4), to fall back
replegué (**replegar**)
repleguemos, etc. (**replegar**)
replicar (8), to answer back, to argue back
repliega, etc. (**replegar**)
repliego (**replegar**)
repliegue, etc. (**replegar**)
replique, etc. (**replicar**)
repliqué (**replicar**)
repoblar (ue) (36), to repopulate
repón (**reponer**)
repondré, etc. (**reponer**)
repondría, etc. (**reponer**)
reponer (98), to replace, to reinstate, to restore, to answer
reponerse (98) (4), to recover, to calm down
reponga, etc. (**reponer**)
repongo (**reponer**)
reportar (1), to report
reposar (1), to rest
repostar (ue) (36), to restock
reprender (2), to reprehend, to scold
representar (1), to represent, to show
reprimir (3), to repress
reprobar (ue) (36), to reprove, to flunk
reprochar (1), to reproach
reproducir (67), to reproduce
reproduje (**reproducir**)
reprodujera, etc. (**reproducir**)
reprodujere, etc. (**reproducir**)
reprodujeron (**reproducir**)
reprodujese, etc. (**reproducir**)
reprodujimos (**reproducir**)
reprodujiste (**reproducir**)
reprodujisteis (**reproducir**)
reprodujo (**reproducir**)
reproduzca, etc. (**reproducir**)
reproduzco (**reproducir**)
reprueba, etc. (**reprobar**)
repruebe, etc. (**reprobar**)
repruebo (**reprobar**)
reptar (1), to crawl
repudiar (1), to repudiate
repuebla, etc. (**repoblar**)
repueble, etc. (**repoblar**)
repueblo (**repoblar**)
repuesta, etc. (**repostar**)
repueste, etc. (**repostar**)
repuesto (**reponer**) (**repostar**)
repugnar (1), to be repugnant, to conflict with, to disgust
repujar (1), to make repoussé work on
repulsar (1), to reject, to refuse
repuntar (1), to begin to appear
repuntarse (1) (4), to begin to turn sour (said of wine)
repuse (**reponer**)
repusiera, etc. (**reponer**)
repusiere, etc. (**reponer**)
repusieron (**reponer**)
repusiese, etc. (**reponer**)

repusimos (reponer)
repusiste (reponer)
repusisteis (reponer)
repuso (reponer)
reputar (1), to repute, to esteem
requebrar (ie) (37), to say flattering things
requerir (ie, i) (41), to need, to require
requiebra, etc. (requebrar)
requiebre, etc. (requebrar)
requiebro (requebrar)
requiera, etc. (requerir)
requiere, etc. (requerir)
requiero (requerir)
requiramos, etc. (requerir)
requiriendo (requerir)
requiriera, etc. (requerir)
requiriere, etc. (requerir)
requirieron (requerir)
requiriese, etc. (requerir)
requirió (requerir)
requisar (1), to confiscate
resaber (105), to know thoroughly
resabré, etc. (resaber)
resabría, etc. (resaber)
resaltar (1), to stand out, to bounce
resarcir (13), to compensate, to repay
resarcirse (13) (4), to make up for
resarza, etc. (resarcir)
resarzo (resarcir)
resbalar (1), to slide, to skid
rescatar (1), to ransom, to rescue
rescindir (3), to rescind
resé (resaber)
resecar (8), to dry thoroughly
resentir (ie, i) (41), to be resentful
resentirse (ie, i) (41) (4), to be resentful, to
    resent, to suffer from
reseñar (1), to sketch, to outline, to review
    (a book)
resepa, etc. (resaber)
reseque, etc. (resecar)
resequé (resecar)
reservar (1), to reserve, to put aside
resfriarse (61) (4), to catch cold
resguardar (1), to protect
resguardarse (1) (4), to take shelter
residir (3), to reside
resienta, etc. (resentir)
resiente, etc. (resentir)
resiento (resentir)
resignar (1), to resign
resintamos, etc. (resentir)
resintiendo (resentir)
resintiera, etc. (resentir)
resintiere, etc. (resentir)
resintieron (resentir)
resintiese, etc. (resentir)
resintió (resentir)
resistir (3), to resist, to bear
resistirse (3) (4), to refuse
resolver (ue) (70), to resolve, to decide on,
    to solve
resollar (ue) (36), to breathe hard
resonar (ue) (36), to resonate, to resound
resoplar (1), to puff, to breathe hard
respaldar (1), to back, endorse
respectar (1), to concern
respetar, to respect
respigar (9), to glean
respigue, etc. (respigar)
respigué (respigar)
respingar (9), to kick, to grunt
respingue, etc. (respingar)
respingué (respingar)
respirar (1), to breathe
resplandecer (73), to shine, to flash

resplandezca, etc. (resplandecer)
resplandezco (resplandecer)
responder (2), to answer, to respond
resquebrajar (1), to crack, to split
restablecer (73), to reestablish, to restore
restablecerse (73) (4), to recover
restablezca, etc. (restablecer)
restablezco (restablecer)
restar (1), to subtract, to be left
restaurar (1), to restore
restituir (71), to return, to give back
restituya, etc. (restituir)
restituye, etc. (restituir)
restituyendo (restituir)
restituyera, etc. (restituir)
restituyere, etc. (restituir)
restituyeron (restituir)
restituyese, etc. (restituir)
restituyo (restituir)
restituyó (restituir)
restregar (ie) (50), to rub or scrub hard
restregué (restregar)
restreguemos, etc. (restregar)
restriega, etc. (restregar)
restriego (restregar)
restriegue, etc. (restregar)
restringir (16), to restrict, to constrict
restrinja, etc. (restringir)
restrinjo (restringir)
restriñendo (restriñir)
restriñera, etc. (restriñir)
restriñere, etc. (restriñir)
restriñeron (restriñir)
restriñese, etc. (restriñir)
restriñir (29), to constrict
restriñó (1), restriñir)
resucitar, to resuscitate, to resurrect, to re-
    vive
resuelto (resolver)
resuelva, etc. (resolver)
resuelve, etc. (resolver)
resuelvo (resolver)
resuella, etc. (resollar)
resuelle, etc. (resollar)
resuello (resollar)
resuena, etc. (resonar)
resuene, etc. (resonar)
resueno (resonar)
resultar (1), to result, to turn out to be, to
    become
resumir (3), to summarize
resumirse (3) (4), to be reduced
resupe (resaber)
resupiera, etc. (resaber)
resupiere, etc. (resaber)
resupieron (resaber)
resupiese, etc. (resaber)
resupimos (resaber)
resupiste (resaber)
resupisteis (resaber)
resupo (resaber)
resurgir (16), to resurge
resurja, etc. (resurgir)
resurjo (resurgir)
retace, etc. (retazar)
retacé (retazar)
retar (1), to challenge, to dare
retardar (1), to retard, to slow down
retazar (11), to separate into small flocks
retemblar (ie) (37), to shake, to quiver
retén (retener)
retendré, etc. (retener)
retendría, etc. (retener)
retener (ie) (108), to retain, to keep, to
    withhold
retenga, etc. (retener)

retengo (retener)
reteñir (i, i) (60), to redye
retiembla, etc. (retemblar)
retiemble, etc. (retemblar)
retiemblo (retemblar)
retiene, etc. (retener)
retiña, etc. (reteñir)
retiñe, etc. (reteñir)
retiñendo (reteñir)
retiñera, etc. (reteñir)
retiñere, etc. (reteñir)
retiñeron (reteñir)
retiñese (reteñir)
retiño (reteñir)
retiñó (reteñir)
retirar (1), to retire, to withdraw, to take
    away
retirarse (1) (4), to retire (go to bed)
retocar (8), to retouch, to touch up
retoce, etc. (retozar)
retocé (retozar)
retoñar (1), to sprout
retoque, etc. (retocar)
retoqué (retocar)
retorcer (ue) (53), to twist
retornar (1), to return, to give back
retortijar (1), to curl up, to twist up
retorzamos, etc. (retorcer)
retostar (ue) (36), to toast again, to toast
    brown
retozar (11), to frolic, to romp
retractar (1), to retract
retraer (109), to dissuade
retraerse (109) (4), to withdraw
retraiga, etc. (retraer)
retraigo (retraer)
retraje (retraer)
retrajera, etc. (retraer)
retrajere, etc. (retraer)
retrajeron (retraer)
retrajese, etc. (retraer)
retrajimos (retraer)
retrajiste (retraer)
retrajisteis (retraer)
retrajo (retraer)
retrasar (1), to delay, to retard, to set or
    turn back (a watch or clock)
retrasarse (1) (4), to be late, to fall behind
    time (a watch or clock)
retratar (1), to photograph, to portray
retrayendo (retraer)
retribuir (71), to repay, to reward
retribuya, etc. (retribuir)
retribuye, etc. (retribuir)
retribuyendo (retribuir)
retribuyera, etc. (retribuir)
retribuyere, etc. (retribuir)
retribuyeron (retribuir)
retribuyese, etc. (retribuir)
retribuyo (retribuir)
retribuyó (retribuir)
retroceder (2), to retrocede, to back away
retronar (ue) (36), to rumble, to thunder
retroque, etc. (retrocar)
retroqué (retrocar)
retrotraer (109), to antedate, to date back
retrotraiga, etc. (retrotraer)
retrotraigo (retrotraer)
retrotraje (retrotraer)
retrotrajera, etc. (retrotraer)
retrotrajere, etc. (retrotraer)
retrotrajeron (retrotraer)
retrotrajese, etc. (retrotraer)
retrotrajimos (retrotraer)
retrotrajiste (retrotraer)
retrotrajisteis (retrotraer)

retrotrajo (retrotraer)
retrotrayendo (retrotraer)
retrucar (8), to kiss (billiards)
retruena, etc. **(retronar)**
retruene, etc. **(retronar)**
retrueno (retronar)
retruque, etc. **(retrucar)**
retruqué (retrucar)
retuerce, etc. **(retorcer)**
retuerza, etc. **(retorcer)**
retuerzo (retorcer)
retuesta, etc. **(retostar)**
retueste, etc. **(retostar)**
retuesto (retostar)
retumbar (1), to rumble, to resound
retuve (retener)
retuviera, etc. **(retener)**
retuviere, etc. **(retener)**
retuvieron (retener)
retuviese, etc. **(retener)**
retuvimos (retener)
retuviste (retener)
retuvisteis (retener)
retuvo (retener)
reunir (66), to join, to unite, to assemble, to gather together, to reunite
revalidar (1), to revalidate, to ratify
revalorar (1), to revalue, to reappraise
revalorice, etc. **(revalorizar)**
revaloricé (revalorizar)
revalorizar (11), to revalorize
revea, etc. **(rever)**
reveía, etc. **(rever)**
revelar (1), to reveal, to develop
revender (2), to resell, to retail
reventar (ie) (37), to burst, to explode, to blow out
reveo (rever)
rever (112), to review, to revise, to look over
reverberar (1), to reverberate
reverdecer (73), to grow green again, to sprout again
reverdezca, etc. **(reverdecer)**
reverdezco (reverdecer)
reverenciar (1), to rever, to reverence
reverter (ie) (39), to oveflow
revertir (ie, i) (41), to revert
revestir (i, i) (42), to put on, to don, to coat
revienta, etc. **(reventar)**
reviente, etc. **(reventar)**
reviento (reventar)
revierta, etc. **(reverter) (revertir)**
revierte, etc. **(reverter) (revertir)**
revierto (reverter) (revertir)
revirtamos, etc. **(revertir)**
revirtiendo (revertir)
revirtiera, etc. **(revertir)**
revirtiere, etc. **(revertir)**
revirtieron (revertir)
revirtiese, etc. **(revertir)**
revirtió (revertir)
revisar (1), to revise, to review, to check
revista, etc. **(revestir)**
reviste, etc. **(revestir)**
revisto (rever) (revestir)
revistiendo (revestir)
revistiera, etc. **(revestir)**
revistiere, etc. **(revestir)**
revistieron (revestir)
revistiese, etc. **(revestir)**
revistió (revestir)
revitalice, etc. **(revitalizar)**
revitalicé (revitalizar)
revitalizar (11), to revitalize
revivir (3), to revive

revocar (8), to revoke, to plaster
revolar (ue) (36), to flutter around
revolcar (ue) (44), to roll over
revolcarse (ue) (44) (4), to wallow
revolotear (1), to flutter around
revolqué, etc. **(revolcar)**
revolquemos, etc. **(revolcar)**
revolucionar (1), to revolutionize, to incite to rebellion
revolucionarse (1) (4), to revolt
revolver (ue) (70), to stir, to revolve
revoque, etc. **(revocar)**
revoqué (revocar)
revuela, etc. **(revolar)**
revuelca, etc. **(revolcar)**
revuelco, etc. **(revolcar)**
revuele, etc. **(revolar)**
revuelo (revolar)
revuelque, etc. **(revolcar)**
revuelto (revolver)
revuelva, etc. **(revolver)**
revuelve, etc. **(revolver)**
revuelvo (revolver)
rezagar (9), to leave behind
rezagarse (9) (4), to fall behind
rezague, etc. **(rezagar)**
rezagué (rezagar)
rezar (11), to pray, to say
rezongar (9), to grumble, to groan
rezongue, etc. **(rezongar)**
rezongué (rezongar)
rezumar (1), to ooze
ría, etc. **(reír)**
ribetear (1), to edge
rice, etc. **(rizar)**
ricé (rizar)
ridiculice, etc. **(ridiculizar)**
ridiculicé (ridiculizar)
ridiculizar (11), to ridicule
ríe, etc. **(reír)**
riega, etc. **(regar)**
riego (regar)
riegue, etc. **(regar)**
rielar (1), to twinkle
riendo (reír)
riera, etc. **(reír)**
riere, etc. **(reír)**
rieron (reír)
riese, etc. **(reír)**
rifar (1), to raffle
rige, etc. **(regir)**
rigiendo (regir)
rigiera, etc. **(regir)**
rigiere, etc. **(regir)**
rigieron (regir)
rigiese, etc. **(regir)**
rigió (regir)
rija, etc. **(regir)**
rijo (regir)
rimar (1), to rhyme
rinda, etc. **(rendir)**
rinde, etc. **(rendir)**
rindiendo (rendir)
rindiera, etc. **(rendir)**
rindiere, etc. **(rendir)**
rindieron (rendir)
rindiese, etc. **(rendir)**
rindió (rendir)
rindo (rendir)
riña, etc. **(reñir)**
riñe, etc. **(reñir)**
riñendo (reñir)
riñera, etc. **(reñir)**
riñere, etc. **(reñir)**
riñeron (reñir)
riñese, etc. **(reñir)**

riño (reñir)
riñó (reñir)
río (reír)
rió (reír)
risotear (1), to laugh boisterously
rivalice, etc. **(rivalizar)**
rivalicé (rivalizar)
rivalizar (11), to compete, to vie
rizar (11), to curl, to ripple
robar (1), to steal, to rob
roborar (1), to corroborate
robustecer (73), to make strong, to strengthen
robustecerse (73) (4), to become strong
robustezca, etc. **(robustecer)**
robustezco (robustecer)
roce, etc. **(rozar)**
rocé (rozar)
rociar (61), to sprinkle, to dew
rodar (ue) (36), to roll, to film, to roll down
rodear (1), to surround, to go around
rodillar (1), to roll
rodrigar (9), to prop, to prop up (plants)
rodrigue, etc. **(rodrigar)**
rodrigué (rodrigar)
roer (103), to gnaw, to pick (a bone)
rogar (ue) (45), to beg
rogué (rogar)
roguemos, etc. **(rogar)**
roiga, etc. **(roer)**
roigo (roer)
rojear (1), to redden, to become reddish
romper (104), to break, to tear
roncar (8), to snore, to roar (an engine)
rondar (1), to go around, to hover around, to serenade
ronque, etc. **(roncar)**
ronqué (roncar)
ronronear (1), to purr
rotar (1), to roll, to belch
roto (romper) (rotar)
rotular (1), to title, to label
roturar (1), to break (untilled ground)
roya, etc. **(roer)**
royendo (roer)
royera, etc. **(roer)**
royere, etc. **(roer)**
royeron (roer)
royese, etc. **(roer)**
royo (roer)
royó (roer)
rozar (11), to pass by touching slightly
rubricar (8), to add one's flourish (with or without one's signature), to sign and seal
rubrique, etc. **(rubricar)**
rubriqué (rubricar)
rueda, etc. **(rodar)**
ruede, etc. **(rodar)**
ruedo (rodar)
ruega, etc. **(rogar)**
ruego (rogar)
ruegue, etc. **(rogar)**
rugir (16), to roar, to bellow, to rumble
ruja, etc. **(rugir)**
rujo (rugir)
rumbear (1), to head (towards), to take a certain direction
rumiar (1), to ruminate, to meditate
rumorear (1), to rumor, to spread by rumor
runrunear (1), to purr
rutilar (1), to sparkle, to shine

S

sabatice, etc. **(sabatizar)**
sabaticé (sabatizar)

sabatizar (11), to keep the Sabbath, to rest on Saturday
saber (105), to know, to know how
saberse (105) (4), to become known
saborear (1), to taste, to savor
sabotear (1), to sabotage
sabré, etc. (**saber**)
sabría, etc. (**saber**)
sacar (8), to draw out, to pull out, to take out, to extract, to stick out (one's chest), to take (pictures)
sacrificar (8), to sacrifice, to slaughter
sacrifique, etc. (**sacrificar**)
sacrifiqué (**sacrificar**)
sacudir (3), to shake, to jolt, to beat (to remove dust), to spank
sahúma, etc. (**sahumar**)
sahumar (34), to perfume with smoke or incense
sahúme, etc. (**sahumar**)
sahúmo (**sahumar**)
sajar (1), to make an incision in, to cut
sal (**salir**)
salar (1), to salt
salariar (1), to fix a salary or wages for
saldar (1), to settle, to liquidate, to sell out at reduced prices
saldré, etc. (**salir**)
saldría, etc. (**salir**)
salga, etc. (**salir**)
salgo (**salir**)
salir (106), to leave, to go out, to come out, to get out, to rise (the sun), to turn out
salirse (106) (4), to leak (said of a liquid or its container), to boil over
salivar (1), to salivate
salmear (1), to sing psalms
salmodiar (1), to sing in a monotone, to sing psalms
salpicar (8), to splash, to sprinkle
salpimentar (ie) (37), to salt and pepper, to make pleasant (with wit, cleverness)
salpimienta, etc. (**salpimentar**)
salpimiente, etc. (**salpimentar**)
salpimiento (**salpimentar**)
salpique, etc. (**salpicar**)
salpiqué (**salpicar**)
saltar (1), to jump, to skip
saltear (1), to hold up
saludar (1), to salute, to greet
salvar (1), to save, to salvage
sanar (1), to cure, to heal
sancionar (1), to sanction
sanear (1), to make sanitary
sangrar (1), to bleed, to drain
santificar (8), to sanctify, to keep (holy days)
santifique, etc. (**santificar**)
santifiqué (**santificar**)
santiguar (10), to make the sign of the cross (over something)
santiguarse (10) (4), to make the sign of the cross (on oneself)
santigüe, etc. (**santiguar**)
santigüé (**santiguar**)
saque, etc. (**sacar**)
saqué (**sacar**)
saquear (1), to sack, to loot
satirice, etc. (**satirizar**)
satiricé (**satirizar**)
satirizar (11), to satirize
satisfacer (68), to satisfy
satisfacerse (68) (4), to take satisfaction, to be satisfied
satisfaga, etc. (**satisfacer**)
satisfago (**satisfacer**)

satisfaré, etc. (**satisfacer**)
satisfaría, etc. (**satisfacer**)
satisfaz (**satisfacer**)
satisfecho (**satisfacer**)
satisfice (**satisfacer**)
satisficiera, etc. (**satisfacer**)
satisficiere, etc. (**satisfacer**)
satisficieron (**satisfacer**)
satisficiese, etc. (**satisfacer**)
satisficimos (**satisfacer**)
satisficiste (**satisfacer**)
satisficisteis (**satisfacer**)
satisfizo (**satisfacer**)
saturar (1), to saturate
sazonar (1), to season, to ripen
sé (**saber**) (**ser**)
sea, etc. (**ser**)
secar (8), to dry, to wipe dry
seccionar (1), to section
secretar (1), to secrete
secuestrar (1), to kidnap
secularice, etc. (**secularizar**)
secularicé (**secularizar**)
secularizar (11), to secularize
sedar (1), to soothe, to quiet
sedimentar (1), to sediment, to settle
seducir (67), to seduce, to tempt, to captivate
seduje (**seducir**)
sedujera, etc. (**seducir**)
sedujere, etc. (**seducir**)
sedujeron (**seducir**)
sedujese, etc. (**seducir**)
sedujimos (**seducir**)
sedujiste (**seducir**)
sedujisteis (**seducir**)
sedujo (**seducir**)
seduzca, etc. (**seducir**)
seduzco (**seducir**)
segar (ie) (50), to reap, to harvest, to cut off
segregar (9), to segregate, to secrete
segregue, etc. (**segregar**)
segregué (**segregar**)
segué (**segar**)
seguemos, etc. (**segar**)
seguetear (1), to saw with a buhl saw
seguir (i, i) (58), to follow, to pursue, to continue
sellar (1), to seal, to stamp
sembrar (ie) (37), to seed, to sow, to spread
semejar (1), to be alike
sementar (ie) (37), to seed, to sow
semienta, etc. (**sementar**)
semiente, etc. (**sementar**)
semiento (**sementar**)
sendear (1), to open a path
sensibilice, etc. (**sensibilizar**)
sensibilicé (**sensibilizar**)
sensibilizar (11), to sensitize
sentar (ie) (37), to seat
sentarse (ie) (37) (4), to sit, to sit down
sentenciar (1), to sentence
sentir (ie, i) (41), to regret, to feel, to hear, to be or feel sorry for, to sense
sentirse (ie, i) (41) (4), to feel
señalar (1), to mark, to indicate, to signal, to point at, to point out, to designate
señorear (1), to dominate
sepa, etc. (**saber**)
separar (1), to separate
sepultar (1), to buy
seque, etc. (**secar**)
sequé (**secar**)
ser (107), to be
serenar (1), to calm, to pacify, to cool

sermonear (1), to lecture, to reprimand
serpentear (1), to wind, to meander
serrar (ie) (37), to saw
servir (i, i) (42), to serve, to help, to wait on
servirse (i, i) (42) (4), to help oneself, to serve oneself
sesear (1), to pronounce Spanish *c* (before *e* or *i*) and *z* like *s*
sesgar (9), to cut (cloth) on the bias
sesgue, etc. (**sesgar**)
sesgué (**sesgar**)
sesionar (1), to be in session
sestear (1), to take a siesta
sicoanalice, etc. (**sicoanalizar**)
sicoanalicé (**sicoanalizar**)
sicoanalizar = **psicoanalizar**
siega (**segar**)
siego (**segar**)
siegue, etc. (**segar**)
siembra, etc. (**sembrar**)
siembre, etc. (**sembrar**)
siembro (**sembrar**)
sienta, etc. (**sentar**) (**sentir**)
siente, etc. (**sentar**) (**sentir**)
siento (**sentar**) (**sentir**)
sierra, etc. (**serrar**)
sierre, etc. (**serrar**)
sierro (**serrar**)
siga, etc. (**seguir**)
signar (1), to put a mark on, to sign, to make the sign of the cross (over something)
signarse (1) (4), to make the sign of the cross (on oneself)
significar (8), to mean, to signify
signifique, etc. (**significar**)
signifiqué (**significar**)
sigo (**seguir**)
sigue, etc. (**seguir**)
siguiendo (**seguir**)
siguiera, etc. (**seguir**)
siguiere, etc. (**seguir**)
siguieron (**seguir**)
siguiese, etc. (**seguir**)
siguió (**seguir**)
silabear (1), to syllable, to syllabify
silbar (1), to whistle, to blow a whistle, to hiss (a performer or a performance)
silenciar (1), to silence
simbolice, etc. (**simbolizar**)
simbolicé (**simbolizar**)
simbolizar (11), to symbolize
simpatice, etc. (**simpatizar**)
simpaticé (**simpatizar**)
simpatizar (11), to be congenial
simplificar (8), to simplify
simplifique, etc. (**simplificar**)
simplifiqué (**simplificar**)
simular (1), to simulate, to feign, to fake
simultanear (1), to carry out simultaneously
sincopar (1), to syncopate, to abridge
sincronice, etc. (**sincroninzar**)
sincronicé (**sincronizar**)
sincronizar (11), to synchronize
sindicar (8), to accuse, to syndicate
sindicarse (8) (4), to syndicate
sindique, etc. (**sindicar**)
sindiqué (**sindicar**)
singularice, etc. (**singularizar**)
singularicé (**singularizar**)
singularizar (11), to single out, to distinguish
sintamos (**sentir**)
sintetice, etc. (**sintetizar**)
sinteticé (**sintetizar**)

sintetizar (11), to synthetize
sintiendo (sentir)
sintiera, etc. (sentir)
sintiere, etc. (sentir)
sintieron (sentir)
sintiese, etc. (sentir)
sintió (sentir)
sintonice, etc. (sintonizar)
sintonicé (sintonizar)
sintonizar (11), to tune (a radio)
sirgar (9), to tow (a boat)
sirgue, etc. (sirgar)
sirgué (sirgar)
sirva, etc. (servir)
sirve, etc. (servir)
sirviendo (servir)
sirviera, etc. (servir)
sirviere, etc. (servir)
sirvieron (servir)
sirviese, etc. (servir)
sirvió (servir)
sirvo (servir)
sisar (1), to snitch, to filch
sisear (1), to hiss (a performer or a performance)
sistematice, etc. (sistematizar)
sistematicé (sistematizar)
sistematizar (11), to systematize
sitiar (1), to siege
situar (62), to situate, to locate, to place
sobar (1), to work something with the hands to soften it
sobornar (1), to bribe
sobrar (1), to be more than enough, to be left
sobreabundar (1), to be in great abundance
sobrealimentar (1), to overfeed, to supercharge
sobreañadir (3), to put in as extra
sobrebarrer (2), to sweep lightly
sobrebeber (2), to drink too much
sobrecalentar (ie) (37), to overheat
sobrecalienta, etc. (sobrecalentar)
sobrecaliente, etc. (sobrecalentar)
sobrecaliento (sobrecalentar)
sobrecargar (9), to overload, to overcharge
sobrecargue, etc. (sobrecargar)
sobrecargué (sobrecargar)
sobrecoger (15), to surprise
sobrecogerse (15) (4), to become afraid or apprehensive
sobrecoja, etc. (sobrecoger)
sobrecojo (sobrecoger)
sobrecrecer (73), to grow too much
sobrecrezca, etc. (sobrecrecer)
sobrecrezco (sobrecrecer)
sobreentender (ie) (39), to understand
sobreentenderse (ie) (39) (4), to be understood, to be implied
sobreentienda, etc. (sobreentender)
sobreentiende, etc. (sobreentender)
sobreentiendo (sobreentender)
sobreexcitar (1), to overexcite
sobreexpón (sobreexponer)
sobreexpondré, etc. (sobreexponer)
sobreexpondría, etc. (sobreexponer)
sobreexponer (98), to overexpose
sobreexponga, etc. (sobreexponer)
sobreexpongo (sobreexponer)
sobreexpuesto (sobreexponer)
sobreexpuse (sobreexponer)
sobreexpusiera, etc. (sobreexponer)
sobreexpusiere, etc. (sobreexponer)
sobreexpusieron (sobreexponer)

sobreexpusiese, etc. (sobreexponer)
sobreexpusimos (sobreexponer)
sobreexpusiste (sobreexponer)
sobreexpusisteis (sobreexponer)
sobreexpuso (sobreexponer)
sobrehíla, etc. (sobrehilar)
sobrehilar (34), to overcast (sewing)
sobrehíle, etc. (sobrehilar)
sobrehílo (sobrehilar)
sobrellenar (1), to fill to overflowing
sobrellevar (1), to bear, to carry, to suffer (annoyances) with patience
sobrenadar (1), to float
sobrenaturalice, etc. (sobrenaturalizar)
sobrenaturalicé (sobrenaturalizar)
sobrenaturalizar (11), to make supernatural
sobrepasar (1), to surpass, to excel
sobrepasarse (1) (4), to go too far
sobrepón (sobreponer)
sobrepondré, etc. (sobreponer)
sobrepondría, etc. (sobreponer)
sobreponer (98), to superpose, to superimpose
sobreponerse (98) (4), to control oneself, to overcome adversity
sobreponga, etc. (sobreponer)
sobrepongo (sobreponer)
sobrepuesto (sobreponer)
sobrepujar (1), to excel, to surpass
sobrepuse (sobreponer)
sobrepusiera, etc. (sobreponer)
sobrepusiere, etc. (sobreponer)
sobrepusieron (sobreponer)
sobrepusiese, etc. (sobreponer)
sobrepusimos (sobreponer)
sobrepusiste (sobreponer)
sobrepusisteis (sobreponer)
sobrepuso (sobreponer)
sobresal (sobresalir)
sobresaldré, etc. (sobresalir)
sobresaldría, etc. (sobresalir)
sobresalga, etc. (sobresalir)
sobresalgo (sobresalir)
sobresalir (106), to stand out, to excel, to jut out
sobresaltar (1), to assail, to frighten, to stand out clearly
sobresaltarse (1) (4), to be frightened
sobrescribir (69), to address (a letter)
sobrescrito (sobrescribir)
sobreseer (20), to supersede, to desist
sobreseyendo (sobreseer)
sobreseyera, etc. (sobreseer)
sobreseyere, etc. (sobreseer)
sobreseyeron (sobreseer)
sobreseyese, etc. (sobreseer)
sobreseyó (sobreseer)
sobrevén (sobrevenir)
sobrevendré, etc. (sobrevenir)
sobrevendría, etc. (sobrevenir)
sobrevenga, etc. (sobrevenir)
sobrevengo (sobrevenir)
sobrevenir (ie, i) (111), to happen, to take place
sobrevestir (i, i) (42), to put (a garment) on over other clothes
sobreviene, etc. (sobrevenir)
sobrevine (sobrevenir)
sobreviniendo (sobrevenir)
sobreviniera, etc. (sobrevenir)
sobreviniere, etc. (sobrevenir)
sobrevinieron (sobrevenir)
sobreviniese, etc. (sobrevenir)
sobrevinimos (sobrevenir)

sobreviniste (sobrevenir)
sobrevinisteis (sobrevenir)
sobrevino (sobrevenir)
sobrevista, etc. (sobrevestir)
sobreviste, etc. (sobrevestir)
sobrevistiendo (sobrevestir)
sobrevistiera, etc. (sobrevestir)
sobrevistiere, etc. (sobrevestir)
sobrevistieron (sobrevestir)
sobrevistiese, etc. (sobrevestir)
sobrevistió (sobrevestir)
sobrevisto (sobrevestir)
sobrevivir (3), to survive
socarrar (1), to singe, to scorch
socavar (1), to undermine
socialice, etc. (socializar)
socialicé (socializar)
socializar (11), to socialize
socorrer (2), to assist, to aid, to help, to succor
sofocar (8), to suffocate, to choke, to extinguish
sofoque, etc. (sofocar)
sofoqué (sofocar)
sofreír (i, i) (88), to fry lightly
sofrenar (1), to check (a horse) suddenly, to control (a passion)
sofría, etc. (sofreír)
sofríe, etc. (sofreír)
sofriendo (sofreír)
sofriera, etc. (sofreír)
sofriere, etc. (sofreír)
sofrieron (sofreír)
sofriese, etc. (sofreír)
sofrío (sofreír)
sofrió (sofreír)
sofrito (sofreír)
sois (ser)
sojuzgar (9), to subjugate, to subdue
sojuzgue, etc. (sojuzgar)
sojuzgué (sojuzgar)
solace, etc. (solazar)
solacé (solazar)
solapar (1), to put lapels on, to conceal
solar (ue) (36), to pave, to floor, to sole (a shoe)
solazar (11), to solace, to console, to amuse, to comfort
solazarse (11) (4), to be comforted, to rejoice
soldar (ue) (36), to solder, to weld
soldarse (ue) (36) (4), to knit (bones)
solear (1), to sun
solemnice, etc. (solemnizar)
solemnicé (solemnizar)
solemnizar (11), to solemnize
soler (ue) (123), to be accustomed to, to be used to
solfear (1), to sing sol-fa
solicitar (1), to solicit, to ask for, to apply for
solidarice, etc. (solidarizar)
solidaricé (solidarizar)
solidarizar (11), to make solidary, to make jointly liable
solidarizarse (11) (4), to make common cause
solidificar (8), to solidify
solidifique, etc. (solidificar)
solidifiqué (solidificar)
soliviantar (1), to rouse, to incite
soltar (ue) (36), to untie, to unfasten, to loosen, to turn loose, to set free, to let go
solucionar (1), to solve, to resolve
solventar (1), to settle (accounts), to solve (a difficulty)

solloce, etc. (sollozar)
sollocé (sollozar)
sollozar (11), to sob
sombrear (1), to shade
someter (2), to subdue, to submit, to subject
someterse (2) (4), to yield, to submit, to surrender
somos (ser)
son (ser)
sonar (ue) (36), to sound, to ring, to strike (clock)
sonarse (ue) (36) (4), to blow one's nose
sondear (1), to sound, to sound out (other's intentions), to fathom
sonorice, etc. (sonorizar)
sonoricé (sonorizar)
sonorizar (11), to record sound effects (on a film)
sonreír (i, i) (59), to smile
sonría, etc. (sonreír)
sonríe, etc. (sonreír)
sonriendo (sonreír)
sonriera, etc. (sonreír)
sonriere, etc. (sonreír)
sonrieron (sonreír)
sonriese, etc. (sonreír)
sonrío (sonreír)
sonrió (sonreír)
sonrosarse (1) (4), to flush, to blush
sonsacar (8), to entice away, to draw out (a secret)
sonsaque, etc. (sonsacar)
sonsaqué (sonsacar)
sonsear (1), to fool around
soñar (ue) (36), to dream
sopesar (1), to try the weight of by lifting
soplar (1), to blow, to prompt, to whisper (an answer to a student), to tip (off)
soplonear (1), to squeal on
soportar (1), to support, to bear, to endure, to put up with
sorber (2), to sip, to absorb
sorocharse (1) (4), to become mountain-sick (altitude sick)
sorprender (2), to surprise, to catch
sortear (1), to raffle, to dodge
sosegar (ie) (50), to calm, to quiet
sosegarse (ie) (50) (4), to calm down
sosegué (sosegar)
soseguemos, etc. (sosegar)
sosiega, etc. (sosegar)
sosiego (sosegar)
sosiegue, etc. (sosegar)
soslayar (1), to place obliquely, to duck (a question)
sospechar (1), to suspect
sospesar (1), to try the weight of by lifting
sostén (sostener)
sostendré, etc. (sostener)
sostendría, etc. (sostener)
sostener (ie) (108), to support, to hold up, to sustain, to maintain
sostenga, etc. (sostener)
sostengo (sostener)
sostiene, etc. (sostener)
sostuve (sostener)
sostuviera, etc. (sostener)
sostuviere, etc. (sostener)
sostuvieron (sostener)
sostuviese, etc. (sostener)
sostuvimos (sostener)
sostuviste (sostener)
sostuvisteis (sostener)
sostuvo (sostener)
soterrar (ie) (37), to bury, to inhume

sotierra, etc. (soterrar)
sotierre, etc. (soterrar)
sotierro (soterrar)
soy (ser)
suavice, etc. (suavizar)
suavicé (suavizar)
suavizar (11), to smooth, to ease, to sweeten, to soften, to strop (a razor)
subarrendar (ie) (37), to sublease, to sublet
subarrienda, etc. (subarrendar)
subarriende, etc. (subarrendar)
subarriendo (subarrendar)
subastar (1), to auction
subcontratar (1), to subcontract
subdividir (3), to subdivide
subir (3), to go up, to come up, to carry up, to raise, to lift, to rise, to increase
sublevar (1), to incite to rebellion
sublevarse (1) (4), to rise in rebellion, to revolt
sublimar (1), to sublimate, to sublime
subordinar (1), to subordinate
subrayar (1), to underline, to emphasize
subrogar (9), to subrogate, to substitute
subrogue, etc. (subrogar)
subrogué (subrogar)
subsanar (1), to correct
subscribir (69), to subscribe, to endorse, to sign
subscrito (subscribir)
subseguir (i, i) (58), to follow next
subsidiar (1), to subsidize
subsiga, etc. (subseguir)
subsigo (subseguir)
subsigue, etc. (subseguir)
subsiguiendo (subseguir)
subsiguiera, etc. (subseguir)
subsiguiere, etc. (subseguir)
subsiguieron (subseguir)
subsiguiese, etc. (subseguir)
subsiguió (subseguir)
subsistir (3), to subsist
substanciar (1), to substantiate, to abstract, to abridge
substantivar (1), to substantivize
substituir (71), to substitute
substituya, etc. (substituir)
substituye, etc. (substituir)
substituyendo (substituir)
substituyera, etc. (substituir)
substituyere, etc. (substituir)
substituyeron (substituir)
substituyese, etc. (substituir)
substituyo (substituir)
substituyó (substituir)
substraer (109), to remove, to deduct, to subtract
substraerse (109) (4), to withdraw
substraiga, etc. (substraer)
substraigo (substraer)
substraje (substraer)
substrajera, etc. (substraer)
substrajere, etc. (substraer)
substrajeron (substraer)
substrajese, etc. (substraer)
substrajimos (substraer)
substrajiste (substraer)
substrajisteis (substraer)
substrajo (substraer)
substrayendo (substraer)
subsumir (3), to subsume
subtender (ie) (39), to subtend
subtienda, etc. (subtender)
subtiende, etc. (subtender)
subtiendo (subtender)

subvén (subvenir)
subvencionar (1), to subsidize
subvendré, etc. (subvenir)
subvendría, etc. (subvenir)
subvenga, etc. (subvenir)
subvengo (subvenir)
subvenir (ie, i) (111), to provide, to assist
subvertir (ie, i) (41), to subvert
subviene, etc. (subvenir)
subvierta, etc. (subvertir)
sunvierte, etc. (subvertir)
subvierto (subvertir)
subvine (subvenir)
subviniendo (subvenir)
subviniera, etc. (subvenir)
subviniere, etc. (subvenir)
subvinieron (subvenir)
subviniese, etc. (subvenir)
subvinimos (subvenir)
subviniste (subvenir)
subvinisteis (subvenir)
subvino (subvenir)
subvirtamos, etc. (subvertir)
subvirtiendo (subvertir)
subvirtiera, etc. (subvertir)
subvirtiere, etc. (subvertir)
subvirtieron (subvertir)
subvirtiese, etc. (subvertir)
subvirtió (subvertir)
subyugar (9), to subjugate, to subdue
subyugue, etc. (subyugar)
subyugué (subyugar)
succionar (1), to suck, to suck in
suceder (2), to succeed, to follow, to happen
sucederse (2) (4), to follow one after the other
sucintarse (1) (4), to be precise, to be brief
sucumbir (3), to succumb
sudar (1), to sweat, to perspire, to transpire
suela, etc. (solar) (soler)
suelda, etc. (soldar)
suelde, etc. (soldar)
sueldo (soldar)
suele, etc. (solar) (soler)
suelo (solar) (soler)
suelta, etc. (soltar)
suelte, etc. (soltar)
suelto (soltar)
suena, etc. (sonar)
suene, etc. (sonar)
sueno (sonar)
sueña, etc. (soñar)
sueñe, etc. (soñar)
sueño (soñar)
sufragar (9), to aid, to favor, to defray, to pay
sufrague, etc. (sufragar)
sufragué (sufragar)
sufrir (3), to suffer, to undergo, to take (an examination)
sugerir (ie, i) (41), to suggest
sugestionar (1), to hypnotize, to influence, to suggest
sugiera, etc. (sugerir)
sugiere, etc. (sugerir)
sugiero (sugerir)
sugiramos, etc. (sugerir)
sugiriendo (sugerir)
sugiriera, etc. (sugerir)
sugiriere, etc. (sugerir)
sugirieron (sugerir)
sugiriese, etc. (sugerir)
sugirió (sugerir)
suicidarse (1) (4), to commit suicide

sujetar (1), to subject, to subdue, to fasten, to hold
sujetarse (1) (4), to submit, to stick to
sulfatar (1), to sulfate
sulfurar (1), to sulfurate, to anger, to annoy
sumar (1), to add, to sum, to sum up, to amount to
sumergir (16), to submerge, to submerse
sumerja, etc. (**sumergir**)
sumerjo (**sumergir**)
suministrar (1), to supply
sumir (3), to sink, to submerge
supe (**saber**)
supeditar (1), to subject
superabundar (1), to be in great abundance
superar (1), to surpass, to overcome
superentender (ie) (39), to supervise
superentienda, etc. (**superentender**)
superentiende, etc. (**superentender**)
superentiendo (**superentender**)
superpón (**superponer**)
superpondré, etc. (**superponer**)
superpondría, etc. (**superponer**)
superponer (98), to superpose
superponga, etc. (**superponer**)
superpongo (**superponer**)
superpuesto (**superponer**)
superpuse (**superponer**)
superpusiera, etc. (**superponer**)
superpusiere, etc. (**superponer**)
superpusieron (**superponer**)
superpusiese, etc. (**superponer**)
superpusimos (**superponer**)
superpusiste (**superponer**)
superpusisteis (**superponer**)
superpuso (**superponer**)
supervén (**supervenir**)
supervendré, etc. (**supervenir**)
supervendría, etc. (**supervenir**)
supervenga, etc. (**supervenir**)
supervengo (**supervenir**)
supervenir (ie, i) (111), to happen, to take place
superviene, etc. (**supervenir**)
supervine (**supervenir**)
superviniendo (**supervenir**)
superviniera, etc. (**supervenir**)
superviniere, etc. (**supervenir**)
supervinieron (**supervenir**)
superviniese, etc. (**supervenir**)
supervinimos (**supervenir**)
superviniste (**supervenir**)
supervinisteis (**supervenir**)
supervino (**supervenir**)
supiera, etc. (**saber**)
supiere, etc. (**saber**)
supieron (**saber**)
supiese, etc. (**saber**)
supimos (**saber**)
supiste (**saber**)
supisteis (**saber**)
suplantar (1), to supplant, to forge (a document)
suplementar (1), to supplement
suplicar (8), to suplicate, to implore, to beg
suplique, etc. (**suplicar**)
supliqué (**suplicar**)
suplir (3), to substitute, to make up for, to supply
supo (**saber**)
supón (**suponer**)
supondré, etc. (**suponer**)
supondría, etc. (**suponer**)
suponer (98), to suppose, to imply

suponga, etc. (**suponer**)
supongo (**suponer**)
suprimir (3), to suppress, to eliminate, to do away with
supuesto (**suponer**)
supurar (1), to fester
supuse (**suponer**)
supusiera, etc. (**suponer**)
supusiere, etc. (**suponer**)
supusieron (**suponer**)
supusiese, etc. (**suponer**)
supusimos (**suponer**)
supusiste (**suponer**)
supusisteis (**suponer**)
supuso (**suponer**)
surcar (8), to move through, to cut through, to furrow
surgir (16), to come forth, to surge, to spurt
surja, etc. (**surgir**)
surjo (**surgir**)
surque, etc. (**surcar**)
surqué (**surcar**)
surtir (3), to furnish, to spout
suscitar (1), to stir up, to provoke
suscribir = **subscribir**
suscrito (**subscribir**)
suspender (2), to hang, to suspend, to flunk
suspirar (1), to sight
sustanciar = **substanciar**
sustantivar = **substantivar**
sustentar (1), to sustain, to feed, to maintain
sustituir = **substituir**
sustituya, etc. (**sustituir**)
sustituye, etc. (**sustituir**)
sustituyendo (**sustituir**)
sustituyera, etc. (**sustituir**)
sustituyere, etc. (**sustituir**)
sustituyeron (**sustituir**)
sustituyese, etc. (**sustituir**)
sustituyo (**sustituir**)
sustituyó (**sustituir**)
sustraer = **substraer**
sustraerse = **substraerse**
sustraiga, etc. (**sustraer**)
sustraigo (**sustraer**)
sustraje (**sustraer**)
sustrajera, etc. (**sustraer**)
sustrajere, etc. (**sustraer**)
sustrajeron (**sustraer**)
sustrajese, etc. (**sustraer**)
sustrajimos (**sustraer**)
sustrajiste (**sustraer**)
sustrajisteis (**sustraer**)
sustrajo (**sustraer**)
sustrayendo (**sustraer**)
susurrar (1), to whisper
sutilice, etc. (**sutilizar**)
sutilicé (**sutilizar**)
sutilizar (11), to split hairs

T

tabalear (1), to drum with the fingers (on a table, etc.)
tabicar (8), to wall up
tabique, etc. (**tabicar**)
tabiqué (**tabicar**)
tablear (1), to cut into boards, to divide (a garden) into sections
tabletear (1), to rattle
tabular (1), to tabulate
tacañear (1), to be stingy
tachar (1), to cross out, to put blame on

tachonar (1), to adorn with ribbon or trimming, to spangle, to stud
taconear (1), to walk making noise with the heels
tafiletear (1), to adorn or finish with Morocco leather
tajar (1), to cut, to slice
taladrar (1), to drill, to bore, to perforate, to pierce, to punch (a ticket)
talar (1), to fell (trees)
talionar (1), to punish by retaliation
talonear (1), to dash along, to tap with one's heels
tallar (1), to carve, to cut (a precious stone), to measure the height of
tamborear (1), to drum with the fingers
tamice, etc. (**tamizar**)
tamicé (**tamizar**)
tamizar (11), to sieve, to screen, to sift
tantear (1), to feel out, to keep score, to grope
tañendo (**tañer**)
tañer (28), to play (musical instrument)
tañera, etc. (**tañer**)
tañere, etc. (**tañer**)
tañeron (**tañer**)
tañese, etc. (**tañer**)
tañó (**tañer**)
tapar (1), to cover, to cover up
tapiar (1), to wall up, to wall in
tapice, etc. (**tapizar**)
tapicé (**tapizar**)
tapizar (11), to tapestry, to upholster
taponar (1), to plug, to stop up
tapujarse (1) (4), to muffle oneself
taquigrafiar (61), to take shorthand, to write in shorthand
tararear (1), to hum
tardar (1), to be late, to delay, to take long
tardecer = **atardecer**
tardezca (**tardecer**)
tartajear (1), to stutter
tartamudear (1), to stutter
tasar (1), to appraise, to tax
tatuar (62), to tattoo
taxear (1), to taxi (aeronautic)
teclear (1), to finger a keyboard
techar (1), to roof
tejar (1), to roof with tiles
tejer (2), to weave
teledifundir (3), to telecast
telefonar (1), to telephone
telefonear (1), to telephone
telefotografiar (61), to telephotograph
telegrafiar (61), to telegraph
televisar (1), to televise
temblar (ie) (37), to tremble, to quiver, to shiver
temer (2), to fear
temperar (1), to temper
tempestear (1), to storm
templar (1), to temper, to moderate
temporalice, etc. (**temporalizar**)
temporalicé (**temporalizar**)
temporalizar (11), to make temporary, to secularize
temporice, etc. (**temporizar**)
temporicé (**temporizar**)
temporizar (11), to temporize
ten (**tener**)
tender (ie) (39), to spread out, to extend, to reach out, to offer, to hang out (clothes to dry), to lay (a cable, etc.), to build (a bridge), to set (a trap)
tendré, etc. (**tener**)
tendría, etc. (**tener**)

tener (ie) (108), to have, to possess, to hold
tenga, etc. (**tener**)
tengo (**tener**)
tensar (1), to tighten
tentar (ie) (37), to touch, to feel (one's way, etc.), to tempt
teñir (i, i) (60), to dye, to color
teorice, etc. (**teorizar**)
teroicé (**teorizar**)
teorizar (11), to theorize
terciar (1), to mediate, to arbitrate, to divide into three parts, to place diagonally
tergiversar (1), to twist (facts, etc.), to tergiversate
terminar (1), to end, to finish, to terminate
terraplenar (1), to bank, to fill (with dirt)
tersar (1), to smooth, to polish
tertuliar (1), to sit around and talk
testar (1), to make a testament or will
testificar (8), to testify
testifique, etc. (**testificar**)
testifiqué (**testificar**)
testimoniar (1), to attest, to testify
tiembla, etc. (**temblar**)
tiemble, etc. (**temblar**)
tiemblo (**temblar**)
tienda, etc. (**tender**)
tiende, etc. (**tender**)
tiendo (**tender**)
tiene (**tener**)
tienta, etc. (**tentar**)
tiente, etc. (**tentar**)
tiento (**tentar**)
tijeretear (1), to cut with scissors
tildar (1), to stigmatize, to put a tilde
timar (1), to snitch, to swindle
timbalear (1), to play the kettledrum
timbrar (1), to stamp
timonear (1), to steer
tintar (1), to tint, to color
tintinear (1), to jingle, to clink
tinturar (1), to tincture
tiña, etc. (**teñir**)
tiñe, etc. (**teñir**)
tiñendo (**teñir**)
tiñera, etc. (**teñir**)
tiñere, etc. (**teñir**)
tiñeron (**teñir**)
tiñese, etc. (**teñir**)
tiño (**teñir**)
tiñó (**teñir**)
tirar (1), to throw, to throw away, to shoot (a gun), to pull, to draw (said of a chimney), to draw (a line)
tiritar (1), to shiver
tironear (1), to pull, to jerk
tirotear (1), to shoot wildly at, to shoot at random
tirotearse (1) (4), to exchange shots
titar (1), to gobble (said of a turkey)
titiritar (1), to shiver
titubear (1), to hesitate
titular (1), to title, to entitle
titularse (1) (4), to receive a title, to be called
tiznar (1), to soil with soot, to smudge, to smut
tizonear (1), to stir up a fire
tocar (8), to touch, to play (musical instrument), to toll, to ring a bell, to be one's turn, to knock, to fall to one's lot
tolerar (1), to tolerate
tomar (1), to take, to sieze, to have (food, drink, a meal), to drink
tonificar (8), to invigorate

tonifique, etc. (**tonificar**)
tonifiqué (**tonificar**)
tonsurar (1), to cut hair, to shear
tontear (1), to talk or act foolishly
topar (1), to bump, to run into, to butt
topetar (1), to butt, to bump into
toque, etc. (**tocar**)
toqué (**tocar**)
torcer (ue) (53), to twist, to bend, to turn
torear (1), to fight bulls
tornar (1), to return, to give back
tornarse (1) (4), to become
tornear (1), to do lathe work
torpedear (1), to torpedo
torrar (1), to toast
torrear (1), to fortify with towers or turrets
torturar (1), to torture
torzamos, etc. (**torcer**)
toser (2), to cough
tosigar = **atosigar**
tosigue, etc. (**tosigar**)
tosigué (**tosigar**)
tostar (ue) (36), to toast, to tan
totalice, etc. (**totalizar**)
totalicé (**totalizar**)
totalizar (11), to totalize, to add up
trabajar (1), to work
trabar (1), to clasp, to join
trabarse (1) (4), to stammer
trabucarse (8) (4), to become confused, to be mixed up
trabuque, etc. (**trabucarse**)
trabuqué (**trabucarse**)
trace (**trazar**)
tracé (**trazar**)
traducir (67), to translate
traduje (**traducir**)
tradujera, etc. (**traducir**)
tradujere, etc. (**traducir**)
tradujeron (**traducir**)
tradujese, etc. (**traducir**)
tradujimos (**traducir**)
tradujiste (**traducir**)
tradujisteis (**traducir**)
tradujo (**traducir**)
traduzca, etc. (**traducir**)
traduzco (**traducir**)
traer (109), to bring, to bring on, to adduce, to wear
traficar (8), to trade, to traffic
trafique, etc. (**traficar**)
trafiqué (**traficar**)
tragar (9), to swallow, to gulp down
trague, etc. (**tragar**)
tragué (**tragar**)
traiga, etc. (**traer**)
traigo (**traer**)
traillar (63), to grade with a scraper
traje (**traer**)
trajera, etc. (**traer**)
trajere, etc. (**traer**)
trajeron (**traer**)
trajese, etc. (**traer**)
trajimos (**traer**)
trajinar (1), to go back and forth, to travel about
trajiste (**traer**)
trajisteis (**traer**)
trajo (**traer**)
tramar (1), to plot, to scheme, to weave
tramitar (1), to take legal or official steps, to negotiate
trampear (1), to trick, to cheat
trancar = **atrancar**
tranque, etc. (**trancar**)
tranqué (**trancar**)

tranquilice (**tranquilizar**)
tranquilicé (**tranquilizar**)
tranquilizar (11), to tranquilize
transbordar (1), to transfer, to change trains
transcender = **trascender**
transcribir (69), to transcribe
transcrito (**transcribir**)
transcurrir (3), to elapse, to pass
transferir (ie, i) (41), to transfer
transfiera, etc. (**transferir**)
transfiere, etc. (**transferir**)
transfiero (**transferir**)
transfigurar (1), to transfigure
transfiramos, etc. (**transferir**)
transfiriendo (**transferir**)
transfiriera, etc. (**transferir**)
transfiriere, etc. (**transferir**)
transfirieron (**transferir**)
transfiriese, etc. (**transferir**)
transfirió (**transferir**)
transformar (1), to tranform
transfundir (3), to transfuse
transgredir (116), to transgress
transigir (16), to compromise, to yield
transija, etc. (**transigir**)
transijo (**transigir**)
transitar (1), to roam back and forth
translucirse = **traslucirse**
transluzca, etc. (**translucir**)
transluzco (**translucir**)
transmigrar (1), to transmigrate
transmitir (3), to transmit
transmutar (1), to transform, to change
transparentar (1), to be transparent
transpirar (1), to transpire
transpón (**transponer**)
transpondré, etc. (**transponer**)
transpondría, etc. (**transponer**)
transponer (98), to transpose
transponga, etc. (**transponer**)
transpongo (**transponer**)
transportar (1), to transport
transpuesto (**transponer**)
transpuse (**transponer**)
transpusiera, etc. (**transponer**)
transpusiere, etc. (**transponer**)
transpusieron (**transponer**)
transpusiese, etc. (**transponer**)
transpusimos (**transponer**)
transpusiste (**transponer**)
transpusisteis (**transponer**)
transpuso (**transponer**)
transubstanciar (1), to transubstantiate, to transform
transvasar (1), to pour from one container to another
trapacear (1), to cheat, to swindle
trapear (1), to mop
trapichear (1), to scheme, to deal at retail, to run a sugarcane mill
traquetear (1), to rattle, to agitate
trascender (ie) (39), to spread, to become known, to smell
trascienda, etc. (**trascender**)
trasciende, etc. (**trascender**)
trasciendo (**trascender**)
trascolar (ue) (36), to strain, to percolate, to butt in
trascribir = **transcribir**
trascrito (**trascribir**)
trascuela, etc. (**trascolar**)
trascuele, etc. (**trascolar**)
trascuelo (**trascolar**)
trasegar (ie) (50), to transfer
trasegué (**trasegar**)

traseguemos, etc. (**trasegar**)
trasgredir = **transgredir**
trashumar (1), to move from winter to summer or from summer to winter pasture
trasiega, etc. (**trasegar**)
trasiego (**trasegar**)
trasiegue, etc. (**trasegar**)
trasladar (1), to transfer
trasladarse (1) (4), to move (to another place, job, etc.)
traslucirse (74) (4), to be transparent, to become evident
trasluzca, etc. (**traslucir**)
trasluzco (**traslucir**)
trasnochar (1), to keep late hours, to spend sleepless nights
trasoiga, etc. (**trasoír**)
trasoigo (**trasoír**)
trasoír (95), to hear wrong
trasoye, etc. (**trasoír**)
trasoyendo (**trasoír**)
trasoyera, etc. (**trasoír**)
trasoyere, etc. (**trasoír**)
trasoyeron (**trasoír**)
trasoyese, etc. (**trasoír**)
trasoyó (**trasoír**)
traspalar (1), to shovel, to transfer
traspapelar (1), to mislay among other papers
traspapelarse (1) (4), to be mislaid among other papers
traspasar (1), to pass over, to go beyond, to pass through, to transfer property, to transgress
trasplantar (1), to transplant
traspón (**trasponer**)
traspondré, etc. (**trasponer**)
traspondría, etc. (**trasponer**)
trasponer = **transponer**
trasponga, etc. (**trasponer**)
traspongo (**trasponer**)
traspuesto (**trasponer**)
traspuse (**trasponer**)
traspusiera, etc. (**trasponer**)
traspusiere, etc. (**trasponer**)
traspusieron (**trasponer**)
traspusiese, etc. (**trasponer**)
traspusimos (**trasponer**)
traspusiste (**trasponer**)
traspusisteis (**trasponer**)
traspuso (**trasponer**)
trastocar (8), to upset, to disturb
trastoque, etc. (**trastocar**)
trastoqué (**trastocar**)
trastornar (1), to upset, to disturb, to overturn
trastrocar (ue) (44), to change the order of, to change the nature of
trastroqué (**trastrocar**)
trastroquemos, etc. (**trastrocar**)
trastrueca, etc. (**trastrocar**)
trastrueco (**trastrocar**)
trastrueque, etc. (**trastrocar**)
trasvolar (ue) (36), to fly over
trasvuela, etc. (**trasvolar**)
trasvuele, etc. (**trasvolar**)
trasvuelo (**trasvolar**)
tratar (1), to deal with, to treat, to handle
trayendo (**traer**)
trazar (11), to trace, to design, to outline, to draw (as a line)
tremer (2), to tremble, to shake
trence, etc. (**trenzar**)
trencé (**trenzar**)
trenzar (11), to braid

trepar (1), to climb
trepidar (1), to shake, to vibrate
tributar (1), to pay or render (homage, admiration, honor, etc.)
trice, etc. (**trizar**)
tricé (**trizar**)
trifurcar (8), to divide into three forks or branches
trifurque, etc. (**trifurcar**)
trifurqué (**trifurcar**)
trillar (1), to thresh
trinar (1), to warble, to get angry
trincar (8), to break up, to tie fast, to drink (wine, liquor)
trinchar (1), to carve (meat), to slice (meat)
trinque, etc. (**trincar**)
trinqué (**trincar**)
triplicar (8), to triple, to triplicate
triplique, etc. (**triplicar**)
tripliqué (**triplicar**)
tripular (1), to man (ships, planes, etc.)
trisecar (8), to trisect
triseque, etc. (**trisecar**)
trisequé (**trisecar**)
triturar (1), to pulverize, to tear to pieces
triunfar (1), to triumph, to trump
trizar (11), to break or tear to pieces
trocar (ue) (44), to exchange
trocarse (ue) (44) (4), to change
troce, etc. (**trozar**)
trocé (**trozar**)
trompar (1), to spin a top
trompear (1), to bump, to spin a top, to hit
trompetear (1), to sound a trumpet
trompicar (8), to trip, to make stumble
trompique, etc. (**trompicar**)
trompiqué (**trompicar**)
tronar (ue) (36), to thunder, to lose one's all
tronce, etc. (**tronzar**)
troncé (**tronzar**)
tronchar (1), to bend or break (a stalk or trunk), to chop off, to break off
tronzar (11), to shatter, to pleat
tropecé (**tropezar**)
tropecemos, etc. (**tropezar**)
tropezar (ie) (51), to stumble, to slip
tropiece, etc. (**tropezar**)
tropieza, etc. (**tropezar**)
tropiezo (**tropezar**)
troqué (**trocar**)
troquemos, etc. (**trocar**)
trozar (11), to break to pieces, to cut into logs
trueca, etc. (**trocar**)
trueco (**trocar**)
truena, etc. (**tronar**)
truene, etc. (**tronar**)
trueno (**tronar**)
trueque, etc. (**trocar**)
trufar (1), to fill or stuff with truffles
truhanear (1), to act like a rascal
truncar (8), to truncate
trunque, etc. (**truncar**)
trunqué (**truncar**)
tuerce, etc. (**torcer**)
tuerza, etc. (**torcer**)
tuerzo (**torcer**)
tuesta, etc. (**tostar**)
tueste, etc. (**tostar**)
tuesto (**tostar**)
tullendo (**tullir**)
tullera, etc. (**tullir**)
tullere, etc. (**tullir**)
tulleron (**tullir**)
tullese, etc. (**tullir**)

tullir (27), to cripple, to maim
tulló (**tullir**)
tumbar (1), to knock down, to knock out
tumbarse (1) (4), to lie down
tumefacer (68), to swell
tumefaga, etc. (**tumefacer**)
tumefago (**tumefacer**)
tumefaré, etc. (**tumefacer**)
tumefaría, etc. (**tumefacer**)
tumefaz (**tumefacer**)
tumefecho (**tumefacer**)
tumefice (**tumefacer**)
tumeficimos (**tumefacer**)
tumeficiste (**tumefacer**)
tumeficisteis (**tumefacer**)
tumeficiera, etc. (**tumefacer**)
tumeficiere, etc. (**tumefacer**)
tumeficieron (**tumefacer**)
tumeficiese, etc. (**tumefacer**)
tumefizo (**tumefacer**)
turbar (1), to disturb, to stir up
tutear (1), to address using "tú," to be on close or intimate terms with
tutearse (1) (4), to be on close or intimate terms with
tuve (**tener**)
tuviera, etc. (**tener**)
tuviere, etc. (**tener**)
tuvieron (**tener**)
tuviese, etc. (**tener**)
tuvimos (**tener**)
tuviste (**tener**)
tuvisteis (**tener**)
tuvo (**tener**)

U

ubicar (8), to place, to locate
ubicarse (8) (4), to be placed, to be located
ubique, etc. (**ubicar**)
ubiqué (**ubicar**)
ufanarse (1) (4), to boast
ultimar (1), to finish, to terminate, to close
ultrajar (1), to offend, to insult
uncir (13), to yoke
ungir (16), to anoint
unificar (8), to unify
unificarse (8) (4), to become unified
unifique, etc. (**unificar**)
unifiqué (**unificar**)
uniformar (1), to uniform
unir (3), to unite, to join
unja, etc. (**ungir**)
unjo (**ungir**)
untar (1), to smear, to grease, to bribe
untarse (1) (4), to get smeared
unza, etc. (**uncir**)
unzo (**uncir**)
uñendo (**uñir**)
uñera, etc. (**uñir**)
uñere, etc. (**uñir**)
uñeron (**uñir**)
uñese, etc. (**uñir**)
uñir (29), to yoke
uñó (**uñir**)
urbanice, etc. (**urbanizar**)
urbanicé (**urbanizar**)
urbanizar (11), to urbanize, to polish (people)
urbanizarse (11) (4), to become urbanized, to become polished (people)
urdir (3), to plot, to scheme, to conspire
urgir (16), to be urgent
urja, etc. (**urgir**)
urjo (**urgir**)
usar (1), to use, to be accustomed

usucapir (121), to obtain by expiration of time set by law
usufructuar (62), to usufruct
usurear (1), to practice usury
usurpar (1), to usurp
utilice, etc. (**utilizar**)
utilicé (**utilizar**)
utilizar (11), to utilize

V

va (**ir**)
vacar (8), to be vacant, to be idle
vaciar (61), to empty, to hollow out, to sharpen on a grind stone
vacilar (1), to vacillate, to hesitate
vacunar (1), to vaccinate
vadear (1), to ford, to overcome
vadearse (1) (4), to behave, to conduct oneself
vagabundear (1), to loaf around
vagar (9), to wander, to roam, to drift
vague, etc. (**vagar**)
vagué (**vagar**)
vaguear (1), to loaf
vahar (1), to exhale, to emit fumes or vapor
vahear (1), to emit fumes or vapor, to exhale
vais (**ir**)
val (**valer**)
valdré, etc. (**valer**)
valdría, etc. (**valer**)
valer (110), to be worth, to cost, to be valid
valerse (110) (4), to help oneself, to take care of oneself
valga, etc. (**valer**)
valgo (**valer**)
valorar (1), to value, to appraise
valorice, etc. (**valorizar**)
valoricé (**valorizar**)
valorizar (11), to valorize
valuar (62), to appraise, to estimate
vallar (1), to fence
vamos (**ir**)
van (**ir**)
vanagloriarse (1) (4), to boast
vaporice, etc. (**vaporizar**)
vaporicé (**vaporizar**)
vaporizar (11), to vaporize, to atomize
vapulear (1), to beat, to whip
vaque, etc. (**vacar**)
vaqué (**vacar**)
varar (1), to beach (a boat), to run aground
varear (1), to beat, to knock (olives, nuts, fruits from a tree)
variar (61), to vary, to change, to be different
vas (**ir**)
vaticinar (1), to predict
vaya, etc. (**ir**)
ve (**ir**)
vea (**ver**)
vece, etc. (**vezar**)
vecé (**vezar**)
vedar (1), to prohibit, to forbid
veía, etc. (**ver**)
vejar (1), to vex, to annoy
velar (1), to watch, to watch over, to hold a wake over, to veil, to stay awake, to work late, to work at night
ven (**venir**)
vencer (12), to defeat, to surpass, to surmount, to win out, to expire
vencerse (12) (4), to control oneself
vendar (1), to bandage, to bind
vender (2), to sell, to betray

vendimiar (1), to gather grapes
vendré, etc. (**venir**)
vendría, etc. (**venir**)
venerar (1), to revere
venga, etc. (**vengar**) (**venir**)
vengar (9), to avenge
vengarse (9) (4), to take revenge
vengo (**vengar**) (**venir**)
vengue, etc. (**vengar**)
vengué (**vengar**)
venir (ie, i) (111), to come, to go
ventar (ie) (37), to blow (said of the wind)
ventear (1), to air, to blow (said of the wind)
ventilar (1), to ventilate
ventiscar (8), to snow with strong wind, to drift (snow)
ventisque (**ventiscar**)
ventisquear (1) = **ventiscar** (8)
ventosear (1), to break the wind
venza, etc. (**vencer**)
venzo (**vencer**)
veo (**ver**)
ver (112), to see, to look at
veranear (1), to summer
verdear (1), to grow green, to show its greenness
verdecer (73), to turn green
verdezca, etc. (**verdecer**)
verdezco (**verdecer**)
verguear (1), to flog, to whip
verificar (8), to verify, to check, to carry out
verifique, etc. (**verificar**)
verifiqué (**verificar**)
versar (1), to deal
versarse (1) (4), to become versed
verse (112) (4), to be seen, to be obvious, to find oneself
versear (1), to versify
versificar (8), to versify
versifique, etc. (**versificar**)
versifiqué (**versificar**)
verter (ie) (39), to pour, to empty, to dump, to flow
vestir (i, i) (42), to dress, to wear, to cover
vestirse (i, i) (42) (4), to get dressed
vetar (1), to veto
vetear (1), to stripe, to grain
vezar = **avezar**
vezarse = **avezarse**
viajar (1), to travel
vibrar (1), to vibrate, to roll (the letter *r*)
viciar (1), to vitiate
viciarse (1) (4), to become vitiated
victimar (1), to assassinate, to kill
viene, etc. (**venir**)
vienta, etc. (**ventar**)
viente, etc. (**ventar**)
viento (**ventar**)
vierta, etc. (**verter**)
vierte, etc. (**verter**)
vierto (**verter**)
vigorice, etc. (**vigorizar**)
vigoricé (**vigorizar**)
vigorizar (11), to invigorate
vilipendiar (1), to vilify
vincular (1), to entail, to found upon, to perpetuate
vindicar (8), to vindicate
vindique, etc. (**vindicar**)
vindiqué (**vindicar**)
vine (**venir**)
viniendo (**venir**)
viniera, etc. (**venir**)
viniere, etc. (**venir**)

vinieron (**venir**)
viniese, etc. (**venir**)
vinimos (**venir**)
viniste (**venir**)
vinisteis (**venir**)
vino (**venir**)
violar (1), to violate, to rape
violentar (1), to do violence to, to break into
virar (1), to turn
visar (1), to give a visa, to put a visa on a passport
visitar (1), to visit
vislumbrar (1), to glimpse, to suspect
vista, etc. (**vestir**)
viste, etc. (**vestir**)
vistiendo (**vestir**)
vistiera, etc. (**vestir**)
vistiere, etc. (**vestir**)
vistieron (**vestir**)
vistiese, etc. (**vestir**)
vistió (**vestir**)
visto (**ver**) (**vestir**)
visualice, etc. (**visualizar**)
visualicé (**visualizar**)
visualizar (11), to visualize
vitalice, etc. (**vitalizar**)
vitalicé (**vitalizar**)
vitalizar (11), to vitalize
vitrificar (8), to vitrify
vitrifique, etc. (**vitrificar**)
vitrifiqué (**vitrificar**)
vituperar (1), to vituperate
vivaquear (1), to bivouac
vivar (1), to cheer, to acclaim
vivir (3), to live
vocalice, etc. (**vocalizar**)
vocalicé (**vocalizar**)
vocalizar (11), to vocalize
vocear (1), to shout
vociferar (1), to shout, to announce boastfully
volar (ue) (36), to blow up, to fly, to disappear rapidly
volatilice, etc. (**volatilizar**)
volatilicé (**volatilizar**)
volatilizar (11), to make volatile
volatilizarse (11), (4), to become volatile
volcar (ue) (44), to tip over, to overturn, to capsize
volear (1), to volley, to sow grain by throwing it in the air with the hand
volqué (**volcar**)
volquemos, etc. (**volcar**)
voltear (1), to overturn, to turn, to turn around, to revolve, to turn inside out, to turn or roll over, to turn a somersault
voltearse (1) (4), to turn over, to change sides
volver (ue) (70), to return, to turn, to turn up, over or inside out
volverse (ue) (70) (4), to become, to turn, to turn around
vomitar (1), to vomit, to throw up
votar (1), to vote
voy (**ir**)
vuela, etc. (**volar**)
vuele, etc. (**volar**)
vuelca, etc. (**volcar**)
vuelco (**volcar**)
vuelo (**volar**)
vuelque, etc. (**volcar**)
vuelto (**volver**)
vuelva, etc. (**volver**)
vuelve, etc. (**volver**)
vuelvo (**volver**)

vulcanice, etc. (vulcanizar)
vulcanicé (vulcanizar)
vulcanizar (11), to vulcanize
vulgarice, etc. (vulgarizar)
vulgaricé (vulgarizar)
vulgarizar (11), to vulgarize, to popularize
vulgarizarse (11) (4), to become common
vulnerar (1), to harm, to injure, to damage (reputation)

X

xilofonear (1), to play the xylophone
xilograbar (1), to xylograph, to wood engrave
xilografiar (61), to make printed impressions from xylographs

Y

yacer (113), to lie in the grave, to be lying down
yaga, etc. (yacer)
yago (yacer)
yantar (1), to eat, to dine
yapar (1), to add something as extra, to give something extra
yaz (yacer)
yazca, etc. (yacer)
yazco (yacer)
yazga, etc. (yacer)
yazgo (yacer)
yendo (ir)
yerbatear (1), to drink maté
yerga, etc. (erguir)
yergo (erguir)
yergue (erguir)
yermar (1), to lay waste, to leave deserted
yerra, etc. (errar)
yerre, etc. (errar)

yerro (errar)
yuxtapón (yuxtaponer)
yuxtapondré, etc. (yuxtaponer)
yuxtapondría, etc. (yuxtaponer)
yuxtaponer (98), to juxtapose
yuxtaponerse (98 (4), to become juxtaposed
yuxtaponga, etc. (yuxtaponer)
yuxtapongo (yuxtaponer)
yuxtapuesto (yuxtaponer)
yuxtapuse (yuxtaponer)
yuxtapusiera, etc. (yuxtaponer)
yuxtapusiere, etc. (yuxtaponer)
yuxtapusieron (yuxtaponer)
yuxtapusiese, etc. (yuxtaponer)
yuxtapusimos (yuxtaponer)
yuxtapusiste (yuxtaponer)
yuxtapusisteis (yuxtaponer)
yuxtapuso (yuxtaponer)

Z

zafar (1), to release, to set free
zafarse (1) (4), to slip away, to get rid of
zaherir (ie, i) (41), to hurt feelings, to reproach, to censure, to blame
zahiera, etc. (zaherir)
zahiere, etc. (zaherir)
zahiero (zaherir)
zahiramos, etc. (zaherir)
zahiriendo (zaherir)
zahiriera, etc. (zaherir)
zahiriere, etc. (zaherir)
zahirieron (zaherir)
zahiriese (zaherir)
zahirió (zaherir)
zambear (1), to be or walk knock-kneed
zambullendo (zambullir)
zambullera, etc. (zambullir)

zambullere, etc. (zambullir)
zambulleron (zambullir)
zambullese, etc. (zambullir)
zambullir (27), to duck, to give a ducking to, to plunge
zambullirse (27) (4), to dive, to plunge
zambulló (zambullir)
zampar (1), to gobble down
zanganear (1), to drone, to loaf, to idle
zangolotear (1), to jiggle, to shake
zangolotearse (1) (4), to sway from side to side
zanjar (1), to settle, to dig a ditch or ditches in
zanquear (1), to waddle, to rush around
zapar (1), to excavate, to mine
zapatear (1), to tap with the feet, to tap dance
zarandear (1), to stir and move nimbly, to winnow
zarandearse (1) (4), to move to and fro
zarpar (1), to weigh anchor, to set sail
zigzaguear (1), to zigzag
zonzear = sonsear
zozobrar (1), to sink, to capsize, to founder, to be in great danger
zulacar (8), to waterproof with tar
zulaque, etc. (zulacar)
zulaqué (zulacar)
zulaquear (1) = zulacar (8)
zumbar (1), to buzz, to hum, to ring (said of the ears), to let (someone) have it (slap)
zurcir (13), to darn, to mend
zurrar (1), to spank
zurriagar (9), to whip
zurriague, etc. (zurriagar)
zurriagué (zurriagar)
zurza, etc. (zurcir)
zurzo (zurcir)

Sample of verbal forms with English translation possibilities A

II. Meaning of Spanish verbal forms

TIEMPOS SIMPLES
SIMPLE TENSES

PRESENTE DE INDICATIVO **PRESENT** *INDICATIVE*	PRETÉRITO IMPERFECTO DE INDICATIVO **IMPERFECT** *INDICATIVE*	PRETÉRITO INDEFINIDO DE INDICATIVO **PRETERITE** *INDICATIVE*	FUTURO IMPERFECTO DE INDICATIVO **FUTURE** *INDICATIVE*	POTENCIAL SIMPLE **CONDITIONAL**

hablo
  - *I speak*
  - *I am speaking*
  - *I do speak*
	hablaba
	  - *I was speaking*
	  - *I used to speak*
	  - *I would speak*
	  - *I spoke*
		hablé
		  - *I spoke*
		  - *I did speak*
			hablaré
			  - *I will speak*
			  - *I shall speak*
				hablaría
				  - *I would speak*
				  - *I should speak*

PRESENTE DE SUBJUNTIVO **PRESENT** *SUBJUNCTIVE*	PRETÉRITO IMPERFECTO DE SUBJUNTIVO **PAST (IMPERFECT)** *SUBJUNCTIVE*		FUTURO IMPERFECTO DE SUBJUNTIVO **FUTURE** *SUBJUNCTIVE*

hable
  - *I speak*
  - *I am speaking*
  - *I do speak*
  - *me to speak*
  - *for me to speak*
  - *I will speak*
  - *I shall speak*
	hablara <u>or</u> hablase
	  - *I spoke*
	  - *I was speaking*
	  - *I used to speak*
	  - *I would speak*
	  - *I did speak*
	  - *me to speak*
	  - *for me to speak*
			hablare
			  - *I will speak*
			  - *I shall speak*
			  - *me to speak*
			  - *for me to speak*

FORMAS IMPERATIVAS, GERUNDIOS Y PARTICIPIO
COMMANDS AND PARTICIPLES

FORMAS IMPERATIVAS *COMMANDS*		GERUNDIO Y PARTICIPIO *PARTICIPLES*		
AFIRMATIVA *AFFIRMATIVE*	NEGATIVA *NEGATIVE*	GERUNDIO SIMPLE *PRESENT PARTICIPLE*	PARTICIPIO *PAST PARTICIPLE*	GERUNDIO COMPUESTO *PERFECT PARTICIPLE*

habla
  - *speak*
	no hables
	  - *don't speak*
		hablando
		  - *speaking*
			hablado
			  - *spoken*
				habiendo hablado
				  - *having spoken*

hablemos
  - *let's speak*
	no hablemos
	  - *let's not speak*			

INFINITIVO COMPUESTO: haber hablado
PERFECT INFINITIVE: to have spoken

TIEMPOS COMPUESTOS
PERFECT (COMPOUND) TENSES

PRETÉRITO PERFECTO DE INDICATIVO **PRESENT PERFECT** *INDICATIVE*	PRETÉRITO PLUSCUAMPERFECTO DE INDICATIVO **PAST PERFECT (PLUPERFECT)** *INDICATIVE*	PRETÉRITO ANTERIOR DE INDICATIVO **PRETERITE PERFECT** *INDICATIVE*	FUTURO PERFECTO DE INDICATIVO **FUTURE PERFECT** *INDICATIVE*	POTENCIAL COMPUESTO **CONDITIONAL PERFECT**

he hablado
  - *I have spoken*
	había hablado
	  - *I had spoken*
		hube hablado
		  - *I had spoken*
			habré hablado
			  - *I will have spoken*
			  - *I shall have spoken*
				habría hablado
				  - *I would have spoken*
				  - *I should have spoken*

PRETÉRITO PERFECTO DE SUBJUNTIVO **PRESENT PERFECT** *SUBJUNCTIVE*	PRETÉRITO PLUSCUAMPERFECTO DE SUBJUNTIVO **PAST PERFECT (PLUPERFECT)** *SUBJUNCTIVE*		FUTURO PERFECTO DE SUBJUNTIVO **FUTURE PERFECT** *SUBJUNCTIVE*	

haya hablado
  - *I have spoken*
  - *me to have spoken*
  - *for me to have spoken*
  - *I will have spoken*
  - *I shall have spoken*
  - *I was speaking*
  - *I used to speak*
  - *I would speak*
  - *I did speak*
	hubiera hablado <u>or</u> hubiese hablado
	  - *I had spoken*
	  - *me to have spoken*
	  - *for me to have spoken*
	  - *I was speaking*
	  - *I used to speak*
	  - *I would speak*
	  - *I did speak*
			hubiere hablado
			  - *I will have spoken*
			  - *I shall have spoken*
			  - *me to have spoken*
			  - *for me to have spoken*	

B Subjects of personal verbal forms

TIEMPOS SIMPLES
SIMPLE TENSES

PRESENTE DE INDICATIVO *PRESENT INDICATIVE*	PRETÉRITO IMPERFECTO DE INDICATIVO *IMPERFECT INDICATIVE*	PRETÉRITO INDEFINIDO DE INDICATIVO *PRETERITE INDICATIVE*	FUTURO IMPERFECTO DE INDICATIVO *FUTURE INDICATIVE*	POTENCIAL SIMPLE *CONDITIONAL*

UNDERSTOOD SUBJECTS OF THE VERBAL FORMS GIVEN IN THE PARADIGMS PRESENTED UNDER THESE HEADINGS IN SUBSEQUENT CHARTS

yo — *I*
tú — *you (familiar singular)*
usted *(abbreviated* Ud.) OR él OR ella OR "it" *(understood)* — *you (polite singular)* OR *he* OR *she* OR *it (understood)*
nosotros OR nosotras — *we (masculine)* OR *we (feminine)*
vosotros OR vosotras — *you (familiar plural masculine)* OR *you (familiar plural feminine)*
ustedes *(abbreviated* Uds.) OR ellos OR ellas OR "they" *(understood)* — *you (polite plural)* OR *they (masculine)* OR *they (feminine)* OR *they (understood)*

PRESENTE DE SUBJUNTIVO *PRESENT SUBJUNCTIVE*	PRETÉRITO IMPERFECTO DE SUBJUNTIVO *PAST (IMPERFECT) SUBJUNCTIVE*	FUTURO IMPERFECTO DE SUBJUNTIVO *FUTURE SUBJUNCTIVE*

UNDERSTOOD SUBJECTS OF THE VERBAL FORMS GIVEN IN THE PARADIGMS PRESENTED UNDER THESE HEADINGS IN SUBSEQUENT CHARTS

yo — *I*
tú — *you (familiar singular)*
usted *(abbreviated* Ud.) OR él OR ella OR "it" *(understood)* — *you (polite singular)* OR *he* OR *she* OR *it (understood)*
nosotros OR nosotras — *we (masculine)* OR *we (feminine)*
vosotros OR vosotras — *you (familiar plural masculine)* OR *you (familiar plural feminine)*
ustedes *(abbreviated* Uds.) OR ellos OR ellas OR "they" *(understood)* — *you (polite plural)* OR *they (masculine)* OR *they (feminine)* OR *they (understood)*

FORMAS IMPERATIVAS, GERUNDIOS Y PARTICIPIO
COMMANDS AND PARTICIPLES

FORMAS IMPERATIVAS *COMMANDS*				
AFIRMATIVA *AFFIRMATIVE*	NEGATIVA *NEGATIVE*			

SUBJECTS OF COMMAND FORMS

tú — *you (familiar singular)*
usted *(abbreviated* Ud.) — *you (polite singular)*
vosotros OR vosotras — *you (familiar plural masculine)* (familiar plural feminine)
ustedes *(abbreviated* Uds.) — *you (polite plural)*

nosotros OR nosotras — *we (masculine)* OR *we (feminine)*

TIEMPOS COMPUESTOS
PERFECT (COMPOUND) TENSES

PRETÉRITO PERFECTO DE INDICATIVO *PRESENT PERFECT INDICATIVE*	PRETÉRITO PLUSCUAMPERFECTO DE INDICATIVO *PAST PERFECT (PLUPERFECT) INDICATIVE*	PRETÉRITO ANTERIOR DE INDICATIVO *PRETERITE PERFECT INDICATIVE*	FUTURO PERFECTO DE INDICATIVO *FUTURE PERFECT INDICATIVE*	POTENCIAL COMPUESTO *CONDITIONAL PERFECT*

UNDERSTOOD SUBJECTS OF THE VERBAL FORMS GIVEN IN THE PARADIGMS PRESENTED UNDER THESE HEADINGS IN SUBSEQUENT CHARTS

yo — *I*
tú — *you (familiar singular)*
usted *(abbreviated* Ud.) OR él OR ella OR "it" *(understood)* — *you (polite singular)* OR *he* OR *she* OR *it (understood)*
nosotros OR nosotras — *we (masculine)* OR *we (feminine)*
vosotros OR vosotras — *you (familiar plural masculine)* OR *you (familiar plural feminine)*
ustedes *(abbreviated* Uds.) OR ellos OR ellas OR "they" *(understood)* — *you (polite plural)* OR *they (masculine)* OR *they (feminine)* OR *they (understood)*

PRETÉRITO PERFECTO DE SUBJUNTIVO *PRESENT PERFECT SUBJUNCTIVE*	PRETÉRITO PLUSCUAMPERFECTO DE SUBJUNTIVO *PAST PERFECT (PLUPERFECT) SUBJUNCTIVE*	FUTURO PERFECTO DE SUBJUNTIVO *FUTURE PERFECT SUBJUNCTIVE*

UNDERSTOOD SUBJECTS OF THE VERBAL FORMS GIVEN IN THE PARADIGMS PRESENTED UNDER THESE HEADINGS IN SUBSEQUENT CHARTS

yo — *I*
tú — *you (familiar singular)*
usted *(abbreviated* Ud.) OR él OR ella OR "it" *(understood)* — *you (polite singular)* OR *he* OR *she* OR *it (understood)*
nosotros OR nosotras — *we (masculine)* OR *we (feminine)*
vosotros OR vosotras — *you (familiar plural masculine)* OR *you (familiar plural feminine)*
ustedes *(abbreviated* Uds.) OR ellos OR ellas OR "they" *(understood)* — *you (polite plural)* OR *they (masculine)* OR *they (feminine)* OR *they (understood)*

Structure of regular verb forms with infinitive ending in -ar

C

TIEMPOS SIMPLES
SIMPLE TENSES

PRESENTE DE INDICATIVO *PRESENT INDICATIVE*	PRETÉRITO IMPERFECTO DE INDICATIVO *IMPERFECT INDICATIVE*	PRETÉRITO INDEFINIDO DE INDICATIVO *PRETERITE INDICATIVE*	FUTURO IMPERFECTO DE INDICATIVO *FUTURE INDICATIVE*	POTENCIAL SIMPLE *CONDITIONAL*
stem: *infinitive minus -ar*	stem: *infinitive minus -ar*	stem: *infinitive minus -ar*	stem: *infinitive*	stem: *infinitive*
endings: -o -as -a -amos -áis -an	endings: -aba -abas -aba -ábamos -abais -aban	endings: -é -aste -ó -amos -asteis -aron	endings: -é -ás -á -emos -éis -án	endings: -ía -ías -ía -íamos -íais -ían

PRESENTE DE SUBJUNTIVO *PRESENT SUBJUNCTIVE*	PRETÉRITO IMPERFECTO DE SUBJUNTIVO *PAST (IMPERFECT) SUBJUNCTIVE*		FUTURO IMPERFECTO DE SUBJUNTIVO *FUTURE SUBJUNCTIVE*
stem: *1st person singular present indicative minus -o*	stem: *3rd person plural preterite minus -ron*		stem: *3rd person plural preterite minus -ron*
endings: -e -es -e -emos -éis -en	endings: -ra -ras -ra -ramos -rais -ran	*or* -se -ses -se -semos -seis -sen	endings: -re -res -re -remos -reis -ren

FORMAS IMPERATIVAS, GERUNDIOS Y PARTICIPIO
COMMANDS AND PARTICIPLES

FORMAS IMPERATIVAS *COMMANDS*		GERUNDIO Y PARTICIPIO *PARTICIPLES*		
AFIRMATIVA *AFFIRMATIVE*	NEGATIVA *NEGATIVE*	GERUNDIO SIMPLE *PRESENT PARTICIPLE*	PARTICIPIO *PAST PARTICIPLE*	GERUNDIO COMPUESTO *PERFECT PARTICIPLE*
tú - *2nd person singular present indicative minus -s* Ud. - *3rd person singular present subjunctive* vosotros - *infinitive minus -r plus -d* Uds. - *3rd person plural present subjunctive* nosotros - *1st person plural present subjunctive*	tú - *2nd person singular present subjunctive* Ud. - *3rd person singular present subjunctive* vosotros - *2nd person plural present subjunctive* Uds. - *3rd person plural present subjunctive* nosotros - *1st person plural present subjunctive*	stem: *infinitive minus -ar* ending: -ando	stem: *infinitive minus -ar* ending: -ado	habiendo + *past participle*

INFINITIVO COMPUESTO: haber + *past participle*
PERFECT INFINITIVE:

TIEMPOS COMPUESTOS
PERFECT (COMPOUND) TENSES

PRETÉRITO PERFECTO DE INDICATIVO *PRESENT PERFECT INDICATIVE*	PRETÉRITO PLUSCUAMPERFECTO DE INDICATIVO *PAST PERFECT (PLUPERFECT) INDICATIVE*	PRETÉRITO ANTERIOR DE INDICATIVO *PRETERITE PERFECT INDICATIVE*	FUTURO PERFECTO DE INDICATIVO *FUTURE PERFECT INDICATIVE*	POTENCIAL COMPUESTO *CONDITIONAL PERFECT*
present indicative of haber *plus past participle*	*imperfect indicative of* haber *plus past participle*	*preterite indicative of* haber *plus past participle*	*future indicative of* haber *plus past participle*	*conditional of* haber *plus past participle*
he + *past participle* has + *past participle* ha + *past participle* hemos + *past participle* habéis + *past participle* han + *past participle*	había + *past participle* habías + *past participle* había + *past participle* habíamos + *past participle* habíais + *past participle* habían + *past participle*	hube + *past participle* hubiste + *past participle* hubo + *past participle* hubimos + *past participle* hubisteis + *past participle* hubieron + *past participle*	habré + *past participle* habrás + *past participle* habrá + *past participle* habremos + *past participle* habréis + *past participle* habrán + *past participle*	habría + *past participle* habrías + *past participle* habría + *past participle* habríamos + *past participle* habríais + *past participle* habrían + *past participle*

PRETÉRITO PERFECTO DE SUBJUNTIVO *PRESENT PERFECT SUBJUNCTIVE*	PRETÉRITO PLUSCUAMPERFECTO DE SUBJUNTIVO *PAST PERFECT (PLUPERFECT) SUBJUNCTIVE*		FUTURO PERFECTO DE SUBJUNTIVO *FUTURE PERFECT SUBJUNCTIVE*
present subjunctive of haber *plus past participle*	*past (imperfect) subjunctive of* haber *plus past participle*		*future subjunctive of* haber *plus past participle*
haya + *past participle* hayas + *past participle* haya + *past participle* hayamos + *past participle* hayáis + *past participle* hayan + *past participle*	hubiera + *past participle* hubieras + *past participle* hubiera + *past participle* hubiéramos + *past participle* hubierais + *past participle* hubieran + *past participle*	*or* hubiese + *past participle* hubieses + *past participle* hubiese + *past participle* hubiésemos + *past participle* hubieseis + *past participle* hubiesen + *past participle*	hubiere + *past participle* hubieres + *past participle* hubiere + *past participle* hubiéremos + *past participle* hubiereis + *past participle* hubieren + *past participle*

D Structure of regular verb forms with infinitive ending in -er

TIEMPOS SIMPLES
SIMPLE TENSES

PRESENTE DE INDICATIVO *PRESENT INDICATIVE*	PRETÉRITO IMPERFECTO DE INDICATIVO *IMPERFECT INDICATIVE*	PRETÉRITO INDEFINIDO DE INDICATIVO *PRETERITE INDICATIVE*	FUTURO IMPERFECTO DE INDICATIVO *FUTURE INDICATIVE*	POTENCIAL SIMPLE *CONDITIONAL*
stem: infinitive minus -er	*stem:* infinitive minus -er	*stem:* infinitive minus -er	*stem:* infinitive	*stem:* infinitive
endings: -o -es -e -emos -éis -en	*endings:* -ía -ías -ía -íamos -íais -ían	*endings:* -í -iste -ió -imos -isteis -ieron	*endings:* -é -ás -á -emos -éis -án	*endings:* -ía -ías -ía -íamos -íais -ían

PRESENTE DE SUBJUNTIVO *PRESENT SUBJUNCTIVE*	PRETÉRITO IMPERFECTO DE SUBJUNTIVO *PAST (IMPERFECT) SUBJUNCTIVE*		FUTURO IMPERFECTO DE SUBJUNTIVO *FUTURE SUBJUNCTIVE*
stem: 1st person singular present indicative minus -o	*stem:* 3rd person plural preterite minus -ron		*stem:* 3rd person plural preterite minus -ron
endings: -a -as -a -amos -áis -an	*endings:* -ra -ras -ra -ramos -rais -ran	*or* -se -ses -se -semos -seis -sen	*endings:* -re -res -re -remos -reis -ren

FORMAS IMPERATIVAS, GERUNDIOS Y PARTICIPIO
COMMANDS AND PARTICIPLES

FORMAS IMPERATIVAS *COMMANDS*		GERUNDIO Y PARTICIPIO *PARTICIPLES*		
AFIRMATIVA *AFFIRMATIVE*	NEGATIVA *NEGATIVE*	GERUNDIO SIMPLE *PRESENT PARTICIPLE*	PARTICIPIO *PAST PARTICIPLE*	GERUNDIO COMPUESTO *PERFECT PARTICIPLE*
tú – 2nd person singular present indicative minus -s Ud. – 3rd person singular present subjunctive vosotros – infinitive minus -r plus -d Uds. – 3rd person plural present subjunctive nosotros – 1st person plural present subjunctive	tú – 2nd person singular present subjunctive Ud. – 3rd person singular present subjunctive vosotros – 2nd person plural present subjunctive Uds. – 3rd person plural present subjunctive nosotros – 1st person plural present subjunctive	*stem:* infinitive minus -er *ending:* -iendo	*stem:* infinitive minus -er *ending:* -ido	habiendo + *past participle*

INFINITIVO COMPUESTO: haber + *past participle*
PERFECT INFINITIVE:

TIEMPOS COMPUESTOS
PERFECT (COMPOUND) TENSES

PRETÉRITO PERFECTO DE INDICATIVO *PRESENT PERFECT INDICATIVE*	PRETÉRITO PLUSCUAMPERFECTO DE INDICATIVO *PAST PERFECT (PLUPERFECT) INDICATIVE*	PRETÉRITO ANTERIOR DE INDICATIVO *PRETERITE PERFECT INDICATIVE*	FUTURO PERFECTO DE INDICATIVO *FUTURE PERFECT INDICATIVE*	POTENCIAL COMPUESTO *CONDITIONAL PERFECT*
present indicative of haber plus past participle	imperfect indicative of haber plus past participle	preterite indicative of haber plus past participle	future indicative of haber plus past participle	conditional of haber plus past participle
he + *past participle* has + *past participle* ha + *past participle* hemos + *past participle* habéis + *past participle* han + *past participle*	había + *past participle* habías + *past participle* había + *past participle* habíamos + *past participle* habíais + *past participle* habían + *past participle*	hube + *past participle* hubiste + *past participle* hubo + *past participle* hubimos + *past participle* hubisteis + *past participle* hubieron + *past participle*	habré + *past participle* habrás + *past participle* habrá + *past participle* habremos + *past participle* habréis + *past participle* habrán + *past participle*	habría + *past participle* habrías + *past participle* habría + *past participle* habríamos + *past participle* habríais + *past participle* habrían + *past participle*

PRETÉRITO PERFECTO DE SUBJUNTIVO *PRESENT PERFECT SUBJUNCTIVE*	PRETÉRITO PLUSCUAMPERFECTO DE SUBJUNTIVO *PAST PERFECT (PLUPERFECT) SUBJUNCTIVE*		FUTURO PERFECTO DE SUBJUNTIVO *FUTURE PERFECT SUBJUNCTIVE*
present subjunctive of haber plus past participle	past (imperfect) subjunctive of haber plus past participle		future subjunctive of haber plus past participle
haya + *past participle* hayas + *past participle* haya + *past participle* hayamos + *past participle* hayáis + *past participle* hayan + *past participle*	hubiera + *past participle* hubieras + *past participle* hubiera + *past participle* hubiéramos + *past participle* hubierais + *past participle* hubieran + *past participle*	hubiese + *past participle* hubieses + *past participle* hubiese + *past participle* hubiésemos + *past participle* hubieseis + *past participle* hubiesen + *past participle*	hubiere + *past participle* hubieres + *past participle* hubiere + *past participle* hubiéremos + *past participle* hubiereis + *past participle* hubieren + *past participle*

III. Structure of Spanish verbal forms

TIEMPOS SIMPLES
SIMPLE TENSES

PRESENTE DE INDICATIVO **PRESENT** *INDICATIVE*	PRETÉRITO IMPERFECTO DE INDICATIVO **IMPERFECT** *INDICATIVE*	PRETÉRITO INDEFINIDO DE INDICATIVO **PRETERITE** *INDICATIVE*	FUTURO IMPERFECTO DE INDICATIVO **FUTURE** *INDICATIVE*	POTENCIAL SIMPLE **CONDITIONAL**
stem: *infinitive minus -ir*	stem: *infinitive minus -ir*	stem: *infinitive minus -ir*	stem: *infinitive*	stem: *infinitive*
endings: -o	endings: -ía	endings: -í	endings: -é	endings: -ía
-es	-ías	-iste	-ás	-ías
-e	-ía	-ió	-á	-ía
-imos	-íamos	-imos	-emos	-íamos
-ís	-íais	-isteis	-éis	-íais
-en	-ían	-ieron	-án	-ían

PRESENTE DE SUBJUNTIVO **PRESENT** *SUBJUNCTIVE*	PRETÉRITO IMPERFECTO DE SUBJUNTIVO **PAST (IMPERFECT)** *SUBJUNCTIVE*		FUTURO IMPERFECTO DE SUBJUNTIVO **FUTURE** *SUBJUNCTIVE*
stem: *1st person singular present indicative minus -o*	stem: *3rd person plural preterite minus -ron*		stem: *3rd person plural preterite minus -ron*
endings: -a	endings: -ra	-se	endings: -re
-as	-ras	-ses	-res
-a	-ra	-se	-re
-amos	-ramos *or* -semos		-remos
-áis	-rais	-seis	-reis
-an	-ran	-sen	-ren

FORMAS IMPERATIVAS, GERUNDIOS Y PARTICIPIO
COMMANDS AND PARTICIPLES

FORMAS IMPERATIVAS **COMMANDS**		GERUNDIO Y PARTICIPIO **PARTICIPLES**		
AFIRMATIVA *AFFIRMATIVE*	NEGATIVA *NEGATIVE*	GERUNDIO SIMPLE *PRESENT PARTICIPLE*	PARTICIPIO *PAST PARTICIPLE*	GERUNDIO COMPUESTO *PERFECT PARTICIPLE*
tú – *2nd person singular present indicative minus -s*	tú – *2nd person singular present subjunctive*	stem: *infinitive minus -ir*	stem: *infinitive minus -ir*	habiendo + *past participle*
Ud. – *3rd person singular present subjunctive*	Ud. – *3rd person singular present subjunctive*	ending: -iendo	ending: -ido	
vosotros – *infinitive minus -r plus -d*	vosotros – *2nd person plural present subjunctive*			
Uds. – *3rd person plural present subjunctive*	Uds. – *3rd person plural present subjunctive*			
nosotros – *1st person plural present subjunctive*	nosotros – *1st person plural present subjunctive*			

INFINITIVO COMPUESTO: haber + *past participle*
PERFECT INFINITIVE:

TIEMPOS COMPUESTOS
PERFECT (COMPOUND) TENSES

PRETÉRITO PERFECTO DE INDICATIVO **PRESENT PERFECT** *INDICATIVE*	PRETÉRITO PLUSCUAMPERFECTO DE INDICATIVO **PAST PERFECT (PLUPERFECT)** *INDICATIVE*	PRETÉRITO ANTERIOR DE INDICATIVO **PRETERITE PERFECT** *INDICATIVE*	FUTURO PERFECTO DE INDICATIVO **FUTURE PERFECT** *INDICATIVE*	POTENCIAL COMPUESTO **CONDITIONAL PERFECT**
present indicative of haber *plus past participle*	*imperfect indicative of* haber *plus past participle*	*preterite indicative of* haber *plus past participle*	*future indicative of* haber *plus past participle*	*conditional of* haber *plus past participle*
he + *past participle*	había + *past participle*	hube + *past participle*	habré + *past participle*	habría + *past participle*
has + *past participle*	habías + *past participle*	hubiste + *past participle*	habrás + *past participle*	habrías + *past participle*
ha + *past participle*	había + *past participle*	hubo + *past participle*	habrá + *past participle*	habría + *past participle*
hemos + *past participle*	habíamos + *past participle*	hubimos + *past participle*	habremos + *past participle*	habríamos + *past participle*
habéis + *past participle*	habíais + *past participle*	hubisteis + *past participle*	habréis + *past participle*	habríais + *past participle*
han + *past participle*	habían + *past participle*	hubieron + *past participle*	habrán + *past participle*	habrían + *past participle*

PRETÉRITO PERFECTO DE SUBJUNTIVO **PRESENT PERFECT** *SUBJUNCTIVE*	PRETÉRITO PLUSCUAMPERFECTO DE SUBJUNTIVO **PAST PERFECT (PLUPERFECT)** *SUBJUNCTIVE*		FUTURO PERFECTO DE SUBJUNTIVO **FUTURE PERFECT** *SUBJUNCTIVE*
present subjunctive of haber *plus past participle*	*past (imperfect) subjunctive of* haber *plus past participle*		*future subjunctive of* haber *plus past participle*
haya + *past participle*	hubiera + *past participle*	hubiese + *past participle*	hubiere + *past participle*
hayas + *past participle*	hubieras + *past participle*	hubieses + *past participle*	hubieres + *past participle*
haya + *past participle*	hubiera + *past participle*	hubiese + *past participle*	hubiere + *past participle*
hayamos + *past participle*	hubiéramos + *past participle* *or*	hubiésemos + *past participle*	hubiéremos + *past participle*
hayáis + *past participle*	hubierais + *past participle*	hubieseis + *past participle*	hubiereis + *past participle*
hayan + *past participle*	hubieran + *past participle*	hubiesen + *past participle*	hubieren + *past participle*

F Comparison of regular forms of -ar, -er, and -ir verbs

TIEMPOS SIMPLES
SIMPLE TENSES

PRESENTE DE INDICATIVO *PRESENT INDICATIVE*	PRETÉRITO IMPERFECTO DE INDICATIVO *IMPERFECT INDICATIVE*	PRETÉRITO INDEFINIDO DE INDICATIVO *PRETERITE INDICATIVE*	FUTURO IMPERFECTO DE INDICATIVO *FUTURE INDICATIVE*	POTENCIAL SIMPLE *CONDITIONAL*
stem: *infinitive minus* -ar -er -ir endings: -o -o -o -as -es -es -a -e -e -amos -emos -imos -áis -éis -ís -an -en -en	stem: *infinitive minus* -ar -er, -ir endings: -aba -ía -abas -ías -aba -ía -ábamos -íamos -abais -íais -aban -ían	stem: *infinitive minus* -ar -er, -ir endings: -é -í -aste -iste -ó -ió -amos -imos -asteis -isteis -aron -ieron	stem: *infinitive* endings for all verbs: -é -ás -á -emos -éis -án	stem: *infinitive* endings for all verbs: -ía -ías -ía -íamos -íais -ían

PRESENTE DE SUBJUNTIVO *PRESENT SUBJUNCTIVE*	PRETÉRITO IMPERFECTO DE SUBJUNTIVO *PAST (IMPERFECT) SUBJUNCTIVE*		FUTURO IMPERFECTO DE SUBJUNTIVO *FUTURE SUBJUNCTIVE*
stem: *1st person singular present indicative minus* -o endings for -ar *verbs* -er, -ir *verbs* -e -a -es -as -e -a -emos -amos -éis -áis -en -an	stem: *3rd person plural preterite minus* -ron endings for all verbs: -ra -ras -ra -ramos -rais -ran	*or* -se -ses -se -semos -seis -sen	stem: *3rd person plural preterite minus* -ron endings for all verbs: -re -res -re -remos -reis -ren

FORMAS IMPERATIVAS, GERUNDIOS Y PARTICIPIO
COMMANDS AND PARTICIPLES

FORMAS IMPERATIVAS *COMMANDS*		GERUNDIO Y PARTICIPIO *PARTICIPLES*		
AFIRMATIVA *AFFIRMATIVE*	NEGATIVA *NEGATIVE*	GERUNDIO SIMPLE *PRESENT PARTICIPLE*	PARTICIPIO *PAST PARTICIPLE*	GERUNDIO COMPUESTO *PERFECT PARTICIPLE*
tú – *2nd person singular present indicative minus* -s Ud.– *3rd person singular present subjunctive* vosotros – *infinitive minus* -r *plus* -d Uds.– *3rd person plural present subjunctive* nosotros – *1st person plural present subjunctive*	tú – *2nd person singular present subjunctive* Ud.– *3rd person singular present subjunctive* vosotros – *2nd person plural present subjunctive* Uds. – *3rd person plural present subjunctive* nosotros – *1st person plural present subjunctive*	stem: *infinitive minus* -ar -er, -ir endings: -ando -iendo	stem: *infinitive minus* -ar -er, -ir endings: -ado -ido	habiendo + *past participle*

INFINITIVO COMPUESTO: haber + *past participle*
PERFECT INFINITIVE:

TIEMPOS COMPUESTOS
PERFECT (COMPOUND) TENSES

PRETÉRITO PERFECTO DE INDICATIVO *PRESENT PERFECT INDICATIVE*	PRETÉRITO PLUSCUAMPERFECTO DE INDICATIVO *PAST PERFECT (PLUPERFECT) INDICATIVE*	PRETÉRITO ANTERIOR DE INDICATIVO *PRETERITE PERFECT INDICATIVE*	FUTURO PERFECTO DE INDICATIVO *FUTURE PERFECT INDICATIVE*	POTENCIAL COMPUESTO *CONDITIONAL PERFECT*
present indicative of haber plus past participle	imperfect indicative of haber plus past participle	preterite indicative of haber plus past participle	future indicative of haber plus past participle	conditional of haber plus past participle
he + *past participle* has + *past participle* ha + *past participle* hemos + *past participle* habéis + *past participle* han + *past participle*	había + *past participle* habías + *past participle* había + *past participle* habíamos + *past participle* habíais + *past participle* habían + *past participle*	hube + *past participle* hubiste + *past participle* hubo + *past participle* hubimos + *past participle* hubisteis + *past participle* hubieron + *past participle*	habré + *past participle* habrás + *past participle* habrá + *past participle* habremos + *past participle* habréis + *past participle* habrán + *past participle*	habría + *past participle* habrías + *past participle* habría + *past participle* habríamos + *past participle* habríais + *past participle* habrían + *past participle*

PRETÉRITO PERFECTO DE SUBJUNTIVO *PRESENT PERFECT SUBJUNCTIVE*	PRETÉRITO PLUSCUAMPERFECTO DE SUBJUNTIVO *PAST PERFECT (PLUPERFECT) SUBJUNCTIVE*		FUTURO PERFECTO DE SUBJUNTIVO *FUTURE PERFECT SUBJUNCTIVE*
present subjunctive of haber plus past participle	past (imperfect) subjunctive of haber plus past participle		future subjunctive of haber plus past participle
haya + *past participle* hayas + *past participle* haya + *past participle* hayamos + *past participle* hayáis + *past participle* hayan + *past participle*	hubiera + *past participle* hubieras + *past participle* hubiera + *past participle* hubiéramos + *past participle* hubierais + *past participle* hubieran + *past participle*	*or* hubiese + *past participle* hubieses + *past participle* hubiese + *past participle* hubiésemos + *past participle* hubieseis + *past participle* hubiesen + *past participle*	hubiere + *past participle* hubieres + *past participle* hubiere + *past participle* hubiéremos + *past participle* hubiereis + *past participle* hubieren + *past participle*

1 Regular verbs ending in -ar } model: HABLAR

PRESENTE DE INDICATIVO *PRESENT INDICATIVE*	PRETÉRITO IMPERFECTO DE INDICATIVO *IMPERFECT INDICATIVE*	PRETÉRITO INDEFINIDO DE INDICATIVO *PRETERITE INDICATIVE*	FUTURO IMPERFECTO DE INDICATIVO *FUTURE INDICATIVE*	POTENCIAL SIMPLE *CONDITIONAL*
I speak, etc.*	*I was speaking, etc.**	*I spoke, etc.**	*I will speak, etc.**	*I would speak, etc.**
hablo	hablaba	hablé	hablaré	hablaría
hablas	hablabas	hablaste	hablarás	hablarías
habla	hablaba	habló	hablará	hablaría
hablamos	hablábamos	hablamos	hablaremos	hablaríamos
habláis	hablabais	hablasteis	hablaréis	hablaríais
hablan	hablaban	hablaron	hablarán	hablarían

PRESENTE DE SUBJUNTIVO *PRESENT SUBJUNCTIVE*	PRETÉRITO IMPERFECTO DE SUBJUNTIVO *PAST (IMPERFECT) SUBJUNCTIVE*		FUTURO IMPERFECTO DE SUBJUNTIVO *FUTURE SUBJUNCTIVE*
I speak, etc.*	*I spoke, etc.**		*I will speak, etc.**
hable	hablara	hablase	hablare
hables	hablaras	hablases	hablares
hable	hablara	hablase	hablare
hablemos	habláramos	*or* hablásemos	habláremos
habléis	hablarais	hablaseis	hablareis
hablen	hablaran	hablasen	hablaren

FORMAS IMPERATIVAS *COMMANDS*		GERUNDIO Y PARTICIPIO *PARTICIPLES*		
AFIRMATIVA *AFFIRMATIVE*	NEGATIVA *NEGATIVE*	GERUNDIO SIMPLE *PRESENT PARTICIPLE*	PARTICIPIO *PAST PARTICIPLE*	GERUNDIO COMPUESTO *PERFECT PARTICIPLE*
speak	*don't speak*	*speaking*	*spoken*	*having spoken*
habla (tú)	no hables (tú)	hablando	hablado	habiendo hablado
hable (Ud.)	no hable (Ud.)			
hablad (vosotros)	no habléis (vosotros)			
hablen (Uds.)	no hablen (Uds.)			
let's speak	*let's not speak*			
hablemos	no hablemos			

INFINITIVO COMPUESTO: haber hablado
PERFECT INFINITIVE: to have spoken

PRETÉRITO PERFECTO DE INDICATIVO *PRESENT PERFECT INDICATIVE*	PRETÉRITO PLUSCUAMPERFECTO DE INDICATIVO *PAST PERFECT (PLUPERFECT) INDICATIVE*	PRETÉRITO ANTERIOR DE INDICATIVO *PRETERITE PERFECT INDICATIVE*	FUTURO PERFECTO DE INDICATIVO *FUTURE PERFECT INDICATIVE*	POTENCIAL COMPUESTO *CONDITIONAL PERFECT*
I have spoken, etc.	*I had spoken, etc.*	*I had spoken, etc.*	*I will have spoken, etc.**	*I would have spoken, etc.**
he hablado	había hablado	hube hablado	habré hablado	habría hablado
has hablado	habías hablado	hubiste hablado	habrás hablado	habrías hablado
ha hablado	había hablado	hubo hablado	habrá hablado	habría hablado
hemos hablado	habíamos hablado	hubimos hablado	habremos hablado	habríamos hablado
habéis hablado	habíais hablado	hubisteis hablado	habréis hablado	habríais hablado
han hablado	habían hablado	hubieron hablado	habrán hablado	habrían hablado

PRETÉRITO PERFECTO DE SUBJUNTIVO *PRESENT PERFECT SUBJUNCTIVE*	PRETÉRITO PLUSCUAMPERFECTO DE SUBJUNTIVO *PAST PERFECT (PLUPERFECT) SUBJUNCTIVE*		FUTURO PERFECTO DE SUBJUNTIVO *FUTURE PERFECT SUBJUNCTIVE*
I have spoken, etc.*	*I had spoken, etc.**		*I will have spoken, etc.**
haya hablado	hubiera hablado	hubiese hablado	hubiere hablado
hayas hablado	hubieras hablado	hubieses hablado	hubieres hablado
haya hablado	hubiera hablado	hubiese hablado	hubiere hablado
hayamos hablado	hubiéramos hablado	*or* hubiésemos hablado	hubiéremos hablado
hayáis hablado	hubierais hablado	hubieseis hablado	hubiereis hablado
hayan hablado	hubieran hablado	hubiesen hablado	hubieren hablado

*For additional translation possibilities see chart A.

1

IV. Regular verbs

Any regular Spanish verb ending in -ar follows this pattern. Since the verbs of this category are so numerous, it is impractical to list them here. Note that all verbs in the alphabetical lists with a (1) belong to this category.

2 Regular verbs ending in -er } model: COMER

TIEMPOS SIMPLES
SIMPLE TENSES

PRESENTE DE INDICATIVO / PRESENT INDICATIVE	PRETÉRITO IMPERFECTO DE INDICATIVO / IMPERFECT INDICATIVE	PRETÉRITO INDEFINIDO DE INDICATIVO / PRETERITE INDICATIVE	FUTURO IMPERFECTO DE INDICATIVO / FUTURE INDICATIVE	POTENCIAL SIMPLE / CONDITIONAL
*I eat, etc.**	*I was eating, etc.**	*I ate, etc.**	*I will eat, etc.**	*I would eat, etc.**
como	comía	comí	comeré	comería
comes	comías	comiste	comerás	comerías
come	comía	comió	comerá	comería
comemos	comíamos	comimos	comeremos	comeríamos
coméis	comíais	comisteis	comeréis	comeríais
comen	comían	comieron	comerán	comerían

PRESENTE DE SUBJUNTIVO / PRESENT SUBJUNCTIVE	PRETÉRITO IMPERFECTO DE SUBJUNTIVO / PAST (IMPERFECT) SUBJUNCTIVE		FUTURO IMPERFECTO DE SUBJUNTIVO / FUTURE SUBJUNCTIVE
*I eat, etc.**	*I ate, etc.**		*I will eat, etc.**
coma	comiera	comiese	comiere
comas	comieras	comieses	comieres
coma	comiera	comiese	comiere
comamos	comiéramos _or_	comiésemos	comiéremos
comáis	comierais	comieseis	comiereis
coman	comieran	comiesen	comieren

FORMAS IMPERATIVAS, GERUNDIOS Y PARTICIPIO
COMMANDS AND PARTICIPLES

FORMAS IMPERATIVAS / COMMANDS		GERUNDIO Y PARTICIPIO / PARTICIPLES		
AFIRMATIVA / AFFIRMATIVE	NEGATIVA / NEGATIVE	GERUNDIO SIMPLE / PRESENT PARTICIPLE	PARTICIPIO / PAST PARTICIPLE	GERUNDIO COMPUESTO / PERFECT PARTICIPLE
eat	*don't eat*	*eating*	*eaten*	*having eaten*
come (tú)	no comas (tú)	comiendo	comido	habiendo comido
coma (Ud.)	no coma (Ud.)			
comed (vosotros)	no comáis (vosotros)			
coman (Uds.)	no coman (Uds.)			
let's eat	*let's not eat*			
comamos	no comamos			

INFINITIVO COMPUESTO: haber comido
PERFECT INFINITIVE: to have eaten

TIEMPOS COMPUESTOS
PERFECT (COMPOUND) TENSES

PRETÉRITO PERFECTO DE INDICATIVO / PRESENT PERFECT INDICATIVE	PRETÉRITO PLUSCUAMPERFECTO DE INDICATIVO / PAST PERFECT (PLUPERFECT) INDICATIVE	PRETÉRITO ANTERIOR DE INDICATIVO / PRETERITE PERFECT INDICATIVE	FUTURO PERFECTO DE INDICATIVO / FUTURE PERFECT INDICATIVE	POTENCIAL COMPUESTO / CONDITIONAL PERFECT
I have eaten, etc.	*I had eaten, etc.*	*I had eaten, etc.*	*I will have eaten, etc.**	*I would have eaten, etc.**
he comido	había comido	hube comido	habré comido	habría comido
has comido	habías comido	hubiste comido	habrás comido	habrías comido
ha comido	había comido	hubo comido	habrá comido	habría comido
hemos comido	habíamos comido	hubimos comido	habremos comido	habríamos comido
habéis comido	habíais comido	hubisteis comido	habréis comido	habríais comido
han comido	habían comido	hubieron comido	habrán comido	habrían comido

PRETÉRITO PERFECTO DE SUBJUNTIVO / PRESENT PERFECT SUBJUNCTIVE	PRETÉRITO PLUSCUAMPERFECTO DE SUBJUNTIVO / PAST PERFECT (PLUPERFECT) SUBJUNCTIVE		FUTURO PERFECTO DE SUBJUNTIVO / FUTURE PERFECT SUBJUNCTIVE
*I have eaten, etc.**	*I had eaten, etc.**		*I will have eaten, etc.**
haya comido	hubiera comido	hubiese comido	hubiere comido
hayas comido	hubieras comido	hubieses comido	hubieres comido
haya comido	hubiera comido	hubiese comido	hubiere comido
hayamos comido	hubiéramos comido _or_	hubiésemos comido	hubiéremos comido
hayáis comido	hubierais comido	hubieseis comido	hubiereis comido
hayan comido	hubieran comido	hubiesen comido	hubieren comido

*For additional translation possibilities see chart A.

IV. Regular verbs

2

VERBS OF THIS CATEGORY

absorber
acceder
acometer
anteceder
aprehender
aprender
arremeter
atreverse 4. (R)
barrer
beber
beberse 4. (R)
ceder
coextender
comer
comerse 4. (R)
cometer
compeler
competer
comprender
comprometer
comprometerse 4. (R)
conceder
correr
correrse 4. (R)
corresponder
corromper
corromperse 4. (R)
coser
deber
depender
descorrer
descoser
desprender
embeber
emprender
entremeter
entremeterse 4. (R)
entretejer
entrometer
entrometerse 4. (R)
esconder
exceder
impeler
interceder
lamer
malvender
meter
ofender
ofenderse 4. (R)
pender
precaver
precaverse 4. (R)
preceder
prender
pretender
proceder
prometer
propender

recorrer
recoser
relamer
relamerse 4. (R)
repeler
reprender
responder
retroceder
revender
sobrebarrer
sobrebeber
socorrer
someter
someterse 4. (R)
sorber
sorprender
suceder
sucederse 4. (R)
suspender
temer
toser
tremer
vender

R = Reflexive

[63]

3 Regular verbs ending in -ir } model: VIVIR

PRESENTE DE INDICATIVO *PRESENT INDICATIVE*	PRETÉRITO IMPERFECTO DE INDICATIVO *IMPERFECT INDICATIVE*	PRETÉRITO INDEFINIDO DE INDICATIVO *PRETERITE INDICATIVE*	FUTURO IMPERFECTO DE INDICATIVO *FUTURE INDICATIVE*	POTENCIAL SIMPLE *CONDITIONAL*
*I live, etc.**	*I was living, etc.**	*I lived, etc.**	*I will live, etc.**	*I would live, etc.**
vivo	vivía	viví	viviré	viviría
vives	vivías	viviste	vivirás	vivirías
vive	vivía	vivió	vivirá	viviría
vivimos	vivíamos	vivimos	viviremos	viviríamos
vivís	vivíais	vivisteis	viviréis	viviríais
viven	vivían	vivieron	vivirán	vivirían

PRESENTE DE SUBJUNTIVO *PRESENT SUBJUNCTIVE*	PRETÉRITO IMPERFECTO DE SUBJUNTIVO *PAST (IMPERFECT) SUBJUNCTIVE*		FUTURO IMPERFECTO DE SUBJUNTIVO *FUTURE SUBJUNCTIVE*
*I live, etc.**	*I lived, etc.**		*I will live, etc.**
viva	viviera	viviese	viviere
vivas	vivieras	vivieses	vivieres
viva	viviera	viviese	viviere
vivamos	viviéramos	*or* viviésemos	viviéremos
viváis	vivierais	vivieseis	viviereis
vivan	vivieran	viviesen	vivieren

FORMAS IMPERATIVAS, GERUNDIOS Y PARTICIPIO
COMMANDS AND PARTICIPLES

FORMAS IMPERATIVAS *COMMANDS*		GERUNDIO Y PARTICIPIO *PARTICIPLES*		
AFIRMATIVA *AFFIRMATIVE*	NEGATIVA *NEGATIVE*	GERUNDIO SIMPLE *PRESENT PARTICIPLE*	PARTICIPIO *PAST PARTICIPLE*	GERUNDIO COMPUESTO *PERFECT PARTICIPLE*
live	*don't live*	*living*	*lived*	*having lived*
vive (tú)	no vivas (tú)	viviendo	vivido	habiendo vivido
viva (Ud.)	no viva (Ud.)			
vivid (vosotros)	no viváis (vosotros)			
vivan (Uds.)	no vivan (Uds.)			
let's live	*let's not live*			
vivamos	no vivamos			

INFINITIVO COMPUESTO: haber vivido
PERFECT INFINITIVE: to have lived

PRETÉRITO PERFECTO DE INDICATIVO *PRESENT PERFECT INDICATIVE*	PRETÉRITO PLUSCUAMPERFECTO DE INDICATIVO *PAST PERFECT (PLUPERFECT) INDICATIVE*	PRETÉRITO ANTERIOR DE INDICATIVO *PRETERITE PERFECT INDICATIVE*	FUTURO PERFECTO DE INDICATIVO *FUTURE PERFECT INDICATIVE*	POTENCIAL COMPUESTO *CONDITIONAL PERFECT*
I have lived, etc.	*I had lived, etc.*	*I had lived, etc.*	*I will have lived, etc.**	*I would have lived, etc.**
he vivido	había vivido	hube vivido	habré vivido	habría vivido
has vivido	habías vivido	hubiste vivido	habrás vivido	habrías vivido
ha vivido	había vivido	hubo vivido	habrá vivido	habría vivido
hemos vivido	habíamos vivido	hubimos vivido	habremos vivido	habríamos vivido
habéis vivido	habíais vivido	hubisteis vivido	habréis vivido	habríais vivido
han vivido	habían vivido	hubieron vivido	habrán vivido	habrían vivido

PRETÉRITO PERFECTO DE SUBJUNTIVO *PRESENT PERFECT SUBJUNCTIVE*	PRETÉRITO PLUSCUAMPERFECTO DE SUBJUNTIVO *PAST PERFECT (PLUPERFECT) SUBJUNCTIVE*		FUTURO PERFECTO DE SUBJUNTIVO *FUTURE PERFECT SUBJUNCTIVE*
*I have lived, etc.**	*I had lived, etc.**		*I will have lived, etc.**
haya vivido	hubiera vivido	hubiese vivido	hubiere vivido
hayas vivido	hubieras vivido	hubieses vivido	hubieres vivido
haya vivido	hubiera vivido	hubiese vivido	hubiere vivido
hayamos vivido	hubiéramos vivido *or*	hubiésemos vivido	hubiéremos vivido
hayáis vivido	hubierais vivido	hubieseis vivido	hubiereis vivido
hayan vivido	hubieran vivido	hubiesen vivido	hubieren vivido

*For additional translation possibilities see chart A.

IV. Regular verbs

VERBS OF THIS CATEGORY

abatir
aburrir
aburrirse 4. (R)
acudir
aludir
añadir
apercibir
apercibirse 4. (R)
aplaudir
asistir
asumir
aturdir
aturdirse 4. (R)
batir
coexistir
coincidir
coludir
combatir
compartir
comprimir
comprimirse 4. (R)
concurrir
confundir
confundirse 4. (R)
consistir
consumir
contundir
convivir
crujir
cumplir
cundir
curtir
curtirse 4. (R)
debatir
debatirse 4. (R)
decidir
definir
deglutir
deludir
departir
deprimir
desabrirse 4. (R)
desasistir
desnutrirse 4. (R)
desvivirse 4. (R)
difundir
dimitir
discurrir
discutir
disidir
disuadir
eludir
embutir
emitir
esculpir
escupir
escurrir

escurrirse 4. (R)
esgrimir
evadir
exhibir
exhibirse 4. (R)
eximir
exprimir
fundir
hundir
impartir
incumbir
incurrir
infundir
inhibir
insistir
intermitir
interrumpir
invadir
irrumpir
latir
manumitir
nutrir
ocurrir
omitir
oprimir
parir
partir
percibir
permitir
persistir
persuadir
persuadirse 4. (R)
preexistir
prescindir
presidir
presumir
prohibir
prorrumpir
pulir
radiodifundir
readmitir
reasumir
rebatir
rebutir
recibir
recurrir
redimir
refundir
reincidir
remitir
repartir
reprimir
rescindir
residir
resistir
resistirse 4. (R)
resumir

resumirse 4. (R)
revivir
sacudir
sobreañadir
sobrevivir
subdividir
subir
subsistir
subsumir
sucumbir
sufrir
sumir
suplir
suprimir
surtir
teledifundir
transcurrir
transfundir
transmitir
unir
urdir
vivir

R = Reflexive

[65]

4 Reflexive verbs } model: LAVARSE

PRESENTE DE INDICATIVO *PRESENT INDICATIVE*	PRETÉRITO IMPERFECTO DE INDICATIVO *IMPERFECT INDICATIVE*	PRETÉRITO INDEFINIDO DE INDICATIVO *PRETERITE INDICATIVE*	FUTURO IMPERFECTO DE INDICATIVO *FUTURE INDICATIVE*	POTENCIAL SIMPLE *CONDITIONAL*
I wash myself, etc.*	*I was washing myself, etc.**	*I washed myself, etc.**	*I will wash myself, etc.**	*I would wash myself, etc.**
me lavo	me lavaba	me lavé	me lavaré	me lavaría
te lavas	te lavabas	te lavaste	te lavarás	te lavarías
se lava	se lavaba	se lavó	se lavará	se lavaría
nos lavamos	nos lavábamos	nos lavamos	nos lavaremos	nos lavaríamos
os laváis	os lavabais	os lavasteis	os lavaréis	os lavaríais
se lavan	se lavaban	se lavaron	se lavarán	se lavarían

PRESENTE DE SUBJUNTIVO *PRESENT SUBJUNCTIVE*	PRETÉRITO IMPERFECTO DE SUBJUNTIVO *PAST (IMPERFECT) SUBJUNCTIVE*		FUTURO IMPERFECTO DE SUBJUNTIVO *FUTURE SUBJUNCTIVE*
I wash myself, etc.*	*I washed myself, etc.**		*I will wash myself, etc.**
me lave	me lavara	me lavase	me lavare
te laves	te lavaras	te lavases	te lavares
se lave	se lavara	se lavase	se lavare
nos lavemos	nos laváramos _or_	nos lavásemos	nos laváremos
os lavéis	os lavarais	os lavaseis	os lavareis
se laven	se lavaran	se lavasen	se lavaren

FORMAS IMPERATIVAS *COMMANDS*		GERUNDIO Y PARTICIPIO *PARTICIPLES*		
AFIRMATIVA *AFFIRMATIVE*	NEGATIVA *NEGATIVE*	GERUNDIO SIMPLE *PRESENT PARTICIPLE*	PARTICIPIO *PAST PARTICIPLE*	GERUNDIO COMPUESTO *PERFECT PARTICIPLE*
wash yourself; *wash yourselves*	*don't wash yourself;* *don't wash yourselves*	*washing myself, etc.*	*washed*	*having washed myself, etc.*
lávate (tú)	no te laves (tú)	lavándome	lavado	habiéndome lavado
lávese (Ud.)	no se lave (Ud.)	lavándote		habiéndote lavado
		lavándose		habiéndose lavado
		lavándonos		habiéndonos lavado
lavaos+ (vosotros)	no os lavéis (vosotros)	lavándoos		habiéndoos lavado
lávense (Uds.)	no se laven (Uds.)	lavándose		habiéndose lavado
let's wash ourselves	*let's not wash ourselves*			
lavémonos†	no nos lavemos			

```
INFINITIVO COMPUESTO:  haberse lavado
PERFECT INFINITIVE:  to have washed oneself
```

PRETÉRITO PERFECTO DE INDICATIVO *PRESENT PERFECT INDICATIVE*	PRETÉRITO PLUSCUAMPERFECTO DE INDICATIVO *PAST PERFECT (PLUPERFECT) INDICATIVE*	PRETÉRITO ANTERIOR DE INDICATIVO *PRETERITE PERFECT INDICATIVE*	FUTURO PERFECTO DE INDICATIVO *FUTURE PERFECT INDICATIVE*	POTENCIAL COMPUESTO *CONDITIONAL PERFECT*
I have washed myself, etc.	*I had washed myself, etc.*	*I had washed myself, etc.*	*I will have washed myself, etc.**	*I would have washed myself, etc.**
me he lavado	me había lavado	me hube lavado	me habré lavado	me habría lavado
te has lavado	te habías lavado	te hubiste lavado	te habrás lavado	te habrías lavado
se ha lavado	se había lavado	se hubo lavado	se habrá lavado	se habría lavado
nos hemos lavado	nos habíamos lavado	nos hubimos lavado	nos habremos lavado	nos habríamos lavado
os habéis lavado	os habíais lavado	os hubisteis lavado	os habréis lavado	os habríais lavado
se han lavado	se habían lavado	se hubieron lavado	se habrán lavado	se habrían lavado

PRETÉRITO PERFECTO DE SUBJUNTIVO *PRESENT PERFECT SUBJUNCTIVE*	PRETÉRITO PLUSCUAMPERFECTO DE SUBJUNTIVO *PAST PERFECT (PLUPERFECT) SUBJUNCTIVE*		FUTURO PERFECTO DE SUBJUNTIVO *FUTURE PERFECT SUBJUNCTIVE*
I have washed myself, etc.*	*I had washed myself, etc.**		*I will have washed myself, etc.**
me haya lavado	me hubiera lavado	me hubiese lavado	me hubiere lavado
te hayas lavado	te hubieras lavado	te hubieses lavado	te hubieres lavado
se haya lavado	se hubiera lavado	se hubiese lavado	se hubiere lavado
nos hayamos lavado	nos hubiéramos lavado _or_	nos hubiésemos lavado	nos hubiéremos lavado
os hayáis lavado	os hubierais lavado	os hubieseis lavado	os hubiereis lavado
se hayan lavado	se hubieran lavado	se hubiesen lavado	se hubieren lavado

*For additional translation possibilities see chart A.
+Note the dropping of the -d of the affirmative vosotros command when the reflexive pronoun os is attached.
†Note the dropping of the -s of the affirmative nosotros command when the reflexive pronoun nos is attached.

IV. Regular verbs

VERBS OF THIS CATEGORY

Any Spanish verb that is reflexive follows this model for its reflexive aspect. See the model verb indicated by the other reference number following any infinitive in this book for the nonreflexive portion of its conjugation pattern.

5 Progressive tenses, nonreflexive verbs } model: ESTAR HABLANDO

TIEMPOS SIMPLES
SIMPLE TENSES

PRESENTE DE INDICATIVO *PRESENT INDICATIVE*	PRETÉRITO IMPERFECTO DE INDICATIVO *IMPERFECT INDICATIVE*	PRETÉRITO INDEFINIDO DE INDICATIVO *PRETERITE INDICATIVE*	FUTURO IMPERFECTO DE INDICATIVO *FUTURE INDICATIVE*	POTENCIAL SIMPLE *CONDITIONAL*
I am speaking, etc.	*I was speaking, etc.**	*I was speaking, etc.*	*I will be speaking, etc.**	*I would be speaking, etc.**
estoy hablando	estaba hablando	estuve hablando	estaré hablando	estaría hablando
estás hablando	estabas hablando	estuviste hablando	estarás hablando	estarías hablando
está hablando	estaba hablando	estuvo hablando	estará hablando	estaría hablando
estamos hablando	estábamos hablando	estuvimos hablando	estaremos hablando	estaríamos hablando
estáis hablando	estabais hablando	estuvisteis hablando	estaréis hablando	estaríais hablando
están hablando	estaban hablando	estuvieron hablando	estarán hablando	estarían hablando

PRESENTE DE SUBJUNTIVO *PRESENT SUBJUNCTIVE*	PRETÉRITO IMPERFECTO DE SUBJUNTIVO *PAST (IMPERFECT) SUBJUNCTIVE*		FUTURO IMPERFECTO DE SUBJUNTIVO *FUTURE SUBJUNCTIVE*
I am speaking, etc.*	*I was speaking, etc.**		*I will be speaking, etc.**
esté hablando	estuviera hablando	estuviese hablando	estuviere hablando
estés hablando	estuvieras hablando	estuvieses hablando	estuvieres hablando
esté hablando	estuviera hablando	estuviese hablando	estuviere hablando
estemos hablando	estuviéramos hablando _or_	estuviésemos hablando	estuviéremos hablando
estéis hablando	estuvierais hablando	estuvieseis hablando	estuviereis hablando
estén hablando	estuvieran hablando	estuviesen hablando	estuvieren hablando

FORMAS IMPERATIVAS, GERUNDIOS Y PARTICIPIO
COMMANDS AND PARTICIPLES

FORMAS IMPERATIVAS *COMMANDS*		GERUNDIO Y PARTICIPIO *PARTICIPLES*		
AFIRMATIVA *AFFIRMATIVE*	NEGATIVA *NEGATIVE*	GERUNDIO SIMPLE *PRESENT PARTICIPLE*	PARTICIPIO *PAST PARTICIPLE*	GERUNDIO COMPUESTO *PERFECT PARTICIPLE*
be speaking	*don't be speaking*	*being speaking*	*been speaking*	*having been speaking*
está hablando (tú)	no estés hablando (tú)	estando hablando	estado hablando	habiendo estado hablando
esté hablando (Ud.)	no esté hablando (Ud.)			
estad hablando (vosotros)	no estéis hablando (vosotros)			
estén hablando (Uds.)	no estén hablando (Uds.)			
let's be speaking	*let's not be speaking*			
estemos hablando	no estemos hablando			

INFINITIVO COMPUESTO: haber estado hablando
PERFECT INFINITIVE: to have been speaking

TIEMPOS COMPUESTOS
PERFECT (COMPOUND) TENSES

PRETÉRITO PERFECTO DE INDICATIVO *PRESENT PERFECT INDICATIVE*	PRETÉRITO PLUSCUAMPERFECTO DE INDICATIVO *PAST PERFECT (PLUPERFECT) INDICATIVE*	PRETÉRITO ANTERIOR DE INDICATIVO *PRETERITE PERFECT INDICATIVE*	FUTURO PERFECTO DE INDICATIVO *FUTURE PERFECT INDICATIVE*	POTENCIAL COMPUESTO *CONDITIONAL PERFECT*
I have been speaking, etc.	*I had been speaking, etc.*	*I had been speaking, etc.*	*I will have been speaking, etc.**	*I would have been speaking, etc.**
he estado hablando	había estado hablando	hube estado hablando	habré estado hablando	habría estado hablando
has estado hablando	habías estado hablando	hubiste estado hablando	habrás estado hablando	habrías estado hablando
ha estado hablando	había estado hablando	hubo estado hablando	habrá estado hablando	habría estado hablando
hemos estado hablando	habíamos estado hablando	hubimos estado hablando	habremos estado hablando	habríamos estado hablando
habéis estado hablando	habíais estado hablando	hubisteis estado hablando	habréis estado hablando	habríais estado hablando
han estado hablando	habían estado hablando	hubieron estado hablando	habrán estado hablando	habrían estado hablando

PRETÉRITO PERFECTO DE SUBJUNTIVO *PRESENT PERFECT SUBJUNCTIVE*	PRETÉRITO PLUSCUAMPERFECTO DE SUBJUNTIVO *PAST PERFECT (PLUPERFECT) SUBJUNCTIVE*		FUTURO PERFECTO DE SUBJUNTIVO *FUTURE PERFECT SUBJUNCTIVE*
I have been speaking, etc.*	*I had been speaking, etc.**		*I will have been speaking, etc.**
haya estado hablando	hubiera estado hablando	hubiese estado hablando	hubiere estado hablando
hayas estado hablando	hubieras estado hablando	hubieses estado hablando	hubieres estado hablando
haya estado hablando	hubiera estado hablando	hubiese estado hablando	hubiere estado hablando
hayamos estado hablando	hubiéramos estado hablando _or_	hubiésemos estado hablando	hubiéremos estado hablando
hayáis estado hablando	hubierais estado hablando	hubieseis estado hablando	hubiereis estado hablando
hayan estado hablando	hubieran estado hablando	hubiesen estado hablando	hubieren estado hablando

*For additional translation possibilities see chart A.

IV. Regular verbs

5

VERBS OF THIS CATEGORY

Any nonreflexive Spanish verb that is used in a progressive form follows this model for its progressive aspect. See the model verb indicated by the reference number following any infinitive in this book for the present participle to use with the appropriate form of **estar** (87) to form the progressive.

6 Progressive tenses, reflexive verbs } model: ESTAR LAVÁNDOSE

TIEMPOS SIMPLES
SIMPLE TENSES

PRESENTE DE INDICATIVO *PRESENT INDICATIVE*	PRETÉRITO IMPERFECTO DE INDICATIVO *IMPERFECT INDICATIVE*	PRETÉRITO INDEFINIDO DE INDICATIVO *PRETERITE INDICATIVE*	FUTURO IMPERFECTO DE INDICATIVO *FUTURE INDICATIVE*	POTENCIAL SIMPLE *CONDITIONAL*
*I am washing myself, etc.**	*I was washing myself, etc.**	*I was washing myself, etc.**	*I will be washing myself, etc.**	*I would be washing myself, etc.**
estoy lavándome	estaba lavándome	estuve lavándome	estaré lavándome	estaría lavándome
estás lavándote	estabas lavándote	estuviste lavándote	estarás lavándote	estarías lavándote
está lavándose	estaba lavándose	estuvo lavándose	estará lavándose	estaría lavándose
estamos lavándonos	estábamos lavándonos	estuvimos lavándonos	estaremos lavándonos	estaríamos lavándonos
estáis lavándoos	estabais lavándoos	estuvisteis lavándoos	estaréis lavándoos	estaríais lavándoos
están lavándose	estaban lavándose	estuvieron lavándose	estarán lavándose	estarían lavándose

PRESENTE DE SUBJUNTIVO *PRESENT SUBJUNCTIVE*	PRETÉRITO IMPERFECTO DE SUBJUNTIVO *PAST (IMPERFECT) SUBJUNCTIVE*		FUTURO IMPERFECTO DE SUBJUNTIVO *FUTURE SUBJUNCTIVE*
*I am washing myself, etc.**	*I was washing myself, etc.**		*I will be washing myself, etc.**
esté lavándome	estuviera lavándome	estuviese lavándome	estuviere lavándome
estés lavándote	estuvieras lavándote	estuvieses lavándote	estuvieres lavándote
esté lavándose	estuviera lavándose	estuviese lavándose	estuviere lavándose
estemos lavándonos	estuviéramos lavándonos *or*	estuviésemos lavándonos	estuviéremos lavándonos
estéis lavándoos	estuvierais lavándoos	estuvieseis lavándoos	estuviereis lavándoos
estén lavándose	estuvieran lavándose	estuviesen lavándose	estuvieren lavándose

FORMAS IMPERATIVAS, GERUNDIOS Y PARTICIPIO
COMMANDS AND PARTICIPLES

FORMAS IMPERATIVAS *COMMANDS*		GERUNDIO Y PARTICIPIO *PARTICIPLES*		
AFIRMATIVA *AFFIRMATIVE*	NEGATIVA *NEGATIVE*	GERUNDIO SIMPLE *PRESENT PARTICIPLE*	PARTICIPIO *PAST PARTICIPLE*	GERUNDIO COMPUESTO *PERFECT PARTICIPLE*
be washing yourself; *be washing yourselves*	*don't be washing yourself;* *don't be washing yourselves*	*being washing myself, etc.*	*been washing myself, etc.*	*having been washing myself, etc.*
estate lavando (tú)	no te estés lavando (tú)	estando lavándome	estado lavándome	habiendo estado lavándome
estese lavando (Ud.)	no se esté lavando (Ud.)	estando lavándote	estado lavándote	habiendo estado lavándote
estaos+ lavando (vosotros)	no os estéis lavando (vosotros)	estando lavándose	estado lavándose	habiendo estado lavándose
estense lavando (Uds.)	no se estén lavando (Uds.)	estando lavándonos	estado lavándonos	habiendo estado lavándonos
		estando lavándoos	estado lavándoos	habiendo estado lavándoos
let's be washing ourselves	*let's not be washing ourselves*	estando lavándose	estado lavándose	habiendo estado lavándose
estémonos† lavando	no nos estemos lavando			

INFINITIVO COMPUESTO: haber estado lavándose
PERFECT INFINITIVE: to have been washing oneself

TIEMPOS COMPUESTOS
PERFECT (COMPOUND) TENSES

PRETÉRITO PERFECTO DE INDICATIVO *PRESENT PERFECT INDICATIVE*	PRETÉRITO PLUSCUAMPERFECTO DE INDICATIVO *PAST PERFECT (PLUPERFECT) INDICATIVE*	PRETÉRITO ANTERIOR DE INDICATIVO *PRETERITE PERFECT INDICATIVE*	FUTURO PERFECTO DE INDICATIVO *FUTURE PERFECT INDICATIVE*	POTENCIAL COMPUESTO *CONDITIONAL PERFECT*
I have been washing myself, etc.	*I had been washing myself, etc.*	*I had been washing myself, etc.*	*I will have been washing myself, etc.**	*I would have been washing myself, etc.**
he estado lavándome	había estado lavándome	hube estado lavándome	habré estado lavándome	habría estado lavándome
has estado lavándote	habías estado lavándote	hubiste estado lavándote	habrás estado lavándote	habrías estado lavándote
ha estado lavándose	había estado lavándose	hubo estado lavándose	habrá estado lavándose	habría estado lavándose
hemos estado lavándonos	habíamos estado lavándonos	hubimos estado lavándonos	habremos estado lavándonos	habríamos estado lavándonos
habéis estado lavándoos	habíais estado lavándoos	hubisteis estado lavándoos	habréis estado lavándoos	habríais estado lavándoos
han estado lavándose	habían estado lavándose	hubieron estado lavándose	habrán estado lavándose	habrían estado lavándose

PRETÉRITO PERFECTO DE SUBJUNTIVO *PRESENT PERFECT SUBJUNCTIVE*	PRETÉRITO PLUSCUAMPERFECTO DE SUBJUNTIVO *PAST PERFECT (PLUPERFECT) SUBJUNCTIVE*		FUTURO PERFECTO DE SUBJUNTIVO *FUTURE PERFECT SUBJUNCTIVE*
*I have been washing myself, etc.**	*I had been washing myself, etc.**		*I will have been washing myself, etc.**
haya estado lavándome	hubiera estado lavándome	hubiese estado lavándome	hubiere estado lavándome
hayas estado lavándote	hubieras estado lavándote	hubieses estado lavándote	hubieres estado lavándote
haya estado lavándose	hubiera estado lavándose	hubiese estado lavándose	hubiere estado lavándose
hayamos estado lavándonos	hubiéramos estado lavándonos *or*	hubiésemos estado lavándonos	hubiéremos estado lavándonos
hayáis estado lavándoos	hubierais estado lavándoos	hubieseis estado lavándoos	hubiereis estado lavándoos
hayan estado lavándose	hubieran estado lavándose	hubiesen estado lavándose	hubieren estado lavándose

*For additional translation possibilities see chart A.
+Note the dropping of the -d of the affirmative vosotros command when the reflexive pronoun os is attached.
†Note the dropping of the -s of the affirmative nosotros command when the reflexive pronoun nos is attached.

6

IV. Regular verbs

Any reflexive Spanish verb that is used in a progressive form follows this model for its progressive aspect. See the model verb indicated by the reference number following any infinitive in this book for the present participle to use with the appropriate form of **estar** (87) to form the progressive.

7 Passive voice } model: SER AMADO

TIEMPOS SIMPLES
SIMPLE TENSES

PRESENTE DE INDICATIVO *PRESENT INDICATIVE*	PRETÉRITO IMPERFECTO DE INDICATIVO *IMPERFECT INDICATIVE*	PRETÉRITO INDEFINIDO DE INDICATIVO *PRETERITE INDICATIVE*	FUTURO IMPERFECTO DE INDICATIVO *FUTURE INDICATIVE*	POTENCIAL SIMPLE *CONDITIONAL*
*I am loved, etc.**	*I was loved, etc.**	*I was loved, etc.**	*I will be loved, etc.**	*I would be loved, etc.**
soy amado (amada)	era amado (amada)	fui amado (amada)	seré amado (amada)	sería amado (amada)
eres amado (amada)	eras amado (amada)	fuiste amado (amada)	serás amado (amada)	serías amado (amada)
es amado (amada)	era amado (amada)	fue amado (amada)	será amado (amada)	sería amado (amada)
somos amados (amadas)	éramos amados (amadas)	fuimos amados (amadas)	seremos amados (amadas)	seríamos amados (amadas)
sois amados (amadas)	erais amados (amadas)	fuisteis amados (amadas)	seréis amados (amadas)	seríais amados (amadas)
son amados (amadas)	eran amados (amadas)	fueron amados (amadas)	serán amados (amadas)	serían amados (amadas)

PRESENTE DE SUBJUNTIVO *PRESENT SUBJUNCTIVE*	PRETÉRITO IMPERFECTO DE SUBJUNTIVO *PAST (IMPERFECT) SUBJUNCTIVE*		FUTURO IMPERFECTO DE SUBJUNTIVO *FUTURE SUBJUNCTIVE*
*I am loved, etc.**	*I was loved, etc.**		*I will be loved, etc.**
sea amado (amada)	fuera amado (amada)	fuese amado (amada)	fuere amado (amada)
seas amado (amada)	fueras amado (amada)	fueses amado (amada)	fueres amado (amada)
sea amado (amada)	fuera amado (amada)	fuese amado (amada)	fuere amado (amada)
seamos amados (amadas)	fuéramos amados (amadas) _or_	fuésemos amados (amadas)	fuéremos amados (amadas)
seáis amados (amadas)	fuerais amados (amadas)	fueseis amados (amadas)	fuereis amados (amadas)
sean amados (amadas)	fueran amados (amadas)	fuesen amados (amadas)	fueren amados (amadas)

FORMAS IMPERATIVAS, GERUNDIOS Y PARTICIPIO
COMMANDS AND PARTICIPLES

FORMAS IMPERATIVAS *COMMANDS*		GERUNDIO Y PARTICIPIO *PARTICIPLES*		
AFIRMATIVA *AFFIRMATIVE*	NEGATIVA *NEGATIVE*	GERUNDIO SIMPLE *PRESENT PARTICIPLE*	PARTICIPIO *PAST PARTICIPLE*	GERUNDIO COMPUESTO *PERFECT PARTICIPLE*
be loved	*don't be loved*	*being loved*	*been loved*	*having been loved*
sé amado (amada) (tú)	no seas amado (amada) (tú)	siendo amado (amada, amados, amadas)	sido amado (amada, amados, amados)	habiendo sido amado (amada, amados, amadas)
sea amado (amada) (Ud.)	no sea amado (amada) (Ud.)			
sed amados (amadas)	no seáis amados (amadas)			
sean amados (amadas) (Uds.)	no sean amados (amadas) (Uds.)			
let's be loved	*let's not be loved*			
seamos amados (amadas)	no seamos amados (amadas)			

INFINITIVO COMPUESTO: haber sido amado (amada, amados, amadas)
PERFECT INFINITIVE: to have been loved

TIEMPOS COMPUESTOS
PERFECT (COMPOUND) TENSES

PRETÉRITO PERFECTO DE INDICATIVO *PRESENT PERFECT INDICATIVE*	PRETÉRITO PLUSCUAMPERFECTO DE INDICATIVO *PAST PERFECT (PLUPERFECT) INDICATIVE*	PRETÉRITO ANTERIOR DE INDICATIVO *PRETERITE PERFECT INDICATIVE*	FUTURO PERFECTO DE INDICATIVO *FUTURE PERFECT INDICATIVE*	POTENCIAL COMPUESTO *CONDITIONAL PERFECT*
I have been loved, etc.	*I had been loved, etc.*	*I had been loved, etc.*	*I will have been loved, etc.**	*I would have been loved, etc.**
he sido amado (amada)	había sido amado (amada)	hube sido amado (amada)	habré sido amado (amada)	habría sido amado (amada)
has sido amado (amada)	habías sido amado (amada)	hubiste sido amado (amada)	habrás sido amado (amada)	habrías sido amado (amada)
ha sido amado (amada)	había sido amado (amada)	hubo sido amado (amada)	habrá sido amado (amada)	habría sido amado (amada)
hemos sido amados (amadas)	habíamos sido amados (amadas)	hubimos sido amados (amadas)	habremos sido amados (amadas)	habríamos sido amados (amadas)
habéis sido amados (amadas)	habíais sido amados (amadas)	hubisteis sido amados (amadas)	habréis sido amados (amadas)	habríais sido amados (amadas)
han sido amados (amadas)	habían sido amados (amadas)	hubieron sido amados (amadas)	habrán sido amados (amadas)	habrían sido amados (amadas)

PRETÉRITO PERFECTO DE SUBJUNTIVO *PRESENT PERFECT SUBJUNCTIVE*	PRETÉRITO PLUSCUAMPERFECTO DE SUBJUNTIVO *PAST PERFECT (PLUPERFECT) SUBJUNCTIVE*		FUTURO PERFECTO DE SUBJUNTIVO *FUTURE PERFECT SUBJUNCTIVE*
*I have been loved, etc.**	*I had been loved, etc.**		*I will have been loved, etc.**
haya sido amado (amada)	hubiera sido amado (amada) _or_	hubiese sido amado (amada)	hubiere sido amado (amada)
hayas sido amado (amada)	hubieras sido amado (amada)	hubieses sido amado (amada)	hubieres sido amado (amada)
haya sido amado (amada)	hubiera sido amado (amada)	hubiese sido amado (amada)	hubiere sido amado (amada)
hayamos sido amados (amadas)	hubiéramos sido amados (amadas)	hubiésemos sido amados (amadas)	hubiéremos sido amados (amadas)
hayáis sido amados (amadas)	hubierais sido amados (amadas)	hubieseis sido amados (amadas)	hubiereis sido amados (amadas)
hayan sido amados (amadas)	hubieran sido amados (amadas)	hubiesen sido amados (amadas)	hubieren sido amados (amadas)

For additional translation possibilities see chart A.

7

IV. Regular verbs

Any Spanish verb that is used in the passive follows this model for its passive aspect. See the model verb indicated by the reference number following any infinitive in this book for the past participle to use with the appropriate form of **ser** (107) to form the passive.

8 Verbs ending in -car } model: TOCAR

TIEMPOS SIMPLES
SIMPLE TENSES

PRESENTE DE INDICATIVO *PRESENT INDICATIVE*	PRETÉRITO IMPERFECTO DE INDICATIVO *IMPERFECT INDICATIVE*	PRETÉRITO INDEFINIDO DE INDICATIVO *PRETERITE INDICATIVE*	FUTURO IMPERFECTO DE INDICATIVO *FUTURE INDICATIVE*	POTENCIAL SIMPLE *CONDITIONAL*
I touch, etc. *	*I was touching, etc.* *	*I touched, etc.* *	*I will touch, etc.* *	*I would touch, etc.* *
toco $^+$	tocaba	toqué	tocaré	tocaría
tocas $^+$	tocabas	tocaste	tocarás	tocarías
toca $^+$	tocaba	tocó	tocará	tocaría
tocamos	tocábamos	tocamos	tocaremos	tocaríamos
tocáis	tocabais	tocasteis	tocaréis	tocaríais
tocan $^+$	tocaban	tocaron	tocarán	tocarían

PRESENTE DE SUBJUNTIVO *PRESENT SUBJUNCTIVE*	PRETÉRITO IMPERFECTO DE SUBJUNTIVO *PAST (IMPERFECT) SUBJUNCTIVE*		FUTURO IMPERFECTO DE SUBJUNTIVO *FUTURE SUBJUNCTIVE*
I touch, etc. *	*I touched, etc.* *		*I will touch, etc.* *
toque $^+$	tocara	tocase	tocare
toques $^+$	tocaras	tocases	tocares
toque $^+$	tocara	tocase	tocare
toquemos	tocáramos _or_	tocásemos	tocáremos
toquéis	tocarais	tocaseis	tocareis
toquen $^+$	tocaran	tocasen	tocaren

FORMAS IMPERATIVAS, GERUNDIOS Y PARTICIPIO
COMMANDS AND PARTICIPLES

FORMAS IMPERATIVAS *COMMANDS*		GERUNDIO Y PARTICIPIO *PARTICIPLES*		
AFIRMATIVA *AFFIRMATIVE*	NEGATIVA *NEGATIVE*	GERUNDIO SIMPLE *PRESENT PARTICIPLE*	PARTICIPIO *PAST PARTICIPLE*	GERUNDIO COMPUESTO *PERFECT PARTICIPLE*
touch	*don't touch*	*touching*	*touched*	*having touched*
toca $^+$ (tú)	no toques $^+$ (tú)	tocando	tocado	habiendo tocado
toque $^+$ (Ud.)	no toque $^+$ (Ud.)			
tocad (vosotros)	no toquéis (vosotros)			
toquen $^+$ (Uds.)	no toquen $^+$ (Uds.)			
let's touch	*let's not touch*			
toquemos	no toquemos			

INFINITIVO COMPUESTO: haber tocado
PERFECT INFINITIVE: to have touched

TIEMPOS COMPUESTOS
PERFECT (COMPOUND) TENSES

PRETÉRITO PERFECTO DE INDICATIVO *PRESENT PERFECT INDICATIVE*	PRETÉRITO PLUSCUAMPERFECTO DE INDICATIVO *PAST PERFECT (PLUPERFECT) INDICATIVE*	PRETÉRITO ANTERIOR DE INDICATIVO *PRETERITE PERFECT INDICATIVE*	FUTURO PERFECTO DE INDICATIVO *FUTURE PERFECT INDICATIVE*	POTENCIAL COMPUESTO *CONDITIONAL PERFECT*
I have touched, etc.	*I had touched, etc.*	*I had touched, etc.*	*I will have touched, etc.* *	*I would have touched, etc.* *
he tocado	había tocado	hube tocado	habré tocado	habría tocado
has tocado	habías tocado	hubiste tocado	habrás tocado	habrías tocado
ha tocado	había tocado	hubo tocado	habrá tocado	habría tocado
hemos tocado	habíamos tocado	hubimos tocado	habremos tocado	habríamos tocado
habéis tocado	habíais tocado	hubisteis tocado	habréis tocado	habríais tocado
han tocado	habían tocado	hubieron tocado	habrán tocado	habrían tocado

PRETÉRITO PERFECTO DE SUBJUNTIVO *PRESENT PERFECT SUBJUNCTIVE*	PRETÉRITO PLUSCUAMPERFECTO DE SUBJUNTIVO *PAST PERFECT (PLUPERFECT) SUBJUNCTIVE*		FUTURO PERFECTO DE SUBJUNTIVO *FUTURE PERFECT SUBJUNCTIVE*
I have touched, etc. *	*I had touched, etc.* *		*I will have touched, etc.* *
haya tocado	hubiera tocado	hubiese tocado	hubiere tocado
hayas tocado	hubieras tocado	hubieses tocado	hubieres tocado
haya tocado	hubiera tocado	hubiese tocado	hubiere tocado
hayamos tocado	hubiéramos tocado _or_	hubiésemos tocado	hubiéremos tocado
hayáis tocado	hubierais tocado	hubieseis tocado	hubiereis tocado
hayan tocado	hubieran tocado	hubiesen tocado	hubieren tocado

*For additional translation possibilities see chart A.
$^+$In these forms ahincar has a written accent on the i. (See 34.)

V. Orthographic/spelling changing verbs

8

VERBS OF THIS CATEGORY

abanicar
abarcar
abdicar
abellacar
abellacarse 4. (R)
abocar
aborrascarse 4. (R)
acercar
acercarse 4. (R)
acidificar
*aclocarse (ue) 44. (RC), 4. (R)
acorrucarse 4. (R)
acurrucar
acurrucarse 4. (R)
achacar
achicar
afincar
afoscarse 4. (R)
ahincar 34. (OC) (see footnote
    on opposite page)
ahocicar
ahorcar
ahuecar
alambicar
alfeñicarse 4. (R)
altercar
amoscarse 4. (R)
amplificar
amurcar
añascar
apalancar
aparcar
aplacar
aplicar
aplicarse 4. (R)
apocar
apriscar
arcar
arrancar
atacar
atascar
atascarse 4. (R)
atracar
atracarse 4. (R)
atrancar
atrancarse 4. (R)
autenticar
becar
bifurcar
bilocar
bisecar
brincar
buscar
caducar
calcar

calcificar
calificar
cascar
centuplicar
cercar
certificar
clarificar
clasificar
claudicar
*clocar (ue) 44. (RC)
codificar
colocar
colocarse 4. (R)
comarcar
complicar
complicarse 4. (R)
comunicar
comunicarse 4. (R)
conculcar
confiscar
contraatacar
contramarcar
convocar
criticar
crucificar
cuadruplicar
cubicar
chamuscar
chancar
chascar
chascarse 4. (R)
chocar
churruscarse 4. (R)
decuplicar
dedicar
dedicarse 4. (R)
defecar
deificar
demarcar
deprecar
derrocar or *derrocar (ue) 44. (RC)
desatascar
desatrancar
desbocarse 4. (R)
desecar
desedificar
desembarcar
desembarrancar
desembocar
desempacar
desenroscar
desfalcar
desnucar
despotricar
destacar

destacarse 4. (R)
diagnosticar
dignificar
dignificarse 4. (R)
disecar
dislocar
diversificar
domesticar
dosificar
dulcificar
duplicar
edificar
educar
ejemplificar
elastificar
electrificar
embarcar
embarrancarse
embaucar
emboscar
empacar
*emporcar (ue) 44. (RC)
*emporcarse (ue) 44. (RC), 4.
    (R)
encharcar
enfocar
enfrascarse 4. (R)
enmarcar
enroscar
ensacar
entresacar
entroncar
equivocar
equivocarse 4. (R)
erradicar
escenificar
especificar
estancar
estancarse 4. (R)
estratificar
evocar
explicar
fabricar
falsificar
fornicar
fortificar
fructificar
gasificar
glorificar
gratificar
hincar
hincarse 4. (R)
hocicar
identificar
implicar

imprecar
incomunicar
inculcar
indicar
intensificar
intoxicar
intrincar
invocar
justificar
lubricar
machacar
machucar
magnificar
mancar
manducar
marcar
mascar
masticar
mercar
modificar
molificar
momificar
mordiscar
mortificar
multiplicar
neviscar
notificar
ofuscar
opacar
opacarse 4. (R)
osificar
pacificar
pacificarse 4. (R)
panificar
pecar
pellizcar
perjudicar
personificar
pescar
petrificar
picar
picarse 4. (R)
pizcar
planificar
plantificar
platicar
pontificar
practicar
predicar
prefabricar
prevaricar
pronosticar
provocar
publicar
purificar
(continued)

R = Reflexive
OC = Orthographic/Spelling Change
RC = Radical/Stem Change
*These verbs have radical/stem changes in addition to the orthographic/spelling changes exemplified by the model verb on the chart given here. The cross reference number following each verb indicates the chart which shows all changes together.

8 Verbs ending } model:
in -car } TOCAR

radicar
radicarse 4. (R)
ramificar
rarificar
rascar
ratificar
rebuscar
recalcar
reciprocar
rectificar
reedificar
reeducar
reembarcar
reempacar
refrescar
reivindicar
remarcar
remolcar
repicar
replicar
resecar
retocar
retrucar
revocar
*revolcar (ue), 44. (RC)
*revolcarse (ue) 44. (RC), 4. (R)
roncar
rubricar
sacar
sacrificar
salpicar
santificar
secar
significar
simplificar
sindicar
sindicarse 4. (R)
sofocar
solidificar
sonsacar
suplicar
surcar
tabicar
testificar
tocar
tonificar
trabucarse 4. (R)
traficar
trastocar
*trastrocar (ue) 44. (RC)
trifurcar
trincar
triplicar
trisecar
*trocar (ue) 44. (RC)
*trocarse (ue) 44. (RC), 4. (R)

trompicar
truncar
ubicar
ubicarse 4. (R)
unificar
unificarse 4. (R)
vacar
ventiscar
verificar
versificar
vindicar
vitrificar
*volcar (ue) 44. (RC)
zulacar

R = Reflexive
RC = Radical/Stem Change
*These verbs have radical/stem changes in addition to the orthographic/spelling changes exemplified by the model verb on the chart given here. The cross reference number following each verb indicates the chart which shows all changes together.

9 Verbs ending in -gar } model: PAGAR

TIEMPOS SIMPLES
SIMPLE TENSES

PRESENTE DE INDICATIVO *PRESENT INDICATIVE*	PRETÉRITO IMPERFECTO DE INDICATIVO *IMPERFECT INDICATIVE*	PRETÉRITO INDEFINIDO DE INDICATIVO *PRETERITE INDICATIVE*	FUTURO IMPERFECTO DE INDICATIVO *FUTURE INDICATIVE*	POTENCIAL SIMPLE *CONDITIONAL*
*I pay, etc.**	*I was paying, etc.**	*I paid, etc.**	*I will pay, etc.**	*I would pay, etc.**
pago	pagaba	pagué	pagaré	pagaría
pagas	pagabas	pagaste	pagarás	pagarías
paga	pagaba	pagó	pagará	pagaría
pagamos	pagábamos	pagamos	pagaremos	pagaríamos
pagáis	pagabais	pagasteis	pagaréis	pagaríais
pagan	pagaban	pagaron	pagarán	pagarían

PRESENTE DE SUBJUNTIVO *PRESENT SUBJUNCTIVE*	PRETÉRITO IMPERFECTO DE SUBJUNTIVO *PAST (IMPERFECT) SUBJUNCTIVE*		FUTURO IMPERFECTO DE SUBJUNTIVO *FUTURE SUBJUNCTIVE*
*I pay, etc.**	*I paid, etc.**		*I will pay, etc.**
pague	pagara	pagase	pagare
pagues	pagaras	pagases	pagares
pague	pagara	pagase	pagare
paguemos	pagáramos *or* pagásemos		pagáremos
paguéis	pagarais	pagaseis	pagareis
paguen	pagaran	pagasen	pagaren

FORMAS IMPERATIVAS, GERUNDIOS Y PARTICIPIO
COMMANDS AND PARTICIPLES

FORMAS IMPERATIVAS *COMMANDS*		GERUNDIO Y PARTICIPIO *PARTICIPLES*		
AFIRMATIVA *AFFIRMATIVE*	NEGATIVA *NEGATIVE*	GERUNDIO SIMPLE *PRESENT PARTICIPLE*	PARTICIPIO *PAST PARTICIPLE*	GERUNDIO COMPUESTO *PERFECT PARTICIPLE*
pay	*don't pay*	*paying*	*paid*	*having paid*
paga (tú)	no pagues (tú)	pagando	pagado	habiendo pagado
pague (Ud.)	no pague (Ud.)			
pagad (vosotros)	no paguéis (vosotros)			
paguen (Uds.)	no paguen (Uds.)			
let's pay	*let's not pay*			
paguemos	no paguemos			

INFINITIVO COMPUESTO: haber pagado
PERFECT INFINITIVE: to have paid

TIEMPOS COMPUESTOS
PERFECT (COMPOUND) TENSES

PRETÉRITO PERFECTO DE INDICATIVO *PRESENT PERFECT INDICATIVE*	PRETÉRITO PLUSCUAMPERFECTO DE INDICATIVO *PAST PERFECT (PLUPERFECT) INDICATIVE*	PRETÉRITO ANTERIOR DE INDICATIVO *PRETERITE PERFECT INDICATIVE*	FUTURO PERFECTO DE INDICATIVO *FUTURE PERFECT INDICATIVE*	POTENCIAL COMPUESTO *CONDITIONAL PERFECT*
I have paid, etc.	*I had paid, etc.*	*I had paid, etc.*	*I will have paid, etc.**	*I would have paid, etc.**
he pagado	había pagado	hube pagado	habré pagado	habría pagado
has pagado	habías pagado	hubiste pagado	habrás pagado	habrías pagado
ha pagado	había pagado	hubo pagado	habrá pagado	habría pagado
hemos pagado	habíamos pagado	hubimos pagado	habremos pagado	habríamos pagado
habéis pagado	habíais pagado	hubisteis pagado	habréis pagado	habríais pagado
han pagado	habían pagado	hubieron pagado	habrán pagado	habrían pagado

PRETÉRITO PERFECTO DE SUBJUNTIVO *PRESENT PERFECT SUBJUNCTIVE*	PRETÉRITO PLUSCUAMPERFECTO DE SUBJUNTIVO *PAST PERFECT (PLUPERFECT) SUBJUNCTIVE*		FUTURO PERFECTO DE SUBJUNTIVO *FUTURE PERFECT SUBJUNCTIVE*	
*I have paid, etc.**	*I had paid, etc.**		*I will have paid, etc.**	
haya pagado	hubiera pagado	hubiese pagado	hubiere pagado	
hayas pagado	hubieras pagado	hubieses pagado	hubieres pagado	
haya pagado	hubiera pagado	hubiese pagado	hubiere pagado	
hayamos pagado	hubiéramos pagado *or* hubiésemos pagado		hubiéremos pagado	
hayáis pagado	hubierais pagado	hubieseis pagado	hubiereis pagado	
hayan pagado	hubieran pagado	hubiesen pagado	hubieren pagado	

*For additional translation possibilities see chart A.

9

V. Orthographic/spelling changing verbs

VERBS OF THIS CATEGORY

*abnegar (ie) 50. (RC)
abogar
abrigar
abrigarse 4. (R)
abrogar
adargar
agregar
agregarse 4. (R)
ahogar
ahogarse 4. (R)
alargar
alargarse 4. (R)
albergar
albergarse 4. (R)
alegar
aletargar
aletargarse 4. (R)
alongar
allegar
allegarse 4. (R)
amagar
amargar
amargarse 4. (R)
amelgar
amusgar
*anegar (ie) 50. (RC)
antepagar
añusgar
apagar
apegarse 4. (R)
arengar
arraigar
arremangar
arremangarse 4. (R)
arrezagar
arriesgar
arriesgarse 4. (R)
*asosegar (ie) 50. (RC)
atarugar
atarugarse 4. (R)
atosigar
bogar
bregar
cabalgar
cagar
cargar
castigar
*cegar (ie) 50. (RC)
*cegarse (ie) 50. (RC), 4. (R)
centrifugar
circunnavegar
*colgar (ue) 45. (RC)
coligarse 4. (R)
comulgar
congregar

conjugar
corrugar
chungar
delegar
*denegar (ie) 50. (RC)
derogar
*derrengar (ie) 50. (RC)
desabrigar
desahogar
desahogarse 4. (R)
desarraigar
desarrugar
*desasosegar (ie) 50. (RC)
*desasosegarse (ie) 50. (RC), 4.
    (R)
descabalgar
descargar
*descolgar (ue) 45. (RC)
*descolgarse (ue) 45. (RC), 4.
    (R)
desembargar
desembragar
desfogarse 4. (R)
desligar
despegar
despegarse 4. (R)
desperdigar
*desplegar (ie) 50. (RC)
dialogar
disgregar
divagar
divulgar
divulgarse 4. (R)
doblegar
dragar
drogar
embargar
embodegar
embragar
embriagar
embriagarse 4. (R)
empalagar
encargar
endomingarse 4. (R)
enfangar
enfangarse 4. (R)
engringarse 4. (R)
enjabelgar
enjuagar
enjugar
entregar
entregarse 4. (R)
epilogar
espigar
espigarse 4. (R)

excomulgar
expurgar
fatigar
fatigarse 4. (R)
fisgar
*fregar (ie) 50. (RC)
fugarse 4. (R)
fumigar
fustigar
halagar
*holgar (ue) 45. (RC)
*holgarse (ue) 45. (RC)
homolgar
hostigar
hurgar
indagar
instigar
interrogar
intrigar
investigar
irrigar
jeringar
*jugar (ue) 93, (RC) (I)
*jugarse (ue) 93. (RC) (I), 4. (R)
juzgar
largar
largarse 4. (R)
legar
ligar
litigar
llegar
madrugar
mendigar
merengar
migar
mitigar
monologar
naufragar
navegar
*negar (ie) 50. (RC)
obligar
obligarse 4. (R)
otorgar
pagar
pegar
plagar
*plegar (ie) 50. (RC)
postergar
prejuzgar
pringar
prodigar
prologar
prolongar
promulgar
propagar

prorrogar
purgar
purgarse 4. (R)
rasgar
rasgarse 4. (R)
recargar
*refregar (ie) 50. (RC)
*regar (ie) 50. (RC)
relegar
remilgarse 4. (R)
*renegar (ie) 50. (RC)
repagar
repantigarse 4. (R)
*replegar (ie) 50. (RC)
*replegarse (ie) 50. (RC), 4. (R)
respigar
respingar
*restregar (ie) 50. (RC)
rezagar
rezagarse 4. (R)
rezongar
rodrigar
*rogar (ue) 45. (RC)
*segar (ie) 50. (RC)
segregar
sesgar
sobrecargar
sojuzgar
*sosegar (ie) 50. (RC)
*sosegarse (ie) 50. (RC), 4.
    (R)
subrogar
subyugar
sufragar
tosigar
tragar
*trasegar (ie) 50. (RC)
vagar
vengarse 4. (R)
zurriagar

R = Reflexive
RC = Radical/Stem Change
I = Irregular
*These verbs have irregularities and/or radical/stem changes in addition to the orthographic/spelling changes exemplified by the model verb on the chart given here. The cross reference number following each verb indicates the chart which shows all irregularities and/or changes together.

10 Verbs ending in -guar } model: AVERIGUAR

TIEMPOS SIMPLES
SIMPLE TENSES

PRESENTE DE INDICATIVO *PRESENT INDICATIVE*	PRETÉRITO IMPERFECTO DE INDICATIVO *IMPERFECT INDICATIVE*	PRETÉRITO INDEFINIDO DE INDICATIVO *PRETERITE INDICATIVE*	FUTURO IMPERFECTO DE INDICATIVO *FUTURE INDICATIVE*	POTENCIAL SIMPLE *CONDITIONAL*
*I find out, etc.**	*I was finding out, etc.**	*I found out, etc.**	*I will find out, etc.**	*I would find out, etc.**
averiguo	averiguaba	averigüé	averiguaré	averiguaría
averiguas	averiguabas	averiguaste	averiguarás	averiguarías
averigua	averiguaba	averiguó	averiguará	averiguaría
averiguamos	averiguábamos	averiguamos	averiguaremos	averiguaríamos
averiguáis	averiguabais	averiguasteis	averiguaréis	averiguaríais
averiguan	averiguaban	averiguaron	averiguarán	averiguarían

PRESENTE DE SUBJUNTIVO *PRESENT SUBJUNCTIVE*	PRETÉRITO IMPERFECTO DE SUBJUNTIVO *PAST (IMPERFECT) SUBJUNCTIVE*		FUTURO IMPERFECTO DE SUBJUNTIVO *FUTURE SUBJUNCTIVE*
*I find out, etc.**	*I found out, etc.**		*I will find out, etc.**
averigüe	averiguara	averiguase	averiguare
averigües	averiguaras	averiguases	averiguares
averigüe	averiguara	averiguase	averiguare
averigüemos	averiguáramos *or*	averiguásemos	averiguáremos
averigüéis	averiguarais	averiguaseis	averiguareis
averigüen	averiguaran	averiguasen	averiguaren

FORMAS IMPERATIVAS, GERUNDIOS Y PARTICIPIO
COMMANDS AND PARTICIPLES

FORMAS IMPERATIVAS *COMMANDS*		GERUNDIO Y PARTICIPIO *PARTICIPLES*		
AFIRMATIVA *AFFIRMATIVE*	NEGATIVA *NEGATIVE*	GERUNDIO SIMPLE *PRESENT PARTICIPLE*	PARTICIPIO *PAST PARTICIPLE*	GERUNDIO COMPUESTO *PERFECT PARTICIPLE*
find out	*don't find out*	*finding out*	*found out*	*having found out*
averigua (tú)	no averigües (tú)	averiguando	averiguado	habiendo averiguado
averigüe (Ud.)	no averigüe (Ud.)			
averiguad (vosotros)	no averigüéis (vosotros)			
averigüen (Uds.)	no averigüen (Uds.)			
let's find out	*let's not find out*			
averigüemos	no averigüemos			

INFINITIVO COMPUESTO: haber averiguado
PERFECT INFINITIVE: to have found out

TIEMPOS COMPUESTOS
PERFECT (COMPOUND) TENSES

PRETÉRITO PERFECTO DE INDICATIVO *PRESENT PERFECT INDICATIVE*	PRETÉRITO PLUSCUAMPERFECTO DE INDICATIVO *PAST PERFECT (PLUPERFECT) INDICATIVE*	PRETÉRITO ANTERIOR DE INDICATIVO *PRETERITE PERFECT INDICATIVE*	FUTURO PERFECTO DE INDICATIVO *FUTURE PERFECT INDICATIVE*	POTENCIAL COMPUESTO *CONDITIONAL PERFECT*
I have found out, etc.	*I had found out, etc.*	*I had found out, etc.*	*I will have found out, etc.**	*I would have found out, etc.**
he averiguado	había averiguado	hube averiguado	habré averiguado	habría averiguado
has averiguado	habías averiguado	hubiste averiguado	habrás averiguado	habrías averiguado
ha averiguado	había averiguado	hubo averiguado	habrá averiguado	habría averiguado
hemos averiguado	habíamos averiguado	hubimos averiguado	habremos averiguado	habríamos averiguado
habéis averiguado	habíais averiguado	hubisteis averiguado	habréis averiguado	habríais averiguado
han averiguado	habían averiguado	hubieron averiguado	habrán averiguado	habrían averiguado

PRETÉRITO PERFECTO DE SUBJUNTIVO *PRESENT PERFECT SUBJUNCTIVE*	PRETÉRITO PLUSCUAMPERFECTO DE SUBJUNTIVO *PAST PERFECT (PLUPERFECT) SUBJUNCTIVE*		FUTURO PERFECTO DE SUBJUNTIVO *FUTURE PERFECT SUBJUNCTIVE*
*I have found out, etc.**	*I had found out, etc.**		*I will have found out, etc.**
haya averiguado	hubiera averiguado	hubiese averiguado	hubiere averiguado
hayas averiguado	hubieras averiguado	hubieses averiguado	hubieres averiguado
haya averiguado	hubiera averiguado	hubiese averiguado	hubiere averiguado
hayamos averiguado	hubiéramos averiguado *or*	hubiésemos averiguado	hubiéremos averiguado
hayáis averiguado	hubierais averiguado	hubieseis averiguado	hubiereis averiguado
hayan averiguado	hubieran averiguado	hubiesen averiguado	hubieren averiguado

*For additional translation possibilities see chart A.

V. Orthographic/spelling changing verbs

VERBS OF THIS CATEGORY

aguar
amenguar
amortiguar
antiguarse 4. (R)
apaciguar
apaciguarse 4. (R)
atestiguar
averiguar
desaguar
fraguar
fraguarse 4. (R)
menguar
santiguar
santiguarse 4. (R)

R = Reflexive

11 Verbs ending in -zar } model: REZAR

TIEMPOS SIMPLES
SIMPLE TENSES

PRESENTE DE INDICATIVO **PRESENT INDICATIVE**	PRETÉRITO IMPERFECTO DE INDICATIVO **IMPERFECT INDICATIVE**	PRETÉRITO INDEFINIDO DE INDICATIVO **PRETERITE INDICATIVE**	FUTURO IMPERFECTO DE INDICATIVO **FUTURE INDICATIVE**	POTENCIAL SIMPLE **CONDITIONAL**
*I pray, etc. * *	*I was praying, etc.* *	*I prayed, etc.* *	*I will pray, etc.* *	*I would pray, etc.* *
rezo	rezaba	recé	rezaré	rezaría
rezas	rezabas	rezaste	rezarás	rezarías
reza	rezaba	rezó	rezará	rezaría
rezamos	rezábamos	rezamos	rezaremos	rezaríamos
rezáis	rezabais	rezasteis	rezaréis	rezaríais
rezan	rezaban	rezaron	rezarán	rezarían

PRESENTE DE SUBJUNTIVO **PRESENT SUBJUNCTIVE**	PRETÉRITO IMPERFECTO DE SUBJUNTIVO **PAST (IMPERFECT) SUBJUNCTIVE**		FUTURO IMPERFECTO DE SUBJUNTIVO **FUTURE SUBJUNCTIVE**
I pray, etc. *	*I prayed, etc.* *		*I will pray, etc.* *
rece	rezara	rezase	rezare
reces	rezaras	rezases	rezares
rece	rezara	rezase	rezare
recemos	rezáramos *or*	rezásemos	rezáremos
recéis	rezarais	rezaseis	rezareis
recen	rezaran	rezasen	rezaren

FORMAS IMPERATIVAS, GERUNDIOS Y PARTICIPIO
COMMANDS AND PARTICIPLES

FORMAS IMPERATIVAS **COMMANDS**		GERUNDIO Y PARTICIPIO **PARTICIPLES**		
AFIRMATIVA **AFFIRMATIVE**	NEGATIVA **NEGATIVE**	GERUNDIO SIMPLE **PRESENT PARTICIPLE**	PARTICIPIO **PAST PARTICIPLE**	GERUNDIO COMPUESTO **PERFECT PARTICIPLE**
pray	*don't pray*	*praying*	*prayed*	*having prayed*
reza (tú)	no reces (tú)	rezando	rezado	habiendo rezado
rece (Ud.)	no rece (Ud.)			
rezad (vosotros)	no recéis (vosotros)			
recen (Uds.)	no recen (Uds.)			
let's pray	*let's not pray*			
recemos	no recemos			

INFINITIVO COMPUESTO: haber rezado
PERFECT INFINITIVE: to have prayed

TIEMPOS COMPUESTOS
PERFECT (COMPOUND) TENSES

PRETÉRITO PERFECTO DE INDICATIVO **PRESENT PERFECT INDICATIVE**	PRETÉRITO PLUSCUAMPERFECTO DE INDICATIVO **PAST PERFECT (PLUPERFECT) INDICATIVE**	PRETÉRITO ANTERIOR DE INDICATIVO **PRETERITE PERFECT INDICATIVE**	FUTURO PERFECTO DE INDICATIVO **FUTURE PERFECT INDICATIVE**	POTENCIAL COMPUESTO **CONDITIONAL PERFECT**
I have prayed, etc.	*I had prayed, etc.*	*I had prayed, etc.*	*I will have prayed, etc.* *	*I would have prayed, etc.* *
he rezado	había rezado	hube rezado	habré rezado	habría rezado
has rezado	habías rezado	hubiste rezado	habrás rezado	habrías rezado
ha rezado	había rezado	hubo rezado	habrá rezado	habría rezado
hemos rezado	habíamos rezado	hubimos rezado	habremos rezado	habríamos rezado
habéis rezado	habíais rezado	hubisteis rezado	habréis rezado	habríais rezado
han rezado	habían rezado	hubieron rezado	habrán rezado	habrían rezado

PRETÉRITO PERFECTO DE SUBJUNTIVO **PRESENT PERFECT SUBJUNCTIVE**	PRETÉRITO PLUSCUAMPERFECTO DE SUBJUNTIVO **PAST PERFECT (PLUPERFECT) SUBJUNCTIVE**		FUTURO PERFECTO DE SUBJUNTIVO **FUTURE PERFECT SUBJUNCTIVE**
I have prayed, etc. *	*I had prayed, etc.* *		*I will have prayed, etc.* *
haya rezado	hubiera rezado	hubiese rezado	hubiere rezado
hayas rezado	hubieras rezado	hubieses rezado	hubieres rezado
haya rezado	hubiera rezado	hubiese rezado	hubiere rezado
hayamos rezado	hubiéramos rezado *or*	hubiésemos rezado	hubiéremos rezado
hayáis rezado	hubierais rezado	hubieseis rezado	hubiereis rezado
hayan rezado	hubieran rezado	hubiesen rezado	hubieren rezado

*For additional translation possibilities see chart A.

V. Orthographic/spelling changing verbs

VERBS OF THIS CATEGORY

abalanzar
abalanzarse 4. (R)
abrazar
academizar
academizarse 4. (R)
acapizarse 4. (R)
acezar
acorazar
acromatizar
acuatizar
adelgazar
adelgazarse 4. (R)
aderezar
adonizarse 4. (R)
adulzar
afianzar
agonizar
agudizar
agudizarse 4. (R)
aguzar
alborozar
alcanzar
alfabetizar
alforzar
*almorzar (ue) 46. (RC)
alzar
alzarse 4. (R)
amenazar
amenizar
americanizar
amordazar
amortazar
amortizar
amostazar
analizar
anarquizar
anatomizar
animalizar
antipatizar
apedazar
apelmazar
aplazar
apologizar
arabizar
atemorizar
atemorizarse 4. (R)
aterrizar
aterrorizar
atezarse 4. (R)
atizar
atomizar
autorizar
avanzar
*avergonzar (ue) 49 (RC)

*avergonzarse (ue) 49 (RC), 4.
    (R)
avezar
avezarse 4. (R)
azuzar
balizar
barnizar
bautizar
brutalizar
calzar
canalizar
canonizar
capitalizar
caracterizar
caramelizar
carbonizar
carduzar
caricaturizar
catequizar
cauterizar
cazar
cicatrizar
civilizar
cloroformizar
colectivizar
colectivizarse 4. (R)
colonizar
*comenzar (ie) 51. (RC)
comercializar
comunizar
comunizarse 4. (R)
confraternizar
connaturalizar
connaturalizarse 4. (R)
contemporizar
cotizar
cristalizar
cristianizar
cruzar
chapuzar
danzar
democratizar
desautorizar
desbrozar
descabezar
descalzar
descortezar
descuartizar
desembarazar
desembarazarse 4. (R)
desenlazar
desguazar
deshumanizar
deslizar

desmenuzar
desmilitarizar
desmoralizar
desmovilizar
desnaturalizar
desorganizar
despedazar
desperezarse 4. (R)
desplazar
desplazarse 4. (R)
despotizar
destrozar
desvalorizar
*desvergonzarse (ue) 49.
    (RC), 4. (R)
diafanizar
disfrazar
divinizar
dogmatizar
dramatizar
economizar
electrizar
electrizarse 4. (R)
electrolizar
elegantizar
embarazar
embarazarse 4. (R)
embozar
empalizar
*empezar (ie) 51. (RC)
emplazar
encabezar
encalabozar
encarnizar
encarnizarse 4. (R)
encauzar
encolerizar
encolerizarse 4. (R)
enderezar
endulzar
enfervorizar
enfervorizarse 4. (R)
engarzar
enjaezar
enlazar
enlodazar
**enraizar 64. (accent shift)
ensalzar
entrelazar
entronizar
enzarzarse 4. (R)
erizar
esbozar
escandalizar

escaramuzar
esclavizar
*esforzar (ue) 46. (RC)
*esforzarse (ue) 46. (RC), 4.
    (R)
espiritualizar
espolvorizar
esquematizar
estabilizar
estabilizarse 4. (R)
estandardizar
esterilizar
estigmatizar
estilizar
eternizar
eternizarse 4. (R)
evangelizar
evaporizar
exorcizar
exteriorizar
extranjerizarse 4. (R)
familiarizar
familiarizarse 4. (R)
fanatizar
fecundizar
fertilizar
finalizar
formalizar
*forzar (ue) 46. (RC)
fraternizar
galvanizar
garantizar
gargarizar
generalizar
generalizarse 4. (R)
gozar
granizar
guturalizar
hechizar
herborizar
hidrolizar
higienizar
hiperbolizar
hipnotizar
homogeneizar
homogenizar
horrorizar
horrorizarse 4. (R)
hospitalizar
hozar
humanizar
idealizar
impermeabilizar
impopularizar
    (continued)

R = Reflexive
RC = Radical/Stem Change
*These verbs have radical/stem changes in addition to the orthographic/spelling changes exemplified by the model verb on the chart given here. The cross reference number following each verb indicates the chart which shows all changes together.
**This verb has an accent shift in addition to the orthographic/spelling changes exemplified by the model verb on the chart given here. The cross reference number following the verb indicates the chart which shows all changes together.

11 Verbs ending in -zar } model: REZAR

impopularizarse 4. (R)
indemnizar
independizar
independizarse 4. (R)
individualizar
industrializar
industrializarse 4. (R)
inmortalizar
inmovilizar
inmunizar
insensibilizar
insensibilizarse 4. (R)
insonorizar
internacionalizar
intranquilizar
inutilizar
inutilizarse 4. (R)
ionizar
izar
laicizar
lanzar
lazar
legalizar
liberalizar
localizar
magnetizar
martirizar
materializar
materializarse 4. (R)
matizar
mecanizar
metalizarse 4. (R)
militarizar
modernizar
monopolizar
moralizar
motorizar
movilizar
nacionalizar
naturalizar
naturalizarse 4. (R)
neutralizar
nominalizar
normalizar
novelizar
obstaculizar
organizar
panegirizar
pantanizarse 4. (R)
paralizar
paralizarse 4. (R)
particularizar
particularizarse 4. (R)
pasterizar
pasteurizar

patentizar
personalizar
pluralizar
poetizar
polarizar
polemizar
polinizar
popularizar
popularizarse 4. (R)
pormenorizar
potabilizar
preconizar
profetizar
profundizar
profundizarse 4. (R)
proletarizar
psicoanalizar
pulverizar
puntualizar
punzar
racionalizar
realizar
realzar
rebozar
rechazar
reemplazar
*reforzar (ue) 46. (RC)
regularizar
remozar
reorganizar
retazar
retozar
revalorizar
revitalizar
rezar
ridiculizar
rivalizar
rizar
rozar
sabatizar
secularizar
sensibilizar
sicoanalizar
simbolizar
simpatizar
sincronizar
singularizar
sintetizar
sintonizar
sistematizar
sobrenaturalizar
socializar
solazar
solazarse 4. (R)
solemnizar

solidarizar
solidarizarse 4. (R)
sollozar
sonorizar
suavizar
sutilizar
tamizar
tapizar
temporalizar
temporizar
teorizar
totalizar
tranquilizar
trazar
trenzar
trizar
tronzar
*tropezar (ie) 51. (RC)
trozar
urbanizar
urbanizarse 4. (R)
utilizar
valorizar
vaporizar
vezar
vezarse 4. (R)
vigorizar
visualizar
vitalizar
vocalizar
volatilizar
volatilizarse 4. (R)
vulcanizar
vulgarizar
vulgarizarse 4. (R)

R = Reflexive
RC = Radical/Stem Change
*These verbs have radical/stem changes in addition to the orthographic/spelling changes exemplified by the model verb on the chart given here. The cross reference number following each verb indicates the chart which shows all changes together.

12 Verbs ending in -consonant + cer } model: VENCER

TIEMPOS SIMPLES
SIMPLE TENSES

PRESENTE DE INDICATIVO PRESENT INDICATIVE	PRETÉRITO IMPERFECTO DE INDICATIVO IMPERFECT INDICATIVE	PRETÉRITO INDEFINIDO DE INDICATIVO PRETERITE INDICATIVE	FUTURO IMPERFECTO DE INDICATIVO FUTURE INDICATIVE	POTENCIAL SIMPLE CONDITIONAL
*I defeat, etc.**	*I was defeating, etc.**	*I defeated, etc.**	*I will defeat, etc.**	*I would defeat, etc.**
venzo	vencía	vencí	venceré	vencería
vences	vencías	venciste	vencerás	vencerías
vence	vencía	venció	vencerá	vencería
vencemos	vencíamos	vencimos	venceremos	venceríamos
vencéis	vencíais	vencisteis	venceréis	venceríais
vencen	vencían	vencieron	vencerán	vencerían

PRESENTE DE SUBJUNTIVO PRESENT SUBJUNCTIVE	PRETÉRITO IMPERFECTO DE SUBJUNTIVO PAST (IMPERFECT) SUBJUNCTIVE		FUTURO IMPERFECTO DE SUBJUNTIVO FUTURE SUBJUNCTIVE
*I defeat, etc.**	*I defeated, etc.**		*I will defeat, etc.**
venza	venciera	venciese	venciere
venzas	vencieras	vencieses	vencieres
venza	venciera	venciese	venciere
venzamos	venciéramos *or*	venciésemos	venciéremos
venzáis	vencierais	vencieseis	venciereis
venzan	vencieran	venciesen	vencieren

FORMAS IMPERATIVAS, GERUNDIOS Y PARTICIPIO
COMMANDS AND PARTICIPLES

FORMAS IMPERATIVAS COMMANDS		GERUNDIO Y PARTICIPIO PARTICIPLES		
AFIRMATIVA AFFIRMATIVE	NEGATIVA NEGATIVE	GERUNDIO SIMPLE PRESENT PARTICIPLE	PARTICIPIO PAST PARTICIPLE	GERUNDIO COMPUESTO PERFECT PARTICIPLE
defeat	*don't defeat*	*defeating*	*defeated*	*having defeated*
vence (tú)	no venzas (tú)	venciendo	vencido	habiendo vencido
venza (Ud.)	no venza (Ud.)			
venced (vosotros)	no venzáis (vosotros)			
venzan (Uds.)	no venzan (Uds.)			
let's defeat	*let's not defeat*			
venzamos	no venzamos			

INFINITIVO COMPUESTO: haber vencido
PERFECT INFINITIVE: *to have defeated*

TIEMPOS COMPUESTOS
PERFECT (COMPOUND) TENSES

PRETÉRITO PERFECTO DE INDICATIVO PRESENT PERFECT INDICATIVE	PRETÉRITO PLUSCUAMPERFECTO DE INDICATIVO PAST PERFECT (PLUPERFECT) INDICATIVE	PRETÉRITO ANTERIOR DE INDICATIVO PRETERITE PERFECT INDICATIVE	FUTURO PERFECTO DE INDICATIVO FUTURE PERFECT INDICATIVE	POTENCIAL COMPUESTO CONDITIONAL PERFECT
I have defeated, etc.	*I had defeated, etc.*	*I had defeated, etc.*	*I will have defeated, etc.**	*I would have defeated, etc.**
he vencido	había vencido	hube vencido	habré vencido	habría vencido
has vencido	habías vencido	hubiste vencido	habrás vencido	habrías vencido
ha vencido	había vencido	hubo vencido	habrá vencido	habría vencido
hemos vencido	habíamos vencido	hubimos vencido	habremos vencido	habríamos vencido
habéis vencido	habíais vencido	hubisteis vencido	habréis vencido	habríais vencido
han vencido	habían vencido	hubieron vencido	habrán vencido	habrían vencido

PRETÉRITO PERFECTO DE SUBJUNTIVO PRESENT PERFECT SUBJUNCTIVE	PRETÉRITO PLUSCUAMPERFECTO DE SUBJUNTIVO PAST PERFECT (PLUPERFECT) SUBJUNCTIVE		FUTURO PERFECTO DE SUBJUNTIVO FUTURE PERFECT SUBJUNCTIVE
*I have defeated, etc.**	*I had defeated, etc.**		*I will have defeated, etc.**
haya vencido	hubiera vencido	hubiese vencido	hubiere vencido
hayas vencido	hubieras vencido	hubieses vencido	hubieres vencido
haya vencido	hubiera vencido	hubiese vencido	hubiere vencido
hayamos vencido	hubiéramos vencido *or*	hubiésemos vencido	hubiéremos vencido
hayáis vencido	hubierais vencido	hubieseis vencido	hubiereis vencido
hayan vencido	hubieran vencido	hubiesen vencido	hubieren vencido

*For additional translation possibilities see chart A.

V. Orthographic/spelling changing verbs

VERBS OF THIS CATEGORY

coercer
*contorcerse (ue) 53. (RC), 4. (R)
convencer
ejercer
*retorcer (ue) 53. (RC)
*torcer (ue) 53. (RC)
vencer
vencerse 4. (R)

R = Reflexive
RC = Radical/Stem Change
*These verbs have radical/stem changes in addition to the orthographic/spelling changes exemplified by the model verb on the chart given here. The cross reference number indicates the chart which shows all changes together.

13 Verbs ending in -consonant + cir } model: ESPARCIR

TIEMPOS SIMPLES
SIMPLE TENSES

PRESENTE DE INDICATIVO *PRESENT* *INDICATIVE*	PRETÉRITO IMPERFECTO DE INDICATIVO *IMPERFECT* *INDICATIVE*	PRETÉRITO INDEFINIDO DE INDICATIVO *PRETERITE* *INDICATIVE*	FUTURO IMPERFECTO DE INDICATIVO *FUTURE* *INDICATIVE*	POTENCIAL SIMPLE *CONDITIONAL*
I scatter, etc.*	*I was scattering, etc.**	*I scattered, etc.**	*I will scatter, etc.**	*I would scatter, etc.**
esparzo	esparcía	esparcí	esparciré	esparciría
esparces	esparcías	esparciste	esparcirás	esparcirías
esparce	esparcía	esparció	esparcirá	esparciría
esparcimos	esparcíamos	esparcimos	esparciremos	esparciríamos
esparcís	esparcíais	esparcisteis	esparciréis	esparciríais
esparcen	esparcían	esparcieron	esparcirán	esparcirían

PRESENTE DE SUBJUNTIVO *PRESENT* *SUBJUNCTIVE*	PRETÉRITO IMPERFECTO DE SUBJUNTIVO *PAST (IMPERFECT)* *SUBJUNCTIVE*		FUTURO IMPERFECTO DE SUBJUNTIVO *FUTURE* *SUBJUNCTIVE*
I scatter, etc.*	*I scattered, etc.**		*I will scatter, etc.**
esparza	esparciera	esparciese	esparciere
esparzas	esparcieras	esparcieses	esparcieres
esparza	esparciera	esparciese	esparciere
esparzamos	esparciéramos _or_	esparciésemos	esparciéremos
esparzáis	esparcierais	esparcieseis	esparciereis
esparzan	esparcieran	esparciesen	esparcieren

FORMAS IMPERATIVAS, GERUNDIOS Y PARTICIPIO
COMMANDS AND PARTICIPLES

FORMAS IMPERATIVAS / *COMMANDS*		GERUNDIO Y PARTICIPIO / *PARTICIPLES*		
AFIRMATIVA *AFFIRMATIVE*	NEGATIVA *NEGATIVE*	GERUNDIO SIMPLE *PRESENT PARTICIPLE*	PARTICIPIO *PAST PARTICIPLE*	GERUNDIO COMPUESTO *PERFECT PARTICIPLE*
scatter	*don't scatter*	*scattering*	*scattered*	*having scattered*
esparce (tú)	no esparzas (tú)	esparciendo	esparcido	habiendo esparcido
esparza (Ud.)	no esparza (Ud.)			
esparcid (vosotros)	no esparzáis (vosotros)			
esparzan (Uds.)	no esparzan (Uds.)			
let's scatter	*let's not scatter*			
esparzamos	no esparzamos			

INFINITIVO COMPUESTO: haber esparcido
PERFECT INFINITIVE: to have scattered

TIEMPOS COMPUESTOS
PERFECT (COMPOUND) TENSES

PRETÉRITO PERFECTO DE INDICATIVO *PRESENT PERFECT* *INDICATIVE*	PRETÉRITO PLUSCUAMPERFECTO DE INDICATIVO *PAST PERFECT (PLUPERFECT)* *INDICATIVE*	PRETÉRITO ANTERIOR DE INDICATIVO *PRETERITE PERFECT* *INDICATIVE*	FUTURO PERFECTO DE INDICATIVO *FUTURE PERFECT* *INDICATIVE*	POTENCIAL COMPUESTO *CONDITIONAL PERFECT*
I have scattered, etc.	*I had scattered, etc.*	*I had scattered, etc.*	*I will have scattered, etc.**	*I would have scattered, etc.**
he esparcido	había esparcido	hube esparcido	habré esparcido	habría esparcido
has esparcido	habías esparcido	hubiste esparcido	habrás esparcido	habrías esparcido
ha esparcido	había esparcido	hubo esparcido	habrá esparcido	habría esparcido
hemos esparcido	habíamos esparcido	hubimos esparcido	habremos esparcido	habríamos esparcido
habéis esparcido	habíais esparcido	hubisteis esparcido	habréis esparcido	habríais esparcido
han esparcido	habían esparcido	hubieron esparcido	habrán esparcido	habrían esparcido

PRETÉRITO PERFECTO DE SUBJUNTIVO *PRESENT PERFECT* *SUBJUNCTIVE*	PRETÉRITO PLUSCUAMPERFECTO DE SUBJUNTIVO *PAST PERFECT (PLUPERFECT)* *SUBJUNCTIVE*		FUTURO PERFECTO DE SUBJUNTIVO *FUTURE PERFECT* *SUBJUNCTIVE*
I have scattered. etc.*	*I had scattered, etc.**		*I will have scattered, etc.**
haya esparcido	hubiera esparcido	hubiese esparcido	hubiere esparcido
hayas esparcido	hubieras esparcido	hubieses esparcido	hubieres esparcido
haya esparcido	hubiera esparcido	hubiese esparcido	hubiere esparcido
hayamos esparcido	hubiéramos esparcido _or_	hubiésemos esparcido	hubiéremos esparcido
hayáis esparcido	hubierais esparcido	hubieseis esparcido	hubiereis esparcido
hayan esparcido	hubieran esparcido	hubiesen esparcido	hubieren esparcido

*For additional translation possibilities see chart A.

V. Orthographic/spelling changing verbs

VERBS OF THIS CATEGORY

---

esparcir
fruncir
resarcir
resarcirse 4. (R)
uncir
zurcir

R = Reflexive

V. Orthographic/spelling changing verbs

VERBS OF THIS CATEGORY

---

esparcir
fruncir
resarcir
resarcirse 4. (R)
uncir
zurcir

R = Reflexive

14 Verbs ending in -vowel + cer* } model: MECER

*Only in mecer, cocer, and their compounds. For others, see 73, 90, 96, 113.

TIEMPOS SIMPLES
SIMPLE TENSES

PRESENTE DE INDICATIVO *PRESENT INDICATIVE*	PRETÉRITO IMPERFECTO DE INDICATIVO *IMPERFECT INDICATIVE*	PRETÉRITO INDEFINIDO DE INDICATIVO *PRETERITE INDICATIVE*	FUTURO IMPERFECTO DE INDICATIVO *FUTURE INDICATIVE*	POTENCIAL SIMPLE *CONDITIONAL*
*I rock, etc.**	*I was rocking, etc.**	*I rocked, etc.**	*I will rock, etc.**	*I would rock, etc.**
mezo	mecía	mecí	meceré	mecería
meces	mecías	meciste	mecerás	mecerías
mece	mecía	meció	mecerá	mecería
mecemos	mecíamos	mecimos	meceremos	meceríamos
mecéis	mecíais	mecisteis	meceréis	meceríais
mecen	mecían	mecieron	mecerán	mecerían

PRESENTE DE SUBJUNTIVO *PRESENT SUBJUNCTIVE*	PRETÉRITO IMPERFECTO DE SUBJUNTIVO *PAST (IMPERFECT) SUBJUNCTIVE*		FUTURO IMPERFECTO DE SUBJUNTIVO *FUTURE SUBJUNCTIVE*
*I rock, etc.**	*I rocked, etc.**		*I will rock, etc.**
meza	meciera	meciese	meciere
mezas	mecieras	mecieses	mecieres
meza	meciera	meciese	meciere
mezamos	meciéramos *or*	meciésemos	meciéremos
mezáis	mecierais	mecieseis	meciereis
mezan	mecieran	meciesen	mecieren

FORMAS IMPERATIVAS, GERUNDIOS Y PARTICIPIO
COMMANDS AND PARTICIPLES

FORMAS IMPERATIVAS *COMMANDS*		GERUNDIO Y PARTICIPIO *PARTICIPLES*		
AFIRMATIVA *AFFIRMATIVE*	NEGATIVA *NEGATIVE*	GERUNDIO SIMPLE *PRESENT PARTICIPLE*	PARTICIPIO *PAST PARTICIPLE*	GERUNDIO COMPUESTO *PERFECT PARTICIPLE*
rock	*don't rock*	*rocking*	*rocked*	*having rocked*
mece (tú)	no mezas (tú)	meciendo	mecido	habiendo mecido
meza (Ud.)	no meza (Ud.)			
meced (vosotros)	no mezáis (vosotros)			
mezan (Uds.)	no mezan (Uds.)			
let's rock	*let's not rock*			
mezamos	no mezamos			

INFINITIVO COMPUESTO: haber mecido
PERFECT INFINITIVE: to have rocked

TIEMPOS COMPUESTOS
PERFECT (COMPOUND) TENSES

PRETÉRITO PERFECTO DE INDICATIVO *PRESENT PERFECT INDICATIVE*	PRETÉRITO PLUSCUAMPERFECTO DE INDICATIVO *PAST PERFECT (PLUPERFECT) INDICATIVE*	PRETÉRITO ANTERIOR DE INDICATIVO *PRETERITE PERFECT INDICATIVE*	FUTURO PERFECTO DE INDICATIVO *FUTURE PERFECT INDICATIVE*	POTENCIAL COMPUESTO *CONDITIONAL PERFECT*
I have rocked, etc.	*I had rocked, etc.*	*I had rocked, etc.*	*I will have rocked, etc.**	*I would have rocked, etc.**
he mecido	había mecido	hube mecido	habré mecido	habría mecido
has mecido	habías mecido	hubiste mecido	habrás mecido	habrías mecido
ha mecido	había mecido	hubo mecido	habrá mecido	habría mecido
hemos mecido	habíamos mecido	hubimos mecido	habremos mecido	habríamos mecido
habéis mecido	habíais mecido	hubisteis mecido	habréis mecido	habríais mecido
han mecido	habían mecido	hubieron mecido	habrán mecido	habrían mecido

PRETÉRITO PERFECTO DE SUBJUNTIVO *PRESENT PERFECT SUBJUNCTIVE*	PRETÉRITO PLUSCUAMPERFECTO DE SUBJUNTIVO *PAST PERFECT (PLUPERFECT) SUBJUNCTIVE*		FUTURO PERFECTO DE SUBJUNTIVO *FUTURE PERFECT SUBJUNCTIVE*
*I have rocked, etc.**	*I had rocked, etc.**		*I will have rocked, etc.**
haya mecido	hubiera mecido	hubiese mecido	hubiere mecido
hayas mecido	hubieras mecido	hubieses mecido	hubieres mecido
haya mecido	hubiera mecido	hubiese mecido	hubiere mecido
hayamos mecido	hubiéramos mecido *or*	hubiésemos mecido	hubiéremos mecido
hayáis mecido	hubierais mecido	hubieseis mecido	hubiereis mecido
han mecido	hubieran mecido	hubiesen mecido	hubieren mecido

...ional translation possibilities see chart A.

V. Orthographic/spelling changing verbs

VERBS OF THIS CATEGORY

*cocer (ue) 54. (RC)
*escocer (ue) 54. (RC)
 mecer
*recocer (ue) 54. (RC)
 remecer

RC = Radical/Stem Change
*These verbs have radical/stem changes in addition to the orthographic/spelling changes exemplified by the model verb on the chart given here. The cross reference number following each verb indicates the chart which shows all changes together.

TIEMPOS SIMPLES
SIMPLE TENSES

PRESENTE DE INDICATIVO *PRESENT INDICATIVE*	PRETÉRITO IMPERFECTO DE INDICATIVO *IMPERFECT INDICATIVE*	PRETÉRITO INDEFINIDO DE INDICATIVO *PRETERITE INDICATIVE*	FUTURO IMPERFECTO DE INDICATIVO *FUTURE INDICATIVE*	POTENCIAL SIMPLE *CONDITIONAL*
I choose, etc.*	*I was choosing, etc.**	*I chose, etc.**	*I will choose, etc.**	*I would choose, etc.**
escojo	escogía	escogí	escogeré	escogería
escoges	escogías	escogiste	escogerás	escogerías
escoge	escogía	escogió	escogerá	escogería
escogemos	escogíamos	escogimos	escogeremos	escogeríamos
escogéis	escogíais	escogisteis	escogeréis	escogeríais
escogen	escogían	escogieron	escogerán	escogerían

PRESENTE DE SUBJUNTIVO *PRESENT SUBJUNCTIVE*	PRETÉRITO IMPERFECTO DE SUBJUNTIVO *PAST (IMPERFECT) SUBJUNCTIVE*		FUTURO IMPERFECTO DE SUBJUNTIVO *FUTURE SUBJUNCTIVE*
I choose, etc.*	*I chose, etc.**		*I will choose, etc.**
escoja	escogiera	escogiese	escogiere
escojas	escogieras	escogieses	escogieres
escoja	escogiera	escogiese	escogiere
escojamos	escogiéramos *or*	escogiésemos	escogiéremos
escojáis	escogierais	escogieseis	escogiereis
escojan	escogieran	escogiesen	escogieren

FORMAS IMPERATIVAS, GERUNDIOS Y PARTICIPIO
COMMANDS AND PARTICIPLES

FORMAS IMPERATIVAS *COMMANDS*		GERUNDIO Y PARTICIPIO *PARTICIPLES*		
AFIRMATIVA *AFFIRMATIVE*	NEGATIVA *NEGATIVE*	GERUNDIO SIMPLE *PRESENT PARTICIPLE*	PARTICIPIO *PAST PARTICIPLE*	GERUNDIO COMPUESTO *PERFECT PARTICIPLE*
choose	*don't choose*	*choosing*	*chosen*	*having chosen*
escoge (tú)	no escojas (tú)	escogiendo	escogido	habiendo escogido
escoja (Ud.)	no escoja (Ud.)			
escoged (vosotros)	no escojáis (vosotros)			
escojan (Uds.)	no escojan (Uds.)			
let's choose	*let's not choose*			
escojamos	no escojamos			

INFINITIVO COMPUESTO: haber escogido
PERFECT INFINITIVE: to have chosen

TIEMPOS COMPUESTOS
PERFECT (COMPOUND) TENSES

PRETÉRITO PERFECTO DE INDICATIVO *PRESENT PERFECT INDICATIVE*	PRETÉRITO PLUSCUAMPERFECTO DE INDICATIVO *PAST PERFECT (PLUPERFECT) INDICATIVE*	PRETÉRITO ANTERIOR DE INDICATIVO *PRETERITE PERFECT INDICATIVE*	FUTURO PERFECTO DE INDICATIVO *FUTURE PERFECT INDICATIVE*	POTENCIAL COMPUESTO *CONDITIONAL PERFECT*
I have chosen, etc.	*I had chosen, etc.*	*I had chosen, etc.*	*I will have chosen, etc.**	*I would have chosen, etc.**
he escogido	había escogido	hube escogido	habré escogido	habría escogido
has escogido	habías escogido	hubiste escogido	habrás escogido	habrías escogido
ha escogido	había escogido	hubo escogido	habrá escogido	habría escogido
hemos escogido	habíamos escogido	hubimos escogido	habremos escogido	habríamos escogido
habéis escogido	habíais escogido	hubisteis escogido	habréis escogido	habríais escogido
han escogido	habían escogido	hubieron escogido	habrán escogido	habrían escogido

PRETÉRITO PERFECTO DE SUBJUNTIVO *PRESENT PERFECT SUBJUNCTIVE*	PRETÉRITO PLUSCUAMPERFECTO DE SUBJUNTIVO *PAST PERFECT (PLUPERFECT) SUBJUNCTIVE*		FUTURO PERFECTO DE SUBJUNTIVO *FUTURE PERFECT SUBJUNCTIVE*
I have chosen, etc.*	*I had chosen, etc.**		*I will have chosen, etc.**
haya escogido	hubiera escogido	hubiese escogido	hubiere escogido
hayas escogido	hubieras escogido	hubieses escogido	hubieres escogido
haya escogido	hubiera escogido	hubiese escogido	hubiere escogido
hayamos escogido	hubiéramos escogido *or*	hubiésemos escogido	hubiéremos escogido
hayáis escogido	hubierais escogido	hubieseis escogido	hubiereis escogido
hayan escogido	hubieran escogido	hubiesen escogido	hubieren escogido

*For additional translation possibilities see chart A.

V. Orthographic/spelling changing verbs

VERBS OF THIS CATEGORY

acoger
acogerse 4. (R)
coger
converger
emerger
encoger
escoger
proteger
recoger
recogerse 4. (R)
sobrecoger
sobrecogerse 4. (R)

R = Reflexive

16 Verbs ending in -gir } model: DIRIGIR

TIEMPOS SIMPLES
SIMPLE TENSES

PRESENTE DE INDICATIVO *PRESENT INDICATIVE*	PRETÉRITO IMPERFECTO DE INDICATIVO *IMPERFECT INDICATIVE*	PRETÉRITO INDEFINIDO DE INDICATIVO *PRETERITE INDICATIVE*	FUTURO IMPERFECTO DE INDICATIVO *FUTURE INDICATIVE*	POTENCIAL SIMPLE *CONDITIONAL*
I direct, etc.	*I was directing, etc.*	*I directed, etc.*	*I will direct, etc.*	*I would direct, etc.*
dirijo	dirigía	dirigí	dirigiré	dirigiría
diriges	dirigías	dirigiste	dirigirás	dirigirías
dirige	dirigía	dirigió	dirigirá	dirigiría
dirigimos	dirigíamos	dirigimos	dirigiremos	dirigiríamos
dirigís	dirigíais	dirigisteis	dirigiréis	dirigiríais
dirigen	dirigían	dirigieron	dirigirán	dirigirían

PRESENTE DE SUBJUNTIVO *PRESENT SUBJUNCTIVE*	PRETÉRITO IMPERFECTO DE SUBJUNTIVO *PAST (IMPERFECT) SUBJUNCTIVE*		FUTURO IMPERFECTO DE SUBJUNTIVO *FUTURE SUBJUNCTIVE*
I direct, etc.	*I directed. etc.*		*I will direct, etc.*
dirija	dirigiera	dirigiese	dirigiere
dirijas	dirigieras	dirigieses	dirigieres
dirija	dirigiera	dirigiese	dirigiere
dirijamos	dirigiéramos *or*	dirigiésemos	dirigiéremos
dirijáis	dirigierais	dirigieseis	dirigiereis
dirijan	dirigieran	dirigiesen	dirigieren

FORMAS IMPERATIVAS, GERUNDIOS Y PARTICIPIO
COMMANDS AND PARTICIPLES

FORMAS IMPERATIVAS *COMMANDS*		GERUNDIO Y PARTICIPIO *PARTICIPLES*		
AFIRMATIVA *AFFIRMATIVE*	NEGATIVA *NEGATIVE*	GERUNDIO SIMPLE *PRESENT PARTICIPLE*	PARTICIPIO *PAST PARTICIPLE*	GERUNDIO COMPUESTO *PERFECT PARTICIPLE*
direct	*don't direct*	*directing*	*directed*	*having directed*
dirige (tú)	no dirijas (tú)	dirigiendo	dirigido	habiendo dirigido
dirija (Ud.)	no dirija (Ud.)			
dirigid (vosotros)	no dirijáis (vosotros)			
dirijan (Uds.)	no dirijan (Uds.)			
let's direct	*let's not direct*			
dirijamos	no dirijamos			

INFINITIVO COMPUESTO: haber dirigido
PERFECT INFINITIVE: to have directed

TIEMPOS COMPUESTOS
PERFECT (COMPOUND) TENSES

PRETÉRITO PERFECTO DE INDICATIVO *PRESENT PERFECT INDICATIVE*	PRETÉRITO PLUSCUAMPERFECTO DE INDICATIVO *PAST PERFECT (PLUPERFECT) INDICATIVE*	PRETÉRITO ANTERIOR DE INDICATIVO *PRETERITE PERFECT INDICATIVE*	FUTURO PERFECTO DE INDICATIVO *FUTURE PERFECT INDICATIVE*	POTENCIAL COMPUESTO *CONDITIONAL PERFECT*
I have directed, etc.	*I had directed, etc.*	*I had directed, etc.*	*I will have directed, etc.*	*I would have directed, etc.*
he dirigido	había dirigido	hube dirigido	habré dirigido	habría dirigido
has dirigido	habías dirigido	hubiste dirigido	habrás dirigido	habrías dirigido
ha dirigido	había dirigido	hubo dirigido	habrá dirigido	habría dirigido
hemos dirigido	habíamos dirigido	hubimos dirigido	habremos dirigido	habríamos dirigido
habéis dirigido	habíais dirigido	hubisteis dirigido	habréis dirigido	habríais dirigido
han dirigido	habían dirigido	hubieron dirigido	habrán dirigido	habrían dirigido

PRETÉRITO PERFECTO DE SUBJUNTIVO *PRESENT PERFECT SUBJUNCTIVE*	PRETÉRITO PLUSCUAMPERFECTO DE SUBJUNTIVO *PAST PERFECT (PLUPERFECT) SUBJUNCTIVE*		FUTURO PERFECTO DE SUBJUNTIVO *FUTURE PERFECT SUBJUNCTIVE*
I have directed, etc.	*I had directed, etc.*		*I will have directed, etc.*
haya dirigido	hubiera dirigido	hubiese dirigido	hubiere dirigido
hayas dirigido	hubieras dirigido	hubieses dirigido	hubieres dirigido
haya dirigido	hubiera dirigido	hubiese dirigido	hubiere dirigido
hayamos dirigido	hubiéramos dirigido *or*	hubiésemos dirigido	hubiéremos dirigido
hayáis dirigido	hubierais dirigido	hubieseis dirigido	hubiereis dirigido
hayan dirigido	hubieran dirigido	hubiesen dirigido	hubieren dirigido

*For additional translation possibilities see chart A.

V. Orthographic/spelling changing verbs

VERBS OF THIS CATEGORY

afligir
afligirse 4. (R)
astringir
*colegir (i, i) 57. (RC)
compungir
compungirse 4. (R)
convergir
*corregir (i, i) 57. (RC)
dirigir
dirigirse 4. (R)
divergir
*elegir (i, i) 57. (RC)
erigir
exigir
fingir
infligir
infringir
inmergir
mugir
*preelegir (i, i) 57. (RC)
pungir
*reelegir (i, i) 57. (RC)
refulgir
*regir (i, i) 57. (RC)
restringir
resurgir
rugir
sumergir
surgir
transigir
ungir
urgir

R = Reflexive
RC = Radical/Stem Change
*These verbs have radical/stem changes in addition to the orthographic/spelling changes exemplified by the model verb on the chart given here. The cross reference number following each verb indicates the chart which shows all changes together.

17 Verbs ending in -guir } model: DISTINGUIR

TIEMPOS SIMPLES
SIMPLE TENSES

PRESENTE DE INDICATIVO *PRESENT INDICATIVE*	PRETÉRITO IMPERFECTO DE INDICATIVO *IMPERFECT INDICATIVE*	PRETÉRITO INDEFINIDO DE INDICATIVO *PRETERITE INDICATIVE*	FUTURO IMPERFECTO DE INDICATIVO *FUTURE INDICATIVE*	POTENCIAL SIMPLE *CONDITIONAL*
I distinguish, etc.*	*I was distinguishing, etc.**	*I distinguished, etc.**	*I will distinguish, etc.**	*I would distinguish, etc.**
distingo	distinguía	distinguí	distinguiré	distinguiría
distingues	distinguías	distinguiste	distinguirás	distinguirías
distingue	distinguía	distinguió	distinguirá	distinguiría
distinguimos	distinguíamos	distinguimos	distinguiremos	distinguiríamos
distinguís	distinguíais	distinguisteis	distinguiréis	distinguiríais
distinguen	distinguían	distinguieron	distinguirán	distinguirían

PRESENTE DE SUBJUNTIVO *PRESENT SUBJUNCTIVE*	PRETÉRITO IMPERFECTO DE SUBJUNTIVO *PAST (IMPERFECT) SUBJUNCTIVE*		FUTURO IMPERFECTO DE SUBJUNTIVO *FUTURE SUBJUNCTIVE*
I distinguish, etc.*	*I distinguished, etc.**		*I will distinguish, etc.**
distinga	distinguiera	distinguiese	distinguiere
distingas	distinguieras	distinguieses	distinguieres
distinga	distinguiera	distinguiese	distinguiere
distingamos	distinguiéramos *or*	distinguiésemos	distinguiéremos
distingáis	distinguierais	distinguieseis	distinguiereis
distingan	distinguieran	distinguiesen	distinguieren

FORMAS IMPERATIVAS, GERUNDIOS Y PARTICIPIO
COMMANDS AND PARTICIPLES

FORMAS IMPERATIVAS *COMMANDS*		GERUNDIO Y PARTICIPIO *PARTICIPLES*		
AFIRMATIVA *AFFIRMATIVE*	NEGATIVA *NEGATIVE*	GERUNDIO SIMPLE *PRESENT PARTICIPLE*	PARTICIPIO *PAST PARTICIPLE*	GERUNDIO COMPUESTO *PERFECT PARTICIPLE*
distinguish	*don't distinguish*	*distinguishing*	*distinguished*	*having distinguished*
distingue (tú)	no distingas (tú)	distinguiendo	distinguido	habiendo distinguido
distinga (Ud.)	no distinga (Ud.)			
distinguid (vosotros)	no distingáis (vosotros)			
distingan (Uds.)	no distingan (Uds.)			
let's distinguish	*let's not distinguish*			
distingamos	no distingamos			

INFINITIVO COMPUESTO: haber distinguido
PERFECT INFINITIVE: to have distinguished

TIEMPOS COMPUESTOS
PERFECT (COMPOUND) TENSES

PRETÉRITO PERFECTO DE INDICATIVO *PRESENT PERFECT INDICATIVE*	PRETÉRITO PLUSCUAMPERFECTO DE INDICATIVO *PAST PERFECT (PLUPERFECT) INDICATIVE*	PRETÉRITO ANTERIOR DE INDICATIVO *PRETERITE PERFECT INDICATIVE*	FUTURO PERFECTO DE INDICATIVO *FUTURE PERFECT INDICATIVE*	POTENCIAL COMPUESTO *CONDITIONAL PERFECT*
I have distinguished, etc.	*I had distinguished, etc.*	*I had distinguished, etc.*	*I will have distinguished, etc.**	*I would have distinguished, etc.**
he distinguido	había distinguido	hube distinguido	habré distinguido	habría distinguido
has distinguido	habías distinguido	hubiste distinguido	habrás distinguido	habrías distinguido
ha distinguido	había distinguido	hubo distinguido	habrá distinguido	habría distinguido
hemos distinguido	habíamos distinguido	hubimos distinguido	habremos distinguido	habríamos distinguido
habéis distinguido	habíais distinguido	hubisteis distinguido	habréis distinguido	habríais distinguido
han distinguido	habían distinguido	hubieron distinguido	habrán distinguido	habrían distinguido

PRETÉRITO PERFECTO DE SUBJUNTIVO *PRESENT PERFECT SUBJUNCTIVE*	PRETÉRITO PLUSCUAMPERFECTO DE SUBJUNTIVO *PAST PERFECT (PLUPERFECT) SUBJUNCTIVE*		FUTURO PERFECTO DE SUBJUNTIVO *FUTURE PERFECT SUBJUNCTIVE*
I have distinguished, etc.*	*I had distinguished, etc.**		*I will have distinguished, etc.**
haya distinguido	hubiera distinguido	hubiese distinguido	hubiere distinguido
hayas distinguido	hubieras distinguido	hubieses distinguido	hubieres distinguido
haya distinguido	hubiera distinguido	hubiese distinguido	hubiere distinguido
hayamos distinguido	hubiéramos distinguido *or*	hubiésemos distinguido	hubiéremos distinguido
hayáis distinguido	hubierais distinguido	hubieseis distinguido	hubiereis distinguido
hayan distinguido	hubieran distinguido	hubiesen distinguido	hubieren distinguido

*For additional translation possibilities see chart A.

V. Orthographic/spelling changing verbs

*conseguir (i, i) 58. (RC)
distinguir
**erguir (ie, i) 86. (OC) (RC) (I)
extinguir
extinguirse 4. (R)
*perseguir (i, i) 58. (RC)
*proseguir (i, i) 58. (RC)
*seguir (i, i) 58. (RC)
*subseguir (i, i) 58. (RC)

R   = Reflexive
OC = Orthographic/Spelling Change
RC = Radical/Stem Change
I   = Irregular
*These verbs have radical/stem changes in addition to the orthographic/spelling changes exemplified by the model verb on the chart given here. The cross reference number following each verb indicates the chart which shows all changes together.
**This verb has other orthographic/spelling changes, radical/stem changes, and irregularities in addition to the orthographic/spelling changes exemplified by the model verb on the chart given here. The cross reference number following the verb indicates the chart which shows all changes and irregularities together.

18 Verb ending in -quir } model: DELINQUIR

TIEMPOS SIMPLES
SIMPLE TENSES

PRESENTE DE INDICATIVO *PRESENT INDICATIVE*	PRETÉRITO IMPERFECTO DE INDICATIVO *IMPERFECT INDICATIVE*	PRETÉRITO INDEFINIDO DE INDICATIVO *PRETERITE INDICATIVE*	FUTURO IMPERFECTO DE INDICATIVO *FUTURE INDICATIVE*	POTENCIAL SIMPLE *CONDITIONAL*
*I transgress, etc.**	*I was transgressing, etc.**	*I transgressed, etc.**	*I will transgress, etc.**	*I would transgress, etc.**
delinco	delinquía	delinquí	delinquiré	delinquiría
delinques	delinquías	delinquiste	delinquirás	delinquirías
delinque	delinquía	delinquió	delinquirá	delinquiría
delinquimos	delinquíamos	delinquimos	delinquiremos	delinquiríamos
delinquís	delinquíais	delinquisteis	delinquiréis	delinquiríais
delinquen	delinquían	delinquieron	delinquirán	delinquirían

PRESENTE DE SUBJUNTIVO *PRESENT SUBJUNCTIVE*	PRETÉRITO IMPERFECTO DE SUBJUNTIVO *PAST (IMPERFECT) SUBJUNCTIVE*		FUTURO IMPERFECTO DE SUBJUNTIVO *FUTURE SUBJUNCTIVE*
*I transgress, etc.**	*I transgressed, etc.**		*I will transgress, etc.**
delinca	delinquiera	delinquiese	delinquiere
delincas	delinquieras	delinquieses	delinquieres
delinca	delinquiera	delinquiese	delinquiere
delincamos	delinquiéramos *or*	delinquiésemos	delinquiéremos
delincáis	delinquierais	delinquieseis	delinquiereis
delincan	delinquieran	delinquiesen	delinquieren

FORMAS IMPERATIVAS, GERUNDIOS Y PARTICIPIO
COMMANDS AND PARTICIPLES

FORMAS IMPERATIVAS *COMMANDS*		GERUNDIO Y PARTICIPIO *PARTICIPLES*		
AFIRMATIVA *AFFIRMATIVE*	NEGATIVA *NEGATIVE*	GERUNDIO SIMPLE *PRESENT PARTICIPLE*	PARTICIPIO *PAST PARTICIPLE*	GERUNDIO COMPUESTO *PERFECT PARTICIPLE*
transgress	*don't transgress*	*transgressing*	*transgressed*	*having transgressed*
delinque (tú)	no delincas (tú)	delinquiendo	delinquido	habiendo delinquido
delinca (Ud.)	no delinca (Ud.)			
delinquid (vosotros)	no delincáis (vosotros)			
delincan (Uds.)	no delincan (Uds.)			
let's transgress	*let's not transgress*			
delincamos	no delincamos			

INFINITIVO COMPUESTO: haber delinquido
PERFECT INFINITIVE: to have transgressed

TIEMPOS COMPUESTOS
PERFECT (COMPOUND) TENSES

PRETÉRITO PERFECTO DE INDICATIVO *PRESENT PERFECT INDICATIVE*	PRETÉRITO PLUSCUAMPERFECTO DE INDICATIVO *PAST PERFECT (PLUPERFECT) INDICATIVE*	PRETÉRITO ANTERIOR DE INDICATIVO *PRETERITE PERFECT INDICATIVE*	FUTURO PERFECTO DE INDICATIVO *FUTURE PERFECT INDICATIVE*	POTENCIAL COMPUESTO *CONDITIONAL PERFECT*
I have transgressed, etc.	*I had transgressed, etc.*	*I had transgressed, etc.*	*I will have transgressed, etc.**	*I would have transgressed, etc.**
he delinquido	había delinquido	hube delinquido	habré delinquido	habría delinquido
has delinquido	habías delinquido	hubiste delinquido	habrás delinquido	habrías delinquido
ha delinquido	había delinquido	hubo delinquido	habrá delinquido	habría delinquido
hemos delinquido	habíamos delinquido	hubimos delinquido	habremos delinquido	habríamos delinquido
habéis delinquido	habíais delinquido	hubisteis delinquido	habréis delinquido	habríais delinquido
han delinquido	habían delinquido	hubieron delinquido	habrán delinquido	habrían delinquido

PRETÉRITO PERFECTO DE SUBJUNTIVO *PRESENT PERFECT SUBJUNCTIVE*	PRETÉRITO PLUSCUAMPERFECTO DE SUBJUNTIVO *PAST PERFECT (PLUPERFECT) SUBJUNCTIVE*		FUTURO PERFECTO DE SUBJUNTIVO *FUTURE PERFECT SUBJUNCTIVE*
*I have transgressed, etc.**	*I had transgressed, etc.**		*I will have transgressed, etc.**
haya delinquido	hubiera delinquido	hubiese delinquido	hubiere delinquido
hayas delinquido	hubieras delinquido	hubieses delinquido	hubieres delinquido
haya delinquido	hubiera delinquido	hubiese delinquido	hubiere delinquido
hayamos delinquido	hubiéramos delinquido *or*	hubiésemos delinquido	hubiéremos delinquido
hayáis delinquido	hubierais delinquido	hubieseis delinquido	hubiereis delinquido
hayan delinquido	hubieran delinquido	hubiesen delinquido	hubieren delinquido

For additional translation possibilities see chart A.

V. Orthographic/spelling changing verbs

VERB OF THIS CATEGORY

delinquir

TIEMPOS SIMPLES
SIMPLE TENSES

PRESENTE DE INDICATIVO *PRESENT INDICATIVE*	PRETÉRITO IMPERFECTO DE INDICATIVO *IMPERFECT INDICATIVE*	PRETÉRITO INDEFINIDO DE INDICATIVO *PRETERITE INDICATIVE*	FUTURO IMPERFECTO DE INDICATIVO *FUTURE INDICATIVE*	POTENCIAL SIMPLE *CONDITIONAL*
*I rear, etc.**	*I was rearing, etc.**	*I reared, etc.**	*I will rear, etc.**	*I would rear, etc.**
crío	criaba	crié	criaré	criaría
crías	criabas	criaste	criarás	criarías
cría	criaba	crió	criará	criaría
criamos	criábamos	criamos	criaremos	criaríamos
criáis	criabais	criasteis	criaréis	criaríais
crían	criaban	criaron	criarán	criarían

PRESENTE DE SUBJUNTIVO *PRESENT SUBJUNCTIVE*	PRETÉRITO IMPERFECTO DE SUBJUNTIVO *PAST (IMPERFECT) SUBJUNCTIVE*		FUTURO IMPERFECTO DE SUBJUNTIVO *FUTURE SUBJUNCTIVE*
*I rear, etc.**	*I reared, etc.**		*I will rear, etc.**
críe	criara	criase	criare
críes	criaras	criases	criares
críe	criara	criase	criare
criemos	criáramos *or* criásemos		criáremos
criéis	criarais	criaseis	criareis
críen	criaran	criasen	criaren

FORMAS IMPERATIVAS, GERUNDIOS Y PARTICIPIO
COMMANDS AND PARTICIPLES

FORMAS IMPERATIVAS *COMMANDS*		GERUNDIO Y PARTICIPIO *PARTICIPLES*		
AFIRMATIVA *AFFIRMATIVE*	NEGATIVA *NEGATIVE*	GERUNDIO SIMPLE *PRESENT PARTICIPLE*	PARTICIPIO *PAST PARTICIPLE*	GERUNDIO COMPUESTO *PERFECT PARTICIPLE*
rear	*don't rear*	*rearing*	*reared*	*having reared*
cría (tú)	no críes (tú)	criando	criado	habiendo criado
críe (Ud.)	no críe (Ud.)			
criad (vosotros)	no criéis (vosotros)			
críen (Uds.)	no críen (Uds.)			
let's rear	*let's not rear*			
criemos	no criemos			

INFINITIVO COMPUESTO: haber criado
PERFECT INFINITIVE: to have reared

TIEMPOS COMPUESTOS
PERFECT (COMPOUND) TENSES

PRETÉRITO PERFECTO DE INDICATIVO *PRESENT PERFECT INDICATIVE*	PRETÉRITO PLUSCUAMPERFECTO DE INDICATIVO *PAST PERFECT (PLUPERFECT) INDICATIVE*	PRETÉRITO ANTERIOR DE INDICATIVO *PRETERITE PERFECT INDICATIVE*	FUTURO PERFECTO DE INDICATIVO *FUTURE PERFECT INDICATIVE*	POTENCIAL COMPUESTO *CONDITIONAL PERFECT*
I have reared, etc.	*I had reared, etc.*	*I had reared, etc.*	*I will have reared, etc.**	*I would have reared, etc.**
he criado	había criado	hube criado	habré criado	habría criado
has criado	habías criado	hubiste criado	habrás criado	habrías criado
ha criado	había criado	hubo criado	habrá criado	habría criado
hemos criado	habíamos criado	hubimos criado	habremos criado	habríamos criado
habéis criado	habíais criado	hubisteis criado	habréis criado	habríais criado
han criado	habían criado	hubieron criado	habrán criado	habrían criado

PRETÉRITO PERFECTO DE SUBJUNTIVO *PRESENT PERFECT SUBJUNCTIVE*	PRETÉRITO PLUSCUAMPERFECTO DE SUBJUNTIVO *PAST PERFECT (PLUPERFECT) SUBJUNCTIVE*		FUTURO PERFECTO DE SUBJUNTIVO *FUTURE PERFECT SUBJUNCTIVE*
*I have reared, etc.**	*I had reared, etc.**		*I will have reared, etc.**
haya criado	hubiera criado	hubiese criado	hubiere criado
hayas criado	hubieras criado	hubieses criado	hubieres criado
haya criado	hubiera criado	hubiese criado	hubiere criado
hayamos criado	hubiéramos criado *or* hubiésemos criado		hubiéremos criado
hayáis criado	hubierais criado	hubieseis criado	hubiereis criado
hayan criado	hubieran criado	hubiesen criado	hubieren criado

*For additional translation possibilities see chart A.

V. Orthographic/spelling changing verbs

VERBS OF THIS CATEGORY

ciar
criar
fiar
fiarse 4. (R)
guiar
liar
liarse 4. (R)
piar
puar

R = Reflexive

20 Verbs ending in -vowel + er } model: CREER

TIEMPOS SIMPLES
SIMPLE TENSES

PRESENTE DE INDICATIVO PRESENT INDICATIVE	PRETÉRITO IMPERFECTO DE INDICATIVO IMPERFECT INDICATIVE	PRETÉRITO INDEFINIDO DE INDICATIVO PRETERITE INDICATIVE	FUTURO IMPERFECTO DE INDICATIVO FUTURE INDICATIVE	POTENCIAL SIMPLE CONDITIONAL
*I believe, etc.**	*I was believing, etc.**	*I believed, etc.**	*I will believe, etc.**	*I would believe, etc.**
creo	creía	creí	creeré	creería
crees	creías	creíste	creerás	creerías
cree	creía	creyó	creerá	creería
creemos	creíamos	creímos	creeremos	creeríamos
creéis	creíais	creísteis	creeréis	creeríais
creen	creían	creyeron	creerán	creerían

PRESENTE DE SUBJUNTIVO PRESENT SUBJUNCTIVE	PRETÉRITO IMPERFECTO DE SUBJUNTIVO PAST (IMPERFECT) SUBJUNCTIVE		FUTURO IMPERFECTO DE SUBJUNTIVO FUTURE SUBJUNCTIVE	
*I believe, etc.**	*I believed, etc.**		*I will believe, etc.**	
crea	creyera	creyese	creyere	
creas	creyeras	creyeses	creyeres	
crea	creyera	creyese	creyere	
creamos	creyéramos *or*	creyésemos	creyéremos	
creáis	creyerais	creyeseis	creyereis	
crean	creyeran	creyesen	creyeren	

FORMAS IMPERATIVAS, GERUNDIOS Y PARTICIPIO
COMMANDS AND PARTICIPLES

FORMAS IMPERATIVAS COMMANDS		GERUNDIO Y PARTICIPIO PARTICIPLES		
AFIRMATIVA AFFIRMATIVE	NEGATIVA NEGATIVE	GERUNDIO SIMPLE PRESENT PARTICIPLE	PARTICIPIO PAST PARTICIPLE	GERUNDIO COMPUESTO PERFECT PARTICIPLE
believe	*don't believe*	*believing*	*believed*	*having believed*
cree (tú)	no creas (tú)	creyendo	creído	habiendo creído
crea (Ud.)	no crea (Ud.)			
creed (vosotros)	no creáis (vosotros)			
crean (Uds.)	no crean (Uds.)			
let's believe	*let's not believe*			
creamos	no creamos			

INFINITIVO COMPUESTO: haber creído
PERFECT INFINITIVE: to have believed

TIEMPOS COMPUESTOS
PERFECT (COMPOUND) TENSES

PRETÉRITO PERFECTO DE INDICATIVO PRESENT PERFECT INDICATIVE	PRETÉRITO PLUSCUAMPERFECTO DE INDICATIVO PAST PERFECT (PLUPERFECT) INDICATIVE	PRETÉRITO ANTERIOR DE INDICATIVO PRETERITE PERFECT INDICATIVE	FUTURO PERFECTO DE INDICATIVO FUTURE PERFECT INDICATIVE	POTENCIAL COMPUESTO CONDITIONAL PERFECT
I have believed, etc.	*I had believed, etc.*	*I had believed, etc.*	*I will have believed, etc.**	*I would have believed, etc.**
he creído	había creído	hube creído	habré creído	habría creído
has creído	habías creído	hubiste creído	habrás creído	habrías creído
ha creído	había creído	hubo creído	habrá creído	habría creído
hemos creído	habíamos creído	hubimos creído	habremos creído	habríamos creído
habéis creído	habíais creído	hubisteis creído	habréis creído	habríais creído
han creído	habían creído	hubieron creído	habrán creído	habrían creído

PRETÉRITO PERFECTO DE SUBJUNTIVO PRESENT PERFECT SUBJUNCTIVE	PRETÉRITO PLUSCUAMPERFECTO DE SUBJUNTIVO PAST PERFECT (PLUPERFECT) SUBJUNCTIVE		FUTURO PERFECTO DE SUBJUNTIVO FUTURE PERFECT SUBJUNCTIVE	
*I have believed, etc.**	*I had believed, etc.**		*I will have believed, etc.**	
haya creído	hubiera creído	hubiese creído	hubiere creído	
hayas creído	hubieras creído	hubieses creído	hubieres creído	
haya creído	hubiera creído	hubiese creído	hubiere creído	
hayamos creído	hubiéramos creído *or*	hubiésemos creído	hubiéremos creído	
hayáis creído	hubierais creído	hubieseis creído	hubiereis creído	
hayan creído	hubieran creído	hubiesen creído	hubieren creído	

*For additional translation possibilities see chart A.

V. Orthographic/spelling changing verbs

VERBS OF THIS CATEGORY

---

*abstraer 109. (I)
*abstraerse 109. (I), 4. (R)
*atraer 109. (I)
*caer 81. (I)
*contraer 109. (I)
*corroer 103. (I)
 creer
*decaer 81. (I)
*desproveer 99. (I)
*detraer 109. (I)
*distraer 109. (I)
*extraer 109. (I)
 leer
*maltraer 109. (I)
 peer
 poseer
*proveer 99. (I)
*raer 102. (I)
*raerse 102. (I), 4. (R)
*recaer 81. (I)
 releer
*retraer 109. (I)
*retraerse 109. (I), 4. (R)
*retrotraer 109. (I)
*roer 103. (I)
 sobreseer
*substraer 109. (I)
*substraerse 109. (I), 4. (R)
*sustraer 109. (I)
*sustraerse 109. (I), 4. (R)
*traer 109. (I)

R = Reflexive
I = Irregular
*These verbs have irregularities in addition to the orthographic/spelling changes exemplified by the model verb on the chart given here. The cross reference number following each verb indicates the chart showing all changes and irregularities together.

21 Verbs ending in -aír } model: EMBAÍR*

*Defective verb

TIEMPOS SIMPLES
SIMPLE TENSES

PRESENTE DE INDICATIVO **PRESENT** *INDICATIVE*	PRETÉRITO IMPERFECTO DE INDICATIVO **IMPERFECT** *INDICATIVE*	PRETÉRITO INDEFINIDO DE INDICATIVO **PRETERITE** *INDICATIVE*	FUTURO IMPERFECTO DE INDICATIVO **FUTURE** *INDICATIVE*	POTENCIAL SIMPLE **CONDITIONAL**
*we trick, etc.**	*I was tricking, etc.**	*I tricked, etc.**	*I will trick, etc.**	*I would trick, etc.**
----	embaía	embaí	embairé	embairía
----	embaías	embaíste	embairás	embairías
----	embaía	embayó	embairá	embairía
embaímos	embaíamos	embaímos	embairemos	embairíamos
embaís	embaíais	embaísteis	embairéis	embairíais
----	embaían	embayeron	embairán	embairían

PRESENTE DE SUBJUNTIVO **PRESENT** *SUBJUNCTIVE*	PRETÉRITO IMPERFECTO DE SUBJUNTIVO **PAST (IMPERFECT)** *SUBJUNCTIVE*		FUTURO IMPERFECTO DE SUBJUNTIVO **FUTURE** *SUBJUNCTIVE*
	*I tricked, etc.**		*I will trick, etc.**
----	embayera	embayese	embayere
----	embayeras	embayeses	embayeres
----	embayera	embayese	embayere
----	embayéramos *or*	embayésemos	embayéremos
----	embayerais	embayeseis	embayereis
----	embayeran	embayesen	embayeren

FORMAS IMPERATIVAS, GERUNDIOS Y PARTICIPIO
COMMANDS AND PARTICIPLES

FORMAS IMPERATIVAS **COMMANDS**		GERUNDIO Y PARTICIPIO **PARTICIPLES**		
AFIRMATIVA *AFFIRMATIVE*	NEGATIVA *NEGATIVE*	GERUNDIO SIMPLE *PRESENT PARTICIPLE*	PARTICIPIO *PAST PARTICIPLE*	GERUNDIO COMPUESTO *PERFECT PARTICIPLE*
trick		*tricking*	*tricked*	*having tricked*
----	----	embayendo	embaído	habiendo embaído
----	----			
embaíd (vosotros)	----			
----	----			
----	----			

INFINITIVO COMPUESTO: haber embaído
PERFECT INFINITIVE: to have tricked

TIEMPOS COMPUESTOS
PERFECT (COMPOUND) TENSES

PRETÉRITO PERFECTO DE INDICATIVO **PRESENT PERFECT** *INDICATIVE*	PRETÉRITO PLUSCUAMPERFECTO DE INDICATIVO **PAST PERFECT (PLUPERFECT)** *INDICATIVE*	PRETÉRITO ANTERIOR DE INDICATIVO **PRETERITE PERFECT** *INDICATIVE*	FUTURO PERFECTO DE INDICATIVO **FUTURE PERFECT** *INDICATIVE*	POTENCIAL COMPUESTO **CONDITIONAL PERFECT**
I have tricked, etc.	*I had tricked, etc.*	*I had tricked, etc.*	*I will have tricked, etc.**	*I would have tricked, etc.**
he embaído	había embaído	hube embaído	habré embaído	habría embaído
has embaído	habías embaído	hubiste embaído	habrás embaído	habrías embaído
ha embaído	había embaído	hubo embaído	habrá embaído	habría embaído
hemos embaído	habíamos embaído	hubimos embaído	habremos embaído	habríamos embaído
habéis embaído	habíais embaído	hubisteis embaído	habréis embaído	habríais embaído
han embaído	habían embaído	hubieron embaído	habrán embaído	habrían embaído

PRETÉRITO PERFECTO DE SUBJUNTIVO **PRESENT PERFECT** *SUBJUNCTIVE*	PRETÉRITO PLUSCUAMPERFECTO DE SUBJUNTIVO **PAST PERFECT (PLUPERFECT)** *SUBJUNCTIVE*		FUTURO PERFECTO DE SUBJUNTIVO **FUTURE PERFECT** *SUBJUNCTIVE*
*I have tricked, etc.**	*I had tricked, etc.**		*I will have tricked, etc.**
haya embaído	hubiera embaído	hubiese embaído	hubiere embaído
hayas embaído	hubieras embaído	hubieses embaído	hubieres embaído
haya embaído	hubiera embaído	hubiese embaído	hubiere embaído
hayamos embaído	hubiéramos embaído *or*	hubiésemos embaído	hubiéremos embaído
hayáis embaído	hubierais embaído	hubieseis embaído	hubiereis embaído
hayan embaído	hubieran embaído	hubiesen embaído	hubieren embaído

*For additional translation possibilities see chart A.

V. Orthographic/spelling changing verbs

desvaír 117. (defective)
embaír 117. (defective)

22 Verbs ending in -oír* } model: OÍR

*Irregular verb

TIEMPOS SIMPLES
SIMPLE TENSES

PRESENTE DE INDICATIVO *PRESENT INDICATIVE*	PRETÉRITO IMPERFECTO DE INDICATIVO *IMPERFECT INDICATIVE*	PRETÉRITO INDEFINIDO DE INDICATIVO *PRETERITE INDICATIVE*	FUTURO IMPERFECTO DE INDICATIVO *FUTURE INDICATIVE*	POTENCIAL SIMPLE *CONDITIONAL*
I hear, etc. *	*I was hearing, etc.* *	*I heard, etc.* *	*I will hear, etc.* *	*I would hear, etc.* *
oigo	oía	oí	oiré	oiría
oyes	oías	oíste	oirás	oirías
oye	oía	oyó	oirá	oiría
oímos	oíamos	oímos	oiremos	oiríamos
oís	oíais	oísteis	oiréis	oiríais
oyen	oían	oyeron	oirán	oirían

PRESENTE DE SUBJUNTIVO *PRESENT SUBJUNCTIVE*	PRETÉRITO IMPERFECTO DE SUBJUNTIVO *PAST (IMPERFECT) SUBJUNCTIVE*		FUTURO IMPERFECTO DE SUBJUNTIVO *FUTURE SUBJUNCTIVE*
I hear, etc. *	*I heard, etc.* *		*I will hear, etc.* *
oiga	oyera	oyese	oyere
oigas	oyeras	oyeses	oyeres
oiga	oyera	oyese	oyere
oigamos	oyéramos _or_	oyésemos	oyéremos
oigáis	oyerais	oyeseis	oyereis
oigan	oyeran	oyesen	oyeren

FORMAS IMPERATIVAS, GERUNDIOS Y PARTICIPIO
COMMANDS AND PARTICIPLES

FORMAS IMPERATIVAS *COMMANDS*		GERUNDIO Y PARTICIPIO *PARTICIPLES*		
AFIRMATIVA *AFFIRMATIVE*	NEGATIVA *NEGATIVE*	GERUNDIO SIMPLE *PRESENT PARTICIPLE*	PARTICIPIO *PAST PARTICIPLE*	GERUNDIO COMPUESTO *PERFECT PARTICIPLE*
hear	*don't hear*	*hearing*	*heard*	*having heard*
oye (tú)	no oigas (tú)	oyendo	oído	habiendo oído
oiga (Ud.)	no oiga (Ud.)			
oíd (vosotros)	no oigáis (vosotros)			
oigan (Uds.)	no oigan (Uds.)			
let's hear	*let's not hear*			
oigamos	no oigamos			

INFINITIVO COMPUESTO: haber oído
PERFECT INFINITIVE: to have heard

TIEMPOS COMPUESTOS
PERFECT (COMPOUND) TENSES

PRETÉRITO PERFECTO DE INDICATIVO *PRESENT PERFECT INDICATIVE*	PRETÉRITO PLUSCUAMPERFECTO DE INDICATIVO *PAST PERFECT (PLUPERFECT) INDICATIVE*	PRETÉRITO ANTERIOR DE INDICATIVO *PRETERITE PERFECT INDICATIVE*	FUTURO PERFECTO DE INDICATIVO *FUTURE PERFECT INDICATIVE*	POTENCIAL COMPUESTO *CONDITIONAL PERFECT*
I have heard, etc.	*I had heard, etc.*	*I had heard, etc.*	*I will have heard, etc.* *	*I would have heard, etc.* *
he oído	había oído	hube oído	habré oído	habría oído
has oído	habías oído	hubiste oído	habrás oído	habrías oído
ha oído	había oído	hubo oído	habrá oído	habría oído
hemos oído	habíamos oído	hubimos oído	habremos oído	habríamos oído
habéis oído	habíais oído	hubisteis oído	habréis oído	habríais oído
han oído	habían oído	hubieron oído	habrán oído	habrían oído

PRETÉRITO PERFECTO DE SUBJUNTIVO *PRESENT PERFECT SUBJUNCTIVE*	PRETÉRITO PLUSCUAMPERFECTO DE SUBJUNTIVO *PAST PERFECT (PLUPERFECT) SUBJUNCTIVE*		FUTURO PERFECTO DE SUBJUNTIVO *FUTURE PERFECT SUBJUNCTIVE*
I have heard, etc. *	*I had heard, etc.* *		*I will have heard, etc.* *
haya oído	hubiera oído	hubiese oído	hubiere oído
hayas oído	hubieras oído	hubieses oído	hubieres oído
haya oído	hubiera oído	hubiese oído	hubiere oído
hayamos oído	hubiéramos oído _or_	hubiésemos oído	hubiéremos oído
hayáis oído	hubierais oído	hubieseis oído	hubiereis oído
hayan oído	hubieran oído	hubiesen oído	hubieren oído

*For additional translation possibilities see chart A.

V. Orthographic/spelling changing verbs

VERBS OF THIS CATEGORY

desoír 95, (I)
entreoír 95. (I)
oír 95. (I)
trasoír 95. (I)

I = Irregular

TIEMPOS SIMPLES
SIMPLE TENSES

PRESENTE DE INDICATIVO *PRESENT INDICATIVE*	PRETÉRITO IMPERFECTO DE INDICATIVO *IMPERFECT INDICATIVE*	PRETÉRITO INDEFINIDO DE INDICATIVO *PRETERITE INDICATIVE*	FUTURO IMPERFECTO DE INDICATIVO *FUTURE INDICATIVE*	POTENCIAL SIMPLE *CONDITIONAL*
I mix, etc.	*I was mixing, etc.*	*I mixed, etc.*	*I will mix, etc.*	*I would mix, etc.*
inmiscuo	inmiscuía	inmiscuí	inmiscuiré	inmiscuiría
inmiscues	inmiscuías	inmiscuiste	inmiscuirás	inmiscuirías
inmiscue	inmiscuía	inmiscuyó	inmiscuirá	inmiscuiría
inmiscuimos	inmiscuíamos	inmiscuimos	inmiscuiremos	inmiscuiríamos
inmiscuís	inmiscuíais	inmiscuisteis	inmiscuiréis	inmiscuiríais
inmiscuen	inmiscuían	inmiscuyeron	inmiscuirán	inmiscuirían

PRESENTE DE SUBJUNTIVO *PRESENT SUBJUNCTIVE*	PRETÉRITO IMPERFECTO DE SUBJUNTIVO *PAST (IMPERFECT) SUBJUNCTIVE*		FUTURO IMPERFECTO DE SUBJUNTIVO *FUTURE SUBJUNCTIVE*
I mix, etc.	*I mixed, etc.*		*I will mix, etc.*
inmiscua	inmiscuyera	inmiscuyese	inmiscuyere
inmiscuas	inmiscuyeras	inmiscuyeses	inmiscuyeres
inmiscua	inmiscuyera	inmiscuyese	inmiscuyere
inmiscuamos	inmiscuyéramos *or*	inmiscuyésemos	inmiscuyéremos
inmiscuáis	inmiscuyerais	inmiscuyeseis	inmiscuyereis
inmiscuan	inmiscuyeran	inmiscuyesen	inmiscuyeren

FORMAS IMPERATIVAS, GERUNDIOS Y PARTICIPIO
COMMANDS AND PARTICIPLES

FORMAS IMPERATIVAS *COMMANDS*		GERUNDIO Y PARTICIPIO *PARTICIPLES*		
AFIRMATIVA *AFFIRMATIVE*	NEGATIVA *NEGATIVE*	GERUNDIO SIMPLE *PRESENT PARTICIPLE*	PARTICIPIO *PAST PARTICIPLE*	GERUNDIO COMPUESTO *PERFECT PARTICIPLE*
mix	*don't mix*	*mixing*	*mixed*	*having mixed*
inmiscue (tú)	no inmiscuas (tú)	inmiscuyendo	inmiscuido	habiendo inmiscuido
inmiscua (Ud.)	no inmiscua (Ud.)			
inmiscuid (vosotros)	no inmiscuáis (vosotros)			
inmiscuan (Uds.)	no inmiscuan (Uds.)			
let's mix	*let's not mix*			
inmiscuamos	no inmiscuamos			

INFINITIVO COMPUESTO: haber inmiscuido
PERFECT INFINITIVE: to have mixed

TIEMPOS COMPUESTOS
PERFECT (COMPOUND) TENSES

PRETÉRITO PERFECTO DE INDICATIVO *PRESENT PERFECT INDICATIVE*	PRETÉRITO PLUSCUAMPERFECTO DE INDICATIVO *PAST PERFECT (PLUPERFECT) INDICATIVE*	PRETÉRITO ANTERIOR DE INDICATIVO *PRETERITE PERFECT INDICATIVE*	FUTURO PERFECTO DE INDICATIVO *FUTURE PERFECT INDICATIVE*	POTENCIAL COMPUESTO *CONDITIONAL PERFECT*
I have mixed, etc.	*I had mixed, etc.*	*I had mixed, etc.*	*I will have mixed, etc.*	*I would have mixed, etc.*
he inmiscuido	había inmiscuido	hube inmiscuido	habré inmiscuido	habría inmiscuido
has inmiscuido	habías inmiscuido	hubiste inmiscuido	habrás inmiscuido	habrías inmiscuido
ha inmiscuido	había inmiscuido	hubo inmiscuido	habrá inmiscuido	habría inmiscuido
hemos inmiscuido	habíamos inmiscuido	hubimos inmiscuido	habremos inmiscuido	habríamos inmiscuido
habéis inmiscuido	habíais inmiscuido	hubisteis inmiscuido	habréis inmiscuido	habríais inmiscuido
han inmiscuido	habían inmiscuido	hubieron inmiscuido	habrán inmiscuido	habrían inmiscuido

PRETÉRITO PERFECTO DE SUBJUNTIVO *PRESENT PERFECT SUBJUNCTIVE*	PRETÉRITO PLUSCUAMPERFECTO DE SUBJUNTIVO *PAST PERFECT (PLUPERFECT) SUBJUNCTIVE*		FUTURO PERFECTO DE SUBJUNTIVO *FUTURE PERFECT SUBJUNCTIVE*
I have mixed, etc.	*I had mixed, etc.*		*I will have mixed, etc.*
haya inmiscuido	hubiera inmiscuido	hubiese inmiscuido	hubiere inmiscuido
hayas inmiscuido	hubieras inmiscuido	hubieses inmiscuido	hubieres inmiscuido
haya inmiscuido	hubiera inmiscuido	hubiese inmiscuido	hubiere inmiscuido
hayamos inmiscuido	hubiéramos inmiscuido *or*	hubiésemos inmiscuido	hubiéremos inmiscuido
hayáis inmiscuido	hubierais inmiscuido	hubieseis inmiscuido	hubiereis inmiscuido
hayan inmiscuido	hubieran inmiscuido	hubiesen inmiscuido	hubieren inmiscuido

*For additional translation possibilities see chart A.

[108]

V. Orthographic/spelling changing verbs

VERBS OF THIS CATEGORY

*afluir 71. (I)
**argüir 72. (OC) (I)
*atribuir 71. (I)
*circuir 71. (I)
*concluir 71. (I)
*confluir 71. (I)
*constituir 71. (I)
*construir 71. (I)
*contribuir 71. (I)
*derruir 71. (I)
*destituir 71. (I)
*destruir 71. (I)
*diluir 71. (I)
*disminuir 71 (I)
*distribuir 71. (I)
*estatuir 71. (I)
*excluir 71. (I)
*fluir 71. (I)
*fruir 71 (I)
*huir 71. (I)
*imbuir 71. (I)
*incluir 71. (I)
*influir 71. (I)
inmiscuir 23. (OC) *or* the commonly used conjugation found in 71. (I)
inmiscuirse 23. (OC) *or* the commonly used conjugation found in 71. (I), 4. (R)
*instituir 71. (I)
*instruir 71. (I)
*intuir 71. (I)
*obstruir 71. (I)
*ocluir 71. (I)
*prostituir 71. (I)
*recluir 71. (I)
*recluirse 71. (I), 4. (R)
*reconstituir 71. (I)
*reconstruir 71. (I)
**rehuir 71. (OC) (I)
*restituir 71. (I)
*retribuir 71. (I)
*substituir 71. (I)
*sustituir 71. (I)

R = Reflexive
OC = Orthographic/Spelling Change
I = Irregular
*These verbs have irregularities other than the orthographic/spelling changes exemplified by the model verb on the chart given here. The cross reference number following each verb indicates the chart which shows all changes and irregularities together.
**These verbs have other orthographic/spelling changes and irregularities in addition to the orthographic/spelling changes exemplified by the model verb on the chart given here. The cross reference number following each verb indicates the chart which shows all changes and irregularities together.

24 Verb ending in -güir } model: ARGÜIR

TIEMPOS SIMPLES
SIMPLE TENSES

PRESENTE DE INDICATIVO *PRESENT INDICATIVE*	PRETÉRITO IMPERFECTO DE INDICATIVO *IMPERFECT INDICATIVE*	PRETÉRITO INDEFINIDO DE INDICATIVO *PRETERITE INDICATIVE*	FUTURO IMPERFECTO DE INDICATIVO *FUTURE INDICATIVE*	POTENCIAL SIMPLE *CONDITIONAL*
*I argue, etc.**	*I was arguing, etc.**	*I argued, etc.**	*I will argue, etc.**	*I would argue, etc.**
arguyo	argüía	argüí	argüiré	argüiría
arguyes	argüías	argüiste	argüirás	argüirías
arguye	argüía	arguyó	argüirá	argüiría
argüimos	argüíamos	argüimos	argüiremos	argüiríamos
argüís	argüíais	argüisteis	argüiréis	argüiríais
arguyen	argüían	arguyeron	argüirán	argüirían

PRESENTE DE SUBJUNTIVO *PRESENT SUBJUNCTIVE*	PRETÉRITO IMPERFECTO DE SUBJUNTIVO *PAST (IMPERFECT) SUBJUNCTIVE*		FUTURO IMPERFECTO DE SUBJUNTIVO *FUTURE SUBJUNCTIVE*
*I argue, etc.**	*I argued, etc.**		*I will argue, etc.**
arguya	arguyera	arguyese	arguyere
arguyas	arguyeras	arguyeses	arguyeres
arguya	arguyera	arguyese	arguyere
arguyamos	arguyéramos *or*	arguyésemos	arguyéremos
arguyáis	arguyerais	arguyeseis	arguyereis
arguyan	arguyeran	arguyesen	arguyeren

FORMAS IMPERATIVAS, GERUNDIOS Y PARTICIPIO
COMMANDS AND PARTICIPLES

FORMAS IMPERATIVAS *COMMANDS*		GERUNDIO Y PARTICIPIO *PARTICIPLES*		
AFIRMATIVA *AFFIRMATIVE*	NEGATIVA *NEGATIVE*	GERUNDIO SIMPLE *PRESENT PARTICIPLE*	PARTICIPIO *PAST PARTICIPLE*	GERUNDIO COMPUESTO *PERFECT PARTICIPLE*
argue	*don't argue*	*arguing*	*argued*	*having argued*
arguye (tú)	no arguyas (tú)	arguyendo	argüido	habiendo argüido
arguya (Ud.)	no arguya (Ud.)			
argüid (vosotros)	no arguyáis (vosotros)			
arguyan (Uds.)	no arguyan (Uds.)			
let's argue	*let's not argue*			
arguyamos	no arguyamos			

INFINITIVO COMPUESTO: haber argüido
PERFECT INFINITIVE: to have argued

TIEMPOS COMPUESTOS
PERFECT (COMPOUND) TENSES

PRETÉRITO PERFECTO DE INDICATIVO *PRESENT PERFECT INDICATIVE*	PRETÉRITO PLUSCUAMPERFECTO DE INDICATIVO *PAST PERFECT (PLUPERFECT) INDICATIVE*	PRETÉRITO ANTERIOR DE INDICATIVO *PRETERITE PERFECT INDICATIVE*	FUTURO PERFECTO DE INDICATIVO *FUTURE PERFECT INDICATIVE*	POTENCIAL COMPUESTO *CONDITIONAL PERFECT*
I have argued, etc.	*I had argued, etc.*	*I had argued, etc.*	*I will have argued, etc.**	*I would have argued, etc.**
he argüido	había argüido	hube argüido	habré argüido	habría argüido
has argüido	habías argüido	hubiste argüido	habrás argüido	habrías argüido
ha argüido	había argüido	hubo argüido	habrá argüido	habría argüido
hemos argüido	habíamos argüido	hubimos argüido	habremos argüido	habríamos argüido
habéis argüido	habíais argüido	hubisteis argüido	habréis argüido	habríais argüido
han argüido	habían argüido	hubieron argüido	habrán argüido	habrían argüido

PRETÉRITO PERFECTO DE SUBJUNTIVO *PRESENT PERFECT SUBJUNCTIVE*	PRETÉRITO PLUSCUAMPERFECTO DE SUBJUNTIVO *PAST PERFECT (PLUPERFECT) SUBJUNCTIVE*		FUTURO PERFECTO DE SUBJUNTIVO *FUTURE PERFECT SUBJUNCTIVE*
*I have argued, etc.**	*I had argued, etc.**		*I will have argued, etc.**
haya argüido	hubiera argüido	hubiese argüido	hubiere argüido
hayas argüido	hubieras argüido	hubieses argüido	hubieres argüido
haya argüido	hubiera argüido	hubiese argüido	hubiere argüido
hayamos argüido	hubiéramos argüido *or*	hubiésemos argüido	hubiéremos argüido
hayáis argüido	hubierais argüido	hubieseis argüido	hubiereis argüido
hayan argüido	hubieran argüido	hubiesen argüido	hubieren argüido

*For additional translation possibilities see chart A.

V. Orthographic/spelling changing verbs

argüir 72. (OC) (I)

OC = Orthographic / Spelling Change
I   = Irregular

25 Verbs ending in -eír } model: REÍR (i, i)

TIEMPOS SIMPLES
SIMPLE TENSES

PRESENTE DE INDICATIVO **PRESENT INDICATIVE**	PRETÉRITO IMPERFECTO DE INDICATIVO **IMPERFECT INDICATIVE**	PRETÉRITO INDEFINIDO DE INDICATIVO **PRETERITE INDICATIVE**	FUTURO IMPERFECTO DE INDICATIVO **FUTURE INDICATIVE**	POTENCIAL SIMPLE **CONDITIONAL**
I laugh, etc.*	*I was laughing, etc.**	*I laughed, etc.**	*I will laugh, etc.**	*I would laugh, etc.**
río	reía	reí	reiré	reiría
ríes	reías	reíste	reirás	reirías
ríe	reía	rió	reirá	reiría
reímos	reíamos	reímos	reiremos	reiríamos
reís	reíais	reísteis	reiréis	reiríais
ríen	reían	rieron	reirán	reirían

PRESENTE DE SUBJUNTIVO **PRESENT SUBJUNCTIVE**	PRETÉRITO IMPERFECTO DE SUBJUNTIVO **PAST (IMPERFECT) SUBJUNCTIVE**		FUTURO IMPERFECTO DE SUBJUNTIVO **FUTURE SUBJUNCTIVE**
I laugh, etc.*	*I laughed, etc.**		*I will laugh, etc.**
ría	riera	riese	riere
rías	rieras	rieses	rieres
ría	riera	riese	riere
riamos	riéramos *or*	riésemos	riéremos
riáis	rierais	rieseis	riereis
rían	rieran	riesen	rieren

FORMAS IMPERATIVAS, GERUNDIOS Y PARTICIPIO
COMMANDS AND PARTICIPLES

FORMAS IMPERATIVAS **COMMANDS**		GERUNDIO Y PARTICIPIO **PARTICIPLES**		
AFIRMATIVA **AFFIRMATIVE**	NEGATIVA **NEGATIVE**	GERUNDIO SIMPLE **PRESENT PARTICIPLE**	PARTICIPIO **PAST PARTICIPLE**	GERUNDIO COMPUESTO **PERFECT PARTICIPLE**
laugh	*don't laugh*	*laughing*	*laughed*	*having laughed*
ríe (tú)	no rías (tú)	riendo	reído	habiendo reído
ría (Ud.)	no ría (Ud.)			
reíd (vosotros)	no riáis (vosotros)			
rían (Uds.)	no rían (Uds.)			
let's laugh	*let's not laugh*			
riamos	no riamos			

INFINITIVO COMPUESTO: haber reído
PERFECT INFINITIVE: to have laughed

TIEMPOS COMPUESTOS
PERFECT (COMPOUND) TENSES

PRETÉRITO PERFECTO DE INDICATIVO **PRESENT PERFECT INDICATIVE**	PRETÉRITO PLUSCUAMPERFECTO DE INDICATIVO **PAST PERFECT (PLUPERFECT) INDICATIVE**	PRETÉRITO ANTERIOR DE INDICATIVO **PRETERITE PERFECT INDICATIVE**	FUTURO PERFECTO DE INDICATIVO **FUTURE PERFECT INDICATIVE**	POTENCIAL COMPUESTO **CONDITIONAL PERFECT**
I have laughed, etc.	*I had laughed, etc.*	*I had laughed, etc.*	*I will have laughed, etc.**	*I would have laughed, etc.**
he reído	había reído	hube reído	habré reído	habría reído
has reído	habías reído	hubiste reído	habrás reído	habrías reído
ha reído	había reído	hubo reído	habrá reído	habría reído
hemos reído	habíamos reído	hubimos reído	habremos reído	habríamos reído
habéis reído	habíais reído	hubisteis reído	habréis reído	habríais reído
han reído	habían reído	hubieron reído	habrán reído	habrían reído

PRETÉRITO PERFECTO DE SUBJUNTIVO **PRESENT PERFECT SUBJUNCTIVE**	PRETÉRITO PLUSCUAMPERFECTO DE SUBJUNTIVO **PAST PERFECT (PLUPERFECT) SUBJUNCTIVE**		FUTURO PERFECTO DE SUBJUNTIVO **FUTURE PERFECT SUBJUNCTIVE**
I have laughed, etc.*	*I had laughed, etc.**		*I had laughed, etc.**
haya reído	hubiera reído	hubiese reído	hubiere reído
hayas reído	hubieras reído	hubieses reído	hubieres reído
haya reído	hubiera reído	hubiese reído	hubiere reído
hayamos reído	hubiéramos reído *or*	hubiésemos reído	hubiéremos reído
hayáis reído	hubierais reído	hubieseis reído	hubiereis reído
hayan reído	hubieran reído	hubiesen reído	hubieren reído

*For additional translation possibilities see chart A.

V. Orthographic/spelling changing verbs

VERBS OF THIS CATEGORY

---

desleír (i, i) 59. (RC)
engreír (i, i) 59. (RC)
engreírse (i, i) 59. (RC), 4. (R)
*freír (i, i) 88. (RC) (I)
*refreír (i, i) 88. (RC) (I)
reír (i, i) 59. (RC)
reírse (i, i) 59. (RC), 4. (R)
*sofreír (i, i) 88. (RC) (I)
sonreír (i, i) 59. (RC)

R = Reflexive
RC = Radical/Stem Change
I   = Irregular
* These verbs have irregularities in addition to the changes exemplified by the model verb on the chart given here. The cross reference number following each verb indicates the chart which shows all changes and irregularities together.

26 Verb ending in -ller } model: EMPELLER

TIEMPOS SIMPLES
SIMPLE TENSES

PRESENTE DE INDICATIVO *PRESENT INDICATIVE*	PRETÉRITO IMPERFECTO DE INDICATIVO *IMPERFECT INDICATIVE*	PRETÉRITO INDEFINIDO DE INDICATIVO *PRETERITE INDICATIVE*	FUTURO IMPERFECTO DE INDICATIVO *FUTURE INDICATIVE*	POTENCIAL SIMPLE *CONDITIONAL*
*I push, etc.**	*I was pushing, etc.**	*I pushed, etc.**	*I will push, etc.**	*I would push, etc.**
empello	empellía	empellí	empelleré	empellería
empelles	empellías	empelliste	empellerás	empellerías
empelle	empellía	empelló	empellerá	empellería
empellemos	empellíamos	empellimos	empelleremos	empelleríamos
empelléis	empellíais	empellisteis	empelleréis	empelleríais
empellen	empellían	empelleron	empellerán	empellerían

PRESENTE DE SUBJUNTIVO *PRESENT SUBJUNCTIVE*	PRETÉRITO IMPERFECTO DE SUBJUNTIVO *PAST (IMPERFECT) SUBJUNCTIVE*		FUTURO IMPERFECTO DE SUBJUNTIVO *FUTURE SUBJUNCTIVE*
*I push, etc.**	*I pushed, etc.**		*I will push, etc.**
empella	empellera	empellese	empellere
empellas	empelleras	empelleses	empelleres
empella	empellera	empellese	empellere
empellamos	empelléramos *or*	empellésemos	empelléremos
empelláis	empellerais	empelleseis	empellereis
empellan	empelleran	empellesen	empelleren

FORMAS IMPERATIVAS, GERUNDIOS Y PARTICIPIO
COMMANDS AND PARTICIPLES

FORMAS IMPERATIVAS *COMMANDS*		GERUNDIO Y PARTICIPIO *PARTICIPLES*		
AFIRMATIVA *AFFIRMATIVE*	NEGATIVA *NEGATIVE*	GERUNDIO SIMPLE *PRESENT PARTICIPLE*	PARTICIPIO *PAST PARTICIPLE*	GERUNDIO COMPUESTO *PERFECT PARTICIPLE*
push	*don't push*	*pushing*	*pushed*	*having pushed*
empelle (tú)	no empellas (tú)	empellendo	empellido	habiendo empellido
empella (Ud.)	no empella (Ud.)			
empelled (vosotros)	no empelláis (vosotros)			
empellan (Uds.)	no empellan (Uds.)			
let's push	*let's not push*			
empellamos	no empellamos			

INFINITIVO COMPUESTO: haber empellido
PERFECT INFINITIVE: to have pushed

TIEMPOS COMPUESTOS
PERFECT (COMPOUND) TENSES

PRETÉRITO PERFECTO DE INDICATIVO *PRESENT PERFECT INDICATIVE*	PRETÉRITO PLUSCUAMPERFECTO DE INDICATIVO *PAST PERFECT (PLUPERFECT) INDICATIVE*	PRETÉRITO ANTERIOR DE INDICATIVO *PRETERITE PERFECT INDICATIVE*	FUTURO PERFECTO DE INDICATIVO *FUTURE PERFECT INDICATIVE*	POTENCIAL COMPUESTO *CONDITIONAL PERFECT*
I have pushed, etc.	*I had pushed, etc.*	*I had pushed, etc.*	*I will have pushed, etc.**	*I would have pushed, etc.**
he empellido	había empellido	hube empellido	habré empellido	habría empellido
has empellido	habías empellido	hubiste empellido	habrás empellido	habrías empellido
ha empellido	había empellido	hubo empellido	habrá empellido	habría empellido
hemos empellido	habíamos empellido	hubimos empellido	habremos empellido	habríamos empellido
habéis empellido	habíais empellido	hubisteis empellido	habréis empellido	habríais empellido
han empellido	habían empellido	hubieron empellido	habrán empellido	habrían empellido

PRETÉRITO PERFECTO DE SUBJUNTIVO *PRESENT PERFECT SUBJUNCTIVE*	PRETÉRITO PLUSCUAMPERFECTO DE SUBJUNTIVO *PAST PERFECT (PLUPERFECT) SUBJUNCTIVE*		FUTURO PERFECTO DE SUBJUNTIVO *FUTURE PERFECT SUBJUNCTIVE*
*I have pushed, etc. **	*I had pushed, etc.**		*I will have pushed, etc.**
haya empellido	hubiera empellido	hubiese empellido	hubiere empellido
hayas empellido	hubieras empellido	hubieses empellido	hubieres empellido
haya empellido	hubiera empellido	hubiese empellido	hubiere empellido
hayamos empellido	hubiéramos empellido *or*	hubiésemos empellido	hubiéremos empellido
hayáis empellido	hubierais empellido	hubieseis empellido	hubiereis empellido
hayan empellido	hubieran empellido	hubiesen empellido	hubieren empellido

*For additional translation possibilities see chart A.

[114]

V. Orthographic/spelling changing verbs

empeller

27 Verbs ending in -llir } model: BULLIR

PRESENTE DE INDICATIVO *PRESENT* *INDICATIVE*	PRETÉRITO IMPERFECTO DE INDICATIVO *IMPERFECT* *INDICATIVE*	PRETÉRITO INDEFINIDO DE INDICATIVO *PRETERITE* *INDICATIVE*	FUTURO IMPERFECTO DE INDICATIVO *FUTURE* *INDICATIVE*	POTENCIAL SIMPLE *CONDITIONAL*
I boil, etc.	*I was boiling, etc.*	*I boiled, etc.*	*I will boil, etc.*	*I would boil, etc.*
bullo	bullía	bullí	bulliré	bulliría
bulles	bullías	bulliste	bullirás	bullirías
bulle	bullía	bulló	bullirá	bulliría
bullimos	bullíamos	bullimos	bulliremos	bulliríamos
bullís	bullíais	bullisteis	bulliréis	bulliríais
bullen	bullían	bulleron	bullirán	bullirían

PRESENTE DE SUBJUNTIVO *PRESENT* *SUBJUNCTIVE*	PRETÉRITO IMPERFECTO DE SUBJUNTIVO *PAST (IMPERFECT)* *SUBJUNCTIVE*		FUTURO IMPERFECTO DE SUBJUNTIVO *FUTURE* *SUBJUNCTIVE*
I boil, etc.	*I boiled, etc.*		*I will boil, etc.*
bulla	bullera	bullese	bullere
bullas	bulleras	bulleses	bulleres
bulla	bullera	bullese	bullere
bullamos	bulléramos *or*	bullésemos	bulléremos
bulláis	bullerais	bulleseis	bullereis
bullan	bulleran	bullesen	bulleren

FORMAS IMPERATIVAS, GERUNDIOS Y PARTICIPIO
COMMANDS AND PARTICIPLES

FORMAS IMPERATIVAS *COMMANDS*		GERUNDIO Y PARTICIPIO *PARTICIPLES*		
AFIRMATIVA *AFFIRMATIVE*	NEGATIVA *NEGATIVE*	GERUNDIO SIMPLE *PRESENT PARTICIPLE*	PARTICIPIO *PAST PARTICIPLE*	GERUNDIO COMPUESTO *PERFECT PARTICIPLE*
boil	*don't boil*	*boiling*	*boiled*	*having boiled*
bulle (tú)	no bullas (tú)	bullendo	bullido	habiendo bullido
bulla (Ud.)	no bulla (Ud.)			
bullid (vosotros)	no bulláis (vosotros)			
bullan (Uds.)	no bullan (Uds.)			
let's boil	*let's not boil*			
bullamos	no bullamos			

INFINITIVO COMPUESTO: haber bullido
PERFECT INFINITIVE: to have boiled

TIEMPOS COMPUESTOS
PERFECT (COMPOUND) TENSES

PRETÉRITO PERFECTO DE INDICATIVO *PRESENT PERFECT* *INDICATIVE*	PRETÉRITO PLUSCUAMPERFECTO DE INDICATIVO *PAST PERFECT (PLUPERFECT)* *INDICATIVE*	PRETÉRITO ANTERIOR DE INDICATIVO *PRETERITE PERFECT* *INDICATIVE*	FUTURO PERFECTO DE INDICATIVO *FUTURE PERFECT* *INDICATIVE*	POTENCIAL COMPUESTO *CONDITIONAL PERFECT*
I have boiled, etc.	*I had boiled, etc.*	*I had boiled, etc.*	*I will have boiled, etc.*	*I would have boiled, etc.*
he bullido	había bullido	hube bullido	habré bullido	habría bullido
has bullido	habías bullido	hubiste bullido	habrás bullido	habrías bullido
ha bullido	había bullido	hubo bullido	habrá bullido	habría bullido
hemos bullido	habíamos bullido	hubimos bullido	habremos bullido	habríamos bullido
habéis bullido	habíais bullido	hubisteis bullido	habréis bullido	habríais bullido
han bullido	habían bullido	hubieron bullido	habrán bullido	habrían bullido

PRETÉRITO PERFECTO DE SUBJUNTIVO *PRESENT PERFECT* *SUBJUNCTIVE*	PRETÉRITO PLUSCUAMPERFECTO DE SUBJUNTIVO *PAST PERFECT (PLUPERFECT)* *SUBJUNCTIVE*		FUTURO PERFECTO DE SUBJUNTIVO *FUTURE PERFECT* *SUBJUNCTIVE*
I have boiled, etc.	*I had boiled, etc.*		*I will have boiled, etc.*
haya bullido	hubiera bullido	hubiese bullido	hubiere bullido
hayas bullido	hubieras bullido	hubieses bullido	hubieres bullido
haya bullido	hubiera bullido	hubiese bullido	hubiere bullido
hayamos bullido	hubiéramos bullido *or*	hubiésemos bullido	hubiéremos bullido
hayáis bullido	hubierais bullido	hubieseis bullido	hubiereis bullido
hayan bullido	hubieran bullido	hubiesen bullido	hubieren bullido

*For additional translation possibilities see chart A.

V. Orthographic/spelling changing verbs

VERBS OF THIS CATEGORY

bullir
engullir
escabullirse 4. (R)
mullir
rebullir
remullir
tullir
zambullir
zambullirse 4. (R)

R = Reflexive

TIEMPOS SIMPLES
SIMPLE TENSES

PRESENTE DE INDICATIVO *PRESENT INDICATIVE*	PRETÉRITO IMPERFECTO DE INDICATIVO *IMPERFECT INDICATIVE*	PRETÉRITO INDEFINIDO DE INDICATIVO *PRETERITE INDICATIVE*	FUTURO IMPERFECTO DE INDICATIVO *FUTURE INDICATIVE*	POTENCIAL SIMPLE *CONDITIONAL*
I play, etc.*	*I was playing, etc.**	*I played, etc.**	*I will play, etc.**	*I would play, etc.**
taño	tañía	tañí	tañeré	tañería
tañes	tañías	tañiste	tañerás	tañerías
tañe	tañía	tañó	tañerá	tañería
tañemos	tañíamos	tañimos	tañeremos	tañeríamos
tañéis	tañíais	tañisteis	tañeréis	tañeríais
tañen	tañían	tañeron	tañerán	tañerían

PRESENTE DE SUBJUNTIVO *PRESENT SUBJUNCTIVE*	PRETÉRITO IMPERFECTO DE SUBJUNTIVO *PAST (IMPERFECT) SUBJUNCTIVE*		FUTURO IMPERFECTO DE SUBJUNTIVO *FUTURE SUBJUNCTIVE*
I play, etc.*	*I played, etc.**		*I will play, etc.**
taña	tañera	tañese	tañere
tañas	tañeras	tañeses	tañeres
taña	tañera	tañese	tañere
tañamos	tañéramos _or_	tañésemos	tañéremos
tañáis	tañerais	tañeseis	tañereis
tañan	tañeran	tañesen	tañeren

FORMAS IMPERATIVAS, GERUNDIOS Y PARTICIPIO
COMMANDS AND PARTICIPLES

FORMAS IMPERATIVAS *COMMANDS*		GERUNDIO Y PARTICIPIO *PARTICIPLES*		
AFIRMATIVA *AFFIRMATIVE*	NEGATIVA *NEGATIVE*	GERUNDIO SIMPLE *PRESENT PARTICIPLE*	PARTICIPIO *PAST PARTICIPLE*	GERUNDIO COMPUESTO *PERFECT PARTICIPLE*
play	*don't play*	*playing*	*played*	*having played*
tañe (tú)	no tañas (tú)	tañendo	tañido	habiendo tañido
taña (Ud.)	no taña (Ud.)			
tañed (vosotros)	no tañáis (vosotros)			
tañan (Uds.)	no tañan (Uds.)			
let's play	*let's not play*			
tañamos	no tañamos			

INFINITIVO COMPUESTO: haber tañido
PERFECT INFINITIVE: to have played

TIEMPOS COMPUESTOS
PERFECT (COMPOUND) TENSES

PRETÉRITO PERFECTO DE INDICATIVO *PRESENT PERFECT INDICATIVE*	PRETÉRITO PLUSCUAMPERFECTO DE INDICATIVO *PAST PERFECT (PLUPERFECT) INDICATIVE*	PRETÉRITO ANTERIOR DE INDICATIVO *PRETERITE PERFECT INDICATIVE*	FUTURO PERFECTO DE INDICATIVO *FUTURE PERFECT INDICATIVE*	POTENCIAL COMPUESTO *CONDITIONAL PERFECT*
I have played, etc.	*I had played, etc.*	*I had played, etc.*	*I will have played, etc.**	*I would have played, etc.**
he tañido	había tañido	hube tañido	habré tañido	habría tañido
has tañido	habías tañido	hubiste tañido	habrás tañido	habrías tañido
ha tañido	había tañido	hubo tañido	habrá tañido	habría tañido
hemos tañido	habíamos tañido	hubimos tañido	habremos tañido	habríamos tañido
habéis tañido	habíais tañido	hubisteis tañido	habréis tañido	habríais tañido
han tañido	habían tañido	hubieron tañido	habrán tañido	habrían tañido

PRETÉRITO PERFECTO DE SUBJUNTIVO *PRESENT PERFECT SUBJUNCTIVE*	PRETÉRITO PLUSCUAMPERFECTO DE SUBJUNTIVO *PAST PERFECT (PLUPERFECT) SUBJUNCTIVE*		FUTURO PERFECTO DE SUBJUNTIVO *FUTURE PERFECT SUBJUNCTIVE*
I have played, etc.*	*I had played, etc.**		*I will have played, etc.**
haya tañido	hubiera tañido	hubiese tañido	hubiere tañido
hayas tañido	hubieras tañido	hubieses tañido	hubieres tañido
haya tañido	hubiera tañido	hubiese tañido	hubiere tañido
hayamos tañido	hubiéramos tañido _or_	hubiésemos tañido	hubiéremos tañido
hayáis tañido	hubierais tañido	hubieseis tañido	hubiereis tañido
hayan tañido	hubieran tañido	hubiesen tañido	hubieren tañido

*For additional translation possibilities see chart A.

V. Orthographic/spelling changing verbs

28

VERBS OF THIS CATEGORY

atañer (This verb is impersonal, and thus is used only in the third persons singular and plural, and in the infinitives, present participle, and past participle)
tañer

[119]

29 Verbs ending in -ñir } model: BRUÑIR

TIEMPOS SIMPLES
SIMPLE TENSES

PRESENTE DE INDICATIVO / PRESENT INDICATIVE	PRETÉRITO IMPERFECTO DE INDICATIVO / IMPERFECT INDICATIVE	PRETÉRITO INDEFINIDO DE INDICATIVO / PRETERITE INDICATIVE	FUTURO IMPERFECTO DE INDICATIVO / FUTURE INDICATIVE	POTENCIAL SIMPLE / CONDITIONAL
*I polish, etc.**	*I was polishing, etc.**	*I polished, etc.**	*I will polish, etc.**	*I would polish, etc.**
bruño	bruñía	bruñí	bruñiré	bruñiría
bruñes	bruñías	bruñiste	bruñirás	bruñirías
bruñe	bruñía	bruñó	bruñirá	bruñiría
bruñimos	bruñíamos	bruñimos	bruñiremos	bruñiríamos
bruñís	bruñíais	bruñisteis	bruñiréis	bruñiríais
bruñen	bruñían	bruñeron	bruñirán	bruñirían

PRESENTE DE SUBJUNTIVO / PRESENT SUBJUNCTIVE	PRETÉRITO IMPERFECTO DE SUBJUNTIVO / PAST (IMPERFECT) SUBJUNCTIVE		FUTURO IMPERFECTO DE SUBJUNTIVO / FUTURE SUBJUNCTIVE
*I polish, etc.**	*I polished, etc.**		*I will polish, etc.**
bruña	bruñera	bruñese	bruñere
bruñas	bruñeras	bruñeses	bruñeres
bruña	bruñera	bruñese	bruñere
bruñamos	bruñéramos *or*	bruñésemos	bruñéremos
bruñáis	bruñerais	bruñeseis	bruñereis
bruñan	bruñeran	bruñesen	bruñeren

FORMAS IMPERATIVAS, GERUNDIOS Y PARTICIPIO
COMMANDS AND PARTICIPLES

FORMAS IMPERATIVAS / COMMANDS		GERUNDIO Y PARTICIPIO / PARTICIPLES		
AFIRMATIVA / AFFIRMATIVE	NEGATIVA / NEGATIVE	GERUNDIO SIMPLE / PRESENT PARTICIPLE	PARTICIPIO / PAST PARTICIPLE	GERUNDIO COMPUESTO / PERFECT PARTICIPLE
polish	*don't polish*	*polishing*	*polished*	*having polished*
bruñe (tú)	no bruñas (tú)	bruñendo	bruñido	habiendo bruñido
bruña (Ud.)	no bruña (Ud.)			
bruñid (vosotros)	no bruñáis (vosotros)			
bruñan (Uds.)	no bruñan (Uds.)			
let's polish	*let's not polish*			
bruñamos	no bruñamos			

INFINITIVO COMPUESTO: haber bruñido
PERFECT INFINITIVE: to have polished

TIEMPOS COMPUESTOS
PERFECT (COMPOUND) TENSES

PRETÉRITO PERFECTO DE INDICATIVO / PRESENT PERFECT INDICATIVE	PRETÉRITO PLUSCUAMPERFECTO DE INDICATIVO / PAST PERFECT (PLUPERFECT) INDICATIVE	PRETÉRITO ANTERIOR DE INDICATIVO / PRETERITE PERFECT INDICATIVE	FUTURO PERFECTO DE INDICATIVO / FUTURE PERFECT INDICATIVE	POTENCIAL COMPUESTO / CONDITIONAL PERFECT
I have polished, etc.	*I had polished, etc.*	*I had polished, etc.*	*I will have polished, etc.**	*I would have polished, etc.**
he bruñido	había bruñido	hube bruñido	habré bruñido	habría bruñido
has bruñido	habías bruñido	hubiste bruñido	habrás bruñido	habrías bruñido
ha bruñido	había bruñido	hubo bruñido	habrá bruñido	habría bruñido
hemos bruñido	habíamos bruñido	hubimos bruñido	habremos bruñido	habríamos bruñido
habéis bruñido	habíais bruñido	hubisteis bruñido	habréis bruñido	habríais bruñido
han bruñido	habían bruñido	hubieron bruñido	habrán bruñido	habrían bruñido

PRETÉRITO PERFECTO DE SUBJUNTIVO / PRESENT PERFECT SUBJUNCTIVE	PRETÉRITO PLUSCUAMPERFECTO DE SUBJUNTIVO / PAST PERFECT (PLUPERFECT) SUBJUNCTIVE		FUTURO PERFECTO DE SUBJUNTIVO / FUTURE PERFECT SUBJUNCTIVE
*I have polished, etc.**	*I had polished, etc.**		*I will have polished, etc.**
haya bruñido	hubiera bruñido	hubiese bruñido	hubiere bruñido
hayas bruñido	hubieras bruñido	hubieses bruñido	hubieres bruñido
haya bruñido	hubiera bruñido	hubiese bruñido	hubiere bruñido
hayamos bruñido	hubiéramos bruñido *or*	hubiésemos bruñido	hubiéremos bruñido
hayáis bruñido	hubierais bruñido	hubieseis bruñido	hubiereis bruñido
hayan bruñido	hubieran bruñido	hubiesen bruñido	hubieren bruñido

*For additional translation possibilities see chart A.

V. Orthographic/spelling changing verbs

bruñir
*ceñir (i, i) 60. (RC)
*ceñirse (i, i) 60. (RC), 4. (R)
*constreñir (i, i) 60. (RC)
*desteñir (i, i) 60. (RC)
*desteñirse (i, i) 60. (RC), 4. (R)
*estreñir (i, i) 60. (RC)
*estreñirse (i, i) 60. (RC), 4. (R)
gruñir
plañir
regañir
*reñir (i, i) 60. (RC)
restriñir
*reteñir (i, i) 60. (RC)
*teñir (i, i) 60. (RC)
uñir

R   = Reflexive
RC = Radical/Stem Change
*These verbs have radical/stem changes in addition to the orthographic/spelling changes exemplified by the model verb on the chart given here. The cross reference number following each verb indicates the chart which shows all changes together.

30 Verb with forms with initial o that becomes ue } model: OLER (ue)

TIEMPOS SIMPLES
SIMPLE TENSES

PRESENTE DE INDICATIVO *PRESENT INDICATIVE*	PRETÉRITO IMPERFECTO DE INDICATIVO *IMPERFECT INDICATIVE*	PRETÉRITO INDEFINIDO DE INDICATIVO *PRETERITE INDICATIVE*	FUTURO IMPERFECTO DE INDICATIVO *FUTURE INDICATIVE*	POTENCIAL SIMPLE *CONDITIONAL*
*I smell, etc.**	*I was smelling, etc.**	*I smelled, etc.**	*I will smell, etc.**	*I would smell, etc.**
huelo	olía	olí	oleré	olería
hueles	olías	oliste	olerás	olerías
huele	olía	olió	olerá	olería
olemos	olíamos	olimos	oleremos	oleríamos
oléis	olíais	olisteis	oleréis	oleríais
huelen	olían	olieron	olerán	olerían

PRESENTE DE SUBJUNTIVO *PRESENT SUBJUNCTIVE*	PRETÉRITO IMPERFECTO DE SUBJUNTIVO *PAST (IMPERFECT) SUBJUNCTIVE*		FUTURO IMPERFECTO DE SUBJUNTIVO *FUTURE SUBJUNCTIVE*
*I smell, etc.**	*I smelled, etc.**		*I will smell, etc.**
huela	oliera	oliese	oliere
huelas	olieras	olieses	olieres
huela	oliera	oliese	oliere
olamos	oliéramos *or*	oliésemos	oliéremos
oláis	olierais	olieseis	oliereis
huelan	olieran	oliesen	olieren

FORMAS IMPERATIVAS, GERUNDIOS Y PARTICIPIO
COMMANDS AND PARTICIPLES

FORMAS IMPERATIVAS *COMMANDS*		GERUNDIO Y PARTICIPIO *PARTICIPLES*		
AFIRMATIVA *AFFIRMATIVE*	NEGATIVA *NEGATIVE*	GERUNDIO SIMPLE *PRESENT PARTICIPLE*	PARTICIPIO *PAST PARTICIPLE*	GERUNDIO COMPUESTO *PERFECT PARTICIPLE*
smell	*don't smell*	*smelling*	*smelled*	*having smelled*
huele (tú)	no huelas (tú)	oliendo	olido	habiendo olido
huela (Ud.)	no huela (Ud.)			
oled (vosotros)	no oláis (vosotros)			
huelan (Uds.)	no huelan (Uds.)			
let's smell	*let's not smell*			
olamos	no olamos			

INFINITIVO COMPUESTO: haber olido
PERFECT INFINITIVE: to have smelled

TIEMPOS COMPUESTOS
PERFECT (COMPOUND) TENSES

PRETÉRITO PERFECTO DE INDICATIVO *PRESENT PERFECT INDICATIVE*	PRETÉRITO PLUSCUAMPERFECTO DE INDICATIVO *PAST PERFECT (PLUPERFECT) INDICATIVE*	PRETÉRITO ANTERIOR DE INDICATIVO *PRETERITE PERFECT INDICATIVE*	FUTURO PERFECTO DE INDICATIVO *FUTURE PERFECT INDICATIVE*	POTENCIAL COMPUESTO *CONDITIONAL PERFECT*
I have smelled, etc.	*I had smelled, etc.*	*I had smelled, etc.*	*I will have smelled, etc.**	*I would have smelled, etc.**
he olido	había olido	hube olido	habré olido	habría olido
has olido	habías olido	hubiste olido	habrás olido	habrías olido
ha olido	había olido	hubo olido	habrá olido	habría olido
hemos olido	habíamos olido	hubimos olido	habremos olido	habríamos olido
habéis olido	habíais olido	hubisteis olido	habréis olido	habríais olido
han olido	habían olido	hubieron olido	habrán olido	habrían olido

PRETÉRITO PERFECTO DE SUBJUNTIVO *PRESENT PERFECT SUBJUNCTIVE*	PRETÉRITO PLUSCUAMPERFECTO DE SUBJUNTIVO *PAST PERFECT (PLUPERFECT) SUBJUNCTIVE*		FUTURO PERFECTO DE SUBJUNTIVO *FUTURE PERFECT SUBJUNCTIVE*
*I have smelled, etc.**	*I had smelled, etc.**		*I will have smelled. etc.**
haya olido	hubiera olido	hubiese olido	hubiere olido
hayas olido	hubieras olido	hubieses olido	hubieres olido
haya olido	hubiera olido	hubiese olido	hubiere olido
hayamos olido	hubiéramos olido *or*	hubiésemos olido	hubiéremos olido
hayáis olido	hubierais olido	hubieseis olido	hubiereis olido
hayan olido	hubieran olido	hubiesen olido	hubieren olido

*For additional translation possibilities see chart A.

V. Orthographic/spelling changing verbs

VERB OF THIS CATEGORY

oler (ue) 55. (RC)

RC = Radical/Stem Change

Verb with forms with internal o that becomes ue and inserts h before ue } **model: DESOSAR (ue)**

TIEMPOS SIMPLES
SIMPLE TENSES

PRESENTE DE INDICATIVO *PRESENT INDICATIVE*	PRETÉRITO IMPERFECTO DE INDICATIVO *IMPERFECT INDICATIVE*	PRETÉRITO INDEFINIDO DE INDICATIVO *PRETERITE INDICATIVE*	FUTURO IMPERFECTO DE INDICATIVO *FUTURE INDICATIVE*	POTENCIAL SIMPLE *CONDITIONAL*
I bone, etc.*	*I was boning. etc.**	*I boned, etc.**	*I will bone, etc.**	*I would bone, etc.**
deshueso	desosaba	desosé	desosaré	desosaría
deshuesas	desosabas	desosaste	desosarás	desosarías
deshuesa	desosaba	desosó	desosará	desosaría
desosamos	desosábamos	desosamos	desosaremos	desosaríamos
desosáis	desosabais	desosasteis	desosaréis	desosaríais
deshuesan	desosaban	desosaron	desosarán	desosarían

PRESENTE DE SUBJUNTIVO *PRESENT SUBJUNCTIVE*	PRETÉRITO IMPERFECTO DE SUBJUNTIVO *PAST (IMPERFECT) SUBJUNCTIVE*		FUTURO IMPERFECTO DE SUBJUNTIVO *FUTURE SUBJUNCTIVE*
I bone, etc.*	*I boned, etc.**		*I will bone, etc.**
deshuese	desosara	desosase	desosare
deshueses	desosaras	desosases	desosares
deshuese	desosara	desosase	desosare
desosemos	desosáramos *or*	desosásemos	desosáremos
desoséis	desosarais	desosaseis	desosareis
deshuesen	desosaran	desosasen	desosaren

FORMAS IMPERATIVAS, GERUNDIOS Y PARTICIPIO
COMMANDS AND PARTICIPLES

FORMAS IMPERATIVAS *COMMANDS*		GERUNDIO Y PARTICIPIO *PARTICIPLES*		
AFIRMATIVA *AFFIRMATIVE*	NEGATIVA *NEGATIVE*	GERUNDIO SIMPLE *PRESENT PARTICIPLE*	PARTICIPIO *PAST PARTICIPLE*	GERUNDIO COMPUESTO *PERFECT PARTICIPLE*
bone	*don't bone*	*boning*	*boned*	*having boned*
deshuesa (tú)	no deshueses (tú)	desosando	desosado	habiendo desosado
deshuese (Ud.)	no deshuese (Ud.)			
desosad (vosotros)	no desoséis (vosotros)			
deshuesen (Uds.)	no deshuesen (Uds.)			
let's bone	*let's not bone*			
desosemos	no desosemos			

INFINITIVO COMPUESTO: haber desosado
PERFECT INFINITIVE: to have boned

TIEMPOS COMPUESTOS
PERFECT (COMPOUND) TENSES

PRETÉRITO PERFECTO DE INDICATIVO *PRESENT PERFECT INDICATIVE*	PRETÉRITO PLUSCUAMPERFECTO DE INDICATIVO *PAST PERFECT (PLUPERFECT) INDICATIVE*	PRETÉRITO ANTERIOR DE INDICATIVO *PRETERITE PERFECT INDICATIVE*	FUTURO PERFECTO DE INDICATIVO *FUTURE PERFECT INDICATIVE*	POTENCIAL COMPUESTO *CONDITIONAL PERFECT*
I have boned, etc.	*I had boned, etc.*	*I had boned, etc.*	*I will have boned, etc.**	*I would have boned, etc.**
he desosado	había desosado	hube desosado	habré desosado	habría desosado
has desosado	habías desosado	hubiste desosado	habrás desosado	habrías desosado
ha desosado	había desosado	hubo desosado	habrá desosado	habría desosado
hemos desosado	habíamos desosado	hubimos desosado	habremos desosado	habríamos desosado
habéis desosado	habíais desosado	hubisteis desosado	habréis desosado	habríais desosado
han desosado	habían desosado	hubieron desosado	habrán desosado	habrían desosado

PRETÉRITO PERFECTO DE SUBJUNTIVO *PRESENT PERFECT SUBJUNCTIVE*	PRETÉRITO PLUSCUAMPERFECTO DE SUBJUNTIVO *PAST PERFECT (PLUPERFECT) SUBJUNCTIVE*		FUTURO PERFECTO DE SUBJUNTIVO *FUTURE PERFECT SUBJUNCTIVE*
I have boned, etc.*	*I had boned, etc.**		*I will have boned, etc.**
haya desosado	hubiera desosado	hubiese desosado	hubiere desosado
hayas desosado	hubieras desosado	hubieses desosado	hubieres desosado
haya desosado	hubiera desosado	hubiese desosado	hubiere desosado
hayamos desosado	hubiéramos desosado *or*	hubiésemos desosado	hubiéremos desosado
hayáis desosado	hubierais desosado	hubieseis desosado	hubiereis desosado
hayan desosado	hubieran desosado	hubiesen desosado	hubieren desosado

*For additional translation possibilities see chart A.

V. Orthographic/spelling changing verbs

VERB OF THIS CATEGORY

desosar (ue) 47. (RC)

RC = Radical/Stem Change

32 Verbs with forms with initial ie sound } model: ERRAR (ie)

TIEMPOS SIMPLES
SIMPLE TENSES

PRESENTE DE INDICATIVO *PRESENT INDICATIVE*	PRETÉRITO IMPERFECTO DE INDICATIVO *IMPERFECT INDICATIVE*	PRETÉRITO INDEFINIDO DE INDICATIVO *PRETERITE INDICATIVE*	FUTURO IMPERFECTO DE INDICATIVO *FUTURE INDICATIVE*	POTENCIAL SIMPLE *CONDITIONAL*
I err, etc.*	*I was erring, etc.**	*I erred, etc.**	*I will err, etc.**	*I would err, etc.**
yerro	erraba	erré	erraré	erraría
yerras	errabas	erraste	errarás	errarías
yerra	erraba	erró	errará	erraría
erramos	errábamos	erramos	erraremos	erraríamos
erráis	errabais	errasteis	erraréis	erraríais
yerran	erraban	erraron	errarán	errarían

PRESENTE DE SUBJUNTIVO *PRESENT SUBJUNCTIVE*	PRETÉRITO IMPERFECTO DE SUBJUNTIVO *PAST (IMPERFECT) SUBJUNCTIVE*		FUTURO IMPERFECTO DE SUBJUNTIVO *FUTURE SUBJUNCTIVE*
I err, etc.*	*I erred, etc.**		*I will err, etc.**
yerre	errara	errase	errare
yerres	erraras	errases	errares
yerre	errara	errase	errare
erremos	erráramos *or*	errásemos	erráremos
erréis	errarais	erraseis	errareis
yerren	erraran	errasen	erraren

FORMAS IMPERATIVAS, GERUNDIOS Y PARTICIPIO
COMMANDS AND PARTICIPLES

FORMAS IMPERATIVAS *COMMANDS*		GERUNDIO Y PARTICIPIO *PARTICIPLES*		
AFIRMATIVA *AFFIRMATIVE*	NEGATIVA *NEGATIVE*	GERUNDIO SIMPLE *PRESENT PARTICIPLE*	PARTICIPIO *PAST PARTICIPLE*	GERUNDIO COMPUESTO *PERFECT PARTICIPLE*
err	*don't err*	*erring*	*erred*	*having erred*
yerra (tú)	no yerres (tú)	errando	errado	habiendo errado
yerre (Ud.)	no yerre (Ud.)			
errad (vosotros)	no erréis (vosotros)			
yerren (Uds.)	no yerren (Uds.)			
let's err	*let's not err*			
erremos	no erremos			

INFINITIVO COMPUESTO: haber errado
PERFECT INFINITIVE: to have erred

TIEMPOS COMPUESTOS
PERFECT (COMPOUND) TENSES

PRETÉRITO PERFECTO DE INDICATIVO *PRESENT PERFECT INDICATIVE*	PRETÉRITO PLUSCUAMPERFECTO DE INDICATIVO *PAST PERFECT (PLUPERFECT) INDICATIVE*	PRETÉRITO ANTERIOR DE INDICATIVO *PRETERITE PERFECT INDICATIVE*	FUTURO PERFECTO DE INDICATIVO *FUTURE PERFECT INDICATIVE*	POTENCIAL COMPUESTO *CONDITIONAL PERFECT*
I have erred, etc.	*I had erred, etc.*	*I had erred, etc.*	*I will have erred, etc.**	*I would have erred, etc.**
he errado	había errado	hube errado	habré errado	habría errado
has errado	habías errado	hubiste errado	habrás errado	habrías errado
ha errado	había errado	hubo errado	habrá errado	habría errado
hemos errado	habíamos errado	hubimos errado	habremos errado	habríamos errado
habéis errado	habíais errado	hubisteis errado	habréis errado	habríais errado
han errado	habían errado	hubieron errado	habrán errado	habrían errado

PRETÉRITO PERFECTO DE SUBJUNTIVO *PRESENT PERFECT SUBJUNCTIVE*	PRETÉRITO PLUSCUAMPERFECTO DE SUBJUNTIVO *PAST PERFECT (PLUPERFECT) SUBJUNCTIVE*		FUTURO PERFECTO DE SUBJUNTIVO *FUTURE PERFECT SUBJUNCTIVE*
I have erred, etc.*	*I had erred, etc.**		*I will have erred, etc.**
haya errado	hubiera errado	hubiese errado	hubiere errado
hayas errado	hubieras errado	hubieses errado	hubieres errado
haya errado	hubiera errado	hubiese errado	hubiere errado
hayamos errado	hubiéramos errado *or*	hubiésemos errado	hubiéremos errado
hayáis errado	hubierais errado	hubieseis errado	hubiereis errado
hayan errado	hubieran errado	hubiesen errado	hubieren errado

*For additional translation possibilities see chart A.

V. Orthographic/spelling changing verbs

---

*erguir (ie, i) 86. (OC) (RC) (I)
 errar (ie) 52. (RC)
**ir (in the form yendo) 92. (I)

OC = Orthographic/Spelling Change
RC = Radical/Stem Change
I   = Irregular
*This verb has other orthographic/spelling changes and irregularities in addition to the changes exemplified by the model verb on the chart given here. The cross reference number following the verb indicates the chart which shows all changes and irregularities together.
**This verb has irregularities in addition to the orthographic/spelling change given here. The cross reference number following the verb indicates the chart which shows this change and all irregularities together.

33 Verbs with g + (o that becomes ue) } model: AGORAR (ue)

TIEMPOS SIMPLES
SIMPLE TENSES

PRESENTE DE INDICATIVO *PRESENT INDICATIVE*	PRETÉRITO IMPERFECTO DE INDICATIVO *IMPERFECT INDICATIVE*	PRETÉRITO INDEFINIDO DE INDICATIVO *PRETERITE INDICATIVE*	FUTURO IMPERFECTO DE INDICATIVO *FUTURE INDICATIVE*	POTENCIAL SIMPLE *CONDITIONAL*
*I predict, etc.**	*I was predicting, etc.**	*I predicted, etc.**	*I will predict, etc.**	*I would predict, etc.**
agüero	agoraba	agoré	agoraré	agoraría
agüeras	agorabas	agoraste	agorarás	agorarías
agüera	agoraba	agoró	agorará	agoraría
agoramos	agorábamos	agoramos	agoraremos	agoraríamos
agoráis	agorabais	agorasteis	agoraréis	agoraríais
agüeran	agoraban	agoraron	agorarán	agorarían

PRESENTE DE SUBJUNTIVO *PRESENT SUBJUNCTIVE*	PRETÉRITO IMPERFECTO DE SUBJUNTIVO *PAST (IMPERFECT) SUBJUNCTIVE*		FUTURO IMPERFECTO DE SUBJUNTIVO *FUTURE SUBJUNCTIVE*
*I predict, etc.**	*I predicted, etc.**		*I will predict, etc.**
agüere	agorara	agorase	agorare
agüeres	agoraras	agorases	agorares
agüere	agorara	agorase	agorare
agoremos	agoráramos *or* agorásemos		agoráremos
agoréis	agorarais	agoraseis	agorareis
agüeren	agoraran	agorasen	agoraren

FORMAS IMPERATIVAS, GERUNDIOS Y PARTICIPIO
COMMANDS AND PARTICIPLES

FORMAS IMPERATIVAS *COMMANDS*		GERUNDIO Y PARTICIPIO *PARTICIPLES*		
AFIRMATIVA *AFFIRMATIVE*	NEGATIVA *NEGATIVE*	GERUNDIO SIMPLE *PRESENT PARTICIPLE*	PARTICIPIO *PAST PARTICIPLE*	GERUNDIO COMPUESTO *PERFECT PARTICIPLE*
predict	*don't predict*	*predicting*	*predicted*	*having predicted*
agüera (tú)	no agüeres (tú)	agorando	agorado	habiendo agorado
agüere (Ud.)	no agüere (Ud.)			
agorad (vosotros)	no agoréis (vosotros)			
agüeren (Uds.)	no agüeren (Uds.)			
let's predict	*let's not predict*			
agoremos	no agoremos			

INFINITIVO COMPUESTO: haber agorado
PERFECT INFINITIVE: to have predicted

TIEMPOS COMPUESTOS
PERFECT (COMPOUND) TENSES

PRETÉRITO PERFECTO DE INDICATIVO *PRESENT PERFECT INDICATIVE*	PRETÉRITO PLUSCUAMPERFECTO DE INDICATIVO *PAST PERFECT (PLUPERFECT) INDICATIVE*	PRETÉRITO ANTERIOR DE INDICATIVO *PRETERITE PERFECT INDICATIVE*	FUTURO PERFECTO DE INDICATIVO *FUTURE PERFECT INDICATIVE*	POTENCIAL COMPUESTO *CONDITIONAL PERFECT*
I have predicted, etc.	*I had predicted, etc.*	*I had predicted, etc.*	*I will have predicted, etc.**	*I would have predicted, etc.**
he agorado	había agorado	hube agorado	habré agorado	habría agorado
has agorado	habías agorado	hubiste agorado	habrás agorado	habrías agorado
ha agorado	había agorado	hubo agorado	habrá agorado	habría agorado
hemos agorado	habíamos agorado	hubimos agorado	habremos agorado	habríamos agorado
habéis agorado	habíais agorado	hubisteis agorado	habréis agorado	habríais agorado
han agorado	habían agorado	hubieron agorado	habrán agorado	habrían agorado

PRETÉRITO PERFECTO DE SUBJUNTIVO *PRESENT PERFECT SUBJUNCTIVE*	PRETÉRITO PLUSCUAMPERFECTO DE SUBJUNTIVO *PAST PERFECT (PLUPERFECT) SUBJUNCTIVE*		FUTURO PERFECTO DE SUBJUNTIVO *FUTURE PERFECT SUBJUNCTIVE*
*I have predicted, etc.**	*I had predicted etc.**		*I will have predicted, etc.**
haya agorado	hubiera agorado	hubiese agorado	hubiere agorado
hayas agorado	hubieras agorado	hubieses agorado	hubieres agorado
haya agorado	hubiera agorado	hubiese agorado	hubiere agorado
hayamos agorado	hubiéramos agorado *or* hubiésemos agorado		hubiéremos agorado
hayáis agorado	hubierais agorado	hubieseis agorado	hubiereis agorado
hayan agorado	hubieran agorado	hubiesen agorado	hubieren agorado

*For additional translation possibilities see chart A.

V. Orthographic/spelling changing verbs

agorar (ue) 48. (RC)
*avergonzar (ue) 49. (OC) (RC)
*avergonzarse (ue) 49. (OC) (RC), 4. (R)
degollar (ue) 48. (RC)
*desvergonzarse (ue) 49. (OC) (RC), 4. (R)
regoldar (ue) 48. (RC)

R = Reflexive
OC = Orthographic/Spelling Change
RC = Radical/Stem Change
*These verbs have other orthographic/spelling changes in addition to the changes exemplified by the model verb on the chart given here. The cross reference number following each verb indicates the chart which shows all changes together.

Verbs with strong vowel (a, e, or o) + h + stressed weak vowel (u or i) } model: AHIJAR

TIEMPOS SIMPLES
SIMPLE TENSES

PRESENTE DE INDICATIVO *PRESENT INDICATIVE*	PRETÉRITO IMPERFECTO DE INDICATIVO *IMPERFECT INDICATIVE*	PRETÉRITO INDEFINIDO DE INDICATIVO *PRETERITE INDICATIVE*	FUTURO IMPERFECTO DE INDICATIVO *FUTURE INDICATIVE*	POTENCIAL SIMPLE *CONDITIONAL*
I adopt, etc.*	*I was adopting, etc.**	*I adopted, etc.**	*I will adopt, etc.**	*I would adopt, etc.**
ahíjo	ahijaba	ahijé	ahijaré	ahijaría
ahíjas	ahijabas	ahijaste	ahijarás	ahijarías
ahíja	ahijaba	ahijó	ahijará	ahijaría
ahijamos	ahijábamos	ahijamos	ahijaremos	ahijaríamos
ahijáis	ahijabais	ahijasteis	ahijaréis	ahijaríais
ahíjan	ahijaban	ahijaron	ahijarán	ahijarían

PRESENTE DE SUBJUNTIVO *PRESENT SUBJUNCTIVE*	PRETÉRITO IMPERFECTO DE SUBJUNTIVO *PAST (IMPERFECT) SUBJUNCTIVE*		FUTURO IMPERFECTO DE SUBJUNTIVO *FUTURE SUBJUNCTIVE*
I adopt, etc.*	*I adopted, etc.**		*I will adopt, etc.**
ahíje	ahijara	ahijase	ahijare
ahíjes	ahijaras	ahijases	ahijares
ahíje	ahijara *or*	ahijase	ahijare
ahijemos	ahijáramos	ahijásemos	ahijáremos
ahijéis	ahijarais	ahijaseis	ahijareis
ahíjen	ahijaran	ahijasen	ahijaren

FORMAS IMPERATIVAS, GERUNDIOS Y PARTICIPIO
COMMANDS AND PARTICIPLES

FORMAS IMPERATIVAS *COMMANDS*		GERUNDIO Y PARTICIPIO *PARTICIPLES*		
AFIRMATIVA *AFFIRMATIVE*	NEGATIVA *NEGATIVE*	GERUNDIO SIMPLE *PRESENT PARTICIPLE*	PARTICIPIO *PAST PARTICIPLE*	GERUNDIO COMPUESTO *PERFECT PARTICIPLE*
adopt	*don't adopt*	*adopting*	*adopted*	*having adopted*
ahíja (tú)	no ahíjes (tú)	ahijando	ahijado	habiendo ahijado
ahíje (Ud.)	no ahíje (Ud.)			
ahijad (vosotros)	no ahijéis (vosotros)			
ahíjen (Uds.)	no ahíjen (Uds.)			
let's adopt	*let's not adopt*			
ahijemos	no ahijemos			

INFINITIVO COMPUESTO: haber ahijado
PERFECT INFINITIVE: to have adopted

TIEMPOS COMPUESTOS
PERFECT (COMPOUND) TENSES

PRETÉRITO PERFECTO DE INDICATIVO *PRESENT PERFECT INDICATIVE*	PRETÉRITO PLUSCUAMPERFECTO DE INDICATIVO *PAST PERFECT (PLUPERFECT) INDICATIVE*	PRETÉRITO ANTERIOR DE INDICATIVO *PRETERITE PERFECT INDICATIVE*	FUTURO PERFECTO DE INDICATIVO *FUTURE PERFECT INDICATIVE*	POTENCIAL COMPUESTO *CONDITIONAL PERFECT*
I have adopted, etc.	*I had adopted, etc.*	*I had adopted, etc.*	*I will have adopted, etc.**	*I would have adopted, etc.**
he ahijado	había ahijado	hube ahijado	habré ahijado	habría ahijado
has ahijado	habías ahijado	hubiste ahijado	habrás ahijado	habrías ahijado
ha ahijado	había ahijado	hubo ahijado	habrá ahijado	habría ahijado
hemos ahijado	habíamos ahijado	hubimos ahijado	habremos ahijado	habríamos ahijado
habéis ahijado	habíais ahijado	hubisteis ahijado	habréis ahijado	habríais ahijado
han ahijado	habían ahijado	hubieron ahijado	habrán ahijado	habrían ahijado

PRETÉRITO PERFECTO DE SUBJUNTIVO *PRESENT PERFECT SUBJUNCTIVE*	PRETÉRITO PLUSCUAMPERFECTO DE SUBJUNTIVO *PAST PERFECT (PLUPERFECT) SUBJUNCTIVE*		FUTURO PERFECTO DE SUBJUNTIVO *FUTURE PERFECT SUBJUNCTIVE*
I have adopted, etc.*	*I had adopted, etc.**		*I will have adopted, etc.**
haya ahijado	hubiera ahijado	hubiese ahijado	hubiere ahijado
hayas ahijado	hubieras ahijado	hubieses ahijado	hubieres ahijado
haya ahijado	hubiera ahijado	hubiese ahijado	hubiere ahijado
hayamos ahijado	hubiéramos ahijado *or*	hubiésemos ahijado	hubiéremos ahijado
hayáis ahijado	hubierais ahijado	hubieseis ahijado	hubiereis ahijado
hayan ahijado	hubieran ahijado	hubiesen ahijado	hubieren ahijado

*For additional translation possibilities see chart A.

V. Orthographic/spelling changing verbs

ahijar
ahilar
ahilarse 4. (R)
**ahincar 8. (OC)
ahitar
ahuchar
ahumar
amohinar
amohinarse 4. (R)
cohibir
*contrahacer 90. (I)
desahijar
prohibir
prohijar
*rehacer 90. (I)
*rehacerse 90. (I), 4. (R)
*rehenchir (i, i) 42. (RC)
rehilar
*rehuir 71. (OC) (I)
rehundir
rehusar
sahumar
sobrehilar

Special note: **desahuciar**

    This verb technically belongs to this group. Though preferred usage has not been established, in current trends the "a" and "u" form a diphthong, causing the stress to fall on the "a" in the forms where it otherwise would fall on the "u." To conjugate **desahuciar** with this stress pattern, follow the model verb of chart 1.

R = Reflexive
OC = Orthographic/Spelling Change
RC = Radical/Stem Change
I = Irregular
* These verbs have changes and/or irregularities in addition to those orthographic/spelling changes exemplified by the model verb on the chart given here. The cross reference number following each verb indicates the chart which shows all irregularities and/or changes together.
**This verb has other orthographic/spelling changes in addition to those exemplified by the model verb on the chart given here. The cross reference number following the verb indicates the chart which exemplifies the other orthographic/spelling changes.

35 Synopsis of orthographic/spelling changes

V. Orthographic/spelling changing verbs

CHART NUMBER	INFINITIVE ENDING	CHANGE THAT OCCURS	FORMS IN WHICH CHANGE OCCURS	REASON FOR CHANGE
8.	-car	c > qu before e	present subjunctive: all forms commands: those coming from the present subjunctive preterite: 1st singular	to preserve initial sound of the c of the infinitive
9.	-gar	g > gu before e		to preserve initial sound of the g of the infinitive
10.	-guar	u > ü before e		to preserve initial pronunciation of the u
11.	-zar	z > c before e		a z should not be followed by e or i
12.	-consonant + cer	c > z before o or a		to preserve initial sound of the c of the infinitive
13.	-consonant + cir	c > z before o or a		to preserve initial sound of the c of the infinitive
14.	-vowel + cer (only in mecer, cocer, and their compounds)*	c > z before o or a		to preserve initial sound of the c of the infinitive
15.	-ger	g > j before o or a	present indicative: 1st singular present subjunctive: all forms commands: those coming from the present subjunctive	to preserve initial sound of the g of the infinitive
16.	-gir	g > j before o or a		to preserve initial sound of the g of the infinitive
17.	-guir	gu > g before o or a		to preserve initial sound of the g of the infinitive (The u in -guir is merely a device to show that g has a hard sound. Since before o or a a g already has a hard sound, the u is no longer needed.)
18.	-quir	qu > c before o or a		qu should not be followed by a or o

	Ending	Change	Forms affected	Purpose
19.	-iar in monosyllabic infinitives	i of verbal stem > í	present indicative: 1st, 2nd, 3rd singular, 3rd plural present subjunctive: 1st, 2nd, 3rd singular, 3rd plural commands: all except nosotros, vosotros, affirmative and negative	to preserve regular verbal stress pattern
19.	-uar in monosyllabic infinitives	u of verbal stem > ú		to preserve regular verbal stress pattern
20.	-aer	a + unaccented i + vowel > a + y + vowel	preterite: 3rd singular and plural imperfect subjunctive: all forms future subjunctive: all forms present participle	An unaccented i in verbal endings is always followed by another vowel. Since in Spanish there should not be an unaccented i between two pronounced vowels, the i changes to y.
		i of verbal endings > í	preterite: 2nd singular, 1st and 2nd plural past participle	see footnote ** to preserve regular verbal stress pattern
20.	-eer	e + unaccented i + vowel > e + y + vowel	preterite: 3rd singular and plural imperfect subjunctive: all forms future subjunctive: all forms present participle	An unaccented i in verbal endings is always followed by another vowel. Since in Spanish there should not be an unaccented i between two pronounced vowels, the i changes to y.
		i of verbal endings > í	preterite: 2nd singular, 1st and 2nd plural past participle	see footnote ** to preserve regular verbal stress pattern
20.	-oer	o + unaccented i + vowel > o + y + vowel	preterite: 3rd singular and plural imperfect subjunctive: all forms future subjunctive: all forms present participle	An unaccented i in verbal endings is always followed by another vowel. Since in Spanish there should not be an unaccented i between two pronounced vowels, the i changes to y.
		i of verbal endings > í	preterite: 2nd singular, 1st and 2nd plural past participle	see footnote ** to preserve regular verbal stress pattern
21.	-aír	a + unaccented i + vowel > a + y + vowel	preterite: 3rd singular and plural imperfect subjunctive: all forms future subjunctive: all forms present participle	An unaccented i in verbal endings is always followed by another vowel. Since in Spanish there should not be an unaccented i between two pronounced vowels, the i changes to y.
		i of verbal endings > í	infinitive present indicative: 1st plural commands: affirmative vosotros preterite: 2nd singular, 1st and 2nd plural past participle	see footnote ** to preserve regular verbal stress pattern

35 Synopsis of orthographic/spelling changes

V. Orthographic/spelling changing verbs

CHART NUMBER	INFINITIVE ENDING	CHANGE THAT OCCURS	FORMS IN WHICH CHANGE OCCURS	REASON FOR CHANGE
22.	-oír	o + unaccented i + vowel > o + y + vowel	preterite: 3rd singular and plural; imperfect subjunctive: all forms; future subjunctive: all forms; present participle	An unaccented i in verbal endings is always followed by another vowel. Since in Spanish there should not be an unaccented i between two pronounced vowels, the i changes to y.
		i of verbal endings > í	infinitive; present indicative: 1st plural; commands: affirmative vosotros; preterite: 2nd singular, 1st and 2nd plural; past participle	see footnote ** to preserve regular verbal stress pattern
23.	-uir where u is pronounced. Note that this category includes verbs in -güir but not verbs in -guir and -quir (see above) since in these two the u is merely an orthographic device and is not pronounced.	u + unaccented i + vowel > u + y + vowel	preterite: 3rd singular and plural; imperfect subjunctive: all forms; future subjunctive: all forms; present participle	An unaccented i in verbal endings is always followed by another vowel. Since in Spanish there should not be an unaccented i between two pronounced vowels, the i changes to y.
24.	-güir	u + unaccented i + vowel > u + y + vowel	preterite: 3rd singular and plural; imperfect subjunctive: all forms; future subjunctive: all forms; present participle	An unaccented i in verbal endings is always followed by another vowel. Since in Spanish there should not be an unaccented i between two pronounced vowels, the i changes to y.
		ü > u before y	present indicative: 1st, 2nd, 3rd singular, 3rd plural; present subjunctive: all forms; commands: those coming from the present subjunctive; preterite: 3rd singular and plural; imperfect subjunctive: all forms; future subjunctive: all forms; present participle	to preserve initial sound of the gu of the infinitive. Normally a g followed by an i or e has a soft sound. To indicate that a g has a hard sound a u must be inserted between the g and the i or e. In verbs of this -güir category the u not only indicates the way in which the g is pronounced but

No.	Ending	Change	Forms affected	Reason
				also is pronounced itself, this pronunciation of the u being indicated with the diaeresis (compare seguir and argüir.) With the appearance of y*** immediately after the u the y, which here has the value of a consonant, makes the u the only vowel in the syllable introduced by g. This thus eliminates the possibility of the u serving merely as an indicator of the way the g is pronounced and forces the pronunciation of the u. The result is the ¨ is not needed to show the u is pronounced.
25.	-eír (i, i) Note that all verbs ending in -eír are radical changing (41).	i (from e of -eír > i) + i of verbal ending > i	preterite: 3rd singular and plural; imperfect subjunctive: all forms; future subjunctive: all forms; present participle	to reflect the single i sound of the spoken word
		i of verbal endings > í	infinitive; present indicative: 1st plural; commands: affirmative vosotros; preterite: 2nd singular, 1st, 2nd plural; past participle	see footnote **; to preserve regular verbal stress pattern
		i (from e of -eír > i) + i of verbal ending > i	present indicative: 1st, 2nd, 3rd singular, 3rd plural; present subjunctive: 1st, 2nd, 3rd singular, 3rd plural; commands: all except nosotros, affirmative and negative; negative vosotros	see footnote **; to preserve regular verbal stress pattern
26.	-ller	i of verbal endings drops	preterite: 3rd singular and plural; imperfect subjunctive: all forms; future subjunctive: all forms; present participle	to reflect the spoken word wherein the i disappears by the force of the preceding palatal sound of the ll
27.	-llir	i of verbal endings drops	preterite: 3rd singular and plural; imperfect subjunctive: all forms; future subjunctive: all forms; present participle	to reflect the spoken word wherein the i disappears by the force of the preceding palatal sound of the ll
28.	-ñer	i of verbal endings drops	preterite: 3rd singular and plural; imperfect subjunctive: all forms; future subjunctive: all forms; present participle	to reflect the spoken word wherein the i disappears by the force of the preceding palatal sound of the ñ
29.	-ñir	i of verbal endings drops	preterite: 3rd singular and plural; imperfect subjunctive: all forms; future subjunctive: all forms; present participle	to reflect the spoken word wherein the i disappears by the force of the preceding palatal sound of the ñ

35 Synopsis of orthographic/spelling changes

V. Orthographic/spelling changing verbs

CHART NUMBER	TYPE OF VERB	CHANGE THAT OCCURS	FORMS IN WHICH CHANGE OCCURS	REASON FOR CHANGE
30.	initial o > ue	ue > hue	present indicative: 1st, 2nd, 3rd singular, 3rd plural present subjunctive: 1st, 2nd, 3rd singular, 3rd plural commands: all except nosotros, vosotros, affirmative and negative	Spanish words cannot begin with ue.
32.	initial e > ie	ie > ye	present indicative: 1st, 2nd, 3rd singular, 3rd plural present subjunctive: 1st, 2nd, 3rd singular, 3rd plural commands: all except nosotros, vosotros, affirmative and negative	Spanish words cannot begin with ie.
32.	initial ie (in the verb ir)	ie > ye	present participle	Spanish words cannot begin with ie.
33.	g + (o > ue)	g + ue > güe	present indicative: 1st, 2nd, 3rd singular, 3rd plural present subjunctive: 1st, 2nd, 3rd singular, 3rd plural commands: all except nosotros, vosotros, affirmative and negative	A u (without a diaeresis) between a g and an e or i serves only as an indicator that the g has a hard sound, and is not itself pronounced. In order to be pronounced, the u must be written ü (with a diaeresis.)
34.	strong vowel (a, e or o) + h + stressed weak vowel (u or i)	stressed vowel (u or i) has written accent	in contrahacer, rehacer and rehacerse: preterite: 1st and 3rd singular in other verbs of this group: present indicative: 1st, 2nd, 3rd singular, 3rd plural present subjunctive: 1st, 2nd, 3rd singular, 3rd plural commands: all except nosotros, vosotros, affirmative and negative	to preserve regular verbal stress pattern Since the h is not pronounced, the preceding strong vowel could otherwise form a diphthong with the u or i and acquire the stress. (This use of the written accent is according to the norms of the Real Academia Española.)

*For all other verbs ending in a -vowel + cer or a -vowel + cir see charts 73 and 74.
**A, e and o are strong vowels. U and i are weak vowels. In a combination of a strong and a weak vowel the strong receives the stress. In a combination of two weak vowels the second receives the stress. (Two strong vowels together belong in two separate syllables.)
***For the origin of this y see 23 above.

Verbs ending in -ar with o that becomes ue } model: RECORDAR (ue)

TIEMPOS SIMPLES
SIMPLE TENSES

PRESENTE DE INDICATIVO *PRESENT INDICATIVE*	PRETÉRITO IMPERFECTO DE INDICATIVO *IMPERFECT INDICATIVE*	PRETÉRITO INDEFINIDO DE INDICATIVO *PRETERITE INDICATIVE*	FUTURO IMPERFECTO DE INDICATIVO *FUTURE INDICATIVE*	POTENCIAL SIMPLE *CONDITIONAL*
*I remember, etc.**	*I was remembering, etc.**	*I remembered, etc.**	*I will remember, etc.**	*I would remember, etc.**
recuerdo	recordaba	recordé	recordaré	recordaría
recuerdas	recordabas	recordaste	recordarás	recordarías
recuerda	recordaba	recordó	recordará	recordaría
recordamos	recordábamos	recordamos	recordaremos	recordaríamos
recordáis	recordabais	recordasteis	recordaréis	recordaríais
recuerdan	recordaban	recordaron	recordarán	recordarían

PRESENTE DE SUBJUNTIVO *PRESENT SUBJUNCTIVE*	PRETÉRITO IMPERFECTO DE SUBJUNTIVO *PAST (IMPERFECT) SUBJUNCTIVE*		FUTURO IMPERFECTO DE SUBJUNTIVO *FUTURE SUBJUNCTIVE*
*I remember, etc.**	*I remembered. etc.**		*I will remember, etc.**
recuerde	recordara	recordase	recordare
recuerdes	recordaras	recordases	recordares
recuerde	recordara	recordase	recordare
recordemos	recordáramos *or*	recordásemos	recordáremos
recordéis	recordarais	recordaseis	recordareis
recuerden	recordaran	recordasen	recordaren

FORMAS IMPERATIVAS, GERUNDIOS Y PARTICIPIO
COMMANDS AND PARTICIPLES

FORMAS IMPERATIVAS *COMMANDS*		GERUNDIO Y PARTICIPIO *PARTICIPLES*		
AFIRMATIVA *AFFIRMATIVE*	NEGATIVA *NEGATIVE*	GERUNDIO SIMPLE *PRESENT PARTICIPLE*	PARTICIPIO *PAST PARTICIPLE*	GERUNDIO COMPUESTO *PERFECT PARTICIPLE*
remember	*don't remember*	*remembering*	*remembered*	*having remembered*
recuerda (tú)	no recuerdes (tú)	recordando	recordado	habiendo recordado
recuerde (Ud.)	no recuerde (Ud.)			
recordad (vosotros)	no recordéis (vosotros)			
recuerden (Uds.)	no recuerden (Uds.)			
let's remember	*let's not remember*			
recordemos	no recordemos			

INFINITIVO COMPUESTO: haber recordado
PERFECT INFINITIVE: to have remembered

TIEMPOS COMPUESTOS
PERFECT (COMPOUND) TENSES

PRETÉRITO PERFECTO DE INDICATIVO *PRESENT PERFECT INDICATIVE*	PRETÉRITO PLUSCUAMPERFECTO DE INDICATIVO *PAST PERFECT (PLUPERFECT) INDICATIVE*	PRETÉRITO ANTERIOR DE INDICATIVO *PRETERITE PERFECT INDICATIVE*	FUTURO PERFECTO DE INDICATIVO *FUTURE PERFECT INDICATIVE*	POTENCIAL COMPUESTO *CONDITIONAL PERFECT*
I have remembered, etc.	*I had remembered, etc.*	*I had remembered, etc.*	*I will have remembered, etc.**	*I would have remembered, etc.**
he recordado	había recordado	hube recordado	habré recordado	habría recordado
has recordado	habías recordado	hubiste recordado	habrás recordado	habrías recordado
ha recordado	había recordado	hubo recordado	habrá recordado	habría recordado
hemos recordado	habíamos recordado	hubimos recordado	habremos recordado	habríamos recordado
habéis recordado	habíais recordado	hubisteis recordado	habréis recordado	habríais recordado
han recordado	habían recordado	hubieron recordado	habrán recordado	habrían recordado

PRETÉRITO PERFECTO DE SUBJUNTIVO *PRESENT PERFECT SUBJUNCTIVE*	PRETÉRITO PLUSCUAMPERFECTO DE SUBJUNTIVO *PAST PERFECT (PLUPERFECT) SUBJUNCTIVE*		FUTURO PERFECTO DE SUBJUNTIVO *FUTURE PERFECT SUBJUNCTIVE*
*I have remembered, etc.**	*I had remembered, etc.**		*I will have remembered, etc.**
haya recordado	hubiera recordado	hubiese recordado	hubiere recordado
hayas recordado	hubieras recordado	hubieses recordado	hubieres recordado
haya recordado	hubiera recordado	hubiese recordado	hubiere recordado
hayamos recordado	hubiéramos recordado *or*	hubiésemos recordado	hubiéremos recordado
hayáis recordado	hubierais recordado	hubieseis recordado	hubiereis recordado
hayan recordado	hubieran recordado	hubiesen recordado	hubieren recordado

*For additional translation possibilities see chart A.

VI. Radical/stem changing verbs

abuñolar (ue)
*aclocarse (ue) 44. (OC), 4. (R)
acordar (ue)
acordarse (ue) 4. (R)
acornar (ue)
acostar (ue)
acostarse (ue) 4. (R)
*agorar (ue) 48. (OC)
*almorzar (ue) 46. (OC)
amoblar (ue)
amolar (ue)
apercollar (ue)
apostar (ue)
aprobar (ue)
asolar (ue)
atronar (ue)
*avergonzar (ue) 49. (OC)
*avergonzarse (ue) 49. (OC), 4. (R)
circunvolar (ue)
*clocar (ue) 44. (OC)
colar (ue)
colarse (ue) 4. (R)
*colgar (ue) 45. (OC)
comprobar (ue)
concordar (ue)
consolar (ue)
consonar (ue)
contar (ue)
costar (ue)
*degollar (ue) 48. (OC)
demostrar (ue)
denostar (ue)
*derrocar (ue) 44. (OC) or 8. (OC)
desamoblar (ue)
desaprobar (ue)
*descolgar (ue) 45. (OC)
*descolgarse (ue) 45. (OC), 4. (R)
descollar (ue)
desconsolar (ue)
desconsolarse (ue) 4. (R)
descontar (ue)
descontarse (ue) 4. (R)
desolar (ue)
desollar (ue)
*desosar (ue) 47. (OC)
despoblar (ue)
*desvergonzarse (ue) 49. (OC), 4. (R)
discordar (ue)
disonar (ue)
*emporcar (ue) 44. (OC)
*emporcarse (ue) 44. (OC)

encontrar (ue)
encontrarse (ue) 4. (R)
encornar (ue)
engrosar (ue)
*esforzar (ue) 46. (OC)
*esforzarse (ue) 46. (OC), 4. (R)
*forzar (ue) 46. (OC)
*holgar (ue) 45. (OC)
*holgarse (ue) 45. (OC), 4. (R)
hollar (ue)
improbar (ue)
*jugar (ue) 93. (OC) (I)
*jugarse (ue) 93. (OC) (I), 4. (R)
mancornar (ue)
moblar (ue)
mostrar (ue)
poblar (ue)
probar (ue)
probarse (ue) 4. (R)
recontar (ue)
recordar (ue)
recostar (ue)
*reforzar (ue) 46. (OC)
*regoldar (ue) 48. (OC)
renovar (ue)
repoblar (ue)
repostar (ue)
reprobar (ue)
resollar (ue)
resonar (ue)
retostar (ue)
retronar (ue)
revolar (ue)
*revolcar (ue) 44. (OC)
*revolcarse (ue) 44. (OC), 4. (R)
rodar (ue)
*rogar (ue) 44. (OC)
solar (ue)
soldar (ue)
soldarse (ue) 4. (R)
*soler (ue) 123.
soltar (ue)
sonar (ue)
sonarse (ue) 4. (R)
soñar (ue)
tostar (ue)
trascolar (ue)
*trastrocar (ue) 44. (OC)
trasvolar (ue)
*trocar (ue) 44. (OC)
*trocarse (ue) 44. (OC), 4. (R)
tronar (ue)
volar (ue)
*volcar (ue) 44. (OC)

R   = Reflexive
OC = Orthographic/Spelling Change
RC = Radical/Stem Change
I   = Irregular
*These verbs have irregularities and/or orthographic/spelling changes in addition to the radical/stem changes exemplified by the model verb on the chart given here. The cross reference number following each verb indicates the chart which shows all irregularities and/or changes together.

37 Verbs ending in -ar with e that becomes ie } model: PENSAR (ie)

TIEMPOS SIMPLES
SIMPLE TENSES

PRESENTE DE INDICATIVO *PRESENT INDICATIVE*	PRETÉRITO IMPERFECTO DE INDICATIVO *IMPERFECT INDICATIVE*	PRETÉRITO INDEFINIDO DE INDICATIVO *PRETERITE INDICATIVE*	FUTURO IMPERFECTO DE INDICATIVO *FUTURE INDICATIVE*	POTENCIAL SIMPLE *CONDITIONAL*
I think, etc.*	*I was thinking, etc.**	*I thought, etc.**	*I will think, etc.**	*I would think, etc.**
pienso	pensaba	pensé	pensaré	pensaría
piensas	pensabas	pensaste	pensarás	pensarías
piensa	pensaba	pensó	pensará	pensaría
pensamos	pensábamos	pensamos	pensaremos	pensaríamos
pensáis	pensabais	pensasteis	pensaréis	pensaríais
piensan	pensaban	pensaron	pensarán	pensarían

PRESENTE DE SUBJUNTIVO *PRESENT SUBJUNCTIVE*	PRETÉRITO IMPERFECTO DE SUBJUNTIVO *PAST (IMPERFECT) SUBJUNCTIVE*		FUTURO IMPERFECTO DE SUBJUNTIVO *FUTURE SUBJUNCTIVE*
I think, etc.*	*I thought, etc.**		*I will think, etc.**
piense	pensara	pensase	pensare
pienses	pensaras	pensases	pensares
piense	pensara	pensase	pensare
pensemos	pensáramos *or*	pensásemos	pensáremos
penséis	pensarais	pensaseis	pensareis
piensen	pensaran	pensasen	pensaren

FORMAS IMPERATIVAS, GERUNDIOS Y PARTICIPIO
COMMANDS AND PARTICIPLES

FORMAS IMPERATIVAS *COMMANDS*		GERUNDIO Y PARTICIPIO *PARTICIPLES*		
AFIRMATIVA *AFFIRMATIVE*	NEGATIVA *NEGATIVE*	GERUNDIO SIMPLE *PRESENT PARTICIPLE*	PARTICIPIO *PAST PARTICIPLE*	GERUNDIO COMPUESTO *PERFECT PARTICIPLE*
think	*don't think*	*thinking*	*thought*	*having thought*
piensa (tú)	no pienses (tú)	pensando	pensado	habiendo pensado
piense (Ud.)	no piense (Ud.)			
pensad (vosotros)	no penséis (vosotros)			
piensen (Uds.)	no piensen (Uds.)			
let's think	*let's not think*			
pensemos	no pensemos			

INFINITIVO COMPUESTO: haber pensado
PERFECT INFINITIVE: to have thought

TIEMPOS COMPUESTOS
PERFECT (COMPOUND) TENSES

PRETÉRITO PERFECTO DE INDICATIVO *PRESENT PERFECT INDICATIVE*	PRETÉRITO PLUSCUAMPERFECTO DE INDICATIVO *PAST PERFECT (PLUPERFECT) INDICATIVE*	PRETÉRITO ANTERIOR DE INDICATIVO *PRETERITE PERFECT INDICATIVE*	FUTURO PERFECTO DE INDICATIVO *FUTURE PERFECT INDICATIVE*	POTENCIAL COMPUESTO *CONDITIONAL PERFECT*
I have thought, etc.	*I had thought, etc.*	*I had thought, etc.*	*I will have thought, etc.**	*I would have thought, etc.**
he pensado	había pensado	hube pensado	habré pensado	habría pensado
has pensado	habías pensado	hubiste pensado	habrás pensado	habrías pensado
ha pensado	había pensado	hubo pensado	habrá pensado	habría pensado
hemos pensado	habíamos pensado	hubimos pensado	habremos pensado	habríamos pensado
habéis pensado	habíais pensado	hubisteis pensado	habréis pensado	habríais pensado
han pensado	habían pensado	hubieron pensado	habrán pensado	habrían pensado

PRETÉRITO PERFECTO DE SUBJUNTIVO *PRESENT PERFECT SUBJUNCTIVE*	PRETÉRITO PLUSCUAMPERFECTO DE SUBJUNTIVO *PAST PERFECT (PLUPERFECT) SUBJUNCTIVE*		FUTURO PERFECTO DE SUBJUNTIVO *FUTURE PERFECT SUBJUNCTIVE*
I have thought, etc.*	*I had thought, etc.**		*I will have thought, etc.**
haya pensado	hubiera pensado	hubiese pensado	hubiere pensado
hayas pensado	hubieras pensado	hubieses pensado	hubieres pensado
haya pensado	hubiera pensado	hubiese pensado	hubiere pensado
hayamos pensado	hubiéramos pensado *or*	hubiésemos pensado	hubiéremos pensado
hayáis pensado	hubierais pensado	hubieseis pensado	hubiereis pensado
hayan pensado	hubieran pensado	hubiesen pensado	hubieren pensado

*For additional translation possibilities see chart A.

VI. Radical/stem changing verbs

VERBS OF THIS CATEGORY

*abnegar (ie) 50. (OC)
acertar (ie)
acrecentar (ie)
alentar (ie)
amentar (ie)
aneblar (ie)
*anegar (ie) 50. (OC)
apacentar (ie)
apacentarse (ie) 4. (R)
apretar (ie)
arrendar (ie)
asentar (ie)
aserrar (ie)
*asosegar (ie) 50. (OC)
**aterrar (ie)
**atestar (ie)
atravesar (ie)
aventar (ie)
calentar (ie)
*cegar (ie) 50. (OC)
*cegarse (ie) 50. (OC), 4. (R)
cerrar (ie)
cimentar (ie) *or* (regular - 1.)
*comenzar (ie) 50. (OC)
concertar (ie)
concertarse (ie) 4. (R)
confesar (ie)
*denegar (ie) 50. (OC)
dentar (ie)
*derrengar (ie) 50. (OC)
desacertar (ie)
desalentar (ie)
desalentarse (ie) 4. (R)
desapretar (ie)
*desasosegar (ie) 50. (OC)
*desasosegarse (ie) 50. (OC), 4. (R)
desconcertar (ie)
desconcertarse (ie) 4. (R)
desdentar (ie)
desenterrar (ie)
deshelar (ie)
desherbar (ie)
desmembrar (ie)
despertar (ie)
despertarse (ie) 4. (R)
*desplegar (ie) 50. (OC)
desterrar (ie)
emparentar (ie)
empedrar (ie)
*empezar (ie) 51. (OC)
encerrar (ie)
encomendar (ie)
endentar (ie)
enhestar (ie)

enmendar (ie)
ensangrentar (ie)
enterrar (ie)
*errar (ie) 52. (OC)
escarmentar (ie)
*fregar (ie) 50. (OC)
gobernar (ie)
hacendarse (ie) 4. (R)
helar (ie)
herrar (ie)
incensar (ie)
invernar (ie)
manifestar (ie)
mentar (ie)
merendar (ie)
*negar (ie) 50. (OC)
nevar (ie)
pensar (ie)
*plegar (ie) 50. (OC)
quebrar (ie)
recalentar (ie)
recomendar (ie)
*refregar (ie) 50. (OC)
*regar (ie) 50. (OC)
regimentar (ie)
remendar (ie)
*renegar (ie) 50. (OC)
repensar (ie)
*replegar (ie) 50. (OC)
*replegarse (ie) 50. (OC), 4. (R)
requebrar (ie)
*restregar (ie) 50. (OC)
retemblar (ie)
reventar (ie)
salpimentar (ie)
*segar (ie) 50. (OC)
sembrar (ie)
sementar (ie)
sentar (ie)
sentarse (ie) 4. (R)
serrar (ie)
sobrecalentar (ie)
*sosegar (ie) 50. (OC)
*sosegarse (ie) 50. (OC), 4. (R)
soterrar (ie)
subarrendar (ie)
temblar (ie)
tentar (ie)
*trasegar (ie) 50. (OC)
*tropezar (ie) 51. (OC)
ventar (ie)

R = Reflexive
OC = Orthographic/Spelling Change
*These verbs have orthographic/spelling changes in addition to the radical/stem changes exemplified by the model verb on the chart given here. The cross reference number following each verb indicates the chart which shows all changes together.
**There also is a homonymous verb which is not radical/stem changing, but follows the regular pattern of 1.

38 Verbs ending in -er with o that becomes ue } model: MORDER (ue)

TIEMPOS SIMPLES
SIMPLE TENSES

PRESENTE DE INDICATIVO *PRESENT INDICATIVE*	PRETÉRITO IMPERFECTO DE INDICATIVO *IMPERFECT INDICATIVE*	PRETÉRITO INDEFINIDO DE INDICATIVO *PRETERITE INDICATIVE*	FUTURO IMPERFECTO DE INDICATIVO *FUTURE INDICATIVE*	POTENCIAL SIMPLE *CONDITIONAL*
I bite, etc.*	*I was biting, etc.**	*I bit, etc.**	*I will bite, etc.**	*I would bite, etc.**
muerdo	mordía	mordí	morderé	mordería
muerdes	mordías	mordiste	morderás	morderías
muerde	mordía	mordió	morderá	mordería
mordemos	mordíamos	mordimos	morderemos	morderíamos
mordéis	mordíais	mordisteis	morderéis	morderíais
muerden	mordían	mordieron	morderán	morderían

PRESENTE DE SUBJUNTIVO *PRESENT SUBJUNCTIVE*	PRETÉRITO IMPERFECTO DE SUBJUNTIVO *PAST (IMPERFECT) SUBJUNCTIVE*		FUTURO IMPERFECTO DE SUBJUNTIVO *FUTURE SUBJUNCTIVE*	
I bite, etc.*	*I bit, etc.**		*I will bite, etc.**	
muerda	mordiera	mordiese	mordiere	
muerdas	mordieras	mordieses	mordieres	
muerda	mordiera	mordiese	mordiere	
mordamos	mordiéramos *or*	mordiésemos	mordiéremos	
mordáis	mordierais	mordieseis	mordiereis	
muerdan	mordieran	mordiesen	mordieren	

FORMAS IMPERATIVAS, GERUNDIOS Y PARTICIPIO
COMMANDS AND PARTICIPLES

FORMAS IMPERATIVAS *COMMANDS*		GERUNDIO Y PARTICIPIO *PARTICIPLES*		
AFIRMATIVA *AFFIRMATIVE*	NEGATIVA *NEGATIVE*	GERUNDIO SIMPLE *PRESENT PARTICIPLE*	PARTICIPIO *PAST PARTICIPLE*	GERUNDIO COMPUESTO *PERFECT PARTICIPLE*
bite	*don't bite*	*biting*	*bitten*	*having bitten*
muerde (tú)	no muerdas (tú)	mordiendo	mordido	habiendo mordido
muerda (Ud.)	no muerda (Ud.)			
morded (vosotros)	no mordáis (vosotros)			
muerdan (Uds.)	no muerdan (Uds.)			
let's bite	*let's not bite*			
mordamos	no mordamos			

INFINITIVO COMPUESTO: haber mordido
PERFECT INFINITIVE: to have bitten

TIEMPOS COMPUESTOS
PERFECT (COMPOUND) TENSES

PRETÉRITO PERFECTO DE INDICATIVO *PRESENT PERFECT INDICATIVE*	PRETÉRITO PLUSCUAMPERFECTO DE INDICATIVO *PAST PERFECT (PLUPERFECT) INDICATIVE*	PRETÉRITO ANTERIOR DE INDICATIVO *PRETERITE PERFECT INDICATIVE*	FUTURO PERFECTO DE INDICATIVO *FUTURE PERFECT INDICATIVE*	POTENCIAL COMPUESTO *CONDITIONAL PERFECT*
I have bitten, etc.	*I had bitten, etc.*	*I had bitten, etc.*	*I will have bitten, etc.**	*I would have bitten, etc.**
he mordido	había mordido	hube mordido	habré mordido	habría mordido
has mordido	habías mordido	hubiste mordido	habrás mordido	habrías mordido
ha mordido	había mordido	hubo mordido	habrá mordido	habría mordido
hemos mordido	habíamos mordido	hubimos mordido	habremos mordido	habríamos mordido
habéis mordido	habíais mordido	hubisteis mordido	habréis mordido	habríais mordido
han mordido	habían mordido	hubieron mordido	habrán mordido	habrían mordido

PRETÉRITO PERFECTO DE SUBJUNTIVO *PRESENT PERFECT SUBJUNCTIVE*	PRETÉRITO PLUSCUAMPERFECTO DE SUBJUNTIVO *PAST PERFECT (PLUPERFECT) SUBJUNCTIVE*		FUTURO PERFECTO DE SUBJUNTIVO *FUTURE PERFECT SUBJUNCTIVE*	
I have bitten, etc.*	*I had bitten, etc.**		*I will have bitten, etc.**	
haya mordido	hubiera mordido	hubiese mordido	hubiere mordido	
hayas mordido	hubieras mordido	hubieses mordido	hubieres mordido	
haya mordido	hubiera mordido	hubiese mordido	hubiere mordido	
hayamos mordido	hubiéramos mordido *or*	hubiésemos mordido	hubiéremos mordido	
hayáis mordido	hubierais mordido	hubieseis mordido	hubiereis mordido	
hayan mordido	hubieran mordido	hubiesen mordido	hubieren mordido	

*For additional translation possibilities see chart A.

VI. Radical/stem changing verbs

*absolver (ue) 70. (I)
amover (ue)
*cocer (ue) 54. (OC)
condoler (ue)
conmover (ue)
conmoverse (ue) 4. (R)
*contorcerse (ue) 53. (OC), 4. (R)
demoler (ue)
*desenvolver (ue) 70. (I)
*desenvolverse (ue) 70. (I), 4. (R)
*devolver (ue) 70. (I)
*disolver (ue) 70. (I)
doler (ue)
*envolver (ue) 70. (I)
*escocer (ue) 54 (OC)
llover (ue)
moler (ue)
morder (ue)
mover (ue)
*oler (ue) 55. (OC)
*poder (ue) 97. (I)
promover (ue)
*recocer (ue) 54. (OC)
remorder (ue)
remover (ue)
*resolver (ue) 70. (I)
*retorcer (ue) 53. (OC)
*revolver (ue) 70. (I)
soler (ue) 123. (defective)
*torcer (ue) 53. (OC)
*volver (ue) 70. (I)
*volverse (ue) 70. (I), 4. (R)

R = Reflexive
OC = Orthographic/Spelling Change
I = Irregular
* These verbs have orthographic/spelling changes or irregularities in addition to the radical/stem changes exemplifed by the model verb on the chart given here. The cross reference number following each verb indicates the chart which shows all irregularities and/or changes together.

TIEMPOS SIMPLES
SIMPLE TENSES

PRESENTE DE INDICATIVO *PRESENT INDICATIVE*	PRETÉRITO IMPERFECTO DE INDICATIVO *IMPERFECT INDICATIVE*	PRETÉRITO INDEFINIDO DE INDICATIVO *PRETERITE INDICATIVE*	FUTURO IMPERFECTO DE INDICATIVO *FUTURE INDICATIVE*	POTENCIAL SIMPLE *CONDITIONAL*
I understand, etc.*	*I was understanding, etc.**	*I understood, etc.**	*I will understand, etc.**	*I would understand, etc.**
entiendo	entendía	entendí	entenderé	entendería
entiendes	entendías	entendiste	entenderás	entenderías
entiende	entendía	entendió	entenderá	entendería
entendemos	entendíamos	entendimos	entenderemos	entenderíamos
entendéis	entendíais	entendisteis	entenderéis	entenderíais
entienden	entendían	entendieron	entenderán	entenderían

PRESENTE DE SUBJUNTIVO *PRESENT SUBJUNCTIVE*	PRETÉRITO IMPERFECTO DE SUBJUNTIVO *PAST (IMPERFECT) SUBJUNCTIVE*		FUTURO IMPERFECTO DE SUBJUNTIVO *FUTURE SUBJUNCTIVE*
I understand, etc.*	*I understood, etc.**		*I will understand, etc.**
entienda	entendiera	entendiese	entendiere
entiendas	entendieras	entendieses	entendieres
entienda	entendiera	entendiese	entendiere
entendamos	entendiéramos *or*	entendiésemos	entendiéremos
entendáis	entendierais	entendieseis	entendiereis
entiendan	entendieran	entendiesen	entendieren

FORMAS IMPERATIVAS, GERUNDIOS Y PARTICIPIO
COMMANDS AND PARTICIPLES

FORMAS IMPERATIVAS *COMMANDS*		GERUNDIO Y PARTICIPIO *PARTICIPLES*		
AFIRMATIVA *AFFIRMATIVE*	NEGATIVA *NEGATIVE*	GERUNDIO SIMPLE *PRESENT PARTICIPLE*	PARTICIPIO *PAST PARTICIPLE*	GERUNDIO COMPUESTO *PERFECT PARTICIPLE*
understand	*don't understand*	*understanding*	*understood*	*having understood*
entiende (tú)	no entiendas (tú)	entendiendo	entendido	habiendo entendido
entienda (Ud.)	no entienda (Ud.)			
entended (vosotros)	no entendáis (vosotros)			
entiendan (Uds.)	no entiendan (Uds.)			
let's understand	*let's not understand*			
entendamos	no entendamos			

INFINITIVO COMPUESTO: haber entendido
PERFECT INFINITIVE: to have understood

TIEMPOS COMPUESTOS
PERFECT (COMPOUND) TENSES

PRETÉRITO PERFECTO DE INDICATIVO *PRESENT PERFECT INDICATIVE*	PRETÉRITO PLUSCUAMPERFECTO DE INDICATIVO *PAST PERFECT (PLUPERFECT) INDICATIVE*	PRETÉRITO ANTERIOR DE INDICATIVO *PRETERITE PERFECT INDICATIVE*	FUTURO PERFECTO DE INDICATIVO *FUTURE PERFECT INDICATIVE*	POTENCIAL COMPUESTO *CONDITIONAL PERFECT*
I have understood, etc.	*I had understood, etc.*	*I had understood, etc.*	*I will have understood, etc.**	*I would have understood, etc.**
he entendido	había entendido	hube entendido	habré entendido	habría entendido
has entendido	habías entendido	hubiste entendido	habrás entendido	habrías entendido
ha entendido	había entendido	hubo entendido	habrá entendido	habría entendido
hemos entendido	habíamos entendido	hubimos entendido	habremos entendido	habríamos entendido
habéis entendido	habíais entendido	hubisteis entendido	habréis entendido	habríais entendido
han entendido	habían entendido	hubieron entendido	habrán entendido	habrían entendido

PRETÉRITO PERFECTO DE SUBJUNTIVO *PRESENT PERFECT SUBJUNCTIVE*	PRETÉRITO PLUSCUAMPERFECTO DE SUBJUNTIVO *PAST PERFECT (PLUPERFECT) SUBJUNCTIVE*		FUTURO PERFECTO DE SUBJUNTIVO *FUTURE PERFECT SUBJUNCTIVE*
I have understood, etc.*	*I had understood, etc.**		*I will have understood, etc.**
haya entendido	hubiera entendido	hubiese entendido	hubiere entendido
hayas entendido	hubieras entendido	hubieses entendido	hubieres entendido
haya entendido	hubiera entendido	hubiese entendido	hubiere entendido
hayamos entendido	hubiéramos entendido *or*	hubiésemos entendido	hubiéremos entendido
hayáis entendido	hubierais entendido	hubieseis entendido	hubiereis entendido
hayan entendido	hubieran entendido	hubiesen entendido	hubieren entendido

*For additional translation possibilities see chart A.

39

VI. Radical/stem changing verbs

VERBS OF THIS CATEGORY

*abstenerse (ie) 108 (I), 4. (R)
ascender (ie)
atender (ie)
*atenerse (ie) 108 (I), 4. (R)
*bienquerer (ie) 101. (I)
cerner (ie)
cernerse (ie) 4. (R)
condescender (ie)
contender (ie)
*contener (ie) 108. (I)
*contenerse (ie) 108. (I), 4. (R)
defender (ie)
desatender (ie)
descender (ie)
desentenderse (ie) 4. (R)
*detener (ie) 108. (I)
distender (ie)
encender (ie)
entender (ie)
*entretener (ie) 108. (I)
extender (ie)
heder (ie)
hender (ie)
*malquerer (ie) 101. (I)
*mantener (ie) 108. (I)
*obtener (ie) 108. (I)
perder (ie)
perderse (ie) 4. (R)
*querer (ie) 101. (I)
reencender (ie)
*retener (ie) 108. (I)
reverter (ie)
sobreentender (ie)
sobreentenderse (ie) 4. (R)
*sostener (ie) 108. (I)
subtender (ie)
superentender (ie)
tender (ie)
*tener (ie) 108. (I)
trascender (ie)
verter (ie)

R = Reflexive
I = Irregular
*These verbs have irregularities in addition to the radical/stem changes exemplified by the model verb on the chart given here. The cross reference number following each verb indicates the chart which shows all irregularities and changes together.

[145]

40 Verbs ending in -ir with o that becomes ue or u } model: DORMIR (ue, u)

TIEMPOS SIMPLES
SIMPLE TENSES

PRESENTE DE INDICATIVO PRESENT INDICATIVE	PRETÉRITO IMPERFECTO DE INDICATIVO IMPERFECT INDICATIVE	PRETÉRITO INDEFINIDO DE INDICATIVO PRETERITE INDICATIVE	FUTURO IMPERFECTO DE INDICATIVO FUTURE INDICATIVE	POTENCIAL SIMPLE CONDITIONAL
I sleep, etc.*	*I was sleeping, etc.**	*I slept, etc.**	*I will sleep, etc.**	*I would sleep, etc.**
duermo	dormía	dormí	dormiré	dormiría
duermes	dormías	dormiste	dormirás	dormirías
duerme	dormía	durmió	dormirá	dormiría
dormimos	dormíamos	dormimos	dormiremos	dormiríamos
dormís	dormíais	dormisteis	dormiréis	dormiríais
duermen	dormían	durmieron	dormirán	dormirían

PRESENTE DE SUBJUNTIVO PRESENT SUBJUNCTIVE	PRETÉRITO IMPERFECTO DE SUBJUNTIVO PAST (IMPERFECT) SUBJUNCTIVE		FUTURO IMPERFECTO DE SUBJUNTIVO FUTURE SUBJUNCTIVE
I sleep, etc.*	*I slept, etc.**		*I will sleep, etc.**
duerma	durmiera	durmiese	durmiere
duermas	durmieras	durmieses	durmieres
duerma	durmiera	durmiese	durmiere
durmamos	durmiéramos *or*	durmiésemos	durmiéremos
durmáis	durmierais	durmieseis	durmiereis
duerman	durmieran	durmiesen	durmieren

FORMAS IMPERATIVAS, GERUNDIOS Y PARTICIPIO
COMMANDS AND PARTICIPLES

FORMAS IMPERATIVAS COMMANDS		GERUNDIO Y PARTICIPIO PARTICIPLES		
AFIRMATIVA AFFIRMATIVE	NEGATIVA NEGATIVE	GERUNDIO SIMPLE PRESENT PARTICIPLE	PARTICIPIO PAST PARTICIPLE	GERUNDIO COMPUESTO PERFECT PARTICIPLE
sleep	*don't sleep*	*sleeping*	*slept*	*having slept*
duerme (tú)	no duermas (tú)	durmiendo	dormido	habiendo dormido
duerma (Ud.)	no duerma (Ud.)			
dormid (vosotros)	no durmáis (vosotros)			
duerman (Uds.)	no duerman (Uds.)			
let's sleep	*let's not sleep*			
durmamos	no durmamos			

INFINITIVO COMPUESTO: haber dormido
PERFECT INFINITIVE: to have slept

TIEMPOS COMPUESTOS
PERFECT (COMPOUND) TENSES

PRETÉRITO PERFECTO DE INDICATIVO PRESENT PERFECT INDICATIVE	PRETÉRITO PLUSCUAMPERFECTO DE INDICATIVO PAST PERFECT (PLUPERFECT) INDICATIVE	PRETÉRITO ANTERIOR DE INDICATIVO PRETERITE PERFECT INDICATIVE	FUTURO PERFECTO DE INDICATIVO FUTURE PERFECT INDICATIVE	POTENCIAL COMPUESTO CONDITIONAL PERFECT
I have slept, etc.	*I had slept, etc.*	*I had slept, etc.*	*I will have slept, etc.**	*I would have slept, etc.**
he dormido	había dormido	hube dormido	habré dormido	habría dormido
has dormido	habías dormido	hubiste dormido	habrás dormido	habrías dormido
ha dormido	había dormido	hubo dormido	habrá dormido	habría dormido
hemos dormido	habíamos dormido	hubimos dormido	habremos dormido	habríamos dormido
habéis dormido	habíais dormido	hubisteis dormido	habréis dormido	habríais dormido
han dormido	habían dormido	hubieron dormido	habrán dormido	habrían dormido

PRETÉRITO PERFECTO DE SUBJUNTIVO PRESENT PERFECT SUBJUNCTIVE	PRETÉRITO PLUSCUAMPERFECTO DE SUBJUNTIVO PAST PERFECT (PLUPERFECT) SUBJUNCTIVE		FUTURO PERFECTO DE SUBJUNTIVO FUTURE PERFECT SUBJUNCTIVE
I have slept, etc.*	*I had slept, etc.**		*I will have slept, etc.**
haya dormido	hubiera dormido	hubiese dormido	hubiere dormido
hayas dormido	hubieras dormido	hubieses dormido	hubieres dormido
haya dormido	hubiera dormido	hubiese dormido	hubiere dormido
hayamos dormido	hubiéramos dormido *or*	hubiésemos dormido	hubiéremos dormido
hayáis dormido	hubierais dormido	hubieseis dormido	hubiereis dormido
hayan dormido	hubieran dormido	hubiesen dormido	hubieren dormido

*For additional translation possibilities see chart A.

VI. Radical/stem changing verbs

VERBS OF THIS CATEGORY

dormir (ue, u)
dormirse (ue, u) 4. (R)
*morir (ue, u) 94. (I)
*premorir (ue, u) 94. (I)

R   = Reflexive
I   = Irregular
*These verbs have an irregularity in addition to the radical/stem changes exemplified by the model verb on the chart given here. The cross reference number following each verb indicates the chart which shows the irregularity and changes together.

41 Verbs ending in -ir with e that becomes ie or i } model: SENTIR (ie, i)

TIEMPOS SIMPLES
SIMPLE TENSES

PRESENTE DE INDICATIVO **PRESENT** **INDICATIVE**	PRETÉRITO IMPERFECTO DE INDICATIVO **IMPERFECT** **INDICATIVE**	PRETÉRITO INDEFINIDO DE INDICATIVO **PRETERITE** **INDICATIVE**	FUTURO IMPERFECTO DE INDICATIVO **FUTURE** **INDICATIVE**	POTENCIAL SIMPLE **CONDITIONAL**
*I regret, etc.**	*I was regretting, etc.**	*I regretted, etc.**	*I will regret, etc.**	*I would regret, etc.**
siento	sentía	sentí	sentiré	sentiría
sientes	sentías	sentiste	sentirás	sentirías
siente	sentía	sintió	sentirá	sentiría
sentimos	sentíamos	sentimos	sentiremos	sentiríamos
sentís	sentíais	sentisteis	sentiréis	sentiríais
sienten	sentían	sintieron	sentirán	sentirían

PRESENTE DE SUBJUNTIVO **PRESENT** **SUBJUNCTIVE**	PRETÉRITO IMPERFECTO DE SUBJUNTIVO **PAST (IMPERFECT)** **SUBJUNCTIVE**		FUTURO IMPERFECTO DE SUBJUNTIVO **FUTURE** **SUBJUNCTIVE**
*I regret, etc.**	*I regretted, etc.**		*I will regret, etc.**
sienta	sintiera	sintiese	sintiere
sientas	sintieras	sintieses	sintieres
sienta	sintiera	sintiese	sintiere
sintamos	sintiéramos *or*	sintiésemos	sintiéremos
sintáis	sintierais	sintieseis	sintiereis
sientan	sintieran	sintiesen	sintieren

FORMAS IMPERATIVAS, GERUNDIOS Y PARTICIPIO
COMMANDS AND PARTICIPLES

FORMAS IMPERATIVAS COMMANDS		GERUNDIO Y PARTICIPIO PARTICIPLES		
AFIRMATIVA *AFFIRMATIVE*	NEGATIVA *NEGATIVE*	GERUNDIO SIMPLE *PRESENT PARTICIPLE*	PARTICIPIO *PAST PARTICIPLE*	GERUNDIO COMPUESTO *PERFECT PARTICIPLE*
regret	*don't regret*	*regretting*	*regretted*	*having regretted*
siente (tú)	no sientas (tú)	sintiendo	sentido	habiendo sentido
sienta (Ud.)	no sienta (Ud.)			
sentid (vosotros)	no sintáis (vosotros)			
sientan (Uds.)	no sientan (Uds.)			
let's regret	*let's not regret*			
sintamos	no sintamos			

INFINITIVO COMPUESTO: haber sentido
PERFECT INFINITIVE: to have regretted

TIEMPOS COMPUESTOS
PERFECT (COMPOUND) TENSES

PRETÉRITO PERFECTO DE INDICATIVO **PRESENT PERFECT** **INDICATIVE**	PRETÉRITO PLUSCUAMPERFECTO DE INDICATIVO **PAST PERFECT (PLUPERFECT)** **INDICATIVE**	PRETÉRITO ANTERIOR DE INDICATIVO **PRETERITE PERFECT** **INDICATIVE**	FUTURO PERFECTO DE INDICATIVO **FUTURE PERFECT** **INDICATIVE**	POTENCIAL COMPUESTO **CONDITIONAL PERFECT**
I have regretted, etc.	*I had regretted, etc.*	*I had regretted, etc.*	*I will have regretted, etc.**	*I would have regretted, etc.**
he sentido	había sentido	hube sentido	habré sentido	habría sentido
has sentido	habías sentido	hubiste sentido	habrás sentido	habrías sentido
ha sentido	había sentido	hubo sentido	habrá sentido	habría sentido
hemos sentido	habíamos sentido	hubimos sentido	habremos sentido	habríamos sentido
habéis sentido	habíais sentido	hubisteis sentido	habréis sentido	habríais sentido
han sentido	habían sentido	hubieron sentido	habrán sentido	habrían sentido

PRETÉRITO PERFECTO DE SUBJUNTIVO **PRESENT PERFECT** **SUBJUNCTIVE**	PRETÉRITO PLUSCUAMPERFECTO DE SUBJUNTIVO **PAST PERFECT (PLUPERFECT)** **SUBJUNCTIVE**		FUTURO PERFECTO DE SUBJUNTIVO **FUTURE PERFECT** **SUBJUNCTIVE**
*I have regretted, etc.**	*I had regretted, etc.**		*I will have regretted, etc.**
haya sentido	hubiera sentido	hubiese sentido	hubiere sentido
hayas sentido	hubieras sentido	hubieses sentido	hubieres sentido
haya sentido	hubiera sentido	hubiese sentido	hubiere sentido
hayamos sentido	hubiéramos sentido *or*	hubiésemos sentido	hubiéremos sentido
hayáis sentido	hubierais sentido	hubieseis sentido	hubiereis sentido
hayan sentido	hubieran sentido	hubiesen sentido	hubieren sentido

*For additional translation possibilities see chart A.

[148]

41

VI. Radical/stem changing verbs

adherir (ie, i)
adherirse (ie, i) 4 (R)
*adquirir (ie) 76. (I)
*advenir (ie, i) 111 (I)
advertir (ie, i)
arrepentirse (ie, i) 4. (R)
asentir (ie, i)
*avenir (ie, i) 111. (I)
*avenirse (ie, i) 111. (I), 4. (R)
*cernir (ie) 85. (I)
concernir (ie) (This verb is
    impersonal, and thus is
    used only in the third per-
    son singular and plural,
    and in the infinitives, pre-
    sent participle, and past
    participle)
conferir (ie, i)
consentir (ie, i)
*contravenir (ie, i) 111. (I)
controvertir (ie, i)
*convenir (ie, i) 111. (I)
convertir (ie, i)
deferir (ie, i)
*desavenir (ie, i) 111. (I)
*desavenirse (ie, i) 111. (I), 4.
    (R)
desmentir (ie, i)
diferir (ie, i)
digerir (ie, i)
*discernir (ie) 85. (I)
*disconvenir (ie, i) 111. (I)
disentir (ie, i)
divertir (ie, i)
divertirse (ie, i) 4. (R)
*erguir (ie, i) 85. (OC) (I)
herir (ie, i)
hervir (ie, i)
inferir (ie, i)
ingerir (ie, i)
ingerirse (ie, i) 4. (R)
injerir (ie, i)
injerirse (ie, i) 4. (R)
*inquirir (ie) 76. (I)
interferir (ie, i)
*intervenir (ie, i) 111. (I)
invertir (ie, i)
malherir (ie, i)
mentir (ie, i)
pervertir (ie, i)
preferir (ie, i)
presentir (ie, i)
preterir (ie, i) 119. (defective)

*prevenir (ie, i) 110 (I)
*prevenirse (ie, i) 110 (I), 4. (R)
proferir (ie, i)
*provenir (ie, i) 110 (I)
*reconvenir (ie, i) 110. (I)
referir (ie, i)
referirse (ie, i) 4. (R)
reinvertir (ie, i)
requerir (ie, i)
resentir (ie, i)
resentirse (ie, i) 4. (R)
revertir (ie, i)
sentir (ie, i)
sentirse (ie, i) 4. (R)
*sobrevenir (i, i) 111. (I)
*subvenir (ie, i) 111. (I)
subvertir (ie, i)
sugerir (ie, i)
*supervenir (ie, i) 111. (I)
transferir (ie, i)
*venir (ie, i) 111. (I)
zaherir (ie, i)

R = Reflexive
OC = Orthographic/Spelling Change
I = Irregular
*These verbs have orthographic/spelling changes and/or irregularities in addition to the radical/stem changes exemplified by the model verb on the chart
given here. The cross reference number following each verb indicates the chart which shows all irregularities and/or changes together.

42 Verbs ending in -ir with } model: e that becomes i } PEDIR (i, i)

TIEMPOS SIMPLES
SIMPLE TENSES

PRESENTE DE INDICATIVO *PRESENT INDICATIVE*	PRETÉRITO IMPERFECTO DE INDICATIVO *IMPERFECT INDICATIVE*	PRETÉRITO INDEFINIDO DE INDICATIVO *PRETERITE INDICATIVE*	FUTURO IMPERFECTO DE INDICATIVO *FUTURE INDICATIVE*	POTENCIAL SIMPLE *CONDITIONAL*
I ask, etc.*	*I was asking, etc.**	*I asked, etc.**	*I will ask, etc.**	*I would ask, etc.**
pido⁺	pedía	pedí	pediré	pediría
pides⁺	pedías	pediste	pedirás	pedirías
pide⁺	pedía	pidió	pedirá	pediría
pedimos	pedíamos	pedimos	pediremos	pediríamos
pedís	pedíais	pedisteis	pediréis	pediríais
piden⁺	pedían	pidieron	pedirán	pedirían

PRESENTE DE SUBJUNTIVO *PRESENT SUBJUNCTIVE*	PRETÉRITO IMPERFECTO DE SUBJUNTIVO *PAST (IMPERFECT) SUBJUNCTIVE*		FUTURO IMPERFECTO DE SUBJUNTIVO *FUTURE SUBJUNCTIVE*
I ask, etc.*	*I asked, etc.**		*I will ask, etc.**
pida⁺	pidiera	pidiese	pidiere
pidas⁺	pidieras	pidieses	pidieres
pida⁺.	pidiera	pidiese	pidiere
pidamos	pidiéramos *or* pidiésemos		pidiéremos
pidáis	pidierais	pidieseis	pidiereis
pidan⁺	pidieran	pidiesen	pidieren

FORMAS IMPERATIVAS, GERUNDIOS Y PARTICIPIO
COMMANDS AND PARTICIPLES

FORMAS IMPERATIVAS *COMMANDS*		GERUNDIO Y PARTICIPIO *PARTICIPLES*		
AFIRMATIVA *AFFIRMATIVE*	NEGATIVA *NEGATIVE*	GERUNDIO SIMPLE *PRESENT PARTICIPLE*	PARTICIPIO *PAST PARTICIPLE*	GERUNDIO COMPUESTO *PERFECT PARTICIPLE*
ask	*don't ask*	*asking*	*asked*	*having asked*
pide⁺ (tú)	no pidas⁺ (tú)	pidiendo	pedido	habiendo pedido
pida⁺ (Ud.)	no pida⁺ (Ud.)			
pedid (vosotros)	no pidáis (vosotros)			
pidan⁺ (Uds.)	no pidan⁺ (Uds.)			
let's ask	*let's not ask*			
pidamos	no pidamos			

INFINITIVO COMPUESTO: haber pedido
PERFECT INFINITIVE: to have asked

TIEMPOS COMPUESTOS
PERFECT (COMPOUND) TENSES

PRETÉRITO PERFECTO DE INDICATIVO *PRESENT PERFECT INDICATIVE*	PRETÉRITO PLUSCUAMPERFECTO DE INDICATIVO *PAST PERFECT (PLUPERFECT) INDICATIVE*	PRETÉRITO ANTERIOR DE INDICATIVO *PRETERITE PERFECT INDICATIVE*	FUTURO PERFECTO DE INDICATIVO *FUTURE PERFECT INDICATIVE*	POTENCIAL COMPUESTO *CONDITIONAL PERFECT*
I have asked, etc.	*I had asked, etc.*	*I had asked, etc.*	*I will have asked, etc.**	*I would have asked, etc.**
he pedido	había pedido	hube pedido	habré pedido	habría pedido
has pedido	habías pedido	hubiste pedido	habrás pedido	habrías pedido
ha pedido	había pedido	hubo pedido	habrá pedido	habría pedido
hemos pedido	habíamos pedido	hubimos pedido	habremos pedido	habríamos pedido
habéis pedido	habíais pedido	hubisteis pedido	habréis pedido	habríais pedido
han pedido	habían pedido	hubieron pedido	habrán pedido	habrían pedido

PRETÉRITO PERFECTO DE SUBJUNTIVO *PRESENT PERFECT SUBJUNCTIVE*	PRETÉRITO PLUSCUAMPERFECTO DE SUBJUNTIVO *PAST PERFECT (PLUPERFECT) SUBJUNCTIVE*		FUTURO PERFECTO DE SUBJUNTIVO *FUTURE PERFECT SUBJUNCTIVE*
I have asked, etc.*	*I had asked, etc.**		*I will have asked, etc.**
haya pedido	hubiera pedido	hubiese pedido	hubiere pedido
hayas pedido	hubieras pedido	hubieses pedido	hubieres pedido
haya pedido	hubiera pedido	hubiese pedido	hubiere pedido
hayamos pedido	hubiéramos pedido *or* hubiésemos pedido		hubiéremos pedido
hayáis pedido	hubierais pedido	hubieseis pedido	hubiereis pedido
hayan pedido	hubieran pedido	hubiesen pedido	hubieren pedido

*For additional translation possibilities see chart A.
⁺In these forms rehenchir (i, i) has a written accent on the i. (See 34.)

42

VI. Radical/stem changing verbs

*antedecir (i, i) 84 (I)
*bendecir (i, i) 79 (I)
*ceñir (i, i) 60 (OC)
*ceñirse (i, i) 60. (OC), 4. (R)
*colegir (i, i) 57. (OC)
 comedirse (i, i) 4. (R)
 competir (i, i)
 concebir (i, i)
*conseguir (i, i) 58. (OC)
*constreñir (i, i) 60. (OC)
*contradecir (i, i) 84. (I)
*corregir (i, i) 57 (OC)
*decir (i, i) 84. (I)
*decirse (i, i) 84. (I), 4. (R)
 derretir (i, i)
 derretirse (i, i) 4. (R)
 descomedirse (i, i) 4. (R)
*desdecir (i, i) 84. (I)
*desleír (i, i) 59. (OC)
 desmedirse (i, i) 4. (R)
 despedir (i, i)
 despedirse (i, i) 4. (R)
*desteñir (i, i) 60. (OC)
*desteñirse (i, i) 60. (OC), 4. (R)
 desvestir (i, i)
*elegir (i, i) 57. (OC)
 embestir (i, i)
*engreír (i, i) 59. (OC)
*engreírse (i, i) 59. (OC), 4. (R)
*estreñir (i, i) 60. (OC)
*estreñirse, (i, i) 60. (OC), 4. (R)
 expedir (i, i)
*freír (i, i) 88. (OC) (I)
 gemir (i, i)
 henchir (i, i)
 impedir (i, i)
*interdecir (i, i) 84. (I)
 investir (i, i)
*maldecir (i, i) 79. (I)
 medir (i, i)
 medirse (i, i), 4. (R)
 pedir (i, i)
*perseguir (i, i) 58. (OC)
 preconcebir (i, i)
*predecir (i, i) 84. (I)
*preelegir (i, i) 57. (OC)
*proseguir (i, i) 58. (OC)
*redecir (i, i) 84. (I)
*reelegir (i, i) 57. (OC)
*refreír (i, i) 88. (OC) (I)
*regir (i, i) 57. (OC)
 rehenchir (i, i) 34. (OC) (see
    footnote on opposite page)
*reír (i, i) 59. (OC)

*reírse (i, i) 59. (OC), 4. (R)
 rendir (i, i)
 rendirse (i, i) 4. (R)
*reñir (i, i) 60. (OC)
 repetir (i, i)
*reteñir (i, i) 60. (OC)
 revestir (i, i)
*seguir (i, i) 60. (OC)
 servir (i, i)
 servirse (i, i) 4. (R)
 sobrevestir (i, i)
*sofreír (i, i) 88. (OC) (I)
*sonreír (i, i) 59. (OC)
*subseguir (i, i) 58. (OC)
*teñir (i, i) 60. (OC)
 vestir (i, i)
 vestirse (i, i) 4. (R)

R = Reflexive
OC = Orthographic/Spelling Change
I   = Irregular
*These verbs have orthographic/spelling changes and/or irregularities in addition to the radical/stem changes exemplified by the model verb on the chart given here. The cross reference number following each verb indicates the chart which shows all irregularities and/or changes together.

VI. Radical/stem changing verbs

GROUP	INFINITIVE ENDING	CHANGE THAT OCCURS	FORMS IN WHICH CHANGE OCCURS
I.	-ar	o > ue e > ie	present indicative: 1st, 2nd, 3rd singular, 3rd plural present subjunctive: 1st, 2nd, 3rd singular, 3rd plural commands: all except affirmative and negative nosotros and vosotros
	-er	o > ue e > ie	present indicative: 1st, 2nd, 3rd singular, 3rd plural present subjunctive: 1st, 2nd, 3rd singular, 3rd plural commands: all except affirmative and negative nosotros and vosotros
II.	-ir*	o > ue e > ie	present indicative: 1st, 2nd, 3rd singular, 3rd plural present subjunctive: 1st, 2nd, 3rd singular, 3rd plural commands: all except affirmative and negative nosotros and vosotros
	-ir*	o > u e > i	present subjunctive: 1st, 2nd, 3rd plural commands: nosotros, affirmative and negative; negative vosotros preterite: 3rd singular and plural imperfect subjunctive: all forms future subjunctive: all forms present participle
III.	-ir*	e > i	present indicative: 1st, 2nd, 3rd singular, 3rd plural present subjunctive: all forms commands: all except affirmative vosotros preterite: 3rd singular and plural imperfect subjunctive: all forms future subjunctive: all forms present participle

[152]

*Note that the changes in both groups of -ir verbs occur in the same places. The only difference is the type of change.

44 Verbs ending in -car with o that becomes ue } model: VOLCAR (ue)

TIEMPOS SIMPLES
SIMPLE TENSES

PRESENTE DE INDICATIVO *PRESENT INDICATIVE*	PRETÉRITO IMPERFECTO DE INDICATIVO *IMPERFECT INDICATIVE*	PRETÉRITO INDEFINIDO DE INDICATIVO *PRETERITE INDICATIVE*	FUTURO IMPERFECTO DE INDICATIVO *FUTURE INDICATIVE*	POTENCIAL SIMPLE *CONDITIONAL*
*I tip over, etc.**	*I was tipping over, etc.**	*I tipped over, etc.**	*I will tip over, etc.**	*I would tip over, etc.**
vuelco	volcaba	volqué	volcaré	volcaría
vuelcas	volcabas	volcaste	volcarás	volcarías
vuelca	volcaba	volcó	volcará	volcaría
volcamos	volcábamos	volcamos	volcaremos	volcaríamos
volcáis	volcabais	volcasteis	volcaréis	volcaríais
vuelcan	volcaban	volcaron	volcarán	volcarían

PRESENTE DE SUBJUNTIVO *PRESENT SUBJUNCTIVE*	PRETÉRITO IMPERFECTO DE SUBJUNTIVO *PAST (IMPERFECT) SUBJUNCTIVE*		FUTURO IMPERFECTO DE SUBJUNTIVO *FUTURE SUBJUNCTIVE*
*I tip over, etc.**	*I tipped over, etc.**		*I will tip over, etc.**
vuelque	volcara	volcase	volcare
vuelques	volcaras	volcases	volcares
vuelque	volcara	volcase	volcare
volquemos	volcáramos *or*	volcásemos	volcáremos
volquéis	volcarais	volcaseis	volcareis
vuelquen	volcaran	volcasen	volcaren

FORMAS IMPERATIVAS, GERUNDIOS Y PARTICIPIO
COMMANDS AND PARTICIPLES

FORMAS IMPERATIVAS *COMMANDS*		GERUNDIO Y PARTICIPIO *PARTICIPLES*		
AFIRMATIVA *AFFIRMATIVE*	NEGATIVA *NEGATIVE*	GERUNDIO SIMPLE *PRESENT PARTICIPLE*	PARTICIPIO *PAST PARTICIPLE*	GERUNDIO COMPUESTO *PERFECT PARTICIPLE*
tip over	*don't tip over*	*tipping over*	*tipped over*	*having tipped over*
vuelca (tú)	no vuelques (tú)	volcando	volcado	habiendo volcado
vuelque (Ud.)	no vuelque (Ud.)			
volcad (vosotros)	no volquéis (vosotros)			
vuelquen (Uds.)	no vuelquen (Uds.)			
let's tip over	*let's not tip over*			
volquemos	no volquemos			

INFINITIVO COMPUESTO: haber volcado
PERFECT INFINITIVE: to have tipped over

TIEMPOS COMPUESTOS
PERFECT (COMPOUND) TENSES

PRETÉRITO PERFECTO DE INDICATIVO *PRESENT PERFECT INDICATIVE*	PRETÉRITO PLUSCUAMPERFECTO DE INDICATIVO *PAST PERFECT (PLUPERFECT) INDICATIVE*	PRETÉRITO ANTERIOR DE INDICATIVO *PRETERITE PERFECT INDICATIVE*	FUTURO PERFECTO DE INDICATIVO *FUTURE PERFECT INDICATIVE*	POTENCIAL COMPUESTO *CONDITIONAL PERFECT*
I have tipped over, etc.	*I had tipped over, etc.*	*I had tipped over, etc.*	*I will have tipped over, etc.**	*I would have tipped over, etc.**
he volcado	había volcado	hube volcado	habré volcado	habría volcado
has volcado	habías volcado	hubiste volcado	habrás volcado	habrías volcado
ha volcado	había volcado	hubo volcado	habrá volcado	habría volcado
hemos volcado	habíamos volcado	hubimos volcado	habremos volcado	habríamos volcado
habéis volcado	habíais volcado	hubisteis volcado	habréis volcado	habríais volcado
han volcado	habían volcado	hubieron volcado	habrán volcado	habrían volcado

PRETÉRITO PERFECTO DE SUBJUNTIVO *PRESENT PERFECT SUBJUNCTIVE*	PRETÉRITO PLUSCUAMPERFECTO DE SUBJUNTIVO *PAST PERFECT (PLUPERFECT) SUBJUNCTIVE*		FUTURO PERFECTO DE SUBJUNTIVO *FUTURE PERFECT SUBJUNCTIVE*
*I have tipped over, etc.**	*I had tipped over, etc.**		*I will have tipped over, etc.**
haya volcado	hubiera volcado	hubiese volcado	hubiere volcado
hayas volcado	hubieras volcado	hubieses volcado	hubieres volcado
haya volcado	hubiera volcado	hubiese volcado	hubiere volcado
hayamos volcado	hubiéramos volcado *or*	hubiésemos volcado	hubiéremos volcado
hayáis volcado	hubierais volcado	hubieseis volcado	hubiereis volcado
hayan volcado	hubieran volcado	hubiesen volcado	hubieren volcado

For additional translation possibilities see chart A.

VII. Radical/stem changing verbs with spelling changes

VERBS OF THIS CATEGORY

*aclocarse (ue) 8. (OC), 36. (RC), 4. (R)
*clocar (ue) 8. (OC), 36. (RC)
*derrocar (ue) 8. (OC), 36. (RC) *or* derrocar 8. (OC)
*emporcar (ue) 8. (OC), 36. (RC)
*emporcarse (ue) 8. (OC), 36. (RC), 4. (R)
*revolcar (ue) 8. (OC), 36. (RC)
*revolcarse (ue) 8. (OC), 36. (RC), 4 (R)
*trastrocar (ue) 8. (OC), 36. (RC)
*trocar (ue) 8. (OC), 36. (RC)
*trocarse (ue) 8. (OC), 36. (RC), 4. (R)
*volcar (ue) 8. (OC), 36. (RC)

R = Reflexive
OC = Orthographic/Spelling Change
RC = Radical/Stem Change
*These verbs have a combination of orthographic/spelling and radical/stem changes. The cross reference numbers following each verb indicate the category of verbs to which each type of change belongs.

45 Verbs ending in -gar with o that becomes ue } model: ROGAR (ue)

PRESENTE DE INDICATIVO *PRESENT INDICATIVE*	PRETÉRITO IMPERFECTO DE INDICATIVO *IMPERFECT INDICATIVE*	PRETÉRITO INDEFINIDO DE INDICATIVO *PRETERITE INDICATIVE*	FUTURO IMPERFECTO DE INDICATIVO *FUTURE INDICATIVE*	POTENCIAL SIMPLE *CONDITIONAL*
*I beg, etc.**	*I was begging, etc.**	*I begged, etc.**	*I will beg, etc.**	*I would beg, etc.**
ruego	rogaba	rogué	rogaré	rogaría
ruegas	rogabas	rogaste	rogarás	rogarías
ruega	rogaba	rogó	rogará	rogaría
rogamos	rogábamos	rogamos	rogaremos	rogaríamos
rogáis	rogabais	rogasteis	rogaréis	rogaríais
ruegan	rogaban	rogaron	rogarán	rogarían

PRESENTE DE SUBJUNTIVO *PRESENT SUBJUNCTIVE*	PRETÉRITO IMPERFECTO DE SUBJUNTIVO *PAST (IMPERFECT) SUBJUNCTIVE*		FUTURO IMPERFECTO DE SUBJUNTIVO *FUTURE SUBJUNCTIVE*	
*I beg, etc.**	*I begged, etc.**		*I will beg, etc.**	
ruegue	rogara	rogase	rogare	
ruegues	rogaras	rogases	rogares	
ruegue	rogara	rogase	rogare	
roguemos	rogáramos *or* rogásemos		rogáremos	
roguéis	rogarais	rogaseis	rogareis	
rueguen	rogaran	rogasen	rogaren	

FORMAS IMPERATIVAS, GERUNDIOS Y PARTICIPIO
COMMANDS AND PARTICIPLES

FORMAS IMPERATIVAS *COMMANDS*		GERUNDIO Y PARTICIPIO *PARTICIPLES*		
AFIRMATIVA *AFFIRMATIVE*	NEGATIVA *NEGATIVE*	GERUNDIO SIMPLE *PRESENT PARTICIPLE*	PARTICIPIO *PAST PARTICIPLE*	GERUNDIO COMPUESTO *PERFECT PARTICIPLE*
beg	*don't beg*	*begging*	*begged*	*having begged*
ruega (tú)	no ruegues (tú)	rogando	rogado	habiendo rogado
ruegue (Ud.)	no ruegue (Ud.)			
rogad (vosotros)	no roguéis (vosotros)			
rueguen (Uds.)	no rueguen (Uds.)			
let's beg	*let's not beg*			
roguemos	no roguemos			

INFINITIVO COMPUESTO: haber rogado
PERFECT INFINITIVE: to have begged

TIEMPOS COMPUESTOS
PERFECT (COMPOUND) TENSES

PRETÉRITO PERFECTO DE INDICATIVO *PRESENT PERFECT INDICATIVE*	PRETÉRITO PLUSCUAMPERFECTO DE INDICATIVO *PAST PERFECT (PLUPERFECT) INDICATIVE*	PRETÉRITO ANTERIOR DE INDICATIVO *PRETERITE PERFECT INDICATIVE*	FUTURO PERFECTO DE INDICATIVO *FUTURE PERFECT INDICATIVE*	POTENCIAL COMPUESTO *CONDITIONAL PERFECT*
I have begged, etc.	*I had begged, etc.*	*I had begged, etc.*	*I will have begged, etc.**	*I would have begged, etc.**
he rogado	había rogado	hube rogado	habré rogado	habría rogado
has rogado	habías rogado	hubiste rogado	habrás rogado	habrías rogado
ha rogado	había rogado	hubo rogado	habrá rogado	habría rogado
hemos rogado	habíamos rogado	hubimos rogado	habremos rogado	habríamos rogado
habéis rogado	habíais rogado	hubisteis rogado	habréis rogado	habríais rogado
han rogado	habían rogado	hubieron rogado	habrán rogado	habrían rogado

PRETÉRITO PERFECTO DE SUBJUNTIVO *PRESENT PERFECT SUBJUNCTIVE*	PRETÉRITO PLUSCUAMPERFECTO DE SUBJUNTIVO *PAST PERFECT (PLUPERFECT) SUBJUNCTIVE*		FUTURO PERFECTO DE SUBJUNTIVO *FUTURE PERFECT SUBJUNCTIVE*	
*I have begged, etc.**	*I had begged, etc.**		*I will have begged, etc.**	
haya rogado	hubiera rogado	hubiese rogado	hubiere rogado	
hayas rogado	hubieras rogado	hubieses rogado	hubieres rogado	
haya rogado	hubiera rogado	hubiese rogado	hubiere rogado	
hayamos rogado	hubiéramos rogado *or* hubiésemos rogado		hubiéremos rogado	
hayáis rogado	hubierais rogado	hubieseis rogado	hubiereis rogado	
hayan rogado	hubieran rogado	hubiesen rogado	hubieren rogado	

*For additional translation possibilities see chart A.

VII. Radical/stem changing verbs with spelling changes

*colgar (ue) 9. (OC), 36. (RC)
*descolgar (ue) 9. (OC), 36. (RC)
*descolgarse (ue) 9. (OC), 36. (RC), 4. (R)
*holgar (ue) 9. (OC), 36. (RC)
*holgarse (ue) 9. (OC), 36. (RC), 4. (R)
**jugar (ue) 9. (OC), 36. (RC), 93. (I)
**jugarse (ue) 9. (OC), 36. (RC), 93. (I), 4. (R)
*rogar (ue) 9. (OC), 36. (RC)

R   = Reflexive
OC = Orthographic/Spelling Change
RC = Radical/Stem Change
I   = Irregular
*These verbs have a combination of orthographic/spelling and radical/stem changes. The cross reference numbers following each verb indicate the category of verbs to which each type of change belongs.
**These verbs have a combination of orthographic/spelling and radical/stem changes. The first two cross reference numbers following each verb indicate the category of verbs to which each type of change belongs. These verbs also have, in addition to the orthographic/spelling changes and radical/stem changes, irregularities not exemplified by the model verb on the chart given here. The third cross reference number following each verb indicates the chart which shows all changes and irregularities together. Note that this is the chart with the highest number.

Verbs ending in -zar with o that becomes ue } model: FORZAR (ue)

TIEMPOS SIMPLES
SIMPLE TENSES

PRESENTE DE INDICATIVO *PRESENT INDICATIVE*	PRETÉRITO IMPERFECTO DE INDICATIVO *IMPERFECT INDICATIVE*	PRETÉRITO INDEFINIDO DE INDICATIVO *PRETERITE INDICATIVE*	FUTURO IMPERFECTO DE INDICATIVO *FUTURE INDICATIVE*	POTENCIAL SIMPLE *CONDITIONAL*
*I force, etc.**	*I was forcing, etc.**	*I forced, etc.**	*I will force, etc.**	*I would force, etc.**
fuerzo	forzaba	forcé	forzaré	forzaría
fuerzas	forzabas	forzaste	forzarás	forzarías
fuerza	forzaba	forzó	forzará	forzaría
forzamos	forzábamos	forzamos	forzaremos	forzaríamos
forzáis	forzabais	forzasteis	forzaréis	forzaríais
fuerzan	forzaban	forzaron	forzarán	forzarían

PRESENTE DE SUBJUNTIVO *PRESENT SUBJUNCTIVE*	PRETÉRITO IMPERFECTO DE SUBJUNTIVO *PAST (IMPERFECT) SUBJUNCTIVE*		FUTURO IMPERFECTO DE SUBJUNTIVO *FUTURE SUBJUNCTIVE*
*I force, etc.**	*I forced, etc.**		*I will force, etc.**
fuerce	forzara	forzase	forzare
fuerces	forzaras	forzases	forzares
fuerce	forzara	forzase	forzare
forcemos	forzáramos *or*	forzásemos	forzáremos
forcéis	forzarais	forzaseis	forzareis
fuercen	forzaran	forzasen	forzaren

FORMAS IMPERATIVAS, GERUNDIOS Y PARTICIPIO
COMMANDS AND PARTICIPLES

FORMAS IMPERATIVAS *COMMANDS*		GERUNDIO Y PARTICIPIO *PARTICIPLES*		
AFIRMATIVA *AFFIRMATIVE*	NEGATIVA *NEGATIVE*	GERUNDIO SIMPLE *PRESENT PARTICIPLE*	PARTICIPIO *PAST PARTICIPLE*	GERUNDIO COMPUESTO *PERFECT PARTICIPLE*
force	*don't force*	*forcing*	*forced*	*having forced*
fuerza (tú)	no fuerces (tú)	forzando	forzado	habiendo forzado
fuerce (Ud.)	no fuerce (Ud.)			
forzad (vosotros)	no forcéis (vosotros)			
fuercen (Uds.)	no fuercen (Uds.)			
let's force	*let's not force*			
forcemos	no forcemos			

INFINITIVO COMPUESTO: haber forzado
PERFECT INFINITIVE: to have forced

TIEMPOS COMPUESTOS
PERFECT (COMPOUND) TENSES

PRETÉRITO PERFECTO DE INDICATIVO *PRESENT PERFECT INDICATIVE*	PRETÉRITO PLUSCUAMPERFECTO DE INDICATIVO *PAST PERFECT (PLUPERFECT) INDICATIVE*	PRETÉRITO ANTERIOR DE INDICATIVO *PRETERITE PERFECT INDICATIVE*	FUTURO PERFECTO DE INDICATIVO *FUTURE PERFECT INDICATIVE*	POTENCIAL COMPUESTO *CONDITIONAL PERFECT*
I have forced, etc.	*I had forced, etc.*	*I had forced, etc.*	*I will have forced, etc.**	*I would have forced, etc.**
he forzado	había forzado	hube forzado	habré forzado	habría forzado
has forzado	habías forzado	hubiste forzado	habrás forzado	habrías forzado
ha forzado	había forzado	hubo forzado	habrá forzado	habría forzado
hemos forzado	habíamos forzado	hubimos forzado	habremos forzado	habríamos forzado
habéis forzado	habíais forzado	hubisteis forzado	habréis forzado	habríais forzado
han forzado	habían forzado	hubieron forzado	habrán forzado	habrían forzado

PRETÉRITO PERFECTO DE SUBJUNTIVO *PRESENT PERFECT SUBJUNCTIVE*	PRETÉRITO PLUSCUAMPERFECTO DE SUBJUNTIVO *PAST PERFECT (PLUPERFECT) SUBJUNCTIVE*		FUTURO PERFECTO DE SUBJUNTIVO *FUTURE PERFECT SUBJUNCTIVE*
*I have forced, etc.**	*I had forced, etc.**		*I will have forced, etc.**
haya forzado	hubiera forzado	hubiese forzado	hubiere forzado
hayas forzado	hubieras forzado	hubieses forzado	hubieres forzado
haya forzado	hubiera forzado	hubiese forzado	hubiere forzado
hayamos forzado	hubiéramos forzado *or*	hubiésemos forzado	hubiéremos forzado
hayáis forzado	hubierais forzado	hubieseis forzado	hubiereis forzado
hayan forzado	hubieran forzado	hubiesen forzado	hubieren forzado

*For additional translation possiblities see chart A.

VII. Radical/stem changing verbs with spelling changes

*almorzar (ue) 11. (OC), 36. (RC)
*esforzar (ue) 11. (OC), 36. (RC)
*esforzarse (ue) 11. (OC), 36. (RC), 4. (R)
*forzar (ue) 11. (OC), 36. (RC)
*reforzar (ue) 11. (OC), 36. (RC)

R   = Reflexive
OC = Orthographic/Spelling Change
RC = Radical/Stem Change
*These verbs have a combination of orthographic/spelling and radical/stem changes. The cross reference numbers following each verb indicate the category of verbs to which each type of change belongs.

47 Verb with forms with internal o that becomes ue and inserts h before ue } model: DESOSAR (ue)

PRESENTE DE INDICATIVO PRESENT INDICATIVE	PRETÉRITO IMPERFECTO DE INDICATIVO IMPERFECT INDICATIVE	PRETÉRITO INDEFINIDO DE INDICATIVO PRETERITE INDICATIVE	FUTURO IMPERFECTO DE INDICATIVO FUTURE INDICATIVE	POTENCIAL SIMPLE CONDITIONAL
*I bone, etc.**	*I was boning, etc.**	*I boned, etc.**	*I will bone, etc.**	*I would bone, etc.**
deshueso	desosaba	desosé	desosaré	desosaría
deshuesas	desosabas	desosaste	desosarás	desosarías
deshuesa	desosaba	desosó	desosará	desosaría
desosamos	desosábamos	desosamos	desosaremos	desosaríamos
desosáis	desosabais	desosasteis	desosaréis	desosaríais
deshuesan	desosaban	desosaron	desosarán	desosarían

PRESENTE DE SUBJUNTIVO PRESENT SUBJUNCTIVE	PRETÉRITO IMPERFECTO DE SUBJUNTIVO PAST (IMPERFECT) SUBJUNCTIVE		FUTURO IMPERFECTO DE SUBJUNTIVO FUTURE SUBJUNCTIVE
*I bone, etc.**	*I boned, etc.**		*I will bone, etc.**
deshuese	desosara	desosase	desosare
deshueses	desosaras	desosases	desosares
deshuese	desosara	desosase	desosare
desosemos	desosáramos *or*	desosásemos	desosáremos
desoséis	desosarais	desosaseis	desosareis
deshuesen	desosaran	desosasen	desosaren

FORMAS IMPERATIVAS COMMANDS		GERUNDIO Y PARTICIPIO PARTICIPLES		
AFIRMATIVA AFFIRMATIVE	NEGATIVA NEGATIVE	GERUNDIO SIMPLE PRESENT PARTICIPLE	PARTICIPIO PAST PARTICIPLE	GERUNDIO COMPUESTO PERFECT PARTICIPLE
bone	*don't bone*	*boning*	*boned*	*having boned*
deshuesa (tú)	no deshueses (tú)	desosando	desosado	habiendo desosado
deshuese (Ud.)	no deshuese (Ud.)			
desosad (vosotros)	no desoséis (vosotros)			
deshuesen (Uds.)	no deshuesen (Uds.)			
let's bone	*let's not bone*			
desosemos	no desosemos			

INFINITIVO COMPUESTO: haber desosado
PERFECT INFINITIVE: to have boned

PRETÉRITO PERFECTO DE INDICATIVO PRESENT PERFECT INDICATIVE	PRETÉRITO PLUSCUAMPERFECTO DE INDICATIVO PAST PERFECT (PLUPERFECT) INDICATIVE	PRETÉRITO ANTERIOR DE INDICATIVO PRETERITE PERFECT INDICATIVE	FUTURO PERFECTO DE INDICATIVO FUTURE PERFECT INDICATIVE	POTENCIAL COMPUESTO CONDITIONAL PERFECT
I have boned, etc.	*I had boned, etc.*	*I had boned, etc.*	*I will have boned, etc.**	*I would have boned, etc.**
he desosado	había desosado	hube desosado	habré desosado	habría desosado
has desosado	habías desosado	hubiste desosado	habrás desosado	habrías desosado
ha desosado	había desosado	hubo desosado	habrá desosado	habría desosado
hemos desosado	habíamos desosado	hubimos desosado	habremos desosado	habríamos desosado
habéis desosado	habíais desosado	hubisteis desosado	habréis desosado	habríais desosado
han desosado	habían desosado	hubieron desosado	habrán desosado	habrían desosado

PRETÉRITO PERFECTO DE SUBJUNTIVO PRESENT PERFECT SUBJUNCTIVE	PRETÉRITO PLUSCUAMPERFECTO DE SUBJUNTIVO PAST PERFECT (PLUPERFECT) SUBJUNCTIVE		FUTURO PERFECTO DE SUBJUNTIVO FUTURE PERFECT SUBJUNCTIVE
*I have boned, etc.**	*I had boned, etc.**		*I will have boned, etc.**
haya desosado	hubiera desosado	hubiese desosado	hubiere desosado
hayas desosado	hubieras desosado	hubieses desosado	hubieres desosado
haya desosado	hubiera desosado	hubiese desosado	hubiere desosado
hayamos desosado	hubiéramos desosado *or*	hubiésemos desosado	hubiéremos desosado
hayáis desosado	hubierais desosado	hubieseis desosado	hubiereis desosado
hayan desosado	hubieran desosado	hubiesen desosado	hubieren desosado

*For additional translation possibilities see chart A.

VII. Radical/stem changing verbs with spelling changes

VERB OF THIS CATEGORY

---

*desosar (ue) 36. (RC)

RC = Radical/Stem Change
*This verb has a combination of orthographic/spelling and radical/stem changes. The cross reference number following the verb indicates the category of verbs to which the radical/stem changes belong.

48 Verbs with g + (o that becomes ue) } model: AGORAR (ue)

TIEMPOS SIMPLES
SIMPLE TENSES

PRESENTE DE INDICATIVO *PRESENT* *INDICATIVE*	PRETÉRITO IMPERFECTO DE INDICATIVO *IMPERFECT* *INDICATIVE*	PRETÉRITO INDEFINIDO DE INDICATIVO *PRETERITE* *INDICATIVE*	FUTURO IMPERFECTO DE INDICATIVO *FUTURE* *INDICATIVE*	POTENCIAL SIMPLE *CONDITIONAL*
I predict, etc.*	*I was predicting, etc.**	*I predicted, etc.**	*I will predict, etc.**	*I would predict, etc.**
agüero	agoraba	agoré	agoraré	agoraría
agüeras	agorabas	agoraste	agorarás	agorarías
agüera	agoraba	agoró	agorará	agoraría
agoramos	agorábamos	agoramos	agoraremos	agoraríamos
agoráis	agorabais	agorasteis	agoraréis	agoraríais
agüeran	agoraban	agoraron	agorarán	agorarían

PRESENTE DE SUBJUNTIVO *PRESENT* *SUBJUNCTIVE*	PRETÉRITO IMPERFECTO DE SUBJUNTIVO *PAST (IMPERFECT)* *SUBJUNCTIVE*		FUTURO IMPERFECTO DE SUBJUNTIVO *FUTURE* *SUBJUNCTIVE*
I predict, etc.*	*I predicted, etc.**		*I will predict, etc.**
agüere	agorara	agorase	agorare
agüeres	agoraras	agorases	agorares
agüere	agorara	agorase	agorare
agoremos	agoráramos *or*	agorásemos	agoráremos
agoréis	agorarais	agoraseis	agorareis
agüeren	agoraran	agorasen	agoraren

FORMAS IMPERATIVAS, GERUNDIOS Y PARTICIPIO
COMMANDS AND PARTICIPLES

FORMAS IMPERATIVAS *COMMANDS*		GERUNDIO Y PARTICIPIO *PARTICIPLES*		
AFIRMATIVA *AFFIRMATIVE*	NEGATIVA *NEGATIVE*	GERUNDIO SIMPLE *PRESENT PARTICIPLE*	PARTICIPIO *PAST PARTICIPLE*	GERUNDIO COMPUESTO *PERFECT PARTICIPLE*
predict	*don't predict*	*predicting*	*predicted*	*having predicted*
agüera (tú)	no agüeres (tú)	agorando	agorado	habiendo agorado
agüere (Ud.)	no agüere (Ud.)			
agorad (vosotros)	no agoréis (vosotros)			
agüeren (Uds.)	no agüeren (Uds.)			
let's predict	*let's not predict*			
agoremos	no agoremos			

INFINITIVO COMPUESTO: haber agorado
PERFECT INFINITIVE: to have predicted

TIEMPOS COMPUESTOS
PERFECT (COMPOUND) TENSES

PRETÉRITO PERFECTO DE INDICATIVO *PRESENT PERFECT* *INDICATIVE*	PRETÉRITO PLUSCUAMPERFECTO DE INDICATIVO *PAST PERFECT (PLUPERFECT)* *INDICATIVE*	PRETÉRITO ANTERIOR DE INDICATIVO *PRETERITE PERFECT* *INDICATIVE*	FUTURO PERFECTO DE INDICATIVO *FUTURE PERFECT* *INDICATIVE*	POTENCIAL COMPUESTO *CONDITIONAL PERFECT*
I have predicted, etc.	*I had predicted, etc.*	*I had predicted, etc.*	*I will have predicted, etc.**	*I would have predicted, etc.**
he agorado	había agorado	hube agorado	habré agorado	habría agorado
has agorado	habías agorado	hubiste agorado	habrás agorado	habrías agorado
ha agorado	había agorado	hubo agorado	habrá agorado	habría agorado
hemos agorado	habíamos agorado	hubimos agorado	habremos agorado	habríamos agorado
habéis agorado	habíais agorado	hubisteis agorado	habréis agorado	habríais agorado
han agorado	habían agorado	hubieron agorado	habrán agorado	habrían agorado

PRETÉRITO PERFECTO DE SUBJUNTIVO *PRESENT PERFECT* *SUBJUNCTIVE*	PRETÉRITO PLUSCUAMPERFECTO DE SUBJUNTIVO *PAST PERFECT (PLUPERFECT)* *SUBJUNCTIVE*		FUTURO PERFECTO DE SUBJUNTIVO *FUTURE PERFECT* *SUBJUNCTIVE*
I have predicted, etc.*	*I had predicted, etc.**		*I will have predicted, etc.**
haya agorado	hubiera agorado	hubiese agorado	hubiere agorado
hayas agorado	hubieras agorado	hubieses agorado	hubieres agorado
haya agorado	hubiera agorado	hubiese agorado	hubiere agorado
hayamos agorado	hubiéramos agorado *or*	hubiésemos agorado	hubiéremos agorado
hayáis agorado	hubierais agorado	hubieseis agorado	hubiereis agorado
hayan agorado	hubieran agorado	hubiesen agorado	hubieren agorado

*For additional translation possibilities see chart A.

VII. Radical/stem changing verbs with spelling changes

  *agorar (ue) 33. (OC), 36. (RC)
**avergonzar (ue) 49. (OC) (RC)
**avergonzarse (ue) 49. (OC) (RC), 4. (R)
  *degollar (ue) 33. (OC), 36. (RC)
**desvergonzarse (ue) 49. (OC) (RC), 4. (R)
  *regoldar (ue) 33. (OC), 36. (RC)

R   = Reflexive
OC = Orthographic/Spelling Change
RC = Radical/Stem Change
*These verbs have a combination of orthographic/spelling and radical/stem changes. The cross reference numbers following each verb indicate the category of verbs to which each type of change belongs.
**These verbs have a combination of radical/stem changes and two types of orthographic/spelling changes. The cross reference number following each verb indicates the chart which shows all changes together.

[163]

TIEMPOS SIMPLES
SIMPLE TENSES

PRESENTE DE INDICATIVO *PRESENT INDICATIVE*	PRETÉRITO IMPERFECTO DE INDICATIVO *IMPERFECT INDICATIVE*	PRETÉRITO INDEFINIDO DE INDICATIVO *PRETERITE INDICATIVE*	FUTURO IMPERFECTO DE INDICATIVO *FUTURE INDICATIVE*	POTENCIAL SIMPLE *CONDITIONAL*
*I shame, etc.**	*I was shaming, etc.**	*I shamed, etc.**	*I will shame, etc.**	*I would shame, etc.**
avergüenzo	avergonzaba	avergoncé	avergonzaré	avergonzaría
avergüenzas	avergonzabas	avergonzaste	avergonzarás	avergonzarías
avergüenza	avergonzaba	avergonzó	avergonzará	avergonzaría
avergonzamos	avergonzábamos	avergonzamos	avergonzaremos	avergonzaríamos
avergonzáis	avergonzabais	avergonzasteis	avergonzaréis	avergonzaríais
avergüenzan	avergonzaban	avergonzaron	avergonzarán	avergonzarían

PRESENTE DE SUBJUNTIVO *PRESENT SUBJUNCTIVE*	PRETÉRITO IMPERFECTO DE SUBJUNTIVO *PAST (IMPERFECT) SUBJUNCTIVE*		FUTURO IMPERFECTO DE SUBJUNTIVO *FUTURE SUBJUNCTIVE*
*I shame, etc.**	*I shamed, etc.**		*I will shame, etc.**
avergüence	avergonzara	avergonzase	avergonzare
avergüences	avergonzaras	avergonzases	avergonzares
avergüence	avergonzara	avergonzase	avergonzare
avergoncemos	avergonzáramos *or*	avergonzásemos	avergonzáremos
avergoncéis	avergonzarais	avergonzaseis	avergonzareis
avergüencen	avergonzaran	avergonzasen	avergonzaren

FORMAS IMPERATIVAS, GERUNDIOS Y PARTICIPIO
COMMANDS AND PARTICIPLES

FORMAS IMPERATIVAS *COMMANDS*		GERUNDIO Y PARTICIPIO *PARTICIPLES*		
AFIRMATIVA *AFFIRMATIVE*	NEGATIVA *NEGATIVE*	GERUNDIO SIMPLE *PRESENT PARTICIPLE*	PARTICIPIO *PAST PARTICIPLE*	GERUNDIO COMPUESTO *PERFECT PARTICIPLE*
shame	*don't shame*	*shaming*	*shamed*	*having shamed*
avergüenza (tú)	no avergüences (tú)	avergonzando	avergonzado	habiendo avergonzado
avergüence (Ud.)	no avergüence (Ud.)			
avergonzad (vosotros)	no avergoncéis (vosotros)			
avergüencen (Uds.)	no avergüencen (Uds.)			
let's shame	*let's not shame*			
avergoncemos	no avergoncemos			

INFINITIVO COMPUESTO: haber avergonzado
PERFECT INFINITIVE: to have shamed

TIEMPOS COMPUESTOS
PERFECT (COMPOUND) TENSES

PRETÉRITO PERFECTO DE INDICATIVO *PRESENT PERFECT INDICATIVE*	PRETÉRITO PLUSCUAMPERFECTO DE INDICATIVO *PAST PERFECT (PLUPERFECT) INDICATIVE*	PRETÉRITO ANTERIOR DE INDICATIVO *PRETERITE PERFECT INDICATIVE*	FUTURO PERFECTO DE INDICATIVO *FUTURE PERFECT INDICATIVE*	POTENCIAL COMPUESTO *CONDITIONAL PERFECT*
I have shamed, etc.	*I had shamed, etc.*	*I had shamed, etc.*	*I will have shamed, etc.**	*I would have shamed, etc.**
he avergonzado	había avergonzado	hube avergonzado	habré avergonzado	habría avergonzado
has avergonzado	habías avergonzado	hubiste avergonzado	habrás avergonzado	habrías avergonzado
ha avergonzado	había avergonzado	hubo avergonzado	habrá avergonzado	habría avergonzado
hemos avergonzado	habíamos avergonzado	hubimos avergonzado	habremos avergonzado	habríamos avergonzado
habéis avergonzado	habíais avergonzado	hubisteis avergonzado	habréis avergonzado	habríais avergonzado
han avergonzado	habían avergonzado	hubieron avergonzado	habrán avergonzado	habrían avergonzado

PRETÉRITO PERFECTO DE SUBJUNTIVO *PRESENT PERFECT SUBJUNCTIVE*	PRETÉRITO PLUSCUAMPERFECTO DE SUBJUNTIVO *PAST PERFECT (PLUPERFECT) SUBJUNCTIVE*		FUTURO PERFECTO DE SUBJUNTIVO *FUTURE PERFECT SUBJUNCTIVE*
*I have shamed, etc.**	*I had shamed, etc.**		*I will have shamed, etc.**
haya avergonzado	hubiera avergonzado	hubiese avergonzado	hubiere avergonzado
hayas avergonzado	hubieras avergonzado	hubieses avergonzado	hubieres avergonzado
haya avergonzado	hubiera avergonzado	hubiese avergonzado	hubiere avergonzado
hayamos avergonzado	hubiéramos avergonzado *or*	hubiésemos avergonzado	hubiéremos avergonzado
hayáis avergonzado	hubierais avergonzado	hubieseis avergonzado	hubiereis avergonzado
hayan avergonzado	hubieran avergonzado	hubiesen avergonzado	hubieren avergonzado

*For additional translation possibilities see chart A.

VII. Radical/stem changing verbs with spelling changes

VERBS OF THIS CATEGORY

*avergonzar (ue) 11. (OC), 33. (OC), 36. (RC)
*avergonzarse (ue) 11. (OC), 33. (OC), 36. (RC), 4. (R)
*desvergonzarse (ue) 11. (OC), 33. (OC), 36. (RC), 4. (R)

R = Reflexive
OC = Orthographic/Spelling Change
RC = Radical/Stem Change
*These verbs have a combination of orthographic/spelling and radical/stem changes. The cross reference numbers following each verb indicate the category of verbs to which each type of change belongs.

TIEMPOS SIMPLES
SIMPLE TENSES

PRESENTE DE INDICATIVO *PRESENT INDICATIVE*	PRETÉRITO IMPERFECTO DE INDICATIVO *IMPERFECT INDICATIVE*	PRETÉRITO INDEFINIDO DE INDICATIVO *PRETERITE INDICATIVE*	FUTURO IMPERFECTO DE INDICATIVO *FUTURE INDICATIVE*	POTENCIAL SIMPLE *CONDITIONAL*
*I blind, etc.**	*I was blinding, etc.**	*I blinded, etc.**	*I will blind, etc.**	*I would blind, etc.**
ciego	cegaba	cegué	cegaré	cegaría
ciegas	cegabas	cegaste	cegarás	cegarías
ciega	cegaba	cegó	cegará	cegaría
cegamos	cegábamos	cegamos	cegaremos	cegaríamos
cegáis	cegabais	cegasteis	cegaréis	cegaríais
ciegan	cegaban	cegaron	cegarán	cegarían

PRESENTE DE SUBJUNTIVO *PRESENT SUBJUNCTIVE*	PRETÉRITO IMPERFECTO DE SUBJUNTIVO *PAST (IMPERFECT) SUBJUNCTIVE*		FUTURO IMPERFECTO DE SUBJUNTIVO *FUTURE SUBJUNCTIVE*
*I blind, etc.**	*I blinded, etc.**		*I will blind, etc.**
ciegue	cegara	cegase	cegare
ciegues	cegaras	cegases	cegares
ciegue	cegara	cegase	cegare
ceguemos	cegáramos *or*	cegásemos	cegáremos
ceguéis	cegarais	cegaseis	cegareis
cieguen	cegaran	cegasen	cegaren

FORMAS IMPERATIVAS, GERUNDIOS Y PARTICIPIO
COMMANDS AND PARTICIPLES

FORMAS IMPERATIVAS *COMMANDS*		GERUNDIO Y PARTICIPIO *PARTICIPLES*		
AFIRMATIVA *AFFIRMATIVE*	NEGATIVA *NEGATIVE*	GERUNDIO SIMPLE *PRESENT PARTICIPLE*	PARTICIPIO *PAST PARTICIPLE*	GERUNDIO COMPUESTO *PERFECT PARTICIPLE*
blind	*don't blind*	*blinding*	*blinded*	*having blinded*
ciega (tú)	no ciegues (tú)	cegando	cegado	habiendo cegado
ciegue (Ud.)	no ciegue (Ud.)			
cegad (vosotros)	no ceguéis (vosotros)			
cieguen (Uds.)	no cieguen (Uds.)			
let's blind	*let's not blind*			
ceguemos	no ceguemos			

INFINITIVO COMPUESTO: haber cegado
PERFECT INFINITIVE: to have blinded

TIEMPOS COMPUESTOS
PERFECT (COMPOUND) TENSES

PRETÉRITO PERFECTO DE INDICATIVO *PRESENT PERFECT INDICATIVE*	PRETÉRITO PLUSCUAMPERFECTO DE INDICATIVO *PAST PERFECT (PLUPERFECT) INDICATIVE*	PRETÉRITO ANTERIOR DE INDICATIVO *PRETERITE PERFECT INDICATIVE*	FUTURO PERFECTO DE INDICATIVO *FUTURE PERFECT INDICATIVE*	POTENCIAL COMPUESTO *CONDITIONAL PERFECT*
I have blinded, etc.	*I had blinded, etc.*	*I had blinded, etc.*	*I will have blinded, etc.**	*I would have blinded, etc.**
he cegado	había cegado	hube cegado	habré cegado	habría cegado
has cegado	habías cegado	hubiste cegado	habrás cegado	habrías cegado
ha cegado	había cegado	hubo cegado	habrá cegado	habría cegado
hemos cegado	habíamos cegado	hubimos cegado	habremos cegado	habríamos cegado
habéis cegado	habíais cegado	hubisteis cegado	habréis cegado	habríais cegado
han cegado	habían cegado	hubieron cegado	habrán cegado	habrían cegado

PRETÉRITO PERFECTO DE SUBJUNTIVO *PRESENT PERFECT SUBJUNCTIVE*	PRETÉRITO PLUSCUAMPERFECTO DE SUBJUNTIVO *PAST PERFECT (PLUPERFECT) SUBJUNCTIVE*		FUTURO PERFECTO DE SUBJUNTIVO *FUTURE PERFECT SUBJUNCTIVE*
*I have blinded, etc.**	*I had blinded, etc.**		*I will have blinded, etc.**
haya cegado	hubiera cegado	hubiese cegado	hubiere cegado
hayas cegado	hubieras cegado	hubieses cegado	hubieres cegado
haya cegado	hubiera cegado	hubiese cegado	hubiere cegado
hayamos cegado	hubiéramos cegado *or*	hubiésemos cegado	hubiéremos cegado
hayáis cegado	hubierais cegado	hubieseis cegado	hubiereis cegado
hayan cegado	hubieran cegado	hubiesen cegado	hubieren cegado

*For additional translation possibilities see chart A.

VII. Radical/stem changing verbs with spelling changes

VERBS OF THIS CATEGORY

*abnegar (ie) 9. (OC), 37. (RC)
*anegar (ie) 9. (OC), 37. (RC)
*asosegar (ie) 9. (OC), 37. (RC)
*cegar (ie) 9. (OC), 37. (RC)
*cegarse (ie) 9. (OC), 37. (RC), 4. (R)
*denegar (ie) 9. (OC), 37. (RC)
*derrengar (ie) 9. (OC), 37. (RC)
*desasosegar (ie) 9. (OC), 37. (RC)
*desasosegarse (ie) 9. (OC), 37. (RC), 4. (R)
*desplegar (ie) 9. (OC), 37. (RC)
*fregar (ie) 9. (OC), 37. (RC)
*negar (ie) 9. (OC), 37. (RC)
*plegar (ie) 9. (OC), 37. (RC)
*regar (ie) 9. (OC), 37. (RC)
*renegar (ie) 9. (OC), 37. (RC)
*replegar (ie) 9. (OC), 37. (RC)
*replegarse (ie) 9. (OC), 37. (RC), 4. (R)
*restregar (ie) 9. (OC), 37. (RC)
*segar (ie) 9. (OC) 37. (RC)
*sosegar (ie) 9. (OC), 37. (RC)
*sosegarse (ie) 9. (OC), 37. (RC), 4. (R)
*trasegar (ie) 9. (OC), 37. (RC)

R = Reflexive
OC = Orthographic/Spelling Change
RC = Radical/Stem Change
*These verbs have a combination of orthographic/spelling and radical/stem changes. The cross reference numbers following each verb indicate the category of verbs to which each type of change belongs.

TIEMPOS SIMPLES
SIMPLE TENSES

PRESENTE DE INDICATIVO *PRESENT INDICATIVE*	PRETÉRITO IMPERFECTO DE INDICATIVO *IMPERFECT INDICATIVE*	PRETÉRITO INDEFINIDO DE INDICATIVO *PRETERITE INDICATIVE*	FUTURO IMPERFECTO DE INDICATIVO *FUTURE INDICATIVE*	POTENCIAL SIMPLE *CONDITIONAL*
*I begin, etc.**	*I was beginning, etc.**	*I began, etc.**	*I will begin, etc.**	*I would begin, etc.**
comienzo	comenzaba	comencé	comenzaré	comenzaría
comienzas	comenzabas	comenzaste	comenzarás	comenzarías
comienza	comenzaba	comenzó	comenzará	comenzaría
comenzamos	comenzábamos	comenzamos	comenzaremos	comenzaríamos
comenzáis	comenzabais	comenzasteis	comenzaréis	comenzaríais
comienzan	comenzaban	comenzaron	comenzarán	comenzarían

PRESENTE DE SUBJUNTIVO *PRESENT SUBJUNCTIVE*	PRETÉRITO IMPERFECTO DE SUBJUNTIVO *PAST (IMPERFECT) SUBJUNCTIVE*		FUTURO IMPERFECTO DE SUBJUNTIVO *FUTURE SUBJUNCTIVE*
*I begin, etc.**	*I began, etc.**		*I will begin, etc.**
comience	comenzara	comenzase	comenzare
comiences	comenzaras	comenzases	comenzares
comience	comenzara	comenzase	comenzare
comencemos	comenzáramos _or_	comenzásemos	comenzáremos
comencéis	comenzarais	comenzaseis	comenzareis
comiencen	comenzaran	comenzasen	comenzaren

FORMAS IMPERATIVAS, GERUNDIOS Y PARTICIPIO
COMMANDS AND PARTICIPLES

FORMAS IMPERATIVAS *COMMANDS*		GERUNDIO Y PARTICIPIO *PARTICIPLES*		
AFIRMATIVA *AFFIRMATIVE*	NEGATIVA *NEGATIVE*	GERUNDIO SIMPLE *PRESENT PARTICIPLE*	PARTICIPIO *PAST PARTICIPLE*	GERUNDIO COMPUESTO *PERFECT PARTICIPLE*
begin	*don't begin*	*beginning*	*begun*	*having begun*
comienza (tú)	no comiences (tú)	comenzando	comenzado	habiendo comenzado
comience (Ud.)	no comience (Ud.)			
comenzad (vosotros)	no comencéis (vosotros)			
comiencen (Uds.)	no comiencen (Uds.)			
let's begin	*let's not begin*			
comencemos	no comencemos			

INFINITIVO COMPUESTO: haber comenzado
PERFECT INFINITIVE: to have begun

TIEMPOS COMPUESTOS
PERFECT (COMPOUND) TENSES

PRETÉRITO PERFECTO DE INDICATIVO *PRESENT PERFECT INDICATIVE*	PRETÉRITO PLUSCUAMPERFECTO DE INDICATIVO *PAST PERFECT (PLUPERFECT) INDICATIVE*	PRETÉRITO ANTERIOR DE INDICATIVO *PRETERITE PERFECT INDICATIVE*	FUTURO PERFECTO DE INDICATIVO *FUTURE PERFECT INDICATIVE*	POTENCIAL COMPUESTO *CONDITIONAL PERFECT*
I have begun, etc.	*I had begun, etc.*	*I had begun, etc.*	*I will have begun, etc.**	*I would have begun, etc.**
he comenzado	había comenzado	hube comenzado	habré comenzado	habría comenzado
has comenzado	habías comenzado	hubiste comenzado	habrás comenzado	habrías comenzado
ha comenzado	había comenzado	hubo comenzado	habrá comenzado	habría comenzado
hemos comenzado	habíamos comenzado	hubimos comenzado	habremos comenzado	habríamos comenzado
habéis comenzado	habíais comenzado	hubisteis comenzado	habréis comenzado	habríais comenzado
han comenzado	habían comenzado	hubieron comenzado	habrán comenzado	habrían comenzado

PRETÉRITO PERFECTO DE SUBJUNTIVO *PRESENT PERFECT SUBJUNCTIVE*	PRETÉRITO PLUSCUAMPERFECTO DE SUBJUNTIVO *PAST PERFECT (PLUPERFECT) SUBJUNCTIVE*		FUTURO PERFECTO DE SUBJUNTIVO *FUTURE PERFECT SUBJUNCTIVE*
*I have begun, etc.**	*I had begun, etc.**		*I will have begun, etc.**
haya comenzado	hubiera comenzado	hubiese comenzado	hubiere comenzado
hayas comenzado	hubieras comenzado	hubieses comenzado	hubieres comenzado
haya comenzado	hubiera comenzado	hubiese comenzado	hubiere comenzado
hayamos comenzado	hubiéramos comenzado _or_	hubiésemos comenzado	hubiéremos comenzado
hayáis comenzado	hubierais comenzado	hubieseis comenzado	hubiereis comenzado
hayan comenzado	hubieran comenzado	hubiesen comenzado	hubieren comenzado

*For additional translation possibilities see chart A.

VII. Radical/stem changing verbs with spelling changes

*comenzar (ie) 11. (OC), 37. (RC)
*empezar (ie) 11. (OC), 37. (RC)
*tropezar (ie) 11. (OC), 37. (RC)

OC = Orthographic/Spelling Change
RC = Radical/Stem Change
*These verbs have a combination of orthographic/spelling and radical/stem changes. The cross reference numbers following each verb indicate the category of verbs to which each type of change belongs.

TIEMPOS SIMPLES
SIMPLE TENSES

PRESENTE DE INDICATIVO PRESENT INDICATIVE	PRETÉRITO IMPERFECTO DE INDICATIVO IMPERFECT INDICATIVE	PRETÉRITO INDEFINIDO DE INDICATIVO PRETERITE INDICATIVE	FUTURO IMPERFECTO DE INDICATIVO FUTURE INDICATIVE	POTENCIAL SIMPLE CONDITIONAL
I err, etc.*	*I was erring, etc.**	*I erred, etc.**	*I will err, etc.**	*I would err, etc.**
yerro	erraba	erré	erraré	erraría
yerras	errabas	erraste	errarás	errarías
yerra	erraba	erró	errará	erraría
erramos	errábamos	erramos	erraremos	erraríamos
erráis	errabais	errasteis	erraréis	erraríais
yerran	erraban	erraron	errarán	errarían

PRESENTE DE SUBJUNTIVO PRESENT SUBJUNCTIVE	PRETÉRITO IMPERFECTO DE SUBJUNTIVO PAST (IMPERFECT) SUBJUNCTIVE		FUTURO IMPERFECTO DE SUBJUNTIVO FUTURE SUBJUNCTIVE
I err, etc.*	*I erred, etc.**		*I will err, etc.**
yerre	errara	errase	errare
yerres	erraras	errases	errares
yerre	errara	errase	errare
erremos	erráramos *or*	errásemos	erráremos
erréis	errarais	erraseis	errareis
yerren	erraran	errasen	erraren

FORMAS IMPERATIVAS, GERUNDIOS Y PARTICIPIO
COMMANDS AND PARTICIPLES

FORMAS IMPERATIVAS COMMANDS		GERUNDIO Y PARTICIPIO PARTICIPLES		
AFIRMATIVA AFFIRMATIVE	NEGATIVA NEGATIVE	GERUNDIO SIMPLE PRESENT PARTICIPLE	PARTICIPIO PAST PARTICIPLE	GERUNDIO COMPUESTO PERFECT PARTICIPLE
err	*don't err*	*erring*	*erred*	*having erred*
yerra (tú)	no yerres (tú)	errando	errado	habiendo errado
yerre (Ud.)	no yerre (Ud.)			
errad (vosotros)	no erréis (vosotros)			
yerren (Uds.)	no yerren (Uds.)			
let's err	*let's not err*			
erremos	no erremos			

INFINITIVO COMPUESTO: haber errado
PERFECT INFINITIVE: to have erred

TIEMPOS COMPUESTOS
PERFECT (COMPOUND) TENSES

PRETÉRITO PERFECTO DE INDICATIVO PRESENT PERFECT INDICATIVE	PRETÉRITO PLUSCUAMPERFECTO DE INDICATIVO PAST PERFECT (PLUPERFECT) INDICATIVE	PRETÉRITO ANTERIOR DE INDICATIVO PRETERITE PERFECT INDICATIVE	FUTURO PERFECTO DE INDICATIVO FUTURE PERFECT INDICATIVE	POTENCIAL COMPUESTO CONDITIONAL PERFECT
I have erred, etc.	*I had erred, etc.*	*I had erred, etc.*	*I will have erred, etc.**	*I would have erred, etc.**
he errado	había errado	hube errado	habré errado	habría errado
has errado	habías errado	hubiste errado	habrás errado	habrías errado
ha errado	había errado	hubo errado	habrá errado	habría errado
hemos errado	habíamos errado	hubimos errado	habremos errado	habríamos errado
habéis errado	habíais errado	hubisteis errado	habréis errado	habríais errado
han errado	habían errado	hubieron errado	habrán errado	habrían errado

PRETÉRITO PERFECTO DE SUBJUNTIVO PRESENT PERFECT SUBJUNCTIVE	PRETÉRITO PLUSCUAMPERFECTO DE SUBJUNTIVO PAST PERFECT (PLUPERFECT) SUBJUNCTIVE		FUTURO PERFECTO DE SUBJUNTIVO FUTURE PERFECT SUBJUNCTIVE
I have erred, etc.*	*I had erred, etc.**		*I will have erred, etc.**
haya errado	hubiera errado	hubiese errado	hubiere errado
hayas errado	hubieras errado	hubieses errado	hubieres errado
haya errado	hubiera errado	hubiese errado	hubiere errado
hayamos errado	hubiéramos errado *or*	hubiésemos errado	hubiéremos errado
hayáis errado	hubierais errado	hubieseis errado	hubiereis errado
hayan errado	hubieran errado	hubiesen errado	hubieren errado

*For additional translation possibilities see chart A.

VII. Radical/stem changing verbs with spelling changes

VERBS OF THIS CATEGORY

**erguir (ie, i) 56. (OC) (RC), 86. (I)
*errar (ie) 32. (OC), 37. (RC)

TIEMPOS SIMPLES
SIMPLE TENSES

PRESENTE DE INDICATIVO *PRESENT INDICATIVE*	PRETÉRITO IMPERFECTO DE INDICATIVO *IMPERFECT INDICATIVE*	PRETÉRITO INDEFINIDO DE INDICATIVO *PRETERITE INDICATIVE*	FUTURO IMPERFECTO DE INDICATIVO *FUTURE INDICATIVE*	POTENCIAL SIMPLE *CONDITIONAL*
I twist, etc.*	*I was twisting, etc.**	*I twisted, etc.**	*I will twist, etc.**	*I would twist, etc.**
tuerzo	torcía	torcí	torceré	torcería
tuerces	torcías	torciste	torcerás	torcerías
tuerce	torcía	torció	torcerá	torcería
torcemos	torcíamos	torcimos	torceremos	torceríamos
torcéis	torcíais	torcisteis	torceréis	torceríais
tuercen	torcían	torcieron	torcerán	torcerían

PRESENTE DE SUBJUNTIVO *PRESENT SUBJUNCTIVE*	PRETÉRITO IMPERFECTO DE SUBJUNTIVO *PAST (IMPERFECT) SUBJUNCTIVE*		FUTURO IMPERFECTO DE SUBJUNTIVO *FUTURE SUBJUNCTIVE*
I twist, etc.*	*I twisted, etc.**		*I will twist, etc.**
tuerza	torciera	torciese	torciere
tuerzas	torcieras	torcieses	torcieres
tuerza	torciera	torciese	torciere
torzamos	torciéramos *or*	torciésemos	torciéremos
torzáis	torcierais	torcieseis	torciereis
tuerzan	torcieran	torciesen	torcieren

FORMAS IMPERATIVAS, GERUNDIOS Y PARTICIPIO
COMMANDS AND PARTICIPLES

FORMAS IMPERATIVAS *COMMANDS*		GERUNDIO Y PARTICIPIO *PARTICIPLES*		
AFIRMATIVA *AFFIRMATIVE*	NEGATIVA *NEGATIVE*	GERUNDIO SIMPLE *PRESENT PARTICIPLE*	PARTICIPIO *PAST PARTICIPLE*	GERUNDIO COMPUESTO *PERFECT PARTICIPLE*
twist	*don't twist*	*twisting*	*twisted*	*having twisted*
tuerce (tú)	no tuerzas (tú)	torciendo	torcido	habiendo torcido
tuerza (Ud.)	no tuerza (Ud.)			
torced (vosotros)	no torzáis (vosotros)			
tuerzan (Uds.)	no tuerzan (Uds.)			
let's twist	*let's not twist*			
torzamos	no torzamos			

```
INFINITIVO COMPUESTO:  haber torcido
PERFECT INFINITIVE:  to have twisted
```

TIEMPOS COMPUESTOS
PERFECT (COMPOUND) TENSES

PRETÉRITO PERFECTO DE INDICATIVO *PRESENT PERFECT INDICATIVE*	PRETÉRITO PLUSCUAMPERFECTO DE INDICATIVO *PAST PERFECT (PLUPERFECT) INDICATIVE*	PRETÉRITO ANTERIOR DE INDICATIVO *PRETERITE PERFECT INDICATIVE*	FUTURO PERFECTO DE INDICATIVO *FUTURE PERFECT INDICATIVE*	POTENCIAL COMPUESTO *CONDITIONAL PERFECT*
I have twisted, etc.	*I had twisted, etc.*	*I had twisted, etc.*	*I will have twisted, etc.**	*I would have twisted, etc.**
he torcido	había torcido	hube torcido	habré torcido	habría torcido
has torcido	habías torcido	hubiste torcido	habrás torcido	habrías torcido
ha torcido	había torcido	hubo torcido	habrá torcido	habría torcido
hemos torcido	habíamos torcido	hubimos torcido	habremos torcido	habríamos torcido
habéis torcido	habíais torcido	hubisteis torcido	habréis torcido	habríais torcido
han torcido	habían torcido	hubieron torcido	habrán torcido	habrían torcido

PRETÉRITO PERFECTO DE SUBJUNTIVO *PRESENT PERFECT SUBJUNCTIVE*	PRETÉRITO PLUSCUAMPERFECTO DE SUBJUNTIVO *PAST PERFECT (PLUPERFECT) SUBJUNCTIVE*		FUTURO PERFECTO DE SUBJUNTIVO *FUTURE PERFECT SUBJUNCTIVE*
I have twisted, etc.*	*I had twisted, etc.**		*I will have twisted, etc.**
haya torcido	hubiera torcido	hubiese torcido	hubiere torcido
hayas torcido	hubieras torcido	hubieses torcido	hubieres torcido
haya torcido	hubiera torcido	hubiese torcido	hubiere torcido
hayamos torcido	hubiéramos torcido *or*	hubiésemos torcido	hubiéremos torcido
hayáis torcido	hubierais torcido	hubieseis torcido	hubiereis torcido
hayan torcido	hubieran torcido	hubiesen torcido	hubieren torcido

*For additional translation possibilities see chart A.

VII. Radical/stem changing verbs with spelling changes

VERBS OF THIS CATEGORY

*contorcerse (ue) 12. (OC), 38. (RC), 4. (R)
*retorcer (ue) 12. (OC), 38. (RC)
*torcer (ue) 12. (OC), 38. (RC)

R   = Reflexive
OC = Orthographic/Spelling Change
RC = Radical/Stem Change
*These verbs have a combination of orthographic/spelling and radical/stem changes. The cross reference numbers following each verb indicate the category of verbs to which each type of change belongs.

54 Verbs ending in -vowel + cer* with o that becomes ue } model: COCER (ue)

*Like mecer

PRESENTE DE INDICATIVO *PRESENT INDICATIVE*	PRETÉRITO IMPERFECTO DE INDICATIVO *IMPERFECT INDICATIVE*	PRETÉRITO INDEFINIDO DE INDICATIVO *PRETERITE INDICATIVE*	FUTURO IMPERFECTO DE INDICATIVO *FUTURE INDICATIVE*	POTENCIAL SIMPLE *CONDITIONAL*
*I cook, etc.**	*I was cooking, etc.**	*I cooked, etc.**	*I will cook, etc.**	*I would cook, etc.**
cuezo	cocía	cocí	coceré	cocería
cueces	cocías	cociste	cocerás	cocerías
cuece	cocía	coció	cocerá	cocería
cocemos	cocíamos	cocimos	coceremos	coceríamos
cocéis	cocíais	cocisteis	coceréis	coceríais
cuecen	cocían	cocieron	cocerán	cocerían

PRESENTE DE SUBJUNTIVO *PRESENT SUBJUNCTIVE*	PRETÉRITO IMPERFECTO DE SUBJUNTIVO *PAST (IMPERFECT) SUBJUNCTIVE*		FUTURO IMPERFECTO DE SUBJUNTIVO *FUTURE SUBJUNCTIVE*
*I cook, etc.**	*I cooked, etc.**		*I will cook, etc.**
cueza	cociera	cociese	cociere
cuezas	cocieras	cocieses	cocieres
cueza	cociera	cociese	cociere
cozamos	cociéramos *or*	cociésemos	cociéremos
cozáis	cocierais	cocieseis	cociereis
cuezan	cocieran	cociesen	cocieren

FORMAS IMPERATIVAS *COMMANDS*		GERUNDIO Y PARTICIPIO *PARTICIPLES*		
AFIRMATIVA *AFFIRMATIVE*	NEGATIVA *NEGATIVE*	GERUNDIO SIMPLE *PRESENT PARTICIPLE*	PARTICIPIO *PAST PARTICIPLE*	GERUNDIO COMPUESTO *PERFECT PARTICIPLE*
cook	*don't cook*	*cooking*	*cooked*	*having cooked*
cuece (tú)	no cuezas (tú)	cociendo	cocido	habiendo cocido
cueza (Ud.)	no cueza (Ud.)			
coced (vosotros)	no cozáis (vosotros)			
cuezan (Uds.)	no cuezan (Uds.)			
let's cook	*let's not cook*			
cozamos	no cozamos			

INFINITIVO COMPUESTO: haber cocido
PERFECT INFINITIVE: to have cooked

PRETÉRITO PERFECTO DE INDICATIVO *PRESENT PERFECT INDICATIVE*	PRETÉRITO PLUSCUAMPERFECTO DE INDICATIVO *PAST PERFECT (PLUPERFECT) INDICATIVE*	PRETÉRITO ANTERIOR DE INDICATIVO *PRETERITE PERFECT INDICATIVE*	FUTURO PERFECTO DE INDICATIVO *FUTURE PERFECT INDICATIVE*	POTENCIAL COMPUESTO *CONDITIONAL PERFECT*
I have cooked, etc.	*I had cooked, etc.*	*I had cooked, etc.*	*I will have cooked, etc.**	*I would have cooked, etc.**
he cocido	había cocido	hube cocido	habré cocido	habría cocido
has cocido	habías cocido	hubiste cocido	habrás cocido	habrías cocido
ha cocido	había cocido	hubo cocido	habrá cocido	habría cocido
hemos cocido	habíamos cocido	hubimos cocido	habremos cocido	habríamos cocido
habéis cocido	habíais cocido	hubisteis cocido	habréis cocido	habríais cocido
han cocido	habían cocido	hubieron cocido	habrán cocido	habrían cocido

PRETÉRITO PERFECTO DE SUBJUNTIVO *PRESENT PERFECT SUBJUNCTIVE*	PRETÉRITO PLUSCUAMPERFECTO DE SUBJUNTIVO *PAST PERFECT (PLUPERFECT) SUBJUNCTIVE*		FUTURO PERFECTO DE SUBJUNTIVO *FUTURE PERFECT SUBJUNCTIVE*
*I have cooked, etc.**	*I had cooked, etc.**		*I will have cooked, etc.**
haya cocido	hubiera cocido	hubiese cocido	hubiere cocido
hayas cocido	hubieras cocido	hubieses cocido	hubieres cocido
haya cocido	hubiera cocido	hubiese cocido	hubiere cocido
hayamos cocido	hubiéramos cocido *or*	hubiésemos cocido	hubiéremos cocido
hayáis cocido	hubierais cocido	hubieseis cocido	hubiereis cocido
hayan cocido	hubieran cocido	hubiesen cocido	hubieren cocido

*For additional translation possibilities see chart A.

[174]

VII. Radical/stem changing verbs with spelling changes

VERBS OF THIS CATEGORY

*cocer (ue) 14. (OC), 38. (RC)
*escocer (ue) 14. (OC), 38. (RC)
*recocer (ue) 14. (OC), 38. (RC)

OC = Orthographic/Spelling Change
RC = Radical/Stem Change
*These verbs have a combination of orthographic/spelling and radical/stem changes. The cross reference numbers following each verb indicate the category of verbs to which each type of change belongs.

55 Verb with forms with initial o that becomes ue } model: OLER (ue)

TIEMPOS SIMPLES
SIMPLE TENSES

PRESENTE DE INDICATIVO **PRESENT INDICATIVE**	PRETÉRITO IMPERFECTO DE INDICATIVO **IMPERFECT INDICATIVE**	PRETÉRITO INDEFINIDO DE INDICATIVO **PRETERITE INDICATIVE**	FUTURO IMPERFECTO DE INDICATIVO **FUTURE INDICATIVE**	POTENCIAL SIMPLE **CONDITIONAL**
I smell, etc.*	*I was smelling, etc.**	*I smelled, etc.**	*I will smell, etc.**	*I would smell, etc.**
huelo	olía	olí	oleré	olería
hueles	olías	oliste	olerás	olerías
huele	olía	olió	olerá	olería
olemos	olíamos	olimos	oleremos	oleríamos
oléis	olíais	olisteis	oleréis	oleríais
huelen	olían	olieron	olerán	olerían

PRESENTE DE SUBJUNTIVO **PRESENT SUBJUNCTIVE**	PRETÉRITO IMPERFECTO DE SUBJUNTIVO **PAST (IMPERFECT) SUBJUNCTIVE**		FUTURO IMPERFECTO DE SUBJUNTIVO **FUTURE SUBJUNCTIVE**
I smell, etc.*	*I smelled, etc.**		*I will smell, etc.**
huela	oliera	oliese	oliere
huelas	olieras	olieses	olieres
huela	oliera	oliese	oliere
olamos	oliéramos *or*	oliésemos	oliéremos
oláis	olierais	olieseis	oliereis
huelan	olieran	oliesen	olieren

FORMAS IMPERATIVAS, GERUNDIOS Y PARTICIPIO
COMMANDS AND PARTICIPLES

FORMAS IMPERATIVAS *COMMANDS*		GERUNDIO Y PARTICIPIO *PARTICIPLES*		
AFIRMATIVA *AFFIRMATIVE*	NEGATIVA *NEGATIVE*	GERUNDIO SIMPLE *PRESENT PARTICIPLE*	PARTICIPIO *PAST PARTICIPLE*	GERUNDIO COMPUESTO *PERFECT PARTICIPLE*
smell	*don't smell*	*smelling*	*smelled*	*having smelled*
huele (tú)	no huelas (tú)	oliendo	olido	habiendo olido
huela (Ud.)	no huela (Ud.)			
oled (vosotros)	no oláis (vosotros)			
huelan (Uds.)	no huelan (Uds.)			
let's smell	*let's not smell*			
olamos	no olamos			

INFINITIVO COMPUESTO: haber olido
PERFECT INFINITIVE: to have smelled

TIEMPOS COMPUESTOS
PERFECT (COMPOUND) TENSES

PRETÉRITO PERFECTO DE INDICATIVO **PRESENT PERFECT INDICATIVE**	PRETÉRITO PLUSCUAMPERFECTO DE INDICATIVO **PAST PERFECT (PLUPERFECT) INDICATIVE**	PRETÉRITO ANTERIOR DE INDICATIVO **PRETERITE PERFECT INDICATIVE**	FUTURO PERFECTO DE INDICATIVO **FUTURE PERFECT INDICATIVE**	POTENCIAL COMPUESTO **CONDITIONAL PERFECT**
I have smelled, etc.	*I had smelled, etc.*	*I had smelled, etc.*	*I will have smelled, etc.**	*I would have smelled, etc.**
he olido	había olido	hube olido	habré olido	habría olido
has olido	habías olido	hubiste olido	habrás olido	habrías olido
ha olido	había olido	hubo olido	habrá olido	habría olido
hemos olido	habíamos olido	hubimos olido	habremos olido	habríamos olido
habéis olido	habíais olido	hubisteis olido	habréis olido	habríais olido
han olido	habían olido	hubieron oldio	habrán olido	habrían olido

PRETÉRITO PERFECTO DE SUBJUNTIVO **PRESENT PERFECT SUBJUNCTIVE**	PRETÉRITO PLUSCUAMPERFECTO DE SUBJUNTIVO **PAST PERFECT (PLUPERFECT) SUBJUNCTIVE**		FUTURO PERFECTO DE SUBJUNTIVO **FUTURE PERFECT SUBJUNCTIVE**
I have smelled, etc.*	*I had smelled, etc.**		*I will have smelled, etc.**
haya olido	hubiera olido	hubiese olido	hubiere olido
hayas olido	hubieras olido	hubieses olido	hubieres olido
haya olido	hubiera olido	hubiese olido	hubiere olido
hayamos olido	hubiéramos olido *or*	hubiésemos olido	hubiéremos olido
hayáis olido	hubierais olido	hubieseis olido	hubiereis olido
hayan olido	hubieran olido	hubiesen olido	hubieren olido

*For additional translation possibilities see chart A.

VII. Radical/stem changing verbs with spelling changes

*oler (ue) 30. (OC), 38. (RC)

OC = Orthographic/Spelling Change
RC = Radical/Stem Change
*This verb has a combination of orthographic/spelling and radical/stem changes. The cross reference numbers following the verb indicate the category of verbs to which each type of change belongs.

TIEMPOS SIMPLES
SIMPLE TENSES

PRESENTE DE INDICATIVO *PRESENT INDICATIVE*	PRETÉRITO IMPERFECTO DE INDICATIVO *IMPERFECT INDICATIVE*	PRETÉRITO INDEFINIDO DE INDICATIVO *PRETERITE INDICATIVE*	FUTURO IMPERFECTO DE INDICATIVO *FUTURE INDICATIVE*	POTENCIAL SIMPLE *CONDITIONAL*
I erect, etc.*	*I was erecting, etc.**	*I erected, etc.**	*I will erect, etc.**	*I would erect, etc.**
yergo irgo yergues irgues yergue irgue erguimos *or* erguimos erguís erguís yerguen irguen	erguía erguías erguía erguíamos erguíais erguían	erguí erguiste irguió erguimos erguisteis irguieron	erguiré erguirás erguirá erguiremos erguiréis erguirán	erguiría erguirías erguiría erguiríamos erguiríais erguirían

PRESENTE DE SUBJUNTIVO *PRESENT SUBJUNCTIVE*	PRETÉRITO IMPERFECTO DE SUBJUNTIVO *PAST (IMPERFECT) SUBJUNCTIVE*		FUTURO IMPERFECTO DE SUBJUNTIVO *FUTURE SUBJUNCTIVE*
I erect, etc.*	*I erected, etc.**		*I will erect, etc.**
yerga irga yergas irgas yerga irga irgamos *or* irgamos irgáis irgáis yergan irgan	irguiera irguieras irguiera irguiéramos *or* irguierais irguieran	irguiese irguieses irguiese irguiésemos irguieseis irguiesen	irguiere irguieres irguiere irguiéremos irguiereis irguieren

FORMAS IMPERATIVAS, GERUNDIOS Y PARTICIPIO
COMMANDS AND PARTICIPLES

FORMAS IMPERATIVAS *COMMANDS*		GERUNDIO Y PARTICIPIO *PARTICIPLES*		
AFIRMATIVA *AFFIRMATIVE*	NEGATIVA *NEGATIVE*	GERUNDIO SIMPLE *PRESENT PARTICIPLE*	PARTICIPIO *PAST PARTICIPLE*	GERUNDIO COMPUESTO *PERFECT PARTICIPLE*
erect	*don't erect*	*erecting*	*erected*	*having erected*
yergue / irgue (tú) yerga / irga (Ud.) erguid (vosotros) yergan / irgan (Uds.)	no yergas / no irgas (tú) no yerga / no irga (Ud.) no irgáis (vosotros) no yergan / no irgan (Uds.)	irguiendo	erguido	habiendo erguido
let's erect irgamos	*let's not erect* no irgamos			

INFINITIVO COMPUESTO: haber erguido
PERFECT INFINITIVE: to have erected

TIEMPOS COMPUESTOS
PERFECT (COMPOUND) TENSES

PRETÉRITO PERFECTO DE INDICATIVO *PRESENT PERFECT INDICATIVE*	PRETÉRITO PLUSCUAMPERFECTO DE INDICATIVO *PAST PERFECT (PLUPERFECT) INDICATIVE*	PRETÉRITO ANTERIOR DE INDICATIVO *PRETERITE PERFECT INDICATIVE*	FUTURO PERFECTO DE INDICATIVO *FUTURE PERFECT INDICATIVE*	POTENCIAL COMPUESTO *CONDITIONAL PERFECT*
I have erected, etc.	*I had erected, etc.*	*I had erected, etc.*	*I will have erected, etc.**	*I would have erected, etc.**
he erguido has erguido ha erguido hemos erguido habéis erguido han erguido	había erguido habías erguido había erguido habíamos erguido habíais erguido habían erguido	hube erguido hubiste erguido hubo erguido hubimos erguido hubisteis erguido hubieron erguido	habré erguido habrás erguido habrá erguido habremos erguido habréis erguido habrán erguido	habría erguido habrías erguido habría erguido habríamos erguido habríais erguido habrían erguido

PRETÉRITO PERFECTO DE SUBJUNTIVO *PRESENT PERFECT SUBJUNCTIVE*	PRETÉRITO PLUSCUAMPERFECTO DE SUBJUNTIVO *PAST PERFECT (PLUPERFECT) SUBJUNCTIVE*		FUTURO PERFECTO DE SUBJUNTIVO *FUTURE PERFECT SUBJUNCTIVE*
I have erected, etc.*	*I had erected, etc.**		*I will have erected, etc.**
haya erguido hayas erguido haya erguido hayamos erguido hayáis erguido hayan erguido	hubiera erguido hubieras erguido hubiera erguido hubiéramos erguido *or* hubierais erguido hubieran erguido	hubiese erguido hubieses erguido hubiese erguido hubiésemos erguido hubieseis erguido hubiesen erguido	hubiere erguido hubieres erguido hubiere erguido hubiéremos erguido hubiereis erguido hubieren erguido

*For additional translation possibilities see chart A.

VII. Radical/stem changing verbs with spelling changes

VERB OF THIS CATEGORY

---

*erguir (ie, i) 17. (OC), 32. (OC), 41. (RC), 86. (I)

OC = Orthographic/Spelling Change
RC = Radical/Stem Change
I = Irregular
*This verb has a combination of orthographic/spelling changes, radical/stem changes, and irregularities. The first three cross reference numbers follow-
ing the verb indicate the category of verbs to which each type of change belongs.

TIEMPOS SIMPLES
SIMPLE TENSES

PRESENTE DE INDICATIVO *PRESENT INDICATIVE*	PRETÉRITO IMPERFECTO DE INDICATIVO *IMPERFECT INDICATIVE*	PRETÉRITO INDEFINIDO DE INDICATIVO *PRETERITE INDICATIVE*	FUTURO IMPERFECTO DE INDICATIVO *FUTURE INDICATIVE*	POTENCIAL SIMPLE *CONDITIONAL*
*I rule, etc.**	*I was ruling, etc.**	*I ruled, etc.**	*I will rule, etc.**	*I would rule, etc.**
rijo	regía	regí	regiré	regiría
riges	regías	registe	regirás	regirías
rige	regía	rigió	regirá	regiría
regimos	regíamos	regimos	regiremos	regiríamos
regís	regíais	registeis	regiréis	regiríais
rigen	regían	rigieron	regirán	regirían

PRESENTE DE SUBJUNTIVO *PRESENT SUBJUNCTIVE*	PRETÉRITO IMPERFECTO DE SUBJUNTIVO *PAST (IMPERFECT) SUBJUNCTIVE*		FUTURO IMPERFECTO DE SUBJUNTIVO *FUTURE SUBJUNCTIVE*
*I rule, etc.**	*I ruled, etc.**		*I will rule, etc.**
rija	rigiera	rigiese	rigiere
rijas	rigieras	rigieses	rigieres
rija	rigiera	rigiese	rigiere
rijamos	rigiéramos *or*	rigiésemos	rigiéremos
rijáis	rigierais	rigieseis	rigiereis
rijan	rigieran	rigiesen	rigieren

FORMAS IMPERATIVAS, GERUNDIOS Y PARTICIPIO
COMMANDS AND PARTICIPLES

FORMAS IMPERATIVAS *COMMANDS*		GERUNDIO Y PARTICIPIO *PARTICIPLES*		
AFIRMATIVA *AFFIRMATIVE*	NEGATIVA *NEGATIVE*	GERUNDIO SIMPLE *PRESENT PARTICIPLE*	PARTICIPIO *PAST PARTICIPLE*	GERUNDIO COMPUESTO *PERFECT PARTICIPLE*
rule	*don't rule*	*ruling*	*ruled*	*having ruled*
rige (tú)	no rijas (tú)	rigiendo	regido	habiendo regido
rija (Ud.)	no rija (Ud.)			
regid (vosotros)	no rijáis (vosotros)			
rijan (Uds.)	no rijan (Uds.)			
let's rule	*let's not rule*			
rijamos	no rijamos			

INFINITIVO COMPUESTO: haber regido
PERFECT INFINITIVE: to have ruled

TIEMPOS COMPUESTOS
PERFECT (COMPOUND) TENSES

PRETÉRITO PERFECTO DE INDICATIVO *PRESENT PERFECT INDICATIVE*	PRETÉRITO PLUSCUAMPERFECTO DE INDICATIVO *PAST PERFECT (PLUPERFECT) INDICATIVE*	PRETÉRITO ANTERIOR DE INDICATIVO *PRETERITE PERFECT INDICATIVE*	FUTURO PERFECTO DE INDICATIVO *FUTURE PERFECT INDICATIVE*	POTENCIAL COMPUESTO *CONDITIONAL PERFECT*
I have ruled, etc.	*I had ruled, etc.*	*I had ruled, etc.*	*I will have ruled, etc.**	*I would have ruled, etc.**
he regido	había regido	hube regido	habré regido	habría regido
has regido	habías regido	hubiste regido	habrás regido	habrías regido
ha regido	había regido	hubo regido	habrá regido	habría regido
hemos regido	habíamos regido	hubimos regido	habremos regido	habríamos regido
habéis regido	habíais regido	hubisteis regido	habréis regido	habríais regido
han regido	habían regido	hubieron regido	habrán regido	habrían regido

PRETÉRITO PERFECTO DE SUBJUNTIVO *PRESENT PERFECT SUBJUNCTIVE*	PRETÉRITO PLUSCUAMPERFECTO DE SUBJUNTIVO *PAST PERFECT (PLUPERFECT) SUBJUNCTIVE*		FUTURO PERFECTO DE SUBJUNTIVO *FUTURE PERFECT SUBJUNCTIVE*
*I have ruled, etc.**	*I had ruled, etc.**		*I will have ruled, etc.**
haya regido	hubiera regido	hubiese regido	hubiere regido
hayas regido	hubieras regido	hubieses regido	hubieres regido
haya regido	hubiera regido	hubiese regido	hubiere regido
hayamos regido	hubiéramos regido *or*	hubiésemos regido	hubiéremos regido
hayáis regido	hubierais regido	hubieseis regido	hubiereis regido
hayan regido	hubieran regido	hubiesen regido	hubieren regido

For additional translation possibilities see chart A.

VII. Radical/stem changing verbs with spelling changes

VERBS OF THIS CATEGORY

---

*colegir (i, i) 16. (OC), 42. (RC)
*corregir (i, i) 16. (OC), 42. (RC)
*elegir (i, i) 16. (OC), 42. (RC)
*preelegir (i, i) 16. (OC), 42. (RC)
*reelegir (i, i) 16. (OC), 42. (RC)
*regir (i, i) 16. (OC), 42. (RC)

OC = Orthographic/Spelling Change
RC = Radical/Stem Change
*These verbs have a combination of orthographic/spelling and radical/stem changes. The cross reference numbers following each verb indicate the category of verbs to which each type of change belongs.

TIEMPOS SIMPLES
SIMPLE TENSES

PRESENTE DE INDICATIVO *PRESENT* *INDICATIVE*	PRETÉRITO IMPERFECTO DE INDICATIVO *IMPERFECT* *INDICATIVE*	PRETÉRITO INDEFINIDO DE INDICATIVO *PRETERITE* *INDICATIVE*	FUTURO IMPERFECTO DE INDICATIVO *FUTURE* *INDICATIVE*	POTENCIAL SIMPLE *CONDITIONAL*
I follow, etc.	*I was following, etc.*	*I followed, etc.*	*I will follow, etc.*	*I would follow, etc.*
sigo	seguía	seguí	seguiré	seguiría
sigues	seguías	seguiste	seguirás	seguirías
sigue	seguía	siguió	seguirá	seguiría
seguimos	seguíamos	seguimos	seguiremos	seguiríamos
seguís	seguíais	seguisteis	seguiréis	seguiríais
siguen	seguían	siguieron	seguirán	seguirían

PRESENTE DE SUBJUNTIVO *PRESENT* *SUBJUNCTIVE*	PRETÉRITO IMPERFECTO DE SUBJUNTIVO *PAST (IMPERFECT)* *SUBJUNCTIVE*		FUTURO IMPERFECTO DE SUBJUNTIVO *FUTURE* *SUBJUNCTIVE*
I follow, etc.	*I followed, etc.*		*I will follow, etc.*
siga	siguiera	siguiese	siguiere
sigas	siguieras	siguieses	siguieres
siga	siguiera	siguiese	siguiere
sigamos	siguiéramos *or*	siguiésemos	siguiéremos
sigáis	siguierais	siguieseis	siguiereis
sigan	siguieran	siguiesen	siguieren

FORMAS IMPERATIVAS, GERUNDIOS Y PARTICIPIO
COMMANDS AND PARTICIPLES

FORMAS IMPERATIVAS *COMMANDS*		GERUNDIO Y PARTICIPIO *PARTICIPLES*		
AFIRMATIVA *AFFIRMATIVE*	NEGATIVA *NEGATIVE*	GERUNDIO SIMPLE *PRESENT PARTICIPLE*	PARTICIPIO *PAST PARTICIPLE*	GERUNDIO COMPUESTO *PERFECT PARTICIPLE*
follow	*don't follow*	*following*	*followed*	*having followed*
sigue (tú)	no sigas (tú)	siguiendo	seguido	habiendo seguido
siga (Ud.)	no siga (Ud.)			
seguid (vosotros)	no sigáis (vosotros)			
sigan (Uds.)	no sigan (Uds.)			
let's follow	*let's not follow*			
sigamos	no sigamos			

INFINITIVO COMPUESTO: haber seguido
PERFECT INFINITIVE: to have followed

TIEMPOS COMPUESTOS
PERFECT (COMPOUND) TENSES

PRETÉRITO PERFECTO DE INDICATIVO *PRESENT PERFECT* *INDICATIVE*	PRETÉRITO PLUSCUAMPERFECTO DE INDICATIVO *PAST PERFECT (PLUPERFECT)* *INDICATIVE*	PRETÉRITO ANTERIOR DE INDICATIVO *PRETERITE PERFECT* *INDICATIVE*	FUTURO PERFECTO DE INDICATIVO *FUTURE PERFECT* *INDICATIVE*	POTENCIAL COMPUESTO *CONDITIONAL PERFECT*
I have followed, etc.	*I had followed, etc.*	*I had followed, etc.*	*I will have followed, etc.*	*I would have followed, etc.*
he seguido	había seguido	hube seguido	habré seguido	habría seguido
has seguido	habías seguido	hubiste seguido	habrás seguido	habrías seguido
ha seguido	había seguido	hubo seguido	habrá seguido	habría seguido
hemos seguido	habíamos seguido	hubimos seguido	habremos seguido	habríamos seguido
habéis seguido	habíais seguido	hubisteis seguido	habréis seguido	habríais seguido
han seguido	habían seguido	hubieron seguido	habrán seguido	habrían seguido

PRETÉRITO PERFECTO DE SUBJUNTIVO *PRESENT PERFECT* *SUBJUNCTIVE*	PRETÉRITO PLUSCUAMPERFECTO DE SUBJUNTIVO *PAST PERFECT (PLUPERFECT)* *SUBJUNCTIVE*		FUTURO PERFECTO DE SUBJUNTIVO *FUTURE PERFECT* *SUBJUNCTIVE*
I have followed, etc.	*I had followed, etc.*		*I will have followed, etc.*
haya seguido	hubiera seguido	hubiese seguido	hubiere seguido
hayas seguido	hubieras seguido	hubieses seguido	hubieres seguido
haya seguido	hubiera seguido	hubiese seguido	hubiere seguido
hayamos seguido	hubiéramos seguido *or*	hubiésemos seguido	hubiéremos seguido
hayáis seguido	hubierais seguido	hubieseis seguido	hubiereis seguido
hayan seguido	hubieran seguido	hubiesen seguido	hubieren seguido

*For additional translation possibilities see chart A.

[182]

VII. Radical/stem changing verbs with spelling changes

VERBS OF THIS CATEGORY

---

*conseguir (i, i) 17. (OC), 42. (RC)
*perseguir (i, i) 17. (OC), 42. (RC)
*proseguir (i, i) 17. (OC), 42. (RC)
*seguir (i, i) 17. (OC), 42. (RC)
*subseguir (i, i) 17. (OC), 42. (RC)

OC = Orthographic/Spelling Change
RC = Radical/Stem Change
*These verbs have a combination of orthographic/spelling and radical/stem changes. The cross reference numbers following each verb indicate the category of verbs to which each type of change belongs.

TIEMPOS SIMPLES
SIMPLE TENSES

PRESENTE DE INDICATIVO PRESENT INDICATIVE	PRETÉRITO IMPERFECTO DE INDICATIVO IMPERFECT INDICATIVE	PRETÉRITO INDEFINIDO DE INDICATIVO PRETERITE INDICATIVE	FUTURO IMPERFECTO DE INDICATIVO FUTURE INDICATIVE	POTENCIAL SIMPLE CONDITIONAL
I laugh, etc. *	*I was laughing, etc.* *	*I laughed, etc.* *	*I will laugh, etc.* *	*I would laugh, etc.* *
río	reía	reí	reiré	reiría
ríes	reías	reíste	reirás	reirías
ríe	reía	rió	reirá	reiría
reímos	reíamos	reímos	reiremos	reiríamos
reís	reíais	reísteis	reiréis	reiríais
ríen	reían	rieron	reirán	reirían

PRESENTE DE SUBJUNTIVO PRESENT SUBJUNCTIVE	PRETÉRITO IMPERFECTO DE SUBJUNTIVO PAST (IMPERFECT) SUBJUNCTIVE		FUTURO IMPERFECTO DE SUBJUNTIVO FUTURE SUBJUNCTIVE
I laugh, etc. *	*I laughed, etc.* *		*I will laugh, etc.* *
ría	riera	riese	riere
rías	rieras	rieses	rieres
ría	riera	riese	riere
riamos	riéramos _or_	riésemos	riéremos
riáis	rierais	rieseis	riereis
rían	rieran	riesen	rieren

FORMAS IMPERATIVAS, GERUNDIOS Y PARTICIPIO
COMMANDS AND PARTICIPLES

FORMAS IMPERATIVAS COMMANDS		GERUNDIO Y PARTICIPIO PARTICIPLES		
AFIRMATIVA AFFIRMATIVE	NEGATIVA NEGATIVE	GERUNDIO SIMPLE PRESENT PARTICIPLE	PARTICIPIO PAST PARTICIPLE	GERUNDIO COMPUESTO PERFECT PARTICIPLE
laugh	*don't laugh*	*laughing*	*laughed*	*having laughed*
ríe (tú)	no rías (tú)	riendo	reído	habiendo reído
ría (Ud.)	no ría (Ud.)			
reíd (vosotros)	no riáis (vosotros)			
rían (Uds.)	no rían (Uds.)			
let's laugh	*let's not laugh*			
riamos	no riamos			

INFINITIVO COMPUESTO: haber reído
PERFECT INFINITIVE: to have laughed

TIEMPOS COMPUESTOS
PERFECT (COMPOUND) TENSES

PRETÉRITO PERFECTO DE INDICATIVO PRESENT PERFECT INDICATIVE	PRETÉRITO PLUSCUAMPERFECTO DE INDICATIVO PAST PERFECT (PLUPERFECT) INDICATIVE	PRETÉRITO ANTERIOR DE INDICATIVO PRETERITE PERFECT INDICATIVE	FUTURO PERFECTO DE INDICATIVO FUTURE PERFECT INDICATIVE	POTENCIAL COMPUESTO CONDITIONAL PERFECT
I have laughed, etc.	*I had laughed, etc.*	*I had laughed, etc.*	*I will have laughed, etc.* *	*I would have laughed, etc.* *
he reído	había reído	hube reído	habré reído	habría reído
has reído	habías reído	hubiste reído	habrás reído	habrías reído
ha reído	había reído	hubo reído	habrá reído	habría reído
hemos reído	habíamos reído	hubimos reído	habremos reído	habríamos reído
habéis reído	habíais reído	hubisteis reído	habréis reído	habríais reído
han reído	habían reído	hubieron reído	habrán reído	habrían reído

PRETÉRITO PERFECTO DE SUBJUNTIVO PRESENT PERFECT SUBJUNCTIVE	PRETÉRITO PLUSCUAMPERFECTO DE SUBJUNTIVO PAST PERFECT (PLUPERFECT) SUBJUNCTIVE		FUTURO PERFECTO DE SUBJUNTIVO FUTURE PERFECT SUBJUNCTIVE
I have laughed, etc. *	*I had laughed, etc.* *		*I will have laughed, etc.* *
haya reído	hubiera reído	hubiese reído	hubiere reído
hayas reído	hubieras reído	hubieses reído	hubieres reído
haya reído	hubiera reído	hubiese reído	hubiere reído
hayamos reído	hubiéramos reído _or_	hubiésemos reído	hubiéremos reído
hayáis reído	hubierais reído	hubieseis reído	hubiereis reído
hayan reído	hubieran reído	hubiesen reído	hubieren reído

*For additional translation possibilities see chart A.

VII. Radical/stem changing verbs with spelling changes

VERBS OF THIS CATEGORY

*desleír (i, i) 25. (OC), 42. (RC)
*engreír (i, i) 25. (OC), 42. (RC)
*engreírse (i, i) 25. (OC), 42. (RC), 4. (R)
**freír (i, i) 25. (OC), 42. (RC), 88. (I)
**refreír (i, i) 25. (OC), 42. (RC), 88. (I)
*reír (i, i) 25. (OC), 42. (RC)
*reírse (i, i) 25. (OC), 42. (RC), 4. (R)
**sofreír (i, i) 25. (OC), 42. (RC), 88. (I)
*sonreír (i, i) 25. (OC), 42. (RC)

R   = Reflexive
OC = Orthographic/Spelling Change
RC = Radical/Stem Change
I   = Irregular
*These verbs have a combination of orthographic/spelling and radical/stem changes. The cross reference numbers following each verb indicate the category of verbs to which each type of change belongs.
**These verbs have a combination of orthographic/spelling and radical/stem changes. The first two cross reference numbers following each verb indicate the category of verbs to which each type of change belongs. These verbs also have, in addition to the orthographic/spelling changes and radical/stem changes, irregularities not exemplified by the model verb on the chart given here. The third cross reference number following each verb indicates the chart which shows all changes and irregularities together. Note that this is the chart with the highest number.

TIEMPOS SIMPLES
SIMPLE TENSES

PRESENTE DE INDICATIVO _PRESENT INDICATIVE_	PRETÉRITO IMPERFECTO DE INDICATIVO _IMPERFECT INDICATIVE_	PRETÉRITO INDEFINIDO DE INDICATIVO _PRETERITE INDICATIVE_	FUTURO IMPERFECTO DE INDICATIVO _FUTURE INDICATIVE_	POTENCIAL SIMPLE _CONDITIONAL_
I scold, etc.*	_I was scolding, etc.*_	_I scolded etc.*_	_I will scold, etc.*_	_I would scold, etc.*_
riño	reñía	reñí	reñiré	reñiría
riñes	reñías	reñiste	reñirás	reñirías
riñe	reñía	riñó	reñirá	reñiría
reñimos	reñíamos	reñimos	reñiremos	reñiríamos
reñís	reñíais	reñisteis	reñiréis	reñiríais
riñen	reñían	riñeron	reñirán	reñirían

PRESENTE DE SUBJUNTIVO _PRESENT SUBJUNCTIVE_	PRETÉRITO IMPERFECTO DE SUBJUNTIVO _PAST (IMPERFECT) SUBJUNCTIVE_		FUTURO IMPERFECTO DE SUBJUNTIVO _FUTURE SUBJUNCTIVE_
I scold, etc.*	_I scolded, etc.*_		_I will scold, etc.*_
riña	riñera	riñese	riñere
riñas	riñeras	riñeses	riñeres
riña	riñera	riñese	riñere
riñamos	riñéramos _or_	riñésemos	riñéremos
riñáis	riñerais	riñeseis	riñereis
riñan	riñeran	riñesen	riñeren

FORMAS IMPERATIVAS, GERUNDIOS Y PARTICIPIO
COMMANDS AND PARTICIPLES

FORMAS IMPERATIVAS _COMMANDS_		GERUNDIO Y PARTICIPIO _PARTICIPLES_		
AFIRMATIVA _AFFIRMATIVE_	NEGATIVA _NEGATIVE_	GERUNDIO SIMPLE _PRESENT PARTICIPLE_	PARTICIPIO _PAST PARTICIPLE_	GERUNDIO COMPUESTO _PERFECT PARTICIPLE_
scold	_don't scold_	_scolding_	_scolded_	_having scolded_
riñe (tú)	no riñas (tú)	riñendo	reñido	habiendo reñido
riña (Ud.)	no riña (Ud.)			
reñid (vosotros)	no riñáis (vosotros)			
riñan (Uds.)	no riñan (Uds.)			
let's scold	_let's not scold_			
riñamos	no riñamos			

INFINITIVO COMPUESTO: haber reñido
PERFECT INFINITIVE: to have scolded

TIEMPOS COMPUESTOS
PERFECT (COMPOUND) TENSES

PRETÉRITO PERFECTO DE INDICATIVO _PRESENT PERFECT INDICATIVE_	PRETÉRITO PLUSCUAMPERFECTO DE INDICATIVO _PAST PERFECT (PLUPERFECT) INDICATIVE_	PRETÉRITO ANTERIOR DE INDICATIVO _PRETERITE PERFECT INDICATIVE_	FUTURO PERFECTO DE INDICATIVO _FUTURE PERFECT INDICATIVE_	POTENCIAL COMPUESTO _CONDITIONAL PERFECT_
I have scolded, etc.	_I had scolded, etc._	_I had scolded, etc._	_I will have scolded, etc.*_	_I would have scolded, etc.*_
he reñido	había reñido	hube reñido	habré reñido	habría reñido
has reñido	habías reñido	hubiste reñido	habrás reñido	habrías reñido
ha reñido	había reñido	hubo reñido	habrá reñido	habría reñido
hemos reñido	habíamos reñido	hubimos reñido	habremos reñido	habríamos reñido
habéis reñido	habíais reñido	hubisteis reñido	habréis reñido	habríais reñido
han reñido	habían reñido	hubieron reñido	habrán reñido	habrían reñido

PRETÉRITO PERFECTO DE SUBJUNTIVO _PRESENT PERFECT SUBJUNCTIVE_	PRETÉRITO PLUSCUAMPERFECTO DE SUBJUNTIVO _PAST PERFECT (PLUPERFECT) SUBJUNCTIVE_		FUTURO PERFECTO DE SUBJUNTIVO _FUTURE PERFECT SUBJUNCTIVE_
I have scolded, etc.*	_I had scolded, etc.*_		_I will have scolded, etc.*_
haya reñido	hubiera reñido	hubiese reñido	hubiere reñido
hayas reñido	hubieras reñido	hubieses reñido	hubieres reñido
haya reñido	hubiera reñido	hubiese reñido	hubiere reñido
hayamos reñido	hubiéramos reñido _or_	hubiésemos reñido	hubiéremos reñido
hayáis reñido	hubierais reñido	hubieseis reñido	hubiereis reñido
hayan reñido	hubieran reñido	hubiesen reñido	hubieren reñido

*For additional translation possibilities see chart A.

60

VII. Radical/stem changing verbs with spelling changes

VERBS OF THIS CATEGORY
_____

*ceñir (i, i) 29. (OC), 42. (RC)
*ceñirse (i, i) 29. (OC), 42. (RC), 4. (R)
*constreñir (i, i) 29. (OC), 42. (RC)
*desteñir (i, i) 29. (OC), 42. (RC)
*desteñirse (i, i) 29. (OC), 42. (RC), 4. (R)
*estreñir (i, i) 29. (OC), 42. (RC)
*estreñirse (i, i) 29. (OC), 42. (RC), 4. (R)
*reñir (i, i) 29. (OC), 42. (RC)
*reteñir (i, i) 29. (OC), 42. (RC)
*teñir (i, i) 29 (OC), 42. (RC)

_____
R   = Reflexive
OC = Orthographic/Stem Change
RC = Radical/Stem Change
*These verbs have a combination of orthographic/spelling and radical/stem changes. The cross reference numbers following each verb indicate the category of verbs to which each type of change belongs.

61 Verbs ending in -iar with accent shift } model: ENVIAR

SIMPLE TENSES

PRESENTE DE INDICATIVO *PRESENT INDICATIVE*	PRETÉRITO IMPERFECTO DE INDICATIVO *IMPERFECT INDICATIVE*	PRETÉRITO INDEFINIDO DE INDICATIVO *PRETERITE INDICATIVE*	FUTURO IMPERFECTO DE INDICATIVO *FUTURE INDICATIVE*	POTENCIAL SIMPLE *CONDITIONAL*
I send, etc.*	*I was sending, etc.**	*I sent, etc.**	*I will send, etc.**	*I would send, etc.**
envío	enviaba	envié	enviaré	enviaría
envías	enviabas	enviaste	enviarás	enviarías
envía	enviaba	envió	enviará	enviaría
enviamos	enviábamos	enviamos	enviaremos	enviaríamos
enviáis	enviabais	enviasteis	enviaréis	enviaríais
envían	enviaban	enviaron	enviarán	enviarían

PRESENTE DE SUBJUNTIVO *PRESENT SUBJUNCTIVE*	PRETÉRITO IMPERFECTO DE SUBJUNTIVO *PAST (IMPERFECT) SUBJUNCTIVE*		FUTURO IMPERFECTO DE SUBJUNTIVO *FUTURE SUBJUNCTIVE*
I send, etc.*	*I sent, etc.**		*I will send, etc.**
envíe	enviara	enviase	enviare
envíes	enviaras	enviases	enviares
envíe	enviara	enviase	enviare
enviemos	enviáramos *or*	enviásemos	enviáremos
enviéis	enviarais	enviaseis	enviareis
envíen	enviaran	enviasen	enviaren

COMMANDS AND PARTICIPLES

FORMAS IMPERATIVAS *COMMANDS*		GERUNDIO Y PARTICIPIO *PARTICIPLES*		
AFIRMATIVA *AFFIRMATIVE*	NEGATIVA *NEGATIVE*	GERUNDIO SIMPLE *PRESENT PARTICIPLE*	PARTICIPIO *PAST PARTICIPLE*	GERUNDIO COMPUESTO *PERFECT PARTICIPLE*
send	*don't send*	*sending*	*sent*	*having sent*
envía (tú)	no envíes (tú)	enviando	enviado	habiendo enviado
envíe (Ud.)	no envíe (Ud.)			
enviad (vosotros)	no enviéis (vosotros)			
envíen (Uds.)	no envíen (Uds.)			
let's send	*let's not send*			
enviemos	no enviemos			

INFINITIVO COMPUESTO: haber enviado
PERFECT INFINITIVE: to have sent

PERFECT (COMPOUND) TENSES

PRETÉRITO PERFECTO DE INDICATIVO *PRESENT PERFECT INDICATIVE*	PRETÉRITO PLUSCUAMPERFECTO DE INDICATIVO *PAST PERFECT (PLUPERFECT) INDICATIVE*	PRETÉRITO ANTERIOR DE INDICATIVO *PRETERITE PERFECT INDICATIVE*	FUTURO PERFECTO DE INDICATIVO *FUTURE PERFECT INDICATIVE*	POTENCIAL COMPUESTO *CONDITIONAL PERFECT*
I have sent, etc.	*I had sent, etc.*	*I had sent, etc.*	*I will have sent, etc.**	*I would have sent, etc.**
he enviado	había enviado	hube enviado	habré enviado	habría enviado
has enviado	habías enviado	hubiste enviado	habrás enviado	habrías enviado
ha enviado	había enviado	hubo enviado	habrá enviado	habría enviado
hemos enviado	habíamos enviado	hubimos enviado	habremos enviado	habríamos enviado
habéis enviado	habíais enviado	hubisteis enviado	habréis enviado	habríais enviado
han enviado	habían enviado	hubieron enviado	habrán enviado	habrían enviado

PRETÉRITO PERFECTO DE SUBJUNTIVO *PRESENT PERFECT SUBJUNCTIVE*	PRETÉRITO PLUSCUAMPERFECTO DE SUBJUNTIVO *PAST PERFECT (PLUPERFECT) SUBJUNCTIVE*		FUTURO PERFECTO DE SUBJUNTIVO *FUTURE PERFECT SUBJUNCTIVE*
I have sent, etc.*	*I had sent, etc.**		*I will have sent, etc.**
haya enviado	hubiera enviado	hubiese enviado	hubiere enviado
hayas enviado	hubieras enviado	hubieses enviado	hubieres enviado
haya enviado	hubiera enviado	hubiese enviado	hubiere enviado
hayamos enviado	hubiéramos enviado *or*	hubiésemos enviado	hubiéremos enviado
hayáis enviado	hubierais enviado	hubieseis enviado	hubiereis enviado
hayan enviado	hubieran enviado	hubiesen enviado	hubieren enviado

*For additional translation possibilities see chart A.

61

VIII. Verbs with a shift in accent

acuantiar
afiliar *or* (regular - 1)
agriarse *or* (regular - 1) 4. (R)
aliar
aliarse 4. (R)
amnistiar
ampliar
ansiar *or* (regular - 1)
arriar
ataviar
ataviarse 4. (R)
autografiar
auxiliar *or* (regular - 1)
averiar
averiarse 4. (R)
aviar
cablegrafiar
cariar
cariarse 4. (R)
cinematografiar
confiar
confiarse 4. (R)
contrariar
chirriar
desafiar
desaviar
descarriar
descarriarse 4. (R)
desconfiar
desvariar
desviar
enfriar
enviar
espiar
esquiar
estriar
expatriar
expiar
extasiar
extasiarse 4. (R)
extraviar
extraviarse 4. (R)
fotografiar
gloriarse 4. (R)
hastiar
litografiar
malcriar
mecanografiar
mimeografiar
multigrafiar
pipiar
porfiar
radiografiar
radiotelegrafiar
repatriar
resfriarse 4. (R)
rociar

taquigrafiar
telefotografiar
telegrafiar
vaciar
variar
xylografiar

R = Reflexive

62

Verbs ending in -consonant (not c or g) + uar with accent shift* } model: CONTINUAR

*Plus anticuar and anticuarse.

PRESENTE DE INDICATIVO *PRESENT INDICATIVE*	PRETÉRITO IMPERFECTO DE INDICATIVO *IMPERFECT INDICATIVE*	PRETÉRITO INDEFINIDO DE INDICATIVO *PRETERITE INDICATIVE*	FUTURO IMPERFECTO DE INDICATIVO *FUTURE INDICATIVE*	POTENCIAL SIMPLE *CONDITIONAL*
I continue, etc.	*I was continuing, etc.*	*I continued, etc.*	*I will continue, etc.*	*I would continue, etc.*
continúo	continuaba	continué	continuaré	continuaría
continúas	continuabas	continuaste	continuarás	continuarías
continúa	continuaba	continuó	continuará	continuaría
continuamos	continuábamos	continuamos	continuaremos	continuaríamos
continuáis	continuabais	continuasteis	continuaréis	continuaríais
continúan	continuaban	continuaron	continuarán	continuarían

PRESENTE DE SUBJUNTIVO *PRESENT SUBJUNCTIVE*	PRETÉRITO IMPERFECTO DE SUBJUNTIVO *PAST (IMPERFECT) SUBJUNCTIVE*		FUTURO IMPERFECTO DE SUBJUNTIVO *FUTURE SUBJUNCTIVE*
I continue, etc.	*I continued, etc.*		*I will continue, etc.*
continúe	continuara	continuase	continuare
continúes	continuaras	continuases	continuares
continúe	continuara	continuase	continuare
continuemos	continuáramos *or*	continuásemos	continuáremos
continuéis	continuarais	continuaseis	continuareis
continúen	continuaran	continuasen	continuaren

FORMAS IMPERATIVAS *COMMANDS*		GERUNDIO Y PARTICIPIO *PARTICIPLES*		
AFIRMATIVA *AFFIRMATIVE*	NEGATIVA *NEGATIVE*	GERUNDIO SIMPLE *PRESENT PARTICIPLE*	PARTICIPIO *PAST PARTICIPLE*	GERUNDIO COMPUESTO *PERFECT PARTICIPLE*
continue	*don't continue*	*continuing*	*continued*	*having continued*
continúa (tú)	no continúes (tú)	continuando	continuado	habiendo continuado
continúe (Ud.)	no continúe (Ud.)			
continuad (vosotros)	no continuéis (vosotros)			
continúen (Uds.)	no continúen (Uds.)			
let's continue	*let's not continue*			
continuemos	no continuemos			

INFINITIVO COMPUESTO: haber continuado
PERFECT INFINITIVE: to have continued

PRETÉRITO PERFECTO DE INDICATIVO *PRESENT PERFECT INDICATIVE*	PRETÉRITO PLUSCUAMPERFECTO DE INDICATIVO *PAST PERFECT (PLUPERFECT) INDICATIVE*	PRETÉRITO ANTERIOR DE INDICATIVO *PRETERITE PERFECT INDICATIVE*	FUTURO PERFECTO DE INDICATIVO *FUTURE PERFECT INDICATIVE*	POTENCIAL COMPUESTO *CONDITIONAL PERFECT*
I have continued, etc.	*I had continued, etc.*	*I had continued, etc.*	*I will have continued, etc.*	*I would have continued, etc.*
he continuado	había continuado	hube continuado	habré continuado	habría continuado
has continuado	habías continuado	hubiste continuado	habrás continuado	habrías continuado
ha continuado	había continuado	hubo continuado	habrá continuado	habría continuado
hemos continuado	habíamos continuado	hubimos continuado	habremos continuado	habríamos continuado
habéis continuado	habíais continuado	hubisteis continuado	habréis continuado	habríais continuado
han continuado	habían continuado	hubieron continuado	habrán continuado	habrían continuado

PRETÉRITO PERFECTO DE SUBJUNTIVO *PRESENT PERFECT SUBJUNCTIVE*	PRETÉRITO PLUSCUAMPERFECTO DE SUBJUNTIVO *PAST PERFECT (PLUPERFECT) SUBJUNCTIVE*		FUTURO PERFECTO DE SUBJUNTIVO *FUTURE PERFECT SUBJUNCTIVE*
I have continued, etc.	*I had continued, etc.*		*I will have continued, etc.*
haya continuado	hubiera continuado	hubiese continuado	hubiere continuado
hayas continuado	hubieras continuado	hubieses continuado	hubieres continuado
haya continuado	hubiera continuado	hubiese continuado	hubiere continuado
hayamos continuado	hubiéramos continuado *or*	hubiésemos continuado	hubiéremos continuado
hayáis continuado	hubierais continuado	hubieseis continuado	hubiereis continuado
hayan continuado	hubieran continuado	hubiesen continuado	hubieren continuado

*For additional translation possibilities see chart A.

VIII. Verbs with a shift in accent

acensuar
acentuar
actuar
adecuar
†anticuar *or* (regular - 1)
†anticuarse *or* (regular - 1), 4. (R)
atenuar
avaluar
conceptuar
contextuar
continuar
descontinuar
deshabituar
desvirtuar
discontinuar
efectuar
efectuarse 4. (R)
evaluar
exceptuar
extenuar
fluctuar
garuar
graduar
graduarse 4. (R)
habituar
infatuar
insinuar
menstruar
perpetuar
perpetuarse 4. (R)
preceptuar
puntuar
situar
tatuar
usufructuar
valuar

R = Reflexive
†Although according to the norms of the Academy these verbs are regular, in general usage they belong to this category.

63 Verbs with ai in penultimate syllable of infinitive } model: AISLAR

PRESENTE DE INDICATIVO *PRESENT INDICATIVE*	PRETÉRITO IMPERFECTO DE INDICATIVO *IMPERFECT INDICATIVE*	PRETÉRITO INDEFINIDO DE INDICATIVO *PRETERITE INDICATIVE*	FUTURO IMPERFECTO DE INDICATIVO *FUTURE INDICATIVE*	POTENCIAL SIMPLE *CONDITIONAL*
I isolate, etc.	*I was isolating, etc.*	*I isolated, etc.*	*I will isolate, etc.*	*I would isolate, etc.*
aíslo	aislaba	aislé	aislaré	aislaría
aíslas	aislabas	aislaste	aislarás	aislarías
aísla	aislaba	aisló	aislará	aislaría
aislamos	aislábamos	aislamos	aislaremos	aislaríamos
aisláis	aislabais	aislasteis	aislaréis	aislaríais
aíslan	aislaban	aislaron	aislarán	aislarían

PRESENTE DE SUBJUNTIVO *PRESENT SUBJUNCTIVE*	PRETÉRITO IMPERFECTO DE SUBJUNTIVO *PAST (IMPERFECT) SUBJUNCTIVE*		FUTURO IMPERFECTO DE SUBJUNTIVO *FUTURE SUBJUNCTIVE*
I isolate, etc.	*I isolated, etc.*		*I will isolate, etc.*
aísle	aislara	aislase	aislare
aísles	aislaras	aislases	aislares
aísle	aislara *or* aislase	aislare
aislemos	aisláramos	aislásemos	aisláremos
aisléis	aislarais	aislaseis	aislareis
aíslen	aislaran	aislasen	aislaren

FORMAS IMPERATIVAS *COMMANDS*		GERUNDIO Y PARTICIPIO *PARTICIPLES*		
AFIRMATIVA *AFFIRMATIVE*	NEGATIVA *NEGATIVE*	GERUNDIO SIMPLE *PRESENT PARTICIPLE*	PARTICIPIO *PAST PARTICIPLE*	GERUNDIO COMPUESTO *PERFECT PARTICIPLE*
isolate	*don't isolate*	*isolating*	*isolated*	*having isolated*
aísla (tú)	no aísles (tú)	aislando	aislado	habiendo aislado
aísle (Ud.)	no aísle (Ud.)			
aislad (vosotros)	no aisléis (vosotros)			
aíslen (Uds.)	no aíslen (Uds.)			
let's isolate	*let's not isolate*			
aislemos	no aislemos			

INFINITIVO COMPUESTO: haber aislado
PERFECT INFINITIVE: to have isolated

PRETÉRITO PERFECTO DE INDICATIVO *PRESENT PERFECT INDICATIVE*	PRETÉRITO PLUSCUAMPERFECTO DE INDICATIVO *PAST PERFECT (PLUPERFECT) INDICATIVE*	PRETÉRITO ANTERIOR DE INDICATIVO *PRETERITE PERFECT INDICATIVE*	FUTURO PERFECTO DE INDICATIVO *FUTURE PERFECT INDICATIVE*	POTENCIAL COMPUESTO *CONDITIONAL PERFECT*
I have isolated, etc.	*I had isolated, etc.*	*I had isolated, etc.*	*I will have isolated, etc.*	*I would have isolated, etc.*
he aislado	había aislado	hube aislado	habré aislado	habría aislado
has aislado	habías aislado	hubiste aislado	habrás aislado	habrías aislado
ha aislado	había aislado	hubo aislado	habrá aislado	habría aislado
hemos aislado	habíamos aislado	hubimos aislado	habremos aislado	habríamos aislado
habéis aislado	habíais aislado	hubisteis aislado	habréis aislado	habríais aislado
han aislado	habían aislado	hubieron aislado	habrán aislado	habrían aislado

PRETÉRITO PERFECTO DE SUBJUNTIVO *PRESENT PERFECT SUBJUNCTIVE*	PRETÉRITO PLUSCUAMPERFECTO DE SUBJUNTIVO *PAST PERFECT (PLUPERFECT) SUBJUNCTIVE*		FUTURO PERFECTO DE SUBJUNTIVO *FUTURE PERFECT SUBJUNCTIVE*
I have isolated, etc.	*I had isolated, etc.*		*I will have isolated, etc.*
haya aislado	hubiera aislado	hubiese aislado	hubiere aislado
hayas aislado	hubieras aislado	hubieses aislado	hubieres aislado
haya aislado	hubiera aislado	hubiese aislado	hubiere aislado
hayamos aislado	hubiéramos aislado *or* hubiésemos aislado	hubiéremos aislado
hayáis aislado	hubierais aislado	hubieseis aislado	hubiereis aislado
hayan aislado	hubieran aislado	hubiesen aislado	hubieren aislado

*For additional translation possibilities see chart A.

63

VIII. Verbs with a shift in accent

airar
airarse 4. (R)
aislar
*enraizar 64. (OC)
traillar

R   = Reflexive
OC = Orthographic/Spelling Change
* This verb has an orthographic/spelling change in addition to the accent shift exemplified by the model verb on the chart given here. The cross reference
number following the verb indicates the chart which shows all changes together.

64 Verb ending in -zar with ai in penultimate syllable of infinitive } model: ENRAIZAR

TIEMPOS SIMPLES
SIMPLE TENSES

PRESENTE DE INDICATIVO *PRESENT* *INDICATIVE*	PRETÉRITO IMPERFECTO DE INDICATIVO *IMPERFECT* *INDICATIVE*	PRETÉRITO INDEFINIDO DE INDICATIVO *PRETERITE* *INDICATIVE*	FUTURO IMPERFECTO DE INDICATIVO *FUTURE* *INDICATIVE*	POTENCIAL SIMPLE *CONDITIONAL*
I take root, etc.*	*I was taking root, etc.**	*I took root, etc.**	*I will take root, etc.**	*I would take root, etc.**
enraízo	enraizaba	enraicé	enraizaré	enraizaría
enraízas	enraizabas	enraizaste	enraizarás	enraizarías
enraíza	enraizaba	enraizó	enraizará	enraizaría
enraizamos	enraizábamos	enraizamos	enraizaremos	enraizaríamos
enraizáis	enraizabais	enraizasteis	enraizaréis	enraizaríais
enraízan	enraizaban	enraizaron	enraizarán	enraizarían

PRESENTE DE SUBJUNTIVO *PRESENT* *SUBJUNCTIVE*	PRETÉRITO IMPERFECTO DE SUBJUNTIVO *PAST (IMPERFECT)* *SUBJUNCTIVE*		FUTURO IMPERFECTO DE SUBJUNTIVO *FUTURE* *SUBJUNCTIVE*
I take root, etc.*	*I took root, etc.**		*I will take root, etc.**
enraíce	enraizara	enraizase	enraizare
enraíces	enraizaras	enraizases	enraizares
enraíce	enraizara	enraizase	enraizare
enraicemos	enraizáramos *or*	enraizásemos	enraizáremos
enraicéis	enraizarais	enraizaseis	enraizareis
enraícen	enraizaran	enraizasen	enraizaren

FORMAS IMPERATIVAS, GERUNDIOS Y PARTICIPIO
COMMANDS AND PARTICIPLES

FORMAS IMPERATIVAS *COMMANDS*		GERUNDIO Y PARTICIPIO *PARTICIPLES*		
AFIRMATIVA *AFFIRMATIVE*	NEGATIVA *NEGATIVE*	GERUNDIO SIMPLE *PRESENT PARTICIPLE*	PARTICIPIO *PAST PARTICIPLE*	GERUNDIO COMPUESTO *PERFECT PARTICIPLE*
take root	*don't take root*	*taking root*	*taken root*	*having taken root*
enraíza (tú)	no enraíces (tú)	enraizando	enraizado	habiendo enraizado
enraíce (Ud.)	no enraíce (Ud.)			
enraizad (vosotros)	no enraicéis (vosotros)			
enraícen (Uds.)	no enraícen (Uds.)			
let's take root	*let's not take root*			
enraicemos	no enraicemos			

INFINITIVO COMPUESTO: haber enraizado
PERFECT INFINITIVE: to have taken root

TIEMPOS COMPUESTOS
PERFECT (COMPOUND) TENSES

PRETÉRITO PERFECTO DE INDICATIVO *PRESENT PERFECT* *INDICATIVE*	PRETÉRITO PLUSCUAMPERFECTO DE INDICATIVO *PAST PERFECT (PLUPERFECT)* *INDICATIVE*	PRETÉRITO ANTERIOR DE INDICATIVO *PRETERITE PERFECT* *INDICATIVE*	FUTURO PERFECTO DE INDICATIVO *FUTURE PERFECT* *INDICATIVE*	POTENCIAL COMPUESTO *CONDITIONAL PERFECT*
I have taken root, etc.	*I had taken root, etc.*	*I had taken root, etc.*	*I will have taken root, etc.**	*I would have taken root, etc.**
he enraizado	había enraizado	hube enraizado	habré enraizado	habría enraizado
has enraizado	habías enraizado	hubiste enraizado	habrás enraizado	habrías enraizado
ha enraizado	había enraizado	hubo enraizado	habrá enraizado	habría enraizado
hemos enraizado	habíamos enraizado	hubimos enraizado	habremos enraizado	habríamos enraizado
habéis enraizado	habíais enraizado	hubisteis enraizado	habréis enraizado	habríais enraizado
han enraizado	habían enraizado	hubieron enraizado	habrán enraizado	habrían enraizado

PRETÉRITO PERFECTO DE SUBJUNTIVO *PRESENT PERFECT* *SUBJUNCTIVE*	PRETÉRITO PLUSCUAMPERFECTO DE SUBJUNTIVO *PAST PERFECT (PLUPERFECT)* *SUBJUNCTIVE*		FUTURO PERFECTO DE SUBJUNTIVO *FUTURE PERFECT* *SUBJUNCTIVE*
I have taken root, etc.*	*I had taken root, etc.**		*I will have taken root, etc.**
haya enraizado	hubiera enraizado	hubiese enraizado	hubiere enraizado
hayas enraizado	hubieras enraizado	hubieses enraizado	hubieres enraizado
haya enraizado	hubiera enraizado	hubiese enraizado	hubiere enraizado
hayamos enraizado	hubiéramos enraizado *or*	hubiésemos enraizado	hubiéremos enraizado
hayáis enraizado	hubierais enraizado	hubieseis enraizado	hubiereis enraizado
hayan enraizado	hubieran enraizado	hubiesen enraizado	hubieren enraizado

**For additional translation possibilities see chart A.*

VIII. Verbs with a shift in accent

VERB OF THIS CATEGORY

---

*enraizar 11. (OC), 63. (accent shift)

OC = Orthographic/Spelling Change
*This verb has a combination of orthographic/spelling changes and accent shift. The cross reference numbers following the verb indicate the category of verbs to which each type of change belongs.

TIEMPOS SIMPLES
SIMPLE TENSES

PRESENTE DE INDICATIVO *PRESENT INDICATIVE*	PRETÉRITO IMPERFECTO DE INDICATIVO *IMPERFECT INDICATIVE*	PRETÉRITO INDEFINIDO DE INDICATIVO *PRETERITE INDICATIVE*	FUTURO IMPERFECTO DE INDICATIVO *FUTURE INDICATIVE*	POTENCIAL SIMPLE *CONDITIONAL*
I meow, etc.*	*I was meowing, etc.**	*I meowed, etc.**	*I will meow, etc.**	*I would meow, etc.**
maúllo	maullaba	maullé	maullaré	maullaría
maúllas	maullabas	maullaste	maullarás	maullarías
maúlla	maullaba	maulló	maullará	maullaría
maullamos	maullábamos	maullamos	maullaremos	maullaríamos
maulláis	maullabais	maullasteis	maullaréis	maullaríais
maúllan	maullaban	maullaron	maullarán	maullarían

PRESENTE DE SUBJUNTIVO *PRESENT SUBJUNCTIVE*	PRETÉRITO IMPERFECTO DE SUBJUNTIVO *PAST (IMPERFECT) SUBJUNCTIVE*		FUTURO IMPERFECTO DE SUBJUNTIVO *FUTURE SUBJUNCTIVE*
I meow, etc.*	*I meowed, etc.**		*I will meow, etc.**
maúlle	maullara	maullase	maullare
maúlles	maullaras	maullases	maullares
maúlle	maullara	maullase	maullare
maullemos	maulláramos _or_	maullásemos	maulláremos
maulléis	maullarais	maullaseis	maullareis
maúllen	maullaran	maullasen	maullaren

FORMAS IMPERATIVAS, GERUNDIOS Y PARTICIPIO
COMMANDS AND PARTICIPLES

FORMAS IMPERATIVAS *COMMANDS*		GERUNDIO Y PARTICIPIO *PARTICIPLES*		
AFIRMATIVA *AFFIRMATIVE*	NEGATIVA *NEGATIVE*	GERUNDIO SIMPLE *PRESENT PARTICIPLE*	PARTICIPIO *PAST PARTICIPLE*	GERUNDIO COMPUESTO *PERFECT PARTICIPLE*
meow	*don't meow*	*meowing*	*meowed*	*having meowed*
maúlla (tú)	no maúlles (tú)	maullando	maullado	habiendo maullado
maúlle (Ud.)	no maúlle (Ud.)			
maullad (vosotros)	no maulléis (vosotros)			
maúllen (Uds.)	no maúllen (Uds.)			
let's meow	*let's not meow*			
maullemos	no maullemos			

INFINITIVO COMPUESTO: haber maullado
PERFECT INFINITIVE: *to have meowed*

TIEMPOS COMPUESTOS
PERFECT (COMPOUND) TENSES

PRETÉRITO PERFECTO DE INDICATIVO *PRESENT PERFECT INDICATIVE*	PRETÉRITO PLUSCUAMPERFECTO DE INDICATIVO *PAST PERFECT (PLUPERFECT) INDICATIVE*	PRETÉRITO ANTERIOR DE INDICATIVO *PRETERITE PERFECT INDICATIVE*	FUTURO PERFECTO DE INDICATIVO *FUTURE PERFECT INDICATIVE*	POTENCIAL COMPUESTO *CONDITIONAL PERFECT*
I have meowed, etc.	*I had meowed, etc.*	*I had meowed, etc.*	*I will have meowed, etc.**	*I would have meowed, etc.**
he maullado	había maullado	hube maullado	habré maullado	habría maullado
has maullado	habías maullado	hubiste maullado	habrás maullado	habrías maullado
ha maullado	había maullado	hubo maullado	habrá maullado	habría maullado
hemos maullado	habíamos maullado	hubimos maullado	habremos maullado	habríamos maullado
habéis maullado	habíais maullado	hubisteis maullado	habréis maullado	habríais maullado
han maullado	habían maullado	hubieron maullado	habrán maullado	habrían maullado

PRETÉRITO PERFECTO DE SUBJUNTIVO *PRESENT PERFECT SUBJUNCTIVE*	PRETÉRITO PLUSCUAMPERFECTO DE SUBJUNTIVO *PAST PERFECT (PLUPERFECT) SUBJUNCTIVE*		FUTURO PERFECTO DE SUBJUNTIVO *FUTURE PERFECT SUBJUNCTIVE*
I have meowed, etc.*	*I had meowed, etc.**		*I will have meowed, etc.**
haya maullado	hubiera maullado	hubiese maullado	hubiere maullado
hayas maullado	hubieras maullado	hubieses maullado	hubieres maullado
haya maullado	hubiera maullado	hubiese maullado	hubiere maullado
hayamos maullado	hubiéramos maullado _or_	hubiésemos maullado	hubiéremos maullado
hayáis maullado	hubierais maullado	hubieseis maullado	hubiereis maullado
hayan maullado	hubieran maullado	hubiesen maullado	hubieren maullado

*For additional translation possibilities see chart A.

VIII. Verbs with a shift in accent

aullar
aunar
embaular *or* (regular-1)
maullar

66 Verb with eu in penultimate syllable of infinitive } model: REUNIR

TIEMPOS SIMPLES
SIMPLE TENSES

PRESENTE DE INDICATIVO *PRESENT INDICATIVE*	PRETÉRITO IMPERFECTO DE INDICATIVO *IMPERFECT INDICATIVE*	PRETÉRITO INDEFINIDO DE INDICATIVO *PRETERITE INDICATIVE*	FUTURO IMPERFECTO DE INDICATIVO *FUTURE INDICATIVE*	POTENCIAL SIMPLE *CONDITIONAL*
*I join, etc.**	*I was joining, etc.**	*I joined, etc.**	*I will join, etc.**	*I would join, etc.**
reúno	reunía	reuní	reuniré	reuniría
reúnes	reunías	reuniste	reunirás	reunirías
reúne	reunía	reunió	reunirá	reuniría
reunimos	reuníamos	reunimos	reuniremos	reuniríamos
reunís	reuníais	reunisteis	reuniréis	reuniríais
reúnen	reunían	reunieron	reunirán	reunirían

PRESENTE DE SUBJUNTIVO *PRESENT SUBJUNCTIVE*	PRETÉRITO IMPERFECTO DE SUBJUNTIVO *PAST (IMPERFECT) SUBJUNCTIVE*		FUTURO IMPERFECTO DE SUBJUNTIVO *FUTURE SUBJUNCTIVE*
*I join, etc.**	*I joined, etc.**		*I will join, etc.**
reúna	reuniera	reuniese	reuniere
reúnas	reunieras	reunieses	reunieres
reúna	reuniera	reuniese	reuniere
reunamos	reuniéramos *or*	reuniésemos	reuniéremos
reunáis	reunierais	reunieseis	reuniereis
reúnan	reunieran	reuniesen	reunieren

FORMAS IMPERATIVAS, GERUNDIOS Y PARTICIPIO
COMMANDS AND PARTICIPLES

FORMAS IMPERATIVAS *COMMANDS*		GERUNDIO Y PARTICIPIO *PARTICIPLES*		
AFIRMATIVA *AFFIRMATIVE*	NEGATIVA *NEGATIVE*	GERUNDIO SIMPLE *PRESENT PARTICIPLE*	PARTICIPIO *PAST PARTICIPLE*	GERUNDIO COMPUESTO *PERFECT PARTICIPLE*
join	*don't join*	*joining*	*joined*	*having joined*
reúne (tú)	no reúnas (tú)	reuniendo	reunido	habiendo reunido
reúna (Ud.)	no reúna (Ud.)			
reunid (vosotros)	no reunáis (vosotros)			
reúnan (Uds.)	no reúnan (Uds.)			
let's join	*let's not join*			
reunamos	no reunamos			

INFINITIVO COMPUESTO: haber reunido
PERFECT INFINITIVE: to have joined

TIEMPOS COMPUESTOS
PERFECT (COMPOUND) TENSES

PRETÉRITO PERFECTO DE INDICATIVO *PRESENT PERFECT INDICATIVE*	PRETÉRITO PLUSCUAMPERFECTO DE INDICATIVO *PAST PERFECT (PLUPERFECT) INDICATIVE*	PRETÉRITO ANTERIOR DE INDICATIVO *PRETERITE PERFECT INDICATIVE*	FUTURO PERFECTO DE INDICATIVO *FUTURE PERFECT INDICATIVE*	POTENCIAL COMPUESTO *CONDITIONAL PERFECT*
I have joined, etc.	*I had joined, etc.*	*I had joined, etc.*	*I will have joined, etc.**	*I would have joined, etc.**
he reunido	había reunido	hube reunido	habré reunido	habría reunido
has reunido	habías reunido	hubiste reunido	habrás reunido	habrías reunido
ha reunido	había reunido	hubo reunido	habrá reunido	habría reunido
hemos reunido	habíamos reunido	hubimos reunido	habremos reunido	habríamos reunido
habéis reunido	habíais reunido	hubisteis reunido	habréis reunido	habríais reunido
han reunido	habían reunido	hubieron reunido	habrán reunido	habrían reunido

PRETÉRITO PERFECTO DE SUBJUNTIVO *PRESENT PERFECT SUBJUNCTIVE*	PRETÉRITO PLUSCUAMPERFECTO DE SUBJUNTIVO *PAST PERFECT (PLUPERFECT) SUBJUNCTIVE*		FUTURO PERFECTO DE SUBJUNTIVO *FUTURE PERFECT SUBJUNCTIVE*
*I have joined, etc.**	*I had joined, etc.**		*I will have joined, etc.**
haya reunido	hubiera reunido	hubiese reunido	hubiere reunido
hayas reunido	hubieras reunido	hubieses reunido	hubieres reunido
haya reunido	hubiera reunido	hubiese reunido	hubiere reunido
hayamos reunido	hubiéramos reunido *or*	hubiésemos reunido	hubiéremos reunido
hayáis reunido	hubierais reunido	hubieseis reunido	hubiereis reunido
hayan reunido	hubieran reunido	hubiesen reunido	hubieren reunido

*For additional translation possibilities see chart A.

VIII. Verbs with a shift in accent

<u>VERB OF THIS CATEGORY</u>

reunir

67 Verbs ending in -ducir } model: TRADUCIR

TIEMPOS SIMPLES
SIMPLE TENSES

PRESENTE DE INDICATIVO PRESENT INDICATIVE	PRETÉRITO IMPERFECTO DE INDICATIVO IMPERFECT INDICATIVE	PRETÉRITO INDEFINIDO DE INDICATIVO PRETERITE INDICATIVE	FUTURO IMPERFECTO DE INDICATIVO FUTURE INDICATIVE	POTENCIAL SIMPLE CONDITIONAL
I translate, etc.*	*I was translating, etc.**	*I translated, etc.**	*I will translate, etc.**	*I would translate, etc.**
traduzco	traducía	traduje	traduciré	traduciría
traduces	traducías	tradujiste	traducirás	traducirías
traduce	traducía	tradujo	traducirá	traduciría
traducimos	traducíamos	tradujimos	traduciremos	traduciríamos
traducís	traducíais	tradujisteis	traduciréis	traduciríais
traducen	traducían	tradujeron	traducirán	traducirían

PRESENTE DE SUBJUNTIVO PRESENT SUBJUNCTIVE	PRETÉRITO IMPERFECTO DE SUBJUNTIVO PAST (IMPERFECT) SUBJUNCTIVE		FUTURO IMPERFECTO DE SUBJUNTIVO FUTURE SUBJUNCTIVE
I translate, etc.*	*I translated, etc.**		*I will translate, etc.**
traduzca	tradujera	tradujese	tradujere
traduzcas	tradujeras	tradujeses	tradujeres
traduzca	tradujera	tradujese	tradujere
traduzcamos	tradujéramos *or*	tradujésemos	tradujéremos
traduzcáis	tradujerais	tradujeseis	tradujereis
traduzcan	tradujeran	tradujesen	tradujeren

FORMAS IMPERATIVAS, GERUNDIOS Y PARTICIPIO
COMMANDS AND PARTICIPLES

FORMAS IMPERATIVAS COMMANDS		GERUNDIO Y PARTICIPIO PARTICIPLES		
AFIRMATIVA AFFIRMATIVE	NEGATIVA NEGATIVE	GERUNDIO SIMPLE PRESENT PARTICIPLE	PARTICIPIO PAST PARTICIPLE	GERUNDIO COMPUESTO PERFECT PARTICIPLE
translate	*don't translate*	*translating*	*translated*	*having translated*
traduce (tú)	no traduzcas (tú)	traduciendo	traducido	habiendo traducido
traduzca (Ud.)	no traduzca (Ud.)			
traducid (vosotros)	no traduzcáis (vosotros)			
traduzcan (Uds.)	no traduzcan (Uds.)			
let's translate	*let's not translate*			
traduzcamos	no traduzcamos			

INFINITIVO COMPUESTO: haber traducido
PERFECT INFINITIVE: to have translated

TIEMPOS COMPUESTOS
PERFECT (COMPOUND) TENSES

PRETÉRITO PERFECTO DE INDICATIVO PRESENT PERFECT INDICATIVE	PRETÉRITO PLUSCUAMPERFECTO DE INDICATIVO PAST PERFECT (PLUPERFECT) INDICATIVE	PRETÉRITO ANTERIOR DE INDICATIVO PRETERITE PERFECT INDICATIVE	FUTURO PERFECTO DE INDICATIVO FUTURE PERFECT INDICATIVE	POTENCIAL COMPUESTO CONDITIONAL PERFECT
I have translated, etc.	*I had translated, etc.*	*I had translated, etc.*	*I will have translated, etc.**	*I would have translated, etc.**
he traducido	había traducido	hube traducido	habré traducido	habría traducido
has traducido	habías traducido	hubiste traducido	habrás traducido	habrías traducido
ha traducido	había traducido	hubo traducido	habrá traducido	habría traducido
hemos traducido	habíamos traducido	hubimos traducido	habremos traducido	habríamos traducido
habéis traducido	habíais traducido	hubisteis traducido	habréis traducido	habríais traducido
han traducido	habían traducido	hubieron traducido	habrán traducido	habrían traducido

PRETÉRITO PERFECTO DE SUBJUNTIVO PRESENT PERFECT SUBJUNCTIVE	PRETÉRITO PLUSCUAMPERFECTO DE SUBJUNTIVO PAST PERFECT (PLUPERFECT) SUBJUNCTIVE		FUTURO PERFECTO DE SUBJUNTIVO FUTURE PERFECT SUBJUNCTIVE
I have translated, etc.*	*I had translated, etc.**		*I will have translated, etc.**
haya traducido	hubiera traducido	hubiese traducido	hubiere traducido
hayas traducido	hubieras traducido	hubieses traducido	hubieres traducido
haya traducido	hubiera traducido	hubiese traducido	hubiere traducido
hayamos traducido	hubiéramos traducido *or*	hubiésemos traducido	hubiéremos traducido
hayáis traducido	hubierais traducido	hubieseis traducido	hubiereis traducido
hayan traducido	hubieran traducido	hubiesen traducido	hubieren traducido

*For additional translation possibilities see chart A.

IX. Irregular verbs

VERBS OF THIS CATEGORY

abducir
aducir
conducir
conducirse 4. (R)
deducir
inducir
introducir
introducirse 4. (R)
producir
producirse 4. (R)
reducir
reducirse 4. (R)
reproducir
seducir
traducir

R = Reflexive

TIEMPOS SIMPLES
SIMPLE TENSES

PRESENTE DE INDICATIVO **PRESENT INDICATIVE**	PRETÉRITO IMPERFECTO DE INDICATIVO **IMPERFECT INDICATIVE**	PRETÉRITO INDEFINIDO DE INDICATIVO **PRETERITE INDICATIVE**	FUTURO IMPERFECTO DE INDICATIVO **FUTURE INDICATIVE**	POTENCIAL SIMPLE **CONDITIONAL**
I satisfy, etc.	*I was satisfying, etc.*	*I satisfied, etc.*	*I will satisfy, etc.*	*I would satisfy, etc.*
satisfago	satisfacía	satisfice	satisfaré	satisfaría
satisfaces	satisfacías	satisficiste	satisfarás	satisfarías
satisface	satisfacía	satisfizo	satisfará	satisfaría
satisfacemos	satisfacíamos	satisficimos	satisfaremos	satisfaríamos
satisfacéis	satisfacíais	satisficisteis	satisfaréis	satisfaríais
satisfacen	satisfacían	satisficieron	satisfarán	satisfarían

PRESENTE DE SUBJUNTIVO **PRESENT SUBJUNCTIVE**	PRETÉRITO IMPERFECTO DE SUBJUNTIVO **PAST (IMPERFECT) SUBJUNCTIVE**		FUTURO IMPERFECTO DE SUBJUNTIVO **FUTURE SUBJUNCTIVE**
I satisfy, etc.	*I satisfied, etc.*		*I will satisfy, etc.*
satisfaga	satisficiera	satisficiese	satisficiere
satisfagas	satisficieras	satisficieses	satisficieres
satisfaga	satisficiera _or_	satisficiese	satisficiere
satisfagamos	satisficiéramos	satisficiésemos	satisficiéremos
satisfagáis	satisficierais	satisficieseis	satisficiereis
satisfagan	satisficieran	satisficiesen	satisficieren

FORMAS IMPERATIVAS, GERUNDIOS Y PARTICIPIO
COMMANDS AND PARTICIPLES

FORMAS IMPERATIVAS **COMMANDS**		GERUNDIO Y PARTICIPIO **PARTICIPLES**		
AFIRMATIVA **AFFIRMATIVE**	NEGATIVA **NEGATIVE**	GERUNDIO SIMPLE **PRESENT PARTICIPLE**	PARTICIPIO **PAST PARTICIPLE**	GERUNDIO COMPUESTO **PERFECT PARTICIPLE**
satisfy	*don't satisfy*	*satisfying*	*satisfied*	*having satisfied*
satisface / satisfaz (tú)	no satisfagas (tú)	satisfaciendo	satisfecho	habiendo satisfecho
satisfaga (Ud.)	no satisfaga (Ud.)			
satisfaced (vosotros)	no satisfagáis (vosotros)			
satisfagan (Uds.)	no satisfagan (Uds.)			
let's satisfy	*let's not satisfy*			
satisfagamos	no satisfagamos			

INFINITIVO COMPUESTO: haber satisfecho
PERFECT INFINITIVE: to have satisfied

TIEMPOS COMPUESTOS
PERFECT (COMPOUND) TENSES

PRETÉRITO PERFECTO DE INDICATIVO **PRESENT PERFECT INDICATIVE**	PRETÉRITO PLUSCUAMPERFECTO DE INDICATIVO **PAST PERFECT (PLUPERFECT) INDICATIVE**	PRETÉRITO ANTERIOR DE INDICATIVO **PRETERITE PERFECT INDICATIVE**	FUTURO PERFECTO DE INDICATIVO **FUTURE PERFECT INDICATIVE**	POTENCIAL COMPUESTO **CONDITIONAL PERFECT**
I have satisfied, etc.	*I had satisfied, etc.*	*I had satisfied, etc.*	*I will have satisfied, etc.*	*I would have satisfied, etc.*
he satisfecho	había satisfecho	hube satisfecho	habré satisfecho	habría satisfecho
has satisfecho	habías satisfecho	hubiste satisfecho	habrás satisfecho	habrías satisfecho
ha satisfecho	había satisfecho	hubo satisfecho	habrá satisfecho	habría satisfecho
hemos satisfecho	habíamos satisfecho	hubimos satisfecho	habremos satisfecho	habríamos satisfecho
habéis satisfecho	habíais satisfecho	hubisteis satisfecho	habréis satisfecho	habríais satisfecho
han satisfecho	habían satisfecho	hubieron satisfecho	habrán satisfecho	habrían satisfecho

PRETÉRITO PERFECTO DE SUBJUNTIVO **PRESENT PERFECT SUBJUNCTIVE**	PRETÉRITO PLUSCUAMPERFECTO DE SUBJUNTIVO **PAST PERFECT (PLUPERFECT) SUBJUNCTIVE**		FUTURO PERFECTO DE SUBJUNTIVO **FUTURE PERFECT SUBJUNCTIVE**
I have satisfied, etc.	*I had satisfied, etc.*		*I will have satisfied, etc.*
haya satisfecho	hubiera satisfecho	hubiese satisfecho	hubiere satisfecho
hayas satisfecho	hubieras satisfecho	hubieses satisfecho	hubieres satisfecho
haya satisfecho	hubiera satisfecho _or_	hubiese satisfecho	hubiere satisfecho
hayamos satisfecho	hubiéramos satisfecho	hubiésemos satisfecho	hubiéremos satisfecho
hayáis satisfecho	hubierais satisfecho	hubieseis satisfecho	hubiereis satisfecho
hayan satisfecho	hubieran satisfecho	hubiesen satisfecho	hubieren satisfecho

*For additional translation possibilities see chart A.

IX. Irregular verbs

licuefacer
rarefacer
satisfacer
satisfacerse 4. (R)
tumefacer

R = Reflexive

TIEMPOS SIMPLES
SIMPLE TENSES

PRESENTE DE INDICATIVO *PRESENT INDICATIVE*	PRETÉRITO IMPERFECTO DE INDICATIVO *IMPERFECT INDICATIVE*	PRETÉRITO INDEFINIDO DE INDICATIVO *PRETERITE INDICATIVE*	FUTURO IMPERFECTO DE INDICATIVO *FUTURE INDICATIVE*	POTENCIAL SIMPLE *CONDITIONAL*
I write, etc.*	*I was writing, etc.**	*I wrote, etc.**	*I will write, etc.**	*I would write, etc.**
escribo	escribía	escribí	escribiré	escribiría
escribes	escribías	escribiste	escribirás	escribirías
escribe	escribía	escribió	escribirá	escribiría
escribimos	escribíamos	escribimos	escribiremos	escribiríamos
escribís	escribíais	escribisteis	escribiréis	escribiríais
escriben	escribían	escribieron	escribirán	escribirían

PRESENTE DE SUBJUNTIVO *PRESENT SUBJUNCTIVE*	PRETÉRITO IMPERFECTO DE SUBJUNTIVO *PAST (IMPERFECT) SUBJUNCTIVE*		FUTURO IMPERFECTO DE SUBJUNTIVO *FUTURE SUBJUNCTIVE*
I write, etc.*	*I wrote, etc.**		*I will write, etc.**
escriba	escribiera	escribiese	escribiere
escribas	escribieras	escribieses	escribieres
escriba	escribiera	escribiese	escribiere
escribamos	escribiéramos *or*	escribiésemos	escribiéremos
escribáis	escribierais	escribieseis	escribiereis
escriban	escribieran	escribiesen	escribieren

FORMAS IMPERATIVAS, GERUNDIOS Y PARTICIPIO
COMMANDS AND PARTICIPLES

FORMAS IMPERATIVAS *COMMANDS*		GERUNDIO Y PARTICIPIO *PARTICIPLES*		
AFIRMATIVA *AFFIRMATIVE*	NEGATIVA *NEGATIVE*	GERUNDIO SIMPLE *PRESENT PARTICIPLE*	PARTICIPIO *PAST PARTICIPLE*	GERUNDIO COMPUESTO *PERFECT PARTICIPLE*
write	*don't write*	*writing*	*written*	*having written*
escribe (tú)	no escribas (tú)	escribiendo	escrito	habiendo escrito
escriba (Ud.)	no escriba (Ud.)			
escribid (vosotros)	no escribáis (vosotros)			
escriban (Uds.)	no escriban (Uds.)			
let's write	*let's not write*			
escribamos	no escribamos			

INFINITIVO COMPUESTO: haber escrito
PERFECT INFINITIVE: to have written

TIEMPOS COMPUESTOS
PERFECT (COMPOUND) TENSES

PRETÉRITO PERFECTO DE INDICATIVO *PRESENT PERFECT INDICATIVE*	PRETÉRITO PLUSCUAMPERFECTO DE INDICATIVO *PAST PERFECT (PLUPERFECT) INDICATIVE*	PRETÉRITO ANTERIOR DE INDICATIVO *PRETERITE PERFECT INDICATIVE*	FUTURO PERFECTO DE INDICATIVO *FUTURE PERFECT INDICATIVE*	POTENCIAL COMPUESTO *CONDITIONAL PERFECT*
I have written, etc.	*I had written, etc.*	*I had written, etc.*	*I will have written, etc.**	*I would have written, etc.**
he escrito	había escrito	hube escrito	habré escrito	habría escrito
has escrito	habías escrito	hubiste escrito	habrás escrito	habrías escrito
ha escrito	había escrito	hubo escrito	habrá escrito	habría escrito
hemos escrito	habíamos escrito	hubimos escrito	habremos escrito	habríamos escrito
habéis escrito	habíais escrito	hubisteis escrito	habréis escrito	habríais escrito
han escrito	habían escrito	hubieron escrito	habrán escrito	habrían escrito

PRETÉRITO PERFECTO DE SUBJUNTIVO *PRESENT PERFECT SUBJUNCTIVE*	PRETÉRITO PLUSCUAMPERFECTO DE SUBJUNTIVO *PAST PERFECT (PLUPERFECT) SUBJUNCTIVE*		FUTURO PERFECTO DE SUBJUNTIVO *FUTURE PERFECT SUBJUNCTIVE*
I have written, etc.*	*I had written, etc.**		*I will have written, etc.**
haya escrito	hubiera escrito	hubiese escrito	hubiere escrito
hayas escrito	hubieras escrito	hubieses escrito	hubieres escrito
haya escrito	hubiera escrito	hubiese escrito	hubiere escrito
hayamos escrito	hubiéramos escrito *or*	hubiésemos escrito	hubiéremos escrito
hayáis escrito	hubierais escrito	hubieseis escrito	hubiereis escrito
hayan escrito	hubieran escrito	hubiesen escrito	hubieren escrito

*For additional translation possibilities see chart A.

IX. Irregular verbs

adscribir
circunscribir
describir
escribir
inscribir (This verb has two past participles, *inscripto* and *inscrito,* but *inscrito* is more frequently used.)
inscribirse 4. (R) (This verb has two past participles, *inscripto* and *inscrito,* but *inscrito* is more frequently used.)
manuscribir
prescribir
proscribir (This verb has two past participles, *proscripto* and *proscrito,* but *proscrito* is more frequently used.)
sobrescribir
subscribir
suscribir
transcribir
trascribir

R = Reflexive

70 Verbs ending in -olver (ue) } model: VOLVER (ue)

TIEMPOS SIMPLES
SIMPLE TENSES

PRESENTE DE INDICATIVO *PRESENT INDICATIVE*	PRETÉRITO IMPERFECTO DE INDICATIVO *IMPERFECT INDICATIVE*	PRETÉRITO INDEFINIDO DE INDICATIVO *PRETERITE INDICATIVE*	FUTURO IMPERFECTO DE INDICATIVO *FUTURE INDICATIVE*	POTENCIAL SIMPLE *CONDITIONAL*
I return, etc.	*I was returning, etc.*	*I returned, etc.*	*I will return, etc.*	*I would return, etc.*
vuelvo	volvía	volví	volveré	volvería
vuelves	volvías	volviste	volverás	volverías
vuelve	volvía	volvió	volverá	volvería
volvemos	volvíamos	volvimos	volveremos	volveríamos
volvéis	volvíais	volvisteis	volveréis	volveríais
vuelven	volvían	volvieron	volverán	volverían

PRESENTE DE SUBJUNTIVO *PRESENT SUBJUNCTIVE*	PRETÉRITO IMPERFECTO DE SUBJUNTIVO *PAST (IMPERFECT) SUBJUNCTIVE*		FUTURO IMPERFECTO DE SUBJUNTIVO *FUTURE SUBJUNCTIVE*
I return, etc.	*I returned, etc.*		*I will return, etc.*
vuelva	volviera	volviese	volviere
vuelvas	volvieras	volvieses	volvieres
vuelva	volviera	volviese	volviere
volvamos	volviéramos *or*	volviésemos	volviéremos
volváis	volvierais	volvieseis	volviereis
vuelvan	volvieran	volviesen	volvieren

FORMAS IMPERATIVAS, GERUNDIOS Y PARTICIPIO
COMMANDS AND PARTICIPLES

FORMAS IMPERATIVAS *COMMANDS*		GERUNDIO Y PARTICIPIO *PARTICIPLES*		
AFIRMATIVA *AFFIRMATIVE*	NEGATIVA *NEGATIVE*	GERUNDIO SIMPLE *PRESENT PARTICIPLE*	PARTICIPIO *PAST PARTICIPLE*	GERUNDIO COMPUESTO *PERFECT PARTICIPLE*
return	*don't return*	*returning*	*returned*	*having returned*
vuelve (tú)	no vuelvas (tú)	volviendo	vuelto	habiendo vuelto
vuelva (Ud.)	no vuelva (Ud.)			
volved (vosotros)	no volváis (vosotros)			
vuelvan (Uds.)	no vuelvan (Uds.)			
let's return	*let's not return*			
volvamos	no volvamos			

INFINITIVO COMPUESTO: haber vuelto
PERFECT INFINITIVE: to have returned

TIEMPOS COMPUESTOS
PERFECT (COMPOUND) TENSES

PRETÉRITO PERFECTO DE INDICATIVO *PRESENT PERFECT INDICATIVE*	PRETÉRITO PLUSCUAMPERFECTO DE INDICATIVO *PAST PERFECT (PLUPERFECT) INDICATIVE*	PRETÉRITO ANTERIOR DE INDICATIVO *PRETERITE PERFECT INDICATIVE*	FUTURO PERFECTO DE INDICATIVO *FUTURE PERFECT INDICATIVE*	POTENCIAL COMPUESTO *CONDITIONAL PERFECT*
I have returned, etc.	*I had returned, etc.*	*I had returned, etc.*	*I will have returned, etc.*	*I would have returned, etc.*
he vuelto	había vuelto	hube vuelto	habré vuelto	habría vuelto
has vuelto	habías vuelto	hubiste vuelto	habrás vuelto	habrías vuelto
ha vuelto	había vuelto	hubo vuelto	habrá vuelto	habría vuelto
hemos vuelto	habíamos vuelto	hubimos vuelto	habremos vuelto	habríamos vuelto
habéis vuelto	habíais vuelto	hubisteis vuelto	habréis vuelto	habríais vuelto
han vuelto	habían vuelto	hubieron vuelto	habrán vuelto	habrían vuelto

PRETÉRITO PERFECTO DE SUBJUNTIVO *PRESENT PERFECT SUBJUNCTIVE*	PRETÉRITO PLUSCUAMPERFECTO DE SUBJUNTIVO *PAST PERFECT (PLUPERFECT)*		FUTURO PERFECTO DE SUBJUNTIVO *FUTURE PERFECT SUBJUNCTIVE*
I have returned, etc.	*I had returned, etc.*		*I will have returned, etc.*
haya vuelto	hubiera vuelto	hubiese vuelto	hubiere vuelto
hayas vuelto	hubieras vuelto	hubieses vuelto	hubieres vuelto
haya vuelto	hubiera vuelto	hubiese vuelto	hubiere vuelto
hayamos vuelto	hubiéramos vuelto *or*	hubiésemos vuelto	hubiéremos vuelto
hayáis vuelto	hubierais vuelto	hubieseis vuelto	hubiereis vuelto
hayan vuelto	hubieran vuelto	hubiesen vuelto	hubieren vuelto

*For additional translation possibilities see chart A.

[206]

IX. Irregular verbs

*absolver (ue) 38. (RC)
*desenvolver (ue) 38. (RC)
*desenvolverse (ue) 38. (RC), 4. (R)
*devolver (ue) 38. (RC)
*disolver (ue) 38. (RC)
*envolver (ue) 38. (RC)
*resolver (ue) 38. (RC)
*revolver (ue) 38. (RC)
*volver (ue) 38. (RC)
*volverse (ue) 38. (RC) 4. (R)

R = Reflexive
RC = Radical/Stem Change
*These verbs have radical/stem changes in addition to their irregularity. The cross reference number following each verb indicates the category of verbs to which these radical/stem changes belong.

71 Verbs ending in -uir with u pronounced } model: HUIR*

TIEMPOS SIMPLES
SIMPLE TENSES

PRESENTE DE INDICATIVO *PRESENT INDICATIVE*	PRETÉRITO IMPERFECTO DE INDICATIVO *IMPERFECT INDICATIVE*	PRETÉRITO INDEFINIDO DE INDICATIVO *PRETERITE INDICATIVE*	FUTURO IMPERFECTO DE INDICATIVO *FUTURE INDICATIVE*	POTENCIAL SIMPLE *CONDITIONAL*
*I flee, etc.**	*I was fleeing, etc.**	*I fled, etc.**	*I will flee, etc.**	*I would flee, etc.**
huyo+	huía	hui	huiré	huiría
huyes+	huías	huiste	huirás	huirías
huye+	huía	huyó	huirá	huiría
huimos	huíamos	huimos	huiremos	huiríamos
huís	huíais	huisteis	huiréis	huiríais
huyen+	huían	huyeron	huirán	huirían

PRESENTE DE SUBJUNTIVO *PRESENT SUBJUNCTIVE*	PRETÉRITO IMPERFECTO DE SUBJUNTIVO *PAST (IMPERFECT) SUBJUNCTIVE*		FUTURO IMPERFECTO DE SUBJUNTIVO *FUTURE SUBJUNCTIVE*
*I flee, etc.**	*I fled, etc.**		*I will flee, etc.**
huya+	huyera	huyese	huyere
huyas+	huyeras	huyeses	huyeres
huya+	huyera	huyese	huyere
huyamos	huyéramos *or*	huyésemos	huyéremos
huyáis	huyerais	huyeseis	huyereis
huyan+	huyeran	huyesen	huyeren

FORMAS IMPERATIVAS, GERUNDIOS Y PARTICIPIO
COMMANDS AND PARTICIPLES

FORMAS IMPERATIVAS *COMMANDS*		GERUNDIO Y PARTICIPIO *PARTICIPLES*		
AFIRMATIVA *AFFIRMATIVE*	NEGATIVA *NEGATIVE*	GERUNDIO SIMPLE *PRESENT PARTICIPLE*	PARTICIPIO *PAST PARTICIPLE*	GERUNDIO COMPUESTO *PERFECT PARTICIPLE*
flee	*don't flee*	*fleeing*	*fled*	*having fled*
huye+ (tú)	no huyas+ (tú)	huyendo	huido	habiendo huido
huya+ (Ud.)	no huya+ (Ud.)			
huid (vosotros)	no huyáis (vosotros)			
huyan+ (Uds.)	no huyan+ (Uds.)			
let's flee	*let's not flee*			
huyamos	no huyamos			

INFINITIVO COMPUESTO: haber huido
PERFECT INFINITIVE: to have fled

TIEMPOS COMPUESTOS
PERFECT (COMPOUND) TENSES

PRETÉRITO PERFECTO DE INDICATIVO *PRESENT PERFECT INDICATIVE*	PRETÉRITO PLUSCUAMPERFECTO DE INDICATIVO *PAST PERFECT (PLUPERFECT) INDICATIVE*	PRETÉRITO ANTERIOR DE INDICATIVO *PRETERITE PERFECT INDICATIVE*	FUTURO PERFECTO DE INDICATIVO *FUTURE PERFECT INDICATIVE*	POTENCIAL COMPUESTO *CONDITIONAL PERFECT*
I have fled, etc.	*I had fled, etc.*	*I had fled, etc.*	*I will have fled, etc.**	*I would have fled, etc.**
he huido	había huido	hube huido	habré huido	habría huido
has huido	habías huido	hubiste huido	habrás huido	habrías huido
ha huido	había huido	hubo huido	habrá huido	habría huido
hemos huido	habíamos huido	hubimos huido	habremos huido	habríamos huido
habéis huido	habíais huido	hubisteis huido	habréis huido	habríais huido
han huido	habían huido	hubieron huido	habrán huido	habrían huido

PRETÉRITO PERFECTO DE SUBJUNTIVO *PRESENT PERFECT SUBJUNCTIVE*	PRETÉRITO PLUSCUAMPERFECTO DE SUBJUNTIVO *PAST PERFECT (PLUPERFECT) SUBJUNCTIVE*		FUTURO PERFECTO DE SUBJUNTIVO *FUTURE PERFECT SUBJUNCTIVE*
*I have fled, etc.**	*I had fled, etc.**		*I will have fled, etc.**
haya huido	hubiera huido	hubiese huido	hubiere huido
hayas huido	hubieras huido	hubieses huido	hubieres huido
haya huido	hubiera huido	hubiese huido	hubiere huido
hayamos huido	hubiéramos huido *or*	hubiésemos huido	hubiéremos huido
hayáis huido	hubierais huido	hubieseis huido	hubiereis huido
hayan huido	hubieran huido	hubiesen huido	hubieren huido

*For additional translation possibilities see chart A.
+In these forms rehuir has a written accent on the u. (See 34.)

VERBS OF THIS CATEGORY

*afluir 23. (OC)
**argüir 72. (OC) (I)
*atribuir 23. (OC)
*circuir 23. (OC)
*concluir 23. (OC)
*confluir 23. (OC)
*constituir 23. (OC)
*construir 23. (OC)
*contribuir 23. (OC)
*derruir 23. (OC)
*destituir 23. (OC)
*destruir 23. (OC)
*diluir 23. (OC)
*diminuir 23. (OC)
*disminuir 23. (OC)
*distribuir 23. (OC)
*estatuir 23. (OC)
*excluir 23. (OC)
*fluir 23. (OC)
*fruir 23. (OC)
*huir 23. (OC)
*imbuir 23. (OC)
*incluir 23. (OC)
*influir 23. (OC)
*inmiscuir This category or the much less commonly used regular conjugation with (OC) 23.
*inmiscuirse This category or the much less commonly used regular conjugation with (OC) 23. 4. (R)
*instituir 23. (OC)
*instruir 23. (OC)
*intuir 23. (OC)
*obstruir 23. (OC)
*ocluir 23. (OC)
*prostituir 23. (OC)
*recluir 23. (OC)
*recluirse 23. (OC), 4. (R)
*reconstituir 23. (OC)
 reconstruir 23. (OC)
*rehuir 23. (OC), 34. (OC) (see footnote on opposite page)
*restituir 23. (OC)
*retribuir 23. (OC)
*substituir 23. (OC)
*sustituir 23. (OC)

R   = Reflexive
OC = Orthographic/Spelling Change
I   = Irregular
* These verbs have orthographic/spelling changes in addition to their irregularities. The cross reference number or numbers following each verb indicate the category of verbs to which these orthographic/spelling changes belong.
** This verb has two types of orthographic/spelling changes in addition to its irregularities. The cross reference number following the verb indicates the chart which shows all changes and irregularities together.

*Orthographic changing

TIEMPOS SIMPLES
SIMPLE TENSES

PRESENTE DE INDICATIVO *PRESENT INDICATIVE*	PRETÉRITO IMPERFECTO DE INDICATIVO *IMPERFECT INDICATIVE*	PRETÉRITO INDEFINIDO DE INDICATIVO *PRETERITE INDICATIVE*	FUTURO IMPERFECTO DE INDICATIVO *FUTURE INDICATIVE*	POTENCIAL SIMPLE *CONDITIONAL*
*I argue, etc.**	*I was arguing, etc.**	*I argued, etc.**	*I will argue, etc.**	*I would argue, etc.**
arguyo	argüía	argüí	argüiré	argüiría
arguyes	argüías	argüiste	argüirás	argüirías
arguye	argüía	arguyó	argüirá	argüiría
argüimos	argüíamos	argüimos	argüiremos	argüiríamos
argüís	argüíais	argüisteis	argüiréis	argüiríais
arguyen	argüían	arguyeron	argüirán	argüirían

PRESENTE DE SUBJUNTIVO *PRESENT SUBJUNCTIVE*	PRETÉRITO IMPERFECTO DE SUBJUNTIVO *PAST (IMPERFECT) SUBJUNCTIVE*		FUTURO IMPERFECTO DE SUBJUNTIVO *FUTURE SUBJUNCTIVE*
*I argue, etc.**	*I argued, etc.**		*I will argue, etc.**
arguya	arguyera	arguyese	arguyere
arguyas	arguyeras	arguyeses	arguyeres
arguya	arguyera	arguyese	arguyere
arguyamos	arguyéramos *or*	arguyésemos	arguyéremos
arguyáis	arguyerais	arguyeseis	arguyereis
arguyan	arguyeran	arguyesen	arguyeren

FORMAS IMPERATIVAS, GERUNDIOS Y PARTICIPIO
COMMANDS AND PARTICIPLES

FORMAS IMPERATIVAS *COMMANDS*		GERUNDIO Y PARTICIPIO *PARTICIPLES*		
AFIRMATIVA *AFFIRMATIVE*	NEGATIVA *NEGATIVE*	GERUNDIO SIMPLE *PRESENT PARTICIPLE*	PARTICIPIO *PAST PARTICIPLE*	GERUNDIO COMPUESTO *PERFECT PARTICIPLE*
argue	*don't argue*	*arguing*	*argued*	*having argued*
arguye (tú)	no arguyas (tú)	arguyendo	argüido	habiendo argüido
arguya (Ud.)	no arguya (Ud.)			
argüid (vosotros)	no arguyáis (vosotros)			
arguyan (Uds.)	no arguyan (Uds.)			
let's argue	*let's not argue*			
arguyamos	no arguyamos			

INFINITIVO COMPUESTO: haber argüido
PERFECT INFINITIVE: to have argued

TIEMPOS COMPUESTOS
PERFECT (COMPOUND) TENSES

PRETÉRITO PERFECTO DE INDICATIVO *PRESENT PERFECT INDICATIVE*	PRETÉRITO PLUSCUAMPERFECTO DE INDICATIVO *PAST PERFECT (PLUPERFECT) INDICATIVE*	PRETÉRITO ANTERIOR DE INDICATIVO *PRETERITE PERFECT INDICATIVE*	FUTURO PERFECTO DE INDICATIVO *FUTURE PERFECT INDICATIVE*	POTENCIAL COMPUESTO *CONDITIONAL PERFECT*
I have argued, etc.	*I had argued, etc.*	*I had argued, etc.*	*I will have argued, etc.**	*I would have argued, etc.**
he argüido	había argüido	hube argüido	habré argüido	habría argüido
has argüido	habías argüido	hubiste argüido	habrás argüido	habrías argüido
ha argüido	había argüido	hubo argüido	habrá argüido	habría argüido
hemos argüido	habíamos argüido	hubimos argüido	habremos argüido	habríamos argüido
habéis argüido	habíais argüido	hubisteis argüido	habréis argüido	habríais argüido
han argüido	habían argüido	hubieron argüido	habrán argüido	habrían argüido

PRETÉRITO PERFECTO DE SUBJUNTIVO *PRESENT PERFECT SUBJUNCTIVE*	PRETÉRITO PLUSCUAMPERFECTO DE SUBJUNTIVO *PAST PERFECT (PLUPERFECT) SUBJUNCTIVE*		FUTURO PERFECTO DE SUBJUNTIVO *FUTURE PERFECT SUBJUNCTIVE*
*I have argued, etc.**	*I had argued, etc.**		*I will have argued, etc.**
haya argüido	hubiera argüido	hubiese argüido	hubiere argüido
hayas argüido	hubieras argüido	hubieses argüido	hubieres argüido
haya argüido	hubiera argüido	hubiese argüido	hubiere argüido
hayamos argüido	hubiéramos argüido *or*	hubiésemos argüido	hubiéremos argüido
hayáis argüido	hubierais argüido	hubieseis argüido	hubiereis argüido
hayan argüido	hubieran argüido	hubiesen argüido	hubieren argüido

*For additional translation possibilities see chart A.

IX. **Irregular verbs**

VERBS OF THIS CATEGORY

---

*argüir 23. (OC), 24. (OC), 71. (I)

OC = Orthographic/Spelling Change
I = Irregular
* This verb has a combination of orthographic/spelling changes and irregularities. The cross reference numbers following the verb indicate the category of verbs to which each type of change belongs.

[211]

73 Verbs ending in -vowel + cer* } model: CONOCER

*Except mecer (14), cocer (54), hacer (90), yacer (113), their compounds, and placer (96).

TIEMPOS SIMPLES
SIMPLE TENSES

PRESENTE DE INDICATIVO PRESENT INDICATIVE	PRETÉRITO IMPERFECTO DE INDICATIVO IMPERFECT INDICATIVE	PRETÉRITO INDEFINIDO DE INDICATIVO PRETERITE INDICATIVE	FUTURO IMPERFECTO DE INDICATIVO FUTURE INDICATIVE	POTENCIAL SIMPLE CONDITIONAL
I know, etc.	*I was knowing, etc.*	*I knew, etc.*	*I will know, etc.*	*I would know, etc.*
conozco	conocía	conocí	conoceré	conocería
conoces	conocías	conociste	conocerás	conocerías
conoce	conocía	conoció	conocerá	conocería
conocemos	conocíamos	conocimos	conoceremos	conoceríamos
conocéis	conocíais	conocisteis	conoceréis	conoceríais
conocen	conocían	conocieron	conocerán	conocerían

PRESENTE DE SUBJUNTIVO PRESENT SUBJUNCTIVE	PRETÉRITO IMPERFECTO DE SUBJUNTIVO PAST (IMPERFECT) SUBJUNCTIVE		FUTURO IMPERFECTO DE SUBJUNTIVO FUTURE SUBJUNCTIVE
I know, etc.	*I knew, etc.*		*I will know, etc.*
conozca	conociera	conociese	conociere
conozcas	conocieras	conocieses	conocieres
conozca	conociera	conociese	conociere
conozcamos	conociéramos *or*	conociésemos	conociéremos
conozcáis	conocierais	conocieseis	conociereis
conozcan	conocieran	conociesen	conocieren

FORMAS IMPERATIVAS, GERUNDIOS Y PARTICIPIO
COMMANDS AND PARTICIPLES

FORMAS IMPERATIVAS COMMANDS		GERUNDIO Y PARTICIPIO PARTICIPLES		
AFIRMATIVA AFFIRMATIVE	NEGATIVA NEGATIVE	GERUNDIO SIMPLE PRESENT PARTICIPLE	PARTICIPIO PAST PARTICIPLE	GERUNDIO COMPUESTO PERFECT PARTICIPLE
know	*don't know*	*knowing*	*known*	*having known*
conoce (tú)	no conozcas (tú)	conociendo	conocido	habiendo conocido
conozca (Ud.)	no conozca (Ud.)			
conoced (vosotros)	no conozcáis (vosotros)			
conozcan (Uds.)	no conozcan (Uds.)			
let's know	*let's not know*			
conozcamos	no conozcamos			

INFINITIVO COMPUESTO: haber conocido
PERFECT INFINITIVE: to have known

TIEMPOS COMPUESTOS
PERFECT (COMPOUND) TENSES

PRETÉRITO PERFECTO DE INDICATIVO PRESENT PERFECT INDICATIVE	PRETÉRITO PLUSCUAMPERFECTO DE INDICATIVO PAST PERFECT (PLUPERFECT) INDICATIVE	PRETÉRITO ANTERIOR DE INDICATIVO PRETERITE PERFECT INDICATIVE	FUTURO PERFECTO DE INDICATIVO FUTURE PERFECT INDICATIVE	POTENCIAL COMPUESTO CONDITIONAL PERFECT
I have known, etc.	*I had known, etc.*	*I had known, etc.*	*I will have known, etc.*	*I would have known, etc.*
he conocido	había conocido	hube conocido	habré conocido	habría conocido
has conocido	habías conocido	hubiste conocido	habrás conocido	habrías conocido
ha conocido	había conocido	hubo conocido	habrá conocido	habría conocido
hemos conocido	habíamos conocido	hubimos conocido	habremos conocido	habríamos conocido
habéis conocido	habíais conocido	hubisteis conocido	habréis conocido	habríais conocido
han conocido	habían conocido	hubieron conocido	habrán conocido	habrían conocido

PRETÉRITO PERFECTO DE SUBJUNTIVO PRESENT PERFECT SUBJUNCTIVE	PRETÉRITO PLUSCUAMPERFECTO DE SUBJUNTIVO PAST PERFECT (PLUPERFECT) SUBJUNCTIVE		FUTURO PERFECTO DE SUBJUNTIVO FUTURE PERFECT SUBJUNCTIVE
I have known, etc.	*I had known, etc.*		*I will have known, etc.*
haya conocido	hubiera conocido	hubiese conocido	hubiere conocido
hayas conocido	hubieras conocido	hubieses conocido	hubieres conocido
haya conocido	hubiera conocido	hubiese conocido	hubiere conocido
hayamos conocido	hubiéramos conocido *or*	hubiésemos conocido	hubiéremos conocido
hayáis conocido	hubierais conocido	hubieseis conocido	hubiereis conocido
hayan conocido	hubieran conocido	hubiesen conocido	hubieren conocido

*For additional translation possibilities see chart A.

IX. Irregular verbs

VERBS OF THIS CATEGORY

abastecer
ablandecer
aborrecer
acaecer (This verb is impersonal, and thus is used only in the third person singular and plural, and the infinitives, present participle, and past participle.)
acontecer (This verb is impersonal, and thus is used only in the third person singular and plural, and the infinitives, present participle, and past participle.)
acrecer
adolecer
adormecer
adormecerse 4. (R)
agradecer
aloquecerse 4. (R)
altivecerse 4. (R)
amanecer
amarillecer
amodorrecer
amohecer
amortecer
anochecer
aparecer
apetecer
aplacer
aridecerse 4. (R)
atardecer
blanquecer
calecer
carecer
clarecer
compadecer
comparecer
complacer
complacerse 4. (R)
conocer
convalecer
crecer
crecerse 4. (R)
decrecer
denegrecer
denegrecerse 4. (R)
desagradecer
desaparecer
desbravecer
desbravecerse 4. (R)
descaecer
desconocer
desentumecer
desentumecerse 4. (R)
desfallecer
desfavorecer
deshumedecer
desmerecer
desobedecer
desplacer
desvanecerse 4. (R)
displacer
embellecer
emblandecer
emblanquecer
embravecer
embrutecer
empecer
empequeñecer
empobrecer
enaltecer
enaltecerse 4. (R)
enamarillecer
enardecer
enardecerse 4. (R)
encalvecer
encanecerse 4. (R)
encarecer
encarecerse 4. (R)
endurecer
enflaquecer
enflaquecerse 4. (R)
enfurecer
enfurecerse 4. (R)
engrandecer
engrumecerse 4. (R)
enloquecer
enloquecerse 4. (R)
enlustrecer
enmohecerse 4 (R)
enmudecer
ennegrecer
ennoblecer
enorgullecer
enorgullecerse 4. (R)
enraecer
enriquecer
enriquecerse 4. (R)
enrojecer
enronquecer
enronquecerse 4. (R)
ensoberbecer
ensombrecer
ensombrecerse 4. (R)
ensordecer
entenebrecer
enternecer
enternecerse 4. (R)
entontecer
entorpecer
entristecer
entumecer
entumecerse 4. (R)
envanecer
envanecerse 4. (R)
envejecer
envejecerse 4. (R)
envilecer
escarnecer
esclarecer
establecer
estremecer
fallecer
favorecer
florecer
florecerse 4. (R)
fortalecer
guarecer
guarecerse 4. (R)
guarnecer
humedecer
humedecerse 4. (R)
languidecer
lobreguecer
merecer
nacer
obedecer
obscurecer
obscurecerse 4. (R)
ofrecer
oscurecer
oscurecerse 4. (R)
pacer
padecer
palidecer
parecer
parecerse 4. (R)
perecer
permanecer
pertenecer
preconocer
prevalecer
reaparecer
reblandecer
reconocer
reconocerse 4. (R)
reflorecer
rejuvenecer
rejuvenecerse 4. (R)
renacer
resplandecer
restablecer
restablecerse 4. (R)
reverdecer
robustecer
robustecerse 4. (R)
sobrecrecer
tardecer
verdecer

R = Reflexive

Verbs ending in } model:
-vowel + cir* } LUCIR

*Except decir (84), bendecir (79), verbs ending in -ducir (67), and their compounds.

TIEMPOS SIMPLES
SIMPLE TENSES

PRESENTE DE INDICATIVO *PRESENT INDICATIVE*	PRETÉRITO IMPERFECTO DE INDICATIVO *IMPERFECT INDICATIVE*	PRETÉRITO INDEFINIDO DE INDICATIVO *PRETERITE INDICATIVE*	FUTURO IMPERFECTO DE INDICATIVO *FUTURE INDICATIVE*	POTENCIAL SIMPLE *CONDITIONAL*
I shine, etc.	*I was shining, etc.*	*I shone, etc.*	*I will shine, etc.*	*I would shine, etc.*
luzco	lucía	lucí	luciré	luciría
luces	lucías	luciste	lucirás	lucirías
luce	lucía	lució	lucirá	luciría
lucimos	lucíamos	lucimos	luciremos	luciríamos
lucís	lucíais	lucisteis	luciréis	luciríais
lucen	lucían	lucieron	lucirán	lucirían

PRESENTE DE SUBJUNTIVO *PRESENT SUBJUNCTIVE*	PRETÉRITO IMPERFECTO DE SUBJUNTIVO *PAST (IMPERFECT) SUBJUNCTIVE*		FUTURO IMPERFECTO DE SUBJUNTIVO *FUTURE SUBJUNCTIVE*
I shine, etc.	*I shone, etc.*		*I will shine, etc.*
luzca	luciera	luciese	luciere
luzcas	lucieras	lucieses	lucieres
luzca	luciera	luciese	luciere
luzcamos	luciéramos *or*	luciésemos	luciéremos
luzcáis	lucierais	lucieseis	luciereis
luzcan	lucieran	luciesen	lucieren

FORMAS IMPERATIVAS, GERUNDIOS Y PARTICIPIO
COMMANDS AND PARTICIPLES

FORMAS IMPERATIVAS *COMMANDS*		GERUNDIO Y PARTICIPIO *PARTICIPLES*		
AFIRMATIVA *AFFIRMATIVE*	NEGATIVA *NEGATIVE*	GERUNDIO SIMPLE *PRESENT PARTICIPLE*	PARTICIPIO *PAST PARTICIPLE*	GERUNDIO COMPUESTO *PERFECT PARTICIPLE*
shine	*don't shine*	*shining*	*shone*	*having shone*
luce (tú)	no luzcas (tú)	luciendo	lucido	habiendo lucido
luzca (Ud.)	no luzca (Ud.)			
lucid (vosotros)	no luzcáis (vosotros)			
luzcan (Uds.)	no luzcan (Uds.)			
let's shine	*let's not shine*			
luzcamos	no luzcamos			

INFINITIVO COMPUESTO: haber lucido
PERFECT INFINITIVE: to have shone

TIEMPOS COMPUESTOS
PERFECT (COMPOUND) TENSES

PRETÉRITO PERFECTO DE INDICATIVO *PRESENT PERFECT INDICATIVE*	PRETÉRITO PLUSCUAMPERFECTO DE INDICATIVO *PAST PERFECT (PLUPERFECT) INDICATIVE*	PRETÉRITO ANTERIOR DE INDICATIVO *PRETERITE PERFECT INDICATIVE*	FUTURO PERFECTO DE INDICATIVO *FUTURE PERFECT INDICATIVE*	POTENCIAL COMPUESTO *CONDITIONAL PERFECT*
I have shone, etc.	*I had shone, etc.*	*I had shone, etc.*	*I will have shone, etc.*	*I would have shone, etc.*
he lucido	había lucido	hube lucido	habré lucido	habría lucido
has lucido	habías lucido	hubiste lucido	habrás lucido	habrías lucido
ha lucido	había lucido	hubo lucido	habrá lucido	habría lucido
hemos lucido	habíamos lucido	hubimos lucido	habremos lucido	habríamos lucido
habéis lucido	habíais lucido	hubisteis lucido	habréis lucido	habríais lucido
han lucido	habían lucido	hubieron lucido	habrán lucido	habrían lucido

PRETÉRITO PERFECTO DE SUBJUNTIVO *PRESENT PERFECT SUBJUNCTIVE*	PRETÉRITO PLUSCUAMPERFECTO DE SUBJUNTIVO *PAST PERFECT (PLUPERFECT) SUBJUNCTIVE*		FUTURO PERFECTO DE SUBJUNTIVO *FUTURE PERFECT SUBJUNCTIVE*
I have shone, etc.	*I had shone, etc.*		*I will have shone, etc.*
haya lucido	hubiera lucido	hubiese lucido	hubiere lucido
hayas lucido	hubieras lucido	hubieses lucido	hubieres lucido
haya lucido	hubiera lucido	hubiese lucido	hubiere lucido
hayamos lucido	hubiéramos lucido *or*	hubiésemos lucido	hubiéremos lucido
hayáis lucido	hubierais lucido	hubieseis lucido	hubiereis lucido
hayan lucido	hubieran lucido	hubiesen lucido	hubieren lucido

*For additional translation possibilities see chart A.

IX. Irregular verbs

VERBS OF THIS CATEGORY

deslucir
deslucirse 4. (R)
lucir
lucirse 4. (R)
relucir
translucirse 4. (R)
traslucirse 4. (R)

R = Reflexive

75 model: ABRIR

TIEMPOS SIMPLES
SIMPLE TENSES

PRESENTE DE INDICATIVO / PRESENT INDICATIVE	PRETÉRITO IMPERFECTO DE INDICATIVO / IMPERFECT INDICATIVE	PRETÉRITO INDEFINIDO DE INDICATIVO / PRETERITE INDICATIVE	FUTURO IMPERFECTO DE INDICATIVO / FUTURE INDICATIVE	POTENCIAL SIMPLE / CONDITIONAL
*I open, etc.**	*I was opening, etc.**	*I opened, etc.**	*I will open, etc.**	*I would open, etc.**
abro	abría	abrí	abriré	abriría
abres	abrías	abriste	abrirás	abrirías
abre	abría	abrió	abrirá	abriría
abrimos	abríamos	abrimos	abriremos	abriríamos
abrís	abríais	abristeis	abriréis	abriríais
abren	abrían	abrieron	abrirán	abrirían

PRESENTE DE SUBJUNTIVO / PRESENT SUBJUNCTIVE	PRETÉRITO IMPERFECTO DE SUBJUNTIVO / PAST (IMPERFECT) SUBJUNCTIVE		FUTURO IMPERFECTO DE SUBJUNTIVO / FUTURE SUBJUNCTIVE
*I open, etc.**	*I opened, etc.**		*I will open, etc.**
abra	abriera	abriese	abriere
abras	abrieras	abrieses	abrieres
abra	abriera	abriese	abriere
abramos	abriéramos *or*	abriésemos	abriéremos
abráis	abrierais	abrieseis	abriereis
abran	abrieran	abriesen	abrieren

FORMAS IMPERATIVAS, GERUNDIOS Y PARTICIPIO
COMMANDS AND PARTICIPLES

FORMAS IMPERATIVAS / COMMANDS		GERUNDIO Y PARTICIPIO / PARTICIPLES		
AFIRMATIVA / AFFIRMATIVE	NEGATIVA / NEGATIVE	GERUNDIO SIMPLE / PRESENT PARTICIPLE	PARTICIPIO / PAST PARTICIPLE	GERUNDIO COMPUESTO / PERFECT PARTICIPLE
open	*don't open*	*opening*	*opened*	*having opened*
abre (tú)	no abras (tú)	abriendo	abierto	habiendo abierto
abra (Ud.)	no abra (Ud.)			
abrid (vosotros)	no abráis (vosotros)			
abran (Uds.)	no abran (Uds.)			
let's open	*let's not open*			
abramos	no abramos			

INFINITIVO COMPUESTO: haber abierto
PERFECT INFINITIVE: to have opened

TIEMPOS COMPUESTOS
PERFECT (COMPOUND) TENSES

PRETÉRITO PERFECTO DE INDICATIVO / PRESENT PERFECT INDICATIVE	PRETÉRITO PLUSCUAMPERFECTO DE INDICATIVO / PAST PERFECT (PLUPERFECT) INDICATIVE	PRETÉRITO ANTERIOR DE INDICATIVO / PRETERITE PERFECT INDICATIVE	FUTURO PERFECTO DE INDICATIVO / FUTURE PERFECT INDICATIVE	POTENCIAL COMPUESTO / CONDITIONAL PERFECT
I have opened, etc.	*I had opened, etc.*	*I had opened, etc.*	*I will have opened, etc.**	*I would have opened, etc.**
he abierto	había abierto	hube abierto	habré abierto	habría abierto
has abierto	habías abierto	hubiste abierto	habrás abierto	habrías abierto
ha abierto	había abierto	hubo abierto	habrá abierto	habría abierto
hemos abierto	habíamos abierto	hubimos abierto	habremos abierto	habríamos abierto
habéis abierto	habíais abierto	hubisteis abierto	habréis abierto	habríais abierto
han abierto	habían abierto	hubieron abierto	habrán abierto	habrían abierto

PRETÉRITO PERFECTO DE SUBJUNTIVO / PRESENT PERFECT SUBJUNCTIVE	PRETÉRITO PLUSCUAMPERFECTO DE SUBJUNTIVO / PAST PERFECT (PLUPERFECT) SUBJUNCTIVE		FUTURO PERFECTO DE SUBJUNTIVO / FUTURE PERFECT SUBJUNCTIVE
*I have opened, etc.**	*I had opened, etc.**		*I will have opened, etc.**
haya abierto	hubiera abierto	hubiese abierto	hubiere abierto
hayas abierto	hubieras abierto	hubieses abierto	hubieres abierto
haya abierto	hubiera abierto	hubiese abierto	hubiere abierto
hayamos abierto	hubiéramos abierto *or*	hubiésemos abierto	hubiéremos abierto
hayáis abierto	hubierais abierto	hubieseis abierto	hubiereis abierto
hayan abierto	hubieran abierto	hubiesen abierto	hubieren abierto

For additional translation possibilities see chart A.

VERBS OF THIS CATEGORY

abrir
entreabrir
reabrir

Compound of abrir *NOT following this pattern:* desabrirse 3., 4. (R)

R = Reflexive

model:
ADQUIRIR (ie)

TIEMPOS SIMPLES
SIMPLE TENSES

PRESENTE DE INDICATIVO *PRESENT INDICATIVE*	PRETÉRITO IMPERFECTO DE INDICATIVO *IMPERFECT INDICATIVE*	PRETÉRITO INDEFINIDO DE INDICATIVO *PRETERITE INDICATIVE*	FUTURO IMPERFECTO DE INDICATIVO *FUTURE INDICATIVE*	POTENCIAL SIMPLE *CONDITIONAL*
I acquire, etc.	*I was acquiring, etc.*	*I acquired, etc.*	*I will acquire, etc.*	*I would acquire, etc.*
adquiero	adquiría	adquirí	adquiriré	adquiriría
adquieres	adquirías	adquiriste	adquirirás	adquirirías
adquiere	adquiría	adquirió	adquirirá	adquiriría
adquirimos	adquiríamos	adquirimos	adquiriremos	adquiriríamos
adquirís	adquiríais	adquiristeis	adquiriréis	adquiriríais
adquieren	adquirían	adquirieron	adquirirán	adquirirían

PRESENTE DE SUBJUNTIVO *PRESENT SUBJUNCTIVE*	PRETÉRITO IMPERFECTO DE SUBJUNTIVO *PAST (IMPERFECT) SUBJUNCTIVE*		FUTURO IMPERFECTO DE SUBJUNTIVO *FUTURE SUBJUNCTIVE*
I acquire, etc.	*I acquired, etc.*		*I will acquire, etc.*
adquiera	adquiriera	adquiriese	adquiriere
adquieras	adquirieras	adquirieses	adquirieres
adquiera	adquiriera _or_ adquiriese	adquiriese	adquiriere
adquiramos	adquiriéramos	adquiriésemos	adquiriéremos
adquiráis	adquirierais	adquirieseis	adquiriereis
adquieran	adquirieran	adquiriesen	adquirieren

FORMAS IMPERATIVAS, GERUNDIOS Y PARTICIPIO
COMMANDS AND PARTICIPLES

FORMAS IMPERATIVAS *COMMANDS*		GERUNDIO Y PARTICIPIO *PARTICIPLES*		
AFIRMATIVA *AFFIRMATIVE*	NEGATIVA *NEGATIVE*	GERUNDIO SIMPLE *PRESENT PARTICIPLE*	PARTICIPIO *PAST PARTICIPLE*	GERUNDIO COMPUESTO *PERFECT PARTICIPLE*
acquire	*don't acquire*	*acquiring*	*acquired*	*having acquired*
adquiere (tú)	no adquieras (tú)	adquiriendo	adquirido	habiendo adquirido
adquiera (Ud.)	no adquiera (Ud.)			
adquirid (vosotros)	no adquiráis (vosotros)			
adquieran (Uds.)	no adquieran (Uds.)			
let's acquire	*let's not acquire*			
adquiramos	no adquiramos			

INFINITIVO COMPUESTO: haber adquirido
PERFECT INFINITIVE: to have acquired

TIEMPOS COMPUESTOS
PERFECT (COMPOUND) TENSES

PRETÉRITO PERFECTO DE INDICATIVO *PRESENT PERFECT INDICATIVE*	PRETÉRITO PLUSCUAMPERFECTO DE INDICATIVO *PAST PERFECT (PLUPERFECT) INDICATIVE*	PRETÉRITO ANTERIOR DE INDICATIVO *PRETERITE PERFECT INDICATIVE*	FUTURO PERFECTO DE INDICATIVO *FUTURE PERFECT INDICATIVE*	POTENCIAL COMPUESTO *CONDITIONAL PERFECT*
I have acquired, etc.	*I had acquired, etc.*	*I had acquired, etc.*	*I will have acquired, etc.*	*I would have acquired, etc.*
he adquirido	había adquirido	hube adquirido	habré adquirido	habría adquirido
has adquirido	habías adquirido	hubiste adquirido	habrás adquirido	habrías adquirido
ha adquirido	había adquirido	hubo adquirido	habrá adquirido	habría adquirido
hemos adquirido	habíamos adquirido	hubimos adquirido	habremos adquirido	habríamos adquirido
habéis adquirido	habíais adquirido	hubisteis adquirido	habréis adquirido	habríais adquirido
han adquirido	habían adquirido	hubieron adquirido	habrán adquirido	habrían adquirido

PRETÉRITO PERFECTO DE SUBJUNTIVO *PRESENT PERFECT SUBJUNCTIVE*	PRETÉRITO PLUSCUAMPERFECTO DE SUBJUNTIVO *PAST PERFECT (PLUPERFECT) SUBJUNCTIVE*		FUTURO PERFECTO DE SUBJUNTIVO *FUTURE PERFECT SUBJUNCTIVE*
I have acquired, etc.	*I had acquired, etc.*		*I will have acquired, etc.*
haya adquirido	hubiera adquirido	hubiese adquirido	hubiere adquirido
hayas adquirido	hubieras adquirido	hubieses adquirido	hubieres adquirido
haya adquirido	hubiera adquirido _or_ hubiese adquirido	hubiese adquirido	hubiere adquirido
hayamos adquirido	hubiéramos adquirido	hubiésemos adquirido	hubiéremos adquirido
hayáis adquirido	hubierais adquirido	hubieseis adquirido	hubiereis adquirido
hayan adquirido	hubieran adquirido	hubiesen adquirido	hubieren adquirido

*For additional translation possibilities see chart A.

IX. Irregular verbs

VERBS   OF   THIS   CATEGORY

*adquirir (ie) 41. (RC)
*inquirir (ie) 41. (RC)

RC = Radical/Stem Change
*These verbs are irregular because they have the radical/stem change of *i* becoming *ie* instead of *e* becoming *ie*. The cross reference number following each verb indicates the chart which shows the regular *e* becoming *ie*, *i* radical/stem changing pattern for verbs ending in *-ir*.

77 model: ANDAR

TIEMPOS SIMPLES
SIMPLE TENSES

PRESENTE DE INDICATIVO **PRESENT** *INDICATIVE*	PRETÉRITO IMPERFECTO DE INDICATIVO **IMPERFECT** *INDICATIVE*	PRETÉRITO INDEFINIDO DE INDICATIVO **PRETERITE** *INDICATIVE*	FUTURO IMPERFECTO DE INDICATIVO **FUTURE** *INDICATIVE*	POTENCIAL SIMPLE *CONDITIONAL*
*I walk, etc.**	*I was walking, etc.**	*I walked, etc.**	*I will walk, etc.**	*I would walk, etc.**
ando	andaba	anduve	andaré	andaría
andas	andabas	anduviste	andarás	andarías
anda	andaba	anduvo	andará	andaría
andamos	andábamos	anduvimos	andaremos	andaríamos
andáis	andabais	anduvisteis	andaréis	andaríais
andan	andaban	anduvieron	andarán	andarían

PRESENTE DE SUBJUNTIVO **PRESENT** *SUBJUNCTIVE*	PRETÉRITO IMPERFECTO DE SUBJUNTIVO **PAST (IMPERFECT)** *SUBJUNCTIVE*		FUTURO IMPERFECTO DE SUBJUNTIVO **FUTURE** *SUBJUNCTIVE*
*I walk, etc.**	*I walked, etc.**		*I will walk, etc.**
ande	anduviera	anduviese	anduviere
andes	anduvieras	anduvieses	anduvieres
ande	anduviera	anduviese	anduviere
andemos	anduviéramos *or* anduviésemos		anduviéremos
andéis	anduvierais	anduvieseis	anduviereis
anden	anduvieran	anduviesen	anduvieren

FORMAS IMPERATIVAS, GERUNDIOS Y PARTICIPIO
COMMANDS AND PARTICIPLES

FORMAS IMPERATIVAS **COMMANDS**		GERUNDIO Y PARTICIPIO *PARTICIPLES*		
AFIRMATIVA *AFFIRMATIVE*	NEGATIVA *NEGATIVE*	GERUNDIO SIMPLE *PRESENT PARTICIPLE*	PARTICIPIO *PAST PARTICIPLE*	GERUNDIO COMPUESTO *PERFECT PARTICIPLE*
walk	*don't walk*	*walking*	*walked*	*having walked*
anda (tú)	no andes (tú)	andando	andado	habiendo andado
ande (Ud.)	no ande (Ud.)			
andad (vosotros)	no andéis (vosotros)			
anden (Uds.)	no anden (Uds.)			
let's walk	*let's not walk*			
andemos	no andemos			

INFINITIVO COMPUESTO: haber andado
PERFECT INFINITIVE: *to have walked*

TIEMPOS COMPUESTOS
PERFECT (COMPOUND) TENSES

PRETÉRITO PERFECTO DE INDICATIVO **PRESENT PERFECT** *INDICATIVE*	PRETÉRITO PLUSCUAMPERFECTO DE INDICATIVO **PAST PERFECT (PLUPERFECT)** *INDICATIVE*	PRETÉRITO ANTERIOR DE INDICATIVO **PRETERITE PERFECT** *INDICATIVE*	FUTURO PERFECTO DE INDICATIVO **FUTURE PERFECT** *INDICATIVE*	POTENCIAL COMPUESTO *CONDITIONAL PERFECT*
I have walked, etc.	*I had walked, etc.*	*I had walked, etc.*	*I will have walked, etc.**	*I would have walked, etc.**
he andado	había andado	hube andado	habré andado	habría andado
has andado	habías andado	hubiste andado	habrás andado	habrías andado
ha andado	había andado	hubo andado	habrá andado	habría andado
hemos andado	habíamos andado	hubimos andado	habremos andado	habríamos andado
habéis andado	habíais andado	hubisteis andado	habréis andado	habríais andado
han andado	habían andado	hubieron andado	habrán andado	habrían andado

PRETÉRITO PERFECTO DE SUBJUNTIVO **PRESENT PERFECT** *SUBJUNCTIVE*	PRETÉRITO PLUSCUAMPERFECTO DE SUBJUNTIVO **PAST PERFECT (PLUPERFECT)** *SUBJUNCTIVE*		FUTURO PERFECTO DE SUBJUNTIVO **FUTURE PERFECT** *SUBJUNCTIVE*
*I have walked, etc.**	*I had walked, etc.**		*I will have walked, etc.**
haya andado	hubiera andado	hubiese andado	hubiere andado
hayas andado	hubieras andado	hubieses andado	hubieres andado
haya andado	hubiera andado	hubiese andado	hubiere andado
hayamos andado	hubiéramos andado *or* hubiésemos andado		hubiéremos andado
hayáis andado	hubierais andado	hubieseis andado	hubiereis andado
hayan andado	hubieran andado	hubiesen andado	hubieren andado

*For additional translation possibilities see chart A.

IX. Irregular verbs

VERBS OF THIS CATEGORY

andar
desandar

78 model: ASIR

PRESENTE DE INDICATIVO *PRESENT INDICATIVE*	PRETÉRITO IMPERFECTO DE INDICATIVO *IMPERFECT INDICATIVE*	PRETÉRITO INDEFINIDO DE INDICATIVO *PRETERITE INDICATIVE*	FUTURO IMPERFECTO DE INDICATIVO *FUTURE INDICATIVE*	POTENCIAL SIMPLE *CONDITIONAL*
*I grasp, etc.**	*I was grasping, etc.**	*I grasped, etc.**	*I will grasp, etc.**	*I would grasp, etc.**
asgo	asía	así	asiré	asiría
ases	asías	asiste	asirás	asirías
ase	asía	asió	asirá	asiría
asimos	asíamos	asimos	asiremos	asiríamos
asís	asíais	asisteis	asiréis	asiríais
asen	asían	asieron	asirán	asirían

PRESENTE DE SUBJUNTIVO *PRESENT SUBJUNCTIVE*	PRETÉRITO IMPERFECTO DE SUBJUNTIVO *PAST (IMPERFECT) SUBJUNCTIVE*		FUTURO IMPERFECTO DE SUBJUNTIVO *FUTURE SUBJUNCTIVE*
*I grasp, etc. **	*I grasped, etc.**		*I will grasp, etc.**
asga	asiera	asiese	asiere
asgas	asieras	asieses	asieres
asga	asiera	asiese	asiere
asgamos	asiéramos *or*	asiésemos	asiéremos
asgáis	asierais	asieseis	asiereis
asgan	asieran	asiesen	asieren

FORMAS IMPERATIVAS *COMMANDS*		GERUNDIO Y PARTICIPIO *PARTICIPLES*		
AFIRMATIVA *AFFIRMATIVE*	NEGATIVA *NEGATIVE*	GERUNDIO SIMPLE *PRESENT PARTICIPLE*	PARTICIPIO *PAST PARTICIPLE*	GERUNDIO COMPUESTO *PERFECT PARTICIPLE*
grasp	*don't grasp*	*grasping*	*grasped*	*having grasped*
ase (tú)	no asgas (tú)	asiendo	asido	habiendo asido
asga (Ud.)	no asga (Ud.)			
asid (vosotros)	no asgáis (vosotros)			
asgan (Uds.)	no asgan (Uds.)			
let's grasp	*let's not grasp*			
asgamos	no asgamos			

INFINITIVO COMPUESTO: haber asido
PERFECT INFINITIVE: to have grasped

PRETÉRITO PERFECTO DE INDICATIVO *PRESENT PERFECT INDICATIVE*	PRETÉRITO PLUSCUAMPERFECTO DE INDICATIVO *PAST PERFECT (PLUPERFECT) INDICATIVE*	PRETÉRITO ANTERIOR DE INDICATIVO *PRETERITE PERFECT INDICATIVE*	FUTURO PERFECTO DE INDICATIVO *FUTURE PERFECT INDICATIVE*	POTENCIAL COMPUESTO *CONDITIONAL PERFECT*
I have grasped, etc.	*I had grasped, etc.*	*I had grapsed, etc.*	*I will have grasped, etc.**	*I would have grasped, etc.**
he asido	había asido	hube asido	habré asido	habría asido
has asido	habías asido	hubiste asido	habrás asido	habrías asido
ha asido	había asido	hubo asido	habrá asido	habría asido
hemos asido	habíamos asido	hubimos asido	habremos asido	habríamos asido
habéis asido	habíais asido	hubisteis asido	habréis asido	habríais asido
han asido	habían asido	hubieron asido	habrán asido	habrían asido

PRETÉRITO PERFECTO DE SUBJUNTIVO *PRESENT PERFECT SUBJUNCTIVE*	PRETÉRITO PLUSCUAMPERFECTO DE SUBJUNTIVO *PAST PERFECT (PLUPERFECT) SUBJUNCTIVE*		FUTURO PERFECTO DE SUBJUNTIVO *FUTURE PERFECT SUBJUNCTIVE*
*I have grasped, etc.**	*I had grasped, etc.**		*I will have grasped, etc.**
haya asido	hubiera asido	hubiese asido	hubiere asido
hayas asido	hubieras asido	hubieses asido	hubieres asido
haya asido	hubiera asido	hubiese asido	hubiere asido
hayamos asido	hubiéramos asido *or*	hubiésemos asido	hubiéremos asido
hayáis asido	hubierais asido	hubieseis asido	hubiereis asido
hayan asido	hubieran asido	hubiesen asido	hubieren asido

*For additional translation possibilities see chart A.

IX. Irregular verbs

asir
asirse 4. (R)
desasir
desasirse 4. (R)

R = Reflexive

79 model:
BENDECIR (i, i)

TIEMPOS SIMPLES
SIMPLE TENSES

PRESENTE DE INDICATIVO *PRESENT* *INDICATIVE*	PRETÉRITO IMPERFECTO DE INDICATIVO *IMPERFECT* *INDICATIVE*	PRETÉRITO INDEFINIDO DE INDICATIVO *PRETERITE* *INDICATIVE*	FUTURO IMPERFECTO DE INDICATIVO *FUTURE* *INDICATIVE*	POTENCIAL SIMPLE *CONDITIONAL*
I bless, etc.*	*I was blessing, etc.**	*I blessed, etc.**	*I will bless, etc.**	*I would bless, etc.**
bendigo	bendecía	bendije	bendeciré	bendeciría
bendices	bendecías	bendijiste	bendecirás	bendecirías
bendice	bendecía	bendijo	bendecirá	bendeciría
bendecimos	bendecíamos	bendijimos	bendeciremos	bendeciríamos
bendecís	bendecíais	bendijisteis	bendeciréis	bendeciríais
bendicen	bendecían	bendijeron	bendecirán	bendecirían

PRESENTE DE SUBJUNTIVO *PRESENT* *SUBJUNCTIVE*	PRETÉRITO IMPERFECTO DE SUBJUNTIVO *PAST (IMPERFECT)* *SUBJUNCTIVE*		FUTURO IMPERFECTO DE SUBJUNTIVO *FUTURE* *SUBJUNCTIVE*	
I bless, etc.*	*I blessed, etc.**		*I will bless, etc.**	
bendiga	bendijera	bendijese	bendijere	
bendigas	bendijeras	bendijeses	bendijeres	
bendiga	bendijera	bendijese	bendijere	
bendigamos	bendijéramos *or*	bendijésemos	bendijéremos	
bendigáis	bendijerais	bendijeseis	bendijereis	
bendigan	bendijeran	bendijesen	bendijeren	

FORMAS IMPERATIVAS, GERUNDIOS Y PARTICIPIO
COMMANDS AND PARTICIPLES

FORMAS IMPERATIVAS *COMMANDS*		GERUNDIO Y PARTICIPIO *PARTICIPLES*		
AFIRMATIVA *AFFIRMATIVE*	NEGATIVA *NEGATIVE*	GERUNDIO SIMPLE *PRESENT PARTICIPLE*	PARTICIPIO *PAST PARTICIPLE*	GERUNDIO COMPUESTO *PERFECT PARTICIPLE*
bless	*don't bless*	*blessing*	*blessed*	*having blessed*
bendice (tú)	no bendigas (tú)	bendiciendo	bendecido	habiendo bendecido
bendiga (Ud.)	no bendiga (Ud.)			
bendecid (vosotros)	no bendigáis (vosotros)			
bendigan (Uds.)	no bendigan (Uds.)			
let's bless	*let's not bless*			
bendigamos	no bendigamos			

INFINITIVO COMPUESTO: haber bendecido
PERFECT INFINITIVE: to have blessed

TIEMPOS COMPUESTOS
PERFECT (COMPOUND) TENSES

PRETÉRITO PERFECTO DE INDICATIVO *PRESENT PERFECT* *INDICATIVE*	PRETÉRITO PLUSCUAMPERFECTO DE INDICATIVO *PAST PERFECT (PLUPERFECT)* *INDICATIVE*	PRETÉRITO ANTERIOR DE INDICATIVO *PRETERITE PERFECT* *INDICATIVE*	FUTURO PERFECTO DE INDICATIVO *FUTURE PERFECT* *INDICATIVE*	POTENCIAL COMPUESTO *CONDITIONAL PERFECT*
I have blessed, etc.	*I had blessed, etc.*	*I had blessed, etc.*	*I will have blessed, etc.**	*I would have blessed, etc.**
he bendecido	había bendecido	hube bendecido	habré bendecido	habría bendecido
has bendecido	habías bendecido	hubiste bendecido	habrás bendecido	habrías bendecido
ha bendecido	había bendecido	hubo bendecido	habrá bendecido	habría bendecido
hemos bendecido	habíamos bendecido	hubimos bendecido	habremos bendecido	habríamos bendecido
habéis bendecido	habíais bendecido	hubisteis bendecido	habréis bendecido	habríais bendecido
han bendecido	habían bendecido	hubieron bendecido	habrán bendecido	habrían bendecido

PRETÉRITO PERFECTO DE SUBJUNTIVO *PRESENT PERFECT* *SUBJUNCTIVE*	PRETÉRITO PLUSCUAMPERFECTO DE SUBJUNTIVO *PAST PERFECT (PLUPERFECT)* *SUBJUNCTIVE*		FUTURO PERFECTO DE SUBJUNTIVO *FUTURE PERFECT* *SUBJUNCTIVE*	
I have blessed, etc.*	*I had blessed, etc.**		*I will have blessed, etc.**	
haya bendecido	hubiera bendecido	hubiese bendecido	hubiere bendecido	
hayas bendecido	hubieras bendecido	hubieses bendecido	hubieres bendecido	
haya bendecido	hubiera bendecido	hubiese bendecido	hubiere bendecido	
hayamos bendecido	hubiéramos bendecido *or*	hubiésemos bendecido	hubiéremos bendecido	
hayáis bendecido	hubierais bendecido	hubieseis bendecido	hubiereis bendecido	
hayan bendecido	hubieran bendecido	hubiesen bendecido	hubieren bendecido	

*For additional translation possibilities see chart A.

VERBS OF THIS CATEGORY

*bendecir (i, i) 42. (RC)
*maldecir (i, i) 42. (RC)

RC = Radical/Stem Change
*These verbs have radical/stem changes in addition to their irregularities. The cross reference number following each verb indicates the category of verbs to which these radical/stem changes belong.

80 model: CABER

TIEMPOS SIMPLES
SIMPLE TENSES

PRESENTE DE INDICATIVO *PRESENT INDICATIVE*	PRETÉRITO IMPERFECTO DE INDICATIVO *IMPERFECT INDICATIVE*	PRETÉRITO INDEFINIDO DE INDICATIVO *PRETERITE INDICATIVE*	FUTURO IMPERFECTO DE INDICATIVO *FUTURE INDICATIVE*	POTENCIAL SIMPLE *CONDITIONAL*
I fit, etc.	*I was fitting, etc.*	*I fit, etc.*	*I will fit, etc.*	*I would fit, etc.*
quepo	cabía	cupe	cabré	cabría
cabes	cabías	cupiste	cabrás	cabrías
cabe	cabía	cupo	cabrá	cabría
cabemos	cabíamos	cupimos	cabremos	cabríamos
cabéis	cabíais	cupisteis	cabréis	cabríais
caben	cabían	cupieron	cabrán	cabrían

PRESENTE DE SUBJUNTIVO *PRESENT SUBJUNCTIVE*	PRETÉRITO IMPERFECTO DE SUBJUNTIVO *PAST (IMPERFECT) SUBJUNCTIVE*		FUTURO IMPERFECTO DE SUBJUNTIVO *FUTURE SUBJUNCTIVE*
I fit, etc.	*I fit, etc.*		*I will fit, etc.*
quepa	cupiera	cupiese	cupiere
quepas	cupieras	cupieses	cupieres
quepa	cupiera	cupiese	cupiere
quepamos	cupiéramos *or*	cupiésemos	cupiéremos
quepáis	cupierais	cupieseis	cupiereis
quepan	cupieran	cupiesen	cupieren

FORMAS IMPERATIVAS, GERUNDIOS Y PARTICIPIO
COMMANDS AND PARTICIPLES

FORMAS IMPERATIVAS *COMMANDS*		GERUNDIO Y PARTICIPIO *PARTICIPLES*		
AFIRMATIVA *AFFIRMATIVE*	NEGATIVA *NEGATIVE*	GERUNDIO SIMPLE *PRESENT PARTICIPLE*	PARTICIPIO *PAST PARTICIPLE*	GERUNDIO COMPUESTO *PERFECT PARTICIPLE*
fit	*don't fit*	*fitting*	*fitted*	*having fitted*
cabe (tú)	no quepas (tú)	cabiendo	cabido	habiendo cabido
quepa (Ud.)	no quepa (Ud.)			
cabed (vosotros)	no quepáis (vosotros)			
quepan (Uds.)	no quepan (Uds.)			
let's fit	*let's not fit*			
quepamos	no quepamos			

INFINITIVO COMPUESTO: haber cabido
PERFECT INFINITIVE: to have fit

TIEMPOS COMPUESTOS
PERFECT (COMPOUND) TENSES

PRETÉRITO PERFECTO DE INDICATIVO *PRESENT PERFECT INDICATIVE*	PRETÉRITO PLUSCUAMPERFECTO DE INDICATIVO *PAST PERFECT (PLUPERFECT) INDICATIVE*	PRETÉRITO ANTERIOR DE INDICATIVO *PRETERITE PERFECT INDICATIVE*	FUTURO PERFECTO DE INDICATIVO *FUTURE PERFECT INDICATIVE*	POTENCIAL COMPUESTO *CONDITIONAL PERFECT*
I have fit, etc.	*I had fit, etc.*	*I had fit, etc.*	*I will have fit, etc.*	*I would have fit, etc.*
he cabido	había cabido	hube cabido	habré cabido	habría cabido
has cabido	habías cabido	hubiste cabido	habrás cabido	habrías cabido
ha cabido	había cabido	hubo cabido	habrá cabido	habría cabido
hemos cabido	habíamos cabido	hubimos cabido	habremos cabido	habríamos cabido
habéis cabido	habíais cabido	hubisteis cabido	habréis cabido	habríais cabido
han cabido	habían cabido	hubieron cabido	habrán cabido	habrían cabido

PRETÉRITO PERFECTO DE SUBJUNTIVO *PRESENT PERFECT SUBJUNCTIVE*	PRETÉRITO PLUSCUAMPERFECTO DE SUBJUNTIVO *PAST PERFECT (PLUPERFECT) SUBJUNCTIVE*		FUTURO PERFECTO DE SUBJUNTIVO *FUTURE PERFECT SUBJUNCTIVE*
I have fit, etc.	*I had fit, etc.*		*I will have fit, etc.*
haya cabido	hubiera cabido	hubiese cabido	hubiere cabido
hayas cabido	hubieras cabido	hubieses cabido	hubieres cabido
haya cabido	hubiera cabido	hubiese cabido	hubiere cabido
hayamos cabido	hubiéramos cabido *or*	hubiésemos cabido	hubiéremos cabido
hayáis cabido	hubierais cabido	hubieseis cabido	hubiereis cabido
hayan cabido	hubieran cabido	hubiesen cabido	hubieren cabido

*For additional translation possibilities see chart A.

IX. Irregular verbs

caber

81 model: CAER*

TIEMPOS SIMPLES
SIMPLE TENSES

PRESENTE DE INDICATIVO *PRESENT INDICATIVE*	PRETÉRITO IMPERFECTO DE INDICATIVO *IMPERFECT INDICATIVE*	PRETÉRITO INDEFINIDO DE INDICATIVO *PRETERITE INDICATIVE*	FUTURO IMPERFECTO DE INDICATIVO *FUTURE INDICATIVE*	POTENCIAL SIMPLE *CONDITIONAL*
*I fall, etc.**	*I was falling, etc.**	*I fell, etc.**	*I will fall, etc.**	*I would fall, etc.**
caigo	caía	caí	caeré	caería
caes	caías	caíste	caerás	caerías
cae	caía	cayó	caerá	caería
caemos	caíamos	caímos	caeremos	caeríamos
caéis	caíais	caísteis	caeréis	caeríais
caen	caían	cayeron	caerán	caerían

PRESENTE DE SUBJUNTIVO *PRESENT SUBJUNCTIVE*	PRETÉRITO IMPERFECTO DE SUBJUNTIVO *PAST (IMPERFECT) SUBJUNCTIVE*		FUTURO IMPERFECTO DE SUBJUNTIVO *FUTURE SUBJUNCTIVE*
*I fall, etc.**	*I fell, etc.**		*I will fall, etc.**
caiga	cayera	cayese	cayere
caigas	cayeras	cayeses	cayeres
caiga	cayera	cayese	cayere
caigamos	cayéramos *or*	cayésemos	cayéremos
caigáis	cayerais	cayeseis	cayereis
caigan	cayeran	cayesen	cayeren

FORMAS IMPERATIVAS, GERUNDIOS Y PARTICIPIO
COMMANDS AND PARTICIPLES

FORMAS IMPERATIVAS *COMMANDS*		GERUNDIO Y PARTICIPIO *PARTICIPLES*		
AFIRMATIVA *AFFIRMATIVE*	NEGATIVA *NEGATIVE*	GERUNDIO SIMPLE *PRESENT PARTICIPLE*	PARTICIPIO *PAST PARTICIPLE*	GERUNDIO COMPUESTO *PERFECT PARTICIPLE*
fall	*don't fall*	*falling*	*fallen*	*having fallen*
cae (tú)	no caigas (tú)	cayendo	caído	habiendo caído
caiga (Ud.)	no caiga (Ud.)			
caed (vosotros)	no caigáis (vosotros)			
caigan (Uds.)	no caigan (Uds.)			
let's fall	*let's not fall*			
caigamos	no caigamos			

INFINITIVO COMPUESTO: haber caído
PERFECT INFINITIVE: to have fallen

TIEMPOS COMPUESTOS
PERFECT (COMPOUND) TENSES

PRETÉRITO PERFECTO DE INDICATIVO *PRESENT PERFECT INDICATIVE*	PRETÉRITO PLUSCUAMPERFECTO DE INDICATIVO *PAST PERFECT (PLUPERFECT) INDICATIVE*	PRETÉRITO ANTERIOR DE INDICATIVO *PRETERITE PERFECT INDICATIVE*	FUTURO PERFECTO DE INDICATIVO *FUTURE PERFECT INDICATIVE*	POTENCIAL COMPUESTO *CONDITIONAL PERFECT*
I have fallen, etc.	*I had fallen, etc.*	*I had fallen, etc.*	*I will have fallen, etc.**	*I would have fallen, etc.**
he caído	había caído	hube caído	habré caído	habría caído
has caído	habías caído	hubiste caído	habrás caído	habrías caído
ha caído	había caído	hubo caído	habrá caído	habría caído
hemos caído	habíamos caído	hubimos caído	habremos caído	habríamos caído
habéis caído	habíais caído	hubisteis caído	habréis caído	habríais caído
han caído	habían caído	hubieron caído	habrán caído	habrían caído

PRETÉRITO PERFECTO DE SUBJUNTIVO *PRESENT PERFECT SUBJUNCTIVE*	PRETÉRITO PLUSCUAMPERFECTO DE SUBJUNTIVO *PAST PERFECT (PLUPERFECT) SUBJUNCTIVE*		FUTURO PERFECTO DE SUBJUNTIVO *FUTURE PERFECT SUBJUNCTIVE*
*I have fallen, etc.**	*I had fallen, etc.**		*I will have fallen, etc.**
haya caído	hubiera caído	hubiese caído	hubiere caído
hayas caído	hubieras caído	hubieses caído	hubieres caído
haya caído	hubiera caído	hubiese caído	hubiere caído
hayamos caído	hubiéramos caído *or*	hubiésemos caído	hubiéremos caído
hayáis caído	hubierais caído	hubieseis caído	hubiereis caído
hayan caído	hubieran caído	hubiesen caído	hubieren caído

*For additional translation possibilities see chart A.

IX. Irregular verbs

*caer 20. (OC)
*decaer 20. (OC)
*recaer 20. (OC)

OC = Orthographic/Spelling Change
*These verbs have orthographic/spelling changes in addition to their irregularities. The cross reference number following each verb indicates the category of verbs to which these orthographic/spelling changes belong.

TIEMPOS SIMPLES
SIMPLE TENSES

PRESENTE DE INDICATIVO *PRESENT INDICATIVE*	PRETÉRITO IMPERFECTO DE INDICATIVO *IMPERFECT INDICATIVE*	PRETÉRITO INDEFINIDO DE INDICATIVO *PRETERITE INDICATIVE*	FUTURO IMPERFECTO DE INDICATIVO *FUTURE INDICATIVE*	POTENCIAL SIMPLE *CONDITIONAL*
*I cover, etc.**	*I was covering, etc.**	*I covered, etc.**	*I will cover, etc.**	*I would cover, etc.**
cubro	cubría	cubrí	cubriré	cubriría
cubres	cubrías	cubriste	cubrirás	cubrirías
cubre	cubría	cubrió	cubrirá	cubriría
cubrimos	cubríamos	cubrimos	cubriremos	cubriríamos
cubrís	cubríais	cubristeis	cubriréis	cubriríais
cubren	cubrían	cubrieron	cubrirán	cubrirían

PRESENTE DE SUBJUNTIVO *PRESENT SUBJUNCTIVE*	PRETÉRITO IMPERFECTO DE SUBJUNTIVO *PAST (IMPERFECT) SUBJUNCTIVE*		FUTURO IMPERFECTO DE SUBJUNTIVO *FUTURE SUBJUNCTIVE*
*I cover, etc.**	*I covered, etc.**		*I will cover, etc.**
cubra	cubriera	cubriese	cubriere
cubras	cubrieras	cubrieses	cubrieres
cubra	cubriera	cubriese	cubriere
cubramos	cubriéramos *or*	cubriésemos	cubriéremos
cubráis	cubrierais	cubrieseis	cubriereis
cubran	cubrieran	cubriesen	cubrieren

FORMAS IMPERATIVAS, GERUNDIOS Y PARTICIPIO
COMMANDS AND PARTICIPLES

FORMAS IMPERATIVAS *COMMANDS*		GERUNDIO Y PARTICIPIO *PARTICIPLES*		
AFIRMATIVA *AFFIRMATIVE*	NEGATIVA *NEGATIVE*	GERUNDIO SIMPLE *PRESENT PARTICIPLE*	PARTICIPIO *PAST PARTICIPLE*	GERUNDIO COMPUESTO *PERFECT PARTICIPLE*
cover	*don't cover*	*covering*	*covered*	*having covered*
cubre (tú)	no cubras (tú)	cubriendo	cubierto	habiendo cubierto
cubra (Ud.)	no cubra (Ud.)			
cubrid (vosotros)	no cubráis (vosotros)			
cubran (Uds.)	no cubran (Uds.)			
let's cover	*let's not cover*			
cubramos	no cubramos			

INFINITIVO COMPUESTO: haber cubierto
PERFECT INFINITIVE: to have covered

TIEMPOS COMPUESTOS
PERFECT (COMPOUND) TENSES

PRETÉRITO PERFECTO DE INDICATIVO *PRESENT PERFECT INDICATIVE*	PRETÉRITO PLUSCUAMPERFECTO DE INDICATIVO *PAST PERFECT (PLUPERFECT) INDICATIVE*	PRETÉRITO ANTERIOR DE INDICATIVO *PRETERITE PERFECT INDICATIVE*	FUTURO PERFECTO DE INDICATIVO *FUTURE PERFECT INDICATIVE*	POTENCIAL COMPUESTO *CONDITIONAL PERFECT*
I have covered, etc.	*I had covered, etc.*	*I had covered, etc.*	*I will have covered, etc.**	*I would have covered, etc.**
he cubierto	había cubierto	hube cubierto	habré cubierto	habría cubierto
has cubierto	habías cubierto	hubiste cubierto	habrás cubierto	habrías cubierto
ha cubierto	había cubierto	hubo cubierto	habrá cubierto	habría cubierto
hemos cubierto	habíamos cubierto	hubimos cubierto	habremos cubierto	habríamos cubierto
habéis cubierto	habíais cubierto	hubisteis cubierto	habréis cubierto	habríais cubierto
han cubierto	habían cubierto	hubieron cubierto	habrán cubierto	habrían cubierto

PRETÉRITO PERFECTO DE SUBJUNTIVO *PRESENT PERFECT SUBJUNCTIVE*	PRETÉRITO PLUSCUAMPERFECTO DE SUBJUNTIVO *PAST PERFECT (PLUPERFECT) SUBJUNCTIVE*		FUTURO PERFECTO DE SUBJUNTIVO *FUTURE PERFECT SUBJUNCTIVE*
*I have covered, etc.**	*I had covered, etc.**		*I will have covered, etc.**
haya cubierto	hubiera cubierto	hubiese cubierto	hubiere cubierto
hayas cubierto	hubieras cubierto	hubieses cubierto	hubieres cubierto
haya cubierto	hubiera cubierto	hubiese cubierto	hubiere cubierto
hayamos cubierto	hubiéramos cubierto *or*	hubiésemos cubierto	hubiéremos cubierto
hayáis cubierto	hubierais cubierto	hubieseis cubierto	hubiereis cubierto
hayan cubierto	hubieran cubierto	hubiesen cubierto	hubieren cubierto

*For additional translation possibilities see chart A.

VERBS OF THIS CATEGORY

cubrir
cubrirse 4. (R)
descubrir
descubrirse 4. (R)
encubrir
recubrir

R = Reflexive

model:
DAR

TIEMPOS SIMPLES
SIMPLE TENSES

PRESENTE DE INDICATIVO *PRESENT INDICATIVE*	PRETÉRITO IMPERFECTO DE INDICATIVO *IMPERFECT INDICATIVE*	PRETÉRITO INDEFINIDO DE INDICATIVO *PRETERITE INDICATIVE*	FUTURO IMPERFECTO DE INDICATIVO *FUTURE INDICATIVE*	POTENCIAL SIMPLE *CONDITIONAL*
*I give, etc.**	*I was giving, etc.**	*I gave, etc.**	*I will give, etc.**	*I would give, etc.**
doy	daba	di	daré	daría
das	dabas	diste	darás	darías
da	daba	dio	dará	daría
damos	dábamos	dimos	daremos	daríamos
dais	dabais	disteis	daréis	daríais
dan	daban	dieron	darán	darían

PRESENTE DE SUBJUNTIVO *PRESENT SUBJUNCTIVE*	PRETÉRITO IMPERFECTO DE SUBJUNTIVO *PAST (IMPERFECT) SUBJUNCTIVE*		FUTURO IMPERFECTO DE SUBJUNTIVO *FUTURE SUBJUNCTIVE*
*I give, etc.**	*I gave, etc.**		*I will give, etc.**
dé	diera	diese	diere
des	dieras	dieses	dieres
dé	diera	diese	diere
demos	diéramos *or* diésemos		diéremos
deis	dierais	dieseis	diereis
den	dieran	diesen	dieren

FORMAS IMPERATIVAS, GERUNDIOS Y PARTICIPIO
COMMANDS AND PARTICIPLES

FORMAS IMPERATIVAS *COMMANDS*		GERUNDIO Y PARTICIPIO *PARTICIPLES*		
AFIRMATIVA *AFFIRMATIVE*	NEGATIVA *NEGATIVE*	GERUNDIO SIMPLE *PRESENT PARTICIPLE*	PARTICIPIO *PAST PARTICIPLE*	GERUNDIO COMPUESTO *PERFECT PARTICIPLE*
give	*don't give*	*giving*	*given*	*having given*
da (tú)	no des (tú)	dando	dado	habiendo dado
dé (Ud.)	no dé (Ud.)			
dad (vosotros)	no deis (vosotros)			
den (Uds.)	no den (Uds.)			
let's give	*let's not give*			
demos	no demos			

```
INFINITIVO COMPUESTO:  haber dado
PERFECT INFINITIVE:  to have given
```

TIEMPOS COMPUESTOS
PERFECT (COMPOUND) TENSES

PRETÉRITO PERFECTO DE INDICATIVO *PRESENT PERFECT INDICATIVE*	PRETÉRITO PLUSCUAMPERFECTO DE INDICATIVO *PAST PERFECT (PLUPERFECT) INDICATIVE*	PRETÉRITO ANTERIOR DE INDICATIVO *PRETERITE PERFECT INDICATIVE*	FUTURO PERFECTO DE INDICATIVO *FUTURE PERFECT INDICATIVE*	POTENCIAL COMPUESTO *CONDITIONAL PERFECT*
I have given, etc.	*I had given, etc.*	*I had given, etc.*	*I will have given, etc.**	*I would have given, etc.**
he dado	había dado	hube dado	habré dado	habría dado
has dado	habías dado	hubiste dado	habrás dado	habrías dado
ha dado	había dado	hubo dado	habrá dado	habría dado
hemos dado	habíamos dado	hubimos dado	habremos dado	habríamos dado
habéis dado	habíais dado	hubisteis dado	habréis dado	habríais dado
han dado	habían dado	hubieron dado	habrán dado	habrían dado

PRETÉRITO PERFECTO DE SUBJUNTIVO *PRESENT PERFECT SUBJUNCTIVE*	PRETÉRITO PLUSCUAMPERFECTO DE SUBJUNTIVO *PAST PERFECT (PLUPERFECT) SUBJUNCTIVE*		FUTURO PERFECTO DE SUBJUNTIVO *FUTURE PERFECT SUBJUNCTIVE*
*I have given, etc.**	*I had given, etc.**		*I will have given, etc.**
haya dado	hubiera dado	hubiese dado	hubiere dado
hayas dado	hubieras dado	hubieses dado	hubieres dado
haya dado	hubiera dado	hubiese dado	hubiere dado
hayamos dado	hubiéramos dado *or* hubiésemos dado		hubiéremos dado
hayáis dado	hubierais dado	hubieseis dado	hubiereis dado
hayan dado	hubieran dado	hubiesen dado	hubieren dado

*For additional translation possibilities see chart A.

IX. Irregular verbs

VERBS OF THIS CATEGORY

dar
darse 4. (R)

R = Reflexive

84 model: DECIR (i, i)

TIEMPOS SIMPLES
SIMPLE TENSES

PRESENTE DE INDICATIVO *PRESENT INDICATIVE*	PRETÉRITO IMPERFECTO DE INDICATIVO *IMPERFECT INDICATIVE*	PRETÉRITO INDEFINIDO DE INDICATIVO *PRETERITE INDICATIVE*	FUTURO IMPERFECTO DE INDICATIVO *FUTURE INDICATIVE*	POTENCIAL SIMPLE *CONDITIONAL*
I tell, etc.*	*I was telling, etc.**	*I told, etc.**	*I will tell, etc.**	*I would tell, etc.**
digo	decía	dije	diré	diría
dices	decías	dijiste	dirás	dirías
dice	decía	dijo	dirá	diría
decimos	decíamos	dijimos	diremos	diríamos
decís	decíais	dijisteis	diréis	diríais
dicen	decían	dijeron	dirán	dirían

PRESENTE DE SUBJUNTIVO *PRESENT SUBJUNCTIVE*	PRETÉRITO IMPERFECTO DE SUBJUNTIVO *PAST (IMPERFECT) SUBJUNCTIVE*		FUTURO IMPERFECTO DE SUBJUNTIVO *FUTURE SUBJUNCTIVE*
I tell, etc.*	*I told, etc.**		*I will tell, etc.**
diga	dijera	dijese	dijere
digas	dijeras	dijeses	dijeres
diga	dijera	dijese	dijere
digamos	dijéramos *or*	dijésemos	dijéremos
digáis	dijerais	dijeseis	dijereis
digan	dijeran	dijesen	dijeren

FORMAS IMPERATIVAS, GERUNDIOS Y PARTICIPIO
COMMANDS AND PARTICIPLES

FORMAS IMPERATIVAS *COMMANDS*		GERUNDIO Y PARTICIPIO *PARTICIPLES*		
AFIRMATIVA *AFFIRMATIVE*	NEGATIVA *NEGATIVE*	GERUNDIO SIMPLE *PRESENT PARTICIPLE*	PARTICIPIO *PAST PARTICIPLE*	GERUNDIO COMPUESTO *PERFECT PARTICIPLE*
tell	*don't tell*	*telling*	*told*	*having told*
di (tú)	no digas (tú)	diciendo	dicho	habiendo dicho
diga (Ud.)	no diga (Ud.)			
decid (vosotros)	no digáis (vosotros)			
digan (Uds.)	no digan (Uds.)			
let's tell	*let's not tell*			
digamos	no digamos			

INFINITIVO COMPUESTO: haber dicho
PERFECT INFINITIVE: to have told

TIEMPOS COMPUESTOS
PERFECT (COMPOUND) TENSES

PRETÉRITO PERFECTO DE INDICATIVO *PRESENT PERFECT INDICATIVE*	PRETÉRITO PLUSCUAMPERFECTO DE INDICATIVO *PAST PERFECT (PLUPERFECT) INDICATIVE*	PRETÉRITO ANTERIOR DE INDICATIVO *PRETERITE PERFECT INDICATIVE*	FUTURO PERFECTO DE INDICATIVO *FUTURE PERFECT INDICATIVE*	POTENCIAL COMPUESTO *CONDITIONAL PERFECT*
I have told, etc.	*I had told, etc.*	*I had told, etc.*	*I will have told, etc.**	*I would have told, etc.**
he dicho	había dicho	hube dicho	habré dicho	habría dicho
has dicho	habías dicho	hubiste dicho	habrás dicho	habrías dicho
ha dicho	había dicho	hubo dicho	habrá dicho	habría dicho
hemos dicho	habíamos dicho	hubimos dicho	habremos dicho	habríamos dicho
habéis dicho	habíais dicho	hubisteis dicho	habréis dicho	habríais dicho
han dicho	habían dicho	hubieron dicho	habrán dicho	habrían dicho

PRETÉRITO PERFECTO DE SUBJUNTIVO *PRESENT PERFECT SUBJUNCTIVE*	PRETÉRITO PLUSCUAMPERFECTO DE SUBJUNTIVO *PAST PERFECT (PLUPERFECT) SUBJUNCTIVE*		FUTURO PERFECTO DE SUBJUNTIVO *FUTURE PERFECT SUBJUNCTIVE*
I have told, etc.*	*I had told, etc.**		*I will have told, etc.**
haya dicho	hubiera dicho	hubiese dicho	hubiere dicho
hayas dicho	hubieras dicho	hubieses dicho	hubieres dicho
haya dicho	hubiera dicho	hubiese dicho	hubiere dicho
hayamos dicho	hubiéramos dicho *or*	hubiésemos dicho	hubiéremos dicho
hayáis dicho	hubierais dicho	hubieseis dicho	hubiereis dicho
hayan dicho	hubieran dicho	hubiesen dicho	hubieren dicho

*For additional translation possibilities see chart A.

IX. Irregular verbs

*antedecir (i, i) 42. (RC)
*contradecir (i, i) 42. (RC)
*decir (i, i) 42. (RC)
*decirse (i, i) 42. (RC), 4. (R)
*desdecir (i, i) 42. (RC)
*interdecir (i, i) 42. (RC)
*predecir (i, i) 42. (RC)
*redecir (i, i) 42. (RC)

Compounds of decir *NOT following this pattern:*
    bendecir (i, i) 79. (RC) (I)
    maldecir (i, i) 79. (RC) (I)

R = Reflexive
RC = Radical/Stem Change
I = Irregular
* These verbs have radical/stem changes in addition to their irregularities. The cross reference number following each verb indicates the category of verbs to which these radical/stem changes belong.

85 model: DISCERNIR (ie)

TIEMPOS SIMPLES
SIMPLE TENSES

PRESENTE DE INDICATIVO **PRESENT INDICATIVE**	PRETÉRITO IMPERFECTO DE INDICATIVO **IMPERFECT INDICATIVE**	PRETÉRITO INDEFINIDO DE INDICATIVO **PRETERITE INDICATIVE**	FUTURO IMPERFECTO DE INDICATIVO **FUTURE INDICATIVE**	POTENCIAL SIMPLE **CONDITIONAL**
*I distinguish, etc.**	*I was distinguishing, etc.**	*I distinguished, etc.**	*I will distinguish, etc.**	*I would distinguish, etc.**
discierno	discernía	discerní	discerniré	discerniría
disciernes	discernías	discerniste	discernirás	discernirías
discierne	discernía	discernió	discernirá	discerniría
discernimos	discerníamos	discernimos	discerniremos	discerniríamos
discernís	discerníais	discernisteis	discerniréis	discerniríais
disciernen	discernían	discernieron	discernirán	discernirían

PRESENTE DE SUBJUNTIVO **PRESENT SUBJUNCTIVE**	PRETÉRITO IMPERFECTO DE SUBJUNTIVO **PAST (IMPERFECT) SUBJUNCTIVE**		FUTURO IMPERFECTO DE SUBJUNTIVO **FUTURE SUBJUNCTIVE**
*I distinguish, etc.**	*I distinguished, etc.**		*I will distinguish, etc.**
discierna	discerniera	discerniese	discerniere
disciernas	discernieras	discernieses	discernieres
discierna	discerniera	discerniese	discerniere
discernamos	discerniéramos *or*	discerniésemos	discerniéremos
discernáis	discernierais	discernieseis	discerniereis
disciernan	discernieran	discerniesen	discernieren

FORMAS IMPERATIVAS, GERUNDIOS Y PARTICIPIO
COMMANDS AND PARTICIPLES

FORMAS IMPERATIVAS **COMMANDS**		GERUNDIO Y PARTICIPIO **PARTICIPLES**		
AFIRMATIVA **AFFIRMATIVE**	NEGATIVA **NEGATIVE**	GERUNDIO SIMPLE **PRESENT PARTICIPLE**	PARTICIPIO **PAST PARTICIPLE**	GERUNDIO COMPUESTO **PERFECT PARTICIPLE**
distinguish	*don't distinguish*	*distinguishing*	*distinguished*	*having distinguished*
discierne (tú)	no disciernas (tú)	discerniendo	discernido	habiendo discernido
discierna (Ud.)	no discierna (Ud.)			
discernid (vosotros)	no discernáis (vosotros)			
disciernan (Uds.)	no disciernan (Uds.)			
let's distinguish	*let's not distinguish*			
discernamos	no discernamos			

INFINITIVO COMPUESTO: haber discernido
PERFECT INFINITIVE: to have distinguished

TIEMPOS COMPUESTOS
PERFECT (COMPOUND) TENSES

PRETÉRITO PERFECTO DE INDICATIVO **PRESENT PERFECT INDICATIVE**	PRETÉRITO PLUSCUAMPERFECTO DE INDICATIVO **PAST PERFECT (PLUPERFECT) INDICATIVE**	PRETÉRITO ANTERIOR DE INDICATIVO **PRETERITE PERFECT INDICATIVE**	FUTURO PERFECTO DE INDICATIVO **FUTURE PERFECT INDICATIVE**	POTENCIAL COMPUESTO **CONDITIONAL PERFECT**
I have distinguished, etc.	*I had distinguished, etc.*	*I had distinguished, etc.*	*I will have distinguished, etc.**	*I would have distinguished, etc.**
he discernido	había discernido	hube discernido	habré discernido	habría discernido
has discernido	habías discernido	hubiste discernido	habrás discernido	habrías discernido
ha discernido	había discernido	hubo discernido	habrá discernido	habría discernido
hemos discernido	habíamos discernido	hubimos discernido	habremos discernido	habríamos discernido
habéis discernido	habíais discernido	hubisteis discernido	habréis discernido	habríais discernido
han discernido	habían discernido	hubieron discernido	habrán discernido	habrían discernido

PRETÉRITO PERFECTO DE SUBJUNTIVO **PRESENT PERFECT SUBJUNCTIVE**	PRETÉRITO PLUSCUAMPERFECTO DE SUBJUNTIVO **PAST PERFECT (PLUPERFECT) SUBJUNCTIVE**		FUTURO PERFECTO DE SUBJUNTIVO **FUTURE PERFECT SUBJUNCTIVE**
*I have distinguished, etc.**	*I had distinguished, etc.**		*I will have distinguished, etc.**
haya discernido	hubiera discernido	hubiese discernido	hubiere discernido
hayas discernido	hubieras discernido	hubieses discernido	hubieres discernido
haya discernido	hubiera discernido	hubiese discernido	hubiere discernido
hayamos discernido	hubiéramos discernido *or*	hubiésemos discernido	hubiéremos discernido
hayáis discernido	hubierais discernido	hubieseis discernido	hubiereis discernido
hayan discernido	hubieran discernido	hubiesen discernido	hubieren discernido

*For additional translation possibilities see chart A.

[236]

85

IX. Irregular verbs

*cernir (ie) 41. (RC)
*concernir (ie) 41. (RC) (This verb is impersonal, and thus is used only in the third person singular and plural, and in the infinitives, present participle, and past participle.)
*discernir (ie) 41. (RC)

RC = Radical/Stem Change
*These verbs are irregular because they are radical/stem changing verbs which end in -ir but have the change of e becoming only ie and never i. The cross reference number following each verb indicates the chart which shows the regular e becoming ie, i radical/stem changing pattern for verbs ending in -ir.

86 model: ERGUIR* (ie, i)

*Orthographic changing

TIEMPOS SIMPLES
SIMPLE TENSES

PRESENTE DE INDICATIVO / PRESENT INDICATIVE	PRETÉRITO IMPERFECTO DE INDICATIVO / IMPERFECT INDICATIVE	PRETÉRITO INDEFINIDO DE INDICATIVO / PRETERITE INDICATIVE	FUTURO IMPERFECTO DE INDICATIVO / FUTURE INDICATIVE	POTENCIAL SIMPLE / CONDITIONAL
I erect, etc.	*I was erecting, etc.*	*I erected, etc.*	*I will erect, etc.*	*I would erect, etc.*
yergo irgo	erguía	erguí	erguiré	erguiría
yergues irgues	erguías	erguiste	erguirás	erguirías
yergue irgue	erguía	irguió	erguirá	erguiría
erguimos _or_ erguimos	erguíamos	erguimos	erguiremos	erguiríamos
erguís erguís	erguíais	erguisteis	erguiréis	erguiríais
yerguen irguen	erguían	irguieron	erguirán	erguirían

PRESENTE DE SUBJUNTIVO / PRESENT SUBJUNCTIVE	PRETÉRITO IMPERFECTO DE SUBJUNTIVO / PAST (IMPERFECT) SUBJUNCTIVE		FUTURO IMPERFECTO DE SUBJUNTIVO / FUTURE SUBJUNCTIVE
I erect, etc.	*I erected, etc.*		*I will erect, etc.*
yerga irga	irguiera	irguiese	irguiere
yergas irgas	irguieras	irguieses	irguieres
yerga irga	irguiera	irguiese	irguiere
irgamos _or_ irgamos	irguiéramos _or_	irguiésemos	irguiéremos
irgáis irgáis	irguierais	irguieseis	irguiereis
yergan irgan	irguieran	irguiesen	irguieren

FORMAS IMPERATIVAS, GERUNDIOS Y PARTICIPIO
COMMANDS AND PARTICIPLES

FORMAS IMPERATIVAS / COMMANDS		GERUNDIO Y PARTICIPIO / PARTICIPLES		
AFIRMATIVA / AFFIRMATIVE	NEGATIVA / NEGATIVE	GERUNDIO SIMPLE / PRESENT PARTICIPLE	PARTICIPIO / PAST PARTICIPLE	GERUNDIO COMPUESTO / PERFECT PARTICIPLE
erect	*don't erect*	*erecting*	*erected*	*having erected*
yergue / irgue (tú)	no yergas / no irgas (tú)	irguiendo	erguido	habiendo erguido
yerga / irga (Ud.)	no yerga / no irga (Ud.)			
erguid (vosotros)	no irgáis (vosotros)			
yergan / irgan (Uds.)	no yergan / no irgan (Uds.)			
let's erect	*let's not erect*			
irgamos	no irgamos			

INFINITIVO COMPUESTO: haber erguido
PERFECT INFINITIVE: to have erected

TIEMPOS COMPUESTOS
PERFECT (COMPOUND) TENSES

PRETÉRITO PERFECTO DE INDICATIVO / PRESENT PERFECT INDICATIVE	PRETÉRITO PLUSCUAMPERFECTO DE INDICATIVO / PAST PERFECT (PLUPERFECT) INDICATIVE	PRETÉRITO ANTERIOR DE INDICATIVO / PRETERITE PERFECT INDICATIVE	FUTURO PERFECTO DE INDICATIVO / FUTURE PERFECT INDICATIVE	POTENCIAL COMPUESTO / CONDITIONAL PERFECT
I have erected, etc.	*I had erected, etc.*	*I had erected, etc.*	*I will have erected, etc.*	*I would have erected, etc.*
he erguido	había erguido	hube erguido	habré erguido	habría erguido
has erguido	habías erguido	hubiste erguido	habrás erguido	habrías erguido
ha erguido	había erguido	hubo erguido	habrá erguido	habría erguido
hemos erguido	habíamos erguido	hubimos erguido	habremos erguido	habríamos erguido
habéis erguido	habíais erguido	hubisteis erguido	habréis erguido	habríais erguido
han erguido	habían erguido	hubieron erguido	habrán erguido	habrían erguido

PRETÉRITO PERFECTO DE SUBJUNTIVO / PRESENT PERFECT SUBJUNCTIVE	PRETÉRITO PLUSCUAMPERFECTO DE SUBJUNTIVO / PAST PERFECT (PLUPERFECT) SUBJUNCTIVE		FUTURO PERFECTO DE SUBJUNTIVO / FUTURE PERFECT SUBJUNCTIVE
I have erected, etc.	*I had erected, etc.*		*I will have erected, etc.*
haya erguido	hubiera erguido	hubiese erguido	hubiere erguido
hayas erguido	hubieras erguido	hubieses erguido	hubieres erguido
haya erguido	hubiera erguido	hubiese erguido	hubiere erguido
hayamos erguido	hubiéramos erguido _or_	hubiésemos erguido	hubiéremos erguido
hayáis erguido	hubierais erguido	hubieseis erguido	hubiereis erguido
hayan erguido	hubieran erguido	hubiesen erguido	hubieren erguido

*For additional translation possibilities see chart A.

86

IX. Irregular verbs

VERB OF THIS CATEGORY

*erguir (ie, i) 56. (OC) (RC)

OC = Orthographic/Spelling Change
RC = Radical/Stem Change
*This verb has radical/stem changes and two types of orthographic/spelling changes in addition to its irregularities. The cross reference number following the verb refers to the "Verbs of This Category" list for chart 56, wherein the individual cross reference numbers which indicate the category of verbs to which each type of change belongs are given.

TIEMPOS SIMPLES
SIMPLE TENSES

PRESENTE DE INDICATIVO *PRESENT* *INDICATIVE*	PRETÉRITO IMPERFECTO DE INDICATIVO *IMPERFECT* *INDICATIVE*	PRETÉRITO INDEFINIDO DE INDICATIVO *PRETERITE* *INDICATIVE*	FUTURO IMPERFECTO DE INDICATIVO *FUTURE* *INDICATIVE*	POTENCIAL SIMPLE *CONDITIONAL*
I am, etc.*	*I was, etc.**	*I was, etc.**	*I will be, etc.**	*I would be, etc.**
estoy	estaba	estuve	estaré	estaría
estás	estabas	estuviste	estarás	estarías
está	estaba	estuvo	estará	estaría
estamos	estábamos	estuvimos	estaremos	estaríamos
estáis	estabais	estuvisteis	estaréis	estaríais
están	estaban	estuvieron	estarán	estarían

PRESENTE DE SUBJUNTIVO *PRESENT* *SUBJUNCTIVE*	PRETÉRITO IMPERFECTO DE SUBJUNTIVO *PAST (IMPERFECT)* *SUBJUNCTIVE*		FUTURO IMPERFECTO DE SUBJUNTIVO *FUTURE* *SUBJUNCTIVE*
I am, etc.*	*I was, etc.**		*I will be, etc.**
esté	estuviera	estuviese	estuviere
estés	estuvieras	estuvieses	estuvieres
esté	estuviera	estuviese	estuviere
estemos	estuviéramos *or*	estuviésemos	estuviéremos
estéis	estuvierais	estuvieseis	estuviereis
estén	estuvieran	estuviesen	estuvieren

FORMAS IMPERATIVAS, GERUNDIOS Y PARTICIPIO
COMMANDS AND PARTICIPLES

FORMAS IMPERATIVAS *COMMANDS*		GERUNDIO Y PARTICIPIO *PARTICIPLES*		
AFIRMATIVA *AFFIRMATIVE*	NEGATIVA *NEGATIVE*	GERUNDIO SIMPLE *PRESENT PARTICIPLE*	PARTICIPIO *PAST PARTICIPLE*	GERUNDIO COMPUESTO *PERFECT PARTICIPLE*
be	*don't be*	*being*	*been*	*having been*
está (tú)	no estés (tú)	estando	estado	habiendo estado
esté (Ud.)	no esté (Ud.)			
estad (vosotros)	no estéis (vosotros)			
estén (Uds.)	no estén (Uds.)			
let's be	*let's not be*			
estemos	no estemos			

INFINITIVO COMPUESTO: haber estado
PERFECT INFINITIVE: to have been

TIEMPOS COMPUESTOS
PERFECT (COMPOUND) TENSES

PRETÉRITO PERFECTO DE INDICATIVO *PRESENT PERFECT* *INDICATIVE*	PRETÉRITO PLUSCUAMPERFECTO DE INDICATIVO *PAST PERFECT (PLUPERFECT)* *INDICATIVE*	PRETÉRITO ANTERIOR DE INDICATIVO *PRETERITE PERFECT* *INDICATIVE*	FUTURO PERFECTO DE INDICATIVO *FUTURE PERFECT* *INDICATIVE*	POTENCIAL COMPUESTO *CONDITIONAL PERFECT*
I have been, etc.	*I had been, etc.*	*I had been, etc.*	*I will have been, etc.**	*I would have been, etc.**
he estado	había estado	hube estado	habré estado	habría estado
has estado	habías estado	hubiste estado	habrás estado	habrías estado
ha estado	había estado	hubo estado	habrá estado	habría estado
hemos estado	habíamos estado	hubimos estado	habremos estado	habríamos estado
habéis estado	habíais estado	hubisteis estado	habréis estado	habríais estado
han estado	habían estado	hubieron estado	habrán estado	habrían estado

PRETÉRITO PERFECTO DE SUBJUNTIVO *PRESENT PERFECT* *SUBJUNCTIVE*	PRETÉRITO PLUSCUAMPERFECTO DE SUBJUNTIVO *PAST PERFECT (PLUPERFECT)* *SUBJUNCTIVE*		FUTURO PERFECTO DE SUBJUNTIVO *FUTURE PERFECT* *SUBJUNCTIVE*
I have been, etc.*	*I had been, etc.**		*I will have been, etc.**
haya estado	hubiera estado	hubiese estado	hubiere estado
hayas estado	hubieras estado	hubieses estado	hubieres estado
haya estado	hubiera estado	hubiese estado	hubiere estado
hayamos estado	hubiéramos estado *or*	hubiésemos estado	hubiéremos estado
hayáis estado	hubierais estado	hubieseis estado	hubiereis estado
hayan estado	hubieran estado	hubiesen estado	hubieren estado

*For additional translation possibilities see chart A.

IX. Irregular verbs

VERB OF THIS CATEGORY

estar

88 model: FREÍR* (i, i)

TIEMPOS SIMPLES
SIMPLE TENSES

PRESENTE DE INDICATIVO *PRESENT INDICATIVE*	PRETÉRITO IMPERFECTO DE INDICATIVO *IMPERFECT INDICATIVE*	PRETÉRITO INDEFINIDO DE INDICATIVO *PRETERITE INDICATIVE*	FUTURO IMPERFECTO DE INDICATIVO *FUTURE INDICATIVE*	POTENCIAL SIMPLE *CONDITIONAL*
*I fry, etc.**	*I was frying, etc.**	*I fried, etc.**	*I will fry, etc.**	*I would fry, etc.**
frío	freía	freí	freiré	freiría
fríes	freías	freíste	freirás	freirías
fríe	freía	frió	freirá	freiría
freímos	freíamos	freímos	freiremos	freiríamos
freís	freíais	freísteis	freiréis	freiríais
fríen	freían	frieron	freirán	freirían

PRESENTE DE SUBJUNTIVO *PRESENT SUBJUNCTIVE*	PRETÉRITO IMPERFECTO DE SUBJUNTIVO *PAST (IMPERFECT) SUBJUNCTIVE*		FUTURO IMPERFECTO DE SUBJUNTIVO *FUTURE SUBJUNCTIVE*
*I fry, etc.**	*I fried, etc.**		*I will fry, etc.**
fría	friera	friese	friere
frías	frieras	frieses	frieres
fría	friera	friese	friere
friamos	friéramos *or*	friésemos	friéremos
friáis	frierais	frieseis	friereis
frían	frieran	friesen	frieren

FORMAS IMPERATIVAS, GERUNDIOS Y PARTICIPIO
COMMANDS AND PARTICIPLES

FORMAS IMPERATIVAS *COMMANDS*		GERUNDIO Y PARTICIPIO *PARTICIPLES*		
AFIRMATIVA *AFFIRMATIVE*	NEGATIVA *NEGATIVE*	GERUNDIO SIMPLE *PRESENT PARTICIPLE*	PARTICIPIO *PAST PARTICIPLE*	GERUNDIO COMPUESTO *PERFECT PARTICIPLE*
fry	*don't fry*	*frying*	*fried*	*having fried*
fríe (tú)	no frías (tú)	friendo	frito+	habiendo frito
fría (Ud.)	no fría (Ud.)			
freid (vosotros)	no friáis (vosotros)			
frían (Uds.)	no frían (Uds.)			
let's fry	*let's not fry*			
friamos	no friamos			

INFINITIVO COMPUESTO: haber frito
PERFECT INFINITIVE: to have fried

TIEMPOS COMPUESTOS
PERFECT (COMPOUND) TENSES

PRETÉRITO PERFECTO DE INDICATIVO *PRESENT PERFECT INDICATIVE*	PRETÉRITO PLUSCUAMPERFECTO DE INDICATIVO *PAST PERFECT (PLUPERFECT) INDICATIVE*	PRETÉRITO ANTERIOR DE INDICATIVO *PRETERITE PERFECT INDICATIVE*	FUTURO PERFECTO DE INDICATIVO *FUTURE PERFECT INDICATIVE*	POTENCIAL COMPUESTO *CONDITIONAL PERFECT*
I have fried, etc.	*I had fried, etc.*	*I had fried, etc.*	*I will have fried, etc.**	*I would have fried, etc.**
he frito	había frito	hube frito	habré frito	habría frito
has frito	habías frito	hubiste frito	habrás frito	habrías frito
ha frito	había frito	hubo frito	habrá frito	habría frito
hemos frito	habíamos frito	hubimos frito	habremos frito	habríamos frito
habéis frito	habíais frito	hubisteis frito	habréis frito	habríais frito
han frito	habían frito	hubieron frito	habrán frito	habrían frito

PRETÉRITO PERFECTO DE SUBJUNTIVO *PRESENT PERFECT SUBJUNCTIVE*	PRETÉRITO PLUSCUAMPERFECTO DE SUBJUNTIVO *PAST PERFECT (PLUPERFECT) SUBJUNCTIVE*		FUTURO PERFECTO DE SUBJUNTIVO *FUTURE PERFECT SUBJUNCTIVE*
*I have fried, etc.**	*I had fried, etc.**		*I will have fried, etc.**
haya frito	hubiera frito	hubiese frito	hubiere frito
hayas frito	hubieras frito	hubieses frito	hubieres frito
haya frito	hubiera frito	hubiese frito	hubiere frito
hayamos frito	hubiéramos frito *or*	hubiésemos frito	hubiéremos frito
hayáis frito	hubierais frito	hubieseis frito	hubiereis frito
hayan frito	hubieran frito	hubiesen frito	hubieren frito

*For additional translation possibilities see chart A.
+This is the irregular form. The regular participio/past participle, freído, exists but is rarely used.

88

IX. Irregular verbs

*freír (i, i) 59. (OC) (RC)
*refreír (i, i) 59. (OC) (RC)
*sofreír (i, i) 59. (OC) (RC)

OC = Orthographic/Spelling Change
RC = Radical/Stem Change
*These verbs have orthographic/spelling and radical/stem changes in addition to their irregularity. The cross reference number following each verb refers to the "Verbs of This Category" list for chart 59, wherein the individual cross reference numbers which indicate the category of verbs to which each type of change belongs are given.

89 model: HABER

TIEMPOS SIMPLES
SIMPLE TENSES

PRESENTE DE INDICATIVO *PRESENT INDICATIVE*	PRETÉRITO IMPERFECTO DE INDICATIVO *IMPERFECT INDICATIVE*	PRETÉRITO INDEFINIDO DE INDICATIVO *PRETERITE INDICATIVE*	FUTURO IMPERFECTO DE INDICATIVO *FUTURE INDICATIVE*	POTENCIAL SIMPLE *CONDITIONAL*
I have, etc.*	*I was having, etc.**	*I had, etc.**	*I will have, etc.**	*I would have, etc.**
he	había	hube	habré	habría
has	habías	hubiste	habrás	habrías
ha	había	hubo	habrá	habría
hemos	habíamos	hubimos	habremos	habríamos
habéis	habíais	hubisteis	habréis	habríais
han	habían	hubieron	habrán	habrían

PRESENTE DE SUBJUNTIVO *PRESENT SUBJUNCTIVE*	PRETÉRITO IMPERFECTO DE SUBJUNTIVO *PAST (IMPERFECT) SUBJUNCTIVE*		FUTURO IMPERFECTO DE SUBJUNTIVO *FUTURE SUBJUNCTIVE*
I have, etc.*	*I had, etc.**		*I will have, etc.**
haya	hubiera	hubiese	hubiere
hayas	hubieras	hubieses	hubieres
haya	hubiera	hubiese	hubiere
hayamos	hubiéramos *or*	hubiésemos	hubiéremos
hayáis	hubierais	hubieseis	hubiereis
hayan	hubieran	hubiesen	hubieren

FORMAS IMPERATIVAS, GERUNDIOS Y PARTICIPIO
COMMANDS AND PARTICIPLES

FORMAS IMPERATIVAS *COMMANDS*		GERUNDIO Y PARTICIPIO *PARTICIPLES*		
AFIRMATIVA *AFFIRMATIVE*	NEGATIVA *NEGATIVE*	GERUNDIO SIMPLE *PRESENT PARTICIPLE*	PARTICIPIO *PAST PARTICIPLE*	GERUNDIO COMPUESTO *PERFECT PARTICIPLE*
have	*don't have*	*having*	*had*	*having had*
he (tú)	no hayas (tú)	habiendo	habido	habiendo habido
haya (Ud.)	no haya (Ud.)			
habed (vosotros)	no hayáis (vosotros)			
hayan (Uds.)	no hayan (Uds.)			
let's have	*let's not have*			
hayamos	no hayamos			

INFINITIVO COMPUESTO: haber habido
PERFECT INFINITIVE: to have had

TIEMPOS COMPUESTOS
PERFECT (COMPOUND) TENSES

PRETÉRITO PERFECTO DE INDICATIVO *PRESENT PERFECT INDICATIVE*	PRETÉRITO PLUSCUAMPERFECTO DE INDICATIVO *PAST PERFECT (PLUPERFECT) INDICATIVE*	PRETÉRITO ANTERIOR DE INDICATIVO *PRETERITE PERFECT INDICATIVE*	FUTURO PERFECTO DE INDICATIVO *FUTURE PERFECT INDICATIVE*	POTENCIAL COMPUESTO *CONDITIONAL PERFECT*
I have had, etc.	*I had had, etc.*	*I had had, etc.*	*I will have had, etc.**	*I would have had, etc.**
he habido	había habido	hube habido	habré habido	habría habido
has habido	habías habido	hubiste habido	habrás habido	habrías habido
ha habido	había habido	hubo habido	habrá habido	habría habido
hemos habido	habíamos habido	hubimos habido	habremos habido	habríamos habido
habéis habido	habíais habido	hubisteis habido	habréis habido	habríais habido
han habido	habían habido	hubieron habido	habrán habido	habrían habido

PRETÉRITO PERFECTO DE SUBJUNTIVO *PRESENT PERFECT SUBJUNCTIVE*	PRETÉRITO PLUSCUAMPERFECTO DE SUBJUNTIVO *PAST PERFECT (PLUPERFECT) SUBJUNCTIVE*		FUTURO PERFECTO DE SUBJUNTIVO *FUTURE PERFECT SUBJUNCTIVE*
I have had, etc.*	*I had had, etc.**		*I will have had, etc.**
haya habido	hubiera habido	hubiese habido	hubiere habido
hayas habido	hubieras habido	hubieses habido	hubieres habido
haya habido	hubiera habido	hubiese habido	hubiere habido
hayamos habido	hubiéramos habido *or*	hubiésemos habido	hubiéremos habido
hayáis habido	hubierais habido	hubieseis habido	hubiereis habido
hayan habido	hubieran habido	hubiesen habido	hubieren habido

*For additional translation possibilities see chart A.

89

IX. Irregular verbs

haber

90 model: HACER

TIEMPOS SIMPLES
SIMPLE TENSES

PRESENTE DE INDICATIVO *PRESENT INDICATIVE*	PRETÉRITO IMPERFECTO DE INDICATIVO *IMPERFECT INDICATIVE*	PRETÉRITO INDEFINIDO DE INDICATIVO *PRETERITE INDICATIVE*	FUTURO IMPERFECTO DE INDICATIVO *FUTURE INDICATIVE*	POTENCIAL SIMPLE *CONDITIONAL*
I do, etc.	*I was doing, etc.*	*I did, etc.*	*I will do, etc.*	*I would do, etc.*
hago	hacía	hice[+]	haré	haría
haces	hacías	hiciste	harás	harías
hace	hacía	hizo[+]	hará	haría
hacemos	hacíamos	hicimos	haremos	haríamos
hacéis	hacíais	hicisteis	haréis	haríais
hacen	hacían	hicieron	harán	harían

PRESENTE DE SUBJUNTIVO *PRESENT SUBJUNCTIVE*	PRETÉRITO IMPERFECTO DE SUBJUNTIVO *PAST (IMPERFECT) SUBJUNCTIVE*		FUTURO IMPERFECTO DE SUBJUNTIVO *FUTURE SUBJUNCTIVE*
I do, etc.	*I did, etc.*		*I will do, etc.*
haga	hiciera	hiciese	hiciere
hagas	hicieras	hicieses	hicieres
haga	hiciera	hiciese	hiciere
hagamos	hiciéramos or	hiciésemos	hiciéremos
hagáis	hicierais	hicieseis	hiciereis
hagan	hicieran	hiciesen	hicieren

FORMAS IMPERATIVAS, GERUNDIOS Y PARTICIPIO
COMMANDS AND PARTICIPLES

FORMAS IMPERATIVAS *COMMANDS*		GERUNDIO Y PARTICIPIO *PARTICIPLES*		
AFIRMATIVA *AFFIRMATIVE*	NEGATIVA *NEGATIVE*	GERUNDIO SIMPLE *PRESENT PARTICIPLE*	PARTICIPIO *PAST PARTICIPLE*	GERUNDIO COMPUESTO *PERFECT PARTICIPLE*
do	*don't do*	*doing*	*done*	*having done*
haz (tú)	no hagas (tú)	haciendo	hecho	habiendo hecho
haga (Ud.)	no haga (Ud.)			
haced (vosotros)	no hagáis (vosotros)			
hagan (Uds.)	no hagan (Uds.)			
let's do	*let's not do*			
hagamos	no hagamos			

INFINITIVO COMPUESTO: haber hecho
PERFECT INFINITIVE: to have done

TIEMPOS COMPUESTOS
PERFECT (COMPOUND) TENSES

PRETÉRITO PERFECTO DE INDICATIVO *PRESENT PERFECT INDICATIVE*	PRETÉRITO PLUSCUAMPERFECTO DE INDICATIVO *PAST PERFECT (PLUPERFECT) INDICATIVE*	PRETÉRITO ANTERIOR DE INDICATIVO *PRETERITE PERFECT INDICATIVE*	FUTURO PERFECTO DE INDICATIVO *FUTURE PERFECT INDICATIVE*	POTENCIAL COMPUESTO *CONDITIONAL PERFECT*
I have done, etc.	*I had done, etc.*	*I had done, etc.*	*I will have done, etc.*	*I would have done, etc.*
he hecho	había hecho	hube hecho	habré hecho	habría hecho
has hecho	habías hecho	hubiste hecho	habrás hecho	habrías hecho
ha hecho	había hecho	hubo hecho	habrá hecho	habría hecho
hemos hecho	habíamos hecho	hubimos hecho	habremos hecho	habríamos hecho
habéis hecho	habíais hecho	hubisteis hecho	habréis hecho	habríais hecho
han hecho	habían hecho	hubieron hecho	habrán hecho	habrían hecho

PRETÉRITO PERFECTO DE SUBJUNTIVO *PRESENT PERFECT SUBJUNCTIVE*	PRETÉRITO PLUSCUAMPERFECTO DE SUBJUNTIVO *PAST PERFECT (PLUPERFECT) SUBJUNCTIVE*		FUTURO PERFECTO DE SUBJUNTIVO *FUTURE PERFECT SUBJUNCTIVE*
I have done, etc.	*I had done, etc.*		*I will have done, etc.*
haya hecho	hubiera hecho	hubiese hecho	hubiere hecho
hayas hecho	hubieras hecho	hubieses hecho	hubieres hecho
haya hecho	hubiera hecho	hubiese hecho	hubiere hecho
hayamos hecho	hubiéramos hecho or	hubiésemos hecho	hubiéremos hecho
hayáis hecho	hubierais hecho	hubieseis hecho	hubiereis hecho
hayan hecho	hubieran hecho	hubiesen hecho	hubieren hecho

*For additional translation possibilities see chart A.
+In these forms contrahacer, rehacer and rehacerse have a written accent on the i. (See 34.)

90

IX. Irregular verbs

contrahacer 34. (OC) (see footnote on opposite page)
deshacer
deshacerse 4. (R)
hacer
rehacer 34. (OC) (see footnote on opposite page)
rehacerse 34. (OC), 4. (R) (see footnote on opposite page)

R = Reflexive
OC = Orthographic/Spelling Change

91 model: IMPRIMIR

TIEMPOS SIMPLES
SIMPLE TENSES

PRESENTE DE INDICATIVO PRESENT INDICATIVE	PRETÉRITO IMPERFECTO DE INDICATIVO IMPERFECT INDICATIVE	PRETÉRITO INDEFINIDO DE INDICATIVO PRETERITE INDICATIVE	FUTURO IMPERFECTO DE INDICATIVO FUTURE INDICATIVE	POTENCIAL SIMPLE CONDITIONAL
I print, etc.	*I was printing, etc.*	*I printed, etc.*	*I will print, etc.*	*I would print, etc.*
imprimo	imprimía	imprimí	imprimiré	imprimiría
imprimes	imprimías	imprimiste	imprimirás	imprimirías
imprime	imprimía	imprimió	imprimirá	imprimiría
imprimimos	imprimíamos	imprimimos	imprimiremos	imprimiríamos
imprimís	imprimíais	imprimisteis	imprimiréis	imprimiríais
imprimen	imprimían	imprimieron	imprimirán	imprimirían

PRESENTE DE SUBJUNTIVO PRESENT SUBJUNCTIVE	PRETÉRITO IMPERFECTO DE SUBJUNTIVO PAST (IMPERFECT) SUBJUNCTIVE		FUTURO IMPERFECTO DE SUBJUNTIVO FUTURE SUBJUNCTIVE
I print, etc.	*I printed, etc.*		*I will print, etc.*
imprima	imprimiera	imprimiese	imprimiere
imprimas	imprimieras	imprimieses	imprimieres
imprima	imprimiera	imprimiese	imprimiere
imprimamos	imprimiéramos *or*	imprimiésemos	imprimiéremos
imprimáis	imprimierais	imprimieseis	imprimiereis
impriman	imprimieran	imprimiesen	imprimieren

FORMAS IMPERATIVAS, GERUNDIOS Y PARTICIPIO
COMMANDS AND PARTICIPLES

FORMAS IMPERATIVAS COMMANDS		GERUNDIO Y PARTICIPIO PARTICIPLES		
AFIRMATIVA AFFIRMATIVE	NEGATIVA NEGATIVE	GERUNDIO SIMPLE PRESENT PARTICIPLE	PARTICIPIO PAST PARTICIPLE	GERUNDIO COMPUESTO PERFECT PARTICIPLE
print	*don't print*	*printing*	*printed*	*having printed*
imprime (tú)	no imprimas (tú)	imprimiendo	impreso[+]	habiendo impreso
imprima (Ud.)	no imprima (Ud.)			
imprimid (vosotros)	no imprimáis (vosotros)			
impriman (Uds.)	no impriman (Uds.)			
let's print	*let's not print*			
imprimamos	no imprimamos			

INFINITIVO COMPUESTO: haber impreso
PERFECT INFINITIVE: to have printed

TIEMPOS COMPUESTOS
PERFECT (COMPOUND) TENSES

PRETÉRITO PERFECTO DE INDICATIVO PRESENT PERFECT INDICATIVE	PRETÉRITO PLUSCUAMPERFECTO DE INDICATIVO PAST PERFECT (PLUPERFECT) INDICATIVE	PRETÉRITO ANTERIOR DE INDICATIVO PRETERITE PERFECT INDICATIVE	FUTURO PERFECTO DE INDICATIVO FUTURE PERFECT INDICATIVE	POTENCIAL COMPUESTO CONDITIONAL PERFECT
I have printed, etc.	*I had printed, etc.*	*I had printed, etc.*	*I will have printed, etc.*	*I would have printed, etc.*
he impreso	había impreso	hube impreso	habré impreso	habría impreso
has impreso	habías impreso	hubiste impreso	habrás impreso	habrías impreso
ha impreso	había impreso	hubo impreso	habrá impreso	habría impreso
hemos impreso	habíamos impreso	hubimos impreso	habremos impreso	habríamos impreso
habéis impreso	habíais impreso	hubisteis impreso	habréis impreso	habríais impreso
han impreso	habían impreso	hubieron impreso	habrán impreso	habrían impreso

PRETÉRITO PERFECTO DE SUBJUNTIVO PRESENT PERFECT SUBJUNCTIVE	PRETÉRITO PLUSCUAMPERFECTO DE SUBJUNTIVO PAST PERFECT (PLUPERFECT) SUBJUNCTIVE		FUTURO PERFECTO DE SUBJUNTIVO FUTURE PERFECT SUBJUNCTIVE
I have printed, etc.	*I had printed, etc.*		*I will have printed, etc.*
haya impreso	hubiera impreso	hubiese impreso	hubiere impreso
hayas impreso	hubieras impreso	hubieses impreso	hubieres impreso
haya impreso	hubiera impreso	hubiese impreso	hubiere impreso
hayamos impreso	hubiéramos impreso *or*	hubiésemos impreso	hubiéremos impreso
hayáis impreso	hubierais impreso	hubieseis impreso	hubiereis impreso
hayan impreso	hubieran impreso	hubiesen impreso	hubieren impreso

*For additional translation possibilities see chart A.
[+]This is the irregular form. The regular participio/past participle, imprimido, exists but is rarely used.

IX. Irregular verbs

VERBS OF THIS CATEGORY

imprimir
reimprimir

92 model: IR*

*Orthographic changing

TIEMPOS SIMPLES
SIMPLE TENSES

PRESENTE DE INDICATIVO PRESENT INDICATIVE	PRETÉRITO IMPERFECTO DE INDICATIVO IMPERFECT INDICATIVE	PRETÉRITO INDEFINIDO DE INDICATIVO PRETERITE INDICATIVE	FUTURO IMPERFECTO DE INDICATIVO FUTURE INDICATIVE	POTENCIAL SIMPLE CONDITIONAL
*I go, etc.**	*I was going, etc.**	*I went, etc.**	*I will go, etc.**	*I would go, etc.**
voy	iba	fui	iré	iría
vas	ibas	fuiste	irás	irías
va	iba	fue	irá	iría
vamos	íbamos	fuimos	iremos	iríamos
vais	ibais	fuisteis	iréis	iríais
van	iban	fueron	irán	irían

PRESENTE DE SUBJUNTIVO PRESENT SUBJUNCTIVE	PRETÉRITO IMPERFECTO DE SUBJUNTIVO PAST (IMPERFECT) SUBJUNCTIVE		FUTURO IMPERFECTO DE SUBJUNTIVO FUTURE SUBJUNCTIVE
*I go, etc.**	*I went, etc.**		*I will go, etc.**
vaya	fuera	fuese	fuere
vayas	fueras	fueses	fueres
vaya	fuera	fuese	fuere
vayamos	fuéramos *or*	fuésemos	fuéremos
vayáis	fuerais	fueseis	fuereis
vayan	fueran	fuesen	fueren

FORMAS IMPERATIVAS, GERUNDIOS Y PARTICIPIO
COMMANDS AND PARTICIPLES

FORMAS IMPERATIVAS COMMANDS		GERUNDIO Y PARTICIPIO PARTICIPLES		
AFIRMATIVA AFFIRMATIVE	NEGATIVA NEGATIVE	GERUNDIO SIMPLE PRESENT PARTICIPLE	PARTICIPIO PAST PARTICIPLE	GERUNDIO COMPUESTO PERFECT PARTICIPLE
go	*don't go*	*going*	*gone*	*having gone*
ve (tú)	no vayas (tú)	yendo	ido	habiendo ido
vaya (Ud.)	no vaya (Ud.)			
id (vosotros)	no vayáis (vosotros)			
vayan (Uds.)	no vayan (Uds.)			
let's go	*let's not go*			
vayamos	no vayamos			

INFINITIVO COMPUESTO: haber ido
PERFECT INFINITIVE: to have gone

TIEMPOS COMPUESTOS
PERFECT (COMPOUND) TENSES

PRETÉRITO PERFECTO DE INDICATIVO PRESENT PERFECT INDICATIVE	PRETÉRITO PLUSCUAMPERFECTO DE INDICATIVO PAST PERFECT (PLUPERFECT) INDICATIVE	PRETÉRITO ANTERIOR DE INDICATIVO PRETERITE PERFECT INDICATIVE	FUTURO PERFECTO DE INDICATIVO FUTURE PERFECT INDICATIVE	POTENCIAL COMPUESTO CONDITIONAL PERFECT
I have gone, etc.	*I had gone, etc.*	*I had gone, etc.*	*I will have gone, etc.**	*I would have gone, etc.**
he ido	había ido	hube ido	habré ido	habría ido
has ido	habías ido	hubiste ido	habrás ido	habrías ido
ha ido	había ido	hubo ido	habrá ido	habría ido
hemos ido	habíamos ido	hubimos ido	habremos ido	habríamos ido
habéis ido	habíais ido	hubisteis ido	habréis ido	habríais ido
han ido	habían ido	hubieron ido	habrán ido	habrían ido

PRETÉRITO PERFECTO DE SUBJUNTIVO PRESENT PERFECT SUBJUNCTIVE	PRETÉRITO PLUSCUAMPERFECTO DE SUBJUNTIVO PAST PERFECT (PLUPERFECT) SUBJUNCTIVE		FUTURO PERFECTO DE SUBJUNTIVO FUTURE PERFECT SUBJUNCTIVE
*I have gone, etc.**	*I had gone, etc.**		*I will have gone, etc.**
haya ido	hubiera ido	hubiese ido	hubiere ido
hayas ido	hubieras ido	hubieses ido	hubieres ido
haya ido	hubiera ido	hubiese ido	hubiere ido
hayamos ido	hubiéramos ido *or*	hubiésemos ido	hubiéremos ido
hayáis ido	hubierais ido	hubieseis ido	hubiereis ido
hayan ido	hubieran ido	hubiesen ido	hubieren ido

*For additional translation possibilities see chart A.

[250]

92

IX. Irregular verbs

VERB OF THIS CATEGORY

*ir 32. (OC)

OC = Orthographic/Spelling Change
*This verb has an orthographic/spelling change in addition to its irregularities. The cross reference number following the verb refers to the "Verbs of This Category" list of chart 32, wherein the orthographic change is specifically indicated.

model:
JUGAR* (ue)

*Orthographic changing

TIEMPOS SIMPLES
SIMPLE TENSES

PRESENTE DE INDICATIVO *PRESENT* *INDICATIVE*	PRETÉRITO IMPERFECTO DE INDICATIVO *IMPERFECT* *INDICATIVE*	PRETÉRITO INDEFINIDO DE INDICATIVO *PRETERITE* *INDICATIVE*	FUTURO IMPERFECTO DE INDICATIVO *FUTURE* *INDICATIVE*	POTENCIAL SIMPLE *CONDITIONAL*
*I play, etc.**	*I was playing, etc.**	*I played, etc.**	*I will play, etc.**	*I would play, etc.**
juego	jugaba	jugué	jugaré	jugaría
juegas	jugabas	jugaste	jugarás	jugarías
juega	jugaba	jugó	jugará	jugaría
jugamos	jugábamos	jugamos	jugaremos	jugaríamos
jugáis	jugabais	jugasteis	jugaréis	jugaríais
juegan	jugaban	jugaron	jugarán	jugarían

PRESENTE DE SUBJUNTIVO *PRESENT* *SUBJUNCTIVE*	PRETÉRITO IMPERFECTO DE SUBJUNTIVO *PAST (IMPERFECT)* *SUBJUNCTIVE*		FUTURO IMPERFECTO DE SUBJUNTIVO *FUTURE* *SUBJUNCTIVE*
*I play, etc.**	*I played, etc.**		*I will play, etc.**
juegue	jugara	jugase	jugare
juegues	jugaras	jugases	jugares
juegue	jugara	jugase	jugare
juguemos	jugáramos *or*	jugásemos	jugáremos
juguéis	jugarais	jugaseis	jugareis
jueguen	jugaran	jugasen	jugaren

FORMAS IMPERATIVAS, GERUNDIOS Y PARTICIPIO
COMMANDS AND PARTICIPLES

FORMAS IMPERATIVAS *COMMANDS*		GERUNDIO Y PARTICIPIO *PARTICIPLES*		
AFIRMATIVA *AFFIRMATIVE*	NEGATIVA *NEGATIVE*	GERUNDIO SIMPLE *PRESENT PARTICIPLE*	PARTICIPIO *PAST PARTICIPLE*	GERUNDIO COMPUESTO *PERFECT PARTICIPLE*
play	*don't play*	*playing*	*played*	*having played*
juega (tú)	no juegues (tú)	jugando	jugado	habiendo jugado
juegue (Ud.)	no juegue (Ud.)			
jugad (vosotros)	no juguéis (vosotros)			
jueguen (Uds.)	no jueguen (Uds.)			
let's play	*let's not play*			
juguemos	no juguemos			

INFINITIVO COMPUESTO: haber jugado
PERFECT INFINITIVE: *to have played*

TIEMPOS COMPUESTOS
PERFECT (COMPOUND) TENSES

PRETÉRITO PERFECTO DE INDICATIVO *PRESENT PERFECT* *INDICATIVE*	PRETÉRITO FLUSCUAMPERFECTO DE INDICATIVO *PAST PERFECT (PLUPERFECT)* *INDICATIVE*	PRETÉRITO ANTERIOR DE INDICATIVO *PRETERITE PERFECT* *INDICATIVE*	FUTURO PERFECTO DE INDICATIVO *FUTURE PERFECT* *INDICATIVE*	POTENCIAL COMPUESTO *CONDITIONAL PERFECT*
I have played, etc.	*I had played, etc.*	*I had played, etc.*	*I will have played, etc.**	*I would have played, etc.**
he jugado	había jugado	hube jugado	habré jugado	habría jugado
has jugado	habías jugado	hubiste jugado	habrás jugado	habrías jugado
ha jugado	había jugado	hubo jugado	habrá jugado	habría jugado
hemos jugado	habíamos jugado	hubimos jugado	habremos jugado	habríamos jugado
habéis jugado	habíais jugado	hubisteis jugado	habréis jugado	habríais jugado
han jugado	habían jugado	hubieron jugado	habrán jugado	habrían jugado

PRETÉRITO PERFECTO DE SUBJUNTIVO *PRESENT PERFECT* *SUBJUNCTIVE*	PRETÉRITO PLUSCUAMPERFECTO DE SUBJUNTIVO *PAST PERFECT (PLUPERFECT)* *SUBJUNCTIVE*		FUTURO PERFECTO DE SUBJUNTIVO *FUTURE PERFECT* *SUBJUNCTIVE*
*I have played, etc.**	*I had played, etc.**		*I will have played, etc.**
haya jugado	hubiera jugado	hubiese jugado	hubiere jugado
hayas jugado	hubieras jugado	hubieses jugado	hubieres jugado
haya jugado	hubiera jugado	hubiese jugado	hubiere jugado
hayamos jugado	hubiéramos jugado *or*	hubiésemos jugado	hubiéremos jugado
hayáis jugado	hubierais jugado	hubieseis jugado	hubiereis jugado
hayan jugado	hubieran jugado	hubiesen jugado	hubieren jugado

*For additional translation possibilities see chart A.

IX. Irregular verbs

VERBS   OF   THIS   CATEGORY

---

*jugar (ue) 45. (OC) (RC)
*jugarse (ue) 45. (OC) (RC), 4. (R)

R = Reflexive
OC = Orthographic/Spelling Change
RC = Radical/Stem Change
*These verbs are irregular because they have the radical/stem change of *u* becoming *ue* instead of *o* becoming *ue*. They also have orthographic/spelling changes in addition to this irregular radical/stem change. The cross reference number following each verb refers to the "Verbs of This Category" list for chart 45, wherein the individual cross reference numbers for the orthographic/spelling changes and for the regular *o* becoming *ue* radical/stem changing pattern for verbs ending in *-ar* are given.

94 model: MORIR (ue, u)

PRESENTE DE INDICATIVO **PRESENT INDICATIVE**	PRETÉRITO IMPERFECTO DE INDICATIVO **IMPERFECT INDICATIVE**	PRETÉRITO INDEFINIDO DE INDICATIVO **PRETERITE INDICATIVE**	FUTURO IMPERFECTO DE INDICATIVO **FUTURE INDICATIVE**	POTENCIAL SIMPLE **CONDITIONAL**
*I die, etc.**	*I was dying, etc.**	*I died, etc.**	*I will die, etc.**	*I would die, etc.**
muero	moría	morí	moriré	moriría
mueres	morías	moriste	morirás	morirías
muere	moría	murió	morirá	moriría
morimos	moríamos	morimos	moriremos	moriríamos
morís	moríais	moristeis	moriréis	moriríais
mueren	morían	murieron	morirán	morirían

PRESENTE DE SUBJUNTIVO **PRESENT SUBJUNCTIVE**	PRETÉRITO IMPERFECTO DE SUBJUNTIVO **PAST (IMPERFECT) SUBJUNCTIVE**		FUTURO IMPERFECTO DE SUBJUNTIVO **FUTURE SUBJUNCTIVE**
*I die, etc.**	*I died, etc.**		*I will die, etc.**
muera	muriera	muriese	muriere
mueras	murieras	murieses	murieres
muera	muriera	muriese	muriere
muramos	muriéramos *or*	muriésemos	muriéremos
muráis	murierais	murieseis	muriereis
mueran	murieran	muriesen	murieren

FORMAS IMPERATIVAS **COMMANDS**		GERUNDIO Y PARTICIPIO **PARTICIPLES**		
AFIRMATIVA **AFFIRMATIVE**	NEGATIVA **NEGATIVE**	GERUNDIO SIMPLE **PRESENT PARTICIPLE**	PARTICIPIO **PAST PARTICIPLE**	GERUNDIO COMPUESTO **PERFECT PARTICIPLE**
die	*don't die*	*dying*	*died*	*having died*
muere (tú)	no mueras (tú)	muriendo	muerto	habiendo muerto
muera (Ud.)	no muera (Ud.)			
morid (vosotros)	no muráis (vosotros)			
mueran (Uds.)	no mueran (Uds.)			
let's die	*let's not die*			
muramos	no muramos			

INFINITIVO COMPUESTO: haber muerto
PERFECT INFINITIVE: to have died

PRETÉRITO PERFECTO DE INDICATIVO **PRESENT PERFECT INDICATIVE**	PRETÉRITO PLUSCUAMPERFECTO DE INDICATIVO **PAST PERFECT (PLUPERFECT) INDICATIVE**	PRETÉRITO ANTERIOR DE INDICATIVO **PRETERITE PERFECT INDICATIVE**	FUTURO PERFECTO DE INDICATIVO **FUTURE PERFECT INDICATIVE**	POTENCIAL COMPUESTO **CONDITIONAL PERFECT**
I have died, etc.	*I had died, etc.*	*I had died, etc.*	*I will have died, etc.**	*I would have died, etc.**
he muerto	había muerto	hube muerto	habré muerto	habría muerto
has muerto	habías muerto	hubiste muerto	habrás muerto	habrías muerto
ha muerto	había muerto	hubo muerto	habrá muerto	habría muerto
hemos muerto	habíamos muerto	hubimos muerto	habremos muerto	habríamos muerto
habéis muerto	habíais muerto	hubisteis muerto	habréis muerto	habríais muerto
han muerto	habían muerto	hubieron muerto	habrán muerto	habrían muerto

PRETÉRITO PERFECTO DE SUBJUNTIVO **PRESENT PERFECT SUBJUNCTIVE**	PRETÉRITO PLUSCUAMPERFECTO DE SUBJUNTIVO **PAST PERFECT (PLUPERFECT) SUBJUNCTIVE**		FUTURO PERFECTO DE SUBJUNTIVO **FUTURE PERFECT SUBJUNCTIVE**
*I have died, etc.**	*I had died, etc.**		*I will have died, etc.**
haya muerto	hubiera muerto	hubiese muerto	hubiere muerto
hayas muerto	hubieras muerto	hubieses muerto	hubieres muerto
haya muerto	hubiera muerto	hubiese muerto	hubiere muerto
hayamos muerto	hubiéramos muerto *or*	hubiésemos muerto	hubiéremos muerto
hayáis muerto	hubierais muerto	hubieseis muerto	hubiereis muerto
hayan muerto	hubieran muerto	hubiesen muerto	hubieren muerto

*For additional translation possibilities see chart A.

[254]

94

IX. Irregular verbs

VERBS OF THIS CATEGORY
---

*morir (ue, u) 40. (RC)
*premorir (ue, u) 40. (RC)

RC = Radical/Stem Change
*These verbs have radical/stem changes in addition to their irregularity. The cross reference number following each verb indicates the category of verbs to which these radical/stem changes belong.

95 model: OÍR*

*Orthographic changing

TIEMPOS SIMPLES
SIMPLE TENSES

PRESENTE DE INDICATIVO *PRESENT* *INDICATIVE*	PRETÉRITO IMPERFECTO DE INDICATIVO *IMPERFECT* *INDICATIVE*	PRETÉRITO INDEFINIDO DE INDICATIVO *PRETERITE* *INDICATIVE*	FUTURO IMPERFECTO DE INDICATIVO *FUTURE* *INDICATIVE*	POTENCIAL SIMPLE *CONDITIONAL*
I hear, etc. *	*I was hearing, etc.* *	*I heard, etc.* *	*I will hear, etc.* *	*I would hear, etc.* *
oigo	oía	oí	oiré	oiría
oyes	oías	oíste	oirás	oirías
oye	oía	oyó	oirá	oiría
oímos	oíamos	oímos	oiremos	oiríamos
oís	oíais	oísteis	oiréis	oiríais
oyen	oían	oyeron	oirán	oirían

PRESENTE DE SUBJUNTIVO *PRESENT* *SUBJUNCTIVE*	PRETÉRITO IMPERFECTO DE SUBJUNTIVO *PAST (IMPERFECT)* *SUBJUNCTIVE*		FUTURO IMPERFECTO DE SUBJUNTIVO *FUTURE* *SUBJUNCTIVE*
I hear, etc. *	*I heard, etc.* *		*I will hear, etc.* *
oiga	oyera	oyese	oyere
oigas	oyeras	oyeses	oyeres
oiga	oyera	oyese	oyere
oigamos	oyéramos *or*	oyésemos	oyéremos
oigáis	oyerais	oyeseis	oyereis
oigan	oyeran	oyesen	oyeren

FORMAS IMPERATIVAS, GERUNDIOS Y PARTICIPIO
COMMANDS AND PARTICIPLES

FORMAS IMPERATIVAS *COMMANDS*		GERUNDIO Y PARTICIPIO *PARTICIPLES*		
AFIRMATIVA *AFFIRMATIVE*	NEGATIVA *NEGATIVE*	GERUNDIO SIMPLE *PRESENT PARTICIPLE*	PARTICIPIO *PAST PARTICIPLE*	GERUNDIO COMPUESTO *PERFECT PARTICIPLE*
hear	*don't hear*	*hearing*	*heard*	*having heard*
oye (tú)	no oigas (tú)	oyendo	oído	habiendo oído
oiga (Ud.)	no oiga (Ud.)			
oíd (vosotros)	no oigáis (vosotros)			
oigan (Uds.)	no oigan (Uds.)			
let's hear	*let's not hear*			
oigamos	no oigamos			

INFINITIVO COMPUESTO: haber oído
PERFECT INFINITIVE: to have heard

TIEMPOS COMPUESTOS
PERFECT (COMPOUND) TENSES

PRETÉRITO PERFECTO DE INDICATIVO *PRESENT PERFECT* *INDICATIVE*	PRETÉRITO PLUSCUAMPERFECTO DE INDICATIVO *PAST PERFECT (PLUPERFECT)* *INDICATIVE*	PRETÉRITO ANTERIOR DE INDICATIVO *PRETERITE PERFECT* *INDICATIVE*	FUTURO PERFECTO DE INDICATIVO *FUTURE PERFECT* *INDICATIVE*	POTENCIAL COMPUESTO *CONDITIONAL PERFECT*
I have heard, etc.	*I had heard, etc.*	*I had heard, etc.*	*I will have heard, etc.* *	*I would have heard, etc.* *
he oído	había oído	hube oído	habré oído	habría oído
has oído	habías oído	hubiste oído	habrás oído	habrías oído
ha oído	había oído	hubo oído	habrá oído	habría oído
hemos oído	habíamos oído	hubimos oído	habremos oído	habríamos oído
habéis oído	habíais oído	hubisteis oído	habréis oído	habríais oído
han oído	habían oído	hubieron oído	habrán oído	habrían oído

PRETÉRITO PERFECTO DE SUBJUNTIVO *PRESENT PERFECT* *SUBJUNCTIVE*	PRETÉRITO PLUSCUAMPERFECTO DE SUBJUNTIVO *PAST PERFECT (PLUPERFECT)* *SUBJUNCTIVE*		FUTURO PERFECTO DE SUBJUNTIVO *FUTURE PERFECT* *SUBJUNCTIVE*
I have heard, etc. *	*I had heard, etc.* *		*I will have heard, etc.* *
haya oído	hubiera oído	hubiese oído	hubiere oído
hayas oído	hubieras oído	hubieses oído	hubieres oído
haya oído	hubiera oído	hubiese oído	hubiere oído
hayamos oído	hubiéramos oído *or*	hubiésemos oído	hubiéremos oído
hayáis oído	hubierais oído	hubieseis oído	hubiereis oído
hayan oído	hubieran oído	hubiesen oído	hubieren oído

*For additional translation possibilities see chart A.

95

IX. Irregular verbs

VERBS OF THIS CATEGORY

desoír 22. (OC)
entreoír 22. (OC)
oír 22. (OC)
trasoír 22. (OC)

OC = Orthographic/Spelling Change

96 model: PLACER

TIEMPOS SIMPLES
SIMPLE TENSES

PRESENTE DE INDICATIVO *PRESENT INDICATIVE*	PRETÉRITO IMPERFECTO DE INDICATIVO *IMPERFECT INDICATIVE*	PRETÉRITO INDEFINIDO DE INDICATIVO *PRETERITE INDICATIVE*	FUTURO IMPERFECTO DE INDICATIVO *FUTURE INDICATIVE*	POTENCIAL SIMPLE *CONDITIONAL*
*I please, etc.**	*I was pleasing, etc.**	*I pleased, etc.**	*I will please, etc.**	*I would please, etc.**
plazco	placía	plací · plací	placeré	placería
places	placías	placiste · placiste	placerás	placerías
place	placía	plació *or* plugo	placerá	placería
placemos	placíamos	placimos · placimos	placeremos	placeríamos
placéis	placíais	placisteis · placisteis	placeréis	placeríais
placen	placían	placieron · pluguieron	placerán	placerían

PRESENTE DE SUBJUNTIVO *PRESENT SUBJUNCTIVE*	PRETÉRITO IMPERFECTO DE SUBJUNTIVO *PAST (IMPERFECT) SUBJUNCTIVE*	FUTURO IMPERFECTO DE SUBJUNTIVO *FUTURE SUBJUNCTIVE*
*I please, etc.**	*I pleased, etc.**	*I will please, etc.**
plazca plazca plazca	placiera placiera placiese placiese	placiere placiere
plazcas plazcas plazcas	placieras placieras placieses placieses	placieres placieres
plazca *or* plega *or* plegue	placiera pluguiera placiese pluguiese	placiere pluguiere
plazcamos/plazcamos/plazcamos	placiéramos *or* placiéramos *or* placiésemos *or* placiésemos	placiéremos *or* placiéremos
plazcáis plazcáis plazcáis	placierais placierais placieseis placieseis	placiereis placiereis
plazcan plazcan plazcan	placieran pluguieran placiesen pluguiesen	placieren pluguieren

FORMAS IMPERATIVAS, GERUNDIOS Y PARTICIPIO
COMMANDS AND PARTICIPLES

FORMAS IMPERATIVAS *COMMANDS*		GERUNDIO Y PARTICIPIO *PARTICIPLES*		
AFIRMATIVA *AFFIRMATIVE*	NEGATIVA *NEGATIVE*	GERUNDIO SIMPLE *PRESENT PARTICIPLE*	PARTICIPIO *PAST PARTICIPLE*	GERUNDIO COMPUESTO *PERFECT PARTICIPLE*
please	*don't please*	*pleasing*	*pleased*	*having pleased*
place (tú)	no plazcas (tú)	placiendo	placido	habiendo placido
plazca / plega / plegue (Ud.)	no plazca/no plega/no plegue			
placed (vosotros)	no plazcáis (vosotros)			
plazcan (Uds.)	no plazcan (Uds.)			
let's please	*let's not please*			
plazcamos	no plazcamos			

```
INFINITIVO COMPUESTO:  haber placido
PERFECT INFINITIVE:  to have pleased
```

TIEMPOS COMPUESTOS
PERFECT (COMPOUND) TENSES

PRETÉRITO PERFECTO DE INDICATIVO *PRESENT PERFECT INDICATIVE*	PRETÉRITO PLUSCUAMPERFECTO DE INDICATIVO *PAST PERFECT (PLUPERFECT) INDICATIVE*	PRETÉRITO ANTERIOR DE INDICATIVO *PRETERITE PERFECT INDICATIVE*	FUTURO PERFECTO DE INDICATIVO *FUTURE PERFECT INDICATIVE*	POTENCIAL COMPUESTO *CONDITIONAL PERFECT*
I have pleased, etc.	*I had pleased, etc.*	*I had pleased, etc.*	*I will have pleased, etc.**	*I would have pleased, etc.**
he placido	había placido	hube placido	habré placido	habría placido
has placido	habías placido	hubiste placido	habrás placido	habrías placido
ha placido	había placido	hubo placido	habrá placido	habría placido
hemos placido	habíamos placido	hubimos placido	habremos placido	habríamos placido
habéis placido	habíais placido	hubisteis placido	habréis placido	habríais placido
han placido	habían placido	hubieron placido	habrán placido	habrían placido

PRETÉRITO PERFECTO DE SUBJUNTIVO *PRESENT PERFECT SUBJUNCTIVE*	PRETÉRITO PLUSCUAMPERFECTO DE SUBJUNTIVO *PAST PERFECT (PLUPERFECT) SUBJUNCTIVE*	FUTURO PERFECTO DE SUBJUNTIVO *FUTURE PERFECT SUBJUNCTIVE*
*I have pleased, etc.**	*I had pleased, etc.**	*I will have pleased, etc.**
haya placido	hubiera placido hubiese placido	hubiere placido
hayas placido	hubieras placido hubieses placido	hubieres placido
haya placido	hubiera placido hubiese placido	hubiere placido
hayamos placido	hubiéramos placido *or* hubiésemos placido	hubiéremos placido
hayáis placido	hubierais placido hubieseis placido	hubiereis placido
hayan placido	hubieran placido hubiesen placido	hubieren placido

*For additional translation possibilities see chart A.

VERB OF THIS CATEGORY

placer

Compounds of placer *NOT following this pattern:*
  aplacer 73. (I)
  complacer 73. (I)
  complacerse 73. (I), 4. (R)
  desplacer 73. (I)

R = Reflexive
I = Irregular

97 model: PODER (ue)

TIEMPOS SIMPLES
SIMPLE TENSES

PRESENTE DE INDICATIVO *PRESENT INDICATIVE*	PRETÉRITO IMPERFECTO DE INDICATIVO *IMPERFECT INDICATIVE*	PRETÉRITO INDEFINIDO DE INDICATIVO *PRETERITE INDICATIVE*	FUTURO IMPERFECTO DE INDICATIVO *FUTURE INDICATIVE*	POTENCIAL SIMPLE *CONDITIONAL*
I am able, etc.*	*I was able, etc.**	*I was able, etc.**	*I will be able, etc.**	*I would be able, etc.**
puedo	podía	pude	podré	podría
puedes	podías	pudiste	podrás	podrías
puede	podía	pudo	podrá	podría
podemos	podíamos	pudimos	podremos	podríamos
podéis	podíais	pudisteis	podréis	podríais
pueden	podían	pudieron	podrán	podrían

PRESENTE DE SUBJUNTIVO *PRESENT SUBJUNCTIVE*	PRETÉRITO IMPERFECTO DE SUBJUNTIVO *PAST (IMPERFECT) SUBJUNCTIVE*		FUTURO IMPERFECTO DE SUBJUNTIVO *FUTURE SUBJUNCTIVE*
I am able, etc.*	*I was able, etc.**		*I will be able, etc.**
pueda	pudiera	pudiese	pudiere
puedas	pudieras	pudieses	pudieres
pueda	pudiera	pudiese	pudiere
podamos	pudiéramos *or*	pudiésemos	pudiéremos
podáis	pudierais	pudieseis	pudiereis
puedan	pudieran	pudiesen	pudieren

FORMAS IMPERATIVAS, GERUNDIOS Y PARTICIPIO
COMMANDS AND PARTICIPLES

FORMAS IMPERATIVAS *COMMANDS*		GERUNDIO Y PARTICIPIO *PARTICIPLES*		
AFIRMATIVA *AFFIRMATIVE*	NEGATIVA *NEGATIVE*	GERUNDIO SIMPLE *PRESENT PARTICIPLE*	PARTICIPIO *PAST PARTICIPLE*	GERUNDIO COMPUESTO *PERFECT PARTICIPLE*
be able	*don't be able*	*being able*	*been able*	*having been able*
puede (tú)	no puedas (tú)	pudiendo	podido	habiendo podido
pueda (Ud.)	no pueda (Ud.)			
poded (vosotros)	no podáis (vosotros)			
puedan (Uds.)	no puedan (Uds.)			
let's be able	*let's not be able*			
podamos	no podamos			

INFINITIVO COMPUESTO: haber podido
PERFECT INFINITIVE: to have been able

TIEMPOS COMPUESTOS
PERFECT (COMPOUND) TENSES

PRETÉRITO PERFECTO DE INDICATIVO *PRESENT PERFECT INDICATIVE*	PRETÉRITO PLUSCUAMPERFECTO DE INDICATIVO *PAST PERFECT (PLUPERFECT) INDICATIVE*	PRETÉRITO ANTERIOR DE INDICATIVO *PRETERITE PERFECT INDICATIVE*	FUTURO PERFECTO DE INDICATIVO *FUTURE PERFECT INDICATIVE*	POTENCIAL COMPUESTO *CONDITIONAL PERFECT*
I have been able, etc.	*I had been able, etc.*	*I had been able, etc.*	*I will have been able, etc.**	*I would have been able, etc.**
he podido	había podido	hube podido	habré podido	habría podido
has podido	habías podido	hubiste podido	habrás podido	habrías podido
ha podido	había podido	hubo podido	habrá podido	habría podido
hemos podido	habíamos podido	hubimos podido	habremos podido	habríamos podido
habéis podido	habíais podido	hubisteis podido	habréis podido	habríais podido
han podido	habían podido	hubieron podido	habrán podido	habrían podido

PRETÉRITO PERFECTO DE SUBJUNTIVO *PRESENT PERFECT SUBJUNCTIVE*	PRETÉRITO PLUSCUAMPERFECTO DE SUBJUNTIVO *PAST PERFECT (PLUPERFECT) SUBJUNCTIVE*		FUTURO PERFECTO DE SUBJUNTIVO *FUTURE PERFECT SUBJUNCTIVE*
I have been able, etc.*	*I had been able, etc.**		*I will have been able, etc.**
haya podido	hubiera podido	hubiese podido	hubiere podido
hayas podido	hubieras podido	hubieses podido	hubieres podido
haya podido	hubiera podido	hubiese podido	hubiere podido
hayamos podido	hubiéramos podido *or*	hubiésemos podido	hubiéremos podido
hayáis podido	hubierais podido	hubieseis podido	hubiereis podido
hayan podido	hubieran podido	hubiesen podido	hubieren podido

*For additional translation possibilities see chart A.

IX. Irregular verbs

VERB OF THIS CATEGORY

*poder (ue) 38. (RC)

RC = Radical/Stem Change
*This verb has radical/stem changes in addition to its irregularities. The cross reference number following the verb indicates the category of verbs to which these radical/stem changes belong.

98 model: PONER

PRESENTE DE INDICATIVO *PRESENT INDICATIVE*	PRETÉRITO IMPERFECTO DE INDICATIVO *IMPERFECT INDICATIVE*	PRETÉRITO INDEFINIDO DE INDICATIVO *PRETERITE INDICATIVE*	FUTURO IMPERFECTO DE INDICATIVO *FUTURE INDICATIVE*	POTENCIAL SIMPLE *CONDITIONAL*
I put, etc.	*I was putting, etc.*	*I put, etc.*	*I will put, etc.*	*I would put, etc.*
pongo	ponía	puse	pondré	pondría
pones	ponías	pusiste	pondrás	pondrías
pone	ponía	puso	pondrá	pondría
ponemos	poníamos	pusimos	pondremos	pondríamos
ponéis	poníais	pusisteis	pondréis	pondríais
ponen	ponían	pusieron	pondrán	pondrían

PRESENTE DE SUBJUNTIVO *PRESENT SUBJUNCTIVE*	PRETÉRITO IMPERFECTO DE SUBJUNTIVO *PAST (IMPERFECT) SUBJUNCTIVE*		FUTURO IMPERFECTO DE SUBJUNTIVO *FUTURE SUBJUNCTIVE*
I put, etc.	*I put, etc.*		*I will put, etc.*
ponga	pusiera	pusiese	pusiere
pongas	pusieras	pusieses	pusieres
ponga	pusiera	pusiese	pusiere
pongamos	pusiéramos _or_	pusiésemos	pusiéremos
pongáis	pusierais	pusieseis	pusiereis
pongan	pusieran	pusiesen	pusieren

FORMAS IMPERATIVAS *COMMANDS*		GERUNDIO Y PARTICIPIO *PARTICIPLES*		
AFIRMATIVA *AFFIRMATIVE*	NEGATIVA *NEGATIVE*	GERUNDIO SIMPLE *PRESENT PARTICIPLE*	PARTICIPIO *PAST PARTICIPLE*	GERUNDIO COMPUESTO *PERFECT PARTICIPLE*
put	*don't put*	*putting*	*put*	*having put*
pon (tú)	no pongas (tú)	poniendo	puesto	habiendo puesto
ponga (Ud.)	no ponga (Ud.)			
poned (vosotros)	no pongáis (vosotros)			
pongan (Uds.)	no pongan (Uds.)			
let's put	*let's not put*			
pongamos	no pongamos			

INFINITIVO COMPUESTO: haber puesto
PERFECT INFINITIVE: to have put

PRETÉRITO PERFECTO DE INDICATIVO *PRESENT PERFECT INDICATIVE*	PRETÉRITO PLUSCUAMPERFECTO DE INDICATIVO *PAST PERFECT (PLUPERFECT) INDICATIVE*	PRETÉRITO ANTERIOR DE INDICATIVO *PRETERITE PERFECT INDICATIVE*	FUTURO PERFECTO DE INDICATIVO *FUTURE PERFECT INDICATIVE*	POTENCIAL COMPUESTO *CONDITIONAL PERFECT*
I have put, etc.	*I had put, etc.*	*I had put, etc.*	*I will have put, etc.*	*I would have put, etc.*
he puesto	había puesto	hube puesto	habré puesto	habría puesto
has puesto	habías puesto	hubiste puesto	habrás puesto	habrías puesto
ha puesto	había puesto	hubo puesto	habrá puesto	habría puesto
hemos puesto	habíamos puesto	hubimos puesto	habremos puesto	habríamos puesto
habéis puesto	habíais puesto	hubisteis puesto	habréis puesto	habríais puesto
han puesto	habían puesto	hubieron puesto	habrán puesto	habrían puesto

PRETÉRITO PERFECTO DE SUBJUNTIVO *PRESENT PERFECT SUBJUNCTIVE*	PRETÉRITO PLUSCUAMPERFECTO DE SUBJUNTIVO *PAST PERFECT (PLUPERFECT) SUBJUNCTIVE*		FUTURO PERFECTO DE SUBJUNTIVO *FUTURE PERFECT SUBJUNCTIVE*
I have put, etc.	*I had put, etc.*		*I will have put, etc.*
haya puesto	hubiera puesto	hubiese puesto	hubiere puesto
hayas puesto	hubieras puesto	hubieses puesto	hubieres puesto
haya puesto	hubiera puesto	hubiese puesto	hubiere puesto
hayamos puesto	hubiéramos puesto _or_	hubiésemos puesto	hubiéremos puesto
hayáis puesto	hubierais puesto	hubieseis puesto	hubiereis puesto
hayan puesto	hubieran puesto	hubiesen puesto	hubieren puesto

*For additional translation possibilities see chart I.

IX. Irregular verbs

anteponer
componer
contraponer
deponer
descomponer
descomponerse 4. (R)
disponer
disponerse 4. (R)
exponer
imponer
indisponer
indisponerse 4. (R)
interponer
oponer
oponerse 4. (R)
poner
ponerse 4. (R)
posponer
predisponer
preponer
presuponer
proponer
proponerse 4. (R)
recomponer
reponer
reponerse 4. (R)
sobreexponer
sobreponer
sobreponerse 4. (R)
superponer
suponer
transponer
trasponer
yuxtaponer
yuxtaponerse 4. (R)

R = Reflexive

99 model: PROVEER*

*Orthographic changing

TIEMPOS SIMPLES
SIMPLE TENSES

PRESENTE DE INDICATIVO **PRESENT** *INDICATIVE*	PRETÉRITO IMPERFECTO DE INDICATIVO **IMPERFECT** *INDICATIVE*	PRETÉRITO INDEFINIDO DE INDICATIVO **PRETERITE** *INDICATIVE*	FUTURO IMPERFECTO DE INDICATIVO **FUTURE** *INDICATIVE*	POTENCIAL SIMPLE **CONDITIONAL**
I provide, etc.*	*I was providing, etc.**	*I provided, etc.**	*I will provide, etc.**	*I would provide, etc.**
proveo	proveía	proveí	proveeré	proveería
provees	proveías	proveíste	proveerás	proveerías
provee	proveía	proveyó	proveerá	proveería
proveemos	proveíamos	proveímos	proveeremos	proveeríamos
proveéis	proveíais	proveísteis	proveeréis	proveeríais
proveen	proveían	proveyeron	proveerán	proveerían

PRESENTE DE SUBJUNTIVO **PRESENT** *SUBJUNCTIVE*	PRETÉRITO IMPERFECTO DE SUBJUNTIVO **PAST (IMPERFECT)** *SUBJUNCTIVE*		FUTURO IMPERFECTO DE SUBJUNTIVO **FUTURE** *SUBJUNCTIVE*
I provide, etc.*	*I provided, etc.**		*I will provide, etc.**
provea	proveyera	proveyese	proveyere
proveas	proveyeras	proveyeses	proveyeres
provea	proveyera	proveyese	proveyere
proveamos	proveyéramos *or*	proveyésemos	proveyéremos
proveáis	proveyerais	proveyeseis	proveyereis
provean	proveyeran	proveyesen	proveyeren

FORMAS IMPERATIVAS, GERUNDIOS Y PARTICIPIO
COMMANDS AND PARTICIPLES

FORMAS IMPERATIVAS — *COMMANDS*		GERUNDIO Y PARTICIPIO — *PARTICIPLES*		
AFIRMATIVA *AFFIRMATIVE*	NEGATIVA *NEGATIVE*	GERUNDIO SIMPLE *PRESENT PARTICIPLE*	PARTICIPIO *PAST PARTICIPLE*	GERUNDIO COMPUESTO *PERFECT PARTICIPLE*
provide	*don't provide*	*providing*	*provided*	*having provided*
provee (tú)	no proveas (tú)	proveyendo	provisto+	habiendo provisto
provea (Ud.)	no provea (Ud.)			
proveed (vosotros)	no proveáis (vosotros)			
provean (Uds.)	no provean (Uds.)			
let's provide	*let's not provide*			
proveamos	no proveamos			

INFINITIVO COMPUESTO: haber provisto
PERFECT INFINITIVE: to have provided

TIEMPOS COMPUESTOS
PERFECT (COMPOUND) TENSES

PRETÉRITO PERFECTO DE INDICATIVO **PRESENT PERFECT** *INDICATIVE*	PRETÉRITO PLUSCUAMPERFECTO DE INDICATIVO **PAST PERFECT (PLUPERFECT)** *INDICATIVE*	PRETÉRITO ANTERIOR DE INDICATIVO **PRETERITE PERFECT** *INDICATIVE*	FUTURO PERFECTO DE INDICATIVO **FUTURE PERFECT** *INDICATIVE*	POTENCIAL COMPUESTO **CONDITIONAL PERFECT**
I have provided, etc.	*I had provided, etc.*	*I had provided, etc.*	*I will have provided, etc.**	*I would have provided, etc.**
he provisto	había provisto	hube provisto	habré provisto	habría provisto
has provisto	habías provisto	hubiste provisto	habrás provisto	habrías provisto
ha provisto	había provisto	hubo provisto	habrá provisto	habría provisto
hemos provisto	habíamos provisto	hubimos provisto	habremos provisto	habríamos provisto
habéis provisto	habíais provisto	hubisteis provisto	habréis provisto	habríais provisto
han provisto	habían provisto	hubieron provisto	habrán provisto	habrían provisto

PRETÉRITO PERFECTO DE SUBJUNTIVO **PRESENT PERFECT** *SUBJUNCTIVE*	PRETÉRITO PLUSCUAMPERFECTO DE SUBJUNTIVO **PAST PERFECT (PLUPERFECT)** *SUBJUNCTIVE*		FUTURO PERFECTO DE SUBJUNTIVO **FUTURE PERFECT** *SUBJUNCTIVE*
I have provided, etc.*	*I had provided, etc.**		*I will have provided, etc.**
haya provisto	hubiera provisto	hubiese provisto	hubiere provisto
hayas provisto	hubieras provisto	hubieses provisto	hubieres provisto
haya provisto	hubiera provisto	hubiese provisto	hubiere provisto
hayamos provisto	hubiéramos provisto *or*	hubiésemos provisto	hubiéremos provisto
hayáis provisto	hubierais provisto	hubieseis provisto	hubiereis provisto
hayan provisto	hubieran provisto	hubiesen provisto	hubieren provisto

For additional translation possibilities see chart A.
+*This is the irregular form. The regular* participio/*past participle,* proveído, *exists but is less commonly used.*

99

IX. Irregular verbs

VERBS OF THIS CATEGORY

*desproveer 20. (OC)
*proveer 20. (OC)

OC = Orthographic/Spelling Change
* These verbs have orthographic/spelling changes in addition to their irregularity. The cross reference number following each verb indicates the category of verbs to which these orthographic/spelling changes belong.

100 model: PUDRIR or PODRIR

TIEMPOS SIMPLES
SIMPLE TENSES

PRESENTE DE INDICATIVO *PRESENT INDICATIVE*	PRETÉRITO IMPERFECTO DE INDICATIVO *IMPERFECT INDICATIVE*	PRETÉRITO INDEFINIDO DE INDICATIVO *PRETERITE INDICATIVE*	FUTURO IMPERFECTO DE INDICATIVO *FUTURE INDICATIVE*	POTENCIAL SIMPLE *CONDITIONAL*
I rot, etc.	*I was rotting, etc.*	*I rotted, etc.*	*I will rot, etc.*	*I would rot, etc.*
pudro	pudría	pudrí	pudriré	pudriría
pudres	pudrías	pudriste	pudrirás	pudrirías
pudre	pudría	pudrió	pudrirá	pudriría
pudrimos	pudríamos	pudrimos	pudriremos	pudriríamos
pudrís	pudríais	pudristeis	pudriréis	pudriríais
pudren	pudrían	pudrieron	pudrirán	pudrirían

PRESENTE DE SUBJUNTIVO *PRESENT SUBJUNCTIVE*	PRETÉRITO IMPERFECTO DE SUBJUNTIVO *PAST (IMPERFECT) SUBJUNCTIVE*		FUTURO IMPERFECTO DE SUBJUNTIVO *FUTURE SUBJUNCTIVE*
I rot, etc.	*I rotted, etc.*		*I will rot, etc.*
pudra	pudriera	pudriese	pudriere
pudras	pudrieras	pudrieses	pudrieres
pudra	pudriera	pudriese	pudriere
pudramos	pudriéramos *or*	pudriésemos	pudriéremos
pudráis	pudrierais	pudrieseis	pudriereis
pudran	pudrieran	pudriesen	pudrieren

FORMAS IMPERATIVAS, GERUNDIOS Y PARTICIPIO
COMMANDS AND PARTICIPLES

FORMAS IMPERATIVAS *COMMANDS*		GERUNDIO Y PARTICIPIO *PARTICIPLES*		
AFIRMATIVA *AFFIRMATIVE*	NEGATIVA *NEGATIVE*	GERUNDIO SIMPLE *PRESENT PARTICIPLE*	PARTICIPIO *PAST PARTICIPLE*	GERUNDIO COMPUESTO *PERFECT PARTICIPLE*
rot	*don't rot*	*rotting*	*rotted*	*having rotted*
pudre (tú)	no pudras (tú)	pudriendo	podrido	habiendo podrido
pudra (Ud.)	no pudra (Ud.)			
pudrid (vosotros)	no pudráis (vosotros)			
pudran (Uds.)	no pudran (Uds.)			
let's rot	*let's not rot*			
pudramos	no pudramos			

INFINITIVO COMPUESTO: haber podrido
PERFECT INFINITIVE: to have rotted

TIEMPOS COMPUESTOS
PERFECT (COMPOUND) TENSES

PRETÉRITO PERFECTO DE INDICATIVO *PRESENT PERFECT INDICATIVE*	PRETÉRITO PLUSCUAMPERFECTO DE INDICATIVO *PAST PERFECT (PLUPERFECT) INDICATIVE*	PRETÉRITO ANTERIOR DE INDICATIVO *PRETERITE PERFECT INDICATIVE*	FUTURO PERFECTO DE INDICATIVO *FUTURE PERFECT INDICATIVE*	POTENCIAL COMPUESTO *CONDITIONAL PERFECT*
I have rotted, etc.	*I had rotted, etc.*	*I had rotted, etc.*	*I will have rotted, etc.*	*I would have rotted, etc.*
he podrido	había podrido	hube podrido	habré podrido	habría podrido
has podrido	habías podrido	hubiste podrido	habrás podrido	habrías podrido
ha podrido	había podrido	hubo podrido	habrá podrido	habría podrido
hemos podrido	habíamos podrido	hubimos podrido	habremos podrido	habríamos podrido
habéis podrido	habíais podrido	hubisteis podrido	habréis podrido	habríais podrido
han podrido	habían podrido	hubieron podrido	habrán podrido	habrían podrido

PRETÉRITO PERFECTO DE SUBJUNTIVO *PRESENT PERFECT SUBJUNCTIVE*	PRETÉRITO PLUSCUAMPERFECTO DE SUBJUNTIVO *PAST PERFECT (PLUPERFECT) SUBJUNCTIVE*		FUTURO PERFECTO DE SUBJUNTIVO *FUTURE PERFECT SUBJUNCTIVE*
I have rotted, etc.	*I had rotted, etc.*		*I will have rotted, etc.*
haya podrido	hubiera podrido	hubiese podrido	hubiere podrido
hayas podrido	hubieras podrido	hubieses podrido	hubieres podrido
haya podrido	hubiera podrido *or*	hubiese podrido	hubiere podrido
hayamos podrido	hubiéramos podrido	hubiésemos podrido	hubiéremos podrido
hayáis podrido	hubierais podrido	hubieseis podrido	hubiereis podrido
hayan podrido	hubieran podrido	hubiesen podrido	hubieren podrido

*For additional translation possibilities see chart A.

100

IX. Irregular verbs

VERBS OF THIS CATEGORY

podrir
pudrir

101 model: QUERER (ie)

TIEMPOS SIMPLES
SIMPLE TENSES

PRESENTE DE INDICATIVO *PRESENT INDICATIVE*	PRETÉRITO IMPERFECTO DE INDICATIVO *IMPERFECT INDICATIVE*	PRETÉRITO INDEFINIDO DE INDICATIVO *PRETERITE INDICATIVE*	FUTURO IMPERFECTO DE INDICATIVO *FUTURE INDICATIVE*	POTENCIAL SIMPLE *CONDITIONAL*
*I want, etc.**	*I was wanting, etc.**	*I wanted, etc.**	*I will want, etc.**	*I would want, etc.**
quiero	quería	quise	querré	querría
quieres	querías	quisiste	querrás	querrías
quiere	quería	quiso	querrá	querría
queremos	queríamos	quisimos	querremos	querríamos
queréis	queríais	quisisteis	querréis	querríais
quieren	querían	quisieron	querrán	querrían

PRESENTE DE SUBJUNTIVO *PRESENT SUBJUNCTIVE*	PRETÉRITO IMPERFECTO DE SUBJUNTIVO *PAST (IMPERFECT) SUBJUNCTIVE*		FUTURO IMPERFECTO DE SUBJUNTIVO *FUTURE SUBJUNCTIVE*
*I want, etc.**	*I wanted, etc.**		*I will want, etc.**
quiera	quisiera	quisiese	quisiere
quieras	quisieras	quisieses	quisieres
quiera	quisiera	quisiese	quisiere
queramos	quisiéramos _or_	quisiésemos	quisiéremos
queráis	quisierais	quisieseis	quisiereis
quieran	quisieran	quisiesen	quisieren

FORMAS IMPERATIVAS, GERUNDIOS Y PARTICIPIO
COMMANDS AND PARTICIPLES

FORMAS IMPERATIVAS *COMMANDS*		GERUNDIO Y PARTICIPIO *PARTICIPLES*		
AFIRMATIVA *AFFIRMATIVE*	NEGATIVA *NEGATIVE*	GERUNDIO SIMPLE *PRESENT PARTICIPLE*	PARTICIPIO *PAST PARTICIPLE*	GERUNDIO COMPUESTO *PERFECT PARTICIPLE*
want	*don't want*	*wanting*	*wanted*	*having wanted*
quiere (tú)	no quieras (tú)	queriendo	querido	habiendo querido
quiera (Ud.)	no quiera (Ud.)			
quered (vosotros)	no queráis (vosotros)			
quieran (Uds.)	no quieran (Uds.)			
let's want	*let's not want*			
queramos	no queramos			

INFINITIVO COMPUESTO: haber querido
PERFECT INFINITIVE: to have wanted

TIEMPOS COMPUESTOS
PERFECT (COMPOUND) TENSES

PRETÉRITO PERFECTO DE INDICATIVO *PRESENT PERFECT INDICATIVE*	PRETÉRITO PLUSCUAMPERFECTO DE INDICATIVO *PAST PERFECT (PLUPERFECT) INDICATIVE*	PRETÉRITO ANTERIOR DE INDICATIVO *PRETERITE PERFECT INDICATIVE*	FUTURO PERFECTO DE INDICATIVO *FUTURE PERFECT INDICATIVE*	POTENCIAL COMPUESTO *CONDITIONAL PERFECT*
I have wanted, etc.	*I had wanted, etc.*	*I had wanted, etc.*	*I will have wanted, etc.**	*I would have wanted, etc.**
he querido	había querido	hube querido	habré querido	habría querido
has querido	habías querido	hubiste querido	habrás querido	habrías querido
ha querido	había querido	hubo querido	habrá querido	habría querido
hemos querido	habíamos querido	hubimos querido	habremos querido	habríamos querido
habéis querido	habíais querido	hubisteis querido	habréis querido	habríais querido
han querido	habían querido	hubieron querido	habrán querido	habrían querido

PRETÉRITO PERFECTO DE SUBJUNTIVO *PRESENT PERFECT SUBJUNCTIVE*	PRETÉRITO PLUSCUAMPERFECTO DE SUBJUNTIVO *PAST PERFECT (PLUPERFECT) SUBJUNCTIVE*		FUTURO PERFECTO DE SUBJUNTIVO *FUTURE PERFECT SUBJUNCTIVE*
*I have wanted, etc.**	*I had wanted, etc.**		*I will have wanted, etc.**
haya querido	hubiera querido	hubiese querido	hubiere querido
hayas querido	hubieras querido	hubieses querido	hubieres querido
haya querido	hubiera querido	hubiese querido	hubiere querido
hayamos querido	hubiéramos querido _or_	hubiésemos querido	hubiéremos querido
hayáis querido	hubierais querido	hubieseis querido	hubiereis querido
hayan querido	hubieran querido	hubiesen querido	hubieren querido

*For additional translation possibilities see chart A.

101

IX. Irregular verbs

*bienquerer (ie) 39. (RC)
*malquerer (ie) 39. (RC)
*querer (ie) 39. (RC)

RC = Radical/Stem Change
* These verbs have radical/stem changes in addition to their irregularities. The cross reference number following each verb indicates the category of verbs to which these radical/stem changes belong.

102 model: RAER*

*Orthographic changing

TIEMPOS SIMPLES
SIMPLE TENSES

PRESENTE DE INDICATIVO *PRESENT INDICATIVE*	PRETÉRITO IMPERFECTO DE INDICATIVO *IMPERFECT INDICATIVE*	PRETÉRITO INDEFINIDO DE INDICATIVO *PRETERITE INDICATIVE*	FUTURO IMPERFECTO DE INDICATIVO *FUTURE INDICATIVE*	POTENCIAL SIMPLE *CONDITIONAL*
I scrape off, etc.	*I was scraping off, etc.*	*I scraped off, etc.*	*I will scrape off, etc.*	*I would scrape off, etc.*
raigo rayo	raía	raí	raeré	raería
raes raes	raías	raíste	raerás	raerías
rae or rae	raía	rayó	raerá	raería
raemos raemos	raíamos	raímos	raeremos	raeríamos
raéis raéis	raíais	raísteis	raeréis	raeríais
raen raen	raían	rayeron	raerán	raerían

PRESENTE DE SUBJUNTIVO *PRESENT SUBJUNCTIVE*	PRETÉRITO IMPERFECTO DE SUBJUNTIVO *PAST (IMPERFECT) SUBJUNCTIVE*		FUTURO IMPERFECTO DE SUBJUNTIVO *FUTURE SUBJUNCTIVE*
I scrape off, etc.	*I scraped off, etc.*		*I will scrape off, etc.*
raiga raya	rayera	rayese	rayere
raigas rayas	rayeras	rayeses	rayeres
raiga raya	rayera	rayese	rayere
raigamos or rayamos	rayéramos or rayésemos		rayéremos
raigáis rayáis	rayerais	rayeseis	rayereis
raigan rayan	rayeran	rayesen	rayeren

FORMAS IMPERATIVAS, GERUNDIOS Y PARTICIPIO
COMMANDS AND PARTICIPLES

FORMAS IMPERATIVAS *COMMANDS*		GERUNDIO Y PARTICIPIO *PARTICIPLES*		
AFIRMATIVA *AFFIRMATIVE*	NEGATIVA *NEGATIVE*	GERUNDIO SIMPLE *PRESENT PARTICIPLE*	PARTICIPIO *PAST PARTICIPLE*	GERUNDIO COMPUESTO *PERFECT PARTICIPLE*
scrape off	*don't scrape off*	*scraping off*	*scraped off*	*having scraped off*
rae (tú)	no raigas / no rayas (tú)	rayendo	raído	habiendo raído
raiga / raya (Ud.)	no raiga / no raya (Ud.)			
raed (vosotros)	no raigáis / no rayáis			
raigan / rayan (Uds.)	no raigan / no rayan (Uds.)			
let's scrape off	*let's not scrape off*			
raigamos / rayamos	no raigamos / no rayamos			

```
INFINITIVO COMPUESTO:  haber raído
PERFECT INFINITIVE:  to have scraped off
```

TIEMPOS COMPUESTOS
PERFECT (COMPOUND) TENSES

PRETÉRITO PERFECTO DE INDICATIVO *PRESENT PERFECT INDICATIVE*	PRETÉRITO PLUSCUAMPERFECTO DE INDICATIVO *PAST PERFECT (PLUPERFECT) INDICATIVE*	PRETÉRITO ANTERIOR DE INDICATIVO *PRETERITE PERFECT INDICATIVE*	FUTURO PERFECTO DE INDICATIVO *FUTURE PERFECT INDICATIVE*	POTENCIAL COMPUESTO *CONDITIONAL PERFECT*
I have scraped off, etc.	*I had scraped off, etc.*	*I had scraped off, etc.*	*I will have scraped off, etc.*	*I would have scraped off, etc.*
he raído	había raído	hube raído	habré raído	habría raído
has raído	habías raído	hubiste raído	habrás raído	habrías raído
ha raído	había raído	hubo raído	habrá raído	habría raído
hemos raído	habíamos raído	hubimos raído	habremos raído	habríamos raído
habéis raído	habíais raído	hubisteis raído	habréis raído	habríais raído
han raído	habían raído	hubieron raído	habrán raído	habrían raído

PRETÉRITO PERFECTO DE SUBJUNTIVO *PRESENT PERFECT SUBJUNCTIVE*	PRETÉRITO PLUSCUAMPERFECTO DE SUBJUNTIVO *PAST PERFECT (PLUPERFECT) SUBJUNCTIVE*		FUTURO PERFECTO DE SUBJUNTIVO *FUTURE PERFECT SUBJUNCTIVE*
I have scraped off, etc.	*I had scraped off, etc.*		*I will have scraped off, etc.*
haya raído	hubiera raído	hubiese raído	hubiere raído
hayas raído	hubieras raído	hubieses raído	hubieres raído
haya raído	hubiera raído	hubiese raído	hubiere raído
hayamos raído	hubiéramos raído or hubiésemos raído		hubiéremos raído
hayáis raído	hubierais raído	hubieseis raído	hubiereis raído
hayan raído	hubieran raído	hubiesen raído	hubieren raído

*For additional translation possibilities see chart A.

102

IX. Irregular verbs

VERBS OF THIS CATEGORY

---

*raer 20. (OC)
*raerse 20. (OC), 4. (R)

R = Reflexive
OC = Orthographic/Spelling Change
*These verbs have orthographic/spelling changes in addition to their irregularities. The cross reference number following each verb indicates the category of verbs to which these orthographic/spelling changes belong.

103 model: ROER*

*Orthographic changing

TIEMPOS SIMPLES
SIMPLE TENSES

PRESENTE DE INDICATIVO *PRESENT INDICATIVE*	PRETÉRITO IMPERFECTO DE INDICATIVO *IMPERFECT INDICATIVE*	PRETÉRITO INDEFINIDO DE INDICATIVO *PRETERITE INDICATIVE*	FUTURO IMPERFECTO DE INDICATIVO *FUTURE INDICATIVE*	POTENCIAL SIMPLE *CONDITIONAL*
*I gnaw, etc.**	*I was gnawing, etc.**	*I gnawed, etc.**	*I will gnaw, etc.**	*I would gnaw, etc.**
roo roigo royo	roía	roí	roeré	roería
roes roes roes	roías	roíste	roerás	roerías
roe roe roe	roía	royó	roerá	roería
roemos _or_ roemos _or_ roemos	roíamos	roímos	roeremos	roeríamos
roéis roéis roéis	roíais	roísteis	roeréis	roeríais
roen roen roen	roían	royeron	roerán	roerían

PRESENTE DE SUBJUNTIVO *PRESENT SUBJUNCTIVE*	PRETÉRITO IMPERFECTO DE SUBJUNTIVO *PAST (IMPERFECT) SUBJUNCTIVE*		FUTURO IMPERFECTO DE SUBJUNTIVO *FUTURE SUBJUNCTIVE*
*I gnaw, etc.**	*I gnawed, etc.**		*I will gnaw, etc.**
roa roiga roya	royera	royese	royere
roas roigas royas	royeras	royeses	royeres
roa roiga roya	royera	royese	royere
roamos _or_ roigamos _or_ royamos	royéramos _or_	royésemos	royéremos
roáis roigáis royáis	royerais	royeseis	royereis
roan roigan royan	royeran	royesen	royeren

FORMAS IMPERATIVAS, GERUNDIOS Y PARTICIPIO
COMMANDS AND PARTICIPLES

FORMAS IMPERATIVAS *COMMANDS*		GERUNDIO Y PARTICIPIO *PARTICIPLES*		
AFIRMATIVA *AFFIRMATIVE*	NEGATIVA *NEGATIVE*	GERUNDIO SIMPLE *PRESENT PARTICIPLE*	PARTICIPIO *PAST PARTICIPLE*	GERUNDIO COMPUESTO *PERFECT PARTICIPLE*
gnaw	*don't gnaw*	*gnawing*	*gnawed*	*having gnawed*
roe (tú)	no roas (tú)	royendo	roído	habiendo roído
roa / roiga / roya (Ud.)	no roa /no roiga /no roya			
roed (vosotros)	no roáis/no roigáis/no royáis			
roan / roigan / royan (Uds.)	no roan /no roigan /no royan			
let's gnaw	*let's not gnaw*			
roamos / roigamos / royamos	no roamos/no roigamos/no royamos			

INFINITIVO COMPUESTO: haber roído
PERFECT INFINITIVE: to have gnawed

TIEMPOS COMPUESTOS
PERFECT (COMPOUND) TENSES

PRETÉRITO PERFECTO DE INDICATIVO *PRESENT PERFECT INDICATIVE*	PRETÉRITO PLUSCUAMPERFECTO DE INDICATIVO *PAST PERFECT (PLUPERFECT) INDICATIVE*	PRETÉRITO ANTERIOR DE INDICATIVO *PRETERITE PERFECT INDICATIVE*	FUTURO PERFECTO DE INDICATIVO *FUTURE PERFECT INDICATIVE*	POTENCIAL COMPUESTO *CONDITIONAL PERFECT*
I have gnawed, etc.	*I had gnawed, etc.*	*I had gnawed, etc.*	*I will have gnawed, etc.**	*I would have gnawed, etc.**
he roído	había roído	hube roído	habré roído	habría roído
has roído	habías roído	hubiste roído	habrás roído	habrías roído
ha roído	había roído	hubo roído	habrá roído	habría roído
hemos roído	habíamos roído	hubimos roído	habremos roído	habríamos roído
habéis roído	habíais roído	hubisteis roído	habréis roído	habríais roído
han roído	habían roído	hubieron roído	habrán roído	habrían roído

PRETÉRITO PERFECTO DE SUBJUNTIVO *PRESENT PERFECT SUBJUNCTIVE*	PRETÉRITO PLUSCUAMPERFECTO DE SUBJUNTIVO *PAST PERFECT (PLUPERFECT) SUBJUNCTIVE*		FUTURO PERFECTO DE SUBJUNTIVO *FUTURE PERFECT SUBJUNCTIVE*
*I have gnawed, etc.**	*I had gnawed, etc.**		*I will have gnawed, etc.**
haya roído	hubiera roído	hubiese roído	hubiere roído
hayas roído	hubieras roído	hubieses roído	hubieres roído
haya roído	hubiera roído	hubiese roído	hubiere roído
hayamos roído	hubiéramos roído _or_	hubiésemos roído	hubiéremos roído
hayáis roído	hubierais roído	hubieseis roído	hubiereis roído
hayan roído	hubieran roído	hubiesen roído	hubieren roído

*For additional translation possibilities see chart A.

103

VERBS OF THIS CATEGORY

*corroer 20. (OC)
*roer 20. (OC)

OC = Orthographic/Spelling Change
*These verbs have orthographic/spelling changes in addition to their irregularities. The cross reference number following each verb indicates the category of verbs to which these orthographic/spelling changes belong.

104 model: ROMPER

TIEMPOS SIMPLES
SIMPLE TENSES

PRESENTE DE INDICATIVO *PRESENT INDICATIVE*	PRETÉRITO IMPERFECTO DE INDICATIVO *IMPERFECT INDICATIVE*	PRETÉRITO INDEFINIDO DE INDICATIVO *PRETERITE INDICATIVE*	FUTURO IMPERFECTO DE INDICATIVO *FUTURE INDICATIVE*	POTENCIAL SIMPLE *CONDITIONAL*
I break, etc.*	*I was breaking, etc.**	*I broke, etc.**	*I will break, etc.**	*I would break, etc.**
rompo	rompía	rompí	romperé	rompería
rompes	rompías	rompiste	romperás	romperías
rompe	rompía	rompió	romperá	rompería
rompemos	rompíamos	rompimos	romperemos	romperíamos
rompéis	rompíais	rompisteis	romperéis	romperíais
rompen	rompían	rompieron	romperán	romperían

PRESENTE DE SUBJUNTIVO *PRESENT SUBJUNCTIVE*	PRETÉRITO IMPERFECTO DE SUBJUNTIVO *PAST (IMPERFECT) SUBJUNCTIVE*		FUTURO IMPERFECTO DE SUBJUNTIVO *FUTURE SUBJUNCTIVE*
I break, etc.*	*I broke, etc.**		*I will break, etc.**
rompa	rompiera	rompiese	rompiere
rompas	rompieras	rompieses	rompieres
rompa	rompiera	rompiese	rompiere
rompamos	rompiéramos *or*	rompiésemos	rompiéremos
rompáis	rompierais	rompieseis	rompiereis
rompan	rompieran	rompiesen	rompieren

FORMAS IMPERATIVAS, GERUNDIOS Y PARTICIPIO
COMMANDS AND PARTICIPLES

FORMAS IMPERATIVAS *COMMANDS*		GERUNDIO Y PARTICIPIO *PARTICIPLES*		
AFIRMATIVA *AFFIRMATIVE*	NEGATIVA *NEGATIVE*	GERUNDIO SIMPLE *PRESENT PARTICIPLE*	PARTICIPIO *PAST PARTICIPLE*	GERUNDIO COMPUESTO *PERFECT PARTICIPLE*
break	*don't break*	*breaking*	*broken*	*having broken*
rompe (tú)	no rompas (tú)	rompiendo	roto	habiendo roto
rompa (Ud.)	no rompa (Ud.)			
romped (vosotros)	no rompáis (vosotros)			
rompan (Uds.)	no rompan (Uds.)			
let's break	*let's not break*			
rompamos	no rompamos			

INFINITIVO COMPUESTO: haber roto
PERFECT INFINITIVE: *to have broken*

TIEMPOS COMPUESTOS
PERFECT (COMPOUND) TENSES

PRETÉRITO PERFECTO DE INDICATIVO *PRESENT PERFECT INDICATIVE*	PRETÉRITO PLUSCUAMPERFECTO DE INDICATIVO *PAST PERFECT (PLUPERFECT) INDICATIVE*	PRETÉRITO ANTERIOR DE INDICATIVO *PRETERITE PERFECT INDICATIVE*	FUTURO PERFECTO DE INDICATIVO *FUTURE PERFECT INDICATIVE*	POTENCIAL COMPUESTO *CONDITIONAL PERFECT*
I have broken, etc.	*I had broken, etc.*	*I had broken, etc.*	*I will have broken, etc.**	*I would have broken, etc.**
he roto	había roto	hube roto	habré roto	habría roto
has roto	habías roto	hubiste roto	habrás roto	habrías roto
ha roto	había roto	hubo roto	habrá roto	habría roto
hemos roto	habíamos roto	hubimos roto	habremos roto	habríamos roto
habéis roto	habíais roto	hubisteis roto	habréis roto	habríais roto
han roto	habían roto	hubieron roto	habrán roto	habrían roto

PRETÉRITO PERFECTO DE SUBJUNTIVO *PRESENT PERFECT SUBJUNCTIVE*	PRETÉRITO PLUSCUAMPERFECTO DE SUBJUNTIVO *PAST PERFECT (PLUPERFECT) SUBJUNCTIVE*		FUTURO PERFECTO DE SUBJUNTIVO *FUTURE PERFECT SUBJUNCTIVE*
I have broken, etc.*	*I had broken, etc.**		*I will have broken, etc.**
haya roto	hubiera roto	hubiese roto	hubiere roto
hayas roto	hubieras roto	hubieses roto	hubieres roto
haya roto	hubiera roto	hubiese roto	hubiere roto
hayamos roto	hubiéramos roto *or*	hubiésemos roto	hubiéremos roto
hayáis roto	hubierais roto	hubieseis roto	hubiereis roto
hayan roto	hubieran roto	hubiesen roto	hubieren roto

VERBS OF THIS CATEGORY

arromper
romper

Compounds of romper *NOT following this pattern:*
corromper (regular-2.)
corromperse (regular-2.), 4. (R)

R = Reflexive

105 model: SABER

TIEMPOS SIMPLES
SIMPLE TENSES

PRESENTE DE INDICATIVO *PRESENT INDICATIVE*	PRETÉRITO IMPERFECTO DE INDICATIVO *IMPERFECT INDICATIVE*	PRETÉRITO INDEFINIDO DE INDICATIVO *PRETERITE INDICATIVE*	FUTURO IMPERFECTO DE INDICATIVO *FUTURE INDICATIVE*	POTENCIAL SIMPLE *CONDITIONAL*
I know, etc. *	*I was knowing, etc.* *	*I knew, etc.* *	*I will know, etc.* *	*I would know, etc.* *
sé	sabía	supe	sabré	sabría
sabes	sabías	supiste	sabrás	sabrías
sabe	sabía	supo	sabrá	sabría
sabemos	sabíamos	supimos	sabremos	sabríamos
sabéis	sabíais	supisteis	sabréis	sabríais
saben	sabían	supieron	sabrán	sabrían

PRESENTE DE SUBJUNTIVO *PRESENT SUBJUNCTIVE*	PRETÉRITO IMPERFECTO DE SUBJUNTIVO *PAST (IMPERFECT) SUBJUNCTIVE*		FUTURO IMPERFECTO DE SUBJUNTIVO *FUTURE SUBJUNCTIVE*
I know, etc. *	*I knew, etc.* *		*I will know, etc.* *
sepa	supiera	supiese	supiere
sepas	supieras	supieses	supieres
sepa	supiera	supiese	supiere
sepamos	supiéramos *or*	supiésemos	supiéremos
sepáis	supierais	supieseis	supiereis
sepan	supieran	supiesen	supieren

FORMAS IMPERATIVAS, GERUNDIOS Y PARTICIPIO
COMMANDS AND PARTICIPLES

FORMAS IMPERATIVAS *COMMANDS*		GERUNDIO Y PARTICIPIO *PARTICIPLES*		
AFIRMATIVA *AFFIRMATIVE*	NEGATIVA *NEGATIVE*	GERUNDIO SIMPLE *PRESENT PARTICIPLE*	PARTICIPIO *PAST PARTICIPLE*	GERUNDIO COMPUESTO *PERFECT PARTICIPLE*
know	*don't know*	*knowing*	*known*	*having known*
sabe (tú)	no sepas (tú)	sabiendo	sabido	habiendo sabido
sepa (Ud.)	no sepa (Ud.)			
sabed (vosotros)	no sepáis (vosotros)			
sepan (Uds.)	no sepan (Uds.)			
let's know	*let's not know*			
sepamos	no sepamos			

INFINITIVO COMPUESTO: haber sabido
PERFECT INFINITIVE: to have known

TIEMPOS COMPUESTOS
PERFECT (COMPOUND) TENSES

PRETÉRITO PERFECTO DE INDICATIVO *PRESENT PERFECT INDICATIVE*	PRETÉRITO PLUSCUAMPERFECTO DE INDICATIVO *PAST PERFECT (PLUPERFECT) INDICATIVE*	PRETÉRITO ANTERIOR DE INDICATIVO *PRETERITE PERFECT INDICATIVE*	FUTURO PERFECTO DE INDICATIVO *FUTURE PERFECT INDICATIVE*	POTENCIAL COMPUESTO *CONDITIONAL PERFECT*
I have known, etc.	*I had known, etc.*	*I had known, etc.*	*I will have known, etc.* *	*I would have known, etc.* *
he sabido	había sabido	hube sabido	habré sabido	habría sabido
has sabido	habías sabido	hubiste sabido	habrás sabido	habrías sabido
ha sabido	había sabido	hubo sabido	habrá sabido	habría sabido
hemos sabido	habíamos sabido	hubimos sabido	habremos sabido	habríamos sabido
habéis sabido	habíais sabido	hubisteis sabido	habréis sabido	habríais sabido
han sabido	habían sabido	hubieron sabido	habrán sabido	habrían sabido

PRETÉRITO PERFECTO DE SUBJUNTIVO *PRESENT PERFECT SUBJUNCTIVE*	PRETÉRITO PLUSCUAMPERFECTO DE SUBJUNTIVO *PAST PERFECT (PLUPERFECT) SUBJUNCTIVE*		FUTURO PERFECTO DE SUBJUNTIVO *FUTURE PERFECT SUBJUNCTIVE*
I have known, etc. *	*I had known, etc.* *		*I will have known, etc.* *
haya sabido	hubiera sabido	hubiese sabido	hubiere sabido
hayas sabido	hubieras sabido	hubieses sabido	hubieres sabido
haya sabido	hubiera sabido	hubiese sabido	hubiere sabido
hayamos sabido	hubiéramos sabido *or*	hubiésemos sabido	hubiéremos sabido
hayáis sabido	hubierais sabido	hubieseis sabido	hubiereis sabido
hayan sabido	hubieran sabido	hubiesen sabido	hubieren sabido

*For additional translation possibilities see chart A.

IX. Irregular verbs

VERBS OF THIS CATEGORY

resaber
saber
saberse 4. (R)

R = Reflexive

106 model: SALIR

PRESENTE DE INDICATIVO *PRESENT INDICATIVE*	PRETÉRITO IMPERFECTO DE INDICATIVO *IMPERFECT INDICATIVE*	PRETÉRITO INDEFINIDO DE INDICATIVO *PRETERITE INDICATIVE*	FUTURO IMPERFECTO DE INDICATIVO *FUTURE INDICATIVE*	POTENCIAL SIMPLE *CONDITIONAL*
*I leave, etc.**	*I was leaving, etc.**	*I left, etc.**	*I will leave, etc.**	*I would leave, etc.**
salgo	salía	salí	saldré	saldría
sales	salías	saliste	saldrás	saldrías
sale	salía	salió	saldrá	saldría
salimos	salíamos	salimos	saldremos	saldríamos
salís	salíais	salisteis	saldréis	saldríais
salen	salían	salieron	saldrán	saldrían

PRESENTE DE SUBJUNTIVO *PRESENT SUBJUNCTIVE*	PRETÉRITO IMPERFECTO DE SUBJUNTIVO *PAST (IMPERFECT) SUBJUNCTIVE*		FUTURO IMPERFECTO DE SUBJUNTIVO *FUTURE SUBJUNCTIVE*
*I leave, etc.**	*I left, etc.**		*I will leave, etc.**
salga	saliera	saliese	saliere
salgas	salieras	salieses	salieres
salga	saliera	saliese	saliere
salgamos	saliéramos *or*	saliésemos	saliéremos
salgáis	salierais	salieseis	saliereis
salgan	salieran	saliesen	salieren

FORMAS IMPERATIVAS *COMMANDS*		GERUNDIO Y PARTICIPIO *PARTICIPLES*		
AFIRMATIVA *AFFIRMATIVE*	NEGATIVA *NEGATIVE*	GERUNDIO SIMPLE *PRESENT PARTICIPLE*	PARTICIPIO *PAST PARTICIPLE*	GERUNDIO COMPUESTO *PERFECT PARTICIPLE*
leave	*don't leave*	*leaving*	*left*	*having left*
sal (tú)	no salgas (tú)	saliendo	salido	habiendo salido
salga (Ud.)	no salga (Ud.)			
salid (vosotros)	no salgáis (vosotros)			
salgan (Uds.)	no salgan (Uds.)			
let's leave	*let's not leave*			
salgamos	no salgamos			

> INFINITIVO COMPUESTO: haber salido
> *PERFECT INFINITIVE: to have left*

PRETÉRITO PERFECTO DE INDICATIVO *PRESENT PERFECT INDICATIVE*	PRETÉRITO PLUSCUAMPERFECTO DE INDICATIVO *PAST PERFECT (PLUPERFECT) INDICATIVE*	PRETÉRITO ANTERIOR DE INDICATIVO *PRETERITE PERFECT INDICATIVE*	FUTURO PERFECTO DE INDICATIVO *FUTURE PERFECT INDICATIVE*	POTENCIAL COMPUESTO *CONDITIONAL PERFECT*
I have left, etc.	*I had left, etc.*	*I had left, etc.*	*I will have left, etc.**	*I would have left, etc.**
he salido	había salido	hube salido	habré salido	habría salido
has salido	habías salido	hubiste salido	habrás salido	habrías salido
ha salido	había salido	hubo salido	habrá salido	habría salido
hemos salido	habíamos salido	hubimos salido	habremos salido	habríamos salido
habéis salido	habíais salido	hubisteis salido	habréis salido	habríais salido
han salido	habían salido	hubieron salido	habrán salido	habrían salido

PRETÉRITO PERFECTO DE SUBJUNTIVO *PRESENT PERFECT SUBJUNCTIVE*	PRETÉRITO PLUSCUAMPERFECTO DE SUBJUNTIVO *PAST PERFECT (PLUPERFECT) SUBJUNCTIVE*		FUTURO PERFECTO DE SUBJUNTIVO *FUTURE PERFECT SUBJUNCTIVE*
*I have left, etc.**	*I had left, etc.**		*I will have left, etc.**
haya salido	hubiera salido	hubiese salido	hubiere salido
hayas salido	hubieras salido	hubieses salido	hubieres salido
haya salido	hubiera salido	hubiese salido	hubiere salido
hayamos salido	hubiéramos salido *or*	hubiésemos salido	hubiéremos salido
hayáis salido	hubierais salido	hubieseis salido	hubiereis salido
hayan salido	hubieran salido	hubiesen salido	hubieren salido

*For additional translation possibilities see chart A.

VERBS OF THIS CATEGORY

salir
salirse 4. (R)
sobresalir

107 model: SER

TIEMPOS SIMPLES
SIMPLE TENSES

PRESENTE DE INDICATIVO *PRESENT INDICATIVE*	PRETÉRITO IMPERFECTO DE INDICATIVO *IMPERFECT INDICATIVE*	PRETÉRITO INDEFINIDO DE INDICATIVO *PRETERITE INDICATIVE*	FUTURO IMPERFECTO DE INDICATIVO *FUTURE INDICATIVE*	POTENCIAL SIMPLE *CONDITIONAL*
I am, etc.	*I was, etc.*	*I was, etc.*	*I will be, etc.*	*I would be, etc.*
soy	era	fui	seré	sería
eres	eras	fuiste	serás	serías
es	era	fue	será	sería
somos	éramos	fuimos	seremos	seríamos
sois	erais	fuisteis	seréis	seríais
son	eran	fueron	serán	serían

PRESENTE DE SUBJUNTIVO *PRESENT SUBJUNCTIVE*	PRETÉRITO IMPERFECTO DE SUBJUNTIVO *PAST (IMPERFECT) SUBJUNCTIVE*		FUTURO IMPERFECTO DE SUBJUNTIVO *FUTURE SUBJUNCTIVE*
I am, etc.	*I was, etc.*		*I will be, etc.*
sea	fuera	fuese	fuere
seas	fueras	fueses	fueres
sea	fuera _or_	fuese	fuere
seamos	fuéramos	fuésemos	fuéremos
seáis	fuerais	fueseis	fuereis
sean	fueran	fuesen	fueren

FORMAS IMPERATIVAS, GERUNDIOS Y PARTICIPIO
COMMANDS AND PARTICIPLES

FORMAS IMPERATIVAS *COMMANDS*		GERUNDIO Y PARTICIPIO *PARTICIPLES*		
AFIRMATIVA *AFFIRMATIVE*	NEGATIVA *NEGATIVE*	GERUNDIO SIMPLE *PRESENT PARTICIPLE*	PARTICIPIO *PAST PARTICIPLE*	GERUNDIO COMPUESTO *PERFECT PARTICIPLE*
be	*don't be*	*being*	*been*	*having been*
sé (tú)	no seas (tú)	siendo	sido	habiendo sido
sea (Ud.)	no sea (Ud.)			
sed (vosotros)	no seáis (vosotros)			
sean (Uds.)	no sean (Uds.)			
let's be	*let's not be*			
seamos	no seamos			

INFINITIVO COMPUESTO: haber sido
PERFECT INFINITIVE: to have been

TIEMPOS COMPUESTOS
PERFECT (COMPOUND) TENSES

PRETÉRITO PERFECTO DE INDICATIVO *PRESENT PERFECT INDICATIVE*	PRETÉRITO PLUSCUAMPERFECTO DE INDICATIVO *PAST PERFECT (PLUPERFECT) INDICATIVE*	PRETÉRITO ANTERIOR DE INDICATIVO *PRETERITE PERFECT INDICATIVE*	FUTURO PERFECTO DE INDICATIVO *FUTURE PERFECT INDICATIVE*	POTENCIAL COMPUESTO *CONDITIONAL PERFECT*
I have been, etc.	*I had been, etc.*	*I had been, etc.*	*I will have been, etc.*	*I would have been, etc.*
he sido	había sido	hube sido	habré sido	habría sido
has sido	habías sido	hubiste sido	habrás sido	habrías sido
ha sido	había sido	hubo sido	habrá sido	habría sido
hemos sido	habíamos sido	hubimos sido	habremos sido	habríamos sido
habéis sido	habíais sido	hubisteis sido	habréis sido	habríais sido
han sido	habían sido	hubieron sido	habrán sido	habrían sido

PRETÉRITO PERFECTO DE SUBJUNTIVO *PRESENT PERFECT SUBJUNCTIVE*	PRETÉRITO PLUSCUAMPERFECTO DE SUBJUNTIVO *PAST PERFECT (PLUPERFECT) SUBJUNCTIVE*		FUTURO PERFECTO DE SUBJUNTIVO *FUTURE PERFECT SUBJUNCTIVE*
I have been, etc.	*I had been, etc.*		*I will have been, etc.*
haya sido	hubiera sido	hubiese sido	hubiere sido
hayas sido	hubieras sido	hubieses sido	hubieres sido
haya sido	hubiera sido	hubiese sido	hubiere sido
hayamos sido	hubiéramos sido _or_	hubiésemos sido	hubiéremos sido
hayáis sido	hubierais sido	hubieseis sido	hubiereis sido
hayan sido	hubieran sido	hubiesen sido	hubieren sido

*For additional translation possibilities see chart A.

IX. Irregular verbs

VERB OF THIS CATEGORY

ser

108 model: TENER (ie)

TIEMPOS SIMPLES
SIMPLE TENSES

PRESENTE DE INDICATIVO *PRESENT INDICATIVE*	PRETÉRITO IMPERFECTO DE INDICATIVO *IMPERFECT INDICATIVE*	PRETÉRITO INDEFINIDO DE INDICATIVO *PRETERITE INDICATIVE*	FUTURO IMPERFECTO DE INDICATIVO *FUTURE INDICATIVE*	POTENCIAL SIMPLE *CONDITIONAL*
I have, etc.*	*I was having, etc.**	*I had, etc.**	*I will have, etc.**	*I would have, etc.**
tengo	tenía	tuve	tendré	tendría
tienes	tenías	tuviste	tendrás	tendrías
tiene	tenía	tuvo	tendrá	tendría
tenemos	teníamos	tuvimos	tendremos	tendríamos
tenéis	teníais	tuvisteis	tendréis	tendríais
tienen	tenían	tuvieron	tendrán	tendrían

PRESENTE DE SUBJUNTIVO *PRESENT SUBJUNCTIVE*	PRETÉRITO IMPERFECTO DE SUBJUNTIVO *PAST (IMPERFECT) SUBJUNCTIVE*		FUTURO IMPERFECTO DE SUBJUNTIVO *FUTURE SUBJUNCTIVE*
I have, etc.*	*I had, etc.**		*I will have, etc.**
tenga	tuviera	tuviese	tuviere
tengas	tuvieras	tuvieses	tuvieres
tenga	tuviera	tuviese	tuviere
tengamos	tuviéramos *or*	tuviésemos	tuviéremos
tengáis	tuvierais	tuvieseis	tuviereis
tengan	tuvieran	tuviesen	tuvieren

FORMAS IMPERATIVAS, GERUNDIOS Y PARTICIPIO
COMMANDS AND PARTICIPLES

FORMAS IMPERATIVAS *COMMANDS*		GERUNDIO Y PARTICIPIO *PARTICIPLES*		
AFIRMATIVA *AFFIRMATIVE*	NEGATIVA *NEGATIVE*	GERUNDIO SIMPLE *PRESENT PARTICIPLE*	PARTICIPIO *PAST PARTICIPLE*	GERUNDIO COMPUESTO *PERFECT PARTICIPLE*
have	*don't have*	*having*	*had*	*having had*
ten (tú)	no tengas (tú)	teniendo	tenido	habiendo tenido
tenga (Ud.)	no tenga (Ud.)			
tened (vosotros)	no tengáis (vosotros)			
tengan (Uds.)	no tengan (Uds.)			
let's have	*let's not have*			
tengamos	no tengamos			

INFINITIVO COMPUESTO: haber tenido
PERFECT INFINITIVE: to have had

TIEMPOS COMPUESTOS
PERFECT (COMPOUND) TENSES

PRETÉRITO PERFECTO DE INDICATIVO *PRESENT PERFECT INDICATIVE*	PRETÉRITO PLUSCUAMPERFECTO DE INDICATIVO *PAST PERFECT (PLUPERFECT) INDICATIVE*	PRETÉRITO ANTERIOR DE INDICATIVO *PRETERITE PERFECT INDICATIVE*	FUTURO PERFECTO DE INDICATIVO *FUTURE PERFECT INDICATIVE*	POTENCIAL COMPUESTO *CONDITIONAL PERFECT*
I have had, etc.	*I had had, etc.*	*I had had, etc.*	*I will have had, etc.**	*I would have had, etc.**
he tenido	había tenido	hube tenido	habré tenido	habría tenido
has tenido	habías tenido	hubiste tenido	habrás tenido	habrías tenido
ha tenido	había tenido	hubo tenido	habrá tenido	habría tenido
hemos tenido	habíamos tenido	hubimos tenido	habremos tenido	habríamos tenido
habéis tenido	habíais tenido	hubisteis tenido	habréis tenido	habríais tenido
han tenido	habían tenido	hubieron tenido	habrán tenido	habrían tenido

PRETÉRITO PERFECTO DE SUBJUNTIVO *PRESENT PERFECT SUBJUNCTIVE*	PRETÉRITO PLUSCUAMPERFECTO DE SUBJUNTIVO *PAST PERFECT (PLUPERFECT) SUBJUNCTIVE*		FUTURO PERFECTO DE SUBJUNTIVO *FUTURE PERFECT SUBJUNCTIVE*
I have had, etc.*	*I had had, etc.**		*I will have had, etc.**
haya tenido	hubiera tenido	hubiese tenido	hubiere tenido
hayas tenido	hubieras tenido	hubieses tenido	hubieres tenido
haya tenido	hubiera tenido	hubiese tenido	hubiere tenido
hayamos tenido	hubiéramos tenido *or*	hubiésemos tenido	hubiéremos tenido
hayáis tenido	hubierais tenido	hubieseis tenido	hubiereis tenido
hayan tenido	hubieran tenido	hubiesen tenido	hubieren tenido

*For additional translation possibilities see chart A.

VERBS OF THIS CATEGORY

---

*abstenerse (ie) 39. (RC) 4. (R)
*atenerse (ie) 39. (RC), 4. (R)
*contener (ie) 39. (RC)
*contenerse (ie) 39. (RC), 4. (R)
*detener (ie) 39. (RC)
*entretener (ie) 39. (RC)
*mantener (ie) 39. (RC)
*obtener (ie) 39. (RC)
*retener (ie) 39. (RC)
*sostener (ie) 39. (RC)
*tener (ie) 39. (RC)

R   = Reflexive
RC = Radical/Stem Change
*These verbs have radical/stem changes in addition to their irregularities. The cross reference number following each verb indicates the category of verbs to which these radical/stem changes belong.

TIEMPOS SIMPLES
SIMPLE TENSES

PRESENTE DE INDICATIVO *PRESENT INDICATIVE*	PRETÉRITO IMPERFECTO DE INDICATIVO *IMPERFECT INDICATIVE*	PRETÉRITO INDEFINIDO DE INDICATIVO *PRETERITE INDICATIVE*	FUTURO IMPERFECTO DE INDICATIVO *FUTURE INDICATIVE*	POTENCIAL SIMPLE *CONDITIONAL*
I bring, etc.*	*I was bringing, etc.**	*I brought, etc.**	*I will bring, etc.**	*I would bring, etc.**
traigo	traía	traje	traeré	traería
traes	traías	trajiste	traerás	traerías
trae	traía	trajo	traerá	traería
traemos	traíamos	trajimos	traeremos	traeríamos
traéis	traíais	trajisteis	traeréis	traeríais
traen	traían	trajeron	traerán	traerían

PRESENTE DE SUBJUNTIVO *PRESENT SUBJUNCTIVE*	PRETÉRITO IMPERFECTO DE SUBJUNTIVO *PAST (IMPERFECT) SUBJUNCTIVE*		FUTURO IMPERFECTO DE SUBJUNTIVO *FUTURE SUBJUNCTIVE*
I bring, etc.*	*I brought, etc.**		*I will bring, etc.**
traiga	trajera	trajese	trajere
traigas	trajeras	trajeses	trajeres
traiga	trajera	trajese	trajere
traigamos	trajéramos _or_	trajésemos	trajéremos
traigáis	trajerais	trajeseis	trajereis
traigan	trajeran	trajesen	trajeren

FORMAS IMPERATIVAS, GERUNDIOS Y PARTICIPIO
COMMANDS AND PARTICIPLES

FORMAS IMPERATIVAS *COMMANDS*		GERUNDIO Y PARTICIPIO *PARTICIPLES*		
AFIRMATIVA *AFFIRMATIVE*	NEGATIVA *NEGATIVE*	GERUNDIO SIMPLE *PRESENT PARTICIPLE*	PARTICIPIO *PAST PARTICIPLE*	GERUNDIO COMPUESTO *PERFECT PARTICIPLE*
bring	*don't bring*	*bringing*	*brought*	*having brought*
trae (tú)	no traigas (tú)	trayendo	traído	habiendo traído
traiga (Ud.)	no traiga (Ud.)			
traed (vosotros)	no traigáis (vosotros)			
traigan (Uds.)	no traigan (Uds.)			
let's bring	*let's not bring*			
traigamos	no traigamos			

INFINITIVO COMPUESTO: haber traído
PERFECT INFINITIVE: to have brought

TIEMPOS COMPUESTOS
PERFECT (COMPOUND) TENSES

PRETÉRITO PERFECTO DE INDICATIVO *PRESENT PERFECT INDICATIVE*	PRETÉRITO PLUSCUAMPERFECTO DE INDICATIVO *PAST PERFECT (PLUPERFECT) INDICATIVE*	PRETÉRITO ANTERIOR DE INDICATIVO *PRETERITE PERFECT INDICATIVE*	FUTURO PERFECTO DE INDICATIVO *FUTURE PERFECT INDICATIVE*	POTENCIAL COMPUESTO *CONDITIONAL PERFECT*
I have brought, etc.	*I had brought, etc.*	*I had brought, etc.*	*I will have brought, etc.**	*I would have brought, etc.**
he traído	había traído	hube traído	habré traído	habría traído
has traído	habías traído	hubiste traído	habrás traído	habrías traído
ha traído	había traído	hubo traído	habrá traído	habría traído
hemos traído	habíamos traído	hubimos traído	habremos traído	habríamos traído
habéis traído	habíais traído	hubisteis traído	habréis traído	habríais traído
han traído	habían traído	hubieron traído	habrán traído	habrían traído

PRETÉRITO PERFECTO DE SUBJUNTIVO *PRESENT PERFECT SUBJUNCTIVE*	PRETÉRITO PLUSCUAMPERFECTO DE SUBJUNTIVO *PAST PERFECT (PLUPERFECT) SUBJUNCTIVE*		FUTURO PERFECTO DE SUBJUNTIVO *FUTURE PERFECT SUBJUNCTIVE*
I have brought, etc.*	*I had brought, etc.**		*I will have brought, etc.**
haya traído	hubiera traído	hubiese traído	hubiere traído
hayas traído	hubieras traído	hubieses traído	hubieres traído
haya traído	hubiera traído	hubiese traído	hubiere traído
hayamos traído	hubiéramos traído _or_	hubiesemos traído	hubiéremos traído
hayáis traído	hubierais traído	hubieseis traído	hubiereis traído
hayan traído	hubieran traído	hubiesen traído	hubieren traído

*For additional translation possibilities see chart A.

VERBS OF THIS CATEGORY

*abstraer 20. (OC)
*abstraerse 20. (OC), 4. (R)
*atraer 20. (OC)
*contraer 20. (OC)
*detraer 20. (OC)
*distraer 20. (OC)
*extraer 20. (OC)
*maltraer 20. (OC)
*retraer 20. (OC)
*retraerse 20. (OC), 4. (R)
*retrotraer 20. (OC)
*substraer 20. (OC)
*substraerse 20. (OC), 4. (R)
*sustraer 20. (OC)
*sustraerse 20. (OC), 4. (R)
*traer 20. (OC)

R = Reflexive
OC = Orthographic/Spelling Change
*These verbs have orthographic/spelling changes in addition to their irregularities. The cross reference number following each verb indicates the category of verbs to which these orthographic/spelling changes belong.

110 model: VALER

TIEMPOS SIMPLES
SIMPLE TENSES

PRESENTE DE INDICATIVO *PRESENT INDICATIVE*	PRETÉRITO IMPERFECTO DE INDICATIVO *IMPERFECT INDICATIVE*	PRETÉRITO INDEFINIDO DE INDICATIVO *PRETERITE INDICATIVE*	FUTURO IMPERFECTO DE INDICATIVO *FUTURE INDICATIVE*	POTENCIAL SIMPLE *CONDITIONAL*
*I am worth, etc.**	*I was worth, etc.**	*I was worth, etc.**	*I will be worth, etc.**	*I would be worth, etc.**
valgo	valía	valí	valdré	valdría
vales	valías	valiste	valdrás	valdrías
vale	valía	valió	valdrá	valdría
valemos	valíamos	valimos	valdremos	valdríamos
valéis	valíais	valisteis	valdréis	valdríais
valen	valían	valieron	valdrán	valdrían

PRESENTE DE SUBJUNTIVO *PRESENT SUBJUNCTIVE*	PRETÉRITO IMPERFECTO DE SUBJUNTIVO *PAST (IMPERFECT) SUBJUNCTIVE*		FUTURO IMPERFECTO DE SUBJUNTIVO *FUTURE SUBJUNCTIVE*
*I am worth, etc.**	*I was worth, etc.**		*I will be worth, etc.**
valga	valiera	valiese	valiere
valgas	valieras	valieses	valieres
valga	valiera	valiese	valiere
valgamos	valiéramos *or*	valiésemos	valiéremos
valgáis	valierais	valieseis	valiereis
valgan	valieran	valiesen	valieren

FORMAS IMPERATIVAS, GERUNDIOS Y PARTICIPIO
COMMANDS AND PARTICIPLES

FORMAS IMPERATIVAS *COMMANDS*		GERUNDIO Y PARTICIPIO *PARTICIPLES*		
AFIRMATIVA *AFFIRMATIVE*	NEGATIVA *NEGATIVE*	GERUNDIO SIMPLE *PRESENT PARTICIPLE*	PARTICIPIO *PAST PARTICIPLE*	GERUNDIO COMPUESTO *PERFECT PARTICIPLE*
be worth	*don't be worth*	*being worth*	*been worth*	*having been worth*
vale / val+ (tú)	no valgas (tú)	valiendo	valido	habiendo valido
valga (Ud.)	no valga (Ud.)			
valed (vosotros)	no valgáis (vosotros)			
valgan (Uds.)	no valgan (Uds.)			
let's be worth	*let's not be worth*			
valgamos	no valgamos			

INFINITIVO COMPUESTO: haber valido
PERFECT INFINITIVE: to have been worth

TIEMPOS COMPUESTOS
PERFECT (COMPOUND) TENSES

PRETÉRITO PERFECTO DE INDICATIVO *PRESENT PERFECT INDICATIVE*	PRETÉRITO PLUSCUAMPERFECTO DE INDICATIVO *PAST PERFECT (PLUPERFECT) INDICATIVE*	PRETÉRITO ANTERIOR DE INDICATIVO *PRETERITE PERFECT INDICATIVE*	FUTURO PERFECTO DE INDICATIVO *FUTURE PERFECT INDICATIVE*	POTENCIAL COMPUESTO *CONDITIONAL PERFECT*
I have been worth, etc.	*I had been worth, etc.*	*I had been worth, etc.*	*I will have been worth, etc.**	*I would have been worth, etc.**
he valido	había valido	hube valido	habré valido	habría valido
has valido	habías valido	hubiste valido	habrás valido	habrías valido
ha valido	había valido	hubo valido	habrá valido	habría valido
hemos valido	habíamos valido	hubimos valido	habremos valido	habríamos valido
habéis valido	habíais valido	hubisteis valido	habréis valido	habríais valido
han valido	habían valido	hubieron valido	habrán valido	habrían valido

PRETÉRITO PERFECTO DE SUBJUNTIVO *PRESENT PERFECT SUBJUNCTIVE*	PRETÉRITO PLUSCUAMPERFECTO DE SUBJUNTIVO *PAST PERFECT (PLUPERFECT) SUBJUNCTIVE*		FUTURO PERFECTO DE SUBJUNTIVO *FUTURE PERFECT SUBJUNCTIVE*
*I have been worth, etc.**	*I had been worth, etc.**		*I will have been worth, etc.**
haya valido	hubiera valido	hubiese valido	hubiere valido
hayas valido	hubieras valido	hubieses valido	hubieres valido
haya valido	hubiera valido	hubiese valido	hubiere valido
hayamos valido	hubiéramos valido *or*	hubiésemos valido	hubiéremos valido
hayáis valido	hubierais valido	hubieseis valido	hubiereis valido
hayan valido	hubieran valido	hubiesen valido	hubieren valido

*For additional translation possibilities see chart A.
+This form is rather archaic.

[286]

110

IX. Irregular verbs

caler (This verb is impersonal, and thus is used only in the third person singular and plural, and in the infinitives, and present and past participles.)
equivaler
prevaler
valer
valerse 4. (R)

R = Reflexive

111 model: VENIR (ie, i)

PRESENTE DE INDICATIVO *PRESENT INDICATIVE*	PRETÉRITO IMPERFECTO DE INDICATIVO *IMPERFECT INDICATIVE*	PRETÉRITO INDEFINIDO DE INDICATIVO *PRETERITE INDICATIVE*	FUTURO IMPERFECTO DE INDICATIVO *FUTURE INDICATIVE*	POTENCIAL SIMPLE *CONDITIONAL*
*I come, etc.**	*I was coming, etc.**	*I came, etc.**	*I will come, etc.**	*I would come, etc.**
vengo	venía	vine	vendré	vendría
vienes	venías	viniste	vendrás	vendrías
viene	venía	vino	vendrá	vendría
venimos	veníamos	vinimos	vendremos	vendríamos
venís	veníais	vinisteis	vendréis	vendríais
vienen	venían	vinieron	vendrán	vendrían

PRESENTE DE SUBJUNTIVO *PRESENT SUBJUNCTIVE*	PRETÉRITO IMPERFECTO DE SUBJUNTIVO *PAST (IMPERFECT) SUBJUNCTIVE*		FUTURO IMPERFECTO DE SUBJUNTIVO *FUTURE SUBJUNCTIVE*
*I come, etc.**	*I came, etc.**		*I will come, etc.**
venga	viniera	viniese	viniere
vengas	vinieras	vinieses	vinieres
venga	viniera	viniese	viniere
vengamos	viniéramos *or*	viniésemos	viniéremos
vengáis	vinierais	vinieseis	viniereis
vengan	vinieran	viniesen	vinieren

FORMAS IMPERATIVAS, GERUNDIOS Y PARTICIPIO
COMMANDS AND PARTICIPLES

FORMAS IMPERATIVAS *COMMANDS*		GERUNDIO Y PARTICIPIO *PARTICIPLES*		
AFIRMATIVA *AFFIRMATIVE*	NEGATIVA *NEGATIVE*	GERUNDIO SIMPLE *PRESENT PARTICIPLE*	PARTICIPIO *PAST PARTICIPLE*	GERUNDIO COMPUESTO *PERFECT PARTICIPLE*
come	*don't come*	*coming*	*come*	*having come*
ven (tú)	no vengas (tú)	viniendo	venido	habiendo venido
venga (Ud.)	no venga (Ud.)			
venid (vosotros)	no vengáis (vosotros)			
vengan (Uds.)	no vengan (Uds.)			
let's come	*let's not come*			
vengamos	no vengamos			

INFINITIVO COMPUESTO: haber venido
PERFECT INFINITIVE: to have come

PRETÉRITO PERFECTO DE INDICATIVO *PRESENT PERFECT INDICATIVE*	PRETÉRITO PLUSCUAMPERFECTO DE INDICATIVO *PAST PERFECT (PLUPERFECT) INDICATIVE*	PRETÉRITO ANTERIOR DE INDICATIVO *PRETERITE PERFECT INDICATIVE*	FUTURO PERFECTO DE INDICATIVO *FUTURE PERFECT INDICATIVE*	POTENCIAL COMPUESTO *CONDITIONAL PERFECT*
I have come, etc.	*I had come, etc.*	*I had come, etc.*	*I will have come, etc.**	*I would have come, etc.**
he venido	había venido	hube venido	habré venido	habría venido
has venido	habías venido	hubiste venido	habrás venido	habrías venido
ha venido	había venido	hubo venido	habrá venido	habría venido
hemos venido	habíamos venido	hubimos venido	habremos venido	habríamos venido
habéis venido	habíais venido	hubisteis venido	habréis venido	habríais venido
han venido	habían venido	hubieron venido	habrán venido	habrían venido

PRETÉRITO PERFECTO DE SUBJUNTIVO *PRESENT PERFECT SUBJUNCTIVE*	PRETÉRITO PLUSCUAMPERFECTO DE SUBJUNTIVO *PAST PERFECT (PLUPERFECT) SUBJUNCTIVE*		FUTURO PERFECTO DE SUBJUNTIVO *FUTURE PERFECT SUBJUNCTIVE*
*I have come, etc.**	*I had come, etc.**		*I will have come, etc.**
haya venido	hubiera venido	hubiese venido	hubiere venido
hayas venido	hubieras venido	hubieses venido	hubieres venido
haya venido	hubiera venido	hubiese venido	hubiere venido
hayamos venido	hubiéramos venido *or*	hubiésemos venido	hubiéremos venido
hayáis venido	hubierais venido	hubieseis venido	hubiereis venido
hayan venido	hubieran venido	hubiesen venido	hubieren venido

*For additional translation possibilities see chart A.

[288]

111

IX. Irregular verbs

VERBS OF THIS CATEGORY

*advenir (ie, i) 41. (RC)
*avenir (ie, i) 41 (RC)
*avenirse (ie, i) 41. (RC), 4. (R)
*contravenir (ie, i) 41. (RC)
*convenir (ie, i) 41. (RC)
*desavenir (ie, i) 41. (RC)
*desavenirse (ie, i) 41. (RC), 4. (R)
*disconvenir (ie, i) 41. (RC)
*intervenir (ie, i) 41. (RC)
*prevenir (ie, i) 41. (RC)
*prevenirse (ie, i) 41. (RC), 4. (R)
*provenir (ie, i) 41. (RC)
*reconvenir (ie, i) 41. (RC)
*sobrevenir (ie, i) 41. (RC)
*subvenir (ie, i) 41. (RC)
*supervenir (ie, i) 41. (RC)
*venir (ie, i) 41. (RC)

R   = Reflexive
RC = Radical/Stem Change
*These verbs have radical/stem changes in addition to their irregularities. The cross reference number following each verb indicates the category of verbs to which these radical/stem changes belong.

112 model: VER

TIEMPOS SIMPLES
SIMPLE TENSES

PRESENTE DE INDICATIVO *PRESENT INDICATIVE*	PRETÉRITO IMPERFECTO DE INDICATIVO *IMPERFECT INDICATIVE*	PRETÉRITO INDEFINIDO DE INDICATIVO *PRETERITE INDICATIVE*	FUTURO IMPERFECTO DE INDICATIVO *FUTURE INDICATIVE*	POTENCIAL SIMPLE *CONDITIONAL*
I see, etc.*	*I was seeing, etc.**	*I saw, etc.**	*I will see, etc.**	*I would see, etc.**
veo	veía	vi	veré	vería
ves	veías	viste	verás	verías
ve	veía	vio	verá	vería
vemos	veíamos	vimos	veremos	veríamos
veis	veíais	visteis	veréis	veríais
ven	veían	vieron	verán	verían

PRESENTE DE SUBJUNTIVO *PRESENT SUBJUNCTIVE*	PRETÉRITO IMPERFECTO DE SUBJUNTIVO *PAST (IMPERFECT) SUBJUNCTIVE*		FUTURO IMPERFECTO DE SUBJUNTIVO *FUTURE SUBJUNCTIVE*
I see, etc.*	*I saw, etc.**		*I will see, etc.**
vea	viera	viese	viere
veas	vieras	vieses	vieres
vea	viera	viese	viere
veamos	viéramos *or*	viésemos	viéremos
veáis	vierais	vieseis	viereis
vean	vieran	viesen	vieren

FORMAS IMPERATIVAS, GERUNDIOS Y PARTICIPIO
COMMANDS AND PARTICIPLES

FORMAS IMPERATIVAS *COMMANDS*		GERUNDIO Y PARTICIPIO *PARTICIPLES*		
AFIRMATIVA *AFFIRMATIVE*	NEGATIVA *NEGATIVE*	GERUNDIO SIMPLE *PRESENT PARTICIPLE*	PARTICIPIO *PAST PARTICIPLE*	GERUNDIO COMPUESTO *PERFECT PARTICIPLE*
see	*don't see*	*seeing*	*seen*	*having seen*
ve (tú)	no veas (tú)	viendo	visto	habiendo visto
vea (Ud.)	no vea (Ud.)			
ved (vosotros)	no veáis (vosotros)			
vean (Uds.)	no vean (Uds.)			
let's see	*let's not see*			
veamos	no veamos			

INFINITIVO COMPUESTO: haber visto
PERFECT INFINITIVE: to have seen

TIEMPOS COMPUESTOS
PERFECT (COMPOUND) TENSES

PRETÉRITO PERFECTO DE INDICATIVO *PRESENT PERFECT INDICATIVE*	PRETÉRITO PLUSCUAMPERFECTO DE INDICATIVO *PAST PERFECT (PLUPERFECT) INDICATIVE*	PRETÉRITO ANTERIOR DE INDICATIVO *PRETERITE PERFECT INDICATIVE*	FUTURO PERFECTO DE INDICATIVO *FUTURE PERFECT INDICATIVE*	POTENCIAL COMPUESTO *CONDITIONAL PERFECT*
I have seen, etc.	*I had seen, etc.*	*I had seen, etc.*	*I will have seen, etc.**	*I would have seen, etc.**
he visto	había visto	hube visto	habré visto	habría visto
has visto	habías visto	hubiste visto	habrás visto	habrías visto
ha visto	había visto	hubo visto	habrá visto	habría visto
hemos visto	habíamos visto	hubimos visto	habremos visto	habríamos visto
habéis visto	habíais visto	hubisteis visto	habréis visto	habríais visto
han visto	habían visto	hubieron visto	habrán visto	habrían visto

PRETÉRITO PERFECTO DE SUBJUNTIVO *PRESENT PERFECT SUBJUNCTIVE*	PRETÉRITO PLUSCUAMPERFECTO DE SUBJUNTIVO *PAST PERFECT (PLUPERFECT) SUBJUNCTIVE*		FUTURO PERFECTO DE SUBJUNTIVO *FUTURE PERFECT SUBJUNCTIVE*
I have seen, etc.*	*I had seen, etc.**		*I will have seen, etc.**
haya visto	hubiera visto	hubiese visto	hubiere visto
hayas visto	hubieras visto	hubieses visto	hubieres visto
haya visto	hubiera visto	hubiese visto	hubiere visto
hayamos visto	hubiéramos visto *or*	hubiésemos visto	hubiéremos visto
hayáis visto	hubierais visto	hubieseis visto	hubiereis visto
hayan visto	hubieran visto	hubiesen visto	hubieren visto

For additional translation possibilities see chart A.

112

IX. Irregular verbs

VERBS OF THIS CATEGORY

antever
entrever
prever
rever
ver
verse 4. (R)

R = Reflexive

113 model: YACER

TIEMPOS SIMPLES
SIMPLE TENSES

PRESENTE DE INDICATIVO *PRESENT* *INDICATIVE*			PRETÉRITO IMPERFECTO DE INDICATIVO *IMPERFECT* *INDICATIVE*	PRETÉRITO INDEFINIDO DE INDICATIVO *PRETERITE* *INDICATIVE*	FUTURO IMPERFECTO DE INDICATIVO *FUTURE* *INDICATIVE*	POTENCIAL SIMPLE *CONDITIONAL*
*I lie, etc.**			*I was lying, etc.**	*I lay, etc.**	*I will lie, etc.**	*I would lie, etc.**
yazco	yazgo	yago	yacía	yací	yaceré	yacería
yaces	yaces	yaces	yacías	yaciste	yacerás	yacerías
yace	yace	yace	yacía	yació	yacerá	yacería
yacemos	yacemos	yacemos	yacíamos	yacimos	yaceremos	yaceríamos
yacéis	yacéis	yacéis	yacíais	yacisteis	yaceréis	yaceríais
yacen	yacen	yacen	yacían	yacieron	yacerán	yacerían

PRESENTE DE SUBJUNTIVO *PRESENT* *SUBJUNCTIVE*			PRETÉRITO IMPERFECTO DE SUBJUNTIVO *PAST (IMPERFECT)* *SUBJUNCTIVE*		FUTURO IMPERFECTO DE SUBJUNTIVO *FUTURE* *SUBJUNCTIVE*
*I lie, etc.**			*I lay, etc.**		*I will lie, etc.**
yazca *or* yazga *or* yaga			yaciera	yaciese	yaciere
yazcas	yazgas	yagas	yacieras	yacieses	yacieres
yazca	yazga	yaga	yaciera	yaciese	yaciere
yazcamos	yazgamos	yagamos	yaciéramos *or*	yaciésemos	yaciéremos
yazcáis	yazgáis	yagáis	yacierais	yacieseis	yaciereis
yazcan	yazgan	yagan	yacieran	yaciesen	yacieren

FORMAS IMPERATIVAS, GERUNDIOS Y PARTICIPIO
COMMANDS AND PARTICIPLES

FORMAS IMPERATIVAS *COMMANDS*		GERUNDIO Y PARTICIPIO *PARTICIPLES*		
AFIRMATIVA *AFFIRMATIVE*	NEGATIVA *NEGATIVE*	GERUNDIO SIMPLE *PRESENT PARTICIPLE*	PARTICIPIO *PAST PARTICIPLE*	GERUNDIO COMPUESTO *PERFECT PARTICIPLE*
lie	*don't lie*	*lying*	*lain*	*having lain*
yace / yaz (tú)	no yazcas/no yazgas/no yagas	yaciendo	yacido	habiendo yacido
yazca / yazga / yaga (Ud.)	no yazca /no yazga /no yaga			
yaced (vosotros)	no yazcáis/no yazgáis/no yagáis			
yazcan / yazgan / yagan (Uds.)	no yazcan / no yazgan/ no yagan			
let's lie	*let's not lie*			
yazcamos/yazgamos/yagamos	no yazcamos/no yazgamos/no yagamos			

INFINITIVO COMPUESTO: haber yacido
PERFECT INFINITIVE: to have lain

TIEMPOS COMPUESTOS
PERFECT (COMPOUND) TENSES

PRETÉRITO PERFECTO DE INDICATIVO *PRESENT PERFECT* *INDICATIVE*	PRETÉRITO PLUSCUAMPERFECTO DE INDICATIVO *PAST PERFECT (PLUPERFECT)* *INDICATIVE*	PRETÉRITO ANTERIOR DE INDICATIVO *PRETERITE PERFECT* *INDICATIVE*	FUTURO PERFECTO DE INDICATIVO *FUTURE PERFECT* *INDICATIVE*	POTENCIAL COMPUESTO *CONDITIONAL PERFECT*
I have lain, etc.	*I had lain, etc.*	*I had lain, etc.*	*I will have lain, etc.**	*I would have lain, etc.**
he yacido	había yacido	hube yacido	habré yacido	habría yacido
has yacido	habías yacido	hubiste yacido	habrás yacido	habrías yacido
ha yacido	había yacido	hubo yacido	habrá yacido	habría yacido
hemos yacido	habíamos yacido	hubimos yacido	habremos yacido	habríamos yacido
habéis yacido	habíais yacido	hubisteis yacido	habréis yacido	habríais yacido
han yacido	habían yacido	hubieron yacido	habrán yacido	habrían yacido

PRETÉRITO PERFECTO DE SUBJUNTIVO *PRESENT PERFECT* *SUBJUNCTIVE*	PRETÉRITO PLUSCUAMPERFECTO DE SUBJUNTIVO *PAST PERFECT (PLUPERFECT)* *SUBJUNCTIVE*		FUTURO PERFECTO DE SUBJUNTIVO *FUTURE PERFECT* *SUBJUNCTIVE*
*I have lain, etc.**	*I had lain, etc.**		*I will have lain, etc.**
haya yacido	hubiera yacido	hubiese yacido	hubiere yacido
hayas yacido	hubieras yacido	hubieses yacido	hubieres yacido
haya yacido	hubiera yacido	hubiese yacido	hubiere yacido
hayamos yacido	hubiéramos yacido *or*	hubiésemos yacido	hubiéremos yacido
hayáis yacido	hubierais yacido	hubieseis yacido	hubiereis yacido
hayan yacido	hubieran yacido	hubiesen yacido	hubieren yacido

*For additional translation possibilities see chart A.

113

IX. Irregular verbs

VERB OF THIS CATEGORY

yacer

Synopsis of location of orthographic changes, radical changes, and irregularities of irregular verbs

IX. Irregular verbs

INFINITIVO SIMPLE / PRESENT INFINITIVE	PRESENTE DE INDICATIVO / PRESENT INDICATIVE	PRESENTE DE SUBJUNTIVO / PRESENT SUBJUNCTIVE	FORMA IMPERATIVA AFIRMATIVA TÚ* / AFFIRMATIVE TÚ COMMAND*	PRETÉRITO IMPERFECTO DE INDICATIVO / IMPERFECT INDICATIVE	PRETÉRITO INDEFINIDO DE INDICATIVO / PRETERITE INDICATIVE	PRETÉRITO IMPERFECTO DE SUBJUNTIVO Y FUTURO IMPERFECTO DE SUBJUNTIVO / PAST (IMPERFECT) SUBJUNCTIVE AND FUTURE SUBJUNCTIVE	FUTURO IMPERFECTO DE INDICATIVO Y POTENCIAL SIMPLE / FUTURE INDICATIVE AND CONDITIONAL	GERUNDIO SIMPLE / PRESENT PARTICIPLE	PARTICIPIO / PAST PARTICIPLE
ending in -ducir (67)	I 1 sing	I all			I all	I all			
ending in -facer (68)	I 1 sing	I all	I		I all	I all			
ending in -scribir (69)									I
ending in -olver (ue) (70)	RC 1,2,3 sing 3 pl	RC 1,2,3 sing 3 pl							I
ending in -uir where u pronounced (71)	I 1,2,3 sing 3 pl				OC 3 sing 3 pl	OC all		OC	

ending in -güir (72)	I 1,2,3 sing 3 pl				OC 3 sing 3 pl	OC all		OC	
ending in vowel + cer (73)	I 1 sing	I all							
ending in vowel + cir (74)	I 1 sing	I all							
abrir (75)									I
adquirir (ie) (76)	RC 1,2,3 sing 3 pl / I because RC	RC 1,2,3 sing 3 pl / I because RC							
andar (77)					I 1,2,3 sing 3 pl	I all			
asir (78)	I 1 sing	I all							
bendecir (i, i) (79)	RC 2,3 sing 3 pl / I 1 sing	I all			I all	I all		RC	

Synopsis of location of orthographic changes, radical changes, and irregularities of irregular verbs

IX. Irregular verbs

INFINITIVO SIMPLE / PRESENT INFINITIVE	PRESENTE DE INDICATIVO / PRESENT INDICATIVE	PRESENTE DE SUBJUNTIVO / PRESENT SUBJUNCTIVE	FORMA IMPERATIVA AFIRMATIVA TÚ* / AFFIRMATIVE TÚ COMMAND*	PRETÉRITO IMPERFECTO DE INDICATIVO / IMPERFECT INDICATIVE	PRETÉRITO INDEFINIDO DE INDICATIVO / PRETERITE INDICATIVE	PRETÉRITO IMPERFECTO DE SUBJUNTIVO Y FUTURO IMPERFECTO DE SUBJUNTIVO / PAST (IMPERFECT) SUBJUNCTIVE AND FUTURE SUBJUNCTIVE	FUTURO IMPERFECTO DE INDICATIVO Y POTENCIAL SIMPLE / FUTURE INDICATIVE AND CONDITIONAL	GERUNDIO SIMPLE / PRESENT PARTICIPLE	PARTICIPIO / PAST PARTICIPLE
caber (80)	I 1 sing	I all			I all	I all	I all		
caer (81)	I 1 sing	I all			OC 2,3 sing 1,2,3 pl	OC all		OC	OC
cubrir (82)									I
dar (83)	I 1 sing	OC 1,3 sing			I all	I all			

Verb								
decir (i, i) (84)	RC 2,3 sing I 1 sing	I all	I all	I all	I	I all	RC	I
discernir (ie) (85)	RC 1,2,3 sing 3 pl	RC 1,2,3 sing 3 pl I not RC (i) 1,2 pl						
erguir (ie, i) (86)	OC 1,2,3 sing 3 pl RC 1,2,3 sing 3 pl I 1,2,3 sing 3 pl	OC 1,2,3 sing 3 pl RC all I 1,2,3 sing 3 pl	RC 3 sing 3 pl	RC all	RC			
estar (87)	I 1,2,3 sing 3 pl	I 1,2,3 sing 3 pl	I all	I all	I			
freír (i, i) (88)	OC 1,2,3 sing 3 pl RC 1,2,3 sing 3 pl	OC all RC all	OC 2,3 sing 1,2,3 pl RC 3 sing 3 pl	OC all RC all		OC RC	I and regular
haber (89)	I 1,2,3 sing 3 pl	I all	I all	I all	I			
hacer (90)	I 1 sing	I all	I all	I all	I	I		I
imprimir (91)								I and regular

[297]

114 Synopsis of location of orthographic changes, radical changes, and irregularities of irregular verbs

IX. Irregular verbs

INFINITIVO SIMPLE / PRESENT INFINITIVE	PRESENTE DE INDICATIVO / PRESENT INDICATIVE	PRESENTE DE SUBJUNTIVO / PRESENT SUBJUNCTIVE	FORMA IMPERATIVA AFIRMATIVA TÚ* / AFFIRMATIVE TÚ COMMAND*	PRETÉRITO IMPERFECTO DE INDICATIVO / IMPERFECT INDICATIVE	PRETÉRITO INDEFINIDO DE INDICATIVO / PRETERITE INDICATIVE	PRETÉRITO IMPERFECTO DE SUBJUNTIVO Y FUTURO IMPERFECTO DE SUBJUNTIVO / PAST (IMPERFECT) SUBJUNCTIVE AND FUTURE SUBJUNCTIVE	FUTURO IMPERFECTO DE INDICATIVO Y POTENCIAL SIMPLE / FUTURE INDICATIVE AND CONDITIONAL	GERUNDIO SIMPLE / PRESENT PARTICIPLE	PARTICIPIO / PAST PARTICIPLE
ir (92)	I all	I all	I	I all	I all	I all		OC	
jugar (ue) (93)	RC 1,2,3 sing 3 pl / I because RC	OC all / RC 1,2,3 sing 3 pl / I because RC			OC 1 sing				
morir (ue, u) (94)	RC 1,2,3 sing 3 pl	RC 1,2,3 sing 3 pl			RC 3 sing 3 pl	RC all		RC	I
oír (95)	OC 1 pl / I 1,2,3 sing 3 pl	I all			OC 2,3 sing 1,2,3 pl	OC all		OC	OC
placer (96)	I 1 sing	I all			regular and I 3 sing 3 pl	regular and I all			

[298]

poder (ue) (97)	RC 1,2,3 sing / 3 pl	RC 1,2,3 sing / 3 pl		I all	I all	I all	I	I
poner (98)	I 1 sing	I all		I all	I all	I all	I	I
proveer (99)			I	OC 3 sing / 3 pl	OC all		OC	OC
pudrir or podrir (100)	I							I
querer (ie) (101)	RC 1,2,3 sing / 3 pl	RC 1,2,3 sing / 3 pl		I all	I all	I all		I
raer (102)	I 1 sing	I all		OC 2,3 sing / 1,2,3 pl	OC all		OC	OC
roer (103)	I 1 sing and regular	I all and regular		OC 2,3 sing / 1,2,3 pl	OC all		OC	OC
romper (104)							I and regular	I

114

Synopsis of location of
orthographic changes, radical changes,
and irregularities of irregular verbs

IX. Irregular verbs

INFINITIVO SIMPLE / PRESENT INFINITIVE	PRESENTE DE INDICATIVO / PRESENT INDICATIVE	PRESENTE DE SUBJUNTIVO / PRESENT SUBJUNCTIVE	FORMA IMPERATIVA AFIRMATIVA TÚ / AFFIRMATIVE TÚ COMMAND*	PRETÉRITO IMPERFECTO DE INDICATIVO / IMPERFECT INDICATIVE	PRETÉRITO INDEFINIDO DE INDICATIVO / PRETERITE INDICATIVE	PRETÉRITO IMPERFECTO DE SUBJUNTIVO Y FUTURO IMPERFECTO DE SUBJUNTIVO / PAST (IMPERFECT) SUBJUNCTIVE AND FUTURE SUBJUNCTIVE	FUTURO IMPERFECTO DE INDICATIVO Y POTENCIAL SIMPLE / FUTURE INDICATIVE AND CONDITIONAL	GERUNDIO SIMPLE / PRESENT PARTICIPLE	PARTICIPIO / PAST PARTICIPLE
saber (105)	I 1 sing	I all			I all	I all	I all		
salir (106)	I 1 sing	I all	I				I all		
ser (107)	I all	I all	I	I all	I all	I all			
tener (ie) (108)	RC 2,3 sing / 3 pl; I 1 sing	I all	I		I all	I all	I all		
traer (109)	I 1 sing	I all			I all	I all		OC	OC

valer (110)	I 1 sing	I all					I all		
venir (ie, i) (111)	RC 2, 3 sing, 3 pl; I 1 sing	I all	I		I all	I all	I all	RC	
ver (112)	I 1 sing	I all		I all					I
yacer (113)	I 1 sing	I all	I and regular						

*Only those affirmative commands that are not derived from the present indicative are indicated here.

OC = Orthographic Change
RC = Radical Change
I = Irregular

[301]

115 Verb lacking various forms } model: ABARSE

TIEMPOS SIMPLES
SIMPLE TENSES

PRESENTE DE INDICATIVO **PRESENT INDICATIVE**	PRETÉRITO IMPERFECTO DE INDICATIVO **IMPERFECT INDICATIVE**	PRETÉRITO INDEFINIDO DE INDICATIVO **PRETERITE INDICATIVE**	FUTURO IMPERFECTO DE INDICATIVO **FUTURE INDICATIVE**	POTENCIAL SIMPLE **CONDITIONAL**
----	----	----	----	----
----	----	----	----	----
----	----	----	----	----
----	----	----	----	----
----	----	----	----	----

PRESENTE DE SUBJUNTIVO **PRESENT SUBJUNCTIVE**	PRETÉRITO IMPERFECTO DE SUBJUNTIVO **PAST (IMPERFECT) SUBJUNCTIVE**		FUTURO IMPERFECTO DE SUBJUNTIVO **FUTURE SUBJUNCTIVE**
----	----	----	----
----	----	----	----
----	----	----	----
----	----	----	----
----	----	----	----
----	----	----	----

FORMAS IMPERATIVAS, GERUNDIOS Y PARTICIPIO
COMMANDS AND PARTICIPLES

FORMAS IMPERATIVAS **COMMANDS**		GERUNDIO Y PARTICIPIO **PARTICIPLES**		
AFIRMATIVA **AFFIRMATIVE**	NEGATIVA **NEGATIVE**	GERUNDIO SIMPLE **PRESENT PARTICIPLE**	PARTICIPIO **PAST PARTICIPLE**	GERUNDIO COMPUESTO **PERFECT PARTICIPLE**
move aside				
ábate (tú)	----	----	----	----
----	----			
abaos[+] (vosotros)	----			

----	----			

INFINITIVO COMPUESTO: ----
PERFECT INFINITIVE: ----

TIEMPOS COMPUESTOS
PERFECT (COMPOUND) TENSES

PRETÉRITO PERFECTO DE INDICATIVO **PRESENT PERFECT INDICATIVE**	PRETÉRITO PLUSCUAMPERFECTO DE INDICATIVO **PAST PERFECT (PLUPERFECT) INDICATIVE**	PRETÉRITO ANTERIOR DE INDICATIVO **PRETERITE PERFECT INDICATIVE**	FUTURO PERFECTO DE INDICATIVO **FUTURE PERFECT INDICATIVE**	POTENCIAL COMPUESTO **CONDITIONAL PERFECT**
----	----	----	----	----
----	----	----	----	----
----	----	----	----	----
----	----	----	----	----
----	----	----	----	----

PRETÉRITO PERFECTO DE SUBJUNTIVO **PRESENT PERFECT SUBJUNCTIVE**	PRETÉRITO PLUSCUAMPERFECTO DE SUBJUNTIVO **PAST PERFECT (PLUPERFECT) SUBJUNCTIVE**		FUTURO PERFECTO DE SUBJUNTIVO **FUTURE PERFECT SUBJUNCTIVE**
----	----	----	----
----	----	----	----
----	----	----	----
----	----	----	----
----	----	----	----

[+]*Note the dropping of the* d *of the* vosotros *command when the reflexive pronoun* os *is attached.*

X. Defective verbs

VERB OF THIS CATEGORY

abarse 4. (R)

R = Reflexive

TIEMPOS SIMPLES
SIMPLE TENSES

PRESENTE DE INDICATIVO *PRESENT INDICATIVE*	PRETÉRITO IMPERFECTO DE INDICATIVO *IMPERFECT INDICATIVE*	PRETÉRITO INDEFINIDO DE INDICATIVO *PRETERITE INDICATIVE*	FUTURO IMPERFECTO DE INDICATIVO *FUTURE INDICATIVE*	POTENCIAL SIMPLE *CONDITIONAL*
we abolish, etc.*	*I was abolishing, etc.**	*I abolished, etc.**	*I will abolish, etc.**	*I would abolish, etc.**
----	abolía	abolí	aboliré	aboliría
----	abolías	aboliste	abolirás	abolirías
----	abolía	abolió	abolirá	aboliría
abolimos	abolíamos	abolimos	aboliremos	aboliríamos
abolís	abolíais	abolisteis	aboliréis	aboliríais
----	abolían	abolieron	abolirán	abolirían

PRESENTE DE SUBJUNTIVO *PRESENT SUBJUNCTIVE*	PRETÉRITO IMPERFECTO DE SUBJUNTIVO *PAST (IMPERFECT) SUBJUNCTIVE*		FUTURO IMPERFECTO DE SUBJUNTIVO *FUTURE SUBJUNCTIVE*
	I abolished, etc.*		*I will abolish, etc.**
----	aboliera	aboliese	aboliere
----	abolieras	abolieses	abolieres
----	aboliera	aboliese	aboliere
----	aboliéramos *or*	aboliésemos	aboliéremos
----	abolierais	abolieseis	aboliereis
----	abolieran	aboliesen	abolieren

FORMAS IMPERATIVAS, GERUNDIOS Y PARTICIPIO
COMMANDS AND PARTICIPLES

FORMAS IMPERATIVAS *COMMANDS*		GERUNDIO Y PARTICIPIO *PARTICIPLES*		
AFIRMATIVA *AFFIRMATIVE*	NEGATIVA *NEGATIVE*	GERUNDIO SIMPLE *PRESENT PARTICIPLE*	PARTICIPIO *PAST PARTICIPLE*	GERUNDIO COMPUESTO *PERFECT PARTICIPLE*
abolish	*don't abolish*	*abolishing*	*abolished*	*having abolished*
----	----	aboliendo	abolido	habiendo abolido
abolid (vosotros)	----			
----	----			
----	----			
----	----			

INFINITIVO COMPUESTO: haber abolido
PERFECT INFINITIVE: to have abolished

TIEMPOS COMPUESTOS
PERFECT (COMPOUND) TENSES

PRETÉRITO PERFECTO DE INDICATIVO *PRESENT PERFECT INDICATIVE*	PRETÉRITO PLUSCUAMPERFECTO DE INDICATIVO *PAST PERFECT (PLUPERFECT) INDICATIVE*	PRETÉRITO ANTERIOR DE INDICATIVO *PRETERITE PERFECT INDICATIVE*	FUTURO PERFECTO DE INDICATIVO *FUTURE PERFECT INDICATIVE*	POTENCIAL COMPUESTO *CONDITIONAL PERFECT*
I have abolished, etc.	*I had abolished, etc.*	*I had abolished, etc.*	*I will have abolished, etc.**	*I would have abolished, etc.**
he abolido	había abolido	hube abolido	habré abolido	habría abolido
has abolido	habías abolido	hubiste abolido	habrás abolido	habrías abolido
ha abolido	había abolido	hubo abolido	habrá abolido	habría abolido
hemos abolido	habíamos abolido	hubimos abolido	habremos abolido	habríamos abolido
habéis abolido	habíais abolido	hubisteis abolido	habréis abolido	habríais abolido
han abolido	habían abolido	hubieron abolido	habrán abolido	habrían abolido

PRETÉRITO PERFECTO DE SUBJUNTIVO *PRESENT PERFECT SUBJUNCTIVE*	PRETÉRITO PLUSCUAMPERFECTO DE SUBJUNTIVO *PAST PERFECT (PLUPERFECT) SUBJUNCTIVE*		FUTURO PERFECTO DE SUBJUNTIVO *FUTURE PERFECT SUBJUNCTIVE*
I have abolished, etc.*	*I had abolished, etc.**		*I will have abolished, etc.**
haya abolido	hubiera abolido	hubiese abolido	hubiere abolido
hayas abolido	hubieras abolido	hubieses abolido	hubieres abolido
haya abolido	hubiera abolido	hubiese abolido	hubiere abolido
hayamos abolido	hubiéramos abolido *or*	hubiésemos abolido	hubiéremos abolido
hayáis abolido	hubierais abolido	hubieseis abolido	hubiereis abolido
hayan abolido	hubieran abolido	hubiesen abolido	hubieren abolido

*For additional translation possibilities see chart A.

X. Defective verbs

abolir
agredir
aguerrir
arrecirse 4. (R)
aterirse 4. (R)
blandir
colorir
denegrir
despavorir
*desvaír 117. (OC) (defective)
*embaír 117. (OC) (defective)
empedernir
garantir
manir
transgredir
trasgredir

R   = Reflexive
OC = Orthographic/Spelling Change
*These verbs, in addition to being defective like the model verb on the chart given here, have orthographic/spelling changes. The cross reference number following each verb indicates the chart which shows the orthographic/spelling changes and the defective aspect of the verb together.

TIEMPOS SIMPLES
SIMPLE TENSES

PRESENTE DE INDICATIVO *PRESENT INDICATIVE*	PRETÉRITO IMPERFECTO DE INDICATIVO *IMPERFECT INDICATIVE*	PRETÉRITO INDEFINIDO DE INDICATIVO *PRETERITE INDICATIVE*	FUTURO IMPERFECTO DE INDICATIVO *FUTURE INDICATIVE*	POTENCIAL SIMPLE *CONDITIONAL*
*we trick, etc.**	*I was tricking, etc.**	*I tricked, etc.**	*I will trick, etc.**	*I would trick, etc.**
----	embaía	embaí	embairé	embairía
----	embaías	embaíste	embairás	embairías
----	embaía	embayó	embairá	embairía
embaímos	embaíamos	embaímos	embairemos	embairíamos
embaís	embaíais	embaísteis	embairéis	embairíais
----	embaían	embayeron	embairán	embairían

PRESENTE DE SUBJUNTIVO *PRESENT SUBJUNCTIVE*	PRETÉRITO IMPERFECTO DE SUBJUNTIVO *PAST (IMPERFECT) SUBJUNCTIVE*		FUTURO IMPERFECTO DE SUBJUNTIVO *FUTURE SUBJUNCTIVE*
	*I tricked, etc.**		*I will trick, etc.**
----	embayera	embayese	embayere
----	embayeras	embayeses	embayeres
----	embayera	embayese	embayere
----	embayéramos *or*	embayésemos	embayéremos
----	embayerais	embayeseis	embayereis
----	embayeran	embayesen	embayeren

FORMAS IMPERATIVAS, GERUNDIOS Y PARTICIPIO
COMMANDS AND PARTICIPLES

FORMAS IMPERATIVAS *COMMANDS*		GERUNDIO Y PARTICIPIO *PARTICIPLES*		
AFIRMATIVA *AFFIRMATIVE*	NEGATIVA *NEGATIVE*	GERUNDIO SIMPLE *PRESENT PARTICIPLE*	PARTICIPIO *PAST PARTICIPLE*	GERUNDIO COMPUESTO *PERFECT PARTICIPLE*
trick		*tricking*	*tricked*	*having tricked*
----	----	embayendo	embaído	habiendo embaído
----	----			
embaíd (vosotros)	----			
----	----			
----	----			

INFINITIVO COMPUESTO: haber embaído
PERFECT INFINITIVE: to have tricked

TIEMPOS COMPUESTOS
PERFECT (COMPOUND) TENSES

PRETÉRITO PERFECTO DE INDICATIVO *PRESENT PERFECT INDICATIVE*	PRETÉRITO PLUSCUAMPERFECTO DE INDICATIVO *PAST PERFECT (PLUPERFECT) INDICATIVE*	PRETÉRITO ANTERIOR DE INDICATIVO *PRETERITE PERFECT INDICATIVE*	FUTURO PERFECTO DE INDICATIVO *FUTURE PERFECT INDICATIVE*	POTENCIAL COMPUESTO *CONDITIONAL PERFECT*
I have tricked, etc.	*I had tricked, etc.*	*I had tricked, etc.*	*I will have tricked, etc.**	*I would have tricked, etc.**
he embaído	había embaído	hube embaído	habré embaído	habría embaído
has embaído	habías embaído	hubiste embaído	habrás embaído	habrías embaído
ha embaído	había embaído	hubo embaído	habrá embaído	habría embaído
hemos embaído	habíamos embaído	hubimos embaído	habremos embaído	habríamos embaído
habéis embaído	habíais embaído	hubisteis embaído	habréis embaído	habríais embaído
han embaído	habían embaído	hubieron embaído	habrán embaído	habrían embaído

PRETÉRITO PERFECTO DE SUBJUNTIVO *PRESENT PERFECT SUBJUNCTIVE*	PRETÉRITO PLUSCUAMPERFECTO DE SUBJUNTIVO *PAST PERFECT (PLUPERFECT) SUBJUNCTIVE*		FUTURO PERFECTO DE SUBJUNTIVO *FUTURE PERFECT SUBJUNCTIVE*
*I have tricked, etc.**	*I had tricked, etc.**		*I will have tricked, etc.**
haya embaído	hubiera embaído	hubiese embaído	hubiere embaído
hayas embaído	hubieras embaído	hubieses embaído	hubieres embaído
haya embaído	hubiera embaído	hubiese embaído	hubiere embaído
hayamos embaído	hubiéramos embaído *or*	hubiésemos embaído	hubiéremos embaído
hayáis embaído	hubierais embaído	hubieseis embaído	hubiereis embaído
hayan embaído	hubieran embaído	hubiesen embaído	hubieren embaído

*For additional translation possibilities see chart A.

X. Defective verbs

*desvaír 21. (OC)
*embaír 21. (OC)

OC = Orthographic/Spelling Change
*These verbs, in addition to being defective, have orthographic/spelling changes. The cross reference number following each verb indicates the category of verbs to which these orthographic/spelling changes belong.

TIEMPOS SIMPLES
SIMPLE TENSES

PRESENTE DE INDICATIVO **PRESENT INDICATIVE**	PRETÉRITO IMPERFECTO DE INDICATIVO **IMPERFECT INDICATIVE**	PRETÉRITO INDEFINIDO DE INDICATIVO **PRETERITE INDICATIVE**	FUTURO IMPERFECTO DE INDICATIVO **FUTURE INDICATIVE**	POTENCIAL SIMPLE **CONDITIONAL**
I stammer, etc.*	*I was stammering, etc.**	*I stammered, etc.**	*I will stammer, etc.**	*I would stammer, etc.**
----+	balbucía	balbucí	balbuciré	balbuciría
balbuces	balbucías	balbuciste	balbucirás	balbucirías
balbuce	balbucía	balbució	balbucirá	balbuciría
balbucimos	balbucíamos	balbucimos	balbuciremos	balbuciríamos
balbucís	balbucíais	balbucisteis	balbuciréis	balbuciríais
balbucen	balbucían	balbucieron	balbucirán	balbucirían

PRESENTE DE SUBJUNTIVO **PRESENT SUBJUNCTIVE**	PRETÉRITO IMPERFECTO DE SUBJUNTIVO **PAST (IMPERFECT) SUBJUNCTIVE**		FUTURO IMPERFECTO DE SUBJUNTIVO **FUTURE SUBJUNCTIVE**
I stammer, etc.*	*I stammered, etc.**		*I will stammer, etc.**
----+	balbuciera	balbuciese	balbuciere
----+	balbucieras	balbucieses	balbucieres
----+	balbuciera	balbuciese	balbuciere
----+	balbuciéramos *or*	balbuciésemos	balbuciéremos
----+	balbucierais	balbucieseis	balbuciereis
----+	balbucieran	balbuciesen	balbucieren

FORMAS IMPERATIVAS, GERUNDIOS Y PARTICIPIO
COMMANDS AND PARTICIPLES

FORMAS IMPERATIVAS **COMMANDS**		GERUNDIO Y PARTICIPIO **PARTICIPLES**		
AFIRMATIVA **AFFIRMATIVE**	NEGATIVA **NEGATIVE**	GERUNDIO SIMPLE **PRESENT PARTICIPLE**	PARTICIPIO **PAST PARTICIPLE**	GERUNDIO COMPUESTO **PERFECT PARTICIPLE**
stammer	*don't stammer*	*stammering*	*stammered*	*having stammered*
balbuce (tú)	----+	balbuciendo	balbucido	habiendo balbucido
----+	----+			
balbucid (vosotros)	----+			
----+	----+			
----+	----+			

INFINITIVO COMPUESTO: haber balbucido
PERFECT INFINITIVE: to have stammered

TIEMPOS COMPUESTOS
PERFECT (COMPOUND) TENSES

PRETÉRITO PERFECTO DE INDICATIVO **PRESENT PERFECT INDICATIVE**	PRETÉRITO PLUSCUAMPERFECTO DE INDICATIVO **PAST PERFECT (PLUPERFECT) INDICATIVE**	PRETÉRITO ANTERIOR DE INDICATIVO **PRETERITE PERFECT INDICATIVE**	FUTURO PERFECTO DE INDICATIVO **FUTURE PERFECT INDICATIVE**	POTENCIAL COMPUESTO **CONDITIONAL PERFECT**
I have stammered, etc.	*I had stammered, etc.*	*I had stammered, etc.*	*I will have stammered, etc.**	*I would have stammered, etc.**
he balbucido	había balbucido	hube balbucido	habré balbucido	habría balbucido
has balbucido	habías balbucido	hubiste balbucido	habrás balbucido	habrías balbucido
ha balbucido	había balbucido	hubo balbucido	habrá balbucido	habría balbucido
hemos balbucido	habíamos balbucido	hubimos balbucido	habremos balbucido	habríamos balbucido
habéis balbucido	habíais balbucido	hubisteis balbucido	habréis balbucido	habríais balbucido
han balbucido	habían balbucido	hubieron balbucido	habrán balbucido	habrían balbucido

PRETÉRITO PERFECTO DE SUBJUNTIVO **PRESENT PERFECT SUBJUNCTIVE**	PRETÉRITO PLUSCUAMPERFECTO DE SUBJUNTIVO **PAST PERFECT (PLUPERFECT) SUBJUNCTIVE**		FUTURO PERFECTO DE SUBJUNTIVO **FUTURE PERFECT SUBJUNCTIVE**
I have stammered, etc.*	*I had stammered, etc.**		*I will have stammered, etc.**
haya balbucido	hubiera balbucido	hubiese balbucido	hubiere balbucido
hayas balbucido	hubieras balbucido	hubieses balbucido	hubieres balbucido
haya balbucido	hubiera balbucido	hubiese balbucido	hubiere balbucido
hayamos balbucido	hubiéramos balbucido *or*	hubiésemos balbucido	hubiéremos balbucido
hayáis balbucido	hubierais balbucido	hubieseis balbucido	hubiereis balbucido
hayan balbucido	hubieran balbucido	hubiesen balbucido	hubieren balbucido

*For additional translation possibilities see chart A.
+The forms of balbucir which are missing are replaced by the corresponding forms of balbucear(1).

X. Defective verbs

balbucir

TIEMPOS SIMPLES
SIMPLE TENSES

PRESENTE DE INDICATIVO *PRESENT INDICATIVE*	PRETÉRITO IMPERFECTO DE INDICATIVO *IMPERFECT INDICATIVE*	PRETÉRITO INDEFINIDO DE INDICATIVO *PRETERITE INDICATIVE*	FUTURO IMPERFECTO DE INDICATIVO *FUTURE INDICATIVE*	POTENCIAL SIMPLE *CONDITIONAL*
----	----	----	----	----
----	----	----	----	----
----	----	----	----	----
----	----	----	----	----
----	----	----	----	----

PRESENTE DE SUBJUNTIVO *PRESENT SUBJUNCTIVE*	PRETÉRITO IMPERFECTO DE SUBJUNTIVO *PAST (IMPERFECT) SUBJUNCTIVE*	FUTURO IMPERFECTO DE SUBJUNTIVO *FUTURE SUBJUNCTIVE*
----	----	----	----
----	----	----	----
----	----	----	----
----	----	----	----
----	----	----	----

FORMAS IMPERATIVAS, GERUNDIOS Y PARTICIPIO
COMMANDS AND PARTICIPLES

FORMAS IMPERATIVAS *COMMANDS*		GERUNDIO Y PARTICIPIO *PARTICIPLES*		
AFIRMATIVA *AFFIRMATIVE*	NEGATIVA *NEGATIVE*	GERUNDIO SIMPLE *PRESENT PARTICIPLE*	PARTICIPIO *PAST PARTICIPLE*	GERUNDIO COMPUESTO *PERFECT PARTICIPLE*
			done without	*having done without*
----	----	----	preterido	habiendo preterido
----	----			
----	----			
----	----			
----	----			

> INFINITIVO COMPUESTO: haber preterido
> *PERFECT INFINITIVE: to have done without*

TIEMPOS COMPUESTOS
PERFECT (COMPOUND) TENSES

PRETÉRITO PERFECTO DE INDICATIVO *PRESENT PERFECT INDICATIVE*	PRETÉRITO PLUSCUAMPERFECTO DE INDICATIVO *PAST PERFECT (PLUPERFECT) INDICATIVE*	PRETÉRITO ANTERIOR DE INDICATIVO *PRETERITE PERFECT INDICATIVE*	FUTURO PERFECTO DE INDICATIVO *FUTURE PERFECT INDICATIVE*	POTENCIAL COMPUESTO *CONDITIONAL PERFECT*
----	----	----	----	----
----	----	----	----	----
----	----	----	----	----
----	----	----	----	----
----	----	----	----	----

PRETÉRITO PERFECTO DE SUBJUNTIVO *PRESENT PERFECT SUBJUNCTIVE*	PRETÉRITO PLUSCUAMPERFECTO DE SUBJUNTIVO *PAST PERFECT (PLUPERFECT) SUBJUNCTIVE*	FUTURO PERFECTO DE SUBJUNTIVO *FUTURE PERFECT SUBJUNCTIVE*
----	----	----	----
----	----	----	----
----	----	----	----
----	----	----	----
----	----	----	----

X. Defective verbs

VERB OF THIS CATEGORY

---

*preterir (ie, i) 41. (RC)

RC = Radical/Stem Change
*This verb, in addition to being defective, has radical/stem changes. The cross reference number following the verb indicates the category of verbs to which these radical/stem changes belong.

TIEMPOS SIMPLES
SIMPLE TENSES

PRESENTE DE INDICATIVO *PRESENT INDICATIVE*	PRETÉRITO IMPERFECTO DE INDICATIVO *IMPERFECT INDICATIVE*	PRETÉRITO INDEFINIDO DE INDICATIVO *PRETERITE INDICATIVE*	FUTURO IMPERFECTO DE INDICATIVO *FUTURE INDICATIVE*	POTENCIAL SIMPLE *CONDITIONAL*
I discolor, etc.*	I was discoloring, etc.*	I discolored, etc.*	I will discolor, etc.*	I would discolor, etc.*
----+	----+	----+	----+	----+
----+	----+	----+	----+	----+
----+	----+	----+	----+	----+
----+	----+	----+	----+	----+
----+	----+	----+	----+	----+
----+	----+	----+	----+	----+

PRESENTE DE SUBJUNTIVO *PRESENT SUBJUNCTIVE*	PRETÉRITO IMPERFECTO DE SUBJUNTIVO *PAST (IMPERFECT) SUBJUNCTIVE*		FUTURO IMPERFECTO DE SUBJUNTIVO *FUTURE SUBJUNCTIVE*
I discolor, etc.*	I discolored, etc.*		I will discolor, etc.*
----+	----+	----+	----+
----+	----+	----+	----+
----+	----+	----+	----+
----+	----+	----+	----+
----+	----+	----+	----+
----+	----+	----+	

FORMAS IMPERATIVAS, GERUNDIOS Y PARTICIPIO
COMMANDS AND PARTICIPLES

FORMAS IMPERATIVAS *COMMANDS*		GERUNDIO Y PARTICIPIO *PARTICIPLES*		
AFIRMATIVA *AFFIRMATIVE*	NEGATIVA *NEGATIVE*	GERUNDIO SIMPLE *PRESENT PARTICIPLE*	PARTICIPIO *PAST PARTICIPLE*	GERUNDIO COMPUESTO *PERFECT PARTICIPLE*
discolor	don't discolor	discoloring	discolored	having discolored
----+	----+	----+	descolorido	habiendo descolorido
----+	----+	----+		
----+	----+	----+		
----+	----+			
let's discolor	let's not discolor			
----+	----+			

INFINITIVO COMPUESTO: haber descolorido
PERFECT INFINITIVE: to have discolored

TIEMPOS COMPUESTOS
PERFECT (COMPOUND) TENSES

PRETÉRITO PERFECTO DE INDICATIVO *PRESENT PERFECT INDICATIVE*	PRETÉRITO PLUSCUAMPERFECTO DE INDICATIVO *PAST PERFECT (PLUPERFECT) INDICATIVE*	PRETÉRITO ANTERIOR DE INDICATIVO *PRETERITE PERFECT INDICATIVE*	FUTURO PERFECTO DE INDICATIVO *FUTURE PERFECT INDICATIVE*	POTENCIAL COMPUESTO *CONDITIONAL PERFECT*
I have discolored, etc.	I had discolored, etc.	I had discolored, etc.	I will have discolored, etc.*	I would have discolored, etc.*
----+	----+	----+	----+	----+
----+	----+	----+	----+	----+
----+	----+	----+	----+	----+
----+	----+	----+	----+	----+
----+	----+	----+	----+	----+
----+	----+	----+	----+	----+

PRETÉRITO PERFECTO DE SUBJUNTIVO *PRESENT PERFECT SUBJUNCTIVE*	PRETÉRITO PLUSCUAMPERFECTO DE SUBJUNTIVO *PAST PERFECT (PLUPERFECT) SUBJUNCTIVE*		FUTURO PERFECTO DE SUBJUNTIVO *FUTURE PERFECT SUBJUNCTIVE*
I have discolored, etc.*	I had discolored, etc.*		I will have discolored, etc.*
----+	----+	----+	----+
----+	----+	----+	----+
----+	----+	----+	----+
----+	----+	----+	----+
----+	----+	----+	----+
----+	----+	----+	----+

*For additional translation possibilities see chart A.
+The forms of descolorir which are missing are replaced by the corresponding forms of descolorar (1).

X. Defective verbs

VERB OF THIS CATEGORY

descolorir

121 Verbs lacking various forms } model: USUCAPIR

TIEMPOS SIMPLES
SIMPLE TENSES

PRESENTE DE INDICATIVO PRESENT INDICATIVE	PRETÉRITO IMPERFECTO DE INDICATIVO IMPERFECT INDICATIVE	PRETÉRITO INDEFINIDO DE INDICATIVO PRETERITE INDICATIVE	FUTURO IMPERFECTO DE INDICATIVO FUTURE INDICATIVE	POTENCIAL SIMPLE CONDITIONAL
----	----	----	----	----
----	----	----	----	----
----	----	----	----	----
----	----	----	----	----
----	----	----	----	----

PRESENTE DE SUBJUNTIVO PRESENT SUBJUNCTIVE	PRETÉRITO IMPERFECTO DE SUBJUNTIVO PAST (IMPERFECT) SUBJUNCTIVE		FUTURO IMPERFECTO DE SUBJUNTIVO FUTURE SUBJUNCTIVE
----	----	----	----
----	----	----	----
----	----	----	----
----	----	----	----
----	----	----	----

FORMAS IMPERATIVAS, GERUNDIOS Y PARTICIPIO
COMMANDS AND PARTICIPLES

FORMAS IMPERATIVAS COMMANDS		GERUNDIO Y PARTICIPIO PARTICIPLES		
AFIRMATIVA AFFIRMATIVE	NEGATIVA NEGATIVE	GERUNDIO SIMPLE PRESENT PARTICIPLE	PARTICIPIO PAST PARTICIPLE	GERUNDIO COMPUESTO PERFECT PARTICIPLE
		obtaining by expiration of time set by law	obtained by expiration of time set by law	having obtained by expiration of time set by law
----	----	usucapiendo+	usucapido+	habiendo usucapido+
----	----			
----	----			
----	----			
----	----			

INFINITIVO COMPUESTO: haber usucapido+
PERFECT INFINITIVE: to have obtained by expiration of time set by law

TIEMPOS COMPUESTOS
PERFECT (COMPOUND) TENSES

PRETÉRITO PERFECTO DE INDICATIVO PRESENT PERFECT INDICATIVE	PRETÉRITO PLUSCUAMPERFECTO DE INDICATIVO PAST PERFECT (PLUPERFECT) INDICATIVE	PRETÉRITO ANTERIOR DE INDICATIVO PRETERITE PERFECT INDICATIVE	FUTURO PERFECTO DE INDICATIVO FUTURE PERFECT INDICATIVE	POTENCIAL COMPUESTO CONDITIONAL PERFECT
----	----	----	----	----
----	----	----	----	----
----	----	----	----	----
----	----	----	----	----
----	----	----	----	----

PRETÉRITO PERFECTO DE SUBJUNTIVO PRESENT PERFECT SUBJUNCTIVE	PRETÉRITO PLUSCUAMPERFECTO DE SUBJUNTIVO PAST PERFECT (PLUPERFECT) SUBJUNCTIVE		FUTURO PERFECTO DE SUBJUNTIVO FUTURE PERFECT SUBJUNCTIVE
----	----	----	----
----	----	----	----
----	----	----	----
----	----	----	----

+This verb is rarely used in forms other than those given.

X. **Defective verbs**

VERBS OF THIS CATEGORY

adir
usucapir

[315]

TIEMPOS SIMPLES
SIMPLE TENSES

PRESENTE DE INDICATIVO PRESENT INDICATIVE	PRETÉRITO IMPERFECTO DE INDICATIVO IMPERFECT INDICATIVE	PRETÉRITO INDEFINIDO DE INDICATIVO PRETERITE INDICATIVE	FUTURO IMPERFECTO DE INDICATIVO FUTURE INDICATIVE	POTENCIAL SIMPLE CONDITIONAL
we initiate, etc.			*I will initiate, etc.*	*I would initiate, etc.*
----	----	----	incoaré	incoaría
----	----	----	incoarás	incoarías
----	----	----	incoará	incoaría
incoamos	----	----	incoaremos	incoaríamos
incoáis	----	----	incoaréis	incoaríais
----	----	----	incoarán	incoarían

PRESENTE DE SUBJUNTIVO PRESENT SUBJUNCTIVE	PRETÉRITO IMPERFECTO DE SUBJUNTIVO PAST (IMPERFECT) SUBJUNCTIVE		FUTURO IMPERFECTO DE SUBJUNTIVO FUTURE SUBJUNCTIVE
I initiate, etc.	*I initiated, etc.*		*I will initiate, etc.*
incoe	incoara	incoase	incoare
incoes	incoaras	incoases	incoares
incoe	incoara	incoase	incoare
incoemos	incoáramos *or*	incoásemos	incoáremos
incoéis	incoarais	incoaseis	incoareis
incoen	incoaran	incoasen	incoaren

FORMAS IMPERATIVAS, GERUNDIOS Y PARTICIPIO
COMMANDS AND PARTICIPLES

FORMAS IMPERATIVAS COMMANDS		GERUNDIO Y PARTICIPIO PARTICIPLES		
AFIRMATIVA AFFIRMATIVE	NEGATIVA NEGATIVE	GERUNDIO SIMPLE PRESENT PARTICIPLE	PARTICIPIO PAST PARTICIPLE	GERUNDIO COMPUESTO PERFECT PARTICIPLE
initiate	*don't initiate*	*initiating*	*initiated*	*having initiated*
incoa (tú)	no incoes (tú)	incoando	incoado	habiendo incoado
incoe (Ud.)	no incoe (Ud.)			
incoad (vosotros)	no incoéis (vosotros)			
incoen (Uds.)	no incoen (Uds.)			
let's initiate	*let's not initiate*			
incoemos	no incoemos			

INFINITIVO COMPUESTO: haber incoado
PERFECT INFINITIVE: to have initiated

TIEMPOS COMPUESTOS
PERFECT (COMPOUND) TENSES

PRETÉRITO PERFECTO DE INDICATIVO PRESENT PERFECT INDICATIVE	PRETÉRITO PLUSCUAMPERFECTO DE INDICATIVO PAST PERFECT (PLUPERFECT) INDICATIVE	PRETÉRITO ANTERIOR DE INDICATIVO PRETERITE PERFECT INDICATIVE	FUTURO PERFECTO DE INDICATIVO FUTURE PERFECT INDICATIVE	POTENCIAL COMPUESTO CONDITIONAL PERFECT
we have initiated, etc.			*I will have initiated, etc.*	*I would have initiated, etc.*
----	----	----	habré incoado	habría incoado
----	----	----	habrás incoado	habrías incoado
----	----	----	habrá incoado	habría incoado
hemos incoado	----	----	habremos incoado	habríamos incoado
habéis incoado	----	----	habréis incoado	habríais incoado
----	----	----	habrán incoado	habrían incoado

PRETÉRITO PERFECTO DE SUBJUNTIVO PRESENT PERFECT SUBJUNCTIVE	PRETÉRITO PLUSCUAMPERFECTO DE SUBJUNTIVO PAST PERFECT (PLUPERFECT) SUBJUNCTIVE		FUTURO PERFECTO DE SUBJUNTIVO FUTURE PERFECT SUBJUNCTIVE
I have initiated, etc.	*I had initiated, etc.*		*I will have initiated, etc.*
haya incoado	hubiera incoado	hubiese incoado	hubiere incoado
hayas incoado	hubieras incoado	hubieses incoado	hubieres incoado
haya incoado	hubiera incoado	hubiese incoado	hubiere incoado
hayamos incoado	hubiéramos incoado *or*	hubiésemos incoado	hubiéremos incoado
hayáis incoado	hubierais incoado	hubieseis incoado	hubiereis incoado
hayan incoado	hubieran incoado	hubiesen incoado	hubieren incoado

*For additional translation possibilities see chart A.

X. Defective verbs

VERB OF THIS CATEGORY

incoar

123 Verb lacking various forms } model: SOLER (ue)

TIEMPOS SIMPLES
SIMPLE TENSES

PRESENTE DE INDICATIVO *PRESENT* *INDICATIVE*	PRETÉRITO IMPERFECTO DE INDICATIVO *IMPERFECT* *INDICATIVE*	PRETÉRITO INDEFINIDO DE INDICATIVO *PRETERITE* *INDICATIVE*	FUTURO IMPERFECTO DE INDICATIVO *FUTURE* *INDICATIVE*	POTENCIAL SIMPLE *CONDITIONAL*
I am accustomed to, etc.*	*I was accustomed to, etc.**	*I was accustomed to, etc.**		
suelo	solía	solí	----	----
sueles	solías	soliste	----	----
suele	solía	solió	----	----
solemos	solíamos	solimos	----	----
soléis	solíais	solisteis	----	----
suelen	solían	solieron	----	----

PRESENTE DE SUBJUNTIVO *PRESENT* *SUBJUNCTIVE*	PRETÉRITO IMPERFECTO DE SUBJUNTIVO *PAST (IMPERFECT)* *SUBJUNCTIVE*		FUTURO IMPERFECTO DE SUBJUNTIVO *FUTURE* *SUBJUNCTIVE*
I am accustomed to, etc.*	*I was accustomed to, etc.**		
suela	soliera	soliese	----
suelas	solieras	solieses	----
suela	soliera	soliese	----
solamos	soliéramos *or*	soliésemos	----
soláis	solierais	solieseis	----
suelan	solieran	soliesen	----

FORMAS IMPERATIVAS, GERUNDIOS Y PARTICIPIO
COMMANDS AND PARTICIPLES

FORMAS IMPERATIVAS *COMMANDS*		GERUNDIO Y PARTICIPIO *PARTICIPLES*		
AFIRMATIVA *AFFIRMATIVE*	NEGATIVA *NEGATIVE*	GERUNDIO SIMPLE *PRESENT PARTICIPLE*	PARTICIPIO *PAST PARTICIPLE*	GERUNDIO COMPUESTO *PERFECT PARTICIPLE*
		being accustomed to	*been accustomed to*	*having been accustomed to*
----	----	soliendo	solido	habiendo solido
----	----			
----	----			
----	----			
----	----			

INFINITIVO COMPUESTO: haber solido
PERFECT INFINITIVE: to have been accustomed to

TIEMPOS COMPUESTOS
PERFECT (COMPOUND) TENSES

PRETÉRITO PERFECTO DE INDICATIVO *PRESENT PERFECT* *INDICATIVE*	PRETÉRITO PLUSCUAMPERFECTO DE INDICATIVO *PAST PERFECT (PLUPERFECT)* *INDICATIVE*	PRETÉRITO ANTERIOR DE INDICATIVO *PRETERITE PERFECT* *INDICATIVE*	FUTURO PERFECTO DE INDICATIVO *FUTURE PERFECT* *INDICATIVE*	POTENCIAL COMPUESTO *CONDITIONAL PERFECT*
I have been accustomed to, etc.*				
he solido	----	----	----	----
has solido	----	----	----	----
ha solido	----	----	----	----
hemos solido	----	----	----	----
habéis solido	----	----	----	----
han solido	----	----	----	----

PRETÉRITO PERFECTO DE SUBJUNTIVO *PRESENT PERFECT* *SUBJUNCTIVE*	PRETÉRITO PLUSCUAMPERFECTO DE SUBJUNTIVO *PAST PERFECT (PLUPERFECT)* *SUBJUNCTIVE*		FUTURO PERFECTO DE SUBJUNTIVO *FUTURE PERFECT* *SUBJUNCTIVE*
----	----	----	----
----	----	----	----
----	----	----	----
----	----	----	----
----	----	----	----

*For additional translation possibilities see chart A.

[318]

X. Defective verbs

VERB OF THIS CATEGORY

---

*soler (ue) 38. (RC)

RC = Radical/Stem Change
*This verb, in addition to being defective, has radical/stem changes. The cross reference number following the verb indicates the category of verbs to which these radical/stem changes belong.

Verb lacking various forms* } model: ANTOJARSE

*Used only in the third person singular and plural, and in the infinitives, present participle, and past participle, and usually with an indirect object.

TIEMPOS SIMPLES
SIMPLE TENSES

PRESENTE DE INDICATIVO **PRESENT INDICATIVE**	PRETÉRITO IMPERFECTO DE INDICATIVO **IMPERFECT INDICATIVE**	PRETÉRITO INDEFINIDO DE INDICATIVO **PRETERITE INDICATIVE**	FUTURO IMPERFECTO DE INDICATIVO **FUTURE INDICATIVE**	POTENCIAL SIMPLE **CONDITIONAL**
*it strikes me, etc.**	*it was striking me, etc.**	*it struck me, etc.**	*it will strike me, etc.*	*it would strike me, etc.*
se me antoja	se me antojaba	se me antojó	se me antojará	se me antojaría
se te antoja	se te antojaba	se te antojó	se te antojará	se te antojaría
se le antoja	se le antojaba	se le antojó	se le antojará	se le antojaría
se nos antoja	se nos antojaba	se nos antojó	se nos antojará	se nos antojaría
se os antoja	se os antojaba	se os antojó	se os antojará	se os antojaría
se les antoja	se les antojaba	se les antojó	se les antojará	se les antojaría
antojan[+]	antojaban[+]	antojaron[+]	antojarán[+]	antojarían[+]

PRESENTE DE SUBJUNTIVO **PRESENT SUBJUNCTIVE**	PRETÉRITO IMPERFECTO DE SUBJUNTIVO **PAST (IMPERFECT) SUBJUNCTIVE**		FUTURO IMPERFECTO DE SUBJUNTIVO **FUTURE SUBJUNCTIVE**
*it strikes me, etc.**	*it struck me, etc.**		*it will strike me, etc.**
se me antoje	se me antojara	se me antojase	se me antojare
se te antoje	se te antojara	se te antojase	se te antojare
se le antoje	se le antojara *or*	se le antojase	se le antojare
se nos antoje	se nos antojara	se nos antojase	se nos antojare
se os antoje	se os antojara	se os antojase	se os antojare
se les antoje	se les antojara	se les antojase	se les antojare
antojen[+]	antojaran[+]	antojasen[+]	antojaren[+]

FORMAS IMPERATIVAS, GERUNDIOS Y PARTICIPIO
COMMANDS AND PARTICIPLES

FORMAS IMPERATIVAS **COMMANDS**		GERUNDIO Y PARTICIPIO **PARTICIPLES**		
AFIRMATIVA **AFFIRMATIVE**	NEGATIVA **NEGATIVE**	GERUNDIO SIMPLE **PRESENT PARTICIPLE**	PARTICIPIO **PAST PARTICIPLE**	GERUNDIO COMPUESTO **PERFECT PARTICIPLE**
		striking me, etc.	*struck*	*having struck me, etc.*
----	----	antojándoseme	antojado	habiéndoseme antojado
----	----	antojándosete		habiéndosete antojado
----	----	antojándosele		habiéndosele antojado
----	----	antojándosenos		habiéndosenos antojado
		antojándoseos		habiéndoseos antojado
		antojándoseles		habiéndoseles antojado
----	----			

INFINITIVO COMPUESTO: haberse antojado
PERFECT INFINITIVE: to have struck

TIEMPOS COMPUESTOS
PERFECT (COMPOUND) TENSES

PRETÉRITO PERFECTO DE INDICATIVO **PRESENT PERFECT INDICATIVE**	PRETÉRITO PLUSCUAMPERFECTO DE INDICATIVO **PAST PERFECT (PLUPERFECT) INDICATIVE**	PRETÉRITO ANTERIOR DE INDICATIVO **PRETERITE PERFECT INDICATIVE**	FUTURO PERFECTO DE INDICATIVO **FUTURE PERFECT INDICATIVE**	POTENCIAL COMPUESTO **CONDITIONAL PERFECT**
it has struck me, etc.	*it had struck me, etc.*	*it had struck me, etc.*	*it will have struck me, etc.*	*it would have struck me, etc.*
se me ha antojado	se me había antojado	se me hubo antojado	se me habrá antojado	se me habría antojado
se te ha antojado	se te había antojado	se te hubo antojado	se te habrá antojado	se te habría antojado
se le ha antojado	se le había antojado	se le hubo antojado	se le habrá antojado	se le habría antojado
se nos ha antojado	se nos había antojado	se nos hubo antojado	se nos habrá antojado	se nos habría antojado
se os ha antojado	se os había antojado	se os hubo antojado	se os habrá antojado	se os habría antojado
se les ha antojado	se les había antojado	se les hubo antojado	se les habrá antojado	se les habría antojado
han antojado[+]	habían antojado[+]	hubieron antojado[+]	habrán antojado[+]	habrían antojado[+]

PRETÉRITO PERFECTO DE SUBJUNTIVO **PRESENT PERFECT SUBJUNCTIVE**	PRETÉRITO PLUSCUAMPERFECTO DE SUBJUNTIVO **PAST PERFECT (PLUPERFECT) SUBJUNCTIVE**		FUTURO PERFECTO DE SUBJUNTIVO **FUTURE PERFECT SUBJUNCTIVE**
*it has struck me, etc.**	*it had struck me, etc.**		*it will have struck me, etc.**
se me haya antojado	se me hubiera antojado	se me hubiese antojado	se me hubiere antojado
se te haya antojado	se te hubiera antojado	se te hubiese antojado	se te hubiere antojado
se le haya antojado	se le hubiera antojado	se le hubiese antojado	se le hubiere antojado
se nos haya antojado	se nos hubiera antojado *or*	se nos hubiese antojado	se nos hubiere antojado
se os haya antojado	se os hubiera antojado	se os hubiese antojado	se os hubiere antojado
se les haya antojado	se les hubiera antojado	se les hubiese antojado	se les hubiere antojado
hayan antojado[+]	hubieran antojado[+]	hubiesen antojado[+]	hubieren antojado[+]

*For additional translation possibilities see chart A.
[+]These plural verbal forms (indicated with +) replace their singular counterpart (given in the paradigm) when what "strikes" is a plurality.

X. Defective verbs

antojarse

XI. English-Spanish Alphabetical Verb List

A

to abandon, abandonar (1)
to abandon, arrinconar (1)
to abandon, dejar (1)
to abandon, desasistir (3)
to abandon oneself to voluptuous living, refocilarse (1) (4)
to abbreviate, abreviar (1)
to abdicate, abdicar (8)
to abduct, abducir (67)
to abhor, renegar (ie, i) (50)
to abide (by), atenerse (ie) (108) (4)
to abjure, abjurar (1)
to abolish, abolir (116)
to abominate, abominar (1)
to abort, abortar (1)
to abound, abundar (1)
to abound, rebosar (1)
to abridge, sincopar (1)
to abridge, substanciar (1)
to abrogate, abrogar (9)
to absent oneself, ausentarse (1) (4)
to absolve, absolver (ue) (70)
to absorb, absorber (2)
to absorb, sorber (2)
to abstain, abstenerse (ie) (108) (4)
to abstract, abstraer (109)
to abstract, substanciar (1)
to abstract (a writing), extractar (1)
to abuse, abusar (1)
to abuse, maltraer (109)
to abuse, maltratar (1)
to accede, acceder (2)
to accelerate, acelerar (1)
to accentuate, acentuar (62)
to accept, aceptar (1)
to accept an inheritance, adir (121)
to acclaim, proclamar (1)
to acclaim, vivar (1)
to acclimatize, aclimatar (1)
to accommodate, acomodar (1)
to accompany, acompañar (1)
to accredit, acreditar (1)
to accumulate, acaudalar (1)
to accumulate, acumular (1)
to accuse, acusar (1)
to accuse, inculpar (1)
to accuse, sindicar (8)
to accustom, acostumbrar (1)
to accustom, avezar (11)
to accustom, habituar (62)
to accustom to war, aguerrir (116)
to ache, doler (ue) (38)
to acidify, acidificar (8)
to acquire, adquirir (ie) (76)
to acquire good manners, desasnarse (1) (4)
to acquire property, hacendarse (ie) (37) (4)
to act, actuar (62)
to act, obrar (1)
to act as a godfather, apadrinar (1)
to act childishly, aniñarse (1) (4)
to act like a child, niñear (1)
to act like a rascal, truhanear (1)
to act or happen before the regular time, anticiparse (1) (4)
to act quixotically, quijotear (1)
to act senile, chochear (1)
to act with grace, gallardear (1)
to act with moderation, medirse (i, i) (42) (4)
to act with restraint, mesurarse (1) (4)
to activate, activar (1)
to adapt, adaptar (1)
to adapt, adecuar (1)
to adapt (a play, a novel), refundir (3)
to add, adicionar (1)
to add, agregar (9)
to add, añadir (3)
to add, sumar (1)
to add a postscript to a letter, posdatar (1)
to add one's flourish (with or without one's signature), rubricar (8)
to add something as extra, yapar (1)
to add up, totalizar (11)
to address, dirigir (16)
to address (a letter, etc.), sobrescribir (69)
to address using "tú", tutear (1)
to adduce, aducir (67)
to adduce, traer (109)
to adhere, adherir (ie, i) (41)
to adhere, adherirse (ie, i) (41) (4)
to admit, reconocer (73)
to admonish, amonestar (1)
to adopt, adoptar (1)
to adopt, ahijar (34)
to adopt, prohijar (34)
to adopt foreign ways, extranjerizarse (11) (4)
to adore, adorar (1)
to adorn, aderezar (11)
to adorn, ataviar (61)
to adorn, engalanar (1)
to adorn, ornamentar (1)
to adorn or finish with Morocco leather, tafiletear (1)
to adorn with bright colors, esmaltar (1)
to adorn with feathers, emplumar (1)
to adorn with ribbon or trimming, tachonar (1)
to adulterate, adulterar (1)
to advance, avanzar (11)
to advance (money), anticipar (1)
to adventure, aventurar (1)
to advertise, anunciar (1)
to advise, aconsejar (1)
to advise, asesorar (1)
to aerate, aerear (1)
to affect, afectar (1)
to affect, conmover (ue) (38)
to affiliate, afiliar (1) or (61)
to affirm, afirmar (1)
to afflict, afligir (16)
to afflict, angustiar (1)
to afflict, aquejar (1)
to afflict, atribular (1)
to affront, afrentar (1)
to affront, baldonar (1)
to affront, deshonrar (1)
to age, añejar (1)
to agglomerate, aglomerar (1)
to agglutinate, aglutinar (1)
to aggravate, agravar (1)
to agitate, agitar (1)
to agitate, traquear (1)
to agitate, traquetear (1)
to agonize, agonizar (11)
to agree, acceder (2)
to agree, acordar (ue) (36)
to agree, avenirse (ie, i) (111) (4)
to agree, compaginarse (1) (4)
to agree, concordar (ue) (36)
to agree, convenir (ie, i) (111)
to agree upon, pactar (1)
to aid, socorrer (2)
to aid, sufragar (9)
to aim, apuntar (1)
to aim, asestar (1)
to air, airear (1)
to air, ventear (1)
to alarm, alarmar (1)
to alert, alertar (1)
to alienate, alienar (1)
to alienate, enajenar (1)
to alienate, malquistar (1)
to alight on water, acuatizar (11)
to alight on water, amarar (1)
to allege, alegar (9)
to alleviate, aliviar (1)
to allow, consentir (ie, i) (41)
to allow, permitir (3)
to alloy, alear (1)
to allude, aludir (3)
to allure, engolosinar (1)
to ally, aliar (61)
to alphabetize, alfabetizar (11)
to alter, alterar (1)
to alternate, alternar (1)
to amalgamate, amalgamar (1)
to amass, amasar (1)
to amaze, asombrar (1)
to ambush, emboscar (8)
to amend, enmendar (ie) (37)
to Americanize, americanizar (11)
to amortize, amortizar (11)
to amount, montar (1)
to amount to, ascender (ie) (39)
to amount to, sumar (1)
to amplify, ampliar (61)
to amplify, amplificar (8)
to amputate, amputar (1)
to amuse, divertir (ie, i) (41)
to amuse, recrear (1)
to amuse, solazar (11)
to analyze, analizar (11)
to anatomize, anatomizar (11)
to anchor, anclar (1)
to anchor, ancorar (1)
to anesthetize, anestesiar (1)
to anger, airar (63)
to anger, amostazar (11)
to anger, encolerizar (11)
to anger, enfadar (1)
to anger, enojar (1)
to anger, indignar (1)
to anger, sulfurar (1)
to animalize, animalizar (11)
to annex, anexar (1)
to annihilate, aniquilar (1)
to announce, anunciar (1)
to announce boastfully, vociferar (1)
to announce in advance, prenunciar (1)
to annoy, amohinar (34)
to annoy, calentar (ie) (37)
to annoy, empalagar (9)
to annoy, estorbar (1)
to annoy, fastidiar (1)
to annoy, fregar (ie) (50)
to annoy, hastiar (61)
to annoy, jeringar (9)
to annoy, jorobar (1)
to annoy, marear (1)
to annoy, mosconear (1)

to **annoy**, sulfurar (1)
to **annoy**, vejar (1)
to **annul**, abrogar (9)
to **annul**, anular (1)
to **anoint**, ungir (16)
to **answer**, contestar (1)
to **answer**, reponer (98)
to **answer**, responder (2)
to **answer back**, replicar (8)
to **answer in chorus**, corear (1)
to **antedate**, retrotraer (109)
to **anticipate**, anticipar (1)
to **antiquate**, anticuar (1) or (62)
to **ape**, remedar (1)
to **apocopate**, apocopar (1)
to **apologize**, disculparse (1) (4)
to **apologize**, excusarse (1) (4)
to **apostatize**, apostatar (1)
to **appeal**, apelar (1)
to **appeal to**, interpelar (1)
to **appear**, aparecer (73)
to **appear**, comparecer (73)
to **appear**, parecer (73)
to **appear**, presentarse (1) (4)
to **appear in person**, apersonarse (1) (4)
to **appear personally**, personarse (1) (4)
to **applaud**, aplaudir (3)
to **apply**, aplicar (8)
to **apply a plaster**, emplastar (1)
to **apply for**, solicitar (1)
to **apply oneself**, aplicarse (8) (4)
to **apply oneself**, dedicarse (8) (4)
to **appoint**, nombrar (1)
to **appoint**, nominar (1)
to **appraise**, aforar (1)
to **appraise**, appreciar (1)
to **appraise**, aquilatar (1)
to **appraise**, avaluar (62)
to **appraise**, preciar (1)
to **appraise**, tasar (1)
to **appraise**, valorar (1)
to **appraise**, valuar (62)
to **appreciate**, appreciar (1)
to **appreciate (in value)**, aquilatar (1)
to **apprehend**, aprehender (2)
to **approach**, acercarse (8) (4)
to **approach**, allegarse (9) (4)
to **approach land**, atracar (8)
to **appropriate**, apropiarse (1) (4)
to **approve**, aprobar (ue) (36)
to **Arabize**, arabizar (11)
to **arbitrate**, terciar (1)
to **arch**, arcar (8)
to **arch**, arquear (1)
to **argue**, altercar (8)
to **argue**, argüir (72)
to **argue**, argumentar (1)
to **argue**, discutir (3)
to **argue**, disputar (1)
to **argue back**, replicar (8)
to **argue stubbornly**, porfiar (61)
to **arise**, provenir (ie, i) (111)
to **arm**, armar (1)
to **armor-plate**, acorazar (11)
to **armor-plate**, blindar (1)
to **arouse**, enfervorizar (11)
to **arouse a strong dislike**, antipatizar (11)
to **arouse passion**, apasionar (1)
to **arouse sexually**, cachondear (1)
to **arrange**, concertar (ie) (37)
to **arrange**, ordenar (1)
to **arrange**, poner (98)
to **arrest**, arrestar (1)
to **arrest**, prender (2)
to **arrive**, advenir (ie, i) (111)

to **arrive**, arribar (1)
to **arrive**, llegar (9)
to **articulate**, articular (1)
to **ascend**, ascender (ie) (39)
to **ascertain**, cerciorarse (1) (4)
to **ask**, pedir (i, i) (42)
to **ask**, preguntar (1)
to **ask for**, encargar (9)
to **ask for**, pedir (i, i) (42)
to **ask for**, solicitar (1)
to **asphalt**, asfaltar (1)
to **asphyxiate**, asfixiar (1)
to **aspire**, aspirar (1)
to **assail**, sobresaltar (1)
to **assassinate**, asesinar (1)
to **assassinate**, victimar (1)
to **assault**, asaltar (1)
to **assay**, aquilatar (1)
to **assemble**, armar (1)
to **assemble**, ensamblar (1)
to **assemble**, reunir (66)
to **assent**, asentir (ie, i) (41)
to **assert**, asegurar (1)
to **assert**, aseverar (1)
to **assign**, adscribir (69)
to **assign**, asignar (1)
to **assign a task**, atarear (1)
to **assimilate**, asimilar (1)
to **assist**, acolitar (1)
to **assist**, asistir (3)
to **assist**, socorrer (2)
to **assist**, subvenir (ie, i) (111)
to **associate**, asociar (1)
to **assume**, asumir (3)
to **assure**, asegurar (1)
to **assure**, cerciorar (1)
to **astonish**, asombrar (1)
to **astonish**, helar (ie) (37)
to **astound**, aplanar (1)
to **astound**, pasmar (1)
to **atomize**, atomizar (11)
to **atomize**, pulverizar (11)
to **atomize**, vaporizar (11)
to **atone for**, expiar (61)
to **atrophy**, atrofiar (1)
to **attack**, acometer (2)
to **attack**, agredir (116)
to **attack**, atacar (8)
to **attack**, embestir (i, i) (42)
to **attack**, opugnar (1)
to **attain seniority**, antiguarse (10) (4)
to **attempt**, atentar (1)
to **attempt**, intentar (1)
to **attend**, atender (ie) (39)
to **attend**, asistir (3)
to **attend to**, despachar (1)
to **attest**, atestar (1)
to **attest**, atestiguar (10)
to **attest**, testimoniar (1)
to **attire**, ataviar (61)
to **attract**, atraer (109)
to **attract**, captar (1)
to **attribute**, achacar (8)
to **attribute**, atribuir (71)
to **attribute**, imputar (1)
to **auction**, almonedar (1)
to **auction**, rematar (1)
to **auction**, subastar (1)
to **augur**, augurar (1)
to **authenticate**, autenticar (8)
to **authorize**, autorizar (11)
to **autograph**, autografiar (61)
to **avenge**, vengar (9)
to **average**, promediar (1)
to **avoid**, evitar (1)
to **avoid**, excusar (1)

to **awaken**, despertarse (ie) (37) (4)

B

to **babble**, balbucear (1)
to **babble**, balbucir (118)
to **back**, apadrinar (1)
to **back**, respaldar (1)
to **back away**, retroceder (2)
to **back down**, arrepentirse (ie, i) (41) (4)
to **back down**, rajarse (1) (4)
to **back up**, cejar (1)
to **back up**, recular (1)
to **back up (said of a horse)**, acular (1)
to **back up (water)**, remansar (1)
to **back water (nautical)**, ciar (19)
to **back with quotations**, contextuar (62)
to **backfire (a car)**, petardear (1)
to **backstitch**, pespuntar (1)
to **bag**, ensacar (8)
to **bait (a fishhook)**, cebar (1)
to **bake**, cocer (ue) (54)
to **bake**, hornear (1)
to **balance**, abalanzar (11)
to **balance**, equilibrar (1)
to **balance (books)**, cuadrar (1)
to **bale**, embalar (1)
to **bamboozle**, embaucar (8)
to **band together**, apandillarse (1) (4)
to **bandage**, vendar (1)
to **banish**, extrañar (1)
to **bank**, terraplenar (1)
to **baptize**, bautizar (11)
to **bar**, atrancar (8)
to **barbecue**, churrasquear (1)
to **bargain**, regatear (1)
to **bark**, ladrar (1)
to **barter**, cambalachear (1)
to **barter**, permutar (1)
to **base**, basar (1)
to **base**, fundar (1)
to **base one's judgment**, basarse (1) (4)
to **base one's opinion**, fundarse (1) (4)
to **baste**, embastar (1)
to **baste (sewing)**, hilvanar (1)
to **bat**, batear (1)
to **bathe**, bañar (1)
to **battle**, batallar (1)
to **be**, estar (87)
to **be**, hallarse (1) (4)
to **be**, quedar (1)
to **be**, ser (107)
to **be abashed**, acholarse (1) (4)
to **be abashed**, azorarse (1) (4)
to **be able**, poder (ue) (97)
to **be absent**, faltar (1)
to **be absorbed**, abstraerse (109) (4)
to **be accustomed**, usar (1)
to **be accustomed to**, soler (ue) (123)
to **be affected**, conmoverse (ue) (38) (4)
to **be alike**, semejar (1)
to **be amazed**, asombrarse (1) (4)
to **be annoyed**, molestarse (1) (4)
to **be ashamed**, afrentarse (1) (4)
to **be ashamed**, avergonzarse (ue) (49) (4)
to **be asphyxiated**, asfixiarse (1) (4)
to **be astonished**, asombrarse (1) (4)
to **be based on**, estribar (1)
to **be best man**, apadrinar (1)
to **be born**, nacer (73)
to **be born again**, renacer (73)
to **be bothered**, molestarse (1) (4)
to **be brief**, sucintarse (1) (4)
to **be brotherly**, confraternar (1)
to **be called**, titularse (1) (4)

to be cautious, precaucionarse (1) (4)
to be certain, constar (1)
to be charmed, embelesarse (1) (4)
to be comforted, solazarse (11) (4)
to be congenial, simpatizar (11)
to be connected, entroncar (8)
to be convenient, convenir (ie, i) (111)
to be crazy about, desvivirse (3 (4)
to be delirious, delirar (1)
to be different, distar (1)
to be different, variar (61)
to be discordant, disonar (ue) (36)
to be displeased, disgustarse (1) (4)
to be disrespectful, descomedirse (i, i) (42) (4)
to be distinguished, particularizarse (11) (4)
to be enough, bastar (1)
to be entangled among brambles, enzarzarse (11) (4)
to be equivalent, equivaler (110)
to be exhalted, enaltecerse (73) (4)
to be extinguished, extinguirse (17) (4)
to be extremely hot, asarse (1) (4)
to be far, distar (1)
to be fast (said of clocks), adelantarse (1) (4)
to be finical, alfeñicarse (8) (4)
to be finicky, melindrear (1)
to be for rent, alquilarse (1) (4)
to be forward, desenvolverse (ue) (70) (4)
to be frightened, sobresaltarse (1) (4)
to be glad, alegrarse (1) (4)
to be glad, holgarse (ue) (45) (4)
to be happy, alegrarse (1) (4)
to be heavy, pesar (1)
to be honored, honrarse (1) (4)
to be horrified, horrorizarse (11) (4)
to be hot, quemar (1)
to be idle, vacar (8)
to be implied, sobreentenderse (ie) (39) (4)
to be important, pintar (1)
to be impudent, desmandarse (1) (4)
to be impudent, desmedirse (i, i) (42) (4)
to be in collusion, coludir (3)
to be in danger, peligrar (1)
to be in ecstasy, extasiarse (61) (4)
to be in force (a rule, a law), regir (i, i) (57)
to be in great abundance, sobreabundar (1)
to be in great abundance, superabundar (1)
to be in great danger, zozobrar (1)
to be in harmony, consonar (ue) (36)
to be in one's dotage, caducar (8)
to be in session, sesionar (1)
to be in style, estilarse (1) (4)
to be in the field, campear (1)
to be in the throes of death, agonizar (11)
to be in the way, estorbar (1)
to be in two places at the same time, bilocar (8)
to be in vogue, privar (1)
to be incumbent on, competer (2)
to be initiated, iniciarse (1) (4)
to be lacking, faltar (1)
to be late, retrasarse (1) (4)
to be late, tardar (1)
to be lazy, flojear (1)
to be left, quedar (1)
to be left, restar (1)
to be left, sobrar (1)
to be left over, quedar (1)

to be located, caer (81)
to be located, radicar (8)
to be located, ubicarse (8) (4)
to be lying down, yacer (113)
to be mislaid among other papers, traspapelarse (1) (4)
to be mistaken, engañarse (1) (4)
to be mistaken, equivocarse (8) (4)
to be moderate, comedirse (i, i) (42) (4)
to be moderate, medirse (i, i) (42) (4)
to be more than enough, sobrar (1)
to be moved, emocionarse (1) (4)
to be moved to pity, enternecerse (73) (4)
to be near to, frisar (1)
to be necessary, caler (110)
to be needless or useless, holgar (ue) (45)
to be obliging, comedirse (i, i) (42) (4)
to be obstinate, obstinarse (1) (4)
to be obvious, verse (112) (4)
to be offended, agraviarse (1) (4)
to be on close or intimate terms with, tutear (1)
to be on close or intimate terms with, tutearse (1) (4)
to be on one's guard, precaverse (2) (4)
to be on the record, constar (1)
to be on the way to, encaminarse (1) (4)
to be one's turn, tocar (8)
to be or act cowardly, cobardear (1)
to be or become cronies, compadrar (1)
to be or become cronies, compadrear (1)
to be or feel sorry for, sentir (ie, i) (41)
to be or walk knock-kneed, zambear (1)
to be out of date, caducar (8)
to be out of tune, desentonar (1)
to be out of tune, discordar (ue) (36)
to be overnice, prudish or finical, remilgarse (9) (4)
to be pedantic, pedantear (1)
to be pending, pender (2)
to be perpetuated, perpetuarse (62) (4)
to be persistent in fulfilling a whim, encapricharse (1) (4)
to be piqued, picarse (8) (4)
to be placed, ubicarse (8) (4)
to be pleased, complacerse (73) (4)
to be pleasing, gustar (1)
to be polite, comedirse (i, i) (42) (4)
to be precise, sucintarse (1) (4)
to be prominent, campear (1)
to be promoted, ascender (ie) (39)
to be proud, enorgullecerse (73) (4)
to be proud, gloriarse (61) (4)
to be recorded, registrarse (1) (4)
to be reduced, resumirse (3) (4)
to be repugnant, repugnar (1)
to be resentful, resentir (ie, i) (41)
to be resentful, resentirse (ie, i) (41) (4)
to be reserved, recatarse (1) (4)
to be resplendent, refulgir (16)
to be ruined, arrearse (1) (4)
to be said, decirse (i, i) (84) (4)
to be satisfied, satisfacerse (68) (4)
to be scarce, escasear (1)
to be seen, verse (112) (4)
to be shipwrecked, naufragar (9)
to be similar, asemejarse (1) (4)
to be stingy, cicatear (1)
to be stingy, tacañear (1)
to be stuck up, endiosarse (1) (4)
to be stunned, aturdirse (3) (4)
to be stunned, pasmarse (1) (4)
to be suitable, acomodar (1)

to be surprised, extrañarse (1) (4)
to be terrified, despavorir (116)
to be touched, emocionarse (1) (4)
to be transparent, transparentar (1)
to be transparent, traslucirse (74) (4)
to be transparent (said of fabric), clarearse (1) (4)
to be trapped, atramparse (1) (4)
to be understood, sobreentenderse (ie) (39) (4)
to be ungrateful, desagradecer (73)
to be urgent, urgir (16)
to be used to, soler (ue) (123)
to be useful, aprovechar (1)
to be vacant, vacar (8)
to be valid, valer (110)
to be very busy, atarearse (1) (4)
to be well received, cuajar (1)
to be widowed, enviudar (1)
to be wily, raposear (1)
to be worth, importar (1)
to be worth, merecer (73)
to be worth, valer (110)
to be worth while, caler (110)
to beach (a boat), varar (1)
to bear, aguantar (1)
to bear, comportar (1)
to bear, portar (1)
to bear, resistir (3)
to bear, sobrellevar (1)
to bear, soportar (1)
to bear fruit, fructificar (8)
to beat, batir (3)
to beat, ganar (1)
to beat, latir (3)
to beat, pegar (9)
to beat, vapulear (1)
to beat, varear (1)
to beat (to remove dust), sacudir (3)
to beat (with a stick), apalear (1)
to beat (wool), arcar (8)
to beat or flap wings or fins, aletear (1)
to beat up, mullir (27)
to beat up (a pillow), remullir (27)
to beautify, embellecer (73)
to beautify, hermosear (1)
to become, ponerse (98) (4)
to become, resultar (1)
to become, tornarse (1) (4)
to become, volverse (ue) (70) (4)
to become a naturalized citizen, naturalizarse (11) (4)
to become absorbed in thought, ensimismarse (1) (4)
to become academic, academizarse (11) (4)
to become accustomed, acostumbrarse (1) (4)
to become accustomed, avezarse (11) (4)
to become accustomed, connaturalizarse (11) (4)
to become afraid or apprehensive, sobrecogerse (15) (4)
to become aggravated, agudizarse (11) (4)
to become alienated, alienarse (1) (4)
to become allied, aliarse (61) (4)
to become angry, encolerizarse (11) (4)
to become angry, indignarse (1) (4)
to become annoyed, amoscarse (8) (4)
to become antiquated, anticuarse (1) or (62) (4)
to become arid, aridecerse (73) (4)
to become attached, apegarse (9) (4)

to **become bitter**, amargarse (9) (4)
to **become black**, denegrecerse (73) (4)
to **become black and blue**, acardenalarse (1) (4)
to **become black and blue**, amoratarse (1) (4)
to **become bold**, encalvecer (73)
to **become bourgeois**, aburguesarse (1) (4)
to **become burnt (food)**, churruscarse (8) (4)
to **become capacitated**, capacitarse (1) (4)
to **become childish**, aniñarse (1) (4)
to **become childish**, chochear (1)
to **become cloudy**, anublarse (1) (4)
to **become cloudy**, encapotarse (1) (4)
to **become cloudy**, nublarse (1) (4)
to **become cloudy**, opacarse (8) (4)
to **become collectivized**, colectivizarse (11) (4)
to **become common**, vulgarizarse (11) (4)
to **become communistic**, comunizarse (11) (4)
to **become complicated**, complicarse (8) (4)
to **become compressed**, comprimirse (3) (4)
to **become compromised**, comprometerse (2) (4)
to **become confident**, confiarse (61) (4)
to **become confused**, confundirse (3) (4)
to **become confused**, cortarse (1) (4)
to **become confused**, desorientarse (1) (4)
to **become confused or mixed up**, trabucarse (8) (4)
to **become constipated**, estreñirse (i, i) (60) (4)
to **become contaminated**, contagiarse (1) (4)
to **become contaminated**, contaminarse (1) (4)
to **become convex**, abombarse (1) (4)
to **become convinced**, persuadirse (3) (4)
to **become crazy**, enloquecerse (73) (4)
to **become damaged**, averiarse (61) (4)
to **become damp**, humdecerse (73) (4)
to **become dark**, atenebrarse (1) (4)
to **become dark**, obscurecerse (73) (4)
to **become decayed**, cariarse (61) (4)
to **become deep**, profundizarse (11) (4)
to **become deeply absorbed**, engolfarse (1) (4)
to **become deformed**, deformarse (1) (4)
to **become dignified**, dignificarse (8) (4)
to **become disappointed**, desengañarse (1) (4)
to **become discouraged**, desalentarse (ie) (37) (4)
to **become disillusioned**, desengañarse (1) (4)
to **become disquieted**, desasosegarse (ie) (50) (4)
to **become drowsy**, amodorrarse (1) (4)
to **become dry**, aridecerse (73) (4)
to **become electrified**, electrizarse (11) (4)
to **become emancipated**, emanciparse (1) (4)
to **become embarrassed**, corrarse (2) (4)
to **become embarrassed**, embarazarse (11) (4)
to **become embittered**, desabrirse (3) (4)
to **become entangled**, complicarse (8) (4)

to **become entangled**, enmarañarse (1) (4)
to **become entangled or involved**, enfrascarse (8) (4)
to **become evident**, traslucirse (74) (4)
to **become excited**, exaltarse (1) (4)
to **become excited**, excitarse (1) (4)
to **become familiar**, familiarizarse (11) (4)
to **become fervorous or heated**, enfervorizarse (11) (4)
to **become fluffy**, esponjarse (1) (4)
to **become fond of**, aficionarse (1) (4)
to **become fond of**, encariñarse (1) (4)
to **become friends**, amistarse (1) (4)
to **become frightened**, aterrarse (1) (4)
to **become generalized**, generalizarse (11) (4)
to **become gray-haired**, encanecerse (73) (4)
to **become grieved**, desconsolarse (ue) (36) (4)
to **become haughty**, altivecerse (73) (4)
to **become heated**, caldearse (1) (4)
to **become hot**, calecer (73)
to **become ill**, enfermar (1)
to **become impassioned**, apasionarse (1) (4)
to **become independent**, independizarse (11) (4)
to **become indifferent**, desganarse (1) (4)
to **become industrialized**, industrializarse (11) (4)
to **become infected**, contagiarse (1) (4)
to **become inflamed (said of the area surrounding a wound)**, enconarse (1) (4)
to **become infuriated**, enfurecerse (73) (4)
to **become insensible**, insensibilizarse (11) (4)
to **become installed**, instalarse (1) (4)
to **become involved in difficulties**, enzarzarse (11) (4)
to **become irritated or aggravated (said of the resentment against someone)**, enconarse (1) (4)
to **become juxtaposed**, yuxtaponerse (98) (4)
to **become known**, saberse (105) (4)
to **become known**, trascender (ie) (39)
to **become lazy**, apoltranarse (1) (4)
to **become less wild**, desbravecerse (73) (4)
to **become lethargic**, aletargarse (9) (4)
to **become magnetized**, imanarse (1) (4)
to **become marshy or swampy**, pantanizarse (11) (4)
to **become materialistic**, materializarse (11) (4)
to **become mean**, abellacarse (8) (4)
to **become mercenary**, metalizarse (11) (4)
to **become metalized**, metalizarse (11) (4)
to **become misty or hazy**, afôscarse (8) (4)
to **become moist**, humdecerse (73) (4)
to **become moldy**, florecerse (73) (4)
to **become moth-eaten**, apolillarse (1) (4)
to **become mountain-sick (altitude sick)**, sorocharse (1) (4)
to **become nauseated**, marearse (1) (4)
to **become numb**, entumcerse (73) (4)
to **become obscure**, opacarse (8) (4)

to **become old**, encanecerse (73) (4)
to **become or feel important**, crecerse (73) (4)
to **become paralyzed**, paralizarse (11) (4)
to **become polished (people)**, urbanizarse (11) (4)
to **become popular**, popularizarse (11) (4)
to **become preoccupied**, preocuparse (1) (4)
to **become qualified**, capacitarse (1) (4)
to **become reconciled**, bienquistarse (1) (4)
to **become reddish**, rojear (1)
to **become reddish (said of clouds)**, arrebolarse (1) (4)
to **become rejuvenated**, rejuvenecerse (73) (4)
to **become related by marriage**, emparentar (ie) (37)
to **become sad and gloomy**, ensombrecerse (73) (4)
to **become seasick**, marearse (1) (4)
to **become scared**, asustarse (1) (4)
to **become sexually aroused**, cachondearse (1) (4)
to **become silent**, callarse (1) (4)
to **become soaked**, calarse (1) (4)
to **become spoiled**, corromperse (2) (4)
to **become spoiled**, malograrse (1) (4)
to **become stabilized**, estabilizarse (11) (4)
to **become stiff in the joints**, anquilosarse (1) (4)
to **become stiff with cold**, aterirse (116) (4)
to **become strong**, robustecerse (73) (4)
to **become stupefied**, atontarse (1) (4)
to **become stupid**, abobarse (1) (4)
to **become swampy**, empantanarse (1) (4)
to **become tan**, curtirse (3) (4)
to **become tanned**, atezarse (11) (4)
to **become torn**, rasgarse (9) (4)
to **become turbid**, enturbiarse (1) (4)
to **become undernourished**, desnutrirse (3) (4)
to **become undisciplined**, indisciplinarse (1) (4)
to **become uneven**, desnivelarse (1) (4)
to **become unified**, unificarse (8) (4)
to **become unpopular**, impopularizarse (11) (4)
to **become unworthy**, desmerecer (73)
to **become unwound (a ball of string, yarn, etc.)**, desovillarse (1) (4)
to **become upset**, descomponerse (98) (4)
to **become urbanized**, urbanizarse (11) (4)
to **become used to difficulty**, curtirse (3) (4)
to **become useless**, inutilizarse (11) (4)
to **become vain**, engreirse (59) (4)
to **become vain**, envanecerse (73) (4)
to **become versed**, versarse (1) (4)
to **become vitiated**, viciarse (1) (4)
to **become volatile**, volatilizarse (11) (4)
to **become widespread**, divulgarse (9) (4)
to **become worn**, raerse (102) (4)
to **become yellow**, amarillecer (73)
to **become yellow**, enamarillecer (73)
to **beg**, mendigar (9)
to **beg**, rogar (ue) (45)
to **beg**, suplicar (8)
to **beg for**, impetrar (1)
to **begin**, comenzar (ie) (51)

to begin, empezar (ie) (51)
to begin, principiar (1)
to begin to act in some capacity, estrenarse (1) (4)
to begin to appear, repuntar (1)
to begin to move, rebullir (27)
to begin to rot, picarse (8) (4)
to begin to show, apuntar (1)
to begin to turn sour (said of wine), repuntarse (1) (4)
to beguile, capear (1)
to beguile, capotear (1)
to behave, comportarse (1) (4)
to behave, conducirse (67) (4)
to behave, portarse (1) (4)
to behave, vadearse (1) (4)
to behead, decapitar (1)
to behead, degollar (ue) (48)
to behead, descabezar (11)
to belch, eructar (1)
to belch, regoldar (ue) (48)
to belch, rotar (1)
to believe, creer (20)
to bellow, bramar (1)
to bellow, rugir (16)
to belong, competer (2)
to belong, pertenecer (73)
to belong to, corresponder (2)
to bend, combar (1)
to bend, corcovar (1)
to bend, doblar (1)
to bend, doblegar (9)
to bend, encorvar (1)
to bend, torcer (ue) (53)
to bend into an elbow, acodillar (1)
to bend or break (a stalk or trunk), tronchar (1)
to bend over, encorvarse (1) (4)
to benefit, beneficiar (1)
to bequeath, legar (9)
to besiege, asediar (1)
to bestow, conferir (ie, i) (41)
to bet, apostar (ue) (36)
to betray, vender (2)
to bevel, biselar (1)
to bewail, plañir (29)
to bewilder, deslumbrar (1)
to bewitch, embrujar (1)
to bewitch, hechizar (11)
to bind, precintar (1)
to bind, vendar (1)
to bind a book, encuadernar (1)
to bind oneself, liarse (19) (4)
to bind oneself, obligarse (9) (4)
to bisect, bisecar (8)
to bite, morder (ue) (38)
to bite, picar (8)
to bite again, remorder (ue) (38)
to bivouac, vivaquear (1)
to blacken, denegrecer (73)
to blacken, denegrir (116)
to blacken, ennegrecer (73)
to blame, afear (1)
to blame, culpar (1)
to blame, zaherir (ie, i) (41)
to blaspheme, blasfemar (1)
to bleat, balar (1)
to bleed, sangrar (1)
to bleed copiously, desangrar (1)
to blend, mezclar (1)
to blend colors, matizar (11)
to bless, bendecir (i, i) (79)
to blind, cegar (ie) (50)
to blink, parpadear (1)
to blink, pestañear (1)
to blister, ampollarse (1) (4)

to block, bloquear (1)
to block up, calzar (11)
to bloom again, renacer (73)
to blossom, florecer (73)
to blossom or flower again, reflorecer (73)
to blot, emborronar (1)
to blow, bufar (1)
to blow, soplar (1)
to blow (said of the wind), ventar (ie) (37)
to blow (said of the wind), ventear (1)
to blow a whistle, pitar (1)
to blow a whistle, pitear (1)
to blow a whistle, silbar (1)
to blow one's nose, sonarse (ue) (36) (4)
to blow out, reventar (ie) (37)
to blow up, volar (ue) (36)
to blunder, desatinar (1)
to blunt, despuntar (1)
to blush, abochornarse (1) (4)
to blush, enrojecer (73)
to blush, sonrosarse (1) (4)
to board, abordar (1)
to board, entablar (1)
to boast, alabarse (1) (4)
to boast, alardear (1)
to boast, blasonar (1)
to boast, bravear (1)
to boast, gloriarse (61) (4)
to boast, jactarse (1) (4)
to boast, ostentar (1)
to boast, presumir (3)
to boast, ufanarse (1) (4)
to boast, vanagloriarse (1) (4)
to boast of being, preciarse (1) (4)
to bob the head, cabecear (1)
to boil, bullir (27)
to boil, cocer (ue) (54)
to boil, hervir (ie, i) (41)
to boil over, salirse (106) (4)
to bolt, acerrojar (1)
to bomb, bombardear (1)
to bone, deshuesar (1)
to bone, desosar (ue) (47)
to boo, abuchear (1)
to border, bordear (1)
to border, colindar (1)
to border, comarcar (8)
to border, confinar (1)
to border, lindar (1)
to border on, rayar (1)
to bore, aburrir (3)
to bore, atediar (1)
to bore, cargar (9)
to bore, taladrar (1)
to bother, chinchar (1)
to bother, jorobar (1)
to bother, molestar (1)
to bottle, envasar (1)
to bounce, botar (1)
to bounce, resaltar (1)
to bounce back, rebotar (1)
to bound, limitar (1)
to bow, encajonar (1)
to bow, inclinar (1)
to bowl, bolear (1)
to box, boxear (1)
to boycott, boicotear (1)
to brag, fanfarronear (1)
to brag, farolear (1)
to braid, trenzar (11)
to brake, frenar (1)
to brand, marcar (8)
to brandish, blandir (116)
to brandish, esgrimir (3)

to bray, rebuznar (1)
to bread, empanar (1)
to break, quebrantar (1)
to break, quebrar (ie) (37)
to break, romper (104)
to break a habit, deshabituar (62)
to break (a ship down), desguazar (11)
to break (untilled ground), roturar (1)
to break forth, prorrumpir (3)
to break in, desbravar (1)
to break in, desbravecer (73)
to break into, irrumpir (3)
to break into, violentar (1)
to break into fragments, fragmentar (1)
to break loose, desatarse (1) (4)
to break loose, desencadenarse (1) (4)
to break loose (said of a horse), desbocarse (8) (4)
to break off, tronchar (1)
to break or tear off the lock of, descerrajar (1)
to break or tear to pieces, trizar (11)
to break out with fury (storm), desencadenarse (1) (4)
to break the neck of, desnucar (8)
to break the tie between, desempatar (1)
to break the wind, peer (20)
to break the wind, ventosear (1)
to break to pieces, despedazar (11)
to break to pieces, trozar (11)
to break up, trincar (8)
to breakfast, desayunar (1)
to breakfast, desayunarse (1) (4)
to breathe, respirar (1)
to breathe hard, resollar (ue) (36)
to breathe hard, resoplar (1)
to breed, criar (19)
to bribe, cohechar (1)
to bribe, sobornar (1)
to bribe, untar (1)
to bridle, enfrenar (1)
to brighten, abrillantar (1)
to brighten, aclarar (1)
to bring, aportar (1)
to bring, traer (109)
to bring close, arrimar (1)
to bring disagreement, desavenir (ie, i) (111)
to bring face to face, carear (1)
to bring in, entrar (1)
to bring near, aproximar (1)
to bring near or nearer, acercar (8)
to bring on, traer (109)
to bring to one's senses, ajuiciar (1)
to bring up, criar (19)
to bring up, educar (8)
to bristle, erizar (11)
to broadcast, difundir (3)
to broadcast, propagar (9)
to broadcast (by radio), perifonear (1)
to brood, aclocarse (ue) (44)
to browse, ramonear (1)
to browse around, curiosear (1)
to bruise, golpear (1)
to bruise, machucar (8)
to bruise, magullar (1)
to brush, cepillar (1)
to brush, escobillar (1)
to brutalize, brutalizar (11)
to brutalize, embrutecer (73)
to bubble, burbujear (1)
to buck (said of horses), corcovear (1)
to bud or sprout, despuntar (1)
to budget, presupuestar (1)
to build, construir (71)

to build, edificar (8)
to build (a bridge), tender (ie) (39)
to bulge, abultar (1)
to bump, topar (1)
to bump, trompear (1)
to bump into, topetar (1)
to bunch together, apelotonar (1)
to burden, gravar (1)
to burn, abrasar (1)
to burn, arder (1)
to burn, quemar (1)
to burn the outside (in the oven) with
    the inside not yet done, ahornarse
    (1) (4)
to burn up, agostar (1)
to burst, reventar (ie) (37)
to burst out, prorrumpir (3)
to burst with, rebosar (1)
to bury, enterrar (ie) (37)
to bury, sepultar (1)
to bury, soterrar (ie) (37)
to busy oneself, atarearse (1) (4)
to butcher, carnear (1)
to butcher, matar (1)
to butt, acornar (ue) (36)
to butt, acornear (1)
to butt, cornear (1)
to butt, topar (1)
to butt, topetar (1)
to butt in, entremeterse (2) (4)
to butt in, entrometerse (2) (4)
to butt in, trascolar (ue) (36)
to button, abotonar (1)
to button, abrochar (1)
to buy, comprar (1)
to buy, mercar (8)
to buy up real estate, afincar (8)
to buzz, zumbar (1)

C

to cable, cablegrafiar (61)
to cackle, cacarear (1)
to cackle, graznar (1)
to cage, enjaular (1)
to cajole, camelar (1)
to cajole, engatusar (1)
to calcify, calcificar (8)
to calcine, calcinar (1)
to calculate, calcular (1)
to calibrate, calibrar (1)
to call, denominar (1)
to call, llamar (1)
to call by one's surname, apellidar (1)
to call names, motejar (1)
to calm, asosegar (ie) (50)
to calm, serenar (1)
to calm, sosegar (ie) (50)
to calm down, apaciguarse (10) (4)
to calm down, desbravecerse (73) (4)
to calm down, desenfadarse (1) (4)
to calm down, pacificarse (8) (4)
to calm down, reponerse (98) (4)
to calm down, sosegarse (ie) (50) (4)
to camouflage, camuflar (1)
to camp, acampar (1)
to camp, campar (1)
to can, enlatar (1)
can (to be able), poder (ue) (97)
to canalize, canalizar (11)
to cancel, cancelar (1)
to candy, confitar (1)
to cannonade, cañonear (1)
to canonize, canonizar (11)
to cap, coronar (1)
to caper, caracolear (1)

to caper and prance, gambetear (1)
to capitalize, capitalizar (11)
to capitulate, capitular (1)
to capsize, volcar (ue) (44)
to capsize, zozobrar (1)
to captivate, seducir (67)
to capture, apresar (1)
to capture, capturar (1)
to capture, cautivar (1)
to caramelize, acaramelar (1)
to caramelize, caramelizar (1)
to carbonate, carbonatar (1)
to carbonize, carbonizar (11)
to card, cardar (1)
to card, carduzar (11)
to caress, acariciar (1)
to caricature, caricaturizar (11)
to carpet, alfombrar (1)
to carry, llevar (1)
to carry, portar (1)
to carry, sobrellevar (1)
to carry on one's back, portear (1)
to carry out, desempeñar (1)
to carry out, verificar (8)
to carry out simultaneously, simul-
    tanear (1)
to carry to an extreme, extremar (1)
to carry up, subir (3)
to cart, acarrear (1)
to cart, carretear (1)
to carve, cincelar (1)
to carve, entallar (1)
to carve, entretallar (1)
to carve, labrar (1)
to carve, tallar (1)
to carve (meat), trinchar (1)
to cash (a check), cobrar (1)
to cast, moldear (1)
to cast the evil eye, aojar (1)
to castrate, capar (1)
to castrate, castrar (1)
to catch, coger (15)
to catch, pescar (8)
to catch, pillar (1)
to catch, prender (2)
to catch, sorprender (2)
to catch a glimpse, atisbar (1)
to catch cold, acatarrarse (1) (4)
to catch cold, constiparse (1) (4)
to catch cold, resfriarse (61) (4)
to catch fire, incendiarse (1) (4)
to catch fire, prender (2)
to catch in a net, enredar (1)
to catch up, alcanzar (11)
to catechize, catequizar (11)
to caulk, calafatear (1)
to cause, causar (1)
to cause, determinar (1)
to cause, ocasionar (1)
to cause, producir (67)
to cause emotion, emocionar (1)
to cause enmity between, enemistar (1)
to cause grief, doler (ue) (38)
to cause indigestion, indigestarse (1) (4)
to cause remorse (to), remorder (ue) (38)
to cause sorrow, apenar (1)
to cause sorrow, pesar (1)
to cause suspicion, escamar (1)
to cause to happen before the regular
    time, anticipar (1)
to cause to like, aficionar (1)
to cauterize, cauterizar (11)
to caution, precautelar (1)
to cavil, cavilar (1)
to cease, cesar (1)
to celebrate, celebrar (1)

to celebrate, festejar (1)
to celebrate with a drink, remojar (1)
to cement, cementar (1)
to censure, zaherir (ie, i) (41)
to censure severely, fustigar (9)
to center, centrar (1)
to centrifuge, centrifugar (9)
to centuple, centuplicar (8)
to certificate, certificar (8)
to certify, certificar (8)
to chain, encadenar (1)
to challenge, retar (1)
to chamfer, chaflanar (1)
to change, cambiar (1)
to change, demudar (1)
to change, inmutar (1)
to change, mudar (1)
to change, transmutar (1)
to change, trocarse (ue) (44) (4)
to change, variar (61)
to change sides, voltearse (1) (4)
to change the nature of, trastrocar (ue)
    (44)
to change the order of, trastrocar (ue)
    (44)
to change thoroughly, permutar (1)
to change trains, transbordar (1)
to channel, acanalar (1)
to channel (stream), encauzar (11)
to chap, cortarse (1) (4)
to char, carbonizar (11)
to characterize, caracterizar (11)
to charge, cobrar (1)
to charge (battery), cargar (9)
to charm, cautivar (1)
to charm, embelesar (1)
to charm, encantar (1)
to charm, hechizar (11)
to charm, prendar (1)
to charter, fletar (1)
to chase away, ahuyentar (1)
to chat, confabular (1)
to chat, charlar (1)
to chat, paliquear (1)
to chat, platicar (8)
to chatter, cotorrear (1)
to chatter, chacharear (1)
to chatter, charlatanear (1)
to chatter, charlotear (1)
to chatter (teeth), castañetear (1)
to cheapen, abaratar (1)
to cheat, trampear (1)
to cheat, trapacear (1)
to check, comprobar (ue) (36)
to check, revisar (1)
to check, verificar (8)
to check (a horse) suddenly, sofrenar
    (1)
to check baggage, facturar (1)
to check over, repasar (1)
to cheer, alegrar (1)
to cheer, regocijar (1)
to cheer, vivar (1)
to cheer (dancers), jalear (1)
to chew, mascar (8)
to chew, masticar (8)
to chip the edge of, desportillar (1)
to chirp, piar (19)
to chirp, pipiar (61)
to chirp, piular (1)
to chirp (said of a cicada), chicharrear
    (1)
to chisel, cincelar (1)
to chloroform, cloroformizar (11)
to choir, corear (1)
to choke, ahogar (9)

to choke, añusgar (9)
to choke, atragantar (1)
to choke, sofocar (8)
to choose, elegir (i, i) (57)
to choose, escoger (15)
to choose, optar (1)
to chop off, tronchar (1)
to chop off (the top or tip), desmochar (1)
to chop up, picar (8)
to Christianize, cristianizar (11)
to cinch, cinchar (1)
to cipher, cifrar (1)
to circle, circuir (73)
to circulate, circular (1)
to circumcise, circuncidar (1)
to circumnavigate, circunnavegar (9)
to circumscribe, circunscribir (69)
to cite, citar (1)
to civilize, civilizar (11)
to civilize, descortezar (11)
to clap, palmear (1)
to clap, palmotear (1)
to clarify, clarear (1)
to clarify, clarificar (8)
to clasp, trabar (1)
to classify, clasificar (8)
to clean, limipar (1)
to clean up, asear (1)
to clean up, adecentar (1)
to clean up (usually a plate, bowl, etc. with a piece of bread), arrebañar (1)
to clear, despejar (1)
to clear (the table), quitar (1)
to clear of stubble, rastrojar (1)
to clear out, escampar (1)
to clear out (debris, rubbish), escombrar (1)
to clear up, clarear (1)
to clear up, despejarse (1) (4)
to clear up (said of the sky), arrasarse (1) (4)
to cleave, hender (ie) (39)
to click (the tongue), chascar (8)
to click castanets, castañetear (1)
to climb, encaramarse (1) (4)
to climb, escalar (1)
to climb, trepar (1)
to climb down, descolgarse (ue) (45)
to clinch (a driven nail), remachar (1)
to clink, tintinear (1)
to cloak, encapotar (1)
to clock, cronometrar (1)
to close, cerrar (ie) (37)
to close, clausurar (1)
to close, ultimar (1)
to close (a wound), cicatrizar (11)
to clot, agrumar (1)
to cloud, aneblar (ie) (37)
to cloud, anieblar (1)
to cloud, anublar (1)
to cloud, nublar (1)
to cloud over, obscurecerse (73) (4)
to clown, bufonear (1)
to clown, payasear (1)
to clown around, apayasarse (1) (4)
to cloy, empalagar (9)
to club, aporrear (1)
to cluck, clocar (ue) (44)
to cluck, cloquear (1)
to cluster, arracimarse (1) (4)
to coagulate, coagular (1)
to coagulate, cuajar (1)
to coat, revestir (i, i) (42)
to codify, codificar (8)
to coerce, coactar (1)

to coerce, coercer (12)
to coexist, coexistir (3)
to coextend, coextender (2)
to coin, acuñar (1)
to coin, amonedar (1)
to coincide, coincidir (3)
to collaborate, colaborar (1)
to collapse, aplomarse (1) (4)
to collapse, desplomarse (1) (4)
to collate, colacionar (1)
to collect, cobrar (1)
to collect, coleccionar (1)
to collect, colectar (1)
to collect, percibir (3)
to collect (taxes, rent), recaudar (1)
to collect a debt, reembolsarse (1) (4)
to collectivize, colectivizar (11)
to collide, chocar (8)
to colonize, colonizar (11)
to color, colorar (1)
to color, colorear (1)
to color, colorir (116)
to color, teñir (i, i) (60)
to color, tintar (1)
to color blue, azular (1)
to comb, peinar (1)
to comb one's hair, peinarse (1) (4)
to combat, combatir (3)
to combine, combinar (1)
to come, acudir (3)
to come, advenir (ie, i) (111)
to come, llegar (9)
to come, provenir (ie, i) (111)
to come, venir (ie, i) (111)
to come along, acompañar (1)
to come close, arrimarse (1) (4)
to come down, bajar (1)
to come face to face, encararse (1) (4)
to come forth, surgir (16)
to come from, descender (ie) (39)
to come off, despegarse (9) (4)
to come off well, lucirse (74) (4)
to come out, salir (106)
to come to grips, acapizarse (11) (4)
to come to terms, concertarse (ie) (37) (4)
to come to the rescue, acudir (3)
to come together, confluir (71)
to come untied, desatarse (1) (4)
to come up, subir (3)
to comfort, confortar (1)
to comfort, reanimar (1)
to comfort, reconfortar (1)
to comfort, solazar (11)
to command, comandar (1)
to command, mandar (1)
to commemorate, conmemorar (1)
to comment, apostillar (1)
to comment, comentar (1)
to commercialize, comercializar (11)
to commission, comisionar (1)
to commit, cometer (2)
to commit perjury, perjurar (1)
to commit suicide, suicidarse (1) (4)
to communicate, comunicar (8)
to communicate, participar (1)
to communize, comunizar (11)
to compare, comparar (1)
to compare, conferir (ie, i) (41)
to compare, contraponer (98)
to compare, cotejar (1)
to compare, equiparar (1)
to compare, parangonar (1)
to compel, compeler (2)
to compel, obligar (9)
to compensate, compensar (1)
to compensate, resarcir (13)

to compete, competir (i, i) (42)
to compete, contender (ie) (39)
to compete, rivalizar (11)
to compile, compilar (1)
to compile, recopilar (1)
to complain, aquejarse (1) (4)
to complain, quejarse (1) (4)
to complain, querellarse (1) (4)
to complement, complementar (1)
to complete, acabar (1)
to complete, completar (1)
to complicate, complicar (8)
to compliment, piropear (1)
to comply, contemporizar (11)
to compose, componer (98)
to compound (interest), capitalizar (11)
to comprehend, comprender (2)
to compress, apelmazar (11)
to compress, comprimir (3)
to compromise, comprometer (2)
to compromise, transigir (16)
to compute, computar (1)
to conceal, celar (1)
to conceal, ocultar (1)
to conceal, solapar (1)
to concede, conceder (2)
to conceive, concebir (i, i) (42)
to conceive, ingeniar (1)
to concentrate, concentrar (1)
to concentrate, reconcentrar (1)
to concern, atañer (28)
to concern, concernir (ie) (85)
to concern, importar (1)
to concern, incumbir (3)
to concern, respectar (1)
to conciliate, conciliar (1)
to conclude, concertar (ie) (37)
to conclude, concluir (71)
to concrete, concretar (1)
to concur, concurrir (3)
to condemn, condenar (1)
to condense, condensar (1)
to condescend, condescender (ie) (39)
to condescend, dignarse (1) (4)
to condition, acondicionar (1)
to condition, condicionar (1)
to condone, condonar (1)
to conduct, conducir (67)
to conduct oneself, portarse (1) (4)
to conduct oneself, vadearse (1) (4)
to confederate, confederar (1)
to confer, conferenciar (1)
to confess, confesar (ie) (37)
to confide, confiar (61)
to confide, fiar (19)
to confine, confinar (1)
to confine oneself, reducirse (67) (4)
to confirm, confirmar (1)
to confirm, convalidar (1)
to confiscate, confiscar (8)
to confiscate, decomisar (1)
to confiscate, requisar (1)
to conflict with, repugnar (1)
to conform, conformar (1)
to confront, afrontar (1)
to confront, confrontar (1)
to confront, cotejar (1)
to confront, enfrentar (1)
to confuse, atolondrar (1)
to confuse, confundir (3)
to confuse, desorientar (1)
to confuse, perturbar (1)
to congeal, helar (ie) (37)
to congest, congestionar (1)
to conglomerate, conglomerar (1)
to congratulate, congratular (1)

to **congratulate**, felicitar (1)
to **congregate**, congregar (9)
to **conjugate**, conjugar (9)
to **conjure**, conjurar (1)
to **connect**, conectar (1)
to **connect**, conexionar (1)
to **connect**, empalmar (1)
to **connect**, enchufar (1)
to **connect**, enlazar (11)
to **connive**, confabularse (1) (4)
to **connote**, connotar (1)
to **conquer**, conquistar (1)
to **consecrate**, consagrar (1)
to **consent**, consentir (ie, i) (41)
to **conserve**, conservar (1)
to **consider**, considerar (1)
to **consider**, reparar (1)
to **consist**, consistir (3)
to **consist**, constar (1)
to **console**, consolar (ue) (36)
to **console**, solazar (11)
to **consolidate**, consolidar (1)
to **consign**, consignar (1)
to **conspire**, conjurar (1)
to **conspire**, conspirar (1)
to **conspire**, urdir (3)
to **constipate**, estreñir (i, i) (60)
to **constitute**, constituir (71)
to **constrain**, constreñir (i, i) (60)
to **constrict**, astringir (16)
to **constrict**, restringir (16)
to **constrict**, restriñir (29)
to **construct**, construir (71)
to **consult**, consultar (1)
to **consumate**, consumar (1)
to **consume**, consumir (3)
to **contain**, contener (ie) (108)
to **contain**, encerrar (ie) (37)
to **contain**, entrañar (1)
to **contaminate**, contagiar (1)
to **contaminate**, contaminar (1)
to **contend**, contender (ie) (39)
to **content**, contentar (1)
to **contemplate**, contemplar (1)
to **contemplate**, meditar (1)
to **continue**, continuar (62)
to **continue**, proseguir (i, i) (58)
to **continue**, seguir (i, i) (58)
to **contract**, contraer (109)
to **contract**, contratar (1)
to **contract (muscles)**, crispar (1)
to **contract and/or have the relationship of father-godfather (with respect to each other)**, compadrar (1)
to **contract and/or have the relationship of father-godfather (with respect to each other)**, compadrear (1)
to **contract with cramps (muscles)**, acalambrarse (1) (4)
to **contradict**, contradecir (i, i) (84)
to **contradict**, desmentir (ie, i) (41)
to **contribute**, aportar (1)
to **contribute**, contribuir (71)
to **contribute one's share**, cotizar (11)
to **control**, controlar (1)
to **control**, moderar (1)
to **control (a passion)**, sofrenar (1)
to **control oneself**, contenerse (ie) (108) (4)
to **control oneself**, dominarse (1) (4)
to **control oneself**, moderarse (1) (4)
to **control oneself**, sobreponerse (98) (4)
to **control oneself**, vencerse (12) (4)
to **contuse**, contundir (3)
to **contuse**, contusionar (1)
to **convalesce**, convalecer (73)

to **convene**, convenir (ie, i) (111)
to **converge**, converger (15)
to **converge**, convergir (16)
to **converse**, conversar (1)
to **converse**, departir (3)
to **converse**, platicar (8)
to **convert**, convertir (ie, i) (41)
to **convince**, convencer (12)
to **convoke**, convocar (8)
to **convulse**, convulsionar (1)
to **coo**, arrullar (1)
to **cook**, cocer (ue) (54)
to **cook**, cocinar (1)
to **cook**, guisar (1)
to **cook a lot**, recocer (ue) (54)
to **cook again**, recocer (ue) (54)
to **cool**, enfriar (61)
to **cool**, refrescar (8)
to **cool**, serenar (1)
to **cool down**, entibiarse (1) (4)
to **cooperate**, cooperar (1)
to **coordinate**, coordinar (1)
to **copulate**, copularse (1) (4)
to **copy**, calcar (8)
to **copy**, contrahacer (90)
to **copy**, copiar (1)
to **copy down**, copiar (1)
to **cordon off**, acordonar (1)
to **corner**, arrinconar (1)
to **corner**, copar (1)
to **corral**, acorralar (1)
to **correct**, corregir (i, i) (57)
to **correct**, enmendar (ie) (37)
to **correct**, subsanar (1)
to **correlate**, correlacionar (1)
to **correspond**, corresponder (2)
to **corroborate**, corroborar (1)
to **corroborate**, roborar (1)
to **corrode**, corroer (103)
to **corrugate**, acanalar (1)
to **corrugate**, corrugar (9)
to **corrupt**, corromper (2)
to **corrupt**, inficionar (1)
to **corrupt**, malear (1)
to **cost**, costar (ue) (36)
to **cost**, valer (110)
to **couch (the lance)**, enristrar (1)
to **cough**, toser (2)
to **count**, contar (ue) (36)
to **counterattack**, contraatacar (8)
to **counterbalance**, contrabalancear (1)
to **counterbalance**, contrapesar (1)
to **counterfeit**, contrahacer (90)
to **counterfeit**, falsificar (8)
to **countermarch**, contramarchar (1)
to **couple**, acoplar (1)
to **court**, cortejar (1)
to **court**, festejar (1)
to **court**, galantear (1)
to **cover**, cobijar (1)
to **cover**, cubrir (82)
to **cover**, forrar (1)
to **cover**, recubrir (82)
to **cover**, tapar (1)
to **cover**, vestir (i, i) (42)
to **cover or soak with tar**, embrear (1)
to **cover the face with a cloak or muffler**, embozar (11)
to **cover up**, cubrir (82)
to **cover up**, tapar (1)
to **cover with an awning**, entoldar (1)
to **cover with batter**, rebozar (11)
to **cover with dust**, empolvar (1)
to **cover with earth**, aterrar (ie) (37)
to **cover with paste**, empastar (1)
to **covet**, acodiciar (1)

to **covet**, codiciar (1)
to **crack**, agrietarse (1) (4)
to **crack**, cascar (8)
to **crack**, rajar (1)
to **crack**, resquebrajar (1)
to **crack (break with a sharp noise)**, chascarse (8) (4)
to **crackle**, crepitar (1)
to **crackle**, decrepitar (1)
to **cram**, atestar (1)
to **cram**, atestar (ie) (37)
to **cram**, atracar (8)
to **crash**, estrellarse (1) (4)
to **crave**, apetecer (73)
to **crawl**, arrastrarse (1) (4)
to **crawl**, gatear (1)
to **crawl**, reptar (1)
to **craze**, enloquecer (73)
to **creak**, crujir (3)
to **creak (door)**, gruñir (29)
to **create**, crear (1)
to **credit**, acreditar (1)
to **cripple**, baldar (1)
to **cripple**, derrengar (ie) (50)
to **cripple**, lisiar (1)
to **cripple**, tullir (27)
to **criticize**, criticar (8)
to **croak**, croar (1)
to **croak**, graznar (1)
to **cross**, atravesar (ie) (37)
to **cross**, cruzar (11)
to **cross**, pasar (1)
to **cross out**, tachar (1)
to **crouch**, agacharse (1) (4)
to **crouch**, agazaparse (1) (4)
to **crowd**, arremolinarse (1) (4)
to **crown**, coronar (1)
to **crucify**, crucificar (8)
to **crumb**, migar (9)
to **crumble**, desmenuzar (11)
to **crumble**, desmoronar (1)
to **crumble down**, desmoronarse (1) (4)
to **crush**, apabullar (1)
to **crush**, apachurrar (1)
to **crush**, machacar (8)
to **crush**, machucar (8)
to **crush (stones)**, chancar (8)
to **cry**, llorar (1)
to **cry out for**, clamar (1)
to **crystallize**, cristalizar (11)
to **cube (math)**, cubicar (8)
to **culminate**, culminar (1)
to **cultivate**, cultivar (1)
to **curd**, agrumar (1)
to **curdle**, cortarse (1) (4)
to **curdle**, engrumecerse (73) (4)
to **cure**, curar (1)
to **cure**, sanar (1)
to **curl**, ensortijar (1)
to **curl**, rizar (11)
to **curl up**, abarquillar (1)
to **curl up**, retortijar (1)
to **curse**, maldecir (i, i) (79)
to **curse**, renegar (ie, i) (50)
to **curtail**, escatimar (1)
to **cushion**, almohadillar (1)
to **cut**, acuchillar (1)
to **cut**, cortar (1)
to **cut**, sajar (1)
to **cut**, tajar (1)
to **cut (a precious stone)**, tallar (1)
to **cut down**, cercenar (1)
to **cut (cloth) on the bias**, sesgar (9)
to **cut hair**, pelar (1)
to **cut hair**, tonsurar (1)
to **cut into boards**, tablear (1)

to cut into logs, trozar (11)
to cut off, cortar (1)
to cut off, segar (ie) (50)
to cut out, recortar (1)
to cut the hair very short, rapar (1)
to cut through, surcar (8)
to cut with scissors, tijeretear (1)

D

to dam, embalsar (1)
to dam, rebalsar (1)
to dam back, rebalsar (1)
to dam up, embalsarse (1) (4)
to damage, averiar (61)
to damage, dañar (1)
to damage, empecer (73)
to damage, perjudicar (8)
to damage (reputation), vulnerar (1)
to dance, bailar (1)
to dance, danzar (11)
to dangle, colgar (ue) (45)
to dangle, pender (2)
to dare, atreverse (2) (4)
to dare, osar (1)
to dare, retar (1)
to darken, ennegrecer (73)
to darken, ensomberecer (73)
to darken, obscurecer (73)
to darken, opacar (8)
to darn, zurcir (13)
to dash along, talonear (1)
to dash off, dispararse (1) (4)
to date, datar (1)
to date (a document, etc.), fechar (1)
to date back, retrotraer (109)
to daub, embadurnar (1)
to daub, pintarrajear (1)
to dawn, alborear (1)
to dawn, amanecer (73)
to dawn, clarecer (73)
to dawn, esclarecer (73)
to daydream, fantasear (1)
to dazzle, deslumbrar (1)
to deafen, asordar (1)
to deafen, ensordecer (73)
to deafen or disturb with thunderlike
　　noise, atronar (ue) (36)
to deal, mercadear (1)
to deal, versar (1)
to deal (cards), repartir (3)
to deal a blow, asestar (1)
to deal at retail, trapichear (1)
to deal with, tratar (1)
to debate, debatir (3)
to debauch, relajar (1)
to decant, decantar (1)
to decay, cariar (61)
to decay, decaer (81)
to deceive, burlar (1)
to deceive, chapucear (1)
to deceive, embaír (117)
to deceive, engañar (1)
to decide, decidir (3)
to decide on, resolver (ue) (70)
to decimate, diezmar (1)
to decipher, descifrar (1)
to deck out, engalanar (1)
to declaim, declamar (1)
to declare, declarar (1)
to declare, manifestar (ie) (37)
to declare a patient past recovery,
　　desahuciar [See special note on (34)]
to decline, declinar (1)
to decline, rehuir (71)
to decompose, descomponer (98)

to decongest, descongestionar (1)
to decorate, decorar (1)
to decorate (with honors, medals,
　　etc.), condecorar (1)
to decorate with flowers, florear (1)
to decrease, decrecer (73)
to decrease, descaecer (73)
to decrease, mermar (1)
to decree, decretar (1)
to dedicate, dedicar (8)
to deduce, deducir (67)
to deduct, deducir (67)
to deduct, substraer (109)
to deepen, ahondar (1)
to defame, detractar (1)
to defame, detraer (109)
to defame, difamar (1)
to defame, infamar (1)
to defeat, derrotar (1)
to defeat, vencer (12)
to defecate, cagar (9)
to defecate, defecar (8)
to defect, defeccionar (1)
to defend, apologizar (11)
to defend, defender (ie) (39)
to defend, propugnar (1)
to defer, diferir (ie, i) (41)
to defer, dilatar (1)
to defer, prorrogar (9)
to defer (yield), deferir (ie, i) (41)
to define, definir (3)
to deflate, deshinchar (1)
to deflate, desinflar (1)
to defoliate, deshojar (1)
to deform, deformar (1)
to defraud, defraudar (1)
to defraud, estafar (1)
to defray, sufragar (9)
to defray or pay cost, costear (1)
to defrost, descongelar (1)
to defy, desafiar (61)
to degenerate, degenerar (1)
to degrade, degradar (1)
to dehumanize, deshumanizar (11)
to dehumidify, deshumedecer (73)
to dehydrate, deshidratar (1)
to deify, deificar (8)
to deify, divinizar (11)
to deify, endiosar (1)
to delay, atrasar (1)
to delay, demorar (1)
to delay, entretener (ie) (108)
to delay, postergar (9)
to delay, retrasar (1)
to delay, tardar (1)
to delegate, delegar (9)
to delegate, diputar (1)
to deliberate, deliberar (1)
to delight, deleitar (1)
to delight, extasiar (61)
to delimit, delimitar (1)
to delineate, delinear (1)
to deliver, entregar (9)
to deliver (a speech), pronunciar (1)
to delude, deludir (3)
to demand, demandar (1)
to demand, exigir (16)
to demand, pedir (i, i) (42)
to demand (one's rights), reivindicar (8)
to demand explanations, interpelar (1)
to demarcate, demarcar (8)
to demilitarize, desmilitarizar (11)
to demobilize, desmovilizar (11)
to democratize, democratizar (11)
to demolish, arrasar (1)
to demolish, demoler (ue) (38)

to demonstrate, demostrar (ue) (36)
to demoralize, desmoralizar (11)
to denaturalize, desnaturalizar (11)
to denigrate, denigrar (1)
to denote, denotar (1)
to denounce, delatar (1)
to denounce, denunciar (1)
to dent, abollar (1)
to dent, mellar (1)
to denude, denudar (1)
to deny, denegar (ie) (50)
to deny, negar (ie) (50)
to deny intensely, renegar (ie, i) (50)
to depart, partir (3)
to depend, depender (2)
to depend, pender (2)
to depict, pintar (1)
to depilate, depilar (1)
to deplore, deplorar (1)
to depopulate, despoblar (ue) (36)
to deport, deportar (1)
to depose, deponer (98)
to deposit, depositar (1)
to deposit, ingresar (1)
to deprave, depravar (1)
to depreciate, depreciar (1)
to depress, deprimir (3)
to deprive, destituir (71)
to deprive, privar (1)
to deprive of, despojar (1)
to deprive of authority or credit, des-
　　autorizar (11)
to deprive of essentials, desproveer (99)
to deprive of shelter, desabrigar (9)
to deprive someone of something nec-
　　essary, desaviar (61)
to derail, descarrilar (1)
to derive, derivar (1)
to descend, descender (ie) (39)
to describe, describir (69)
to desecrate, profanar (1)
to desert, defeccionar (1)
to desert, desertar (1)
to deserve, merecer (73)
to desiccate, desecar (8)
to design, trazar (11)
to designate, designar (1)
to designate, señalar (1)
to desire, desear (1)
to desire, querer (ie) (101)
to desire eagerly, anhelar (1)
to desist, desistir (3)
to desist, sobreseer (20)
to despair, desesperar (1)
to despise, despreciar (1)
to despoil, despojar (1)
to destine, destinar (1)
to destroy, anonadar (1)
to destroy, desbaratar (1)
to destroy, destruir (71)
to destroy completely, extirpar (1)
to detail, detallar (1)
to detain, detener (ie) (108)
to detect, detectar (1)
to deteriorate, deteriorar (1)
to determine, determinar (1)
to determine the volume of, cubicar (8)
to detest, detestar (1)
to dethrone, destronar (1)
to detonate, detonar (1)
to detonate, fulminar (1)
to detract, detractar (1)
to detract, detraer (109)
to devaluate, desvalorar (1)
to devaluate, desvalorizar (11)
to devastate, devastar (1)

to **develop**, desarrollar (1)
to **develop**, revelar (1)
to **deviate**, desviar (61)
to **deviate**, ladear (1)
to **devise**, excogitar (1)
to **devise**, idear (1)
to **devote**, consagrar (1)
to **devote oneself**, aplicarse (8) (4)
to **devote oneself**, consagrarse (1) (4)
to **devote oneself**, darse (83) (4)
to **devour**, devorar (1)
to **dew**, rociar (61)
to **diagnose**, diagnosticar (8)
to **dial**, marcar (8)
to **dialogue**, dialogar (9)
to **dictate**, dictar (1)
to **die**, fallecer (73)
to **die**, morir (ue, u) (94)
to **die**, perecer (73)
to **die away**, morir (ue, u) (94)
to **die first**, premorir (ue, u) (94)
to **differ**, diferenciarse (1) (4)
to **differ**, diferir (ie, i) (41)
to **differentiate**, diferenciar (1)
to **diffuse**, difundir (3)
to **dig**, cavar (1)
to **dig a ditch or ditches in**, zanjar (1)
to **dig holes**, ahoyar (1)
to **digest**, digerir (ie, i) (41)
to **dignify**, dignificar (8)
to **digress**, divagar (9)
to **dilapidate**, dilapidar (1)
to **dilate**, dilatar (1)
to **dilute**, deslefr (i, i) (59
to **dilute**, diluir (71)
to **dim**, obscurecer (73)
to **diminish**, amenguar (10)
to **diminish**, aminorar (1)
to **diminish**, diminuir (71)
to **diminish**, disminuir (71)
to **diminish**, menguar (10)
to **diminish**, menoscabar (1)
to **diminish the quality or value of**, desvirtuar (62)
to **dine**, yantar (1)
to **dip**, remojar (1)
to **direct**, dirigir (16)
to **direct**, encarrilar (1)
to **direct**, encauzar (11)
to **direct**, regentar (1)
to **direct**, regir (i, i) (57)
to **dirty**, emporcar (ue) (44)
to **dirty**, ensuciar (1)
to **disable**, imposibilitar (1)
to **disaccustom**, deshabituar (62)
to **disagree**, desavenirse (ie, i) (111) (4)
to **disagree**, disconvenir (ie, i) (111)
to **disagree**, discordar (ue) (36)
to **disagree**, discrepar (1)
to **disappear**, desaparecer (73)
to **disappear**, esfumarse (1) (4)
to **disappear rapidly**, volar (ue) (36)
to **disappoint**, decepcionar (1)
to **disappoint**, defraudar (1)
to **disappoint**, desengañar (1)
to **disappoint**, desilusionar (1)
to **disapprove**, desaprobar (ue) (36)
to **disapprove**, improbar (ue) (36)
to **disapprove**, oponerse (98) (4)
to **disarm**, desarmar (1)
to **disassociate**, desasociar (1)
to **disassociate**, disociar (1)
to **disband**, desbandar (1)
to **disband**, desabandarse (1) (4)
to **disburse**, desembolsar (1)
to **discard**, descartar (1)

to **discard**, desechar (1)
to **discern**, discernir (ie) (85)
to **discharge**, descargar (9)
to **discipline**, disciplinar (1)
to **discolor**, descolorar (1)
to **discolor**, descolorir (120)
to **discolor**, desteñir (i, i) (60)
to **discolor**, desteñirse (i, i) (60) (4)
to **disconcert**, desconcertar (ie) (37)
to **disconnect**, desconectar (1)
to **discontinue**, descontinuar (62)
to **discontinue**, discontinuar (62)
to **discount**, descontar (ue) (36)
to **discourage**, desalentar (ie) (37)
to **discourage**, desanimar (1)
to **discourse**, disertar (1)
to **discourse at large**, explayarse (1) (4)
to **discover**, descubrir (82)
to **discredit**, desacreditar (1)
to **discredit**, desautorizar (11)
to **discredit**, desprestigiar (1)
to **discriminate against**, discriminar (1)
to **discuss**, discutir (3)
to **discuss a doubtful point**, cuestionar (1)
to **disdain**, desdeñar (1)
to **disembark**, desembarcar (8)
to **disembarrass**, desembarazar (11)
to **disenchant**, desencantar (1)
to **disengage**, desembragar (9)
to **disengage**, desenganchar (1)
to **disentangle**, desembarrancar (8)
to **disentangle**, desenmarañar (1)
to **disentangle**, desenredar (1)
to **disfavor**, desfavorecer (73)
to **disfigure**, desfigurar (1)
to **disguise**, disfrazar (11)
to **disgust**, asquear (1)
to **disgust**, repugnar (1)
to **dishearten**, descorazonar (1)
to **dishonor**, deshonorar (1)
to **dishonor**, mancillar (1)
to **dishonor**, profanar (1)
to **disinfect**, desinfectar (1)
to **disillusion**, desencantar (1)
to **disillusion**, desengañar (1)
to **disinherit**, desheredar (1)
to **disintegrate**, disgregar (9)
to **disjoint**, desarticular (1)
to **dislike**, malquerer (ie) (101)
to **dislocate**, descoyuntar (1)
to **dislocate**, desencajar (1)
to **dislocate**, dislocar (8)
to **dislodge**, desalojar (1)
to **dismantle**, desmantelar (1)
to **dismember**, desmembrar (ie) (37)
to **dismiss from office**, destituir (71)
to **dismount**, apear (1)
to **dismount**, descabalgar (9)
to **dismount**, desmontar (1)
to **disorder**, desbarajustar (1)
to **disorganize**, desorganizar (11)
to **dispatch**, despachar (1)
to **disperse**, dispersar (1)
to **displace (nautical)**, desplazar (11)
to **display**, desplegar (ie) (50)
to **displease**, desagradar (1)
to **displease**, descontentar (1)
to **displease**, desplacer (73)
to **displease**, disgustar (1)
to **dispose**, disponer (98)
to **disproportion**, desproporcionar (1)
to **disprove**, desmentir (ie, i) (41)
to **dispute**, controvertir (ie, i) (41)
to **dispute**, disputar (1)
to **disobey**, desobedecer (73)

to **disquiet**, desasosegar (ie) (50)
to **disquiet**, intranquilizar (11)
to **disregard**, desatender (ie) (39)
to **dissatisfy**, descontentar (1)
to **disseminate**, diseminar (1)
to **dissent**, disentir (ie) i) (41)
to **dissent**, disidir (3)
to **dissipate**, disipar (1)
to **dissolve**, deshacerse (90) (4)
to **dissolve**, deslefr (i, i) (59)
to **dissolve**, disolver (ue) (70)
to **dissuade**, disuadir (3)
to **dissuade**, retraer (109)
to **distend**, distender (ie) (39)
to **distill**, alambicar (8)
to **distill**, destilar (1)
to **distinguish**, discernir (ie) (85)
to **distinguish**, distinguir (17)
to **distinguish**, divisar (1)
to **distinguish**, singularizar (11)
to **distort**, desfigurar (1)
to **distract**, distraer (109)
to **distribute**, distribuir (71)
to **distribute**, repartir (3)
to **distribute proportionally**, prorratear (1)
to **distribute proportionally**, ratear (1)
to **distrust**, desconfiar (61)
to **disturb**, disturbar (1)
to **disturb**, inquietar (1)
to **disturb**, molestar (1)
to **disturb**, perturbar (1)
to **disturb**, trastocar (8)
to **disturb**, trastornar (1)
to **disturb**, turbar (1)
to **dive**, bucear, (1)
to **dive**, chapuzar (11)
to **dive**, zambullirse (27) (4)
to **diverge**, divergir (16)
to **diversify**, diversificar (8)
to **divert one's mind**, despreocuparse (1) (4)
to **divide**, compartir (3)
to **divide**, partir (3)
to **divide (a garden) into sections**, tablear (1)
to **divide into equal parts**, comediar (1)
to **divide into fractions**, fraccionar (1)
to **divide into lots**, lotear (1)
to **divide into squares**, cuadricular (1)
to **divide into three forks or branches**, trifurcar (8)
to **divide into three parts**, terciar (1)
to **divide into two (branches, roads, etc.)**, bifurcar (8)
to **divorce**, divorciar (1)
to **divulge**, propalar (1)
to **do**, hacer (90)
to **do away with**, suprimir (3)
to **do frequently**, menudear (1)
to **do in a disorderly way**, embarullar (1)
to **do lathe work**, tornear (1)
to **do missionary work**, misionar (1)
to **do one's best**, esmerarse (1) (4)
to **do one's best for**, desvivirse (3) (4)
to **do or make something fast and poorly**, chapucear (1)
to **do or wear for the first time**, estrenar (1)
to **do over**, rehacer (90)
to **do poorly**, deslucirse (74) (4)
to **do violence to**, violentar (1)
to **do without**, prescindir (3)
to **do without**, preterir (ie, i) (119)
to **document**, documentar (1)

to document or support with evidence, razonar (1)
to dodge, esquivar (1)
to dodge, sortear (1)
to dogmatize, dogmatizar (11)
to doll up, adonizarse (11) (4)
to domesticate, domesticar (8)
to dominate, avasallar (1)
to dominate, dominar (1)
to dominate, señorear (1)
to don, revestir (i, i) (42)
to donate, donar (1)
to dot, puntear (1)
to double, doblar (1)
to double, redoblar (1)
to doubt, dudar (1)
to down (a steer) and hold his horns on the ground, mancornar (ue) (36)
to doze, adormilarse (1) (4)
to drag, arrastrar (1)
to drag, rastrear (1)
to drain, achicar (8)
to drain, desaguar (10)
to drain, drenar (1)
to drain, escurrir (3)
to drain, sangrar (1)
to dramatize, dramatizar (11)
to draw, delinear (1)
to draw, dibujar (1)
to draw (a curtain), descorrer (2)
to draw (a line), tirar (1)
to draw (as a line), trazar (11)
to draw (said of a chimney), tirar (1)
to draw out, sacar (8)
to draw out (a secret), sonsacar (8)
to draw towards evening, atardecer (73)
to draw up (a document), extender (ie) (39)
to dream, soñar (ue) (36)
to dredge, dragar (9)
to dredge, rastrear (1)
to dress, ponerse (98) (4)
to dress, vestir (i, i) (42)
to dress in mourning, enlutar (1)
to dress too fancily, atusarse (1) (4)
to dress up, adecentarse (1) (4)
to dress up, ataviarse (61) (4)
to dress up, emperejilar (1)
to dress up in one's Sunday (best) clothes, endomingarse (9) (4)
to dribble, driblar (1)
to dribble (soccer), regatear (1)
to drift, vagar (9)
to drift (snow), ventiscar (8)
to drill, barrenar (1)
to drill, fresar (1)
to drill, taladrar (1)
to drink, beber (2)
to drink, tomar (1)
to drink (wine, liquor), trincar (8)
to drink maté, matear (1)
to drink maté, yerbatear (1)
to drink too much, sobrebeber (2)
to drink up, beberse (2) (4)
to drip, chorrear (1)
to drip, escurrir (3)
to drip, gotear (1)
to drive, conducir (67)
to drive, manejar (1)
to drive (into), hincar (8)
to drive back, rechazar (11)
to drizzle, garuar (62)
to drizzle, lloviznar (1)
to drizzle, molliznar (1)

to drizzle, molliznear (1)
to drone, zanganear (1)
to drop in, descolgarse (ue) (45) (4)
to drown, ahogarse (9) (4)
to drug, drogar (9)
to drum with the fingers, tamborear (1)
to drum with the fingers (on a table, etc.), tabalear (1)
to dry, enjugar (9)
to dry, secar (9)
to dry thoroughly, resecar (8)
to dry up like cardboard, acartonarse (1) (4)
to duck, capear (1)
to duck, capotear (1)
to duck, zambullir (27)
to duck (a question), soslayar (1)
to duck under water, chapuzar (11)
to duck work or effort, remolonear (1)
to dull, embotar (1)
to dull, entorpecer (73)
to dump, verter (ie) (39)
to duplicate, duplicar (8)
to dust, desempolvar (1)
to dwell, morar (1)
to dye, teñir (i, i) (60)
to dynamite, dinamitar (1)

E

to earn, ganar (1)
to earnestly desire, ambicionar (1)
to ease, suavizar (11)
to ease up, escampar (1)
to eat, comer (2)
to eat, manducar (8)
to eat, yantar (1)
to eat breakfast, desayunar (1)
to eat breakfast, desayunarse (1) (4)
to eat dinner, cenar (1)
to eat lunch, almorzar (ue) (46)
to eat up, comerse (2) (4)
to eat without chewing, papar (1)
to eclipse, eclipsar (1)
to economize, economizar (11)
to eddy, remolinar (1)
to eddy, remolinarse (1) (4)
to edge, ribetear (1)
to edit, editar (1)
to educate, educar (8)
to educate and polish, desbastar (1)
to effect, efectuar (62)
to effeminate, afeminar (1)
to ejaculate, eyacular (1)
to elaborate, elaborar (1)
to elapse, transcurrir (3)
to elbow, codear (1)
to elect, elegir (i, i) (57)
to elect beforehand, preelegir (i, i) (57)
to electrify, electrificar (8)
to electrify, electrizar (11)
to electrocute, electrocutar (1)
to electrolyze, electrolizar (11)
to elevate, elevar (1)
to elevate, levantar (1)
to eliminate, eliminar (1)
to eliminate, suprimir (3)
to elucidate, dilucidar (1)
to elude, eludir (3)
to emanate, dimanar (1)
to emanate, emanar (1)
to emancipate, emancipar (1)
to emancipate, manumitir (3)
to embalm, embalsamar (1)
to embargo, embargar (9)

to embark, embarcar (8)
to embarrass, correr (2)
to embarrass, embarazar (11)
to embed, empotrar (1)
to embezzle, desfalcar (8)
to embezzle, malversar (1)
to embitter, acibarar (1)
to embrace, abarcar (8)
to embrace, abrazar (11)
to embroider in relief, recamar (1)
to embroil, embrollar (1)
to embroil, liar (19)
to emerge, emerger (15)
to emigrate, emigrar (1)
to emit, arrojar (1)
to emit, desprender (2)
to emit, emitir (3)
to emit, exhalar (1)
to emit fumes or vapor, vahar (1)
to emit fumes or vapor, vahear (1)
to emphasize, realzar (11)
to emphasize, subrayar (1)
to employ, emplear (1)
to empower, diputar (1)
to empty, desocupar (1)
to empty, desvaír (117)
to empty, vaciar (61)
to empty, verter (ie) (39)
to emulate, emular (1)
to enable, capacitar (1)
to enable, habilitar (1)
to enamel, esmaltar (1)
to enamor, enamorar (1)
to enchant, embobar (1)
to enchase, engastar (1)
to encircle, ceñir (i, i) (60)
to encircle, cercar (8)
to encircle with a halo, nimbar (1)
to enclose, incluir (71)
to encourage, alentar (ie) (37)
to encourage, animar (1)
to encourage, esforzar (ue) (46)
to encourage, jalear (1)
to end, acabar (1)
to end, finalizar (11)
to end, terminar (1)
to endeavor, procurar (1)
to endorse, endorsar (1)
to endorse, endosar (1)
to endorse, respaldar (1)
to endorse, subscribir (69)
to endow, dotar (1)
to endure, durar (1)
to endure, padecer (73)
to engage in a monologue, monologar (9)
to engage in guerrilla warfare, guerrillear (1)
to engage or throw in the clutch, embragar (9)
to engender, engendrar (1)
to engrave, entallar (1)
to engrave, entretallar (1)
to engrave, grabar (1)
to engrave with a burin, burilar (1)
to enhance, engrandecer (73)
to enjoy, disfrutar (1)
to enjoy, gozar (11)
to enjoy oneself, fruir (71)
to enlarge, agrandar (1)
to enlarge, engrandecer (73)
to enlarge, engrosar (ue) (36)
to enlist, alistar (1)
to enliven, avivar (1)
to ennoble, ennoblecer (73)

to enrage, ensañar (1)
to enrapture, embriagar (9)
to enrapture, enajenar (1)
to enrich, enriquecer (73)
to enroll, inscribirse (69) (4)
to enroll, matricular (1)
to ensilage, ensilar (1)
to enslave, esclavizar (11)
to entail, vincular (1)
to entangle, enbarrancarse (8) (4)
to entangle, enmarañar (1)
to entangle, intrincar (8)
to enter, entrar (1)
to enter, ingresar (1)
to entertain, entretener (ie) (108)
to enthrone, entronizar (11)
to enthuse, entusiasmar (1)
to entice away, sonsacar (8)
to entitle, titular (1)
to entrust, confiar (61)
to entrust, encargar (9)
to entrust, encomendar (ie) (37)
to entwine, entrelazar (11)
to enumerate, connumerar (1)
to enumerate, enumerar (1)
to enunciate, enunciar (1)
to envy, envidiar (1)
to epitomize, epitomar (1)
to equal, equivaler (110)
to equalize, igualar (1)
to equip, dotar (1)
to equip, equipar (1)
to equip, pertrechar (1)
to eradicate, erradicar (8)
to erase, borrar (1)
to erect, enhestar (ie) (37)
to erect, erguir (ie, i) (86)
to erect, erigir (16)
to erode, erosionar (1)
to err, aberrar (1)
to err, errar (ie) (52)
to err, pifiar (1)
to escape, escapar (1)
to escape, fugarse (9) (4)
to escort, escoltar (1)
to establish, establecer (73)
to establish, estatuir (71)
to establish, fundar (1)
to esteem, apreciar (1)
to esteem, estimar (1)
to esteem, reputar (1)
to estimate, avalorar (1)
to estimate, estimar (1)
to estimate, valuar (62)
to eulogize, panegirizar (11)
to evacuate, evacuar (1)
to evade, evadir (3)
to evaluate, evaluar (62)
to evangelize, evangelizar (11)
to evaporate, evaporar (1)
to even, igualar (1)
to even, nivelar (1)
to evict, desahuciar [See special note on (34)]
to evict, desalojar (1)
to evoke, evocar (8)
to evolve, evolucionar (1)
to exacerbate, exacerbar (1)
to exaggerate, exagerar (1)
to exaggerate, cacarear (1)
to exaggerate, decantar (1)
to exaggerate, inflar (1)
to exaggerate, macanear (1)
to exaggerate, ponderar (1)
to exalt, enaltecer (73)

to exalt, exaltar (1)
to examine, examinar (1)
to examine with a stethoscope, auscultar (1)
to excavate, excavar (1)
to excavate, zapar (1)
to exceed, exceder (2)
to exceed, rebasar (1)
to excel, aventajar (1)
to excel, descollar (ue) (36)
to excel, despuntar (1)
to excel, sobrepasar (1)
to excel, sobrepujar (1)
to excel, sobresalir (106)
to except, exceptuar (62)
to exchange, cambiar (1)
to exchange, canjear (1)
to exchange, conmutar (1)
to exchange, intercambiar (1)
to exchange, trocar (ue) (44)
to exchange shots, tirotearse (1) (4)
to excite, enardecer (73)
to excite, excitar (1)
to exclaim, exclamar (1)
to exclude, excluir (71)
to excommunicate, excomulgar (9)
to excuse, disculpar (1)
to excuse, dispensar (1)
to excuse, excusar (1)
to excuse, paliar (1)
to excuse, perdonar (1)
to execute, ejecutar (1)
to execute by shooting, fusilar (1)
to exemplify, ejemplificar (8)
to exempt, excusar (1)
to exempt, eximir (3)
to exempt, franquear (1)
to exempt, librar (1)
to exercise, ejercitar (1)
to exert, ejercer (12)
to exert oneself to the utmost, extremarse (1) (4)
to exhale, espirar (1)
to exhale, exhalar (1)
to exhale, vahar (1)
to exhale, vahear (1)
to exhaust, agotar (1)
to exhaust, apurar (1)
to exhibit, exhibir (3)
to exhibit, ostentar (1)
to exhort, exhortar (1)
to exhume, exhumar (1)
to exile, desterrar (ie) (37)
to exonerate, exonerar (1)
to exorcise, exorcizar (11)
to expand, expansionar (1)
to expatriate, expatriar (61)
to expect, esperar (1)
to expectorate phlegm, gargajear (1)
to expedite, expedir (i, i) (42)
to expel, echar (1)
to expel, expulsar (1)
to experience, experimentar (1)
to experiment, experimentar (1)
to expiate, expiar (61)
to expire, caducar (8)
to expire, expirar (1)
to expire, vencer (12)
to explain, explanar (1)
to explain, explicar (8)
to explode, estallar (1)
to explode, explotar (1)
to explode, reventar (ie) (37)
to exploit, explotar (1)
to explore, explorar (1)

to export, exportar (1)
to expose, exponer (98)
to express, expresar (1)
to express an opinion, opinar (1)
to express with hyperbole, hiperbolizar (11)
to expropriate, expropiar (1)
to expurgate, expurgar (9)
to extend, explayar (1)
to extend, extender (ie) (39)
to extend, prolongar (9)
to extend, tender (ie) (39)
to extenuate, extenuar (62)
to extenuate, paliar (1)
to exterminate, exterminar (1)
to extinguish, apagar (9)
to extinguish, extinguir (17)
to extinguish, sofocar (8)
to extol, encarecer (73)
to extol, engrandecer (73)
to extol, ensalzar (11)
to extort, extorsionar (1)
to extract, extraer (109)
to extract, sacar (8)
to extrapolate, extrapolar (1)
to exult in cruelty, ensañarse (1) (4)
to eye, ojear (1)

F

to fabricate, fabricar (8)
to face, arrostrar (1)
to face, encarar (1)
to facilitate, facilitar (1)
to fade, desteñir (i, i) (60)
to fade, desteñirse (i, i) (60) (4)
to fail, fallar (1)
to fail, fracasar (1)
to fail (a student), catear (1)
to fail to recognize, desconocer (73)
to faint, desfallecer (73)
to faint, desmayarse (1) (4)
to faint, desvanecerse (73) (4)
to faint from hunger, ahilarse (34) (4)
to fake, simular (1)
to fall, caer (81)
to fall again, recaer (81)
to fall asleep, dormirse (ue, u) (40) (4)
to fall back, replegarse (ie) (50) (4)
to fall behind, atrasarse (1) (4)
to fall behind, rezagarse (9) (4)
to fall behind time (a watch or clock), retratarse (1) (4)
to fall down a precipice, despeñarse (1) (4)
to fall in love, enamorarse (1) (4)
to fall in love, prendarse (1) (4)
to fall into pieces, desbaratarse (1) (4)
to fall to one's lot, tocar (8)
to fall to the ground, aplomarse (1) (4)
to falsify, falsificar (8)
to familiarize, familiarizar (11)
to fan, abanicar (8)
to fan, abaniquear (1)
to fan, aventar (ie) (37)
to fascinate, embobar (1)
to fascinate, fascinar (1)
to fascinate, ilusionar (1)
to fast, ayunar (1)
to fasten, abrochar (1)
to fasten, sujetar (1)
to fasten with a strap, amentar (ie) (37)
to fathom, sondear (1)
to fatigue, fatigar (9)
to fatten, cebar (1)

to fatten, engordar (1)
to favor, favorecer (73)
to favor, sufragar (9)
to fear, recelar (1)
to fear, temer (2)
to feast, festejar (1)
to feather, emplumar (1)
to feather (carpentry), machihembrar (1)
to fecundate, fecundar (1)
to fecundate, fecundizar (11)
to feed, alimentar (1)
to feed, sustentar (1)
to feed on, apacentarse (ie) (37) (4)
to feed with milk, lactar (1)
to feel, palpar (1)
to feel, sentir (ie, i) (41)
to feel, sentirse (ie, i) (41) (4)
to feel (one's way, etc.), tentar (ie) (37)
to feel out, tantear (1)
to feel remorse, compungirse (16) (4)
to feel sorry for, compadecer (73)
to feel the pulse of, pulsar (1)
to feign, simular (1)
to fell (trees), talar (1)
to fence, esgrimir (3)
to fence, vallar (1)
to fence in, cercar (8)
to fence with wire, alambrar (1)
to ferment, fermentar (1)
to fertilize, abonar (1)
to fertilize, fertilizar (11)
to fester, supurar (1)
to fictionalize, novelizar (11)
to fight, chocar (8)
to fight, luchar (1)
to fight, pelear (1)
to fight, pugnar (1)
to fight, reñir (i, i) (60
to fight (bulls), lidiar (1)
to fight bulls, torear (1)
to fight with fury, encarnizarse (11) (4)
to figure, figurar (1)
to filch, birlar (1)
to filch, ratear (1)
to filch, sisar (1)
to file, archivar (1)
to file, limar (1)
to fill, henchir (i, i) (42)
to fill, llenar (1)
to fill a tooth, empastar (1)
to fill or cover with straw, empajar (1)
to fill or stuff with truffles, trufar (1)
to fill to overflowing, sobrellenar (1)
to fill to the brim, colmar (1)
to fill up, rellenar (1)
to fill (with dirt), terraplenar (1)
to film, cinematografiar (61)
to film, filmar (1)
to film, rodar (ue) (36)
to filter, filtrar (1)
to finalize, finalizar (11)
to finance, financiar (1)
to find, encontrar (ue) (36)
to find, hallar (1)
to find a job, colocarse (8) (4)
to find oneself, hallarse (1) (4)
to find oneself, verse (112) (4)
to find out, averiguar (10)
to find out, enterarse (1) (4)
to find out where, localizar (11)
to find relief or release, desahogarse (9) (4)
to finger a keyboard, teclear (1)
to finish, acabar (1)
to finish, arrematar (1)

to finish, concluir (71)
to finish, finalizar (11)
to finish, pulir (3)
to finish, terminar (1)
to finish, ultimar (1)
to finish off, rematar (1)
to fire (dismiss), despedir (i, i) (42)
to fire (bricks), cocer (ue) (54)
to fish, pescar (8)
to fit, ajustar (1)
to fit, caber (80)
to fit, encuadrar (1)
to fit into, encajar (1)
to fit tightly, apretar (ie) (37)
to fit together, entretallarse (1) (4)
to fix, arreglar (1)
to fix, componer (98)
to fix, fijar (1)
to fix a salary, asalariar (1)
to fix a salary or wages for, salariar (1)
to fix in one's mind, puntualizar (11)
to fix or set amount of, acuantiar (61)
to flame, flamear (1)
to flame, llamear (1)
to flank, flanquear (1)
to flash, fulgurar (1)
to flash, resplandecer (73)
to flatten, achatar (1)
to flatten, chafar (1)
to flatter, adular (1)
to flatter, halagar (9)
to flatter, incensar (ie) (37)
to flatter, lisonjear (1)
to flee, fugarse (9) (4)
to flee, huir (71)
to flee, pirarse (1) (4)
to fling down, derrocar [(ue) (44)] or (8)
to fling down a precipice, despeñar (1)
to flirt, camelar (1)
to flirt, coquetear (1)
to flirt, flirtear (1)
to float, flotar (1)
to float, sobrenadar (1)
to flog, verguear (1)
to flood, anegar (ie) (50)
to floor, solar (ue) (36)
to floor with boards, entarimar (1)
to flourish, florecer (73)
to flow, afluir (71)
to flow, desembocar (8)
to flow, discurrir (3)
to flow, fluir (71)
to flow, verter (ie) (39)
to flow back, regolfar (1)
to fluctuate, fluctuar (62)
to fluff, mullir (27)
to fluff, remullir (27)
to flunk, catear (1)
to flunk, reprobar (ue) (36)
to flunk, suspender (2)
to flush, sonrosarse (1) (4)
to flute, estriar (61)
to flutter around, mariposear (1)
to flutter around, revolar (ue) (36)
to flutter around, revolotear (1)
to fly, volar (ue) (36)
to fly around, circunvolar (ue) (36)
to fly over, trasvolar (ue) (36)
to foam, espumar (1)
to focus, enfocar (8)
to fog, empañar (1)
to fold, doblar (1)
to fold, plegar (ie) (50)
to fold over and over, replegar (ie) (50)
to follow, seguir (i, i) (58)
to follow, suceder (2)

to follow foreign customs, engringarse (9) (4)
to follow next, subseguir (i, i) (58)
to follow one after the other, sucederse (2) (4)
to foment, fomentar (1)
to fool around, sonsear (1)
to forbid, prohibir (34)
to forbid, vedar (1)
to force, forzar (ue) (46)
to force, obligar (9)
to ford, vadear (1)
to foresee, antever (112)
to foresee, prever (112)
to foretell, augurar (1)
to foretell, predecir (i, i) (84)
to foretell, pronosticar (8)
to forge, falsificar (8)
to forge, forjar (1)
to forge, fraguar (10)
to forge (a document), suplantar (1)
to forget, olvidar (1)
to form, configurar (1)
to form, formar (1)
to form a crowd, arremolinarse (1) (4)
to form an idea, idear (1)
to form ears (said of cereals), espigar (9)
to form into a ball (yarn, string, etc.), ovillar (1)
to form pockets, abolsar (1)
to formalize, formalizar (11)
to formulate, formalizar (11)
to formulate, formular (1)
to fornicate, fornicar (8)
to fortify, fortificar (8)
to fortify with towers or turrets, torrear (1)
to found, cimentar [(ie) (37)] or (1)
to found, fundar (1)
to found upon, vincular (1)
to founder, zozobrar (1)
to fracture, fracturar (1)
to fracture one's skull, descalabrarse (1) (4)
to fragment, fragmentarse (1) (4)
to frame, encuadrar (1)
to frame, enmarcar (8)
to frank (a letter), franquear (1)
to fraternize, confraternizar (11)
to fraternize, fraternizar (11)
to fray, deshilachar (1)
to free, franquear (1)
to free, independizar (11)
to free, liberar (1)
to free, librar (1)
to free from slavery, manumitir (3)
to free oneself, desembarazarse (11) (4)
to freeze, congelar (1)
to freeze, helar (ie) (37)
to frequent, frecuentar (1)
to frighten, amedrentar (1)
to frighten, atemorizar (11)
to frighten, sobresaltar (1)
to frighten away, espantar (1)
to frisk, cachear (1)
to frizzle, frisar (1)
to frolic, retozar (11)
to frost, escarchar (1)
to frustrate, frustrar (1)
to fry, freír (i, i) (88)
to fry again, refreír (i, i) (88)
to fry (eggs) fluffy and brown, abuñolar (36)
to fry (eggs) fluffy and brown, abuñuelar (1)
to fry lightly, sofreír (i, i) (88)

to **fry well**, refreír (i, i) (88)
to **fulfill**, cumplir (3)
to **fulfill**, desempeñar (1)
to **fulfill**, realizar (11)
to **fulfill an obligation**, cumplir (3)
to **fumigate**, fumigar (9)
to **function**, funcionar (1)
to **furnish**, amoblar (ue) (36)
to **furnish**, amueblar (1)
to **furnish**, moblar (ue) (36)
to **furnish**, surtir (3)
to **furnish with teeth**, endentar (ie) (37)
to **furrow**, acaballonar (1)
to **furrow**, surcar (8)
to **fuse**, fundir (3)
to **fuse**, fusionar (1)

G

to **gain**, ganar (1)
to **gain (said of clocks)**, adelantarse (1) (4)
to **gain access**, introducirse (67) (4)
to **gain by entreaty**, recabar (1)
to **gallop**, cabalgar (9)
to **gallop**, galopar (1)
to **galvanize**, galvanizar (11)
to **gamble (one's life, money, etc.)**, jugarse (ue) (93) (4)
to **gangrene**, gangrenarse (1) (4)
to **gargle**, gargarear (1)
to **gargle**, gargarizar (11)
to **garnish**, aderezar (11)
to **garnish**, guarnecer (73)
to **gasify**, gasificar (8)
to **gasp**, acezar (11)
to **gather**, allegar (9)
to **gather**, colegir (i, i) (57)
to **gather**, concurrir (3)
to **gather**, juntar (1)
to **gather**, recoger (15)
to **gather (sheep) into the fold**, apriscar (8)
to **gather grapes**, vendimiar (1)
to **gather herbs**, herborizar (11)
to **gather together**, acopiar (1)
to **gather together**, reunir (66)
to **gather together bit by bit**, añascar (8)
to **gear**, engranar (1)
to **generalize**, generalizar (11)
to **generate**, generar (1)
to **germinate**, germinar (1)
to **gesticulate**, accionar (1)
to **gesture**, gesticular (1)
to **gesture**, manotear (1)
to **get**, coger (15)
to **get**, conseguir (i, i) (58)
to **get**, granjearse (1) (4)
to **get**, lograr (1)
to **get a haircut**, pelarse (1) (4)
to **get ahead of**, aventajarse (1) (4)
to **get alarmed**, alarmarse (1) (4)
to **get along**, congeniar (1)
to **get angry**, airarse (63) (4)
to **get angry**, atufarse (1) (4)
to **get angry**, enfadarse (1) (4)
to **get angry**, enfurruñarse (1) (4)
to **get angry**, enojarse (1) (4)
to **get angry**, trinar (1)
to **get annoyed**, amohinarse (34) (4)
to **get annoyed**, incomodarse (1) (4)
to **get better**, mejorarse (1) (4)
to **get bored**, aburrirse (3) (4)
to **get bored**, atediarse (1) (4)
to **get cleaned up**, asearse (1) (4)

to **get closer**, acercarse (8) (4)
to **get cocky**, envalentonarse (1) (4)
to **get conceited**, encopetarse (1) (4)
to **get confused**, atarugarse (9) (4)
to **get confused**, atolondrarse (1) (4)
to **get customers**, aparroquiar (1)
to **get damaged**, dañarse (1) (4)
to **get dirty**, ensuciarse (1) (4)
to **get dressed**, vestirse (i, i) (42) (4)
to **get dressed up**, acicalarse (1) (4)
to **get drunk**, ajumarse (1) (4)
to **get drunk**, curarse (1) (4)
to **get drunk**, chuparse (1) (4)
to **get drunk**, emborracharse (1) (4)
to **get drunk**, embriagarse (9) (4)
to **get drunk**, mamarse (1) (4)
to **get entangled**, encallar (1)
to **get even**, desquitarse (1) (4)
to **get excited**, acalorarse (1) (4)
to **get excited**, alborotarse (1) (4)
to **get excited**, enardecerse (73) (4)
to **get fat**, engordarse (1) (4)
to **get filthy**, emporcarse (ue) (44) (4)
to **get frightened**, atemorizarse (11) (4)
to **get furious**, encarnizarse (11) (4)
to **get hoarse**, enronquecerse (73) (4)
to **get hurt**, dañarse (1) (4)
to **get in touch**, comunicarse (8) (4)
to **get indisposed**, indisponerse (98) (4)
to **get insured**, asegurarse (1) (4)
to **get into debt**, endeudarse (1) (4)
to **get into the good graces (of)**, congraciarse (1) (4)
to **get irritated**, alterarse (1) (4)
to **get knotted**, anudarse (1) (4)
to **get lost**, extraviarse (61) (4)
to **get lost**, perderse (ie) (39) (4)
to **get mad**, rabiar (1)
to **get married**, casarse (1) (4)
to **get moldy**, enmohecerse (73) (4)
to **get muddied**, enlodarse (1) (4)
to **get near**, aproximarse (1) (4)
to **get numb**, adormecerse (73) (4)
to **get off**, apearse (1) (4)
to **get off**, bajar (1)
to **get off center**, descentrarse (1) (4)
to **get on to**, montar (1)
to **get on top**, encaramarse (1) (4)
to **get one's bearings**, orientarse (1) (4)
to **get one's hopes up**, ilusionarse (1) (4)
to **get out**, apearse (1) (4)
to **get out**, salir (106)
to **get out of a difficult or tight spot**, desatascar (8)
to **get out of adjustment**, desajustarse (1) (4)
to **get out of order**, descomponerse (98) (4)
to **get out of order**, desconcertarse (ie) (37) (4)
to **get out of the way**, abarse (115) (4)
to **get out of tune**, desafinarse (1) (4)
to **get placed**, colocarse (8) (4)
to **get prepared**, prepararse (1) (4)
to **get prepared**, prevenirse (ie, i) (111) (4)
to **get rattled**, azararse (1) (4)
to **get ready**, alistarse (1) (4)
to **get ready**, apercibirse (3) (4)
to **get ready**, aprestarse (1) (4)
to **get ready**, aviar (61)
to **get ready**, disponerse (98) (4)
to **get ready**, prepararse (1) (4)
to **get rich**, enriquecerse (73) (4)
to **get rid of**, desasirse (78) (4)
to **get rid of**, zafarse (1) (4)
to **get scared**, amedrentarse (1) (4)

to **get sleepy**, adormecerse (73) (4)
to **get smeared**, untarse (1) (4)
to **get soiled with mud**, enfangarse (9) (4)
to **get stopped up**, atascarse (8) (4)
to **get stormy**, aborrascarse (8) (4)
to **get stubborn**, emperrarse (1) (4)
to **get stuck**, atascarse (8) (4)
to **get stuck**, atollarse (1) (4)
to **get stuck**, atrancarse (8) (4)
to **get stuck in the mud**, apantanarse (1) (4)
to **get sunburned**, asolearse (1) (4)
to **get swampy**, apantanarse (1) (4)
to **get tangled**, enmarañarse (1) (4)
to **get thin**, adelgazarse (11) (4)
to **get thin**, enflaquecerse (73) (4)
to **get tied up**, atarse (1) (4)
to **get tipsy**, achisparse (1) (4)
to **get tipsy**, alumbrarse (1) (4)
to **get tired**, cansarse (1) (4)
to **get tired**, fatigarse (9) (4)
to **get to the bottom**, profundizar (11)
to **get uncovered**, destaparse (1) (4)
to **get up**, levantarse (1) (4)
to **get up early**, madrugar (9)
to **get upset**, indisponerse (98) (4)
to **get used to**, acostumbrarse (1) (4)
to **get well**, curarse (1) (4)
to **get well groomed**, encopetarse (1) (4)
to **get worse**, agudizarse (11) (4)
to **get worse**, empeorarse (1) (4)
to **get worse again**, reagravarse (1) (4)
to **gild**, dorar (1)
to **gird**, ceñir (i, i) (60)
to **girdle**, fajar (1)
to **give**, dar (83)
to **give (beating, kick, slap)**, propinar (1)
to **give a bad example to**, desedificar (8)
to **give a detailed account of**, puntualizar (11)
to **give a dowry to**, dotar (1)
to **give a ducking to**, zambullir (27)
to **give a present**, obsequiar (1)
to **give a shower**, duchar (1)
to **give a tip**, propinar (1)
to **give a visa**, visar (1)
to **give as a present**, regalar (1)
to **give as a security, pledge**, pignorar (1)
to **give atmosphere to**, ambientar (1)
to **give back**, devolver (ue) (70)
to **give back**, restituir (71)
to **give back**, retornar (1)
to **give back**, tornar (1)
to **give birth**, parir (3)
to **give good manners to**, desasnar (1)
to **give indigestion**, empachar (1)
to **give off**, despedir (i, i) (42)
to **give or issue a precept**, preceptuar (62)
to **give possession**, aposesionar (1)
to **give possession**, posesionar (1)
to **give refuge**, asilar (1)
to **give rein to (passions, desires)**, desahogar (9)
to **give shelter**, guarecer (73)
to **give signs of life**, rebullir (27)
to **give something extra**, yapar (1)
to **give special tint to**, matizar (11)
to **give up**, ceder (2)
to **give up**, claudicar (8)
to **give up**, darse (83) (4)
to **give up**, rendirse (i, i) (42) (4)
to **gladden**, regocijar (1)

to glean, rebuscar (8)
to glean, respigar (9)
to glide, planear (1)
to glimpse, avistar (1)
to glimpse, columbrar (1)
to glimpse, vislumbrar (1)
to glitter, relucir (74)
to glitter, relumbrar (1)
to glorify, glorificar (8)
to glue, encolar (1)
to glue, pegar (9)
to gnash, rechinar (1)
to gnaw, roer (103)
to go, andar (77)
to go, caminar (1)
to go, dirigirse (16) (4)
to go, marchar (1)
to go, ir (92)
to go, venir (ie, i) (111)
to go around, contornear (1)
to go around, rodear (1)
to go around, rondar (1)
to go around gossiping, comadrear (1)
to go around in slippers, chancletear (1)
to go around thieving, ladronear (1)
to go as far as, llegar (9)
to go astray, descarriarse (61) (4)
to go astray, extraviarse (61) (4)
to go astray, marrar (1)
to go away, alargarse (9) (4)
to go away, largarse (9) (4)
to go away, marcharse (1) (4)
to go away, pirarse (1) (4)
to go back and forth, trajinar (1)
to go beyond, traspasar (1)
to go blind, cegarse (ie) (50) (4)
to go crazy, aloquecerse (73) (4)
to go deep, profundizar (11)
to go down, bajar (1)
to go downstairs, bajar (1)
to go in debt, empeñarse (1) (4)
to go into, adentrar (1)
to go into, adentrarse (1) (4)
to go into seclusion, recluirse (71) (4)
to go merrymaking, jaranear (1)
to go off, dispararse (1)
to go on a pilgrimage, peregrinar (1)
to go out, asomarse (1) (4)
to go out, extinguirse (17) (4)
to go out, salir (106)
to go out on a spree, parrandear (1)
to go over, recorrer (2)
to go serenading, jacarear (1)
to go single file, ahilar (34)
to go slow, atrasarse (1) (4)
to go through, atravesar (ie) (37)
to go to bed, acostarse (ue) (36) (4)
to go to pasture, campear (1)
to go to ruin, arruinarse (1) (4)
to go too far, propasarse (1) (4)
to go too far, sobrepasarse (1) (4)
to go up, subir (3)
to go uphill, repechar (1)
to goad, acuciar (1)
to gobble (said of a turkey), titar (1)
to gobble down, zampar (1)
to gore, acornear (1)
to gore, encornar (ue) (36)
to gorge, atiborrarse (1) (4)
to gorge to the point of feeling sick,
    ahitar (34)
to gossip, comentar (1)
to gossip, cotillear (1)
to gossip, cotorrear (1)
to gossip, chismear (1)
to gossip, chismorrear (1)

to gossip, chispar (1)
to gossip, paliquear (1)
to govern, gobernar (ie) (37)
to govern, regir (i, i) (57)
to grab by the neck, apercollar (ue) (36)
to grace, agraciar (1)
to grade, calificar (8)
to grade, graduar (62)
to grade with a scraper, traillar (63)
to graduate, graduar (62)
to graduate, graduarse (62) (4)
to graft, injertar (1)
to grain, vetear (1)
to grant, conceder (2)
to grant, dispensar (1)
to grant, otorgar (9)
to grant a scholarship or fellowship,
    becar (8)
to grant amnesty, amnistiar (61)
to granulate, granular (1)
to grasp, agarrar (1)
to grasp, asir (78)
to grate, rallar (1)
to grate (one's teeth), crujir (3)
to gratify, halagar (9)
to gratify, gratificar (8)
to gravitate, gravitar (1)
to graze, pacer (73)
to grease, engrasar (1)
to grease, untar (1)
to greet, saludar (1)
to grieve, acongojar (1)
to grieve, afligirse (16) (4)
to grieve, apenarse (1) (4)
to grieve, apesadumbrar (1)
to grieve, desconsolar (ue) (36)
to grieve, plañir (29)
to grind, moler (ue) (38)
to groan, rezongar (9)
to groove, estriar (61)
to groove, ranurar (1)
to grope, palpar (1)
to grope, tantear (1)
to group, agrupar (1)
to grow, crecer (73)
to grow dark (day), anochecer (73)
to grow dark (day), atardecer (73)
to grow dark, lobreguecer (73)
to grow dark, obscurecer (73)
to grow green, campear (1)
to grow green, verdear (1)
to grow green again, reverdecer (73)
to grow hair, cabellar (1)
to grow horns, encornudar (1)
to grow late, atardecer (73)
to grow old, envejecerse (73) (4)
to grow stiff with cold, arrecirse (116)
    (4)
to grow tall, espigarse (9) (4)
to grow too much, sobrecrecer (73)
to grow weak, desfallecer (73)
to grow worse, arreciar (1)
to growl, gruñir (29)
to grumble, gruñir (29)
to grumble, refunfuñar (1)
to grumble, regañar (1)
to grumble, rezongar (9)
to grunt, gruñir (29)
to grunt, respingar (9)
to guarantee, afianzar (11)
to guarantee, garantir (116)
to guarantee, garantizar (11)
to guarantee with a letter of credit or
    similar document, avalar (1)
to guard, custodiar (1)
to guard, guardar (1)

to guess, adivinar (1)
to guess, barruntar (1)
to guess, columbrar (1)
to guess, conjeturar (1)
to guess right, acertar (ie) (37)
to guess right, atinar (1)
to guide, guiar (19)
to guillotine, guillotinar (1)
to gulp down, engullir (27)
to gulp down, tragar (9)
to gum, engomar (1)

H

to habituate, habituar (62)
to haggle over, regatear (1)
to hail, granizar (11)
to hail large hail stones, acantalear (1)
to half-close, juntar (1)
to half-close (door, eyes), entornar (1)
to half-open (door, eyes), entreabrir (75)
to hallucinate, alucinar (1)
to hammer, amartillar (1)
to hammer, martillar (1)
to hammer, martillear (1)
to hand, dar (83)
to hand, entregar (9)
to hand over, entregar (9)
to hand over without delay, aprontar
    (1)
to hand-wrestle, pulsear (1)
to handcuff, esposar (1)
to handle, manejar (1)
to handle, tratar (1)
to handle perfectly, dominar (1)
to hang, ahorcar (8)
to hang, colgar (ue) (45)
to hang, pender (2)
to hang, suspender (2)
to hang one's head, amorrar (1)
to hang out (clothes to dry), tender (ie)
    (39)
to hang over, cernerse (ie) (39) (4)
to happen, acaecer (73)
to happen, acontecer (73)
to happen, ocurrir (3)
to happen, producirse (67) (4)
to happen, sobrevenir (ie, i) (111)
to happen, suceder (2)
to happen, supervenir (ie, i) (111)
to harangue, arengar (9)
to harass, acosar (1)
to harass, apremiar (1)
to harass, hostigar (9)
to harden, acerarse (1) (4)
to harden, empedernir (116)
to harden, endurecer (73)
to harm, dañar (1)
to harm, vulnerar (1)
to harmonize, concertar (ie) (37)
to harmonize, hermanar (1)
to harness, aparejar (1)
to harness, enjaezar (11)
to harpoon, arponear (1)
to harvest, cosechar (1)
to harvest, segar (ie) (50)
to hasten, aligerar (1)
to hatch, empollar (1)
to hate, aborrecer (73)
to haul up, izar (11)
to have, poseer (20)
to have, tener (ie) (108)
to have (auxiliary), haber (89)
to have (food, drink, a meal), tomar (1)
to have a drink, copear (1)

to have a good time, divertirse (ie, i) (41) (4)
to have a high time, loquear (1)
to have a presentiment of, presentir (ie, i) (41)
to have a thorough knowledge of, dominar (1)
to have an accident, accidentarse (1) (4)
to have an afternoon snack, merendar (ie) (37)
to have an untimely end, malograrse (1) (4)
to have as a characteristic, particularizarse (11) (4)
to have enough room, caber (80)
to have indigestion, indigestarse (1) (4)
to have pity, apiadarse (1) (4)
to have rabies, rabiar (1)
to have recourse, apelar (1)
to have recourse, recurrir (3)
to have repercussion, repercutir (3)
to have supper, cenar (1)
to have the same thoughts and feelings, compenetrarse (1) (4)
to have to, deber (2)
to have weight, pesar (1)
to head, encabezar (11)
to head (towards), rumbear (1)
to heal, cicatrizar (11)
to heal, curar (1)
to heal, sanar (1)
to heap up, coacervar (1)
to hear, oír (95)
to hear, sentir (ie, i) (41)
not to hear, desoír (95)
to hear vaguely, entreoír (95)
to hear wrong, trasoír (95)
to heat, calefaccionar (1)
to heat, calentar (ie) (37)
to heat up, caldear (1)
to heed, escuchar (1)
to help, auxiliar (1) or (61)
to help, ayudar (1)
to help, coadyuvar (1)
to help, remediar (1)
to help, servir (i, i) (42)
to help, socorrer (2)
to help oneself, servirse (i, i) (42) (4)
to help oneself, valerse (110) (4)
to hesitate, oscilar (1)
to hesitate, titubear (1)
to hesitate, vacilar (1)
to hibernate, hibernar (1)
to hide, encubrir (82)
to hide, esconder (2)
to hide, ocultar (1)
to hide behind a parapet, parapetarse (1) (4)
to hide from danger, achantarse (1) (4)
to hide one's feelings, disimular (1)
to hint, amagar (9)
to hire by the day, ajornalar (1)
to hire oneself out, alquilarse (1) (4)
to hiss, chichear (1)
to hiss, pitar (1)
to hiss, pitear (1)
to hiss (a performer or a performance), silbar (1)
to hiss (a performer or a performance), sisear (1)
to hit, dar (83)
to hit, pegar (9)
to hit, trompear (1)
to hit in the head, descalabrar (1)
to hit upon, acertar (ie) (37)
to hit with the horns, amurcar (8)

to hoard up, atesorar (1)
to hobnob, codearse (1) (4)
to hoist, izar (11)
to hold, aguantar (1)
to hold, coger (15)
to hold, sujetar (1)
to hold, tener (ie) (108)
to hold a wake over, velar (1)
to hold in low esteem, desestimar (1)
to hold tightly with the fist, empuñar (1)
to hold up, atracar (8)
to hold up, saltear (1)
to hold up, sostener (ie) (108)
to hollow, ahuecar (8)
to hollow out, vaciar (61)
to homogenize, homogeneizar (11)
to homogenize, homogenizar (11)
to honor, honrar (1)
to hook, enganchar (1)
to hop, brincar (8)
to hope, esperar (1)
to horrify, horrorizar (11)
to hospitalize, hospitalizar (11)
to hover, cernerse (ie) (39) (4)
to hover around, rondar (1)
to howl, aullar (65)
to huddle up, acorrucarse (8) (4)
to huddle up, acurrucarse (8) (4)
to hull, pelar (1)
to hum, tararear (1)
to hum, zumbar (1)
to humanize, humanizar (11)
to humble, apocar (8)
to humidify, humedecer (73)
to humiliate, apocar (8)
to humiliate, hollar (ue) (36)
to humiliate, humillar (1)
to hunt, cazar (11)
to hurl, abalanzar (11)
to hurry, apresurar (1)
to hurry, apurar (1)
to hurry, apurarse (1) (4)
to hurt, dañar (1)
to hurt, herir (ie, i) (41)
to hurt, lastimar (1)
to hurt, perjudicar (8)
to hurt feelings, zaherir (ie, i) (41)
to hurt one's head, descalabrarse (1) (4)
to husk, pelar (1)
to hydrate, hidratar (1)
to hydrogenate, hidrogenar (1)
to hydrolize, hidrolizar (11)
to hypnotize, hipnotizar (11)
to hypnotize, sugestionar (1)

I

to idealize, idealizar (11)
to identify, identificar (8)
to idle, gandulear (1)
to idle, ociar (1)
to idle, zanganear (1)
to idolize, idolatrar (1)
to ignore, desentenderse (ie) (39) (4)
to illuminate, alumbrar (1)
to illuminate, iluminar (1)
to illustrate, ilustrar (1)
to imagine, fantasear (1)
to imagine, figurarse (1) (4)
to imagine, imaginar (1)
to imagine, imaginarse (1) (4)
to imbibe, embeber (2)
to imbue, imbuir (71)
to imitate, imitar (1)
to imitate, remedar (1)

to immerse, inmergir (16)
to immigrate, inmigrar (1)
to immobilize, inmovilizar (11)
to immortalize, inmortalizar (11)
to immunize, inmunizar (11)
to impair, desmejorar (1)
to impair, menoscabar (1)
to impale, empalar (1)
to impart, impartir (3)
to impede, embargar (9)
to impede, empachar (1)
to impel, impeler (2)
to implore, deprecar (8)
to implore, suplicar (8)
to imply, envolver (ue) (70)
to imply, implicar (8)
to imply, importar (1)
to imply, inferir (ie, i) (41)
to imply, suponer (98)
to import, importar (1)
to importune, importunar (1)
to importune, perseguir (i, i) (58)
to impose, imponer (98)
to impoverish, empobrecer (73)
to impregnate, impregnar (1)
to impress, impresionar (1)
to imprison, aprisionar (1)
to improve, mejorar (1)
to improve, perfeccionar (1)
to improve soil by adding clay, arcillar (1)
to improvise, improvisar (1)
to impugn, impugnar (1)
to inaugurate, inaugurar (1)
to incapacitate, incapacitar (1)
to incapacitate, inhabilitar (1)
to incarcerate, encarcelar (1)
to incense, incensar (ie) (37)
to incinerate, incinerar (1)
to incite, achuchar (1)
to incite, azuzar (11)
to incite, concitar (1)
to incite, incitar (1)
to incite, provocar (8)
to incite, soliviantar (1)
to incite to insubordination, insubordinar (1)
to incite to rebellion, insurreccionar (1)
to incite to rebellion, revolucionar (1)
to incite to rebellion, sublevar (1)
to incite to riot or mutiny, amotinar (1)
to incline, inclinar (1)
to include, abarcar (8)
to include, englobar (1)
to include, incluir (71)
to inconvenience, incomodar (1)
to incorporate, incorporar (1)
to incorporate, incorporarse (1) (4)
to increase, acrecentar (ie) (37)
to increase, acrecer (73)
to increase, aumentar (1)
to increase, incrementar (1)
to increase, subir (3)
to incriminate, acriminar (1)
to incriminate, incriminar (1)
to incrust, incrustar (1)
to incubate, incubar (1)
to inculcate, inculcar (8)
to incur, incurrir (3)
to indemnify, indemnizar (11)
to indent, endentar (ie) (37)
to indicate, indicar (8)
to indicate, señalar (1)
to indict, procesar (1)
to indispose, indisponer (98)
to individualize, individualizar (11)

to indoctrinate, adoctrinar (1)
to induce, inducir (67)
to industrialize, industrializar (11)
to infatuate, infatuar (62)
to infect, contagiar (1)
to infect, infectar (1)
to infect, inficionar (1)
to infer, colegir (i, i) (57)
to infer, inferir (ie, i) (41)
to infest, infestar (1)
to infest, plagar (9)
to infiltrate, infiltrar (1)
to inflame, inflamar (1)
to inflate, inflar (1)
to inflict, infligir (16)
to influence, influir (71)
to influence, sugestionar (1)
to inform, avisar (1)
to inform, enterar (1)
to inform, informar (1)
to infringe, infringir (16)
to infuriate, embravecer (73)
to infuriate, encarnizar (11)
to infuriate, enfurecer (73)
to infuse, infundir (3)
to ingest, ingerir (ie, i) (41)
to ingest, injerir (ie, i) (41)
to inhabit, habitar (1)
to inhale, aspirar (1)
to inhale, inhalar (1)
to inhale, inspirar (1)
to inherit, heredar (1)
to inhibit, inhibir (3)
to inhume, inhumar (1)
to inhume, soterrar (ie) (37)
to initiate, incoar (122)
to initiate, iniciar (1)
to inject, inyectar (1)
to inject with a syringe, jeringar (9)
to injure, injuriar (1)
to injure, lesionar (1)
to injure, vulnerar (1)
to innovate, innovar (1)
to inoculate, inocular (1)
to inquire, inquirir (ie) (76)
to inquire, preguntar (1)
to insalivate, insalivar (1)
to inscribe, inscribir (69)
to inseminate, inseminar (1)
to insert, embutir (3)
to insert, entremeter (2)
to insert, entrometer (2)
to insert, insertar (1)
to insert, introducir (67)
to insert, meter (2)
to insert, rebutir (3)
to insert a page or pages, interpaginar (1)
to insinuate, insinuar (62)
to insist, aferrarse (1) (4)
to insist, empeñarse (1) (4)
to insist, insistir (3)
to insist, instar (1)
to inspect, examinar (1)
to inspect, inspeccionar (1)
to inspire, inspirar (1)
to install, instalar (1)
to instigate, instigar (9)
to instill, infundir (3)
to instill, instilar (1)
to institute, instituir (71)
to instruct, instruir (71)
to insult, denostar (ue) (36)
to insult, deshonrar (1)
to insult, injuriar (1)
to insult, insultar (1)

to insult, ultrajar (1)
to insure, asegurar (1)
to integrate, integrar (1)
to intend, intentar (1)
to intensify, intensificar (8)
to intercede, interceder (2)
to intercept, atajar (1)
to intercept, interceptar (1)
to interconnect, interconectar (1)
to interdict, interdecir (i, i) (84)
to interest, interesar (1)
to interfere, ingerirse (ie, i) (41) (4)
to interfere, injerirse (ie, i) (41) (4)
to interfere, inmiscuirse (23) (4)
to interfere, interferir (ie, i) (41)
to interfere, introducirse (67) (4)
to intermediate, intermediar (1)
to intermit, intermitir (3)
to intern, internar (1)
to intern, recluir (71)
to internationalize, internacionalizar (11)
to interpenetrate, compenetrarse (1) (4)
to interpolate, interpolar (1)
to interpret, interpretar (1)
to interrogate, interrogar (9)
to interrupt, interrumpir (3)
to intervene, intervenir (ie, i) (111)
to intervene, mediar (1)
to interview, entrevistar (1)
to intimate, intimar (1)
to intimidate, acoquinar (1)
to intimidate, amilanar (1)
to intimidate, intimidar (1)
to intone, entonar (1)
to intoxicate, emborrachar (1)
to intoxicate, embriagar (9)
to intoxicate, intoxicar (8)
to intrigue, intrigar (9)
to introduce, introducir (67)
to introduce, presentar (1)
to intrude, entremeterse (2) (4)
to intrude, entrometerse (2) (4)
to inundate, inundar (1)
to invade, invadir (3)
to invade, irrumpir (3)
to invalidate, invalidar (1)
to invent, descubrir (82)
to invent, inventar (1)
to invert, invertir (ie, i) (41)
to invest, invertir (ie, i) (41)
to invest, investir (i, i) (42)
to invest in (an undertaking) as a silent partner, comanditar (1)
to investigate, indagar (9)
to investigate, investigar (9)
to invigorate, tonificar (8)
to invigorate, vigorizar (11)
to invite, convidar (1)
to invite, invitar (1)
to invoice, facturar (1)
to invoke, invocar (8)
to involve, complicar (8)
to involve, envolver (ue) (70)
to ionize, ionizar (11)
to iron, planchar (1)
to irradiate, irradiar (1)
to irradiate, radiar (1)
to irrigate, irrigar (9)
to irrigate, regar (ie) (50)
to irritate, contrariar (61)
to irritate, encrespar (1)
to irritate, irritar (1)
to isolate, incomunicar (8)
to isolate, aislar (63)
to issue, expedir (i, i) (42)

it is said, diz (**apocope of** dícese **from** decirse)
to itch, picar (8)
to itemize, pormenorizar (11)
to iterate, iterar (1)

J

to jab a bull with a short lance, breaking it off at its notch, rejonear (1)
to jam, apretujar (1)
to jeer, chotear (1)
to jeer, mofar (1)
to jeer, pitorrear (1)
to jerk, tironear (1)
to jest, chufletear (1)
to jest, chungar (9)
to jiggle, zangolotear (1)
to jingle, cascabelear (1)
to jingle, tintinear (1)
to jingle cowbells continuously, cencerrear (1)
to join, agregarse (9) (4)
to join, conchabar (1)
to join, hermanar (1)
to join, juntar (1)
to join, ligar (9)
to join, reunir (66)
to join, trabar (1)
to join, unir (3)
to join closely together, coadunar (1)
to join forces, acomunar (1)
to join forces, coligarse (9) (4)
to join one thing with another, copular (1)
to join two things of the same species, mancornar (ue) (36)
to joint, ensamblar (1)
to joke, bromear (1)
to joke, cuchufletear (1)
to joke, chancear (1)
to joke, macanear (1)
to joke, regodearse (1) (4)
to jolt, sacudir (3)
to judge, juzgar (9)
to judge (form a concept of something), conceptuar (62)
to jumble together, rebujar (1)
to jump, brincar (8)
to jump, saltar (1)
to justify, justificar (8)
to jut out, sobresalir (106)
to juxtapose, yuxtaponer (98)

K

to keep, guardar (1)
to keep, retener (ie) (108)
to keep (a promise), cumplir (3)
to keep (holy days), santificar (8)
to keep (silence), prestar (1)
to keep an eye or check on, celar (1)
to keep awake, desvelar (1)
to keep busy, ocupar (1)
to keep late hours, trasnochar (1)
to keep meat until it becomes gamy, manir (116)
to keep oneself confined, confinarse (1) (4)
to keep score, tantear (1)
to keep the Sabbath, sabatizar (11)
to keep time (rhythm), acompasar (1)
to keep up, mantener (ie) (108)
to kick, patear (1)
to kick, respingar (9)
to kick (said of horses), acocear (1)

to kick (said of horses), cocear (1)
to kick a ball, chutar (1)
to kidnap, raptar (1)
to kidnap, secuestrar (1)
to kill, matar (1)
to kill, victimar (1)
to kill off, rematar (1)
to kindle, quemar (1)
to kiss, besar (1)
to kiss (billiards), retrucar (8)
to knead, amasar (1)
to kneel, arrodillarse (1) (4)
to kneel down, hincarse (8) (4)
to knife, acuchillar (1)
to knit (bones), soldarse (ue) (36) (4)
to knock, golpear (1)
to knock, tocar (8)
to knock (olives, nuts, fruits from a tree), varear (1)
to knock a ball around (without playing a game, without effort or interest), pelotear (1)
to knock down, abatir (3)
to knock down, derrumbar (1)
to knock down, tumbar (1)
to knock out, tumbar (1)
to knock the dents out, desabollar (1)
to knot, anudar (1)
to know, conocer (73)
to know, saber (105)
not to know, ignorar (1)
to know how, saber (105)
to know in advance, preconocer (73)
to know oneself, reconocerse (73) (4)
to know or perceive by intuition, intuir (71)
to know thoroughly, resaber (105)

L

to label, rotular (1)
to lace, acordonar (1)
to lacerate, lacerar (1)
to lack, carecer (73)
to laicize, laicizar (11)
to lament, lamentar (1)
to lament, plañir (29)
to laminate, laminar (1)
to land, aterrizar (11)
to languish, languidecer (73)
to lard, mechar (1)
to lash, chicotear (1)
to lasso, enlazar (11)
to lasso, lazar (11)
to last, durar (1)
to last a long time, perdurar (1)
to laugh, reír (i, i) (59)
to laugh, reírse (i, i) (59) (4)
to laugh and make a lot of noise, chacotear (1)
to laugh boisterously, risotear (1)
to launch, lanzar (11)
to launch (an enterprise), embarcar (8)
to lavish, prodigar (9)
to lay (a cable, etc.), tender (ie) (39)
to lay aside (as useless), arrumbar (1)
to lay down, acostar (ue) (36)
to lay hold of, reivindicar (8)
to lay seige to, cercar (8)
to lay the foundation, cimentar [(ie) (37)] or (1)
to lay waste, yermar (1)
to lead, acaudillar (1)
to lead, capitanear (1)
to lead, desembocar (8)
to lead astray, desaviar (61)

to lead astray, descarriar (61)
to leaf through (a book, etc.), hojear (1)
to leak (said of a liquid or its container), salirse (106) (4)
to lean, adosar (1)
to lean, apoyar (1)
to lean, inclinarse (1) (4)
to lean, recostar (ue) (36)
to lean out, asomarse (1) (4)
to learn, aprender (2)
to learn by one's experience, escarmentar (ie) (37)
to leave, ausentarse (1) (4)
to leave, dejar (1)
to leave, largarse (9) (4)
to leave, marcharse (1) (4)
to leave, salir (106)
to leave a margin on, marginar (1)
to leave behind, rezagar (9)
to leave deserted, yermar (1)
to leave dumbfounded, plantar (1)
to leave out, prescindir (3)
to leave someone speechless, aplastar (1)
to leave someone waiting, planchar (1)
to lecture, dictar (1)
to lecture, sermonear (1)
to legalize, formalizar (11)
to legalize, legalizar (11)
to legalize, refrendar (1)
to legislate, legislar (1)
to legitimate, legitimar (1)
to lend, anticipar (1)
to lend, dejar (1)
to lend, prestar (1)
to lengthen, alargar (9)
to lengthen, alongar (9)
to lessen, apocar (8)
to lessen, atenuar (62)
to let, dejar (1)
to let go, desasir (78)
to let go, largar (9)
to let go, soltar (ue) (36)
to let (someone) have it (slap, kick, etc.), atizar (11)
to let (someone) have it (slap), zumbar (1)
to let know, avisar (1)
to let loose, desasirse (78) (4)
to level, allanar (1)
to level, aplanar (1)
to level, arrasar (1)
to level, explanar (1)
to level, nivelar (1)
to liberalize, liberalizar (11)
to liberate, libertar (1)
to license, licenciar (1)
to lick, lamer (1)
to lick again, relamer (2)
to lick one's lips, relamerse (2) (4)
to lie, mentir (ie, i) (41)
to lie down, acostarse (ue) (36) (4)
to lie down, tumbarse (1) (4)
to lie in the grave, yacer (113)
to lift, levantar (1)
to lift, subir (3)
to lift an embargo, desembargar (9)
to light, encender (ie) (39)
to lighten, aligerar (1)
to lighten, esclarecer (73)
to lightning, relampaguear (1)
to like, bienquerer (ie) (101)
to like, gustar (1)
to like, querer (ie) (101)
to limit, coartar (1)
to limit, limitar (1)

to limit oneself, ceñirse (i, i) (60) (4)
to limit oneself, concretarse (1) (4)
to limp, cojear (1)
to limp, renguear (1)
to limp, renquear (1)
to line, aforrar (1)
to line, forrar (1)
to line, rayar (1)
to line up, ahilar (34)
to link, enlazar (11)
to link, eslabonar (1)
to link together, concadenar (1)
to link together, concatenar (1)
to liquefy, liquefacer (68)
to liquefy, liquidar (1)
to liquidate, liquidar (1)
to liquidate, saldar (1)
to lisp, cecear (1)
to listen to, escuchar (1)
to listen to, oír (95)
to lithograph, litografiar (61)
to litigate, litigar (9)
to litigate, pleitear (1)
to live, habitar (1)
to live, morar (1)
to live, vivir (3)
to live together, cohabitar (1)
to live together, convivir (3)
to load, cargar (9)
to loaf, gandulear (1)
to loaf, haranganear (1)
to loaf, holgar (ue) (45)
to loaf, vaguear (1)
to loaf, zanganear (1)
to loaf around, vagabundear (1)
to loaf around the streets, callejear (1)
to localize, localizar (11)
to locate, localizar (11)
to locate, situar (62)
to locate, ubicar (8)
to lock, cerrar (ie) (37)
to lock up, encerrar (ie) (37)
to lodge, alojar (1)
to lodge, aposentar (1)
to lodge, hospedar (1)
to lodge, posar (1)
to long for, ansiar (1) or (61)
to long for, añorar (1)
to look alike, parecerse (73) (4)
to look at, mirar (1)
to look at, ver (112)
to look cautiously, atisbar (1)
to look for, buscar (8)
to look fresh and luxuriant, lozanear (1)
to look over, rever (112)
to look through papers, papelear (1)
to look to be, aparentar (1)
to loosen, aflojar (1)
to loosen, desapretar (ie) (37)
to loosen, desprender (2)
to loosen, soltar (ue) (36)
to loot, saquear (1)
to lord, enseñorear (1)
to lose, perder (ie) (39)
to lose all one's money, arrearse (1) (4)
to lose interest, desinteresarse (1) (4)
to lose its inflamation, desinflamarse (1) (4)
to lose moderation or self-control, desmandarse (1) (4)
to lose one's all, tronar (ue) (36)
to lose one's appetite, desganarse (1) (4)
to lose one's head, chalarse (1) (4)
to lose one's head, chiflarse (1) (4)
to lose one's way, desorientarse (1) (4)

to lose weight, rebajarse (1) (4)
to love, amar (1)
to love, querer (ie) (101)
to lower, agachar (1)
to lower, arriar (61)
to lower, bajar (1)
to lower, descender (ie) (39)
to lower, rebajar (1)
to lubricate, engrasar (1)
to lubricate, lubricar (8)
to lump together, englobar (1)
to lunch, lonchear (1)
to lurk, acechar (1)

M

to mace, macear (1)
to macerate, macerar (1)
to machine-gun, ametrallar (1)
to madden, enloquecer (73)
to magnetize, imanar (1)
to magnetize, imantar (1)
to magnetize, magnetizar (11)
to magnify, magnificar (8)
to maim, mancar (8)
to maim, tullir (27)
to maintain, mantener (ie) (108)
to maintain, sostener (ie) (108)
to maintain, sustentar (1)
to make, hacer (90)
to make a cuckold, encornudar (1)
to make a hole or holes in, agujerear (1)
to make a mess of, embarullar (1)
to make a mistake, desacertar (ie) (37)
to make a mistake, equivocarse (8) (4)
to make a racket, alborotar (1)
to make a testament or will, testar (1)
to make academic, academizar (11)
to make agile, agilitar (1)
to make agreeable, amenizar (11)
to make amends, desagraviar (1)
to make an appointment with, citar (1)
to make an impassioned speech, pe-
    rorar (1)
to make an incision in, sajar (1)
to make Arabic, arabizar (11)
to make better, mejorar (1)
to make bitter, amargar (9)
to make black and blue, acardenalar (1)
to make black and blue, amoratar (1)
to make blush, abochornar (1)
to make bread, panificar (8)
to make charcoal, carbonear (1)
to make clear, aclarar (1)
to make clear, esclarecer (73)
to make cocky, envalentonar (1)
to make commensurate, conmensurar
    (1)
to make common cause, solidarizarse
    (11) (4)
to make convex, abombar (1)
to make dark, entenebrecer (73)
to make dark, lobreguecer (73)
to make decent, adecentar (1)
to make deeper, profundizar (11)
to make desolate, desolar (ue) (36)
to make diaphanous, diafanizar (11)
to make difficult, dificultar (1)
to make disappear by sleight of hand,
    escamotear (1)
to make drinkable, potabilizar (11)
to make drowsy, amodorrecer (73)
to make elastic, elastificar (8)
to make elegant, elegantizar (11)
to make endless, eternizar (11)
to make equal, homologar (9)

to make even, aparear (1)
to make evident, evidenciar (1)
to make evident, patentizar (11)
to make faces, monear (1)
to make famous, afamar (1)
to make fanatical, fanatizar (11)
to make fed up, hartar (1)
to make flourishes (on the guitar,
    with a pen), rasguear (1)
to make fluffy, esponjar (1)
to make foolish, entontecer (73)
to make fun, burlarse (1) (4)
to make fun, cuchufletear (1)
to make fun of, coñearse (1) (4)
to make fun of, chotear (1)
to make fun of someone, cachondearse
    (1) (4)
to make gloomy, lobreguecer (73)
to make guttural sounds, guturalizar
    (11)
to make hoarse, enronquecer (73)
to make huge, agigantar (1)
to make hygienic, higienizar (11)
to make impatient, impacientar (1)
to make impossible, imposibilitar (1)
to make insensible, insensibilizar (11)
to make insolent, insolentar (1)
to make into bread, panificar (8)
to make into rings, anillar (1)
to make jealous, amartelar (1)
to make lethargic, aletargar (9)
to make like, asemejar (1)
to make lines on, rayar (1)
to make look old, envejecer (73)
to make lukewarm, entibiar (1)
to make manifest, exteriorizar (11)
to make mean, abellacar (8)
to make more acute, agudizar (11)
to make natural, connaturalizar (11)
to make numb, entumecer (73)
to make old, envejecer (73)
to make one's debut, debutar (1)
to make oneself comfortable, acomo-
    darse (1) (4)
to make oneself sure, asegurarse (1) (4)
to make out, descifrar (1)
to make over, rehacer (90)
to make pleasant (with wit, clever-
    ness), salpimentar (ie) (37)
to make possible, posibilitar (1)
to make pregnant, embarazar (11)
to make printed impressions from
    xylographs, xilografiar (61)
to make prominent, realzar (11)
to make proud, enorgullecer (73)
to make proud, ensoberbecer (73)
to make public, divulgar (9)
to make ready, aprestar (1)
to make real, realizar (11)
to make red, enrojecer (73)
to make red-hot, enrojecer (73)
to make remorseful, compungir (16)
to make repoussé work on, repujar (1)
to make round, redondear (1)
to make sanitary, sanear (1)
to make secure, asegurar (1)
to make sleepy, adormecer (73)
to make smaller, achicar (8)
to make smaller, empequeñecer (73)
to make solidary, solidarizar (11)
to make someone be quiet, atarugar (9)
to make someone lose his head, chalar
    (1)
to make sour, acidular (1)
to make speeches, discursear (1)
to make stand out, destacar (8)

to make straight with a plumb, aplo-
    mar (1)
to make strong, robustecer (73)
to make stumble, trompicar (8)
to make stupid, abobar (1)
to make supernatural, sobrenaturalizar
    (11)
to make swampy, apantanar (1)
to make temporary, temporalizar (11)
to make the sign of the cross (on one-
    self), persignarse (1) (4)
to make the sign of the cross (on
    oneself), santiguarse (10) (4)
to make the sign of the cross (on
    oneself), signarse (1) (4)
to make the sign of the cross (over
    something), santiguar (10)
to make the sign of the cross (over
    something), signar (1)
to make thin, adelgazar (11)
to make thin, enflaquecer (73)
to make turbid, enturbiar (1)
to make ugly, afear (1)
to make unequal, desigualar (1)
to make uneven, desemparejar (1)
to make uneven, desnivelar (1)
to make unpopular, impopularizar (11)
to make up for, resarcirse (13) (4)
to make up for, suplir (3)
to make use, aprovechar (1)
to make used to difficulty, curtir (3)
to make useless, inutilizar (11)
to make vain, engreír (59)
to make vain, envanecer (73)
to make volatile, volatilizar (11)
to make waterproof, impermeabilizar
    (11)
to make worse, desmejorar (1)
to make worse, empeorar (1)
to make worse again, reagravar (1)
to man (ships, planes, etc.), tripular (1)
to manage, agenciar (1)
to manage, gestionar (1)
to manage, ingeniarse (1) (4)
to manage, manejar (1)
to manage, procurar (1)
to manage, regentar (1)
to manage, regir (i, i) (57)
to manage the situation, desenvolverse
    (ue) (70) (4)
to maneuver, apañarse (1) (4)
to maneuver, maniobrar (1)
to manifest, manifestar (ie) (37)
to manipulate, manipular (1)
to manufacture, fabricar (8)
to manufacture, manufacturar (1)
to maraud, merodear (1)
to march, desfilar (1)
to march, marchar (1)
to marinate, marinar (1)
to mark, marcar (8)
to mark, señalar (1)
to mark (exam paper), calificar (8)
to mark a plot of ground for planting,
    marquear (1)
to mark again, remarcar (8)
to mark boundaries of, deslindar (1)
to mark off, acotar (1)
to mark off, alindar (1)
to mark with buoys, aboyar (1)
to mark with buoys or flares, balizar
    (11)
to marry, casar (1)
to marry, desposar (1)
to martyrize, martirizar (11)
to mask, enmascarar (1)

to masquerade, enmascararse (1) (4)
to massage, friccionar (1)
to masturbate, masturbarse (1) (4)
to match, parear (1)
to materialize, cuajar (1)
to materialize, materializar (11)
to matriculate, matricular (1)
to mature, madurar (1)
may, poder (ue) (97)
to mean, significar (8)
to meander, serpentear (1)
to measure, aforar (1)
to measure, medir (i, i) (42)
to measure, mensurar (1)
to measure out the doses of, dosificar (8)
to measure the height of, tallar (1)
to measure with a compass, compasar (1)
to mechanize, mecanizar (11)
to meddle (pretending to have authority), mangonear (1)
to mediate, mediar (1)
to mediate, promediar (1)
to meditate, meditar (1)
to meditate, rumiar (1)
to meditate, terciar (1)
to meet, avistarse (1) (4)
to meet, conocer (73)
to meet, encontrar (ue) (36)
to meet, encontrarse (ue) (36) (4)
to meet, recibir (3)
to meet face to face, enfrentarse (1) (4)
to melt, derretir (ie, i) (42)
to melt down, derretirse (i, i) (42) (4)
to mend, apedazar (11)
to mend, recomponer (98)
to mend, recoser (2)
to mend, reformar (1)
to mend, remendar (ie) (37)
to mend, zurcir (13)
to mend (by reweaving; stockings, nets, etc.), remallar (1)
to menstruate, menstruar (62)
to mention, mencionar (1)
to mention, mentar (ie) (37)
not to mention, callar (1)
to meow, maullar (65)
to meow, mayar (1)
to merge, fusionar (1)
to mess up, desarreglar (1)
to mess up the hair, despeinar (1)
to migrate, emigrar (1)
to militarize, militarizar (11)
to militate (for or against), militar (1)
to milk, ordeñar (1)
to mill, fresar (1)
to mimeograph, mimeografiar (61)
to mimic, remedar (1)
to mine, minar (1)
to mine, zapar (1)
to misapply funds, malversar (1)
to miscount, descontarse (ue) (36) (4)
to misdirect, desorientar (1)
to misfire, fallar (1)
to mislay among other papers, traspapelar (1)
to mislead, desaviar (61)
to mislead, descarriar (61)
to mislead, extraviar (61)
to mismate in marriage, malcasar (1)
to misplace, extraviar (61)
to misrepresent, falsear (1)
to miss, desacertar (ie) (37)
to miss, errar (ie) (52)
to miss, extrañar (1)

to miss, marrar (1)
to miss, perder (ie) (39)
to miss, pifiar (1)
to misspend, malgastar (1)
to mistake, equivocar (8)
to mistreat, maltraer (109)
to mistreat, maltratar (1)
to mitigate, mitigar (9)
to mix, inmiscuir (23)
to mix, mezclar (1)
to moan, gemir (i, i) (42)
to mobilize, movilizar (11)
to mock, burlar (1)
to mock, mofar (1)
to model, modelar (1)
to moderate, amortiguar (10)
to moderate, moderar (1)
to moderate, templar (1)
to modernize, modernizar (11)
to modify, modificar (8)
to modulate, modular (1)
to moisten, humedecer (73)
to mold, amohecer (73)
to mold, amoldar (1)
to mold, moldear (1)
to mold, plasmar (1)
to monkey around, monear (1)
to monopolize, abarcar (8)
to monopolize, acaparar (1)
to monopolize, monopolizar (11)
to moo, mugir (16)
to mop, trapear (1)
to moralize, moralizar (11)
to mortify, mortificar (8)
to mortise, machihembrar (1)
to motivate, motivar (1)
to motorize, motorizar (11)
to mount, montar (1)
to move, ir (92)
to move, menear (1)
to move, mover (ue) (38)
to move, mudar (1)
to move (to another place, job, etc.), trasladarse (1) (4)
to move about, ambular (1)
to move about, deambular
to move about, navegar (9)
to move aside, abarse (115) (4)
to move away, alejar (1)
to move forward, adelantar (1)
to move forward, adelantarse (1) (4)
to move from winter to summer or from summer to winter pasture, trashumar (1)
to move or raise with a crowbar, apalancar (8)
to move, talk or act hastily, atropellarse (1) (4)
to move through, surcar (8)
to move to and fro, zarandearse (1) (4)
to move to pity, apiadar (1)
to move to pity, enternecer (73)
to muddy, enlodar (1)
to muddy, enlodazar (11)
to muffle oneself, tapujarse (1) (4)
to multigraph, multigrafiar (61)
to multiply, multiplicar (8)
to multiply by ten, decuplicar (8)
to mumble, chistar (1)
to mumble, mascullar (1)
to mummify, momificar (8)
to murmur, murmurar (1)
must, deber (2)
to mutilate, mutilar (1)
to mutter, mumurar (1)
to muzzle, amordazar (11)

N

to nail, clavar (1)
to nail, clavetear (1)
to nail something down with wooden pegs, atarugar (9)
to name, denominar (1)
to name, nombrar (1)
to name, proponer (98)
to narrow, angostar (1)
to narrow, estrechar (1)
to nationalize, nacionalizar (11)
to naturalize, nacionalizar (11)
to naturalize, naturalizar (11)
to nauseate, asquear (1)
to navigate, navegar (9)
to navigate along the coast, costear (1)
to necessitate, necesitar (1)
to need, necesitar (1)
to need, precisar (1)
to need, requerir (ie, i) (41)
to neglect, descuidar (1)
to neglect, omitir (3)
to negotiate, negociar (1)
to negotiate, tramitar (1)
to neigh, relinchar (1)
to nestle, anidar (1)
to net, redar (1)
to neutralize, neutralizar (11)
never to finish, eternizarse (11) (4)
to nibble, morder (ue) (38)
to nibble at, mordiscar (8)
to nibble grass, twigs or leaves, ramonear (1)
to nick, mellar (1)
to nickname, apodar (1)
to nod (in sleep), cabecear (1)
to nominalize, nominalizar (11)
to normalize, normalizar (11)
to nose, husmear (1)
to notch, mellar (1)
to note, anotar (1)
to note, apostillar (1)
to note, notar (1)
to note in advance, prenotar (1)
to notice, advertir (ie, i) (41)
to notice, notar (1)
to notice, reparar (1)
to notify, notificar (8)
to notify, participar (1)
to nourish, nutrir (3)
to novelize, novelizar (11)
to number, numerar (1)
to numerate, numerar (1)
to nurse, amamantar (1)
to nurse, lactar (1)
to nuzzle, hocicar (8)
to nuzzle, hociquear (1)
to nuzzle, hozar (11)

O

to obey, obedecer (73)
to obfuscate, ofuscar (8)
to object, objetar (1)
to obligate, obligar (9)
to obscure, anublar (1)
to obscure, nublar (1)
to observe, observar (1)
to obsess, obsesionar (1)
to obstruct, atorar (1)
to obstruct, atrancar (8)
to obstruct, entorpecer (73)
to obstruct, estorbar (1)
to obstruct, obstruir (71)
to obtain, conseguir (i, i) (58)

to obtain, lograr (1)
to obtain, obtener (ie) (108)
to obtain, recabar (1)
to obtain by expiration of time set by law, usucapir (121)
to occlude, ocluir (71)
to occupy, ocupar (1)
to occur, ocurrir (3)
to offend, agraviar (1)
to offend, atropellar (1)
to offend, faltar (1)
to offend, lastimar (1)
to offend, ofender (2)
to offend, ultrajar (1)
to offer, brindar (1)
to offer, ofrecer (73)
to offer, tender (ie) (39)
to offer or lend oneself, prestarse (1) (4)
to officiate, oficiar (1)
to oil, aceitar (1)
to omit, cortar (1)
to omit, omitir (3)
to ooze, rezumar (1)
to open, abrir (75)
to open, destapar (1)
to open a path, sendear (1)
to open one's heart, expansionarse (1) (4)
to open the first time (store, bridge, etc.), inaugurar (1)
to operate, operar (1)
to oppose, contraponer (98)
to oppose, contrariar (61)
to oppose, oponer (98)
to oppress, abrumar (1)
to oppress, oprimir (3)
to orchestrate, orquestar (1)
to order, disponer (98)
to order, encargar (9)
to order, mandar (1)
to order, ordenar (1)
to order, pedir (i, i) (42)
to organize, organizar (11)
to organize, estructurar (1)
to orient, orientar (1)
to orientate, orientar (1)
to originate, nacer (73)
to originate, originar (1)
to originate, proceder (2)
to originate, provenir (ie, i) (111)
to ornament, ornamentar (1)
to oscillate, oscilar (1)
to ossify, osificar (8)
to oust, desalojar (1)
to outbid, pujar (1)
to outline, esquematizar (11)
to outline, plantificar (8)
to outline, reseñar (1)
to outline, trazar (11)
to outshine, eclipsar (1)
to outshine, lucir (74)
to overburden, agobiar (1)
to overcast (sewing), sobrehilar (34)
to overcharge, recargar (9)
to overcharge, sobrecargar (9)
to overcome, superar (1)
to overcome, vadear (1)
to overcome adversity, sobreponerse (98) (4)
to overeat, atracarse (8) (4)
to overexcite, sobrexcitar (1)
to overexpose, sobreexponer (98)
to overfeed, sobrealimentar (1)
to overflow, derramarse (1) (4)
to overflow, desbordar (1)
to overflow, rebasar (1)

to overflow, redundar (1)
to overflow, reverter (ie) (39)
to overheat, recalentar (ie) (37)
to overheat, sobrecalentar (ie) (37)
to overjoy, alborozar (11)
to overload, sobrecargar (9)
to overlook, preterir (ie, i) (119)
to overpay, repagar (9)
to overstep, extralimitarse (1) (4)
to overstock, abarrotar (1)
to overthrow, derrocar [(ue) (44)] or (8)
to overturn, trastornar (1)
to overturn, volcar (ue) (44)
to overturn, voltear (1)
to overwhelm, abismar (1)
to overwhelm, abrumar (1)
to overwhelm, anonadar (1)
to overwhelm, colmar (1)
to owe, adeudar (1)
to owe, deber (2)
to own, poseer (20)
to oxidize, oxidar (1)
to oxygenate, oxigenar (1)

P

to pacify, apaciguar (10)
to pacify, pacificar (8)
to pacify, serenar (1)
to pack, empacar (8)
to pack, empaquetar (1)
to pack into a trunk, embaular (1) or (65)
to package in a container, envasar (1)
to pad, almohadillar (1)
to paint, pincelar (1)
to paint, pintar (1)
to paint in motley colors, abigarrar (1)
to pair, emparejar (1)
to pair off, aparear (1)
to pair off, parearse (1) (4)
to palliate, paliar (1)
to pamper, mimar (1)
to pant, acezar (11)
to pant, jadear (1)
to paper, empapelar (1)
to parade, desfilar (1)
to paralyze, embargar (9)
to paralyze, paralizar (11)
to paraphrase, parafrasear (1)
to parcel out, parcelar (1)
to parch, quemar (1)
to pardon, disculpar (1)
to pardon, indultar (1)
to pardon, perdonar (1)
to park, aparcar (8)
to park, estacionar (1)
to park, parquear (1)
to parody, parodiar (1)
to participate, participar (1)
to particularize, particularizar (11)
to pass, pasar (1)
to pass, transcurrir (3)
to pass an examination, aprobar (ue) (36)
to pass a judgment, opinar (1)
to pass by touching slightly, rozar (11)
to pass judgment, dictaminar (1)
to pass judgment on, enjuiciar (1)
to pass over, traspasar (1)
to pass over (disregard seniority), postergar (9)
to pass through, traspasar (1)
to pasteurize, pasterizar (11)
to pasteurize, pasteurizar (11)
to pasture, apacentar (ie) (37)
to pasture, pacer (73)

to patch, apedazar (11)
to patch, parchar (1)
to patch, remendar (ie) (37)
to patent, patentar (1)
to patrol, patrullar (1)
to pause, pausar (1)
to pave, pavimentar (1)
to pave, solar (ue) (36)
to pave with bricks, enladrillar (1)
to pave with bricks, ladrillar (1)
to pave with cobblestones, adoquinar (1)
to pave with slabs, enlosar (1)
to pave with stones, empedrar (ie) (37)
to pave with tile, embaldosar (1)
to paw (said of a horse), piafar (1)
to pawn, empeñar (1)
to pawn, prendar (1)
to pay, abonar (1)
to pay, pagar (9)
to pay, sufragar (9)
to pay (attention), prestar (1)
to pay attention, atender (ie) (39)
to pay attention, fijarse (1) (4)
to pay back, reintegrar (1)
to pay for, pagar (9)
to pay for itself, costearse (1) (4)
to pay in advance, antepagar (9)
to pay or render (homage, admiration, honor, etc.), tributar (1)
to peck, picar (8)
to pedal, pedalear (1)
to peel, mondar (1)
to peel, pelar (1)
to peel bark, pelar (1)
to peel off, pelarse (1) (4)
to peep, pipiar (61)
to peep, piular (1)
to penalize, penar (1)
to penetrate, penetrar (1)
to pension, pensionar (1)
to perceive, percibir (3)
to perch, posar (1)
to perch (birds), posarse (1) (4)
to percolate, trascolar (ue) (36)
to perfect, afinar (1)
to perfect, perfeccionar (1)
to perfect, perfilar (1)
to perforate, horadar (1)
to perforate, perforar (1)
to perforate, punzar (11)
to perforate, taladrar (1)
to perform, desempeñar (1)
to perform, ejecutar (1)
to perfume, perfumar (1)
to perfume with smoke or incense, sahumar (34)
to periphrase, perifrasear (1)
to perish, perecer (73)
to permit, permitir (3)
to perpetrate, perpetrar (1)
to perpetuate, perpetuar (62)
to perpetuate, vincular (1)
to persecute, perseguir (i, i) (58)
to persevere, perseverar (1)
to persist, persistir (3)
to persist, porfiar (61)
to personalize, personalizar (11)
to personify, personificar (8)
to perspire, perspirar (1)
to perspire, sudar (1)
to persuade, persuadir (3)
to pertain, pertenecer (73)
to perturb, perturbar (1)
to pervert, pervertir (ie, i) (41)
to petition, peticionar (1)

to petrify, petrificar (8)
to philosophize, filosofar (1)
to photoengrave, fotograbar (1)
to photograph, fotografiar (61)
to photograph, retratar (1)
to phrase, frasear (1)
to pick, coger (15)
to pick (a bone), roer (103)
to pick out, entresacar (8)
to pick up, apañar (1)
to pick up, recoger (15)
to pickle, escabechar (1)
to piece out, apedazar (11)
to pierce, atravesar (ie) (37)
to pierce, calar (1)
to pierce, taladrar (1)
to pigeonhole, encasillar (1)
to pigment, pigmentar (1)
to pile, amontonar (1)
to pile, apilar (1)
to pile, coacervar (1)
to pile up, apelontonar (1)
to pilot, pilotar (1)
to pilot, pilotear (1)
to pin, alfilerar (1)
to pin, prender (2)
to pinch, pellizcar (8)
to pinch, pizcar (8)
to pique, picar (8)
to pirate, piratear (1)
to pirouette, piruetear (1)
to pity, compadecer (73)
to pivot, pivotar (1)
to placate, aplacar (8)
to place, colocar (8)
to place, emplazar (11)
to place, meter (2)
to place, poner (98)
to place, situar (62)
to place, ubicar (8)
to place a long, flexible thing in vibrating motion, cimbrear (1)
to place a second mark on something for reverification, contramarcar (8)
to place at a distance, distanciar (1)
to place between, intercalar (1)
to place between, interponer (98)
to place confidence in, fiarse (19) (4)
to place diagonally, terciar (1)
to place in an asylum, asilar (1)
to place in an upright position, parar (1)
to place in front, anteponer (98)
to place obliquely, soslayar (1)
to plagiarize, plagiar (1)
to plague, plagar (9)
to plan, pensar (ie) (37)
to plan, planear (1)
to plan, planificar (8)
to plan, plantear (1)
to plan, plantificar (8)
to plan, proyectar (1)
to plan or outline again, replantear (1)
to plane, cepillar (1)
to plane, garlopar (1)
to plant, plantar (1)
to plaster, enyesar (1)
to plaster, revocar (8)
to plate with silver, platear (1)
to play, jugar (ue) (93)
to play (harp, lyre, etc.), pulsar (1)
to play (musical instrument), tañer (28)
to play (musical instrument), tocar (8)
to play a trick on, chasquear (1)
to play in politics, politiquear (1)
to play or sing out of tune, desafinar (1)

to play the guitar, guitarrear (1)
to play the kettledrum, timbalear (1)
to play the tambourine, panderetear (1)
to play the xylophone, xylofonear (1)
to plead, abogar (9)
to please, agradar (1)
to please, aplacer (73)
to please, complacer (73)
to please, placer (96)
to pleat, alforzar (11)
to pleat, plegar (ie) (50)
to pleat, tronzar (11)
to pledge, empeñar (1)
to plot, complotar (1)
to plot, maquinar (1)
to plot, tramar (1)
to plot, urdir (3)
to plot against, insidiar (1)
to plow, arar (1)
to plow, labrar (1)
to plow (untilled ground), arromper (104)
to plow regularly, amelgar (9)
to pluck, desplumar (1)
to pluck, pelar (1)
to plug, cegar (ie) (50)
to plug, enchufar (1)
to plug, obturar (1)
to plug, taponar (1)
to plug up, atascar (8)
to plumb, aplomar (1)
to plunder, rapiñar (1)
to plunge, zambullir (27)
to plunge, zambullirse (27) (4)
to pluralize, pluralizar (11)
to poach (eggs), escalfar (1)
to poetize, poetizar (11)
to point at, apuntar (1)
to point at, señalar (1)
to point out, apuntar (1)
to point out, señalar (1)
to poison, atosigar (9)
to poison, envenenar (1)
to poison, intoxicar (8)
to poison, tosigar (9)
to poke, hurgar (9)
to poke (a fire), atizar (11)
to polarize, polarizar (11)
to polish, abrillantar (1)
to polish, bruñir (29)
to polish, charolar (1)
to polish, enlustrecer (73)
to polish, lustrar (1)
to polish, perfilar (1)
to polish, pulir (3)
to polish, tersar (1)
to polish (people), urbanizar (11)
to pollinate, polinizar (11)
to ponder, ponderar (1)
to ponder over, ponderar (1)
to pontificate, pontificar (8)
to pool (resources), mancomunar (1)
to popularize, popularizar (11)
to popularize, vulgarizar (11)
to populate, poblar (ue) (36)
to portray, pincelar (1)
to portray, retratar (1)
to pose, posar (1)
to possess, poseer (20)
to possess, tener (108)
to postpone, aplazar (11)
to postpone, posponer (98)
to postpone, prorrogar (9)
to postulate, postular (1)
to pour, diluviar (1)
to pour, echar (1)

to pour, verter (ie) (39)
to pour at intervals, chaparrear (1)
to pour forth, manar (1)
to pour from one container to another, transvasar (1)
to pour wine, escanciar (1)
to powder, empolvar (1)
to practice, ejercer (12)
to practice, ejercitar (1)
to practice, practicar (8)
to practice usury, usurear (1)
to praise, alabar (1)
to praise, apologizar (11)
to praise, elogiar (1)
to praise, encomiar (1)
to praise, loar (1)
to pray, rezar (11)
to preach, predicar (8)
to precede, anteceder (2)
to precede, preceder (2)
to precipitate, precipitar (1)
to preconceive, preconcebir (i, i) (42)
to predestine, predestinar (1)
to predict, agorar (ue) (48)
to predict, antedecir (i, i) (84)
to predict, predecir (i, i) (84)
to predict, presagiar (1)
to predict, vaticinar (1)
to predispose, predisponer (98)
to predominate, predominar (1)
to preexist, preexistir (3)
to prefabricate, prefabricar (8)
to prefer, anteponer (98)
to prefer, preferir (ie, i) (41)
to prefix, prefijar (1)
to prejudge, prejuzgar (9)
to prelude, preludiar (1)
to premeditate, premeditar (1)
to preoccupy, preocupar (1)
to prepare, aderezar (11)
to prepare, aparejar (1)
to prepare, apercibir (3)
to prepare, aviar (61)
to prepare, preparar (1)
to prepare, prevenir (ie, i) (111)
to prepare quickly, aprontar (1)
to prepare something for the road, aviar (61)
to prescribe, prescribir (69)
to prescribe, recetar (1)
to present, presentar (1)
to present (a candidate), proponer (98)
to present offerings, ofrendar (1)
to preserve, confitar (1)
to preserve, preservar (1)
to preserve in syrup, almibarar (1)
to preside over, presidir (3)
to press, ahincar (8)
to press, aprensar (1)
to press, apretar (ie) (37)
to press, prensar (1)
to press (clothes), planchar (1)
to press hard, apretujar (1)
to presume, presumir (3)
to presuppose, presuponer (98)
to pretend, aparentar (1)
to pretend, fingir (16)
to pretend, pretender (2)
to pretend not to know, desentenderse (ie) (39) (4)
to prevail, imperar (1)
to prevail, preponderar (1)
to prevail, prevalecer (73)
to prevail, prevaler (110)
to prevail, reinar (1)
to prevaricate, prevaricar (8)

to prevent, aviar (61)
to prevent, impedir (i, i) (42)
to prevent, imposibilitar (1)
to prevent, obstaculizar (11)
to prevent, precaver (2)
to prevent, prevenir (ie, i) (111)
to prevent, remediar (1)
to prick, pinchar (1)
to prick, pungir (16)
to prick, punzar (11)
to prime (a pump, a furnace), cebar (1)
to print, imprimir (91)
to privilege, privilegiar (1)
to proceed, proceder (2)
to proceed, proseguir (i, i) (58)
to proclaim, preconizar (11)
to proclaim, pregonar (1)
to proclaim, proclamar (1)
to proclaim, promulgar (8)
to procrastinate, procrastinar (1)
to procreate, procrear (1)
to procure, procurar (1)
to prod, acuciar (1)
to produce, engendrar (1)
to produce, producir (67)
to produce income, rentar (1)
to profess, profesar (1)
to profile, perfilar (1)
to profit, beneficiarse (1) (4)
to profit, lucrarse (1) (4)
to prognosticate, pronosticar (8)
to program, programar (1)
to progress, progresar (1)
to prohibit, prohibir (34)
to prohibit, vedar (1)
to project, proyectar (1)
to proletarianize, proletarizar (11)
to prolong, prolongar (9)
to promenade, pasear (1)
to promise, prometer (2)
to promote, ascender (ie) (39)
to promote, fomentar (1)
to promote, promover (ue) (38)
to promote, provocar (8)
to prompt, apuntar (1)
to prompt, soplar (1)
to promulgate, promulgar (9)
to pronounce, pronunciar (1)
to pronounce Spanish c (before e or i)
    and z like s, sesear (1)
to pronounce Spanish s like c (before
    e or i) and z, cecear (1)
to prop, apuntalar (1)
to prop, rodrigar (9)
to prop up (plants), rodrigar (9)
to propagate, cundir (3)
to propagate, propagar (9)
to propel, propulsar (1)
to prophesy, profetizar (11)
to propitiate, propiciar (1)
to proportion, proporcionar (1)
to propose, proponer (98)
to prorate, prorratear (1)
to proscribe, proscribir (69)
to prosecute, procesar (1)
to prosper, medrar (1)
to prosper, prosperar (1)
to prostitute, prostituir (71)
to prostrate, postrar (1)
to prostrate oneself, prosternarse (1) (4)
to protect, amparar (1)
to protect, defender (ie) (39)
to protect, propugnar (1)
to protect, proteger (15)
to protect, resguardar (1)
to protect oneself, parapetarse (1) (4)
to protest, protestar (1)

to prove, comprobar (ue) (36)
to prove, probar (ue) (36)
to provide, apercibir (3)
to provide, aviar (61)
to provide, deparar (1)
to provide, proporcionar (1)
to provide, proveer (99)
to provide, subvenir (ie, i) (111)
to provoke, provocar (8)
to provoke, suscitar (1)
to pry, fisgar (9)
to pry into, escarbar (1)
to pry into, escudriñar (1)
to psychoanalyze, psicoanalizar (11)
to publicize, publicar (8)
to publish, editar (1)
to publish, publicar (8)
to puff, resoplar (1)
to pull, jalar (1)
to pull, tirar (1)
to pull, tironear (1)
to pull or break the teeth of, desdentar
    (ie) (37)
to pull out, arrancar (8)
to pull out, sacar (8)
to pull out hair, mesar (1)
to pull out of the mud, desatascar (8)
to pulverize, pulverizar (11)
to pulverize, triturar (1)
to pump, bombear (1)
to punch, taladrar (1)
to punch with the fist, apuñetear (1)
to punctuate, puntuar (62)
to puncture, pinchar (1)
to punish, castigar (9)
to punish, penar (1)
to punish as a lesson, escarmentar (ie)
    (37)
to punish by retaliation, talionar (1)
to punish with death, ajusticiar (1)
to purge, purgar (9)
to purify, acrisolar (1)
to purify, depurar (1)
to purify, purgar (9)
to purify, purificar (8)
to purr, ronronear (1)
to purr, runrunear (1)
to pursue, perseguir (i, i) (58)
to pursue, seguir (i, i) (58)
to pursue relentlessly, acosar (1)
to push, empeller (26)
to push, empujar (1)
to push ahead, pujar (1)
to put, meter (2)
to put, poner (98)
to put a border or edge, orillar (1)
to put a heading, encabezar (11)
to put a mark on, signar (1)
to put a tilde, tildar (1)
to put a visa on a passport, visar (1)
to put after, posponer (98)
to put an end to, rematar (1)
to put aside, reservar (1)
to put before, preponer (98)
to put blame on, tachar (1)
to put crumbles in (a liquid), migar (9)
to put hinges on, abisagrar (1)
to put in a case, enfundar (1)
to put in as extra, sobreañadir (3)
to put in mourning, enlutar (1)
to put in order, compaginar (1)
to put in order, enderezar (11)
to put in the cradle, encunar (1)
to put in the oven, ahornar (1)
to put lapels on, solapar (1)
to put obstacles, obstaculizar (11)
to put off, posponer (98)

to put off center, descentrar (1)
to put on, chantar (1)
to put on, ponerse (98) (4)
to put on, revestir (i, i) (42)
to put on a diet, adietar (1)
to put on a mask, enmascararse (1) (4)
to put on edge, crispar (1)
to put on false hair, cabellar (1)
to put on one's cloak, encapotarse (1)(4)
to put (a garment) on over other
    clothes, sobrevestir (i, i) (42)
to put on the right track, encarrilar (1)
to put one's hat on, cubrirse (82) (4)
to put or lay across, atravesar (ie) (37)
to put out, apagar (9)
to put out of adjustment, desajustar (1)
to put out of order, descomponer (98)
to put pressure (on a person), presionar
    (1)
to put shoes on, calzar (11)
to put teeth on (e.g. comb), puar (19)
to put to bed, acostar (ue) (36)
to put up with, soportar (1)
to put vinegar on or in, envinagrar (1)

Q

to quadruple, cuadruplicar (8)
to qualify, calificar (8)
to qualify, capacitar (1)
to quarrel, pelear (1)
to quarter, cuartear (1)
to quarter (divide into pieces), des-
    cuartizar (11)
to quarter (troops), acantonar (1)
to quarter (troops), acuartelar (1)
to question, interrogar (9)
to quibble, cavilar (1)
to quiet, aquietar (1)
to quiet, sedar (1)
to quiet, sosegar (ie) (50)
to quiet down, aquietarse (1) (4)
to quilt, acojinar (1)
to quilt, acolchar (1)
to quilt, colchar (1)
to quit, cesar (1)
to quiver, retemblar (ie) (37)
to quiver, temblar (ie) (37)
to quote (price), cotizar (11)

R

to radiate, irradiar (1)
to radiate, radiar (1)
to radio, radiar (1)
to radio, radiografiar (61)
to radiobroadcast, radiodifundir (3)
to radiotelegraph, radiotelegrafiar (61)
to radiotelephone, radiotelefonear (1)
to raffle, rifar (1)
to raffle, sortear (1)
to rage, rabiar (1)
to rain, llover (ue) (38)
to rain gently, chispear (1)
to rain hard, chaparrear (1)
to rain hard, diluviar (1)
to raise, alzar (11)
to raise, criar (19)
to raise, empinar (1)
to raise, encaramar (1)
to raise, encumbrar (1)
to raise, enhestar (ie) (37)
to raise, levantar (1)
to raise, subir (3)
to raise (an issue), plantear (1)
to raise (difficulties), objetar (1)

to raise on high, enarbolar (1)
to raise the price of, encarecer (73)
to rake, rastrillar (1)
to ramify, ramificar (8)
to ransom, rescatar (1)
to rape, forzar (ue) (46)
to rape, violar (1)
to rarefy, enraecer (73)
to rarefy, rarefacer (68)
to rarefy, rarificar (8)
to rate, calificar (8)
to ratify, ratificar (8)
to ratify, refirmar (1)
to ratify, revalidar (1)
to ratiocinate, raciocinar (1)
to ration, racionar (1)
to rationalize, racionalizar (11)
to rattle, cencerrear (1)
to rattle, tabletear (1)
to rattle, traquear (1)
to rattle, traquetear (1)
to rave, rabiar (1)
to rave, desvariar (61)
to ravel, deshilachar (1)
to raze, asolar (ue) (36)
to reach, alcanzar (11)
to reach, llegar (9)
to reach out, tender (ie) (39)
to react, reaccionar (1)
to reactivate, reactivar (1)
to read, leer (20)
to readapt, readaptar (1)
to readjust, reajustar (1)
to readmit, readmitir (3)
to reaffirm, reafirmar (1)
to realize, percatarse (1) (4)
to reap, segar (ie) (50)
to reappear, reaparecer (73)
to reappraise, revalorar (1)
to rear, criar (19)
to rear (said of a horse), encabritarse (1)
   (4)
to rearm, rearmar (1)
to rearrange, reordenar (1)
to rearrange the order or sequence
   of, permutar (1)
to reason, discurrir (3)
to reason, razonar (1)
to reassume, reasumir (3)
to rebel, insubordinarse (1) (4)
to rebel, insurreccionarse (1) (4)
to rebel, levantarse (1) (4)
to rebel, rebelar (1)
to rebind, reencuadernar (1)
to rebound, rebotar (1)
to rebound, repercutir (3)
to rebuild, reconstruir (71)
to rebuild, reedificar (8)
to rebut, rebatir (3)
to recall, rememorar (1)
to recap, recauchutar (1)
to recap, regomar (1)
to recapitulate, epilogar (9)
to recapitulate, recapitular (1)
to recast, refundir (3)
to receive, acoger (15)
to receive, recibir (3)
to receive a title, titularse (1) (4)
to recharge, recargar (9)
to reciprocate, corresponder (2)
to reciprocate, reciprocar (8)
to recite, recitar (1)
to reclaim, reclamar (1)
to recline, recostar (ue) (36)
to recognize, reconocer (73)
to recognize one's own faults, errors,
   etc., reconocerse (73) (4)

to recommend, encomendar (ie) (37)
to recommend, recomendar (ie) (37)
to recompense, recompensar (1)
to recompose, recomponer (98)
to reconcile, avenir (ie, i) (111)
to reconcile, bienquistar (1)
to reconcile, reconciliar (1)
to recondition, reacondicionar (1)
to reconquer, reconquistar (1)
to reconsider, reconsiderar (1)
to reconstitute, reconstituir (71)
to record, registrar (1)
to record sound effects (on a film),
   sonorizar (11)
to recount, recontar (ue) (36)
to recouple, reenganchar (1)
to recover, recobrar (1)
to recover, reconquistar (1)
to recover, recuperar (1)
to recover, reponerse (98) (4)
to recover, restablecerse (73) (4)
to recover (cover again), recubrir (82)
to recover oneself, rehacerse (90) (4)
to recreate, recrear (1)
to recriminate, recriminar (1)
to recruit, reclutar (1)
to rectify, rectificar (8)
to recuperate, recuperar (1)
to redden, colorearse (1) (4)
to redden, rojear (1)
to redeem, redimir (3)
to redound, redundar (1)
to reduce, rebajar (1)
to reduce, reducir (67)
to redye, reteñir (i, i) (60)
to reeducate, reeducar (8)
to reel, rehilar (34)
to reelect, reelegir (i, i) (57)
to reembark, reembarcar (8)
to reenlist, reenganchar (1)
to reestablish, restablecer (73)
to reexamine, reexaminar (1)
to refer, referir (ie, i) (41)
to refer, referirse (ie, i) (41) (4)
to refer, remitir (3)
to referee, arbitrar (1)
to refill, rehenchir (i, i) (42)
to refill, rellenar (1)
to reflect, reflejar (1)
to reflect, reflexionar (1)
to reform, reformar (1)
to refract, refractar (1)
to refresh, refrescar (8)
to refresh one's memory, recapacitar
   (1)
to refrigerate, refrigerar (1)
to refry, refreír (i, i) (88)
to refund, reembolsar (1)
to refuse, desoír (95)
to refuse, negar (ie) (50)
to refuse, rehusar (34)
to refuse, repulsar (1)
to refuse, resistirse (3) (4)
to refute, rebatir (3)
to refute, refutar (1)
to regenerate, reengendrar (1)
to regenerate, regenerar (1)
to regiment, regimentar (ie) (37)
to register, inscribirse (69) (4)
to register, matricular (1)
to register, matricularse (1) (4)
to register, registrarse (1) (4)
to register (a letter), certificar (8)
to register in the census, empadronar
   (1)
to regret, lamentar (1)
to regret, sentir (ie, i) (41)

to regularize, regularizar (11)
to regulate, normalizar (11)
to regulate, reglar (1)
to regulate, regular (1)
to regurgitate, regurgitar (1)
to rehabilitate, rehabilitar (1)
to rehearse, ensayar (1)
to reheat, recalentar (ie) (37)
to reign, reinar (1)
to reimburse, reembolsar (1)
to rein, refrenar (1)
to reincarnate, reencarnar (1)
to reinforce, reforzar (ue) (46)
to reinstate, reponer (98)
to reinsure, reasegurar (1)
to reintegrate, reintegrar (1)
to reinvest, reinvertir (ie, i) (41)
to reiterate, reiterar (1)
to reject, desechar (1)
to reject, rechazar (11)
to reject, repulsar (1)
to rejoice, alegrarse (1) (4)
to rejoice, jubilar (1)
to rejoice, regocijarse (1) (4)
to rejoice, solazarse (11) (4)
to rejuvenate, rejuvenecer (73)
to rejuvenate, rejuvenecerse (73) (4)
to rejuvenate, remozar (11)
to rekindle, reencender (ie) (39)
to relapse, recaer (81)
to relapse (into vice or error), reincidir
   (3)
to relate, contar (ue) (36)
to relate, relacionar (1)
to relax, relajar (1)
to release, zafar (1)
to relegate, relegar (9)
to relieve, relevar (1)
to relieve from pain or trouble, desahogar (9)
to relieve of numbness, desentumecer
   (73)
to relight, reencender (ie) (39)
to relish, paladear (1)
to relish, relamerse (2) (4)
to reload, recargar (9)
to remain, permanecer (73)
to remain, quedar (1)
to remake, rehacer (90)
to remedy, remediar (1)
to remelt, refundir (3)
to remember, acordarse (ue) (36) (4)
to remember, memorar (1)
to remember, recordar (ue) (36)
to remember, rememorar (1)
to remind, recordar (ue) (36)
to remit, remesar (1)
to remit, remitir (3)
to remove, amover (ue) (38)
to remove, quitar (1)
to remove, remover (ue) (38)
to remove, substraer (109)
to remove bark, bread crust, descortezar (11)
to remove from office, deponer (98)
to remove grass, rotten branches,
   leaves on the ground, desbrozar (11)
to remove impediments from, desembargar (9)
to remove obstacles, despejar (1)
to remove obstructions from, desatrancar (8)
to remove roofing tiles, destejar (1)
to remove seeds, despepitar (1)
to remove the furniture, desamoblar
   (ue) (36)

to **remove the grain from**, desgranar (1)
to **remove the inflammation from**, desinflamar (1)
to **remove wedges or chocks from**, descalzar (11)
to **remunerate**, remunerar (1)
to **render (a service)**, prestar (1)
to **renew**, reanudar (1)
to **renew**, renovar (ue) (36)
to **renounce**, abnegar (ie) (50)
to **renounce**, renunciar (1)
to **renovate**, rehacer (90)
to **renovate**, renovar (ue) (36)
to **rent**, alquilar (1)
to **rent**, arrendar (ie) (37)
to **rent**, rentar (1)
to **reopen**, reabrir (75)
to **reorganize**, reorganizar (11)
to **repack**, reempacar (8)
to **repair**, apañar (1)
to **repair**, arreglar (1)
to **repair**, refaccionar (1)
to **repair**, remendar (ie) (37)
to **repair**, reparar (1)
to **repatriate**, repatriar (61)
to **repay**, repagar (9)
to **repay**, resarcir (13)
to **repay**, retribuir (71)
to **repeal**, abrogar (9)
to **repeat**, reiterar (1)
to **repeat**, repetir (i, i) (42)
to **repeat an offense**, reincidir (3)
to **repeatedly touch or handle something**, manosear (1)
to **repel**, repeler (2)
to **repent**, arrepentirse (ie, i) (41) (4)
to **replace**, reemplazar (11)
to **replace**, relevar (1)
to **replace**, reponer (98)
to **repopulate**, repoblar (ue) (36)
to **report**, reportar (1)
to **reprehend**, increpar (1)
to **reprehend**, reprender (2)
to **represent**, figurar (1)
to **represent**, representar (1)
to **repress**, cohibir (34)
to **repress**, reprimir (3)
to **reprimand**, sermonear (1)
to **reprint**, reimprimir (91)
to **reproach**, reconvenir (ie, i) (111)
to **reproach**, reprochar (1)
to **reproach**, zaherir (ie, i) (41)
to **reproduce**, reproducir (67)
to **reprove**, reprobar (ue) (36)
to **repudiate**, repudiar (1)
to **repulse**, repeler (2)
to **repute**, reputar (1)
to **require**, exigir (16)
to **require**, requerir (ie, i) (41)
to **reread**, releer (20)
to **rescind**, rescindir (3)
to **rescue**, rescatar (1)
to **resell**, revender (2)
to **resemble**, asimilarse (1) (4)
to **resemble each other**, parecerse (73) (4)
to **resent**, resentirse (ie, i) (41) (4)
to **reserve**, apalabrar (1)
to **reserve**, reservar (1)
to **reside**, avecindar (1)
to **reside**, residir (3)
to **resign**, dimitir (3)
to **resign**, renunciar (1)
to **resign**, resignar (1)
to **resist**, contrarrestar (1)
to **resist**, contrastar (1)

to **resist**, rebelar (1)
to **resist**, resistir (3)
to **resolve**, proponerse (98) (4)
to **resolve**, resolver (ue) (70)
to **resolve**, solucionar (1)
to **resonate**, resonar (ue) (36)
to **resort**, recorrer (2)
to **resort**, recurrir (3)
to **resound**, resonar (ue) (36)
to **resound**, retumbar (1)
to **respect**, respetar (1)
to **respond**, responder (2)
to **rest**, descansar (1)
to **rest**, gravitar (1)
to **rest**, holgar (ue) (45)
to **rest**, reposar (1)
to **rest on**, estribar (1)
to **rest on Saturday**, sabatizar (11)
to **restate**, replantear (1)
to **restock**, repostar (ue) (36)
to **restore**, instaurar (1)
to **restore**, reintegrar (1)
to **restore**, reponer (98)
to **restore**, restablecer (73)
to **restore**, restaurar (1)
to **restrain**, cohibir (34)
to **restrain**, embargar (9)
to **restrain**, frenar (1)
to **restrain**, refrenar (1)
to **restrain oneself**, aguantarse (1) (4)
to **restrict**, restringir (16)
to **resuscitate**, resucitar (1)
to **result**, resultar (1)
to **resume**, reanudar (1)
to **resume**, reasumir (3)
to **resurge**, resurgir (16)
to **resurrect**, resucitar (1)
to **retail**, revender (2)
to **retain**, retener (ie) (108)
to **retard**, retardar (1)
to **retard**, retrasar (1)
to **retire**, jubilar (1)
to **retire**, jubilarse (1) (4)
to **retire**, retirar (1)
to **retire (go to bed)**, recogerse (15) (4)
to **retire (go to bed)**, retirarse (1) (4)
to **retouch**, retocar (8)
to **retrace**, desandar (77)
to **retract**, desdecir (i, i) (84)
to **retract**, retractar (1)
to **retread**, regomar (1)
to **retrocede**, retroceder (2)
to **return**, devolver (ue) (70)
to **return**, regresar (1)
to **return**, restituir (71)
to **return**, retornar (1)
to **return**, tornar (1)
to **return**, volver (ue) (70)
to **reunite**, reunir (66)
to **revalidate**, revalidar (1)
to **revalorize**, revalorizar (11)
to **revalue**, revalorar (1)
to **reveal**, desvelar (1)
to **reveal**, patentizar (11)
to **reveal**, revelar (1)
to **reverberate**, repercutir (3)
to **reverberate**, reverberar (1)
to **revere**, reverenciar (1)
to **revere**, venerar (1)
to **reverence**, reverenciar (1)
to **revert**, revertir (ie, i) (41)
to **review**, repasar (1)
to **review**, rever (112)
to **review**, revisar (1)
to **review (a book)**, reseñar (1)
to **revise**, rever (112)

to **revise**, revisar (1)
to **revise (a book)**, refundir (3)
to **revitalize**, revitalizar (11)
to **revive**, reanimar (1)
to **revive**, reavivar (1)
to **revive**, resucitar (1)
to **revive**, revivir (3)
to **revoke**, abolir (116)
to **revoke**, derogar (9)
to **revoke**, revocar (8)
to **revolt**, revolucionarse (1) (4)
to **revolt**, sublevarse (1) (4)
to **revolutionize**, revolucionar (1)
to **revolve**, girar (1)
to **revolve**, revolver (ue) (70)
to **revolve**, voltear (1)
to **reward**, galardonar (1)
to **reward**, gratificar (8)
to **reward**, premiar (1)
to **reward**, recompensar (1)
to **reward**, retribuir (71)
to **rhyme**, rimar (1)
to **rid of color**, acromatizar (11)
to **riddle**, acribillar (1)
to **ride**, montar (1)
to **ride horseback**, cabalgar (9)
to **ridicule**, escarnecer (73)
to **ridicule**, ridiculizar (11)
to **ring**, sonar (ue) (36)
to **ring (a bell)**, tocar (8)
to **ring (said of the ears)**, zumbar (1)
to **ring bells**, repicar (8)
to **ring gaily**, repiquetear (1)
to **ring the bells**, campanear (1)
to **rinse**, enjuagar (9)
to **rip**, rasgar (9)
to **ripen**, madurar (1)
to **ripen**, sazonar (1)
to **ripple**, rizar (11)
to **rise**, alzarse (11) (4)
to **rise**, elevarse (1) (4)
to **rise**, encumbrarse (1) (4)
to **rise (the sun)**, salir (106)
to **rise early**, madrugar (9)
to **rise high**, empinarse (1) (4)
to **rise in price**, encarecerse (73) (4)
to **rise in rebellion**, sublevarse (1) (4)
to **rise up on the hind legs (said of a horse)**, encabritarse (1) (4)
to **risk**, arriesgar (9)
to **risk**, jugarse (ue) (93) (4)
to **rivet**, remachar (1)
to **roam**, vagar (9)
to **roam back and forth**, transitar (1)
to **roar**, rugir (16)
to **roar (an engine)**, roncar (8)
to **roast**, asar (1)
to **roast**, tostar (ue) (36)
to **rob**, desvalijar (1)
to **rob**, robar (1)
to **rock**, balancear (1)
to **rock**, mecer (14)
to **rock in a cradle**, acunar (1)
to **roll**, rodar (ue) (36)
to **roll**, rodillar (1)
to **roll**, rotar (1)
to **roll (the letter r)**, vibrar (1)
to **roll a drum**, redoblar (1)
to **roll down**, rodar (ue) (36)
to **roll over**, revolcar (ue) (44)
to **roll up**, enrollar (1)
to **roll with a roller**, apisonar (1)
to **romp**, corretear (1)
to **romp**, retozar (11)
to **romp around**, enredar (1)
to **roof**, techar (1)

to roof with tiles, tejar (1)
to root out, desarraigar (9)
to root out, extirpar (1)
to rot, corromper (2)
to rot, corromperse (2) (4)
to rot, descomponerse (98) (4)
to rot, pudrir (100)
to rough out, desbastar (1)
to round off, redondear (1)
to rouse, atizar (11)
to rouse, soliviantar (1)
to row, bogar (9)
to row, remar (1)
to row ineffectively, paletear (1)
to rub, fregar (ie) (50)
to rub, friccionar (1)
to rub, frotar (1)
to rub, refregar (ie) (50)
to rub elbows with, codearse (1) (4)
to rub or scrub hard, restregar (ie) (50)
to ruffle, encrespar (1)
to ruin, arruinar (1)
to ruin, descalabrar (1)
to rule, imperar (1)
to rule, regir (i, i) (57)
to rule (paper), reglar (1)
to rumble, retronar (ue) (36)
to rumble, retumbar (1)
to rumble, rugir (16)
to ruminate, rumiar (1)
to rumor, rumorear (1)
to run, correr (2)
to run, funcionar (1)
to run, marchar (1)
to run (clock), andar (77)
to run a sugarcane mill, trapichear (1)
to run aground, embarrancarse (8) (4)
to run aground, encallar (1)
to run aground, varar (1)
to run around, corretear (1)
to run away, ahuyentarse (1) (4)
to run away (said of a horse), desbocarse (8) (4)
to run into, topar (1)
to run over, atropellar (1)
to run over in one's mind, recapacitar (1)
to run through, ensartar (1)
to run through a narrow ravine, encajonarse (1) (4)
to rush, precipitar (1)
to rush ahead boldly, arrestarse (1) (4)
to rush around, zanquear (1)
to rush forth, arremeter (2)
to rush upon, abalanzarse (11) (4)
to rust, aherrumbrar (1)

S

to sabotage, sabotear (1)
to sack, ensacar (8)
to sack, saquear (1)
to sacrifice, inmolar (1)
to sacrifice, sacrificar (8)
to sadden, contristar (1)
to sadden, entristecer (73)
to saddle, ensillar (1)
to salivate, salivar (1)
to salt, salar (1)
to salt and pepper, salpimentar (ie) (37)
to salute, saludar (1)
to salvage, salvar (1)
to sample, probar (ue) (36)
to sanctify, santificar (8)
to sanction, sancionar (1)
to sandpaper, alijar (1)

to satiate, hartar (1)
to satirize, satirizar (11)
to satisfy, aplacar (8)
to satisfy, hartar (1)
to satisfy, satisfacer (68)
to saturate, saturar (1)
to save, ahorrar (1)
to save, salvar (1)
to savor, saborear (1)
to saw, aserrar (ie) (37)
to saw, serrar (ie) (37)
to saw with a buhl saw, seguetear (1)
to say, decir (i, i) (84)
to say, rezar (11)
to say flattering things, requebrar (ie) (37)
to say good-by, despedirse (i, i) (42) (4)
to say over and over again, redecir (i, i) (84)
says, diz (apocope of dice from decir)
to scald, escaldar (1)
to scale, escalar (1)
to scale, escamar (1)
to scandalize, escandalizar (11)
to scar, cicatrizar (11)
to scare, asustar (1)
to scare, asustarse (1) (4)
to scare, espantar (1)
to scatter, desparramar (1)
to scatter, desperdigar (9)
to scatter, esparcir (13)
to scent, husmear (1)
to scheme, apañarse (1) (4)
to scheme, confabularse (1) (4)
to scheme, fraguar (10)
to scheme, maquinar (1)
to scheme, tramar (1)
to scheme, trapichear (1)
to scheme, urdir (3)
to scoff, befar (1)
to scoff, mofar (1)
to scoff, pitorrear (1)
to scold, regañar (1)
to scold, reñir (i, i) (60)
to scold, reprender (2)
to scorch, achicharrar (1)
to scorch, chicharrar (1)
to scorch, socarrar (1)
to score, marcar (8)
to scorn, menospreciar (1)
to scrape, raer (102)
to scrape, rascar (8)
to scrape, raspar (1)
to scrape a bone, legrar (1)
to scrape off, raer (102)
to scrape off, raspar (1)
to scratch, arañar (1)
to scratch, rascar (8)
to scratch, rasguñar (1)
to scratch (mar), rayar (1)
to scratch up, escarbar (1)
to scream, chillar (1)
to screen, tamizar (11)
to screw, atornillar (1)
to screw a nut on a bolt, enroscar (8)
to scribble, garabatear (1)
to scribble, garrapatear (1)
to scrub, fregar (ie) (50)
to scrutinize, alambicar (8)
to scrutinize, escrutar (1)
to sculpture, esculpir (3)
to seal, precintar (1)
to seal, sellar (1)
to search, registrar (1)
to season, condimentar (1)
to season, sazonar (1)

to season with chili, enchilar (1)
to seat, asentar (ie) (37)
to seat, sentar (ie) (37)
to seclude, recluir (71)
to secrete, segregar (9)
to secrete, secretar (1)
to section, seccionar (1)
to secularize, temporalizar (11)
to secularize, secularizar (11)
to sediment, sedimentar (1)
to seduce, seducir (67)
to seduce (a woman), deshonrar (1)
to see, ver (112)
to see imperfectly, entrever (112)
to see off, despedir (i, i) (42)
to see vaguely, entrever (112)
to seed, sembrar (ie) (37)
to seed, sementar (ie) (37)
to seek advice, asesorarse (1) (4)
to seek after, rebuscar (8)
to seek protection, ampararse (1) (4)
to seem, parecer (73)
to segregate, segregar (9)
to seize, aferrar (1)
to seize, apresar (1)
to seize, coger (15)
to seize, incautar (1)
to seize, tomar (1)
to select, escoger (15)
to sell, vender (2)
to sell at a bargain, baratear (1)
to sell at retail, menudear (1)
to sell on credit, fiar (19)
to sell out at reduced prices, saldar (1)
to sell wine and liquor by the glass, copear (1)
to send, enviar (61)
to send, mandar (1)
to send, pasar (1)
to send, remesar (1)
to send, remitir (3)
to send away, ausentar (1)
to send, issue or draw checks, girar (1)
to send something on its way through channels, cursar (1)
to sense, sentir (ie, i) (41)
to sensitize, sensibilizar (11)
to sentence, sentenciar (1)
to separate, apartar (1)
to separate, separar (1)
to separate into small flocks, retazar (11)
to separate young from their mothers in a herd, desahijar (34)
to serenade, rondar (1)
to serve, servir (i, i) (42)
to serve as an acolyte, acolitar (1)
to serve in the army, militar (1)
to serve oneself, servirse (i, i) (42) (4)
to serve wine, escanciar (1)
to set (a trap), tender (ie) (39)
to set (cement), fraguarse (10) (4)
to set (said of the sun), ponerse (98) (4)
to set (the table), poner (98)
to set afloat, desembarrancar (8)
to set back, atrasar (1)
to set free, soltar (ue) (36)
to set free, zafar (1)
to set off petards, petardear (1)
to set on fire, encender (ie) (39)
to set on fire, incendiar (1)
to set or turn back (a watch or clock), retrasar (1)
to set sail, zarpar (1)
to set up, constituir (71)
to set up, montar (1)

to set up straight, erguir (ie, i) (86)
to set upright, erguir (ie, i) (86)
to settle, colonizar (11)
to settle, instalarse (1) (4)
to settle, saldar (1)
to settle, sedimentar (1)
to settle, zanjar (1)
to settle down, radicarse (8) (4)
to settle (accounts), solventar (1)
to settle (sediment), posarse (1) (4)
to sew, coser (2)
to sew again, recoser (2)
to shade, sombrear (1)
to shake, cimbrearse (1) (4)
to shake, conmover (ue) (38)
to shake, estremecer (73)
to shake, menear (1)
to shake, remecer (14)
to shake, retemblar (ie) (37)
to shake, sacudir (3)
to shake, tremer (2)
to shake, trepidar (1)
to shake, zangolotear (1)
to shake off the numbness, desentumecerse (73) (4)
to shame, avergonzar (49)
to shape, configurar (1)
to shape, plasmar (1)
to share, compartir (3)
to share, participar (1)
to sharpen, afilar (1)
to sharpen, agudizar (11)
to sharpen, aguzar (11)
to sharpen, amolar (ue) (36)
to sharpen on a grind stone, vaciar (61)
to shatter, destrozar (11)
to shatter, estrellar (1)
to shatter, tronzar (11)
to shave, afeitar (1)
to shave, rapar (1)
to shave, rasurar (1)
to shear, esquilar (1)
to shear, tonsurar (1)
to shell, descascarar (1)
to shelter, abrigar (9)
to shelter, albergar (9)
to shepherd, pastorear (1)
to shield, adargar (9)
to shift, desplazarse (11) (4)
to shift for oneself, bandearse (1) (4)
to shine, abrillantar (1)
to shine, brillar (1)
to shine, lucir (74)
to shine, lustrar (1)
to shine, refulgir (16)
to shine, relucir (74)
to shine, relumbrar (1)
to shine, resplandecer (73)
to shine, rutilar (1)
to ship, embarcar (8)
to ship, expedir (i, i) (42)
to shiver, tiritar (1)
to shiver, titiritar (1)
to shiver, tremblar (ie) (37)
to shock, chocar (8)
to shoe (a horse, etc.), herrar (ie) (37)
to shoot, balear (1)
to shoot, disparar (1)
to shoot, grillarse (1) (4)
to shoot (a gun), tirar (1)
to shoot at random, tirotear (1)
to shoot billiard balls (but not as part of a game), bolear (1)
to shoot wildly at, tirotear (1)
to shoot with arrows, asaetear (1)
to shorten, acortar (1)
to shout, gritar (1)

to shout, vocear (1)
to shout, vociferar (1)
to shout (decrees, etc.) thunderously, fulminar (1)
to shovel, apalear (1)
to shovel, palear (1)
to shovel, traspalar (1)
to show, enseñar (1)
to show, exponer (98)
to show, mostrar (ue) (36)
to show, reflejar (1)
to show, representar (1)
to show cruelty, encarnizarse (11) (4)
to show disrespect and lack of submission, desacatar (1)
to show gratitude (for), regraciar (1)
to show its greenness, verdear (1)
to show off, exhibirse (3) (4)
to show off, lucir (74)
to show off, ostentar (1)
to show off, pavonearse (1) (4)
to show one's profile, perfilarse (1) (4)
to show or prove the relationship between, entroncar (8)
to show respect and submission, acatar (1)
to show something out through an opening or from behind something, asomar (1)
to show the way, encaminar (1)
to show through, clarearse (1) (4)
to show yellow, amarillear (1)
to shower with, colmar (1)
to shower with attentions, agasajar (1)
to shrink, aovillarse (1) (4)
to shrink, encoger (15)
to shroud, amortazar (11)
to shuffle, barajar (1)
to shun, rehuir (71)
to sick, azuzar (11)
to siege, sitiar (1)
to sieve, cribar (1)
to sieve, tamizar (11)
to sift, cerner (ie) (39)
to sift, cernir (ie) (85)
to sift, tamizar (11)
to sigh, suspirar (1)
to sight, divisar (1)
to sign, firmar (1)
to sign, signar (1)
to sign, subscribir (69)
to sign and seal, rubricar (8)
to signal, señalar (1)
to signify, significar (8)
to silence, acallar (1)
to silence, callar (1)
to silence, enmudecer (73)
to silence, silenciar (1)
to silo, asilar (1)
to silver, argentar (1)
to simplify, simplificar (8)
to simulate, simular (1)
to sin, pecar (8)
to sing, cantar (1)
to sing in a low voice, canturrear (1)
to sing in a monotone, salmodiar (1)
to sing in tune, entonar (1)
to sing or play in tune, afinar (1)
to sing psalms, salmear (1)
to sing psalms, salmodiar (1)
to sing sol-fa, solfear (1)
to singe, chamuscar (8)
to singe, socarrar (1)
to single out, singularizar (11)
to sink, hundir (3)
to sink, sumir (3)
to sink, zozobrar (1)

to sink (something) to the bottom, rehundir (34)
to sip, sorber (2)
to sit, sentarse (ie) (37) (4)
to sit around and talk, tertuliar (1)
to sit astride, ahorcajarse (1) (4)
to sit down, sentarse (ie) (37) (4)
to sit up (from a reclining position), incorporarse (1) (4)
to situate, situar (62)
to size up a person, calar (1)
to skate, patinar (1)
to sketch, abocetar (1)
to sketch, diseñar (1)
to sketch, esbozar (11)
to sketch, esquematizar (11)
to sketch, reseñar (1)
to ski, esquiar (61)
to skid, patinar (1)
to skid, resbalar (1)
to skim, desnatar (1)
to skin, desollar (ue) (36)
to skin, despellejar (1)
to skin, pelar (1)
to skip, saltar (1)
to skipper, patronar (1)
to skipper, patronear (1)
to skirmish, escaramuzar (11)
to slacken, aflojar (1)
to slacken, flojear (1)
to slacken, relajar (1)
to slap in the face, abofetear (1)
to slaughter, carnear (1)
to slaughter, sacrificar (8)
to sleep, dormir (ue, u) (40)
to sleet, cellisquear (1)
to sleet, neviscar (8)
to slice, rebanar (1)
to slice (meat), trinchar (1)
to slice, tajar (1)
to slide, deslizar (11)
to slide, escurrir (3)
to slide, resbalar (1)
to slip, patinar (1)
to slip, tropezar (ie) (51)
to slip away, escabullirse (27) (4)
to slip away, escurrirse (3) (4)
to slip away, zafarse (1) (4)
to slip in, entrarse (1) (4)
to slip or sneak in, colarse (ue) (36) (4)
to slobber, babear (1)
to slow down, atrasar (1)
to slow down, retardar (1)
to smart, escocer (ue) (54)
to smash, despachurrar (1)
to smear, untar (1)
to smear with paint, pintarrajear (1)
to smell, oler (ue) (55)
to smell, olfatear (1)
to smell, trascender (ie) (39)
to smelt, fundir (3)
to smile, sonreír (i, i) (59)
to smoke, ahumar (34)
to smoke, fumar (1)
to smoke, humear (1)
to smooth, alisar (1)
to smooth, suavizar (11)
to smooth, tersar (1)
to smooth hair with hand or comb, atusar (1)
to smudge, tiznar (1)
to smuggle, contrabandear (1)
to smut, tiznar (1)
to snap one's fingers, castañetear (1)
to snatch, arrebatar (1)
to sneeze, estornudar (1)
to sniff, olfatear (1)

to sniff out, oler (ue) (55)
to snitch, sisar (1)
to snitch, timar (1)
to snoop, curiosear (1)
to snoop, fisgar (9)
to snore, roncar (8)
to snort, bufar (1)
to snow, nevar (ie) (37)
to snow lightly, neviscar (8)
to snow with strong winds, ventiscar (8)
to snuff, espabilar (1)
to soak, empapar (1)
to soak, remojar (1)
to soak through, calar (1)
to soap, enjabonar (1)
to soap, jabonar (1)
to sob, sollozar (11)
to sober up, desemborrachar (1)
to socialize, socializar (11)
to soften, ablandar (1)
to soften, ablandecer (73)
to soften, amortiguar (10)
to soften, blandear (1)
to soften, emblandecer (73)
to soften, molificar (8)
to soften, reblandecer (73)
to soften, suavizar (11)
to soil, emporcar (ue) (44)
to soil, ensuciar (1)
to soil oneself, ensuciarse (1) (4)
to soil with mud, enfangar (9)
to soil with soot, tiznar (1)
to solace, solazar (11)
to solder, estañar (1)
to solder, soldar (ue) (36)
to sole (a shoe), solar (ue) (36)
to solemnize, solemnizar (11)
to solicit, solicitar (1)
to solidify, solidificar (8)
to solve, resolver (ue) (70)
to solve (a difficulty), solventar (1)
to soothe, sedar (1)
to sound, sonar (ue) (36)
to sound, sondear (1)
to sound a trumpet, trompetear (1)
to sound out, pulsar (1)
to sound out, sondear (1)
to soundproof, insonorizar (11)
to sour, agriarse (1) or (61) (4)
to sour, avinagrar (1)
to sow, sembrar (ie) (37)
to sow, sementar (ie) (37)
to sow discord, cizañar (1)
to sow grain by throwing it in the air with the hand, volear (1)
to space, espaciar (1)
to spangle, tachonar (1)
to spank, sacudir (3)
to spank, zurrar (1)
to spare, ahorrar (1)
to spark, chispear (1)
to sparkle, centellear (1)
to sparkle, chispear (1)
to sparkle, relampaguear (1)
to sparkle, rutilar (1)
to spawn, desovar (1)
to speak, hablar (1)
to speak (a language) brokenly, chapurrear (1)
to speak for, apalabrar (1)
to speak or act in an impudent or insolent manner, desvergonzarse (ue) (49) (4)
to speak or behave in an impudent or insolent manner, descararse (1) (4)
to spear, alancear (1)

to specify, especificar (8)
to speckle, motear (1)
to speculate, especular (1)
to spell, deletrear (1)
to spend, gastar (1)
to spend sleepless nights, trasnochar (1)
to spend the night, pernoctar (1)
to spin (thread, etc.), hilar (1)
to spin a top, trompar (1)
to spin a top, trompear (1)
to spill, derramar (1)
to spiritualize, espiritualizar (11)
to spit, escupir (3)
to splash, chapalear (1)
to splash, chapotear (1)
to splash, salpicar (8)
to splice, empalmar (1)
to splinter, astillar (1)
to split, partir (3)
to split, rajar (1)
to split, resquebrajar (1)
to split hairs, sutilizar (11)
to spoil, aguar (10)
to spoil, cagar (9)
to spoil, corromper (2)
to spoil, dañarse (1) (4)
to spoil, estropear (1)
to spoil, malear (1)
to spoil, malograr (1)
to spoil, malograrse (1) (4)
to spoil (a child), malcriar (61)
to spoil (a child), mimar (1)
to sponsor, patrocinar (1)
to spoon, cucharear (1)
to spot or stain with grease, pringar (9)
to spout, chorrear (1)
to spout, surtir (3)
to sprawl in a chair, apoltronarse (1) (4)
to sprawl in one's seat, arrellanarse (1) (4)
to sprawl out, repantigarse (9) (4)
to spray, pulverizar (11)
to spread, cundir (3)
to spread, difundir (3)
to spread, propagar (9)
to spread, sembrar (ie) (37)
to spread, trascender (ie) (39)
to spread anarchism, anarquizar (11)
to spread by rumor, rumorear (1)
to spread out, tender (ie) (39)
to spread sand, arenar (1)
to spring up, dimanar (1)
to sprinkle, gotear (1)
to sprinkle, rociar (61)
to sprinkle, salpicar (8)
to sprinkle with dust or powder, polvorear (1)
to sprinkle with powder, espolvorear (1)
to sprinkle with powder, espolvorizar (11)
to sprout, brotar (1)
to sprout, grillarse (1) (4)
to sprout, rebrotar (1)
to sprout, retoñar (1)
to sprout again, reverdecer (73)
to sprout ears (corn), jilotear (1)
to spruce up, atildar (1)
to spur, aguijonear (1)
to spur, espolear (1)
to spurt, surgir (16)
to spy, espiar (61)
to squander, derrochar (1)
to squander, despilfarrar (1)
to squander, malbaratar (1)
to squander, malgastar (1)

to squander, prodigar (9)
to square, cuadrar (1)
to squash, despachurrar (1)
to squat, aclocarse (ue) (44) (4)
to squat, acuclillarse (1) (4)
to squat, agacharse (1) (4)
to squat, agazaparse (1) (4)
to squeak, chirriar (61)
to squeak, rechinar (1)
to squeal on, soplonear (1)
to squeeze, apretar (ie) (37)
to squeeze, estrujar (1)
to squeeze, exprimir (3)
to squeeze, oprimir (3)
to squeeze together, apiñar (1)
to squint to see better, amusgar (9)
to stab, apuñalar (1)
to stabilize, estabilizar (11)
to stage, escenificar (8)
to stagger, rehilar (34)
to stagnate, estancarse (8) (4)
to stain, amancillar (1)
to stain, manchar (1)
to stain or smear with mud, embarrar (1)
to stain with blood, ensangrentar (ie) (37)
to stammer, balbucear (1)
to stammer, balbucir (118)
to stammer, trabarse (1) (4)
to stamp, estampar (1)
to stamp, estampillar (1)
to stamp, marcar (8)
to stamp, sellar (1)
to stamp, timbrar (1)
to stamp (said of a horse), piafar (1)
to stamp the feet, patalear (1)
to stanch, estancar (8)
to stand, plantarse (1) (4)
to stand at attention, cuadrarse (1) (4)
to stand in the way, obstar (1)
to stand in the way, obviar (1)
to stand out, campar (1)
to stand out, destacarse (8) (4)
to stand out, predominar (1)
to stand out, recortarse (1) (4)
to stand out, resaltar (1)
to stand out, sobresalir (106)
to stand out clearly, sobresaltar (1)
to stand out in relief, relevarse (1) (4)
to stand up, levantarse (1) (4)
to stand up, pararse (1) (4)
to standardize, estandardizar (11)
to standardize, normalizar (11)
to staple, engrapar (1)
to starch, almidonar (1)
to start, arrancar (8)
to start, comenzar (ie) (51)
to start (a conversation), entablar (1)
to start a polemic, polemizar (11)
to start forming kernels or seed, granar (1)
to starve, hambrear (1)
to stash away (in a piggy bank or safe place), ahuchar (34)
to state, plantear (1)
to state precisely, precisar (1)
to station, estacionar (1)
to stay, permanecer (73)
to stay, quedarse (1) (4)
to stay awake, velar (1)
to stay on the edge, bordear (1)
to steal, hurtar (1)
to steal, rapiñar (1)
to steal, robar (1)
to steer, dirigir (16)
to steer, gobernar (ie) (37)

to steer, guiar (19)
to steer, timonear (1)
to step, escalonar (1)
to step on, pisar (1)
to stereotype, estereotipar (1)
to sterilize, esterilizar (11)
to stew, estofar (1)
to stick, pegar (9)
to stick out (one's chest), sacar (8)
to stick to, sujetarse (1) (4)
to stick together, aglutinar (1)
to stiffen, atiesar (1)
to stigmatize, estigmatizar (11)
to stigmatize, tildar (1)
to stimulate, estimular (1)
to sting, picar (8)
to sting, pungir (16)
to stink, apestar (1)
to stink, heder (ie) (39)
to stipulate, estipular (1)
to stipulate, pactar (1)
to stir, agitar (1)
to stir, conmover (ue) (38)
to stir, menear (1)
to stir, mover (ue) (38)
to stir, rebullir (27)
to stir, remover (ue) (38)
to stir, revolver (70)
to stir and move nimbly, zarandear (1)
to stir up, atizar (11)
to stir up, suscitar (1)
to stir up, turbar (1)
to stir up a fire, tizonear (1)
to stitch, embastar (1)
to stitch, puntear (1)
to stockade, empalizar (11)
to stone, apedrear (1)
to stone to death, lapidar (1)
to stop, cesar (1)
to stop, detener (ie) (108)
to stop, parar (1)
to stop, pararse (1) (4)
to stop raining, escampar (1)
to stop up, atascar (8)
to stop up, obturar (1)
to stop up, taponar (1)
to store, almacenar (1)
to store away, embodegar (9)
to storm, tempestear (1)
to straighten, enderezar (11)
to strain, colar (ue) (36)
to strain, trascolar (ue) (36)
to strangle, estrangular (1)
to strap, precintar (1)
to stratify, estratificar (8)
to strengthen, afirmar (1)
to strengthen, fortalecer (71)
to strengthen, reforzar (ue) (46)
to strengthen, robustecer (73)
to stress, acentuar (62)
to stress, remarcar (8)
to stress (one's words), recalcar (8)
to stretch, desperezarse (11) (4)
to stretch, estirar (1)
to striate, estriar (61)
to strike, antojarse (124)
to strike, golpear (1)
to strike (clock), sonar (ue) (36)
to strike with the beak, picotear (1)
to strike with the hands, manotear (1)
to string (beads, etc.), ensartar (1)
to string (mainly jewelry), engarzar (11)
to string (onions, etc.), enristrar (1)
to stripe, vetear (1)
to strive, pugnar (1)
to strive to, afanarse (1) (4)

to stroll, pasear (1)
to strop (a razor), suavizar (11)
to struggle, bregar (9)
to struggle, debatirse (3) (4)
to struggle, luchar (1)
to struggle, pelear (1)
to struggle, pugnar (1)
to strut, contornearse (1) (4)
to strut, pavonearse (1) (4)
to stud, clavetear (1)
to stud, tachonar (1)
to study, estudiar (1)
to stuff, atestar (1)
to stuff, atestar (ie) (37)
to stuff, atiborrar (1)
to stuff, embutir (3)
to stuff, llenar (1)
to stuff, rebutir (3)
to stuff, rellenar (1)
to stuff (furniture), rehenchir (i, i) (42)
to stuff and mount, disecar (8)
to stumble, tropezar (ie) (51)
to stun, atarantar (1)
to stun, aturdir (3)
to stun, pasmar (1)
to stupefy, alelar (1)
to stupefy, atontar (1)
to stupefy, entorpecer (73)
to stutter, balbucear (1)
to stutter, balbucir (118)
to stutter, tartajear (1)
to stutter, tartamudear (1)
to stylize, estilizar (11)
to subcontract, subcontratar (1)
to subdivide, subdividir (3)
to subdue, acogotar (1)
to subdue, sojuzgar (9)
to subdue, someter (2)
to subdue, subyugar (9)
to subdue, sujetar (1)
to subject, someter (2)
to subject, sujetar (1)
to subject, supeditar (1)
to subjugate, sojuzgar (9)
to sublease, subarrendar (ie) (37)
to sublet, subarrendar (ie) (37)
to sublimate, sublimar (1)
to sublime, sublimar (1)
to submerge, sumergir (16)
to submerge, sumir (3)
to submerse, sumergir (16)
to submit, someter (2)
to submit, someterse (2) (4)
to submit, sujetarse (1) (4)
to subordinate, subordinar (1)
to subrogate, subrogar (9)
to subscribe, subscribir (69)
to subsidize, subsidiar (1)
to subsidize, subvencionar (1)
to subsist, subsistir (3)
to substantiate, substanciar (1)
to substantivize, substantivar (1)
to substitute, reemplazar (11)
to substitute, subrogar (9)
to substitute, substituir (71)
to substitute, suplir (3)
to subsume, subsumir (3)
to subtend, subtender (ie) (39)
to subtract, restar (1)
to subtract, substraer (109)
to subvert, subvertir (ie, i) (41)
to succeed, suceder (2)
to succor, socorrer (2)
to succumb, sucumbir (3)
to suck, chupar (1)
to suck, mamar (1)

to suck, succionar (1)
to suck gently and by starts, chupetear (1)
to suck in, succionar (1)
to suckle, mamar (1)
to sue, enjuiciar (1)
to sue, procesar (1)
to suffer, padecer (73)
to suffer, penar (1)
to suffer, sufrir (3)
to suffer (annoyances) with patience, sobrellevar (1)
to suffer (from illness, defect, etc.), adolecer (73)
to suffer from, resentirse (ie, i) (41) (4)
to suffocate, sofocar (8)
to sugar, azucarar (1)
to suggest, sugerir (ie, i) (41)
to suggest, sugestionar (1)
to sulfate, sulfatar (1)
to sulfurate, sulfurar (1)
to sulk, amorrarse (1) (4)
to sum, sumar (1)
to sum up, sumar (1)
to summarize, compendiar (1)
to summarize, resumir (3)
to summer, veranear (1)
to sun, asolear (1)
to sun, solear (1)
to supercharge, sobrealimentar (1)
to superimpose, sobreponer (98)
to superpose, sobreponer (98)
to superpose, superponer (98)
to supersede, sobreseer (20)
to supervise, superentender (ie) (39)
to supplant, suplantar (1)
to supplement, suplementar (1)
to supplicate, suplicar (8)
to supply, abastecer (73)
to supply, aprovisionar (1)
to supply, facilitar (1)
to supply, suministrar (1)
to supply, suplir (3)
to supply with ammunition, amunicionar (1)
to support, apoyar (1)
to support, auspiciar (1)
to support, refirmar (1)
to support, soportar (1)
to support, sostener (ie) (108)
to suppose, suponer (98)
to suppress, suprimir (3)
to surge, surgir (16)
to surmount, vencer (12)
to surpass, sobrepasar (1)
to surpass, sobrepujar (1)
to surpass, superar (1)
to surpass, vencer (12)
to surprise, sobrecoger (15)
to surprise, sorprender (2)
to surprise by defeating or outsmarting, planchar (1)
to surrender, entregarse (9) (4)
to surrender, rendir (i, i) (42)
to surrender, rendirse (i, i) (42) (4)
to surrender, someterse (2) (4)
to surround, cercar (8)
to surround, circundar (1)
to surround, circunvalar (1)
to surround, rodear (1)
to survive, sobrevivir (3)
to suspect, entrever (112)
to suspect, recelar (1)
to suspect, sospechar (1)
to suspect, vislumbrar (1)
to suspend, suspender (2)

to sustain, sostener (ie) (108)
to sustain, sustentar (1)
to swallow, deglutir (3)
to swallow, pasar (1)
to swallow, tragar (9)
to swamp, empantanar (1)
to swap, cambalachear (1)
to swarm, hormiguear (1)
to swarm, pulular (1)
to sway, bambolear (1)
to sway, mimbrear (1)
to sway from side to side, zangolotearse (1) (4)
to swear, jurar (1)
to swear, perjurar (1)
to sweat, perspirar (1)
to sweat, sudar (1)
to sweep, barrer (2)
to sweep away, arramblar (1)
to sweep lightly, sobrebarrer (2)
to sweeten, adulzar (11)
to sweeten, dulcificar (8)
to sweeten, endulzar (11)
to sweeten, suavizar (11)
to swell, hinchar (1)
to swell, tumefacer (68)
to swell (stream), crecer (73)
to swim, nadar (1)
to swindle, escamotear (1)
to swindle, estafar (1)
to swindle, petardear (1)
to swindle, timar (1)
to swindle, trapacear (1)
to swing, balancear (1)
to swing, columpiar (1)
to swing, remecer (14)
to swing one's arms, bracear (1)
to swipe, apandar (1)
to syllabify, silabear (1)
to syllable, silabear (1)
to symbolize, simbolizar (11)
to sympathize, condoler (ue) (38)
to synchronize, sincronizar (11)
to syncopate, sincopar (1)
to syndicate, sindicar (8)
to syndicate, sindicarse (8) (4)
to synthesize, sintetizar (11)
to systematize, sistematizar (11)

T

to tabulate, tabular (1)
to tag, etiquetar (1)
to take, llevar (1)
to take, tomar (1)
to take (an examination), sufrir (3)
to take (pictures), sacar (8)
to take a bath, bañarse (1) (4)
to take a bribe, cohechar (1)
to take a certain direction, rumbear (1)
to take a course or courses in, cursar (1)
to take a laxative, purgarse (9) (4)
to take a liking to or for, prendarse (1) (4)
to take a pinch of, pellizcar (8)
to take a risk, arriesgarse (9) (4)
to take a shortcut, atajar (1)
to take a shower, ducharse (1) (4)
to take a siesta, sestear (1)
to take a stand, plantarse (1) (4)
to take a walk, pasear (1)
to take a walk, pasearse (1) (4)
to take across, pasar (1)
to take advantage of, aprovecharse (1) (4)

to take an examination, examinarse (1) (4)
to take apart, deshacer (90)
to take apart, desmontar (1)
to take away, quitar (1)
to take away, retirar (1)
to take by storm, expugnar (1)
to take care, atender (ie) (39)
to take care of, cuidar (1)
to take care of oneself, valerse (110) (4)
to take communion, comulgar (9)
to take delight in, regodearse (1) (4)
to take down, bajar (1)
to take form, configurarse (1) (4)
to take good care of, cuidar (1)
to take hold, asirse (78) (4)
to take in, injerir (ie, i) (41)
to take into account, atender (ie) (39)
to take legal or official steps, tramitar (1)
to take lodging, aposentarse (1) (4)
to take long, tardar (1)
to take note, apuntar (1)
to take notice, percatar (1)
to take off clothing, desarropar (1)
to take off, despegar (9)
to take off (article of clothing), quitarse (1) (4)
to take off one's clothing, desarroparse (1) (4)
to take off one's hat, etc., descubrirse (82) (4)
to take off outer clothing (coat, sweater, etc.), desabrigar (9)
to take offense, ofenderse (2) (4)
to take out, sacar (8)
to take out of the cage, desenjaular (1)
to take pains, esmerarse (1) (4)
to take place, efectuarse (62) (4)
to take place, producirse (67) (4)
to take place, sobrevenir (ie, i) (111)
to take place, supervenir (ie, i) (111)
to take pleasure or satisfaction, holgar (ue) (45)
to take possession, adueñarse (1) (4)
to take possession, apoderarse (1) (4)
to take possession, aposesionarse (1) (4)
to take possession, enseñorearse (1) (4)
to take possession, posesionarse (1) (4)
to take refuge, acogerse (15) (4)
to take refuge, asilarse (1) (4)
to take revenge, vengarse (9) (4)
to take root, arraigar (9)
to take root, enraizar (64)
to take root, prender (2)
to take satisfaction, satisfacerse (68) (4)
to take shape, configurarse (1) (4)
to take shelter, abrigarse (9) (4)
to take shelter, albergarse (9) (4)
to take shelter, guarecerse (73) (4)
to take shelter, recogerse (15) (4)
to take shelter, resguardarse (1) (4)
to take shoes off, descalzar (11)
to take shorthand, taquigrafiar (61)
to take someone or something from its place in order to put it in another, desplazar (11)
to take steps to accomplish, diligenciar (1)
to take the brakes off, desfrenar (1)
to take undue liberty, propasarse (1) (4)
to take up residence (in a city or town), avecindarse (1) (4)
to talk, hablar (1)
to talk, platicar (8)
to talk fast and loud, chirlar (1)

to talk nonsense, bobear (1)
to talk nonsense, desatinar (1)
to talk nonsense, desbarrar (1)
to talk nonsense, desvariar (61)
to talk nonsense, disparatar (1)
to talk nonsense, rebuznar (1)
to talk or act foolishly, tontear (1)
to talk politics, politiquear (1)
to talk with, entrevistarse (1) (4)
to talk without restraint, despotricar (8)
to tame, amaestrar (1)
to tame, amansar (1)
to tame, desbravar (1)
to tame, desbravecer (73)
to tame, domar (1)
to tame, domeñar (1)
to tan, broncear (1)
to tan, curtir (3)
to tan, tostar (ue) (36)
to tangle, enmarañar (1)
to tangle up, enredar (1)
to tap dance, zapatear (1)
to tap with one's heels, talonear (1)
to tap with the feet, zapatear (1)
to tape-record, grabar (1)
to tapestry, tapizar (11)
to tar, alquitranar (1)
to tarnish, deslucir (74)
to tarnish, deslustrar (1)
to tarnish, empañar (1)
to taste, catar (1)
to taste, degustar (1)
to taste, gustar (1)
to taste, probar (ue) (36)
to taste, saborear (1)
to tattoo, tatuar (62)
to tax, tasar (1)
to tax a possession, acensuar (62)
to taxi (aeronautic), taxear (1)
to teach, aleccionar (1)
to teach, enseñar (1)
to tear, desgarrar (1)
to tear, rasgar (9)
to tear, romper (104)
to tear down, derribar (1)
to tear down, derruir (71)
to tear to pieces, triturar (1)
to tease, embromar (1)
to telecast, teledifundir (3)
to telegraph, telegrafiar (61)
to telephone, telefonar (1)
to telephone, telefonear (1)
to telephotograph, telefotografiar (61)
to televise, televisar (1)
to tell, decir (i, i) (84)
to tell, referir (ie, i) (41)
to tell coarse jokes, chocarrear (1)
to tell in detail, menudear (1)
to tell in detail, pormenorizar (11)
to tell lies, bolear (1)
to tell someone he or she is lying, desmentir (ie, i) (41)
to tell stories, novelizar (11)
to temper, atemperar (1)
to temper, temperar (1)
to temper, templar (1)
to temporize, temporizar (11)
to tempt, seducir (67)
to tempt, tentar (ie) (37)
to tend, propender (2)
to tergiversate, tergiversar (1)
to terminate, terminar (1)
to terminate, ultimar (1)
to terrify, aterrar (1)
to terrify, aterrorizar (11)

to terrify, consternar (1)
to test, probar (ue) (36)
to testify, atestiguar (10)
to testify, testificar (8)
to testify, testimoniar (1)
to thank, agradecer (73)
to thaw, deshelar (ie) (37)
to theorize, teorizar (11)
to thicken, espesar (1)
to think, creer (20)
to think, opinar (1)
to think, pensar (ie) (37)
to think, reflexionar (1)
to think out, excogitar (1)
to think over, pensar (ie) (37)
to think over again, repensar (ie) (37)
to think up, ingeniar (1)
to thread, enhebrar (1)
to threaten, amenazar (11)
to threaten, cernerse (ie) (39) (4)
to threaten, conminar (1)
to thresh, trillar (1)
to thrive, medrar (1)
to throb, latir (3)
to throb, palpitar (1)
to throng, agolparse (1) (4)
to throw, arrojar (1)
to throw, echar (1)
to throw, lanzar (11)
to throw, tirar (1)
to throw (into the street, prison), plantar (1)
to throw a bouquet, piropear (1)
to throw away, botar (1)
to throw away, tirar (1)
to throw back the ears (said of animals), amusgar (9)
to throw into disorder, desordenar (1)
to throw into jail, encalabozar (11)
to throw off sparks, chisporrotear (1)
to throw off the trail or course, despistar (1)
to throw up, vomitar (1)
to thunder, retronar (ue) (36)
to thunder, tronar (ue) (36)
to tickle, cosquillear (1)
to tie, anudar (1)
to tie, atar (1)
to tie, liar (19)
to tie, ligar (9)
to tie (in games, etc.), empatar (1)
to tie fast, trincar (8)
to tie the hands, maniatar (1)
to tie up, amarrar (1)
to tighten, tensar (1)
to tile, azulejar (1)
to tile, baldosar (1)
to till, labrar (1)
to tilt, ladear (1)
to tincture, tinturar (1)
to tint, tintar (1)
to tip off, soplar (1)
to tip over, volcar (ue) (44)
to tire, cansar (1)
to tire, fatigar (9)
to tire, hartar (1)
to tithe, diezmar (1)
to title, rotular (1)
to title, titular (1)
to toast (before drinking), brindar (1)
to toast, torrar (1)
to toast, tostar (ue) (36)
to toast again, retostar (ue) (36)
to toast brown, retostar (ue) (36)
to tolerate, comportar (1)
to tolerate, tolerar (1)

to toll, tocar (8)
to tone down, amortecer (73)
to tone down, atenuar (62)
to tone down, esfumar (1)
to tooth, dentar (ie) (37)
to top (chop off the tip or head of), descabezar (11)
to torment, atormentar (1)
to torpedo, torpedear (1)
to torture, torturar (1)
to toss in a blanket, mantear (1)
to totalize, totalizar (11)
to touch, palpar (1)
to touch, tentar (ie) (37)
to touch, tocar (8)
to touch up, retocar (8)
to tour, recorrer (2)
to tow, remolcar (8)
to tow (a boat), sirgar (9)
to trace, calcar (8)
to trace, trazar (11)
to trace the contour of, contornear (1)
to track, rastrear (1)
to trade, comerciar (1)
to trade, mercadear (1)
to trade, traficar (8)
to traffic, traficar (8)
to trail, rastrear (1)
to train, adiestrar (1)
to train, amaestrar (1)
to train, entrenar (1)
to trample underfoot, conculcar (8)
to trample underfoot, pisar (1)
to trample underfoot, pisotear (1)
to trample upon, arrollar (1)
to tranquilize, tranquilizar (11)
to transcribe, transcribir (69)
to transfer, transbordar (1)
to transfer, transferir (ie, i) (41)
to transfer, trasegar (ie) (50)
to transfer, trasladar (1)
to transfer, traspalar (1)
to transfer by pouring, abocar (8)
to transfer property, traspasar (1)
to transfigure, transfigurar (1)
to transform, transformar (1)
to transform, transmutar (1)
to transform, transubstanciar (1)
to transfuse, transfundir (3)
to transgress, contravenir (ie, i) (111)
to transgress, delinquir (18)
to transgress, transgredir (116)
to transgress, traspasar (1)
to translate, traducir (67)
to transmigrate, transmigrar (1)
to transmit, transmitir (3)
to transpire, sudar (1)
to transpire, transpirar (1)
to transplant, trasplantar (1)
to transport (for a price), portear (1)
to transport, transportar (1)
to transpose, transponer (98)
to transubstantiate, transubstanciar (1)
to trap, atrapar (1)
to trap, entrampar (1)
to travel, recorrer (2)
to travel, viajar (1)
to travel about, trajinar (1)
to travel around foreign lands, peregrinar (1)
to tread all over, pisotear (1)
to tread upon, hollar (ue) (36)
to treasure, atesorar (1)
to treat, obsequiar (1)
to treat, tratar (1)
to treat (a sick person), curar (1)

to treat roughly, patear (1)
to tremble, temblar (ie) (37)
to tremble, tremer (2)
to trick, embaír (117)
to trick, entrampar (1)
to trick, trampear (1)
to trim, atusar (1)
to trim, cercenar (1)
to trim, recortar (1)
to trim with a fringe, orlar (1)
to trip, trompicar (8)
to triple, triplicar (8)
to triplicate, triplicar (8)
to trisect, trisecar (8)
to triumph, triunfar (1)
to trump, triunfar (1)
to truncate, truncar (8)
to trust, confiarse (61) (4)
to trust, fiar (19)
to try, probar (ue) (36)
to try hard, esforzarse (ue) (46) (4)
to try on (clothes), probarse (ue) (36) (4)
to try out, ensayar (1)
to try out, probar (ue) (36)
to try the weight of by lifting, sopesar (1)
to try the weight of by lifting, sospesar (1)
to tuck up, arremangar (9)
to tuck up, arrezagar (9)
to tuck up one's dress, arremangarse (9) (4)
to tune, afinar (1)
to tune (a radio), sintonizar (11)
to turn, doblar (1)
to turn, girar (1)
to turn, ponerse (98) (4)
to turn, torcer (ue) (53)
to turn, virar (1)
to turn, voltear (1)
to turn, volver (ue) (70)
to turn, volverse (ue) (70) (4)
to turn a deaf ear, desoír (95)
to turn a somersault, voltear (1)
to turn around, voltear (1)
to turn around, volverse (ue) (70) (4)
to turn blue, azularse (1) (4)
to turn down, rehusar (34)
to turn green, verdecer (73)
to turn inside out, voltear (1)
to turn into a puddle, encharcar (8)
to turn loose, soltar (ue) (36)
to turn off, apagar (9)
to turn on, encender (ie) (39)
to turn on, prender (2)
to turn or roll over, voltear (1)
to turn out, quedar (1)
to turn out, salir (106)
to turn out to be, resultar (1)
to turn over, voltearse (1) (4)
to turn pale, palidecer (73)
to turn sour, avinagrarse (1) (4)
to turn sour, envinagrarse (1) (4)
to turn up (sleeves), arremangar (9)
to turn up one's sleeves, arremangarse (9) (4)
to turn up, over or inside out, volver (ue) (70)
to twang (a guitar, etc.), rasguear (1)
to twinkle, destellar (1)
to twinkle, rielar (1)
to twist, enroscar (8)
to twist, retorcer (ue) (53)
to twist, torcer (ue) (53)
to twist (facts, etc.), tergiversar (1)
to twist too much, rehilar (34)

to twist up, retortijar (1)
to type, mecanografiar (61)
to tyrannize, despotizar (11)

U

to unauthorize, desautorizar (11)
to unbalance, desequilibrar (1)
to unbar, desatrancar (8)
to unbaste, deshilvanar (1)
to unbolt, desenroscar (8)
to unbutton, desabotonar (1)
to unbutton, desabrochar (1)
to unchain, desencadenar (1)
to unclog, desatascar (8)
to unclutch, desembragar (9)
to uncork, descorchar (1)
to uncover, descubrir, (82)
to uncover, destapar (1)
to underestimate, menospreciar (1)
to undergo, sufrir (3)
to underline, subrayar (1)
to undermine, minar (1)
to undermine, socavar (1)
to undersell, malbaratar (1)
to undersell, malvender (2)
to understand, comprender (2)
to understand, entender (ie) (39)
to understand, sobreentender (ie) (39)
to undertake, emprender (2)
to undo, deshacer (90)
to undress, desnudar (1)
to undress, desvestir (i, i) (42)
to undulate, ondular (1)
to unearth, desenterrar (ie) (37)
to unfasten, desabrochar (1)
to unfasten, desprender (2)
to unfasten, soltar (ue) (36)
to unfold, desplegar (ie) (50)
to unglue, despegar (9)
to unhang, descolgar (ue) (45)
to unharness, desaparejar (1)
to unhitch, desenganchar (1)
to uniform, uniformar (1)
to unify, unificar (8)
to unite, aunar (65)
to unite, mancomunar (1)
to unite, reunir (66)
to unite, unir (3)
to unknot, desanudar (1)
to unknot, desatar (1)
to unload, descargar (9)
to unlock, abrir (75)
to unmask, desenmascarar (1)
to unnail, desclavar (1)
to unnerve, enervar (1)
to unpack, desembalar (1)
to unpack, desempacar (8)
to unplug, desenchufar (1)
to unravel, desenlazar (11)
to unravel, deshilar (1)
to unroll, desarrollar (1)
to unroll, desenrollar (1)
to unscrew, destornillar (1)
to unsheath, desenvainar (1)
to unstitch, descoser (2)
to untie, desanudar (1)
to untie, desatar (1)
to untie, desenlazar (11)
to untie, deshacer (90)
to untie, desligar (9)
to untie, soltar (ue) (36)
to untile (roofing tiles), destejar (1)
to unwind (a ball of string, yarn, etc.), desovillar (1)
to unwrap, desenvolver (ue) (70)

to unwrinkle, desarrugar (9)
to upbraid, refregar (ie) (50)
to upholster, tapizar (11)
to upset, conturbar (1)
to upset, desbaratar (1)
to upset, descomponer (98)
to upset, indisponer (98)
to upset, trastocar (8)
to upset, trastornar (1)
to urbanize, urbanizar (11)
to urge, acuciar (1)
to urge, ahincar (8)
to urge, apremiar (1)
to urge, encarecer (73)
to urge, instar (1)
to urge on, aguijar (1)
to urge on (horses, etc.), arrear (1)
to urge with insistence, atosigar (9)
to urinate, mear (1)
to urinate, orinar (1)
to use, emplear (1)
to use, usar (1)
to use as a pretext, pretextar (1)
to use as an adjective, adjetivar (1)
to use bluing (on clothes), añilar (1)
to use for the first time, estrenar (1)
to use roughly, maltraer (109)
to use roughly, maltratar (1)
to use to no advantage, desaprovechar (1)
to use up, gastar (1)
to usufruct, usufructuar (62)
to usurp, usurpar (1)
to utilize, utilizar (11)
to utter, proferir (ie, i) (41)

V

to vacate, desocupar (1)
to vacate, desvaír (117)
to vaccinate, vacunar (1)
to vacillate, vacilar (1)
to valorize, valorizar (11)
to value, valorar (1)
to vanish, desvanecerse (73) (4)
to vaporize, evaporizar (11)
to vaporize, vaporizar (11)
to varnish, barnizar (11)
to varnish, charolar (1)
to vary, variar (61)
to veil, velar (1)
to vent, aerear (1)
to vent one's anger, desfogarse (9) (4)
to ventilate, airear (1)
to ventilate, ventilar (1)
to verify, comprobar (ue) (36)
to verify, constatar (1)
to verify, verificar (8)
to versify, versear (1)
to versify, versificar (8)
to veto, vetar (1)
to vex, crucificar (8)
to vex, vejar (1)
to vibrate, cimbrearse (1) (4)
to vibrate, trepidar (1)
to vibrate, vibrar (1)
to vie, rivalizar (11)
to vilify, envilecer (73)
to vilify, vilipendiar (1)
to vindicate, vindicar (8)
to violate, conculcar (8)
to violate, violar (1)
to violate (a law), quebrantar (1)
to visit, visitar (1)
to visualize, visualizar (11)
to vitalize, vitalizar (11)

to vitiate, enviciar (1)
to vitiate, viciar (1)
to vitrify, vitrificar (8)
to vituperate, vituperar (1)
to vocalize, vocalizar (11)
to volley, volear (1)
to vomit, devolver (ue) (70)
to vomit, vomitar (1)
to vote, votar (1)
to vulcanize, vulcanizar (11)
to vulgarize, vulgarizar (11)

W

to waddle, anadear (1)
to waddle, zanquear (1)
to wag, menear (1)
to wag, mover (ue) (38)
to wag the tail, colear (1)
to wait, aguardar (1)
to wait, esperar (1)
to wait on, atender (ie) (39)
to wait on, despachar (1)
to wait on, servir (i, i) (42)
to wake up, despertar (ie) (37)
to wake up, despertarse (ie) (37) (4)
to waken, despertar (ie) (37)
to walk, ambular (1)
to walk, andar (77)
to walk, caminar (1)
to walk, deambular (1)
to walk, pasear (1)
to walk making noise with the heels, taconear (1)
to wall, amurallar (1)
to wall in, tapiar (1)
to wall up, tabicar (8)
to wall up, tapiar (1)
to wallow, revolcarse (ue) (44) (4)
to wallpaper, empapelar (1)
to wander, errar (ie) (52)
to wander, vagar (9)
to want, querer (ie) (101)
to war, guerrear (1)
to warble, gorjear (1)
to warble, trinar (1)
to warm, calentar (ie) (37)
to warn, advertir (ie, i) (41)
to warn, percatar (1)
to warn, prevenir (ie, i) (111)
to warp, combarse (1) (4)
to wash, lavar (1)
to wash (dishes), fregar (ie) (50)
to wash oneself, lavarse (1) (4)
to wash with pails of water (decks, floors, etc.), baldear (1)
to waste, desperdiciar (1)
to waste, gastar (1)
to waste, malgastar (1)
to waste, malograr (1)
to waste, perder (ie) (39)
to watch, mirar (1)
to watch, velar (1)
to watch over, cuidar (1)
to watch over, custodiar (1)
to watch over, guardar (1)
to watch over, velar (1)
to water, aguar (10)
to water, regar (ie) (50)
to water (cattle), abrevar (1)
to wave, ondear (1)
to wave (the hair), ondular (1)
to wax, encerar (1)
to weaken, claudicar (8)
to weaken, debilitar (1)

to weaken, flaquear (1)
to weaken, flojear (1)
to wean, destetar (1)
to wear, gastar (1)
to wear, traer (109)
to wear, vestir (i, i) (42)
to wear (a certain size of shoe), calzar (11)
to wear away, desgastar (1)
to wear down or away, desgastarse (1) (4)
to wear out, gastar (1)
to wear well, durar (1)
to weave, tejer (2)
to weave, tramar (1)
to weave together, entretejer (2)
to weed, desherbar (ie) (37)
to weed out, escardar (1)
to weep, lagrimar (1)
to weep, llorar (1)
to weep easily, lagrimear (1)
to weigh (anchor), levar (1)
to weigh, pesar (1)
to weigh anchor, zarpar (1)
to weight with great care, repesar (1)
to welcome, acoger (15)
to welcome, recibir (3)
to weld, soldar (ue) (36)
to wet, humedecer (73)
to wet, mojar (1)
to whimsically set one's mind upon, encapricharse (1) (4)
to whine, gemir (i, i) (42)
to whine, gimotear (1)
to whine, lloriquear (1)
to whine, piar (19)
to whine, quejarse (1) (4)
to whip, azotar (1)
to whip, chicotear (1)
to whip, flagelar (1)
to whip, fustigar (9)
to whip, vapulear (1)
to whip, verguear (1)
to whip, zurriagar (9)
to whip (cream), merengar (9)
to whirl, arremolinarse (1) (4)
to whirl about, remolinar (1)
to whirl about, remolinarse (1) (4)
to whisper, susurrar (1)
to whisper (an answer to a student), soplar (1)
to whistle, chiflar (1)

to whistle, pitar (1)
to whistle, pitear (1)
to whiten, blanquear (1)
to whiten, blanquecer (73)
to whiten, emblanquecer (73)
to whitewash, encalar (1)
to whitewash, enjabelgar (9)
to whiz, rehilar (34)
to widen, anchar (1)
to widen, ensanchar (1)
to wiggle, culebrear (1)
to wilt, marchitarse (1) (4)
to win, ganar (1)
to win (as the good will of another), granjearse (1) (4)
to win by a fluke, chiripear (1)
to win out, vencer (12)
to win out over someone in a discussion, ahocicar (8)
to win over, conquistar (1)
to win the favor of someone, congraciar (1)
to wind, serpentear (1)
to wink, guiñar (1)
to winnow, zarandear (1)
to winter, invernar (ie) (37)
to wipe dry, secar (8)
to wipe off, raer (102)
to wish, querer (ie) (101)
to withdraw, retirar (1)
to withdraw, retraerse (109) (4)
to withdraw, substraerse (109) (4)
to wither, ajar (1)
to wither, marchitarse (1) (4)
to withhold, retener (ie) (108)
to witness, presenciar (1)
to wobble, cojear (1)
to wood engrave, xilograbar (1)
to work, funcionar (1)
to work, laborar (1)
to work, laborear (1)
to work, labrar (1)
to work, marchar (1)
to work, obrar (1)
to work, operar (1)
to work, trabajar (1)
to work at night, velar (1)
to work for a salary, asalariarse (1) (4)
to work late, velar (1)
to work something with the hands to soften it, sobar (1)
to worry, apurarse (1) (4)

to worry, inquietar (1)
to worry, intranquilizar (11)
to worry, preocuparse (1) (4)
to worship, adorar (1)
to worship, idolatrar (1)
to wound, herir (ie, i) (41)
to wound badly, malherir (ie, i) (41)
to wrap, envolver (ue) (70)
to wrap oneself all up, rebujarse (1) (4)
to wrap oneself up, abrigarse (9) (4)
to wrap up, acurrucar (8)
to wrap up with clothing, arropar (1)
to wrestle, luchar (1)
to wring, escurrir (3)
to wrinkle, arrugar (1)
to wrinkle, fruncir (13)
to write, escribir (69)
to write a preface for, prologar (9)
to write between lines, interlinear (1)
to write by hand, manuscribir (69)
to write in shorthand, taquigrafiar (61)
to write marginal notes, marginar (1)
to write up, redactar (1)
to writhe, contorcerse (ue) (53) (4)

X

to xylograph, xilograbar (1)

Y

to yearn to, ansiar (1) or (61)
to yelp, regañir (29)
to yield, ceder (2)
to yield, claudicar (8)
to yield, dar (83)
to yield, producir (67)
to yield, rendir (i, i) (42)
to yield, someterse (2) (4)
to yield, transigir (16)
to yield abundantly, cundir (3)
to yoke, uncir (13)
to yoke, uñir (29)
to yowl, regañir (29)

Z

to zigzag, zigzaguear (1)